Exploring Social Psychology

Exploring Social Psychology

FOURTH EDITION

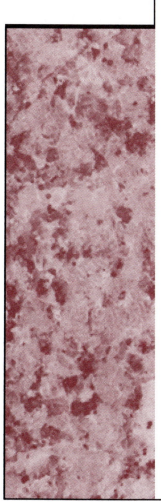

Robert A. Baron
Rensselaer Polytechnic Institute

Donn Byrne
The University at Albany, SUNY

Blair T. Johnson
Syracuse University

Allyn and Bacon
BOSTON • LONDON • TORONTO • SYDNEY • TOKYO • SINGAPORE

Senior Series Editor: Carolyn Merrill
Series Editorial Assistant: Amy Goldmacher
Production Coordinator: Chris Rawlings
Editorial Production Service: Omegatype Typography, Inc.
Text Designer: Carol Somberg for Omegatype Typography, Inc.
Composition and Prepress Buyer: Linda Cox
Manufacturing Buyer: Megan Cochran
Cover Administrator: Linda Knowles
Photo Researcher: Sue C. Howard

Copyright ©1998, 1988, 1982, 1979 by Allyn and Bacon
A Viacom Company
160 Gould Street
Needham Heights, MA 02194

Internet: www.abacon.com
America Online: keyword: College Online

Library of Congress Cataloging-in-Publication Data
Baron, Robert A.
    Exploring social psychology / Robert A. Baron, Donn Byrne, Blair
T. Johnson. — 4th ed.
        p.   cm.
    Includes bibliographical references and index.
    ISBN O-205-27112-X
    1. Social Psychology.   I. Byrne, Donn Erwin.   II. Johnson, Blair
T.   III. Title
HM251.B435   1998
302–dc21   97-22782
                                                                      CIP

Photo Credits: Photo credits can be found on page 364, which should be considered
an extension of the copyright page.

Printed in the United States of America
10 9 8 7 6 5 4 3   RRDV   02   01   00

Dedication

To Jessica, who definitely
inherited her father's optimism!

—*R. A. B.*

———————

To Keven Singleton Byrne
Robin Lynn Byrne
Lindsey Kelley Byrne
Rebecka Byrne Kelley
My four soul-satisfying accomplishments.

—*D. B.*

———————

To Mary Rose,
for intensive instruction
in the art of social psychology.

—*B. T. J.*

Brief Contents

Contents

chapter 3

Social Cognition: Understanding
the Social World   49

chapter 4

The Self   74

chapter 5

Attitudes: Evaluating the Social World   99

chapter 6

Prejudice and Discrimination   125

chapter 7

Interpersonal Attraction: Friendship, Love, and Relationships   152

chapter 8

Social Influence: Changing Others' Behavior   182

chapter 9

Helping and Hurting: The Nature of Prosocial Behavior and Aggression   207

chapter 10

Groups and Individuals: The Consequences of Belonging   236

chapter 11

Applying Social Psychology to
Law, Work, and Health   262

 # Preface

Social Psychology: An Integrated View

In writing the fourth edition of *Exploring Social Psychology*, it dawned on us that there are strong parallels between human behavior and fingerprints. People of all races have fingerprints, yet no two fingerprints are identical. By the same token, individuals often act very similarly to each other, yet at other times can act quite differently. In physically interacting with their environment, all humans leave fingerprints on their surroundings, usually without taking notice. Likewise, people often make indelible impressions on others via their actions and appearance, often without intending to do so.

A close look at the contents of this book will expose the fingerprints of previous editions of *Exploring Social Psychology*, our previous efforts to summarize our field in a succinct yet comprehensive way. Nonetheless, we can honestly state that this edition is anything but a superficial revision: On the contrary, this book is entirely new from previous editions. By the same token, this edition also bears more than a coincidental similarity to the most recent edition of Baron and Byrne's *Social Psychology*. *Exploring Social Psychology* was completed just 15 months after finishing the eighth edition of *Social Psychology*, and the material in the latter served as the starting point for the current book. The result is that the coverage of material is very similar between the two texts, except that the current book has done so in a more succinct fashion, while still incorporating about a year's worth of new social psychological research not included in the bigger text.

Changes in Content: Reflecting Major Trends

In writing this book, our goal was a concise yet comprehensive text that reflects the current state and knowledge-base of social psychology. Thus, we have made many changes from the third edition of *Exploring Social Psychology*, which was published ten years ago. In our view, one of the most significant trends in social psychology in recent years has been toward a level of integration—unity, coherence, and cross-fertilization between its various subfields—that it has not enjoyed since its very earliest days. Theories and principles developed in discrete areas of the field are "spilling over" more and more to other areas, and researchers who specialize in studying various topics are drawing on the findings of colleagues working in other areas of the field to an increasing degree.

What is the basis for this movement toward increased integration? Several factors appear to be playing a role. One, we suspect, is the atmosphere of coherence within all fields of science. Boundaries among traditional fields have continued to weaken, and the volume of research involving collaboration between scientists from several different fields has continued to increase. Social psychology, as a scientific discipline, has been influenced by these trends, and as a result has sought greater integration within itself.

Another factor is the real and rapid progress made by social psychology during the past six decades. During this time, basic principles of social behavior and social thought have begun to emerge with startling clarity. Moreover, in contrast to conditions prevailing in the past, many of these principles are applicable to many different contexts and many forms of social interaction. Thus, they help to connect previously separate areas of our field.

Finally, social psychologists have tried with increasing success to examine whether their principles are equally applicable to members of culturally and ethnically diverse groups. In many cases, these group memberships have no bearing on behavior, but in other instances, they do. We have incorporated two separate features to highlight the integration and the diversity of the field of social psychology.

Integration: Principles and Concepts that Apply to More than One Area

Since we view this rapid movement toward increased integration as very important, we have made strenuous efforts to represent them adequately in this text. In fact, we have made *integration* a major theme of the fourth edition. In order to bring these internal linkages into sharper focus, we have included three special features:

1. *Integrating Principles.* At several points within each chapter, we highlight major integrating principles of social psychology— principles that have emerged out of specific lines of research but which apply to many different areas of our field. As each *Integrating Principle* is presented, we also call attention to other topics in this text to which it is related. (See examples scattered throughout the book.)
2. *Connections: Integrating Social Psychology.* In order to illustrate how research in each area of social psychology is related to research in other areas, chapters are followed by special tables titled *Connections: Integrating Social Psychology.* These tables indicate how topics covered in the current chapter are related to topics covered in other chapters. *Connections* tables serve two major functions. First, they provide a kind of global review, reminding readers of related topics already covered in the text. Second, they emphasize the fact that many aspects of social behavior and social thought are closely interlinked—they do not occur in isolation from each other. (For examples, turn to the ends of Chapters 2 through 11.)
3. *Thinking about Connections.* Each of the *Connections* tables are followed by what we view as a crucial additional feature: questions designed to get readers thinking about the links described in the preceding

table. These questions, called *Thinking about Connections*, focus on specific ways in which various aspects of social behavior and social thought are linked. In other words, they bring our claims about the importance of integration within our field into sharp, concrete focus. (For examples, turn to the ends of Chapters 2 through 11.)

Together, the *Integrating Principles*, *Connections* tables, and *Thinking about Connections* questions help us to represent social psychology as it really is: an integrated field with multiple links between its diverse areas of research.

Diversity: The Multicultural Perspective in Social Psychology

An important trend within social psychology at present is its growing *multicultural perspective*. This perspective examines differences between ethnic groups within a given society, or differences across various cultures. We have attempted to highlight such research at various points throughout the text. In particular, we have also added a special section near the end of each chapter called *Social Diversity: A Critical Analysis*. These sections examine key aspects of social behavior and thought from a multicultural perspective, closely linked to the content of the chapters in which they occur. A few examples:

■ Cultural Differences in Concern about Weight (Chapter 4)
■ How Memory Loss in Our Later Years Is Influenced by Cultural Age Stereotypes (Chapter 6)
■ Love and Intimacy: Individualistic versus Collectivistic Perspectives (Chapter 7)
■ Gender Differences in Social Influence: More Apparent Than Real (Chapter 8)
■ U. S. Geographical Differences in "The Culture of Honor" (Chapter 9)
■ Differences between Asians and Americans in Responding to Stress (Chapter 11)

It is important to note that we have integrated many topics that were previously treated in special sections into the regular text. This, too, is consistent with our theme of greater integration both within and across topics. The result is a smaller number of special sections and, we believe, a less "busy" look for the book.

Changes in Content: Reflecting Recent Research

In addition to the major changes outlined above, we have attempted to keep abreast of, and describe, many new lines of research. As a result, many topics not covered in the third edition of *Exploring Social Psychology* are now included, such as:

- How face shape is related to perceptions of honesty
- The kinds of behavior people try to explain
- Counterfactual thinking (thinking about what might have been)
- Automatic priming effects in social judgments and behaviors
- Pluralistic ignorance (errors in perceiving the group judgment)
- Neuropsychological views about emotion
- Motives for evaluating the self
- Automatic identity shifts based on environmental cues
- Whether thoughts about mortality affect social judgments
- Evolutionary social psychology principles as they relate to various behaviors
- Genetic influences on attitudes
- Defense, accuracy, and impression motives in processing information
- Effects of message framing on acceptance of messages
- The "ultimate attribution error" in judging individuals based on their group membership
- The role of affects or feelings in stereotyping
- The role of social dominance orientation in employment contexts
- How need for accuracy affects conformity to false group judgments
- Cultural influences on social conformity

- The influence of group pressure on individual judgments
- The role of empathy in helping stigmatized persons
- The role of sensitivity to others' needs in sexual aggression
- Cultural differences in aggression

Continuity: What Remains the Same

As our comments above suggest, there is indeed much that is new in the content of the fourth edition. Yet we have retained several important features and perspectives. First, as in the previous edition, we have tried to be as eclectic, accurate, and up-to-date as possible in our presentation of social psychology. We perceive our role as that of describing our field as it currently exists—not expounding our own approaches or interests.

Second, as in the previous edition, we have tried to include the most significant principles of the field while still keeping the text concise. The text's brevity should make it especially useful for instructors who wish to assign additional outside readings, or those who feel that a briefer text is more appropriate to their time-frame or students.

Third, the style of writing and presentation remains unchanged. As in the past, we have aimed for clarity—softened here and there by a touch of humor. Research suggests that an occasional smile can indeed be helpful in the learning process (as well as in many other contexts), so we have retained this as a feature of our general approach.

Other Learning Aids

In addition to these features, we have included many others that are specifically designed to help students learn about—and use—social psychology. These features include:

- A user-friendly writing style in which we address readers directly and often relate experiences from our own lives.
- Annotated "For More Information" sections at the end of each chapter that de-

scribe several sources interested readers can consult.

Our own students have told us that these features are useful, and we have attempted to expand and refine them in this new edition.

Acknowledgments

In preparing this, the fourth edition of our text, many hard-working, talented people have assisted us. In some cases they literally have left their fingerprints all over this book, as the striking cover art suggests. Thus, our first thank you is for the striking cover art, which the Haley Johnson Design Company in Minneapolis, Minnesota, produced; senior designers Haley A. Johnson and Richard Boynton, production assistant Gerrard D'Amour, and research assistant Pipén D'Amour did a splendid job in graphically capturing the essence of social psychology.

Second, we wish to thank Carolyn O. Merrill, our Editor at Allyn and Bacon, for her advice and support throughout the process of writing this book.

Third, we thank Diana R. Nichols, of Syracuse University, without whose help the references would be woefully inadequate. Third, we wish to thank the persons listed below, who either read and commented on various portions of the manuscript, or made reports of their research available to us: John F. Dovidio (Colgate University), Kenneth D. Levin (Syracuse University), Bertram Malle (University of Oregon), Caroline Moseley (University of North Carolina at Greensboro), Paige A. Muellerleile (Syracuse University), Brian Mullen (Syracuse University), Diana R. Nichols (Syracuse University), Thomas Pettigrew (University of California, Santa Cruz), Charles A. Pierce (Montana State University), Richard W. Robins (University of California, Berkeley), Ralph Rosnow (Temple University), Mark Schaller (University of British Columbia), M. Blanche Serban (Syracuse University), and Wendy Wood (Texas A&M University).

Fourth, our special thanks to Omegatype Typography for editing the manuscript and designing the finished book.

Fifth, Amy Goldmacher for helping to facilitate and coordinate our efforts. Finally, our thanks to George E. Schreer of Plymouth State College for preparing an excellent instructor's manual, and to Tom Jackson of Ft. Hayes State University, for preparing an extensive test bank.

To all of these outstanding people, a warm "Thank you."

A Concluding Comment

It is our hope that you, our colleagues and readers, will find the fourth edition changes to be helpful ones. We have spared no effort in preparing this new edition. Yet we are certain that now, as in the past, there is still room for improvement. We would appreciate it greatly, therefore, if you would share your reactions with us. We do pay close attention to such feedback and always find it helpful. So please don't hesitate—send us your comments and suggestions whenever you can and as often as you wish.

Robert A. Baron
315 Lally,
Rensselaer Polytechnic Institute
Troy, NY 12180–3590
Phone: 518/276–2864
Fax: 518/276–8661
E-mail: baronr@rpi.edu

Donn Byrne
Department of Psychology
University at Albany, SUNY
Albany, NY 12222
Phone: 518/442–4827
Fax: 518/442–4867
E-mail: db034@cnsibm.albany.edu

Blair T. Johnson
Department of Psychology
430 Huntington Hall
Syracuse University
Syracuse, NY 13244–2340
Phone: 315/443–3087
Fax: 315/443–4085
E-mail: bjohnson@syr.edu
Page on the World Wide Web:
http://web.syr.edu/~bjohnson

About the Authors

Robert A. Baron is Professor of Psychology and Professor of Management at Rensselaer Polytechnic Institute. Former Chair of the Department of Psychology, he received his Ph.D. from the University of Iowa in 1968. Professor Baron has held faculty appointments at Purdue University, the University of Minnesota, University of Texas, University of South Carolina, and Princeton University. In 1982 he was a Visiting Fellow at Oxford University. From 1979 to 1981 he served as a Program Director at the National Science Foundation (Washington, D.C.). He has been a Fellow of the American Psychological Association since 1978.

Professor Baron has published more than ninety articles in professional journals and twenty-five chapters in edited volumes. He is the author or co-author of thirty books, including *Psychology* (3rd ed.), *Behavior in Organizations* (6th ed.), *Social Psychology* (8th ed.), *Human Aggression* (2nd ed.), and *Understanding Human Relations* (3rd ed.). Textbooks by Professor Baron have been used by more than 1,400,000 students in colleges and universities throughout the world.

Professor Baron served on the Board of Directors of the Albany Symphony Orchestra (1993–1996), and is President of Innovative Environmental Products, Inc., a company engaged in the design of equipment intended to enhance the physical environment of work settings and living spaces through improved air quality, elimination of distracting noise, etc. He holds three U.S. patents, two of which apply to the P. P. S.®, a desk-top device combining air filtration, noise control, and other features. This device, and the basic psychological research behind it, were featured in the APA *Monitor* (March, 1995).

Professor Baron's research currently focuses primarily on the following topics: (1) workplace aggression, (2) impact of the physical environ-ment (e.g., lighting, air quality, temperature) on social behavior and task performance, and (3) interpersonal conflict.

Donn Byrne is currently Professor of Psychology and Chairman of the Department of Psychology at the University at Albany, State University of New York. He received his Ph.D. degree in 1958 from Stanford University and has held academic positions at the California State University at San Francisco, the University of Texas, Stanford University, the University of Hawaii, and Purdue University. A past president of the Midwestern Psychological Association and a Fellow of three divisions of the American Psychological Association, he has written more than twenty books, twenty-five invited chapters, and one-hundred thirty articles. He was invited to deliver a G. Stanley Hall lecture at the 1981 meeting of the American Psychological Association in Los Angeles and a State of the Science address at the 1981 meeting of the Society for the Scientific Study of Sex. In 1987, he received an Excellence in Research Award from the University at Albany. He has served on the Editorial Boards of thirteen journals, including *Psychological Monographs*, *Journal of Experimental Social Psychology*, *Journal of Research in Personality*, *Journal of Applied Social Psychology*, *Journal of Personality*, and *Motivation and Emotion*. His current research interests include interpersonal attraction and the prediction of sexually coercive behavior. Leisure-time activities include literature, the theatre, and landscaping.

Blair T. Johnson is currently Associate Professor of Psychology and Director of Graduate Studies in Social Psychology at Syracuse University. Professor Johnson, who received his Ph.D degree in 1988 from Purdue University, has also taught at Cornell University. He has directed the graduate work of more than ten students, including 4 who have completed the Ph.D. Professor Johnson has over 35 publications in such outlets as *Personality and Social Psychology Bulletin, Journal of Experimental Social Psychology, Psychological Bulletin, AIDS and Behavior, Journal of Applied Psychology,* and *The Journal of the American Medical Association.* He currently serves on the editorial boards of the *Journal of Personality and Social Psychology,* and begins a term as associate editor of *Personality and Social Psychology Bulletin* in 1998. He has received support for his research from the National Institute of Mental Health. In general, his research focuses on theoretical and applied aspects of the psychology of attitudes and stereotypes. Professor Johnson is also an expert on the science of research synthesis, a set of quantitative techniques used to integrate the results of studies on a given topic. Professor Johnson has authored a popular computer program named *DSTAT,* which simplifies the process of research synthesis. He has also published papers that help to develop the process of doing research syntheses, which are also called meta-analyses. Currently, Professor Johnson and his colleagues have been examining what sorts of interventions provide the best protection against infection with HIV, the virus that causes AIDS. They have also been examining how social-cognitive factors, such as a person's involvement with an issue, can affect persuasion. In his leisure time, Professor Johnson enjoys art, music, sports, reading fiction, and fine dining.

chapter 1

Understanding Social Behavior: An Introduction

Why do people fall in—and out of—love? What makes relationships last—or disintegrate?

Are first impressions really as important as many people believe? And if so, what can you do to make sure that you make a good impression on others?

Are some people destined to become leaders because they possess special traits? What makes some leaders charismatic—able to exert truly amazing control over their followers?

Is aggression a built-in part of human nature, or can it somehow be reduced? Why is there so much more violence in some societies than in others?

What are the best ways of influencing other people—of changing their attitudes or their behavior? Why are we so successful at resisting efforts at persuasion most of the time?

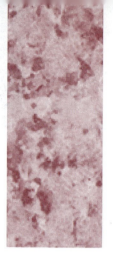

If you've ever wondered about questions like these, welcome: you've come to the right place. These questions, and hundreds like them, form the core of social psychology—the field you are about to study.

Social psychology is a branch of psychology; and, as its name suggests, it focuses on *social behavior*—how people interact with, and think about, others. This means that every form of social behavior or social thought you can imagine—including unusual ones such as that shown in Figure 1.1—falls within its scope. Because other people and our relations with them are such an important part of our lives, we believe that social psychology, too, is very important. In fact, we don't mind stating that in many respects, we view it as the *most* central part of psychology. After all, isn't a field that investigates everything from love, cooperation, and helping on the one hand through prejudice, conflict, and violence on the other, intrinsically important?

"OK," we can almost hear you saying, "so social behavior is interesting—who could disagree? But can you tell me anything about it that I don't already know? After all, I've been interacting with other people all my life." Our answer to this question comes close to capturing the essence of modern social psychology—its fundamental nature, if you will. Two points are crucial in this respect:

1. The conclusions suggested by everyday experience, and by the accumulated wisdom of poets, philosophers, and novelists, are often insightful and informative, but also quite *inconclusive*. For example, consider the following pair of well-known sayings: "Absence makes the heart grow fonder" and "Out of sight, out of mind." Can both be true, and if so, how? Common sense often leaves us facing such dilemmas and unsolved mysteries where human social behavior is concerned.

2. If so, social psychologists reason, why not use the methods of science to attain answers to age-old questions about the social side of human life? These methods have worked extremely well in helping us understand other aspects of human behavior, such as how memory works and how psychological disorders like depression can be relieved; so why not apply them to social behavior, too?

Social psychologists have operated within this scientific framework since the earliest days of their field, and the results have been, we feel, very impressive. Through systematic research, social psychologists have uncovered a great deal of interesting and useful information about practically all aspects of human social behavior. Before turning to this fascinating body of knowledge, however, it is important to provide you with some background information—some basic information about the origins, nature, and methods of social psychology. Why is such information important? Because research findings in psychology indicate that people have a much better chance of understanding, remembering, and

FIGURE 1.1 Social Behavior: The Focus of Social Psychology.

As shown in this cartoon, social behavior is tremendously varied in form—and often highly surprising!

(*Source:* Reprinted with special permission of King Features Syndicate.)

using new information if they are first provided with a framework for organizing it. That's what this introductory chapter is all about: providing you with a framework for interpreting and understanding social psychology. Specifically, we'll use the remainder of this introductory chapter for completing three preliminary tasks.

First, we'll present a more formal and complete *definition* of social psychology. Every field has basic assumptions, and it is important to recognize these and make them explicit. Doing so will help you understand why social psychologists have chosen certain topics for intensive study and why they have studied them in certain ways.

Second, we'll offer a brief overview of social psychology's *history*—how it began and developed, and where it is today. No scientific activity occurs in a vacuum: On the contrary, it generally stands on the shoulders of work that went before. Social psychology is no exception to this basic rule, so knowing something about the history of the field can help you to understand the research social psychologists are conducting today.

Finally, we will examine some of the methods used by social psychologists to answer questions about social behavior. Knowledge of these *research methods* will help you to understand and critically evaluate later discussions of specific research projects, and it will also help you to understand how the knowledge and conclusions we present throughout this text were obtained.

Social Psychology: A Working Definition

Providing a formal definition of almost any field is a complex task. In the case of social psychology, this difficulty is increased by two factors: the field's great diversity, and its rapid rate of change. Despite their diverse interests, however, most social psychologists seem to focus their attention on the following central task: Understanding how and why individuals behave, think, and feel as they do in situations involving other persons. Reflecting this fact, we will define **social psychology** as follows: *Social psychology is the scientific field that seeks to understand the nature and causes of individual behavior and thought in social situations.* In other words, social psychologists seek to understand how we think about and interact with others. We will now clarify several aspects of this definition.

Social Psychology Is Scientific in Nature

Many persons seem to believe that the term *science* refers primarily to fields such as chemistry, physics, and biology. Such persons may find somewhat puzzling our view that social psychology, too, is scientific. How can a field that seeks to investigate the nature of love, the causes of aggression, and everything in between be scientific in the same sense as astronomy, biochemistry, or geophysics? The answer is surprisingly simple. In reality, the term *science* does not refer to a select group of highly advanced fields. Rather, it refers to a general set of methods—techniques that can be used to study a wide range of topics. In deciding whether a given field is or is not scientific, therefore, the crucial question is: *Does it make use of scientific procedures?* To the extent that it does, it can be viewed as scientific in orientation. To the extent that it does not, it falls outside the realm of science.

What are these techniques and procedures? We'll describe them in detail in a later section of this chapter. Here, we'll merely note that they involve efforts to gather systematic information about issues or processes of interest, plus an attitude of *skepticism.* It is a basic premise of science that *all* assertions about the natural world should be tested, retested, and tested again before they are accepted as accurate. For example, consider the following statement made by Samuel Butler, a famous English author of the nineteenth century: "We are not won by arguments that we can analyze but by tone and temper, by . . . manner. . . ." These words suggest that persuasion rests more on the *style* of would-be persuaders than on the arguments they present. Is this true? According to the basic rules of science, we can tell

only by subjecting this idea to careful, systematic research. In fact, such research has been conducted, and we'll examine it in Chapter 5, where we consider the process of *persuasion* in detail.

In contrast, fields that are not generally regarded as scientific in nature make assertions about the natural world, and about people, that are *not* subjected to careful test. In such fields, intuition, beliefs, and special skills of practitioners are considered to be sufficient.

So, is social psychology scientific? Our reply is a definite *yes.* Although the topics that social psychologists study are very different from those in the physical or biological sciences, the methods we employ are similar in nature and orientation. For this reason, it makes sense to describe social psychology as basically scientific in nature.

Social Psychology Focuses on the Behavior of Individuals

Societies differ greatly in terms of their views concerning courtship and marriage; yet it is still individuals who fall in—and out of—love. Similarly, societies vary greatly in terms of their overall levels of violence; still, though, it is individuals who perform aggressive actions or refrain from doing so. The same argument applies to virtually all other aspects of social behavior, from prejudice to helping: The actions and cognitions in question are ultimately performed or held by individuals. Because of this basic fact, the focus, in social psychology, is squarely on individuals. Social psychologists realize, of course, that individuals do not exist in isolation from social and cultural influences—far from it. But the field's major interest lies in understanding the factors that shape the actions and thoughts of individual human beings within social settings. In contrast, the closely related field of *sociology,* which you may have studied in other courses, focuses on many of the same topics as social psychology, but its primary focus is on groups or whole societies—*not* individuals. For example, both social psychologists and sociologists study human aggression, but while social psychologists focus on factors that may cause specific individuals to engage in acts of aggression (e.g., being frustrated by another person, being in a rotten mood), sociologists tend to focus on societal causes of aggression (e.g., poor economic conditions).

Social Psychology Examines the Causes of Social Behavior and Thought

In a key sense, the heading of this section states the most central aspect of our definition. What it means is that social psychologists are principally concerned with understanding the wide range of conditions that shape the social behavior and thought of individuals—their actions, feelings, beliefs, memories, and inferences—with respect to other persons. Obviously, a huge number of different factors play a role in this regard. It is also clear, however, that most factors affecting social interaction fall into five major categories: (1) the *actions and characteristics of others*—what others say and do; (2) basic *cognitive processes* such as memory and reasoning—processes that underlie our thoughts, beliefs, ideas, and judgments about others; (3) *ecological variables*— direct and indirect influences of the physical environment, such as temperature, crowding, privacy, and related factors; (4) the *cultural context* in which social behavior and thought occur; and (5) *biological factors* and processes that are relevant to social behavior, including certain aspects of our genetic inheritance. Perhaps a few words about each of these categories will help clarify their nature, and their importance in shaping social thought and social behavior.

The Actions and Characteristics of Others. Consider the following incidents:

> You are standing in line outside a movie theater; suddenly, another person walks up and cuts in line in front of you.
>
> The person you've been dating exclusively for six months suddenly and unexpectedly says: "I think we should see other people."
>
> You make a presentation in one of your classes; after it is over, the professor remarks: "That was great—the best presentation I've heard in years!"

Will these actions by others have any impact on your behavior and thought? Absolutely. So it is clear that often we are strongly affected by the actions of other persons.

Now, be honest: Have you ever felt uneasy in the presence of a person with a physical disability? Do you ever behave differently toward highly attractive persons than toward less attractive ones? Toward elderly persons than toward young ones? Toward persons belonging to racial and ethnic groups different from your own? Your answer to some of these questions is probably *yes*, for we are often strongly influenced by the visible characteristics and appearance of others, too.

Cognitive Processes. Suppose that you are meeting a friend and this person is late. In fact, after thirty minutes, you begin to suspect that your friend will never arrive. Finally, your friend appears on the scene and says: "Sorry . . . meeting you just slipped my mind!" How will you react? Probably with considerable annoyance and irritation. Imagine that instead, however, your friend said: "I'm so sorry to be late. . . . There was a big accident, and the traffic was tied up for miles." Now how will you react? Probably with less annoyance, although not necessarily. If your friend is habitually late and has used similar excuses before, you may well be suspicious about whether this explanation is true. In contrast, if this is the first time your friend has been late for an appointment, or if the friend has never used such an excuse before, you may accept the explanation as true. In other words, your reactions in this situation will depend strongly upon your *memories* of your friend's past behavior, and will also involve your *inferences* concerning the true explanation for your friend's lateness. Instances like this, which are very common, call attention to the important role of *cognitive processes*—memory, inference, judgment, and so on—in social behavior and social thought. Social psychologists are well aware of the importance of such processes and realize that they must be taken into careful account in our efforts to understand many, if not most, aspects of social behavior (Wyer & Srull, 1994).

Ecological Variables: Impact of the Physical Environment. Do we become more irritable and aggressive when the weather is hot and steamy than when it is cool and comfortable (Anderson, Deuser, & DeNeve, 1995)? Does exposure to high levels of noise, air pollution, or excessive levels of crowding have any impact on our social behavior or performance of various tasks? Research findings indicate that the physical environment does indeed influence our feelings, thoughts, and behavior, so ecological variables certainly fall within the realm of modern social psychology (R. A. Baron, 1994; P. A. Bell et al., 1995).

Cultural Context. Social behavior, it is important to note, does not occur in a cultural vacuum. On the contrary, it is often strongly affected by cultural norms (social rules concerning how people should behave in specific situations), membership in various groups, and shifting societal values. Whom should people marry? How many children should they have? Should people keep their emotional reactions to themselves or demonstrate them openly? How close should they stand to others when talking to them? Is it appropriate to offer gifts to public officials in order to obtain their favorable action on various requests? Do people from different geographic regions within a country differ in their social behavior? These are only a small sampling of the aspects of social behavior that can be—and are—influenced by cultural factors. By *culture* we simply mean the organized system of shared meanings, perceptions, and beliefs held by persons belonging to some group (P. B. Smith & Bond, 1993).

As we'll note below, attention to the effects of cultural factors is an increasingly important trend in modern social psychology as our field attempts to take account of the growing cultural diversity that is a hallmark of the late twentieth century.

Biological Factors. Is social behavior influenced by biological processes and by genetic factors? Ten years ago, most social psychologists would have

answered *no*, at least to the genetic factors part of this question. Now, however, the pendulum of scientific opinion has swung in the other direction, and many believe that our preferences, behaviors, emotional reactions, and even attitudes and values are affected to some extent by the genes passed on to us by our parents (Buss, 1990; Nisbett, 1990).

The most dramatic argument for the belief that genetic factors have a large and unchangeable influence on human social behavior has been voiced by those in the field of **sociobiology.** In essence, this perspective suggests that we all exist primarily to serve our genes—to ensure that our genetic material is passed on to as many offspring as possible (Barkow, 1989; E. O. Wilson, 1975). This basic assumption, in turn, is used to explain many aspects of social behavior. In contrast, **evolutionary social psychology** (Buss, 1996, in press) suggests that social behavior is indeed affected by natural selection; tendencies toward behaviors that are most adaptive from the point of view of survival often increase in strength over time within a given population. But it also recognizes the fact that such tendencies are definitely not set in stone. On the contrary, they can—and do—change in response to shifting environmental and social conditions, and they can even be altered or overridden by cognitive processes.

Although evolutionary social psychology is a relatively new field, researchers in it have already gathered intriguing evidence pointing to the potential role of genetic or evolutionary factors in human behavior. For example, recent research on *mate preference*—the characteristics individuals seek in potential romantic partners—indicates that males and females may differ in some intriguing ways. Females tend to place greater emphasis on such characteristics as dominance and status, while males place greater emphasis on youth and physical attractiveness (Kenrick et al., 1994; see Figure 1.2). This difference is consistent with an evolutionary perspective noting that females invest greater resources in bearing children than males do in fathering them. Thus, from the standpoint of successfully passing one's genes on to the next generation, it makes sense for fe-

FIGURE 1.2   Mate Preference: Do Genetic Factors Play a Role?

In many societies, males place greater emphasis than females on the physical attractiveness of potential romantic partners, while females place greater emphasis than males on status or dominance. Research findings suggest that such differences may stem, at least in part, from genetic predispositions.

males to seek mates who will be able to provide the resources needed for child rearing (mates high in status or dominance). For males, in contrast, it makes sense to seek mates who are young and healthy, and so capable of bearing many offspring. We should emphasize that while findings pointing to such differences are consistent with an evolutionary approach, they do not in any way prove its accuracy. However, a growing number of social psychologists believe that an evolutionary perspective is an informative one, so we'll refer to this approach at several points within this book (for instance, see our discussion of this topic in Chapter 7).

Social Psychology: Summing Up

To conclude: Social psychology focuses mainly on understanding the causes of social behavior and social thought—on identifying factors that shape our feelings, behavior, and thought in social situations. It seeks to accomplish this goal through the use of scientific methods, and it takes careful note of the fact that social behavior and thought are influenced by a wide range of social, cognitive, environmental, cultural, and biological factors.

The remainder of this text describes some of the key findings of social psychology. This information is truly fascinating, so we're certain that you will find it of interest. We're equally sure, however, that you will find some of it to be surprising, and that it will challenge many of your current ideas about people and social relations. So please get ready for some new insights. We predict that after learning about social psychology, you'll never think about social behavior in quite the same way as before.

The Origins and Development of Social Psychology

When, precisely, did social psychology begin? This question is difficult to answer, for speculation about social behavior stretches back to ancient times (G. W. Allport, 1985). Any attempt to present a complete survey of the historical roots of our field would quickly bog us down in more detail than is necessary. For this reason, we'll focus, in this discussion, on the emergence of social psychology as an independent field, its growth in recent decades, and current trends that appear to be shaping its present—and future—form.

The Early Years: Social Psychology Emerges

Few fields of science mark their beginnings with formal ribbon-cutting ceremonies. Instead they develop gradually, as growing numbers of scientists become interested in specific topics or develop new methods for studying existing ones. This pattern applies to social psychology: No bottles of champagne were uncorked to mark its entry on the scene, so it is difficult to choose a specific date for its official launching. Nonetheless, most social psychologists mark 1924 as the year when social psychology first attained status as an independent entity. In that year, an important text named *Social Psychology* was published by Floyd H. Allport. In contrast to several other earlier texts, this book is much closer to the modern orientation of our field. Allport argued that social behavior results from many different factors, including the presence of other persons and their specific actions. Further, his book emphasized the value of experimentation and contained discussions of actual research that had already been conducted on such topics as conformity, the ability to recognize others' emotions from their facial expressions, and the impact of audiences

on task performance. All of these topics have been studied by social psychologists in recent years, so the following conclusion seems justified: By the middle of the Roaring Twenties, social psychology had appeared on the scene and had begun to investigate many of the topics it still studies today (D. Katz, Johnson, & Nichols, in press).

The two decades following publication of Allport's text were marked by rapid growth. New issues were studied and new methods for investigating them were devised. Important milestones in the development of the field during this period include research by two of its founders—Muzafer Sherif and Kurt Lewin. Sherif (1935) studied the nature and impact of *social norms*—rules indicating how individuals ought to behave—and so contributed basic insights to our understanding of pressures toward *conformity*. Kurt Lewin and his colleagues (e.g., Lewin, Lippitt, & White, 1939) carried out revealing research on the nature of leadership and other group processes. Quite apart from this research, Lewin's influence on social psychology was profound, for many of his students went on to become very prominent contributors to the field. Their names—Leon Festinger, Harold Kelley, Morton Deutsch, Stanley Schachter, John Thibaut—read like a "Who's Who" of famous social psychologists during the 1950s, 1960s, and even 1970s. In short, by the close of the 1930s, social psychology was an active, growing field that had already contributed much to our knowledge of social behavior.

Social Psychology's Youth: The 1940s, 1950s, and 1960s

Spurred in part by World War II, social psychology continued its growth during the 1940s and 1950s. Social psychologists focused attention on the influence that groups and group membership exert on individual behavior, on the links between personality traits and behavior, and on techniques to alter attitudes. Each of these areas of research was important to the efforts to win the War or to understand what happened in it. For example, social psychologists examined various ways to increase the rate at which U.S. citizens bought war bonds.

One of the most important events of this period was the development of the theory of **cognitive dissonance** (Festinger, 1957). This theory proposed that human beings dislike inconsistency and strive to reduce it. Briefly, the theory argues that people seek to eliminate inconsistency between different attitudes that they hold, or between their attitudes and their behavior. While this theory may strike you as being quite sensible, it actually leads to many unexpected predictions. For example, dissonance theory suggests that offering individuals small rewards for stating views they don't really hold is often more effective in getting them to change these opinions than offering them larger rewards for the same actions. We'll examine the explanation of this surprising fact, sometimes known as the *less-leads-to-more effect,* in detail in Chapter 5.

In an important sense the 1960s can be viewed as the time when social psychology came of age. During this turbulent decade of rapid social change, the number of social psychologists rose dramatically, and the field expanded to include practically every aspect of social interaction you might imagine. So many lines of research either began or expanded during these years that it is impossible to list them all here, but among the most important were these: *interpersonal attraction* and *romantic love; impression formation, attribution,* and other aspects of *social perception;* and many different aspects of *social influence,* such as *obedience, conformity*, and *compliance.*

The 1970s, 1980s, and 1990s: A Maturing Field

The rapid pace of change did not slacken during the 1970s; if anything, it accelerated. Many lines of research begun during the 1960s were expanded, and several new topics rose to prominence. Among the most important of these were *attribution* (the process through which we seek to understand the causes of others' behavior— *why* they act as they do; see Chapter 2); *gender differences* and *sex discrimination* (investigation

of the extent to which the behavior of women and men actually differs, and the impact of negative stereotypes concerning the traits supposedly possessed by both genders; see Chapters 4 and 6). In addition, three larger-scale important trends took shape during the 1980s and 1990s:

1. Growing Influence of a Cognitive Perspective. As noted earlier, social psychologists have long recognized the importance of cognitive factors— attitudes, beliefs, values, inferences—in social behavior. Starting in the late 1970s, however, interest in such topics took an important new form. At this time, many social psychologists concluded that our understanding of virtually all aspects of social behavior could be greatly enhanced by attention to the cognitive processes that underlie them. The cognitive approach involves efforts to apply basic knowledge about cognitive processes such as *memory* and *reasoning* to the task of understanding many aspects of social thought and behavior. For example, within this context, social psychologists have recently sought to determine whether various forms of prejudice may stem, at least in part, from the operation of basic cognitive processes, such as the tendency to remember only information consistent with stereotypes of various groups, or tendencies to process information about one's own social group differently from information about other social groups (Forgas & Fiedler, 1996; see Chapter 6). The results of research conducted within this cognitive perspective have been impressive, and have added greatly to our understanding of many aspects of social behavior.

2. Growing Emphasis on Application: Using Social Knowledge. Recent decades have also been marked by a second major trend in social psychology: growing concern with the *application* of social knowledge. An increasing number of social psychologists have turned their attention to practical questions concerning *personal health, the legal process, social behavior in work settings,* and a host of other issues. This theme is certainly not new in our field; Kurt Lewin, one of its founders, once remarked, "There's nothing as practical as a good theory," by which he meant that theories of social behavior and thought developed through systematic research often turn out to be extremely useful in solving practical problems. There seems little doubt, however, that interest in applying the knowledge of social psychology to practical issues has increased greatly in recent years, with many beneficial results. We'll examine this work in detail in Chapter 11.

3. Growing Emphasis on Social Diversity: Adopting a Multicultural Perspective. A final major trend is the development of a *multicultural perspective* in social psychology. In the 1950s, about 90 percent of the population of the United States was of European descent; the figure is about 75 percent now. The

United States is thus becoming far more diverse racially and ethnically than it once was (see Figure 1.3).

This growing diversity raises some important questions for social psychology. At the present time, a large majority of the world's practicing social psychologists live and work in North America. As a result, a large proportion of all research in social psychology has been conducted in the United States and Canada. Can the findings of these studies be generalized to other cultures? In other words, are the principles established in North American research applicable to people all around the world? As noted by P. B. Smith and Bond (1993), this is an open question. Most social psychologists have assumed that the findings of their research are generalizable across cultures, and

---

FIGURE 1.3   Increasing Diversity: Definitely the Wave of the Future in the United States.

As shown here, the proportion of various minority groups is projected to increase sharply in the United States in the future. Similar trends are also occurring in many other countries.

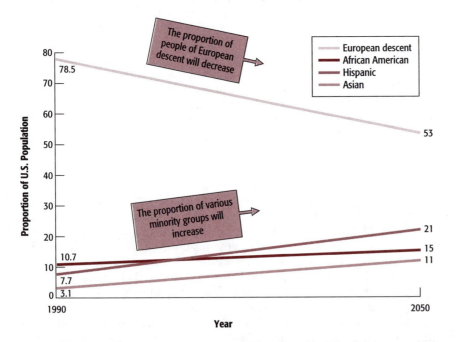

(*Source:* Based on data collected by the U.S. Department of Labor as reported by Carnevale & Stone, 1995.)

that the processes they study are ones operating among human beings everywhere. At first glance, this seems to be a very reasonable view. After all, why should love and attraction, conformity, persuasion, or prejudice operate differently on different continents? On closer examination, however, it may be that even these basic processes are strongly affected by cultural factors (P. B. Smith & Bond, 1993). For example, some cultures do not seem to possess the notion of *romantic love* that is so prevalent in Western cultures. Do people in these cultures form long-term relationships in the same manner as people in cultures where the idea of romantic love is popular? Perhaps; but perhaps they do not. In any case, it is increasingly clear to social psychologists that such questions are important, and that they should be carefully investigated. Merely assuming that basic aspects of social behavior are much the same around the globe is not acceptable.

Mirroring this concern, social psychology has moved in recent years toward a **multicultural perspective**—increased recognition of the importance of cultural factors and human diversity. For example, social psychologists have increasingly recognized that study results obtained with one gender may not apply to the other gender (Eagly, 1995). As one concrete indicator of this realization, studies in one important research journal, the *Journal of Personality and Social Psychology*, have been more and more likely to include both male and female participants. In 1968, only 51 percent of the studies included both genders; by 1988 this figure had risen to 82 percent (West, Newsom, & Fenaughty, 1992). This way, the possibility of gender differences in social behavior can be examined. Similarly, the proportion of published articles with a female senior author has also risen in this journal.

To reflect this new emphasis on multiculturalism, every chapter in this text (after this one) contains a special section titled Social Diversity. These sections highlight research dealing with cultural diversity and its effects, and relate such research to other topics covered within the chapter. They reflect our belief that interest in cultural differences, and in their origins, is a rising trend in social psychology.

How Social Psychology Attains Knowledge

Now that you know what social psychology is and how it developed, it is appropriate for us to turn to another essential issue: How do social psychologists attempt to answer questions about social behavior and social thought? How do they seek to expand our knowledge of these topics? To provide you with a useful overview of this process, we will examine three related issues. First, we will describe two key *methods of research in social psychology*. Next, we will consider the role of *theory* in such research. Finally, we will examine some of the complex *ethical issues* that arise in social psychological research and that, to a degree, are unique to such research.

The Experimental Method

Because the subject matter of our field is so diverse, social psychologists actually use many different methods in their research. Two, however, are used much more frequently than all the others: the *experimental method* of research and the *correlational method* of research. Because the experimental method is generally the one preferred by social psychologists, we'll begin with this powerful tool for understanding social behavior, and then turn to the correlational method.

Experience with our own students tells us that many view the *experimental method* (or *experimentation* for short) as somewhat mysterious and complex. In fact, in its essential logic, it is quite simple. To help you understand its use in social psychological research, we will first describe the basic nature of experimentation and then comment on two conditions essential for its successful use.

Experimentation: Its Basic Nature. A researcher who decides to employ **experimentation** (or the experimental method) generally begins with a clear-cut goal: to determine whether (and to what extent) a specific factor (variable) influences some aspect of social behavior. To find out, the researcher then (1) systematically varies the presence or strength of this factor, and (2) tries to determine whether those variations have any impact on the aspect of social behavior or thought under investigation. The central idea behind these procedures is this: If the factor varied *does* exert such effects, individuals exposed to different amounts (levels) of the factor should show different patterns of behavior. Exposure to a small amount of the factor should result in one level or pattern of behavior, exposure to a larger amount should result in another pattern, and so on.

Generally, the factor systematically varied by the researcher is termed the **independent variable,** while the aspect of behavior studied is termed the **dependent variable.** In a simple experiment, then, participants in different groups are exposed to contrasting levels of the independent variable (low, moderate, high). The researcher then carefully compares the behavior of persons in these various groups (sometimes known as *conditions*) to determine whether behavior does in fact vary with different levels of the independent variable. If it does—and if two other conditions described below are also met— the researcher can tentatively conclude that the independent variable does indeed affect the aspect of behavior or cognition being studied.

Perhaps a concrete example will help you to grasp the basic nature of this process. Let's consider an experiment designed to examine the *hypothesis* (an as yet unverified suggestion) that when people are in a good mood, they are more willing to help others. In such research, the independent variable would be some factor designed to put people into a good mood—for example, providing them with an unexpected gift. The dependent variable would be some measure of their willingness to help others—for example, the amount of time they are willing to donate to a researcher who asks for their help as an unpaid volunteer. How would such a study proceed? Something like this:

1. Participants would come to the place where the study was being conducted one at a time, and then, as part of the general procedures, would receive either a small gift (perhaps a small bag of candy) or no gift. The latter condition would serve as a *control condition,* since in it the variable expected to influence participants' behavior is absent. Control conditions provide a baseline against which the effects of different levels of an independent variable can be compared.

2. After receiving or not receiving a gift, participants would perform various activities; for instance, they might work on various puzzles or fill out questionnaires.

3. As part of these procedures, they would also be given an opportunity to help one or more other persons. For instance, they might receive a request for help from a work partner, or be asked by the researcher to donate some of their time for another study. The same opportunities to engage in helping behavior would be given to participants in both of the experimental conditions—small gift, no gift. Whether participants said yes or no, and the amount of help they offered, would then serve as *dependent variables*—measures of their willingness to help others.

4. If the hypothesis were correct, the results might look something like those in Figure 1.4: Those receiving a gift would say yes more often and offer more of their time than those not receiving a gift (those in the control condition). Researchers usually use statistics to examine whether a given hypothesis holds up. In fact, research very much like this hypothetical experiment has been conducted, and the results do resemble those shown in Figure 1.4 (e.g., M. S. Clark, 1991). We'll examine such research in Chapter 9.

At this point, we should note that this example describes an extremely simple case—the simplest type of experiment social psychologists ever conduct. In many instances, researchers wish to

FIGURE 1.4 Experimentation: A Simple Example.

In the experiment illustrated here, participants in one group are given a small gift—a procedure designed to enhance their current mood—before receiving a request for help. In contrast, the control group does not receive the gift before receiving the request for help. Results indicate that those receiving the gift are more likely to say yes and to donate more time. This finding provides support for the hypothesis that persons in a good mood are more willing to help others.

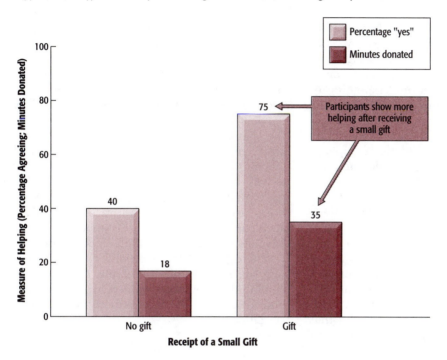

examine the impact of several independent variables at once. For example, in the study just described, they might want to consider not only the effects of mood on helping, but also perhaps the effects of the effort involved. This is because it seems possible that being in a good mood may well increase willingness to help others, but only when the effort involved is quite low. When a high degree of effort is involved, even feeling "on top of the world" may not be enough to increase overt helping. How could this possibility be studied? One possibility would involve varying the size of the request made. In a *low-effort* condition, the researcher would explain that helping would involve completing some simple questionnaires. In a *high-effort* condition, in contrast, the researcher might explain that helping would involve a more effortful (and potentially embarrassing) task, such as calling people on the phone and asking them for money. When two or more variables are included in an experiment, a larger amount of information about the topic of interest can usually be obtained. In real social situations, after all, our behavior and thought are usually influenced by many different factors acting concurrently, not simply by one factor. Even more important, potential **interactions** between variables can be examined—we can determine whether the impact of one independent variable is affected in some manner by one or more other variables. For example, consider the amount of effort involved in helping: Does being in a good mood increase helping regardless of the amount of effort involved? Or do such effects occur only when effort is fairly low?

Successful Experimentation: Two Basic Requirements. Earlier, we mentioned that before we can conclude that an independent variable has affected some form of behavior, two important conditions must be met. A basic understanding of these conditions is essential for evaluating the usefulness of any experiment.

The first condition involves what is usually termed the **random assignment of participants to groups.** According to this principle, each person taking part in a study must have an equal chance of being exposed to each level of the independent variable. The reason for this rule is simple: If participants are *not* randomly assigned to each group, it may prove impossible to determine whether differences in their behavior in the study stem from differences they brought with them, from the impact of the independent variable, or from both. For instance, continuing with our study of mood and helping, suppose that most of the participants who receive a small gift participate in the study late in the afternoon, when they are tired and somewhat grumpy as a result of having sat in four or five classes. In contrast, those in the no-gift condition participate in the early afternoon, right after having eaten lunch. Now, assume that results indicate that there is no difference between the two conditions in terms of helping. Does this mean that helping is *not* affected by mood? Perhaps; but it may also reflect the fact that persons who take part in the study in the late afternoon are so tired and irritable that a small gift is not sufficient to improve their mood—or at least, not sufficient to improve their mood to the point where it influences their willingness to help others. Such problems can be avoided if, instead, persons who participate early and late in the afternoon are equally distributed across the two conditions (gift, no-gift). So, as you can see, it is crucial that all participants in

an experiment have an equal chance of being assigned to different experimental groups.

The second condition may be stated as follows: Insofar as possible, all other factors that might also affect participants' behavior, aside from the independent variable, must be held constant. To see why, consider what would happen if, in the study on mood and helping, two different researchers who differ greatly in personal attractiveness collected data. Further, imagine that the highly attractive one conducted the gift condition, while the less attractive one conducted the no-gift condition. Now, assume that results indicate more helping by participants who received a small gift. What is the cause of this result? The gift? The researcher's high level of attractiveness? Both? Obviously, in this situation, it is impossible to tell. In this case, the independent variable (receipt of a small gift) is *confounded* with another variable—researcher's attractiveness. When such **confounding** occurs, it is impossible to determine the cause of any differences among the various experimental conditions. The result: findings are largely uninterpretable. (In this case, confounding could be avoided by assuring that both researchers conducted both experimental conditions.)

The Correlational Method

Earlier, we noted that experimentation is the preferred method of research in social psychology. (We'll see why below.) For two reasons, however, there are instances when experimentation simply cannot be used. First, systematic variation in some factor of interest may be beyond the experimenter's control. Imagine, for example, that a researcher believes that politicians who use certain techniques of persuasion in their speeches are more likely to win elections than ones who do not. Obviously, it would be very difficult for the researchers to convince one group of candidates to use these techniques, and another to refrain from using them, so that the researchers could then see how many in each condition would win their elections.

Second, ethical constraints may prevent a researcher from conducting what might otherwise be a feasible experiment. In other words, it might be possible to vary some factor of interest, but doing so would violate ethical standards accepted by scientists or society. Suppose a researcher had good reason to believe that certain factors increase the likelihood of violence in intimate relationships—for example, exposure to a large number of films containing such violence. In this case, although the researcher could imagine ways of testing this hypothesis, doing so would be unethical. After all, researchers clearly do not have the right to expose individuals to conditions that might increase the chances that they, or their romantic partners, would become the victims of violent assaults. Certainly, no ethical social psychologist would consider conducting such research, and anyone who *did* perform such research would be strongly censured by his or her colleagues for doing so.

When confronted with such problems, social psychologists often adopt an alternative research technique known as the **correlational method.** In this approach, researchers make no efforts to change one or more variables in order to observe the effects of these changes on some other variable. Instead, they merely observe naturally occurring changes in the variables of interest to learn if changes in one are associated with changes in the other. Such associations are known as *correlations*, and the stronger the association, the higher the correlation. (Correlations range from –1.00 to +1.00, and the greater the departure from 0.00, the stronger the relationship between the variables in question.)

To illustrate the correlational method, let's return once again to our study of mood and helping. A researcher wishing to examine this issue by means of the correlational method might proceed as follows. The researcher might stand near persons seeking donations for charities and then might ask passersby to rate their current moods. The researcher could simply ask: "On a scale of 1 to 7, where 1 is sad and 7 is happy, how do you feel right now?" If mood is related to helping, then the researcher might find a positive correlation between people's self-reported moods, the likelihood that they would make a donation, and the amount given if they did choose to donate. Note that in this case, the researcher makes no effort to vary the moods of passersby; rather, the researcher obtains information about two variables—the current mood of passersby and their level of generosity—to determine if these variables are related.

The correlational method offers several advantages. For one thing, social psychologists can use it to study behavior in many real-life settings. The findings obtained can then serve as the basis for more refined laboratory research. For another, this method is often highly efficient and can yield a large amount of interesting data in a short time. Moreover, it can be extended to include many different variables at once. Thus, in the study described above, information about the age and gender of passersby, as well as whether they donate, could be obtained. Through a statistical procedure known as *regression analysis*, the extent to which each of these variables is related to—and therefore predicts—helping behavior could then be examined.

Unfortunately, however, the correlational method suffers from one major drawback: *In contrast to experimentation, the findings it yields are almost always ambiguous with respect to cause-and-effect associations.* The fact that changes in one variable are accompanied by changes in another in no way guarantees that a causal link exists between them—that changes in the first caused changes in the second. Rather, in many cases, the fact that two variables tend to rise or fall together simply reflects the fact that both are caused by a third variable. For example, among males, yearly income is *negatively* related to the amount of hair on men's heads. Does this mean that wealth causes baldness? Hardly. Instead, it is clear, both variables are related to a third factor—*age*. As age increases, hair decreases, while experience and salary tend to increase. Perhaps this key point about correlations can best be clarified by a few additional examples. These are listed in Table 1.1. Can you identify the third factors that may underlie the relationships shown in the table? (Possible answers are provided.)

TABLE 1.1 ■ Correlation Doesn't Imply Causation: Some Examples

All of the correlations shown here have been observed. However, none indicates that the two factors are causally linked. Can you suggest one or more additional factors that might underlie each of the relationships shown here? (Some possible answers appear below.)

OBSERVED CORRELATION	POSSIBLE UNDERLYING CAUSE
The more money people earn, the fewer children they tend to have.	
The greater degree of crowding in cities, the higher their crime rates.	
People with larger feet have higher IQ scores.	

Answers:

1. The more people earn, the more education they have and the more effective methods of birth control they tend to use. *Or:* The more people earn, the more readily they can afford to purchase effective means of birth control, which often are expensive.

2. The greater the degree of crowding, the greater the poverty, and poverty is related to crime. *Or:* The greater the degree of crowding, the larger the number of people out on the streets, so the greater the number of potential victims.

3. Children have smaller feet than adults and score worse on IQ tests.

By now the main point should be clear. The existence of even a strong correlation between two factors is *not* a definite indication that they are causally related. Such conclusions are justified only in the presence of additional confirming evidence.

Issues in Interpreting—and Trusting—Research Findings

Let's return once again to the research question we have addressed several times already: *Does being in a good mood increase the tendency to help others?* Suppose that we conducted a very careful experiment on this topic that yielded very clear results: Participants exposed to a treatment designed to elevate their mood did in fact offer more help than those not exposed to such a treatment. On the basis of these results, can we conclude that our hypothesis has been confirmed?

While it might be tempting to answer yes, social psychologists would take a somewhat different stand. They'd agree that we are off to a good start and that initial findings are indeed consistent with the hypothesis. However, before concluding that this hypothesis represents *truth*—an accurate description of the social world—they would require additional evidence. Social psychologists would require that many other investigators, too, *confirm* these results in subsequent studies. In other words, they would insist that the initial findings be *replicated* (reproduced) over and over again—preferably in studies employing a wide range of methods, different measures of helping, different determinants of mood, and different populations. So, for example, before accepting the hypothesis that being in a good mood increases helping, they would want to see this finding replicated not just in several laboratory studies but out in the "real world" as well—in what social psychologists often term *natural field settings*.

And here's where a serious problem enters the picture: only rarely do the results of any behavioral research yield totally consistent findings. A more common pattern is for some studies to offer support for a given hypothesis while others fail to offer such support. Why is this so? In part, because different researchers may use different methods. For example, some may seek to induce a good mood by providing participants with a small gift, while others may attempt to accomplish the same goal by praising participants' work on some task. It is possible that these different procedures elevate mood to a different extent, and that only when mood is raised above some threshold does helping increase. This is only one example; there are many other reasons why research results may differ from study to study. Whatever the cause, such inconsistent results raise important questions that must be addressed.

Interpreting Diverse Results: The Role of Research Synthesis.

What do social psychologists do when the results of different studies designed to test the same hypothesis don't agree? In the past, they would review all existing evidence and then, on the basis of what can best be described as insight and personal judgment, would try to reach some conclusion about the meaning of these diverse results. In other words, they would try to determine, in a relatively informal manner, whether most of the studies they reviewed showed one particular pattern of results. This approach, which involved what are sometimes known as *narrative reviews* clearly left a lot to be desired.

Fortunately, there is now a better means of dealing with such situations—of combining the results of independent studies in order to reach conclusions about the hypotheses they all investigate. This technique is known as **research synthesis**—procedures for systematically combining the results of many different studies in order to estimate the *direction* and *size* of the effects of the independent variables in these studies. In other words, after performing an appropriate research synthesis, a social psychologist can reach conclusions about whether, and to what extent, a particular variable influenced some aspect of social behavior *across many different studies*. Because this type of research, which is also known as **meta-analysis**, relies on mathematical procedures, many social psychologists believe that its results are more conclusive than those of informal narrative reviews (e.g., B. T. Johnson & Eagly, in press). Thus, research synthesis is an important tool for understanding

the results of social psychological research, and so for understanding social behavior and social cognition.

Beyond Replication: Converging Operations in Social Psychology.

Earlier, we noted that the mere fact that a research finding can be replicated—reproduced under the same conditions—is not sufficient to overcome scientific skepticism. Before social psychologists accept a finding as valid, they prefer that it be obtained in other settings and under other conditions that, although different from the original context, *are logically related to it*. This principle is known as **converging operations,** and is often used by social psychologists. Briefly, it suggests that if a particular variable affects some aspect of social behavior by influencing an underlying psychological mechanism (for example, elevations in mood), then other variables that influence the same psychological mechanism should produce similar effects *even if they seem very different from the initial variable.*

To illustrate the value of converging operations, let's return once more to the hypothesis that persons in a good mood are more helpful than those in a neutral mood. Assume that initial studies designed to test this hypothesis all seek to place some participants in a good mood by giving them a small gift. So far, so good. But if this hypothesis is really accurate, then shouldn't increased helpfulness be found in response to *any variable* that puts people in a good mood? In other words, the mood–helping relationship should not be restricted to receipt of a small gift. It should also be evident if, for example, participants are praised for their work or are shown a very funny comedy film. If research findings indicate that this is the case, then confidence in the accuracy of the hypothesis is strengthened further.

The Role of Theory in Social Psychology

Over the years, students in our classes have often asked: "How do social psychologists come up with such interesting ideas for their research?" There is no simple answer. Some research projects are suggested by informal observation of the social worlds around us. Social psychologists take note of some puzzling aspect of social behavior or social thought and plan investigations to increase their understanding of that aspect. On other occasions, the idea for a research project is suggested by the findings of an earlier study. Successful experiments in social psychology do not simply answer questions—they raise new ones as well (Wegner, 1992). Perhaps the most important basis for research ideas in social psychology, however, is formal **theories.**

In simple terms, theories represent efforts by scientists in any field to answer the question *Why?* Theories involve attempts to understand precisely why certain events or processes occur as they do. Theories go beyond mere observation or description of aspects of social behavior; they seek to *explain* them as well. The development of comprehensive, accurate theories is a primary goal of all science, and social psychology is no exception (Schaller, Crandall, Stangor, & Neuberg, 1995). Thus, a great deal of research in our field is concerned with efforts to construct, test, and refine theoretical frameworks. But what are theories, and how are they used in social psychological research?

To answer this question, imagine that a social psychologist is interested in the following question: *Why* are people in a good mood more willing to help others than people in a neutral mood? After examining existing literature, the researcher finds that several possibilities exist. For example, perhaps people in a good mood want to "keep a good thing going," and since helping others tends to make us feel good, they are more likely to help for this reason. Another possibility is that being in a good mood causes people to think positive thoughts about themselves; and because "nice people" help others when they need aid, this factor, too, may contribute to increased helping when people are in a good mood. However, the researcher may also note some findings suggesting that such effects occur only when the effort involved in helping others is not too great.

Putting these ideas together, the social psychologist now formulates a preliminary theory: *People in a good mood help others in order to maintain their good moods and to maintain their own positive self-image. However, they will do so*

only when the effort required is not very great. In fields of science such as physics or chemistry, theories are often stated as mathematical equations. In social psychology, however, they are usually phrased as verbal statements or assertions such as the ones above. Regardless of how they are expressed, theories consist of two main parts: (1) several basic concepts (in this example, mood, helping, mood maintenance, self-image, cost of helping), and (2) statements concerning relationships among these concepts ("People in a good mood try to maintain their happy state by helping others when the cost is not high").

Formulation of a theory is just the first step in a continuing process; several procedures normally follow. First, predictions are derived from the theory. These predictions are formulated in accordance with basic principles of logic and are known as *hypotheses.* For example, one hypothesis from the theory we just described is as follows: If people in a good mood can maintain their mood in some other way than by helping others and this alternative requires less effort, they will *not* be more helpful than people in a more neutral mood.

Next, hypotheses are tested in actual research. If they are confirmed, confidence in the accuracy of the theory is increased. If they are disconfirmed, however, confidence in the theory is reduced. Then the theory may be altered so as to generate new predictions. These are subjected to test, and the process continues. If the modified predictions are confirmed, confidence in the revised theory is increased; if they are disconfirmed, the theory may be modified again or, ultimately, rejected. Figure 1.5 summarizes this process.

Confirming evidence obtained in careful research is a crucial feature of useful theories in any field of science. In addition, however, successful theories—ones that are viewed as useful by scientists—have several other features. First, they help to organize and explain a wide range of findings. For example, the theory above would help explain why people in a good mood are more helpful to others in some situations (when the effort required is low), but not more helpful in others (when the effort required is very high). Second, successful theories can be expanded so

FIGURE 1.5   Theory: An Important Basis for Research in Social Psychology.

Once a theory has been formulated, predictions derived from it are tested through actual research. If these are confirmed, confidence in the theory's accuracy is increased. If they are disconfirmed, confidence in the theory's accuracy is reduced. The theory may then be modified to generate new predictions or, ultimately, may be rejected.

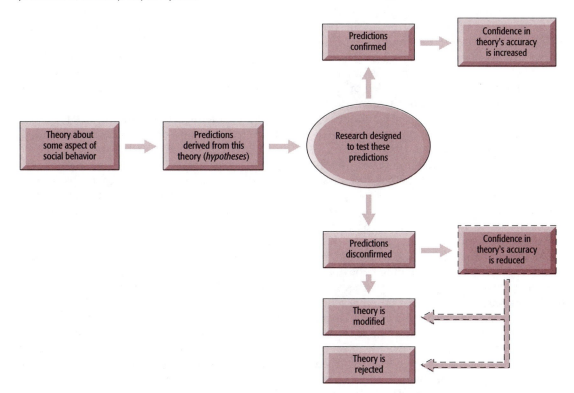

as to explain an increasingly broad range of phenomena. For instance, a useful theory concerned with how current moods affect helping might, ultimately, deal with the effects of bad moods as well as of good ones.

Two final points: First, theories are never *proven* in any final, ultimate sense. Rather, they are always open to test, and are accepted with more or less confidence depending on the weight of available evidence. Second, research is *not* undertaken to prove or verify a theory: It is performed to gather evidence relevant to the theory. If a researcher sets out to "prove" her or his pet theory correct, this is a serious violation of scientific skepticism!

Balancing the Quest for Knowledge with Study Participants' Rights

In their use of experimentation and systematic observation, and in their emphasis on theory construction, social psychologists do not differ from researchers in many other fields. One technique, however, does seem to be unique to research in social psychology: **deception.** This technique involves efforts by researchers to withhold or conceal information about the purposes of a study from participants. The reason for using this procedure is simple: Many social psychologists believe that if participants know the true purposes of an investigation, their behavior will be changed by that knowledge. Then the research will have little chance of providing valid information.

In fact, some kinds of research do seem to require the use of temporary deception. For example, imagine that in a study designed to examine the effects of physical attractiveness on first impressions, participants were informed of this purpose. Would they now react differently to a highly attractive stranger than they would have in the absence of this information? Perhaps, for now, they would bend over backwards to demonstrate that *they* are not affected by others' appearance. In this and many other cases, social psychologists feel compelled to employ temporary deception in their research (Suls & Rosnow, 1988).

However, the use of deception raises important ethical issues that cannot be ignored. First, of course, there is the chance, however slim, that deception may result in some kind of harm to the persons exposed to it (Baumrind, 1985). They may be upset by the procedures used, or by their own reactions to them. For example, in many early studies concerned with helping behavior, a topic we'll cover in Chapter 9, participants were exposed to staged, but seemingly real, emergency situations. For instance, they were exposed to an apparent fire in the laboratory (Latané & Darley, 1970). Many participants were strongly upset by these staged events; others were later disturbed by the fact that although they recognized the need to help in these situations, they failed to do so. Clearly, these procedures had powerful effects on research participants, and raise important ethical issues about just how far researchers can go when studying even very important topics such as this one.

Of course, such research as this represented an extreme use of deception; generally, deception takes much milder and less emotion-provoking forms. For example, participants may receive a request for help from a "partner" who is actually an accomplice of the researcher; or they may be informed that most other students in their university hold certain views when in fact they do not. Still, the potential for some kind of harmful effects to participants exists, and this is a potentially serious drawback to the use of deception.

Second, there is the possibility that participants will resent being "fooled" during a study, and that as a result they will acquire negative attitudes toward social psychology and psychological research generally (Kelman, 1967). To the extent such reactions occur, they would have negative implications for the future of social psychology, which places a heavy emphasis on the value of scientific research.

Because of such possibilities, the use of deception poses something of a dilemma to social psychologists. On the one hand, it seems essential to their research. On the other, its use raises serious problems. How can this issue be resolved? At present, opinion remains divided. Some of our colleagues feel that deception, no matter how useful, is inappropriate (e.g., Baumrind, 1979). Yet many others (perhaps a large majority) believe that temporary deception *is* acceptable provided that certain safeguards are adopted (e.g., Baron, 1981). First, participants should go through an **informed consent** procedure, receiving as much information as possible about the procedures to be followed *before* making their decision to take part in a study. In this way, researchers ensure that participants know pretty much what they are getting into—what they will be asked to do in the study—before making a commitment to participate. Second, at the end of a study, participants should be provided with full **debriefing**—they should receive a full explanation of all aspects of the study, including its true goals, plus an explanation of the need for temporary deception.

Fortunately, a growing body of evidence indicates that together, informed consent and thorough debriefing can substantially reduce the potential dangers of deception (S. S. Smith & Richardson, 1985). For example, most participants report that they view temporary deception as acceptable, provided potential benefits outweigh potential costs and if there is no other means of obtaining the information sought (Sharpe, Adair, & Roese, 1992). Further, persons who have participated in research employing deception report generally favorable attitudes about psychological research—attitudes just as favorable as those who have not participated in such research (Sharpe et al., 1992). Indeed, as long as they are debriefed after the study and told why they were deceived, research participants do not seem to mind being misled (Christensen, 1988). Finally, fears that continued use of deception would "turn people off" about psychological research and make them suspicious of psychologists appear unjustified; on the contrary, research participants in 1990 appeared to be just as favorable in their views about such research as those in 1970.

In sum, existing evidence does seem to suggest that a large majority of research participants do not react negatively to temporary deception and actually endorse its use in social psychological research. However, these findings do *not* mean that the safety or appropriateness of deception should be taken for granted (Rubin, 1985). On the contrary, the guiding principles for all researchers planning to use this procedure should be these: (1) Use deception only when it is absolutely essential to do so—when no other means for conducting a study exist, (2) always proceed with great caution, and (3) make certain that every possible precaution is taken to protect the rights, safety, and welfare of research participants. Many institutions have institutional review boards to approve and monitor research and act as a further safeguard to research participants.

Using This Book: Special Features

Research findings show that having a framework to hold new information makes it easier to remember and use this information. Echoing that theme, we'd like to conclude this opening chapter by calling your attention to several features of this text. All are designed to increase your understanding of social psychology, and to make your studying easier.

First, each chapter begins with an outline of the major topics covered and ends with a detailed summary. Please read the outline before starting the chapter, and be sure to use the summary as a review after you have finished: both features will help you to remember the materials covered. Because figures and charts contained in original research reports are often quite complex, every graph and table in this text has been specially created for it. In addition, all graphs contain special labels designed to call your attention to the key findings presented (see Figure 1.5 for an example).

Second, we've included two distinct types of special sections throughout the text. These appear at the ends of major sections, so they *don't* interrupt the flow of chapter content. All are designed to highlight information we feel is especially important and interesting.

Because research in each area of social psychology is related to research in other areas, we've included two additional features. The first involves what we term *Integrating Principles*. These are major principles of social psychology that have emerged out of specific lines of research but which seem to cut across many different areas of our field. Each *Integrating Principles* box also calls attention to other topics in this text to which it is related. Second, important links between chapters are summarized in special tables titled *Connections: Integrating Social Psychology*, which appear at the end of each chapter. These *Connections* tables indicate how topics covered in the current chapter are related to topics covered in other chapters. *Connections* tables serve two major functions. First, they provide a kind of global review, reminding you of related topics discussed elsewhere in the book. Second, they emphasize the fact that many aspects of social behavior and social thought are closely *interlinked:* they do *not* occur in isolation from each other. Finally, *Connections* tables are followed by a series of in-depth questions, called *Thinking about Connections*, designed to get you thinking about these links and how they actually operate. Together, the *Integrating Principles* and *Connections* tables help us to represent social psychology as it really is: an integrated field with multiple links between its diverse areas of research.

A second type of special section occurs near the end of each chapter and is titled *Social Diversity: A Critical Analysis*. These sections represent the growing multicultural perspective in social psychology to which we referred earlier. They present information concerning differences between ethnic groups within a given society, or differences across various cultures. *Social Diversity* sections are closely linked to the content of the chapters in which they occur, and seek to examine key aspects of social behavior and thought from a multicultural perspective.

All of the features described above are designed to help you get the most out of your first encounter with social psychology. But in a key sense, only *you* can transfer the information on the pages of this book into your own memory— and into your own life. So please do *use* this book. Read the summaries and chapter outlines, review the *Key Terms*, and pay special attention to the *Integrating Principles*. Doing so, we truly believe, will improve your understanding of social psychology. Finally, please *do* think of this book as a reference source—a practical guide to

social behavior to which you can refer over and over again in the years ahead. In contrast to some other fields you will study in college, social psychology really *is* directly relevant to your daily life: to understanding others and getting along better with them. Please consider keeping this text as part of your permanent library; we're certain that you'll find it useful long after the course is over.

To sum up: We truly hope that together, these features of our text will help to enhance your first encounter with social psychology. We also hope that they will help us communicate our own excitement with the field. Despite the fact that between us we have more than seventy-five years of combined teaching and research experience, we still find social psychology as fascinating as ever. To the extent we achieve these goals, and only to that extent, will we feel that as authors, teachers, and representatives of social psychology, we have succeeded.

 # Summary and Review

Social Psychology: A Working Definition

Social psychology is the scientific field that seeks to understand the nature and causes of individual behavior in social situations. It uses scientific methods to obtain new information about how we interact with and think about other persons.

The Origins and Development of Social Psychology

Although speculation about social behavior and thought has continued since antiquity, a science-oriented field of social psychology emerged only during the twentieth century. Once established it grew rapidly, and social psychology currently investigates every conceivable aspect of social behavior and social thought. Three recent trends in the field have involved the growing influence of a *cognitive perspective* (efforts to apply knowledge about cognitive processes to the task of understanding social behavior), an increasing emphasis on *applying* the principles and findings of social psychology to a wide range of practical problems,

and a movement toward a *multicultural perspective* that both studies and takes careful account of ethnic and cultural factors as determinants of social behavior.

Research Methods in Social Psychology

In conducting their research, social psychologists often employ *experimentation* and the *correlational method*. Experimentation involves procedures in which researchers systematically vary one or more factors (variables) to examine the impact of such changes on one or more aspects of social behavior or thought. In the correlational method, scientists carefully observe and measure two or more variables to determine whether changes in one are accompanied by changes in the other.

Like other scientists, social psychologists are skeptical about research findings until these have been replicated many times. To compare the findings of many studies on a given topic, social psychologists often use a statistical procedure known as *research synthesis* or *meta-analysis.* In addition to replication of research findings, social psychologists often also use the principle of *converging operations:* If a particular variable affects some aspect of social behavior by influencing an underlying psychological mechanism, then other variables that influence the same psychological mechanism should produce similar effects.

In choosing the topics of their research and in planning specific studies, social psychologists are often guided by formal *theories,* which are logical frameworks that seek to explain various aspects of social behavior and thought. Predictions from theories are tested in research. If these predictions are confirmed, confidence in the accuracy of the theories is increased. If they are disconfirmed, such confidence is reduced.

Social psychologists often withhold information about the purpose of their studies from the persons participating in them. Such temporary *deception* is deemed necessary because knowledge of the hypotheses behind an experiment may alter participants' behavior in various ways. Although the use of deception raises important ethical issues, most social psychologists believe that it is permissible, provided that proper safeguards such as *informed consent* and thorough *debriefing* are adopted.

Key Terms

Cognitive Dissonance (p. 9)
Confounding (p. 14)
Converging Operations (p. 17)
Correlational Method (p. 15)
Debriefing (p. 20)
Deception (p. 19)
Dependent Variable (p. 12)
Evolutionary Social Psychology (p. 6)
Experimentation (p. 11)
Independent Variable (p. 12)

Informed Consent (p. 20)
Interactions (p. 13)
Meta-Analysis (p. 17)
Multicultural Perspective (p. 11)
Random Assignment of Participants
    to Groups (p. 14)
Research Synthesis (p. 17)
Social Psychology (p. 4)
Sociobiology (p. 6)
Theories (p. 18)

For More Information

Cherry, F. (1995). *The 'stubborn particulars' of social psychology: Essays on the research process.* New York: Routledge.

A provoking discussion of multiculturalism as it relates to the history and practice of social psychology. This book examines classic studies in the history of the field and reinterprets them from divergent viewpoints.

Jackson, J. M. (1993). *Social psychology, past and present.* Hillsdale, NJ: Erlbaum.

A thoughtful overview of the roots and development of social psychology. Organized around major themes in social psychological research, the book emphasizes the multidisciplinary roots of social psychology. The chapter on current trends is especially interesting.

Peplau, L. A., & Taylor, S. E. (1997). *Sociocultural perspectives in social psychology: Current readings.* Upper Saddle River, NJ: Prentice Hall.

A collection of essays written by social psychologists on a range of cross-cultural topics, including perceptions of people and events, social selves, relating to others, and other aspects of social life. The editors provide a useful introduction to research and an informative summary of alternative media for sociocultural perspectives.

chapter 2

Social Perception: Knowing Others

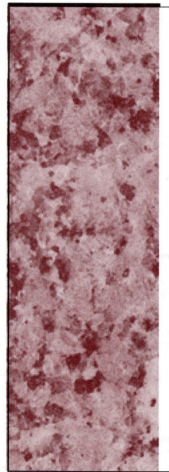

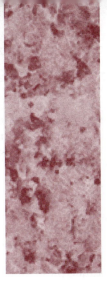

You're at a party; an attractive person glances in your direction and smiles. Is it an invitation to come over and start a conversation? Or is this person smiling because he or she has just heard an amusing remark?

You are buying a used car. You ask the owner whether there is anything wrong with it. He looks you in the eye and says, "No way! This car is in perfect shape." Do you believe him?

Imagine that you are a professor. The day after you give a midterm exam to your class, one of the students comes to see you and, with a look of pure innocence, says: "I'm sorry I missed the exam, but I was away on a field trip for one of my other classes, and we got back much later than I expected. Can I take a makeup exam?" Do you accept this story?

You are going for a job interview. You really need this job, so you want to do everything you can to make a good impression on the interviewer. How do you act? What do you say?

At first glance, these situations might seem totally unrelated. If you think about them for a moment, though, you'll soon realize that there's a common thread tying them together: In each, you are faced with the task of understanding other persons—deciding whether to believe what they say, and, on a more basic level, trying to figure out their intentions and their motives. As you know from your own experience, this is a complex task. Despite all our experience with other people, they sometimes remain one of the true mysteries of life. They say and do things we don't expect, have motives we don't understand, and seem to see the world through eyes very different from our own. Yet, because other persons play such a key role in our lives, this is one mystery we can't afford to leave unsolved. Because of this basic fact, we often engage in what social psychologists describe as social perception—an active process (or set of processes) through which we seek to know and understand others.

Social perception is one of the most basic—and important—aspects of social life, so our efforts to understand the persons around us are truly a part of our daily lives, and take many different forms. Among these, though, two seem to be most important. First, we try to understand other persons' current feelings, moods, and emotions—how they are feeling right now. Such information is often provided by *nonverbal cues* involving facial expressions, eye contact, body posture, and movements. Was that smile a come-on (first example above)? Is that used-car owner lying (second example)? Nonverbal cues often help us reach such decisions.

Second, we attempt to understand the more lasting causes behind others' behavior—the reasons *why* they have acted in certain ways. This generally involves efforts to understand their motives, intentions, and traits. Information relating to this second task is acquired through *attribution*—a complex process in which we observe others' behavior and then attempt to *infer* the causes behind it from this basic information (H. H. Kelley, 1972). Was that student telling the truth (third example), or is the student just a slick manipulator who frequently lies like the proverbial rug? We ask ourselves questions like this every day.

Because they are important aspects of social perception, we'll examine both nonverbal communication and attribution in detail in this chapter. It's important to realize, though, that these processes are not the entire story where social perception is concerned. In addition, such perception often involves efforts to form unified *impressions* of other persons. Common sense suggests that such *first impressions* are very important; and, as we'll soon see, research findings tend to confirm this belief. But how, precisely, do we form such impressions of others? And how do these impressions change over time, in the face of new information? Recent research by social psychologists provides some intriguing answers to these questions (Ruscher & Hammer, 1994). In addition, such research has focused on the opposite side of the impression–formation coin—the question of how we ourselves attempt to make a good first impression on others. Research on this process, known as *impression management* or *self-presentation* (Ruscher & Hammer, 1994; Wyer et al., 1994), has helped clarify which techniques work best, and why. Given the important role of impression formation and impression management in our everyday social life, we'll examine these topics, too, in the present chapter.

Nonverbal Communication: The Unspoken Language

Often, social behavior is strongly affected by temporary factors or causes. Changing moods, shifting emotions, fatigue, illness, drugs—all can influence the ways in which we think and behave. For example, most persons are more willing to do favors for others when in a good mood than when in a bad mood (R. A. Baron & Bronfen, 1994). Similarly, most people are more likely to lose their tempers and lash out at others in some manner when feeling irritable than when feeling pleasant (C. A. Anderson, Anderson, & Deuser, 1996).

Because such temporary factors often exert important effects on social behavior and thought, we often seek knowledge about them: we try to find out how others are feeling right now. How do we go about this process? Sometimes, in a very straightforward way: We ask people directly. Unfortunately, this strategy sometimes fails, because others are often unwilling or unable to reveal their inner feelings to us. In some instances, they may actively seek to conceal such information, or even to mislead us about their current emotions. For example, negotiators often hide their reactions to offers from their opponents; and salespersons frequently show more liking and friendliness toward potential customers than they really feel.

In situations like these, we often fall back upon another, less direct method for information about others' reactions: we pay careful attention to their *nonverbal behaviors*—changes in facial expressions, eye contact, posture, body movements, and other expressive actions. As noted by DePaulo (1992), such behavior is relatively *irrepressible*—difficult to control—so that even when others try to conceal their inner feelings from us, these often "leak out" in many ways through nonverbal cues.

To illustrate, a recent study by Gregory and Webster (1996) examined the "Larry King Show" during the period April 1992 to July 1993 and analyzed the low-frequency, nonverbal expressions of the host and the guests, something that is unlikely to be under intentional control. The researchers showed that many of the guests changed their vocalization patterns to match Mr. King's style of speaking, but that in other cases Mr. King accommodated his guests' vocalization patterns. In a follow-up study, the researchers asked college students to judge the power and social status of the guests King interviewed and then examined whether these ratings predicted the vocalization change patterns. Consistent with their expectations, Gregory and Webster found that guests with low power and social status (e.g., out-of-office politicians such as Dan Quayle and Jimmy Carter) accommodated Mr. King. However, Mr. King's speech patterns changed to match guests with high power and social status (e.g., Bill Clinton, Ross Perot, Barbara Streisand). Thus, vocalization patterns may provide a clue to the relative dominance of each speaker.

Thus, in an important sense, nonverbal behaviors constitute a silent but eloquent language. The information they convey, and our efforts to interpret this input, are often described by the term **nonverbal communication.** Here, we'll examine the basic channels through which nonverbal communication takes place; then we'll turn to some interesting findings about individual differences in the extent to which people display their inner feelings in such cues—individual differences in *emotional expressiveness* (Kring, Smith, & Neale, 1994).

Nonverbal Communication: The Basic Channels

Think for a moment: do you act differently when you are feeling elated than you do when you are feeling really "down"? Most likely, you do. People do tend to behave differently when experiencing different emotional states. But precisely how do differences in your inner states—your emotions, feelings, and moods—show up in your behavior? This key question in the study of nonverbal communication focuses on the *basic channels* of such communication. Research findings indicate in fact, information about our inner states is often revealed through five basic channels: *facial expressions, eye contact, body movements, posture,* and *touching.*

Unmasking the Face: Facial Expressions As Clues to Others' Emotions.
More than two thousand years ago, the Roman orator Cicero stated: "The face is the image of the soul." By this he meant that human feelings and emotions are often reflected in the face and can be read there in specific expressions. Modern research suggests that Cicero—and many other observers of human behavior—were correct in this view: It *is* possible to learn much

about others' current moods and feelings from their facial expressions. In fact, it appears that six different basic emotions are represented clearly, and from a very early age, on the human face: anger, fear, happiness, sadness, surprise, and disgust (Izard, 1991; Rozin, Lowery, & Ebert, 1994). Additional findings suggest that another expression—contempt—may also be quite basic (e.g., Ekman & Heider, 1988). Because this emotion is harder to define verbally, however, it seems to be difficult to establish clear relationships between contempt and specific facial expressions. In contrast, it is easier to establish such links for other emotions—for example, smiles and happiness (Rosenberg & Ekman, 1995).

It's important to realize that these findings concerning a relatively small number of basic facial expressions in no way imply that human beings can show only a small number of facial expressions. On the contrary, emotions occur in many combinations (for example, joy tinged with sorrow, surprise combined with fear), and each of these reactions can vary greatly in strength. Thus, while there may be only a small number of basic themes in facial expression, the number of variations on these themes is immense (see Figure 2.1).

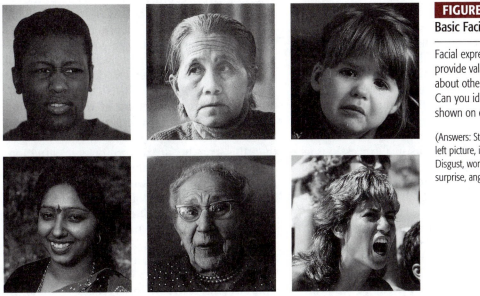

FIGURE 2.1
Basic Facial Expressions.

Facial expressions such as these provide valuable information about others' emotional states. Can you identify the emotion shown on each face?

(Answers: Starting with the upper left picture, in clockwise order: Disgust, worry, sadness, happiness, surprise, anger)

Now for another important question: Do facial expressions really reflect individuals' underlying emotions? Research findings suggest that they do (e.g., Cacioppo et al., 1988). For example, in several studies participants have been asked to move various parts of their faces so as to produce configurations resembling certain facial expressions. For instance, they are asked to wrinkle their nose while opening their mouth (an expression resembling that of disgust), or to crease their brow (as in a frown). They are *not* told to show happiness, anger, fear, and so on; rather, they are merely asked to move parts of their faces in very specific ways. Results indicate that different facial movements are accompanied by changes in physiological activity. The facial expression of fear, for instance, is associated with high heart rate and short periods between breaths, while facial expressions of happiness are associated with lower heart rate and longer periods between breaths. In addition—and this is a key point—the more closely the facial movements resemble expressions associated with specific emotions, the greater the tendency of participants to report experiencing those emotions (e.g., Levenson, Ekman, & Friesen, 1990; Levenson et al., 1992). Findings such as these suggest that the link between emotional experiences and certain facial expressions is a real and very basic one.

Are Facial Expressions Universal? Suppose that you traveled to a remote part of the world and visited a group of people who had never before met an outsider. Would their facial expressions in various situations resemble your own? Would they smile when they encountered events that made them happy, frown when exposed to conditions that made them angry, and so on? Further, would you be able to recognize these distinct expressions as readily as those shown by persons belonging to your own culture? Research findings generally suggest that the answer to both questions is *yes*—although, we should note, not all social psychologists accept this conclusion (e.g., J. A. Russell, 1994). In other words, people living in widely separated geographic areas do seem to show similar facial expressions in similar emotion-provoking situations, and these can be readily—

and accurately—recognized by persons from outside their own cultural group (Ekman, 1989).

Although human beings all over the world tend to show highly similar facial expressions, different cultures have contrasting rules about when and how various emotions should be expressed (these are known as *display rules*). For example, in many Asian countries, it is considered rude to show direct disagreement with or disapproval of another person's words or deeds in many situations. In European and North American cultures, in contrast, open disagreement and disapproval are considered more appropriate, and are shown during negotiations, meetings, and so on. Similarly, in many cultures, it is considered impolite to "gloat" after defeating an opponent; for this reason, expressions of pleasure may be strongly inhibited in such situations (Friedman & Miller-Herringer, 1991). When such display rules don't intervene, however, the link between specific emotions and facial expressions appears to be quite universal.

Similar conclusions have been reached with respect to recognition of such facial expressions: this, too, appears to be quite universal. Systematic research confirms that when individuals living in widely separated countries are shown photos of strangers demonstrating anger, fear, happiness, sadness, surprise, and disgust, they are quite accurate in identifying the strangers' underlying emotions (e.g., Ekman, 1989). Thus, it appears that a smile is indeed interpreted as a sign of happiness, a frown as a sign of anger, and so on, all over the world (Rosenberg & Ekman, 1995).

Gazes and Stares: Eye Contact As a Nonverbal Cue. Have you ever had a conversation with someone wearing mirror-lensed glasses? If so, you realize that this can be an uncomfortable situation. Since you can't see the other person's eyes, you are uncertain about how she or he is reacting. Taking note of the importance of cues provided by others' eyes, ancient poets often described the eyes as "windows to the soul." In one important sense, they were right: We do often learn much about others' feelings from their eyes. For example, we interpret a high level of gazing from another as a sign of liking or friendliness (Kleinke, 1986). In contrast, if others avoid eye contact with us, we may conclude that they are unfriendly, don't like us, or are simply shy (Zimbardo, 1977).

While a high level of eye contact from others is usually interpreted as a sign of liking or positive feelings, there is one important exception to this general rule. If another person gazes at us continuously and maintains such contact regardless of what we do, she or he can be said to be **staring.** A stare is often interpreted as a sign of anger or hostility—as in *cold stare*—and most people attempt to minimize their exposure to this particular nonverbal cue (Ellsworth & Carlsmith, 1973). Thus, we may quickly terminate social interaction with someone who stares at us and may even leave the scene. In view of these facts, it is clear that staring is one form of nonverbal behavior that should be used with great caution in most situations.

Body Language: Gestures, Posture, and Movements.

Try this simple demonstration:

> *First, remember some incident that made you angry—the angrier the better. Think about it for a minute.*
>
> *Now, try to remember another incident, one that made you feel sad—again, the sadder the better.*

Compare your behavior in the two contexts. Did you change your posture or move your hands, arms, or legs as your thoughts shifted from the first event to the second? There is a good chance that you did, for our current moods or emotions are often reflected in the position, posture, and movement of our bodies. Together, such nonverbal behaviors are termed **body language,** and they too can provide us with useful information about others. Large numbers of movements—especially ones in which one part of the body does something to another part (touching, rubbing, scratching)—suggest emotional arousal. The greater the frequency of such behavior, the higher the level of arousal or nervousness (Harrigan et al., 1991).

Larger patterns of movements, involving the whole body, can also be informative. Such phrases as "she adopted a *threatening posture*" and "he greeted her with *open arms*" suggest that different body orientations or postures can indicate contrasting emotional reactions. For example, Ballet dancers who play dangerous or threatening roles (e.g., MacBeth, the Angel of Death) adopt more diagonal or angular postures whereas dancers who play warm, sympathetic roles (e.g., Juliet, Romeo) tend to show more rounded postures (Aronoff, Woike, & Hyman, 1992). Similarly, Lynn and Mynier (1993) conducted a study in a busy restaurant and arranged for waiters and waitresses, when taking drink orders from customers, either to stand upright or to crouch down next to the customers. Lynn and Mynier predicted that crouching down would be interpreted as a sign of friendliness, because in that position the waiters and waitresses would make more eye contact with customers and would be physically closer to them. As a result, they expected servers to receive larger tips when they crouched down than when they did not. Regardless of servers' gender, they received larger tips when they bent down than when they did not.

Finally, we should add that more specific information about others' feelings is often provided by gestures. These fall into several categories, but perhaps the most important are *emblems*—body movements carrying specific meanings in a given culture. For example, in several countries holding one's hand with the thumb pointing up is a sign of "OK." Similarly, seizing one's nose between the thumb and index finger is a sign of displeasure or disgust. Emblems vary greatly from culture to culture, but every human society seems to have at least some signals of this type for greetings, departures, insults, and the descriptions of many different physical states.

Touching: The Most Intimate Nonverbal Cue.

Suppose that during a brief conversation with another person, she or he touched you briefly. How would you react? What information would this behavior convey? The answer to both questions is, *it depends.* And what it depends on is several factors relating to who does the touching (a friend or a stranger, a member of your own or the other gender); the nature of this physical contact (brief or prolonged, gentle or rough, what part of the body is touched); and the context in which it takes place (a business or social setting, a doctor's office). Depending on such factors, touch can suggest affection, sexual interest, dominance, caring, or even aggression. Despite such complexities, existing evidence indicates that when touching is considered acceptable, positive reactions often result (e.g., D. E. Smith, Gier, & Willis, 1982). This fact is illustrated by yet another ingenious study performed in restaurants. The researchers (Crusco & Wetzel, 1984) arranged for waitresses working in two different restaurants to interact with customers in one of three different ways when giving them their change: They either refrained from touching these persons in any manner, touched them briefly on the hand, or touched for a somewhat longer period on the shoulder. Size of tips left for the waitresses was, again, the dependent measure. Results were clear: Both a brief touch on the hand (about 0.5 second) and a longer touch on the shoulder (1.0 to 1.5 seconds) significantly increased tipping over the no-touch condition. So, consistent with other findings, being touched in an innocuous, nonthreatening way seemed to generate positive rather than negative reactions among recipients. Of course, touching does not always produce such effects. If it is perceived as a status or power play, or if it is too prolonged or intimate, or occurs in a context where touching is not viewed as appropriate, this form of nonverbal

behavior may evoke anxiety, anger, and other negative reactions (see Figure 2.2).

Individual Differences in the Expression of Emotions

Think back over the many persons you have known. Can you remember one who showed very clear facial expressions, used gestures freely, and engaged in a great deal of body movement? In contrast, can you recall someone who made little use of such nonverbal cues? Probably you have little difficulty in bringing examples of both types to mind, for informal experience suggests that human beings differ greatly along a dimension of **emotional expressiveness**—the extent to which they show outward displays of emotion (Kring, Smith, & Neale, 1994). Overall, women tend to be more facially expressive than men. Also, people living in southern areas tend to be more facially expressive than those in northern climates, and those who live in "New World" countries (e.g., the United States, Australia) tend to be more facially expressive than those who live in Old World countries (e.g., Germany, Scotland; see Pennebaker, Rimé, & Blankenship, 1996).

Do such differences play a role in social behavior? Research findings suggest that they do.

FIGURE 2.2   Touching: A Potentially Risky Nonverbal Cue.

Touching can communicate many different messages. What do you think is being communicated in the left-hand photo? The right-hand photo?

For example, some years ago, Friedman and his colleagues (Friedman et al., 1980) administered a test of emotional expressivity to several hundred college students. The students then answered questions about their personal lives, such as "Have you ever given a lecture?" "Have you ever been elected to office in an organization?" and "Have you ever held a major part in a play?" Friedman and his coworkers predicted that students who scored high on expressiveness would be more likely to answer "Yes" to such questions, and results confirmed this prediction. In additional research, the same team of investigators related scores on the test of expressiveness to success in several occupations. They found that among physicians, those scoring high on expressiveness were more popular with their patients than those scoring low on this dimension. And for automobile salespersons, they found that those scoring high on expressiveness actually sold more cars!

Emotional expressiveness is also related to psychological adjustment, but not in a simple or direct manner. What seems to be crucial here is not whether individuals are high or low in emotional expressiveness, but the extent to which they experience concern over expressing their emotions. Thus, persons who would like to express their emotions openly but cannot, and individuals who express their emotions openly but would prefer to hold them inside, are both high in ambivalence. Those who do not experience such feelings, in contrast, are low in such ambivalence (King & Emmons, 1991). Research findings suggest that to the extent individuals experience ambivalence over the expression of their emotions, they may experience psychological difficulties. For example, I. M. Katz and Campbell (1994) found that the greater the ambivalence over the expression of emotion, the more stress and negative moods respondents reported, and the lower their psychological well-being (for example, the more likely they were to feel depressed). These findings indicate that there is no overall "edge" to being high or low in expressiveness: Both nonverbal styles can be advantageous or disadvantageous, depending on the specific social context in which they appear. However, the greater the ambivalence individuals experience over the level of expressiveness they actually do show, the more likely they are to experience negative life outcomes.

Nonverbal Cues and the Detection of Deception

It is a sad fact of life that lies thrive in social interactions. For example, in one study (Kashy & DePaulo, 1996), college students appeared to lie in about one third of their interactions with others! Although lies are sometimes told to protect the target's self-esteem, more often the purpose of lying is to benefit the liar. (See Figure 2.3.) Social

FIGURE 2.3   Detection of Deception.

Often lies are detected because the potential victim knows the facts well enough to avoid being fooled; other times, more subtle, nonverbal means may be necessary.

IN THE BLEACHERS   By Steve Moore

psychologists have conducted many studies to examine what they term *detection of deception*. These studies have capitalized on the fact that there are many different channels of nonverbal communication and that it is virtually impossible to monitor and control all these channels at once—even for highly practiced liars such as salespeople and negotiators (DePaulo, 1992). For example, if a liar focuses on regulating facial expressions and eye contact, then the lying may be revealed through body movements and posture, or through nonverbal aspects of speech such as tone of voice. Research on the detection of deception provides several important clues to determine whether another person is lying.

- Rapid facial expressions known as **microexpressions** can be a marker of deception. Such reactions last only a fraction of a second and appear very quickly after an emotion-producing event. Because they are difficult to suppress, they can be quite revealing about others' true feelings or emotions (Ekman, 1985). So, when you have reason to suspect other people may be lying, say something you think they'll find surprising or upsetting, and then *watch their faces very carefully as you say it.* If one expression is followed very quickly by another, different expression, it may mean their intent is to deceive you.

- A second nonverbal cue that someone is lying is the presence of *interchannel discrepancies*. Because it is difficult to control expressions through all channels at once, inconsistencies between nonverbal cues from different basic channels may signal deceptive intent. For example, a defendant on the witness stand may manage her facial expressions and maintain a high level of eye contact with the jury, but may shift her body so that it reveals the high level of emotional arousal she is experiencing.

- A third nonverbal cue involves nonverbal aspects of people's speech, which is sometimes termed *paralanguage*. When people lie, the pitch of their voices often rises (Zuckerman, DePaulo, & Rosenthal, 1981)

and they tend to speak more slowly and with less fluency. They also engage in more *sentence repairs*—starting a sentence, interrupting it, and then starting again.

- A fourth nonverbal cue can derive from aspects of eye contact. People who are lying often blink more frequently and show pupils that are more dilated than persons who are telling the truth. They may also make an unusually low level of eye contact or—surprisingly—an unusually high one, as they attempt to feign honesty by looking others right in the eye (Kleinke, 1986).

- A fifth and final cue that someone is lying is the presence of exaggerated facial expressions, such as more smiling, greater sorrow, or more emotion than is typically necessary for that type of situation.

Careful attention to these nonverbal cues can often help to tell when others are lying. Other research has shown that people who smile a lot, are attractive, have symmetrical and babyfaced faces with large eyes, tend to be *viewed* as honest (Zebrowitz, Voinescu, & Collins, 1996); for example, a person who smiles while lying is more believed even when the target of the lie does not believe that smiling signals honesty (Zuckerman, DePaulo, & Rosenthal, 1981). Consistent with this evidence, other research shows little or no relation of *perceived* honesty to *actual* honesty (Zebrowitz et al., 1996). The Social Diversity box on pages 42–43 discusses perceptions of politicians' non-verbal cues in different cultures. It is to the topic of these interpretations, or attributions, that we turn next.

Integrating Principles

1. Nonverbal cues often provide valuable information about others' current feelings, moods, and emotions.
2. People around the world readily recognize others' facial expressions.
3. Nonverbal cues play an important role in many forms of social interaction, including interpersonal attraction (Chapter 7), social influence (Chapter 8), helping and aggression (Chapter 9), reactions to illness (Chapter 11).

Attribution: Understanding the Causes of Others' Behavior

Accurately interpreting another person's feelings by recognizing his or her facial expressions is often only the first step to gaining an understanding of that person. In many instances, the mystery lies not so much in others' facial expressions as it does in their behavior. Imagine that another student helps you solve a tough homework problem: Does this behavior indicate that the person is genuinely nice—or does it mean that he has a lot of time on his hands? Perhaps it means that he is trying to do you a favor so he can hit you up for a loan later. In other words, we don't simply want to know *how* others have acted; we want to understand *why* they have done so, too. We usually want to understand what attitudes and traits—or sometimes what situational factors—underlie another person's behavior. The process through which we seek such information is known as **attribution.** More formally, *attribution* refers to our efforts to understand the causes behind others' behavior and, on some occasions, the causes behind *our* behavior, too. Social psychologists have studied attribution for several decades, and as you'll soon see, their research has yielded many intriguing insights into this important process (e.g., Graham & Folkes, 1990; Heider, 1958; Pittman, 1993).

How We Form Attributions for Others' Behavior

Because attribution is complex, many theories have been proposed to explain its operation. Here, we will focus on two that have been especially influential, plus recent efforts to extend and refine them.

From Acts to Dispositions: Using Others' Behavior As a Guide to Their Lasting Traits. The first of these theories—Jones and Davis's (1965) theory of **cor-**respondent inference—asks how we use information about others' behavior as a basis for inferring that they possess various traits or attitudes. In other words, the theory is concerned with how we decide, on the basis of others' overt actions, that they possess dispositions that they carry with them from situation to situation, and that remain fairly stable over time. According to Jones and Davis's theory (E. E. Jones & Davis, 1965; E. E. Jones & McGillis, 1976), we accomplish this task by focusing our attention on certain types of actions—those most likely to prove informative.

First, we consider only behaviors that seem to have been freely chosen, while largely ignoring behaviors that were somehow forced on the person in question (Malle & Knobe, 1997a). Second, we pay careful attention to actions that show what Jones and Davis term **noncommon effects**—effects that can be caused by one specific factor, but not by others. (Don't confuse this word with *uncommon*, which simply means infrequent.) Why are such actions informative? Consider the following example. Imagine that one of your casual friends has just gotten engaged. Her future spouse is very handsome, has a great personality, is wildly in love with your friend, and is very rich. What can you learn about your friend from her decision to marry this man? Obviously, not much. There are so many good reasons that you can't choose among them. In contrast, imagine that your friend's fiance is very handsome, but that he treats her with indifference and is known to be extremely boring; also, he has no visible means of support and intends to live on your friend's salary. Does the fact that she is marrying him tell you anything about her personal characteristics? Now, it does; in fact, you can probably conclude that she places more weight on physical attractiveness in a husband than on personality or considerateness or wealth. As you can see, therefore, we can usually learn more about others from actions on their part that yield noncommon effects than from ones that do not.

Finally, Jones and Davis suggest that we also pay greater attention to actions by others that are low in *social desirability* than to actions that are high on this dimension. In other words, we learn more about others' traits from actions they perform that are somehow out of the ordinary than from actions that are very much like those performed by most other persons.

In sum, according to the theory proposed by Jones and Davis, we are most likely to conclude that others' behavior reflects their stable traits (that is, we are likely to reach *correspondent* inferences about them) when that behavior (1) is freely chosen; (2) yields distinctive, noncommon effects; and (3) is low in social desirability.

Attentional Resources and Trait Attribution: What We Learn—and Don't Learn—from Obscure Behavior.

Jones and Davis's theory offers a useful framework for understanding how we use others' behavior to identify their key traits. However, recent research has extended the theory in several ways. Perhaps the most important of these extensions involves efforts to understand the role of *conscious attentional resources* in trait attribution. As we'll see in more detail in Chapter 3, modern conceptions of social thought generally assume that we have limited cognitive resources—limited capacity to process social information (e.g., Gilbert & Osborne, 1989). Thus, if we devote attention to one cognitive task, we have less remaining for other tasks.

What is the relevance of this principle to Jones and Davis's theory? The answer involves the fact that when we infer others' traits and attitudes from their behavior, we actually accomplish three distinct tasks (Gilbert, Pelham, & Krull, 1988; Gilbert & Malone, 1995). First, we *categorize* an individual's behavior—decide what it is all about. Next, we *characterize* the behavior—use it to infer specific traits. Finally, and this is crucial, we *correct* our inferences about this person's traits in the light of information about the situation in which it has occurred. For example, suppose we see a motorist talking to a state trooper who is standing next to his car. We recognize this as a specific kind of interaction: one between an officer and a driver he or she has just stopped. Suppose we also notice that the person is being very humble—he is practically groveling at the trooper's feet. At first glance, we might use this information to infer that the driver is a very meek person (characterization). Since we realize that the driver is

trying to avoid a ticket, however, we may quickly correct this inference and avoid jumping to this particular conclusion.

Under normal circumstances, we generally have sufficient cognitive resources available to engage in all three tasks. But in some cases, we don't: Others' behavior may be *obscure*, so that it is difficult to tell precisely what they are doing, or we simply don't have enough time to make necessary corrections. In such situations, we use up our limited resources on the first two tasks—categorization and characterization—and don't have enough left to correct our initial trait inferences. As a result, we may make errors in this respect. Indeed, consistent with this theory, research has shown that when perceivers have little ability to correct their initial views, little correction will occur (Gilbert & Malone, 1995; see Figure 2.4).

Kelley's Theory of Causal Attributions: How We Answer the Question *Why*? Consider the following events:

> You meet an attractive person at a party, and she or he promises to phone you the next day, but doesn't.
>
> You receive a much lower grade on an exam than you were expecting.
>
> You arrange to meet one of your friends at 5:00 p.m. You are there on time, but fifteen minutes later, your friend still hasn't arrived.

What question would arise in our mind in each of these situations? The answer is clear: *Why?* You'd want to know *why* that person didn't call you, *why* you got a lower grade than you expected, and *why* your friend is late. In many situations, this is the central attributional task we face. We want to know why other people have acted as they have or why events have turned out in a specific way. Such knowledge is crucial, for only if we understand the causes behind others' actions can we hope to make sense out of the social world. Obviously, the number of specific causes behind others' behavior is very large. To make the task more manageable, therefore, we often begin with a preliminary question: Did others' behavior stem mainly from *internal* causes (their own traits, motives, intentions); mainly

FIGURE 2.4 Information Overload, Clarity of Behavior, and Inferring Traits.

If another person's behavior is clear, we usually have the capacity to complete the entire attribution process (Case 1), including categorization, characterization, and correction (if necessary). If, however, the person's behavior is obscure, or if we are overloaded, we may not be able to complete the attribution process, yet categorization and characterization may still occur (Case 2).

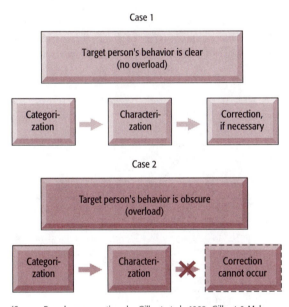

Case 1

Target person's behavior is clear (no overload)

Categorization → Characterization → Correction, if necessary

Case 2

Target person's behavior is obscure (overload)

Categorization → Characterization ✕ Correction cannot occur

(*Source:* Based on suggestions by Gilbert et al., 1992; Gilbert & Malone, 1995.)

from *external* causes (some aspect of the social or physical world); or from a combination of the two? For example, you might wonder whether your received a lower grade than expected because you didn't study enough (an internal cause), because the questions were too difficult (an external cause), or perhaps because of both factors. Revealing insights into how we carry out this initial attributional task are provided by a theory proposed by Kelley (1972; H. H. Kelley & Michela, 1980).

According to Kelley, in our attempts to answer the question *Why* about others' behavior, we focus on information relating to three major dimensions. First, we consider **consensus**—the extent to which others react to some stimulus or

event in the same manner as the person we are considering. The higher the proportion of other people who react in the same way, the higher the consensus. Second, we consider **consistency**—the extent to which the person in question reacts to the stimulus or event in the same way on other occasions, that is, across time. And third, we examine **distinctiveness**—the extent to which this person reacts in the same manner to other, different stimuli or events.

How do we use such information? According to Kelley's theory, we are most likely to attribute another's behavior to *internal* causes under conditions in which consensus and distinctiveness are low, but consistency is high. In contrast, we are most likely to attribute another's behavior to *external* causes under conditions in which consensus, consistency, and distinctiveness are all high. Finally, we usually attribute another's behavior to a combination of internal and external factors under conditions in which consensus is low, but consistency and distinctiveness are high. Perhaps a concrete example will help illustrate the very reasonable nature of these suggestions.

Imagine that a student in one of your classes suddenly gets up, shouts angrily at the professor, and then throws a big, ripe tomato at her. Why did the student act this way? Because of internal causes or external causes? Is this student a weirdo with a violent temper? Or was this person responding to some external cause—something the professor did or said? According to Kelley's theory, your decision (as an observer of this scene) would depend on information relating to the three factors mentioned above. First, assume that the following conditions prevail:

1. No other student shouts or throws tomatoes (*consensus is low*)
2. You have seen this student lose his temper in this same class on other occasions (*consistency is high*)
3. You have seen this student lose his temper outside the classroom—for example, in response to slow waiters and traffic jams (*distinctiveness is low*)

In this case, Kelley's theory suggests that the student blew up because of internal causes: He is a person with a very short fuse! (See the upper part of Figure 2.5.)

Now, in contrast, assume that the following conditions hold:

1. Several other students also shout at the professor *(consensus is high)*
2. You have seen this student lose his temper in this same class on other occasions *(consistency is high)*
3. You have not seen this student lose his temper outside the classroom *(distinctiveness is high)*

Under these conditions, you would probably attribute the student's behavior to external causes—perhaps arrogant or unreasonable behavior by the professor (see the lower part of Figure 2.5).

The basic assumptions of Kelley's theory have been confirmed in a wide range of social situations, so it seems to provide important insights into the nature of causal attributions. However, recent research on the theory also suggests the need for certain modifications. When precisely, does the kind of careful analysis described by Kelley occur? Primarily under two conditions: (1) when people are confronted with

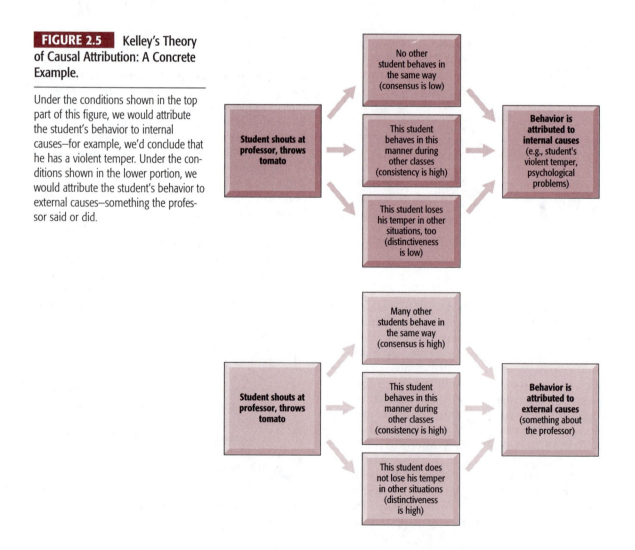

FIGURE 2.5   Kelley's Theory of Causal Attribution: A Concrete Example.

Under the conditions shown in the top part of this figure, we would attribute the student's behavior to internal causes—for example, we'd conclude that he has a violent temper. Under the conditions shown in the lower portion, we would attribute the student's behavior to external causes—something the professor said or did.

unexpected events—ones they can't readily explain in terms of what they know about a specific situation or person, and (2) when they encounter unpleasant outcomes or events (e.g., Lupfer, Clark, & Hutcherson, 1990). In sum, Kelley's theory appears to be an accurate description of causal attributions *when they occur*. It may not describe people's behavior in many situations, though, because they simply don't try.

Attribution: Some Basic Sources of Error

Our discussion of attribution so far seems to imply that it is a highly rational process in which individuals seeking to identify the causes of others' behavior follow orderly cognitive steps. In general, this is so. We should note, however, that attribution is also subject to several forms of error—tendencies that can lead us into serious errors concerning the causes of others' behavior. Several of these errors are described below.

Correspondence Bias: Overestimating the Role of Dispositional Causes. Imagine that you witness the following scene. A man arrives at a meeting one hour late. On entering, he drops his notes on the floor. While he is trying to pick them up, his glasses fall off and break. Later, he spills coffee all over his tie. How would you explain these events? The chances are good that you would reach conclusions such as "This person is disorganized and clumsy." Are such attributions accurate? Perhaps; but it is also possible that the man was late because of unavoidable delays at the airport, dropped his notes because they were printed on slick paper, and spilled the coffee because the cup was too hot to hold. The fact that you would be *less* likely to consider such potential external causes illustrates what Jones (1979) labeled **correspondence bias**—the tendency to explain others' actions as corresponding to dispositions even in the presence of situational causes (see Gilbert & Malone, 1995). This bias has been found in so many different settings that many social psychologists call it the **fundamental attribution error**. In short, we tend to perceive others as acting as they do because they are "that kind of person," rather than because of the

many external factors that may have affected their behavior.

Social psychologists have conducted many studies in efforts to explain correspondence bias (Gilbert & Malone, 1995; E. E. Jones, 1979; Robins, Spranca, & Mendelsohn, 1996). One explanation is that when we observe another person's behavior, we tend to focus on his or her actions; the context in which the person behaves often fades into the background. As a result, dispositions are more salient explanations of behavior than situation. Another explanation is that we notice such situational causes, but give them insufficient weight in the attribution. Yet another explanation appears in Figure 2.5: People may often insufficiently correct for the possibility of situational causes of behavior, due to processing limitations (Gilbert & Malone, 1995). This explanation implies that situational causes require more cognitive resources, but that people infer traits or attitudes of target people with little or no effort. We will again address these possibilities in Chapter 3.

Whatever the basis for the fundamental attribution error, it has important implications. For example, it suggests that even if individuals are made aware of the situational forces that adversely affect members of disadvantaged groups in a society (inadequate educational opportunities, shattered family life), they may still perceive these persons as "bad," "lazy," or "dumb," and therefore responsible for their own plight. In such cases, the fundamental attribution error can have serious social consequences, as we'll discuss in Chapter 6.

Interestingly, our tendency to attribute others' actions to dispositional causes tends to weaken with the passage of time following the action (Burger, 1991; Frank & Gilovich, 1989). For example, Burger and Pavelich's (1993) study showed that people's explanations of election results change across time: within a few days of the elections, nearly two-thirds of the explanations for the outcome were personal. Two or three years later, however, the opposite was true: two-thirds of the explanations referred to situational factors. So, over time, the fundamental attribution error was reversed. In sum, it appears that our attributions often shift over time, and that as a result, the tendency to explain others' actions in terms of internal causes may fade with the passage of time. When such shifts lead us to more accurate conclusions about why others acted as they did, of course, these shifts may be viewed as beneficial ones.

The Actor–Observer Effect: You Fell; I Was Pushed.

Another and closely related type of attributional bias involves our tendency to attribute our own behavior to situational factors, but that of others to dispositional (internal) causes. Thus, when we see another person trip and fall, we tend to attribute this event to his or her clumsiness. If we trip, in contrast, we are more likely to attribute this event to situational causes: ice on the sidewalk or slippery shoes. This "tilt" in our attributions is known as the **actor–observer effect** (E. E. Jones & Nisbett, 1971), and has been observed in many different contexts

In a series of five experiments, Malle and Knobe (1997b) have shown that the actor–observer difference also emerges in terms of *what kinds of behavior* people try to explain. Their systematic research showed that, as actors, people tend to be more concerned with explaining unintentional and unobservable behaviors. In short, our own intended and public behaviors seem intuitively rational to us—because we've played a role in causing them, whereas our unintended and private behaviors force us to think about what caused them. In contrast, as observers people tend to be concerned with other people's actions that are intentional and observable. Their private behaviors are removed from our sight. Moreover, their intended behaviors seem to matter more to understanding their dispositions.

Why does the actor–observer effect occur? In part because we are quite aware of the many situational factors affecting our own actions, but are less aware of such factors when we turn our attention to the actions of other persons. Thus, we tend to perceive our own behavior as arising largely from situational causes, but that of others as deriving mainly from their traits or dispositions.

The Self-Serving Bias: "I'm good; you're lucky." Suppose that you write a term paper for one of your courses. When you get it back you find the following comment on the first page: "An outstanding paper—one of the best I've seen in years. A+." To what will you attribute this success? If you are like most people, you will explain it in terms of internal causes—your high level of talent, the effort you invested in writing the paper, and so on.

Now, in contrast, imagine that when you get the paper back, *these* comments are written on it: "Horrible paper—one of the worst I've seen in years. D–." How will you interpret *this* outcome? The chances are good that you will be tempted to focus mainly on external (situational) factors—the difficulty of the task, your professor's inability to understand what you were trying to say, the fact that your professor is prejudiced against members of your gender, and so on.

This tendency to attribute our own positive outcomes to internal causes but negative ones to external factors is known as the **self-serving bias,** and it appears to be both general in its occurrence and powerful in its effects (Brown & Rogers, 1991; D. T. Miller & Ross, 1975; see Figure 2.6).

Why does this tilt in our attributions occur? Several possibilities have been suggested, but most of these fall into two categories: cognitive and motivational explanations. The cognitive model suggests that the self-serving bias stems mainly from certain tendencies in the way we process social information (Ross, 1977). Specifically, it suggests that we attribute positive outcomes to internal causes, but negative ones to external causes, because we *expect* to succeed and have a tendency to attribute expected outcomes to internal more than to external causes. In contrast, the motivational explanation suggests that the self-serving bias stems from our need to protect and enhance our self-esteem, or the related desire to look good in the eyes of others (Greenberg, Pyszczynski, & Solomon, 1982). While both cognitive and motivational factors may well play a role in this type of attributional error, research evidence seems to offer more support for the motivational interpretation (e.g., Brown & Rogers, 1991).

FIGURE 2.6   The Self-Serving Bias ... ...ration.

The tendency to accept the credit for success but to blame other factors for failures is known as *the self-serving bias.* Thus, we tend to accept more credit for success than we'll give to others, and pin more blame for failures on others than we would for our own failures. The self-serving bias has obvious implications for interpersonal relations, as this comic strip illustrates.

FoxTrot   by Bill Amend

Whatever the precise origins of the self-serving bias, it can be the cause of much interpersonal friction. It often leads persons who work with others on a joint task to perceive that *they,* not their partners, have made the major contributions. Similarly, it leads individuals to perceive that while their own successes stem from internal causes and are well deserved, the successes of others stem from external factors and are less merited. Also, because of the self-serving bias, many persons perceive negative actions on their own part as reasonable and excusable, but identical actions on the part of others as irrational and inexcusable (Baumeister, Stillwell, & Wotman, 1990). Thus, the self-serving bias is clearly one type of attributional error with serious implications for interpersonal relations.

Applications of Attribution Theory: Insights and Interventions

Consistent with the idea that increases in the scientific understanding of social behavior should potentially yield practical applications, attribu-

tion theory has served as a useful framework for understanding of issues and topics as diverse as the causes of marital dissatisfaction, women's reactions to miscarriage, depression, reactions to affirmative action programs, and the causes of interpersonal conflict. Here, we'll examine one especially important, and timely, application of attribution theory, blaming innocent victims of rape.

It has been estimated that in the United States a rape—forced sexual intercourse—occurs every eleven minutes (R. A. Baron & Richardson, 1994). In a national survey, approximately 15 percent of female college students reported that they had been raped—in most cases, by persons they knew (Koss et al., 1988). Clearly, these are frightening statistics. Perhaps even more unsettling, however, is the strong tendency of many persons to hold the victims of rape responsible for this crime (Fischer, 1986; Shotland & Goodstein, 1983). "She must have led him on." "What was she doing in a bar or on the street at that hour of the night, anyway? She was asking for trouble!" These are the kind of comments frequently heard in conversations concerning media reports of rapes. From the perspective of attribution theory, in short, blame is often attributed to victims as much as, or even more than, to perpetrators. As you might guess, males are more likely to make such attributions than females (Cowan & Curtis, 1994); but women, too, often show some tendency to attribute responsibility for rape to its victims.

What accounts for this tendency? One possibility involves what has been termed *belief in a just world*—our desire to assume that the world is basically a fair place (Lerner, 1980). According to this reasoning, if a woman is sexually assaulted, then she "must" have done something to deserve it; thinking the opposite—that she is a completely blameless victim—is too threatening an idea for some persons to entertain. Put another way, believing that totally blameless persons can be made to suffer such degradation is very threatening, so some persons find comfort from such thoughts by concluding that rape victims are *not* blameless and must somehow have invited the assault (S. T. Bell, Kuriloff, & Lottes, 1994).

The findings of many studies have important implications with respect to rape prevention. First, they suggest that the victims of date rape—an alarmingly common event (Koss et al., 1988)—are especially likely to be blamed by other persons. Perhaps this is one reason why so many women who are assaulted by dates are reluctant to report this crime (Koss & Harvey, 1991). Second, the fact that men tend to blame rape victims to a greater extent than women is consistent with recent findings indicating that men—especially those who engage in sexual violence—often misinterpret female communication. Specifically, they are suspicious of, and mistrust, women's communication about sexual interest (Malamuth & Brown, 1994), so that they don't believe it when a woman says no. Obviously, such misperceptions can play a role in some instances of date rape: The woman declines sex in terms that she views as clear and definitive, but her refusals are misinterpreted by her date. To the extent such misperceptions contribute to date rape, it seems important for rape prevention programs to focus on eliminating

their occurrence. In other words, programs that focus on improving communication between males and females with respect to sexual matters may prove quite effective.

Integrating Principles

1. Because we are often interested not only in *what* other people do, but in *why* they do it, attribution is a key aspect of social perception.
2. The conclusions we reach about the causes of others' behavior can strongly influence our relationships with them. Thus, attributions play an important role in many aspects of social behavior, including persuasion (Chapter 5), prejudice (Chapter 6), long-term relationships (Chapter 7), social influence (Chapter 8), and conflict (Chapter 9).

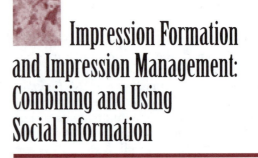 # Impression Formation and Impression Management: Combining and Using Social Information

First impressions, it is widely believed, are very important. Most of us assume that the initial impressions we make on others will shape the course of our future relations with them in crucial ways. Further, we believe that such impressions may be quite resistant to change once they are formed. It is for these reasons that most people prepare carefully for first dates, job interviews, and other situations in which they will meet others for the first time. Are these assumptions about the nature of first impressions accurate? The answer provided by several decades of research is at least a qualified *yes:* First impressions *do* seem to exert a lasting effect on both social thought and social behavior (N. H. Anderson, 1981; Wyer et al., 1994).

Impression Formation: A Cognitive Approach

The first research on **impression formation,** which is the process through which we form impressions of others, was published in 1946 by Solomon Asch. He emphasized the quickness and apparent completeness with which individuals judge what a person is like. These ideas have continued to inspire person perception researchers. Initially, research on impression formation focused on the question of how we combine so much diverse information about others into unified impressions. One answer, suggested by early studies, was as follows: We combine this information into a *weighted average,* in which each piece of information about another person is weighted in terms of its relative importance (N. H. Anderson, 1981). Research conducted within this general framework then focused on identifying the factors that influence this relative weighting. Among the most important factors identified were these: (1) the source of the input—information from sources we trust or admire is weighted more heavily than information from sources we distrust (Rosenbaum & Levin, 1969), (2) whether the information is positive or negative in nature—we tend to weight negative information about others more heavily than positive information (Mellers, Richards, & Birnbaum, 1992), (3) the extent to which the information describes behaviors or traits that are unusual or extreme—the more unusual, the greater the weight placed on information; and finally, as Asch found, (4) information received first tends to be weighted more heavily than information received later (this is known as a *primacy effect*).

While this research certainly added to our knowledge of impression formation, modern investigations of first impressions have adopted a very different approach. Drawing on basic knowledge of *social cognition*—the topic we'll consider in detail in Chapter 3—recent research has sought to understand impression formation in terms of the ways in which we notice, store, remember, and integrate social information (e.g., Wyer et al., 1994; Ruscher & Hammer, 1994). This cognitive approach has proved to be extremely productive,

and has changed our basic ideas about how impressions are formed and changed. For example, it now seems clear that impressions of others involve both concrete examples of behaviors others have performed that are consistent with a given trait—*exemplars*—and mental summaries that are abstracted from repeated observations of others' behavior—*abstractions* (e.g., Klein, Loftus, & Plog, 1992; E. R. Smith & Zárate, 1992). Models of impression formation that stress the role of behavioral exemplars suggest that when we make judgments about others, we recall examples of their behavior and base our judgments—and our impressions—on these. For example, we recall that during our first conversation with a certain woman, she interrupted us repeatedly, made nasty comments about other people, and failed to hold open a door for someone whose arms were loaded with packages. The result: As we recall these pieces of information, we include the trait "inconsiderate" in our first impression of this person.

In contrast, models that stress the role of abstractions suggest that when we make judgments about others, we simply bring our previously formed abstractions to mind, and then use these as the basis for our impressions and our decisions (e.g., Rosnow, Skleder, Jaeger & Rind, 1994). We recall that we have previously judged a person to be inconsiderate or considerate, friendly or unfriendly, optimistic or pessimistic, and combine these traits into an impression of this individual.

That both types of information—concrete examples of behavior and mental abstractions—play a role in impression formation is supported by a growing body of evidence (e.g., Klein et al., 1992). In fact, it appears that the nature of impressions may shift as we gain increasing experience with others. At first, an impression consists largely of exemplars (behavioral examples); but later, as our experience with another person increases, our impression consists mainly of mental abstractions derived from observations of the person's behavior. Convincing evidence for this view is provided by research conducted by J. W. Sherman and Klein (1994).

These investigators exposed research participants either to a relatively small amount of information about another person or to a larger

Social Diversity:
A Critical Analysis

Reactions to Politicians' Nonverbal Behaviors in the United States and France

In the past, political leaders were seen in the flesh only by small numbers of people who attended political rallies or watched as these persons drove by or waved from the back of railroad trains. However, television has made it possible for virtually every citizen in developed countries to watch political leaders in action—debating rivals, delivering speeches, or kissing babies. Such coverage of politicians often zeros in on their faces while they speak, and this in turn gives millions of viewers a close-up view of the facial expressions and other nonverbal cues shown by these persons. Does this information influence reactions to political leaders, attitudes toward them, and perhaps even voting decisions? A growing body of evidence indicates that it does. Moreover, mirroring differences in the political process in various countries, the precise nature of these effects appears to differ across different cultures.

Perhaps the most revealing information on such cross-cultural differences is that reported by Masters and his colleagues (e.g., Masters & Sullivan, 1989, 1990) in a series of studies conducted in the United States and France. In these experiments, participants are shown videotapes of well-known political leaders—Ronald Reagan, Jacques Chirac—delivering speeches or debating with other candidates. These segments are carefully chosen to show the leaders demonstrating three contrasting kinds of facial expressions: happiness/ reassurance, anger/threat, and fear/evasion. Before watching the tapes, participants report on their political attitudes and party affiliation. Immediately after watching each taped excerpt, participants rate the leaders' behavior, and then report on their own emotional reactions to the leaders.

Careful analysis of these ratings indicates, first, that French and American participants distinguish between these three types of facial

expression equally well, and that they tend to react to them in much the same manner. Specifically, they generally report more positive reactions to expressions showing happiness/reassurance than to ones showing fear/evasion or anger/threat. There is one interesting difference, however: French participants react significantly more favorably to facial expressions showing anger/threat. Apparently, because of cultural differences, they find such expressions more appropriate for political candidates than do Americans.

Other intriguing cultural differences arise with respect to the extent to which political attitudes and party affiliation influence viewers' reactions to the candidates' nonverbal cues. In the United States, there are only two major political parties. As a result, both cover a wide range of political opinion. In France, in contrast, there are many parties, so each one tends to reflect a fairly specific set of views; each party, in other words, occupies a well-defined and fairly narrow location on the left–right political spectrum. These differences in the political process lead to the following intriguing predictions. In France, viewers' political attitudes would probably be more predictive of their reactions to political candidates' than the candidates' nonverbal cues, while in the United States, the opposite would be true. Why? Because in France, each candidate is identified with a specific set of positions and a particular spot on the political spectrum. Thus, viewers would pay careful attention to this information, and less attention to candidates' personal characteristics or behaviors. In the United States, in contrast, political candidates go out of their way to represent many different groups, and are not so clearly linked to a specific political ideology. As a result, viewers focus to a greater extent on their personal traits and behaviors. The results of several studies (Masters &

Sullivan, 1989, 1990) offer support for these predictions.

In sum, it seems clear that nonverbal cues play an important role in reactions to political leaders across different cultures. However, the precise nature of these effects varies with the political process in different countries, and with norms indicating what kinds of nonverbal displays are or are not appropriate in public settings. This finding, in turn, provides us with yet another illustration of the complex interplay between seemingly universal human tendencies and specific cultural factors in the determination of social behavior and social thought.

amount of information. In both cases, the information consisted of examples of behaviors by this person indicative of two different traits: intelligence and kindness. (An example of behavior indicative of kindness: "Bob stopped to let another car into the line of traffic." An example of behavior indicative of intelligence: "Bob studies photography in his spare time"). After receiving this information, participants performed one of two different tasks. Some were asked to decide whether various traits described the stranger (the *describe* task), while others were asked to define each trait (the *define* task). Finally, they performed a recall task in which they were asked to remember specific behaviors by the stranger. Sherman and Klein (1994) reasoned that if impressions consist largely of exemplars of behavior, then the task of deciding whether various traits described the stranger would activate these exemplars in memory and so would improve performance on the recall task: participants would recall these more quickly. However, if impressions consist largely of mental abstractions, the describe task would *not* facilitate later recall. Results indicated that for participants who received only a small amount of information about the stranger, the describe task *did* facilitate recall relative to the define task. However, for those who received a larger amount of information about the stranger, the describe task did *not* produce such effects (see Figure 2.7). These findings offer support for the view that at first, impressions of

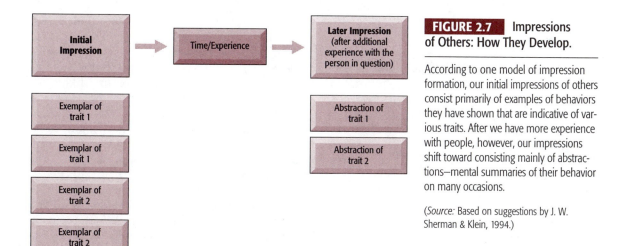

FIGURE 2.7 Impressions of Others: How They Develop.

According to one model of impression formation, our initial impressions of others consist primarily of examples of behaviors they have shown that are indicative of various traits. After we have more experience with people, however, our impressions shift toward consisting mainly of abstractions—mental summaries of their behavior on many occasions.

(*Source:* Based on suggestions by J. W. Sherman & Klein, 1994.)

others consist mainly of concrete behavioral exemplars, but that later, they consist mainly of mental abstractions that have been extracted from experience.

In sum, existing evidence indicates that impression formation does not occur in a cognitive vacuum. On the contrary, mental frameworks representing our previous experience in many social situations, and basic cognitive processes relating to the storage, recall, and integration of social information, play a role in it. So, while the task of forming impressions often seems virtually effortless, there's a lot going on beneath the surface as this process unfolds.

Impression Management: The Fine Art of Looking Good

The desire to make a favorable impression on others is a strong one, so most of us do our best to "look good" to others when we meet them for the first time. Our efforts to make a good impression on others are known as **impression management** (or *self-presentation*), and growing evidence suggests that these efforts are well worth the trouble: Persons who can perform impression management successfully do often gain important advantages in many situations. What tactics do individuals use to create favorable impressions on others? And which of these are most successful? These are the issues we'll consider next.

Impression Management: Some Basic Tactics. As your own experience probably suggests, impression management takes many different forms. Most of these, however, seem to fall into two major categories: *self-enhancement*—efforts to boost our own image, and *other-enhancement*—efforts to make the target person feel good in our presence. As we'll see in Chapter 7, such positive feelings often play an important role in attraction and liking.

Specific tactics of *self-enhancement* include efforts to improve our own appearance. This can be accomplished through alterations in dress,

through personal grooming (cosmetics, hairstyles, the use of perfume or cologne), and through the judicious use of nonverbal cues. Research findings indicate that all of these tactics work, at least under some conditions. For example, women who dress in a professional manner (business suit or dress, subdued jewelry) are often evaluated more favorably for management positions than women who dress in a more traditionally feminine manner (Forsythe, Drake, & Cox, 1985). Similarly, eyeglasses have been found to encourage impressions of intelligence, while long hair for women or beards for men tend to reduce such impressions (Terry & Krantz, 1993). And wearing perfume or cologne can enhance first impressions, provided this particular grooming aid is not overdone (R. A. Baron, 1989a). Most of these efforts to improve personal appearance are not potentially dangerous to the persons who use them; but others *are*. For instance, one reason why at least some young people consume alcohol is that it gives them the right "image" (Sharp & Getz, 1996). In other words, they engage in such potentially dangerous behavior partly for purposes of impression management: to help look good in the eyes of others.

Turning to *other-enhancement*, individuals use many different tactics to induce positive moods and reactions in others. Among the most important of these tactics are *flattery*—heaping praise on target persons, even if they don't deserve it; expressing agreement with their views; showing a high degree of interest in them (hanging on their every word); doing small favors for them; asking for their advice and feedback (Morrison & Bies, 1991); and expressing liking for *them* either verbally or nonverbally (Wayne & Ferris, 1990). All of these tactics seem to work, at least to a degree. They cause target persons to experience positive reactions, and these, in turn, can elevate liking for, and impressions of, the persons who use such tactics.

Impression Management: To What Extent Does It Succeed? Now for the key question: Are efforts to engage in impression management worthwhile? In other words, can they enhance the impressions we make upon others enough to make a difference in terms of their judgments of us or their behavior toward us? A large body of evidence suggests that they can: if used with skill and care, the tactics listed above can indeed be very helpful—at least to the persons who use them. Convincing evidence for this conclusion—and for the view that impression management can influence important judgments based on impressions of others—is provided by a recent synthesis of the studies in this area. Gordon (1996) examined sixty-nine studies of the success of various ingratiation tactics. As Figure 2.8 shows, these tactics varied widely in their success. Making the target person look good, also known as other-enhancement,

was the most successful tactic, followed by expressing similar opinions to the target, promotion of one's positive virtues—or self-presentation, and a combination of these tactics. A fifth tactic, giving favors to the target, was least successful. Importantly, Gordon also found that although ingratiation efforts *are* successful in getting another person to like you, they have a much smaller effect in getting another person to think you are competent. Finally, Gordon also showed that extremely transparent ingratiation efforts tended to boomerang on the ingratiator, with the target reacting negatively to such attempts. Apparently, when it comes to making others appreciate you, a little bit goes a long way!

FIGURE 2.8   Tactics of Ingratiation Differ in Their Effectiveness.

Ingratiation refers to various tactics that people can use to get other people to like them. As this figure shows, the most successful tactic tends to be other-enhancement, followed by expressing similar opinions, promotion of one's virtues, and a combination of these tactics. A fifth tactic, giving favors to the target, was least successful.

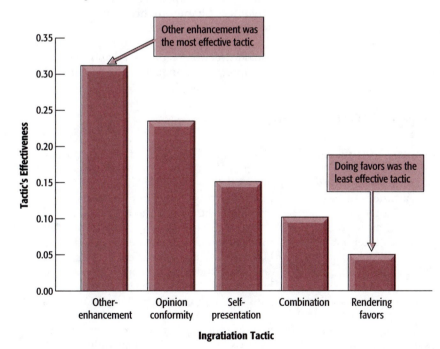

(*Source:* Based on data from Gordon, 1996.)

These findings and other related studies (e.g., Paulhus, Bruce, & Trapnell, 1995) indicate that impression management tactics often do succeed in enhancing the appeal of persons who use them. Given this fact, should *you* resort to such procedures? In all probability, you already apply some of them in your daily life. Whether you should seek to get ahead in life through cal-

culated use of impression management tactics, however, depends on the extent to which you feel comfortable with such a strategy. Social psychologists can study impression management systematically and can help identify its most successful tactics; but the decision as to whether to put these tactics to use is an ethical one that individuals must reach for themselves.

Connections   Integrating Social Psychology

In this chapter, you read about . . .

- basic channels of nonverbal communication

- theories of attribution

- first impressions and impression management

In other chapters, you will find related discussions of . . .

- the role of nonverbal cues in mutual liking (Chapter 7), and in charismatic leadership (Chapter 10)
- the role of attribution in persuasion (Chapter 5), social identity and self-perception (Chapter 4), and the role of attribution in prejudice (Chapter 6), prosocial behavior and aggression (Chapter 9)
- the role of first impressions in interpersonal attraction (Chapter 7), and the role of impression management in job interviews (Chapter 11)

Thinking about Connections

1. As we will discuss in Chapters 5 (Attitudes) and 8 (Social Influence), influence is an important fact of social life: Each day, we attempt to change others' attitudes or behavior and they attempt to change ours. Having read about attribution in this chapter, do you think that influence attempts that conceal their true goal will be more successful than ones that do not? If so, why? If not, why?
2. In Chapter 9 (Hurting and Helping), we'll see that some persons experience much more than their fair share of aggressive encounters. Such persons, it appears, are lacking in basic social skills, such as the

ability to accurately "read" other nonverbal cues. On the basis of the discussion of nonverbal cues in this chapter, can you explain how this could contribute to their problems with respect to aggression?
3. Suppose you meet two persons for the first time and quickly conclude that you like one but don't like the other. Now, imagine you arrange to meet these people again and both are late. Will you be more annoyed with one than the other? Will you assume different possible causes for their being late? In other words, will your contrasting impressions of these persons influence your later thinking about them (Chapter 3)?

Summary and Review

Nonverbal Communication

Social perception is the process through which we attempt to understand other persons. To obtain information about the temporary causes of others' behavior (e.g., their emotions or feelings), we focus on *nonverbal cues*. These are provided by others' facial expressions, eye contact, body posture or movements, and touching. Although *display rules* concerning when and how individuals should demonstrate their emotions differ from culture to culture, evidence suggests that some aspects of nonverbal communication—for example, facial expressions—are fairly universal around the world and across many cultures. Individuals differ greatly in terms of *emotional expressiveness*—the extent to which they show outward displays of emotion; and these differences are related to social behavior, to personal psychological adjustment, and to geographic region. Through the use of nonverbal cues, we can often tell when others are attempting to deceive us.

Attribution: Understanding the Causes of Others' Behavior

Knowledge about the lasting causes of others' behavior is acquired through *attribution*. In this process, we infer others' traits, attitudes, motives, and intentions from observation of their behavior, being careful to focus on those aspects of behavior that are most likely to be revealing in this regard. In order to determine whether others' behavior stems mainly from internal or external causes, we focus on information relating to *consensus*, *consistency*, and *distinctiveness*. However, we engage this kind of careful causal analysis only under some circumstances—for example, when others behave in unexpected ways.

Attribution is subject to several forms of error, including the *correspondence bias* or *fundamental attribution error*, the *actor–observer effect*, and the *self-serving bias*. Attribution theory has been applied to a wide range of practical problems. For example, it has shed important light on why the victims of rape are often blamed for these assaults.

Impression Formation and Impression Management

Common sense seems to be correct in suggesting that first impressions are important. Early views of impression formation viewed this process as one in which information about others is combined into a weighted average. More recent research, however, has stressed the cognitive processes that play a role in impression formation. The findings of such research suggest, for example, that impressions of others involve memories of specific behaviors they have performed, as well as abstractions derived from observing their behavior on many occasions. Individuals engage in many tactics to make favorable impressions on others, but most of these tactics of *impression management* fall into two categories: *self-enhancement*, which includes efforts to enhance one's personal appearance, and *other-enhancement*, which involves efforts to induce positive feelings or reactions in target persons. Growing evidence suggests that impression management often succeeds in its major goal: producing a favorable impression on another person.

Social Diversity: Reactions to Nonverbal Displays by Political Leaders in the United States and France

In the past, relatively few persons could see the nonverbal cues emitted by political leaders in a firsthand manner. Modern technology, however, allows almost all citizens to see close-up views of the faces of political candidates. Studies comparing the reactions to such cues of viewers in the United States and France indicate that cultural factors play an important role in this process. For example, French viewers react more favorably than American viewers to facial expressions by candidates showing anger/threat. In addition, French viewers' reactions to candidates' nonverbal cues are more strongly affected by the viewers' political attitudes and party identification. These findings indicate that reactions to leaders' nonverbal cues involve a complex interaction between basic human tendencies and specific cultural factors.

Key Terms

 # For More Information

Kenny, D. A. (1994). *Interpersonal perception: A social relations analysis.* New York: Guilford.

This well-written and relatively brief book provides an excellent overview of what social psychologists have discovered about many different aspects of interpersonal perception. The book focuses on the key questions of how we see other people, how we see ourselves, and how we think we are seen by others. All in all, a very thoughtful and useful volume.

Martin, L. L., & Tesser, B. (Eds.). (1992). *The construction of social judgments.* Hillsdale, NJ: Erlbaum.

Examines many aspects of how we make judgments about others. The chapters on impression formation and the role of moods and emotions in social judgments are especially relevant to this chapter.

Malandro, L. A., Barker, L., & Barker, D. A. (1994). *Nonverbal communication* (3rd ed). New York: Random House.

A basic and very readable text that examines all aspects of nonverbal communication. Body movements and gestures, facial expression, eye contact, touching, smell, and voice characteristics are among the topics considered.

Social Cognition: Understanding the Social World

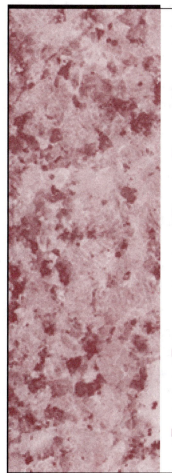

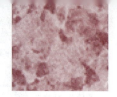

How many times each day do you think about other persons? Your answer may well be "Who can keep count?" because in fact, other persons occupy our attention many times each day—from the moment we open our eyes in the morning until we close them and go to sleep at night. And even then, people are often the focus of those private, internal videos we call dreams. What do we think about where other people are concerned? Partly, we try to understand them by identifying their major traits and the causes behind their behavior—by figuring out why they do or say what they do. As you'll certainly recall, we examined these aspects of social thought in Chapter 2. Thinking about others, however, involves much more than this. When we interact with other persons, we acquire a tremendous amount of information about them—how they look, what they say, what they do. Somehow we must sort this information and enter parts of it—those portions that seem most useful—into memory. And later, we must combine this previously stored information about others in order to make judgments about them, predict their future actions, and draw inferences about their behavior (S. T. Fiske, 1993). It is only by accomplishing these tasks that we can make sense out of the social world in which we live—a world that, we learn quite early in life, is anything but simple (see Figure 3.1).

What is such **social cognition** like? Is it accurate or subject to many errors? And how, given its obvious complexity, do we manage to accomplish social cognition so effortlessly much of the time? Research by social psychologists on these and related questions has yielded findings that are frequently as surprising as they are fascinating. A few samples, to whet your appetite for what follows:

Why are people often overoptimistic in predicting when they'll complete various tasks?

Does thinking too much get us confused and interfere with our ability to make accurate judgments?

Do our mental images of "the kind of person who . . . [smokes, takes risks, uses drugs, gets pregnant]" influence our behavior?

Do our expectations about various events or experiences shape our reactions to them when they actually occur?

After being exposed to persons we find highly attractive, do we feel more dissatisfied with our own romantic relationships?

We'll examine these and many other intriguing questions in the pages that follow. Specifically, our discussion of social cognition will proceed as follows. First, we'll examine two basic components of social thought—*schemas* and *prototypes*, which are mental structures or frameworks that allow us to organize large amounts of diverse information in an efficient manner (S. T. Fiske & Taylor, 1991). Once formed, however, these frameworks exert strong effects on social thought—effects

---

FIGURE 3.1 Understanding the Social World: No Easy Task!

As these youngsters are beginning to realize, understanding the social world is a very complex task.

(*Source:* FOR BETTER OR FOR WORSE copyright 1987 Lynn Johnston Prod., Inc. Reprinted with permission of UNIVERSAL PRESS SYNDICATE. All rights reserved.)

that are not always beneficial from the standpoint of accuracy. Second, we'll turn to several shortcuts and strategies we use to help us in our efforts to make sense out of the social world. A basic finding of research on social cognition is that generally, we try to accomplish this task with the least amount of effort possible—in part because we often find ourselves having to deal with more information than we can readily handle (Macrae, Milne, & Bodenhausen, 1994). Mental shortcuts and strategies that we adopt allow us to cope with this state of affairs and to make sense out of the complex social world in an efficient manner. Such shortcuts often succeed—but, as we'll soon see, only to a degree and only at some cost to accuracy. Third, we'll examine several tendencies or "tilts" in social thought, tendencies that cause us to pay more attention to some kinds of input than to others and, therefore, to reach conclusions that are different, and sometimes less accurate, than would otherwise be the case. The discussion of these effects will emphasize another basic principle established by research on social cognition: while we are certainly impressive social-information processors, we are definitely *not* perfect in this respect (S. T. Fiske, 1993). On the contrary, our social thought is often far less rational, reasonable, and accurate than we would like to believe (e.g., Denes-Raj & Epstein, 1994). Finally, we will examine the complex interplay between **affect**—our current feelings or moods—and various aspects of social cognition. This relationship is indeed a two-way street, with feeling influencing cognition and cognition, in turn, shaping affect (e.g., Forgas, 1995). Please note: Another key aspect of social cognition—our efforts to understand *ourselves*—will be discussed in Chapter 4.

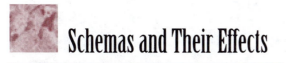

Schemas and Their Effects

Suppose that you are at a party and that you start talking to another person. As you do, you notice that she or he continues to look around the room and only half listens to what you are saying. Will it take you long to figure out what's going on?

Probably not. You'll quickly realize that this person does not find you interesting or attractive and is looking for an excuse to make a quick exit. How are you able to reach such conclusions so quickly and easily? Part of the answer involves the fact that you have been in many other situations like this one; as a result of those experiences, you have formed a kind of mental framework for understanding such situations and others' behavior in them. These frameworks, or **schemas,** contain information relevant to specific situations or events and, once established, help us interpret these situations and what's happening in them. For example, in this situation, you may have a schema for "meeting people at parties," containing information on how people behave in this context, and how they signal liking—or boredom—to each other. When your schema for such encounters is activated, it lets you decide, quickly and effortlessly, that you are probably wasting your time with this person. As we'll soon see, schemas exert powerful effects on several aspects of social cognition, and therefore on our behavior as well.

Now let's consider a related concept: **prototypes.** Prototypes constitute another type of mental framework that we use to interpret the social world. Basically, prototypes involve models of the typical qualities of members of some group or category. For example, you probably have prototypes for *leaders*, for *sports heroes/heroines*, for *criminals*, and for countless other social categories. In a sense, prototypes describe the truly typical member of such categories—the "pattern" to which we compare new persons as we meet them, in order to determine if they do or do not fit into the category. When they fit quite well, we can readily place them in various categories. When they do not, the situation is more puzzling. For example, suppose you met a young woman who told you that she climbed mountains as a hobby and who was dressed in very flashy clothes. When you discovered that she was an accountant, you would probably be surprised. The reason is simple: She does not seem to fit well with the prototype of *accountant* that you have built up through past experience. Prototypes, too, exert important effects on social thought and, as we'll see below, on important aspects of social behavior as well.

Types of Schemas: Persons, Roles, and Events

Let's return to the party mentioned above. Suppose that the stranger you met who was so obviously bored with you had these characteristics: this person was very physically attractive, was dressed in extremely stylish clothes, and was sporting large diamonds on both ears. Would this help you to interpret his or her behavior? In all likelihood it would, because you already have a well-established *person schema* for individuals like this one: a schema for the *super-cool*. Person schemas are mental frameworks suggesting that certain traits and behaviors go together and that individuals having them represent a certain *type*. Once such a schema comes into operation, you don't have to think very long or hard about why this stranger is bored with you: You aren't super-cool yourself and rarely have much success with this kind of person. When the stranger walks off, therefore, you aren't very surprised.

This isn't the only kind of schema we have, however. In addition, we have schemas relating to specific social roles—*role schemas*. These schemas contain information about how persons playing specific roles generally act, and what they are like. For example, consider your role schema for *professors*. You expect professors to stand in front of the room; to talk about the topic of the course; to answer questions from students,

prepare exams, and so on. You *don't* expect them to try to sell you a product or to do magic tricks; such actions are definitely not part of your role schema for *professor*.

A third type of schema involves mental frameworks relating to specific situations. Such schemas relate to events, or sequences of events, and are known as *scripts*. They indicate what is expected to happen in a given setting. For example, when you walk into a restaurant, you expect someone to greet you and either lead you to a seat or put your name on a list. Then you expect a server to come to your table to offer drinks and to take your order. Next on the agenda is the appearance of the food, followed, ultimately, by the bill (see Figure 3.2). Think how surprised you'd be if instead of following this orderly and expected sequence of events, the server sat down at your table and began a friendly conversation; or if this person announced, after bringing your food, "Sorry, I've got to leave now." Scripts, like other schemas, provide us with a mental scaffold: a structure for understanding social information in the context of information we already have. Once established, scripts save us a great deal of mental effort, because they tell us what to expect, how other persons are likely to behave, and what will happen next in a wide range of social situations. (We'll consider another, and very important, type of schema—the *self-schema*—in Chapter 4.)

FIGURE 3.2   Scripts: Schemas That Tell Us "What Should Happen Next."

When you go to a restaurant, you have a *script* for the events that should occur and the order in which they should take place. The activity shown here fits this schema. If a server sat down at the table with you, however, this action would *not* fit your schema.

The Impact of Schemas on Attention, Encoding, Retrieval

How do schemas influence social thought? Research findings suggest that they exert strong effects on three processes that are a basic part of social cognition—and of all cognition: attention, encoding, and retrieval. **Attention** refers to what information we notice; clearly, we are more likely to notice some things about other persons and their actions than others. **Encoding** refers to the processes through which information, once it is noticed, gets stored in memory. Again, not everything we notice about the social world is stored for future use. Finally, **retrieval** refers to the processes through which we recover information from memory in order to use it in some manner—for example, in making judgments about other people, such as whether they would make a good roommate.

Schemas have been found to influence all of these basic aspects of social cognition (Wyer & Srull, 1994). With respect to attention, we often notice information or events inconsistent with existing schemas to a greater extent than information or events that are consistent with these schemas. This is not surprising, since schemas tell us what to expect, and it is usually *unexpected* events or actions that draw our attention. For example, if your dentist tells you to sit down and open your mouth, you don't pay much attention to her actions. If she stands away from the chair and begins to sing loudly, however, you will certainly notice *that* behavior; it doesn't fit with your *script* (event schema) for this situation.

Turning to encoding, the effects of schemas are a bit more complex. Existing evidence indicates that once schemas have been formed, information consistent with them is easier to remember than information that is inconsistent. However, earlier in the process, when schemas are first being formed, information *inconsistent* with them may be more readily noticed, and thus encoded (e.g., Stangor & Ruble, 1989). Finally, schemas also influence what information is retrieved from memory. In particular, to the extent schemas are activated when we are trying to recall some information, they determine what information is actually brought to mind—in

general, information that is part of these schemas or at least consistent with them (e.g., Stangor & McMillan, 1992).

In sum, schemas influence many aspects of social cognition. And since social thought is intimately related to social behavior, they play an important role in many forms of social interaction, too, as we'll see throughout this book.

Integrating Principles

1. Through experience, we acquire *schemas*—mental frameworks containing information relevant to specific situations or events, and *prototypes*—mental representations of the typical members of various groups.
2. Once formed, these mental frameworks help us to understand other persons and events occurring in social situations. They strongly affect what social information we notice (attention), store in memory (encoding), and later remember (retrieval). Thus, they have powerful effects on social behavior in many different settings.
3. Attitudes (which we'll consider in Chapter 5) and stereotypes (Chapter 6) often function as schemas, and both exert strong effects on important forms of social behavior.

Heuristics: Mental Shortcuts

Earlier, we called attention to a basic principle of social cognition: In general, we expend the least possible amount of effort in thinking about other persons and the social world. This principle is hardly surprising because as you know from your own experience, thinking is often very hard work. Our tendency to exert minimal effort in this respect, however, is also related to another basic fact of social life: We have *limited* rather than unlimited cognitive resources, as we discussed in Chapter 2. In fact, we often find ourselves in the situation of having more demands on these resources than we have resources available—a situation known as **information overload.** If you've ever tried to talk on the phone while cooking, or to hold a conversation while driving in heavy traffic, you know what we mean about limited cognitive resources, and how frustrating—or even dangerous—it can be to try to do more than we can handle at one time.

To help stretch our cognitive resources, we employ many strategies to reduce our cognitive effort and decrease the possibility of information overload. To be successful, such strategies must meet two requirements: They must provide a quick and simple way of dealing with large amounts of social information, and they must be reasonably accurate much of the time. Many potential shortcuts for reducing mental effort exist, but among these perhaps the most useful are **heuristics**—simple rules for making complex decisions or drawing complex inferences in a rapid manner. We'll now examine two such heuristics that are used frequently in everyday life.

Representativeness: Judging by Resemblance

Suppose that you have just met your next-door neighbor for the first time. While chatting with her, you notice that she dresses in a conservative manner, is very neat in her personal habits, has a very large library in her home, and has a gentle, shy manner. Later, you realize that she never mentioned what she does for a living. Is she a business executive, a physician, a waitress, an attorney, a dancer, or a librarian? One quick way of making a guess is to compare her with other members of each of these occupations. How well does she resemble persons you have in each of these fields? If you proceed in this manner, you may well conclude that she is a librarian. After all, her traits seem to resemble those that many people associate with librarians more than the traits associated with dancers, executives, or physicians. If you made your judgment about her occupation in this manner, you would be using the **representativeness heuristic.** In other words, you would make your judgment on the basis of a relatively simple rule: *The more similar an individual is to "typical" members of a given group, the more likely she or he is to belong to that group.*

Are such judgments accurate? Often they are, because belonging to certain groups does affect the behavior and mannerisms of persons in them, and because persons with certain characteristics

or "styles" are attracted to particular groups in the first place. But sometimes judgments based on representativeness are wrong. Some librarians are extroverted and lead exciting social lives; some dancers are shy and read lots of books; some professors sky-dive for a hobby! Because of such exceptions, the representativeness heuristic, although useful, can lead to serious errors in at least some instances. In addition, reliance on this heuristic can cause us to overlook other types of information that may potentially be very useful. The most important type is information relating to *base rates*—the frequency with which given events or patterns occur in the general population. Our tendency to overlook such information when relying on the representativeness heuristic is illustrated quite clearly by a famous study performed by Tversky and Kahneman (1973).

Participants in this investigation were told that an imaginary person named Jack had been selected from a group of one hundred men. They were then asked to guess the probability that Jack was an engineer. Some participants were told that thirty of the one hundred men were engineers (the base rate for engineers was 30 percent). Others were told that seventy of the men were engineers. Half of the participants received no further information. The others, however, were also given a personal description of Jack that either resembled or did not resemble the common stereotype of engineers (e.g., they are practical, like to work with numbers, and so on). When participants received only information relating to base rates, their estimates of the likelihood that Jack was an engineer reflected this information. They thought it more likely that Jack was an engineer when the base rate was 70 percent than when it was 30 percent. When participants received personal information about Jack, however, they tended to ignore the important base rate information. They made their estimates primarily on the basis of whether Jack seemed to resemble their stereotype of an engineer. In sum, participants tended to overlook a valuable form of information when they operated in terms of representativeness. This tendency to ignore useful base rate information is known as the **base rate fallacy,** and we'll meet it again at several points in this chapter.

Availability: What Comes to Mind First?

Which are more common: words that start with the letter k (e.g., king) or words with k as the third letter (e.g., awkward)? In English, there are more than twice as many words with k in third place as there are with k in first place. Yet despite this fact, when asked this question a majority of persons guess incorrectly: They assume that there are more words beginning with k (Tversky & Kahneman, 1982). Why? In part, because of the operation of another heuristic—the **availability heuristic.** According to this heuristic, the easier it is to bring instances of some group, category, or event to mind, the more prevalent or important these are judged to be. This heuristic, too, makes good sense: Events or objects that are common *are* usually easier to think of than ones that are less common. But relying on availability in making such judgments can also lead to errors such as the one involving words with the letter k. In this and many other situations, the fact that information is easy to remember does *not* guarantee that it is more important or more common. Yet our subjective feeling that something is easy to bring to mind may lead us to assume that it is important (Rothman & Hardin, 1997). In such cases, the availability heuristic reduces our cognitive effort but may also cause us to reach erroneous conclusions. Since information that is easier to remember *is* often more important or prevalent, however, the availability heuristic is useful in many contexts, and we do often use it—with some very interesting effects, which we'll now consider.

Judging Whether One's Own Views Are Similar to Other People's Views. People often assume that others share their views even when there is little direct support for the assumption, which is known as the **false consensus effect.** In other words, we assume that others are more like us than they actually are. For example, smokers tend to overestimate the proportion of other persons who smoke (Suls, Wan, & Sanders, 1988). One explanation of the false consensus effect is that we sometimes want to believe that others agree with us because the support of others enhances our confidence in our own judgments (Marks & Miller, 1987). A second explanation for the false consensus effect

stems from the availability heuristic (Ross & Nisbett, 1991): cognitively speaking, one's own views will almost always be accessed from memory faster and more easily than our memories of other people's views. Second, people tend to choose friends and associates who share similar views (see Chapter 7); thus, their experiences may provide intuitive evidence that others typically agree. Finally, we sometimes better remember instances in which others agreed with us than instances in which others disagreed. All of these factors will result in more instances of agreement than disagreement and a higher likelihood of the false consensus effect.

Recent evidence suggests that the false consensus effect is very common (e.g., Krueger & Clement, 1994; Mullen et al., 1985), but far from universal. People may perceive themselves as more unique than they really are in terms of their possessing highly desirable attributes, which is known as the **false uniqueness effect** (e.g., Bosveld, Koomen, van der Plight, & Plaiseier, 1995). For example, most people think that they are smarter than average. Similarly, people sometimes privately reject an idea but believe that everyone else in the community privately accepts it, which is known as **pluralistic ignorance** (Prentice & Miller, 1996). For example, college students often describe themselves as being less comfortable about drinking alcohol than they think other students are (Prentice & Miller, 1993). Both false uniqueness and pluralistic ignorance have been explained in terms of the decreased availability of others' views compared to one's own views. Finally, these demonstrations again highlight how error-prone people can be in some cases.

Priming: Some Effects of Increased Availability. During the first year of medical school, many students experience what is known as the "medical student syndrome." They begin to suspect that they or their friends or families are suffering from serious illnesses. An ordinary headache may cause them to wonder if they have a brain tumor, while a mild sore throat may lead to anxiety over the possibility of some rare but fatal type of infection. What accounts for these effects? It appears that the students are exposed to descriptions of diseases day after day in their classes and in assigned readings.

As a result, such information is high in availability. Thus, when a mild symptom occurs, related disease-information is readily brought to mind, with the result that the students imagine the worst about their current health. Such effects are termed **priming.** Specifically, priming involves any stimuli that heighten the availability of certain types or categories of information so that they come more readily to mind. Many instances of priming occur in everyday life. For example, after watching an especially frightening horror movie, many persons react strongly to stimuli that would previously have had little impact upon them ("What's that dark shape at the end of the driveway?" "What's that creak on the stairs?").

The occurrence of priming effects has been demonstrated in many studies, so it seems to be a very real aspect of social thought. Indeed, such effects are so common that they may support the conclusion that there is a **law of cognitive structure activation** (Sedikides & Skowronski, 1991), such that encountering some object or other entity brings related memories to mind automatically, although we may not always be

aware of this happening. In fact, research evidence suggests that priming may occur even when individuals are unaware of the priming stimuli—an effect known as **automatic priming** (e.g., Bargh & Pietromonaco, 1982; Greenwald, Klinger, & Schuh, 1995).

For example, two clever studies (Bargh, Chen, & Burrows, 1996 Experiments 2a and 2b) used the guise of a language-proficiency experiment to examine the effects of exposure to a prime category. These researchers asked college students to complete a series of sentences that involved making sentences from groups of words. Some individuals were assigned to form sentences from *elderly primes* such as old, grey, and bingo; other individuals formed sentences from more *neutral primes* such as thirsty or private. The experimenter then debriefed and dismissed the students, who then left the laboratory area, walking down a hall. However, the study was not yet over: The experimenter then used a hidden stopwatch to time how long it took the students to walk the distance of the hallway. As Figure 3.3 shows, consistent with college students' schema of elderly people, those who had worked with the

FIGURE 3.3   Priming Affects Related Behavior.

Participants in two experiments walked more slowly after being exposed to prime words related to the concept of "elderly" than after being exposed to neutral words. The fact that participants thought the study was already over makes the demonstration even more striking.

(*Source:* Based on data from Bargh, Chen, & Burrows, 1996.)

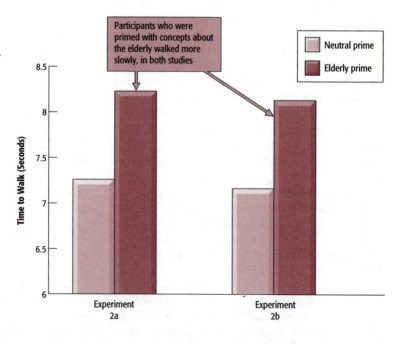

Participants who were primed with concepts about the elderly walked more slowly, in both studies

Neutral prime
Elderly prime

elderly primes walked more slowly after finishing their task than did individuals who formed sentences from neutral primes. Because people tend to have negative views about the elderly (relative to younger people; see Kite & Johnson, 1988), it's reasonable to wonder whether thinking about old people made the participants in the elderly-prime group more depressed, which might have made the participants walk more slowly. However, further research by Bargh and his colleagues ruled out this possibility—individuals in the elderly-prime condition were no more sad (or happy) than individuals in the neutral-prime condition.

In sum, it appears that priming is a basic fact of social thought and behavior. External events and conditions—and even our own thoughts—can increase the availability in memory of specific types of information. And increased availability, in turn, influences our judgments with respect to such information. "If I can think of it," we seem to reason, "then it must be important, frequent, or true"; and we often reach such conclusions even if they are not supported by social reality.

Potential Sources of Error: Why Total Rationality Is So Rare

Human beings are definitely not computers. While we can *imagine* being able to reason in a perfectly logical manner, we know from our own experience that often, we fall short of this goal. This is definitely true with respect to many aspect of social thought, we are subject to a wide range of tendencies that, together, can lead us into serious error. In this section, we'll consider several of these "tilts" in social cognition. Before turning to these sources of potential error, however, we should carefully emphasize the following point: While these aspects of social thought do sometimes result in errors, they are also quite adaptive. They help us to focus on the kinds of information that are usually most informative, and they reduce the effort required for understanding the social world. As is true of virtually

all important aspects of human behavior, then, these tendencies can be beneficial as well as potentially damaging.

Giving Extra Attention to Inconsistent Information

Imagine the following situation: You are watching an evening talk show on television. One of the guests is Newt Gingrich, Speaker of the House of Representatives in the United States Congress. You only half listen as he makes several fairly extreme but, for him, not surprising comments about taxes, welfare reform, and government generally. Then, in a quiet voice, he says something totally unexpected: He has lost interest in politics, and has decided to retire to grow roses at the end of his current two-year term. You sit up straight in disbelief; can you believe your ears? Did he really say that?

This somewhat bizarre example illustrates an important fact about social cognition: In general, we tend to pay much more attention to information that is *unexpected* or somehow *inconsistent* with our expectations than to information that is expected or consistent. Thus, a statement by Newt Gingrich to the effect that he has lost interest in politics would literally leap out at you, demanding close and careful attention.

This tendency to pay greater attention to information inconsistent with our expectations than to information consistent with them is an important and basic aspect of social cognition. It is apparent in a wide range of contexts (e.g., Hilton, Klein, & von Hippel, 1991), and seems to stem from the fact that inconsistent information is unexpected and surprising, with the result that we work harder to understand it (e.g., Stangor & McMillan, 1992). And since the greater the amount of attention we pay to information, the better its chance of entering into long-term memory and influencing our later social judgments (Fiske & Neuberg, 1990), this tendency to notice what's inconsistent has important implications.

Although this tendency to notice what's inconsistent isn't universal (see, e.g., Srull et al., 1985), it does appear to be quite general. For example, it applies to groups as well as individuals, especially if we hold strong stereotypes about a group. Finally, while it is usually the case that information to which we pay particular attention exerts stronger effects on our social thought and judgments than other information, it's important to note that this is not always so. Sometimes, although we readily *notice* information that is inconsistent with our expectations, we tend to discount it or downplay it: It's simply too unexpected to accept. For example, you probably can't help noticing the weird headlines on the tabloid newspapers displayed near the check-out lines in supermarkets ("Woman marries monster from outer space!" "Woman gives birth to dinosaur!"). These headlines are unexpected and inconsistent with views you already hold. But the chances of their influencing your thinking in any serious way are slight, because they are *so* bizarre that you discount them. So the fact that we often pay careful attention to information inconsistent with our current views or thinking does not mean that such information is necessarily more influential with respect to social thought.

Automatic Vigilance: Noticing the Negative

Do you ever notice that political campaigns seem to use many negative advertisements, like the one pictured in Figure 3.4? Similarly, if another person smiles at us twenty times during a conversation but frowns once, it is the frown that we notice most. If one of our friends describes someone to us and mentions twenty positive things about the person but one negative thing, *this* is the information on which we focus and which we are later most likely to remember. So strong is this tendency to pay attention to negative information that some researchers call it **automatic vigilance**—a powerful tendency to pay attention to negative information or stimuli (e.g, Shiffrin, 1988).

In one sense, this tendency makes a great deal of sense. After all, negative information may alert us to potential danger, and it is crucial that we recognize it—and respond to it—as quickly as possible (Pratto & John, 1991). But since our attentional capacity is limited, when we direct attention to negative social information, we run

FIGURE 3.4   Political Campaigns Often "Go Negative."

Political campaigns often rely on negative advertisements such as this one because they tend to get noticed. Such effects show how quickly we identify negative information and pay attention to it.

the risk of overlooking or ignoring other valuable forms of input. As is true with all the tendencies in social cognition we will consider in this chapter, therefore, it is possible for automatic vigilance to cause us difficulties.

How strong is this tendency to focus on negative social information? Very strong, it appears. For example, consider what social psychologists describe as the *face-in-the-crowd effect* (Hansen & Hansen, 1988). We are especially sensitive to negative facial expressions on the part of others—so sensitive that we can very quickly pick out the angry face in a crowd of persons showing neutral or happy expressions. Interestingly, we are somewhat slower to identify a happy face in a crowd of angry faces (Hansen & Hansen, 1988). These findings are consistent with the principles of *evolutionary psychology* (Buss, 1996), since angry persons do indeed represent a greater threat to our safety—or survival—than happy ones.

In any case, the findings of many different studies indicate that where social information is concerned, we are indeed especially sensitive to negative input, which helps explain why political advertisements are often so negative. Campaign managers obviously realize that such attempts to influence are more likely to succeed. And since the information to which we pay most attention often exerts the strongest effects on thought and judgments about others, the *automatic vigilance* effect also helps explain why, as we noted in Chapter 2, making a favorable first impression on others can be so important.

Counterfactual Thinking and Regret: How "What Might Have Been" Matters

Imagine the following events:

> *Ms. Caution never picks up hitchhikers. Yesterday, however, she broke her rule and gave a stranger a lift. He repaid her kindness by robbing her.*

Now, in contrast, consider the following events:

> *Ms. Risk frequently picks up hitchhikers. Yesterday she gave yet another stranger a ride. He repaid her kindness by robbing her.*

Which of these two persons will experience greater regret? If you answered, "Ms. Caution, of course," your thinking in this instance is very much like that of other persons. An overwhelming majority of respondents identify Ms. Caution as experiencing more regret (Kahneman & Miller, 1986). Why is this the case? Both individuals have suffered precisely the same negative outcome: they have been robbed. Thus, from a totally rational point of view, there's no reason to expect most people to choose Ms. Caution. Why, then, do we perceive her as experiencing greater regret? The answer involves some intriguing facts about social thought and the judgments resulting from it. In the most general terms, it appears that our reactions to events depend not only on the events themselves, but also on what these events bring to mind (D. T. Miller, Turnbull, & McFarland, 1990). When we have some experience, we do not think about the experience itself only; we also engage in *mental simulation* with respect to it. This often results in what social psychologists describe as **counterfactual thinking**—bringing alternative events and outcomes to mind. In this

particular instance, we might think, "If only Ms. Caution had not broken her rule against picking up hitchhikers, she'd be okay." Alternatively, we may imagine that "If Ms. Risk read the papers, she would probably act differently."

Why does such counterfactual thinking lead us to believe that Ms. Caution will experience more regret? In part, because it is easier to imagine alternatives to unusual behavior, such as Ms. Caution's picking up the hitchhiker, than it is to imagine alternatives to usual, normal behavior (e.g., Ms. Risk's picking up the hitchhiker). So we conclude that Ms. Caution will experience more regret because it is easier to imagine her acting in a different way—sticking to her standard rule—than it is to imagine Ms. Risk acting differently.

This reasoning leads to the interesting prediction that negative outcomes that follow unusual behavior will generate more sympathy for the persons who experience such outcomes than ones that follow usual behavior. And in fact, these predictions have been confirmed in many different studies (e.g., D. T. Miller et al., 1990; McMullen, 1997). Indeed, consistent with the view that negative affect signals the presence of a hazard, the evidence is even beginning to suggest that people *automatically* engage in counterfactual reasoning whenever negative affect arises (Roese, 1997; Roese & Olson, in press). Thus, when we experience negative outcomes of our actions, we may be especially likely to think of what might have been. So counterfactual thinking does occur, and does influence social judgments and reactions in predictable ways.

So far, so good. But now, before you read on, try this: List the three biggest regrets in your life—the things you wish most strongly you could change. What were they? If you are like most people, you may be surprised to realize that these regrets do not relate to things you did—actions that produced negative outcomes. Rather, they probably relate to things you did not do, but wish you had: the romantic interest you didn't pursue, the job you didn't take, the trip you didn't make. These are the kinds of things most people list when asked about their biggest regrets.

At first glance, this fact seems inconsistent with a key finding of research on counterfactual thinking: In general, people express more regret for things they did—especially unusual actions—than for things they didn't do. How can this inconsistency be explained? Gilovich and Medvec (1994) offer an intriguing answer. They propose that, shortly after the event, people may be more upset by actions they performed that yielded negative outcomes than by actions they didn't perform. The actions we perform may trigger more thoughts about "what might have been" or "should have been." Later, however, we may come to regret the things we didn't do—failures to act that led us to experience reduced or negative outcomes.

Why should our reactions in this respect change over time? Gilovich and Medvec (1994) offer several possibilities. First, they note that there are several factors that, over time, diminish our regrets for specific actions. An action that yielded negative results can sometimes be reversed. Missed opportunities stemming from failure to act, however, may never come again. Similarly, we may be better at rationalizing away actions that produced negative consequences—finding good reasons for these actions—than we are at rationalizing failures to act. Second, Gilovich and Medvec (1994) call attention to factors that, over time, tend to *increase* our regrets about things we didn't do. Often, we fail to act because of fears or lack of confidence; later, looking back, we may feel that these fears were not justified and that we *should have* acted. Similarly, once we have performed an action, we are faced with the consequences: we know what these are. In contrast, if we fail to act, we continue to speculate about what *would have* happened if we had taken some action. Such speculation is limitless, and can serve to magnify our regret. In sum, there are many reasons why the pattern of our regrets for action and inaction may shift greatly over time.

Do such shifts actually occur? To find out, Gilovich and Medvec (1994) asked individuals to describe the biggest regrets of their lives. Results indicated that a large majority reported failures to act; a smaller number listed regrets over past actions (see Table 3.1). In a follow-up study, the same researchers asked individuals to report their single most regrettable action or inaction during the past week, and from their entire lives, and to report on which they regretted more—the action or the inaction. For regrets from the past week, actions and inactions were mentioned about equally by participants. For regrets from their entire lives, however, a large majority of participants (84 percent) focused on inactions. So, consistent with what Gilovich and Medvec (1994) predicted, there was a major shift in the pattern of regrets over time.

In sum, it appears that when we think about various events in our lives, we do engage in coun-

TABLE 3.1 ■ What People Regret

As shown here, when asked to describe the biggest regrets of their lives, individuals are more likely to describe things they didn't do rather than things they did do.

FAILURES TO ACT	NUMBER	ACTIONS	NUMBER
Missed educational opportunities	21	Bad educational choice	3
Failure to seize the moment	21	Rushed in too soon	17
Not spending enough time with friends and relatives	15	Spent time badly	4
Missed romantic opportunity	13	Unwise romantic adventure	10
Not pursuing interest in something	11	Wasted time on something	0
Missed career opportunity	7	Bad career decision	3

(*Source:* Based on data from Gilovich & Medvec, 1994.)

terfactual thinking: We imagine what might have been or should have been in these situations. Moreover, as we noted earlier, we seem to produce counterfactual thoughts automatically in response to negative events (McMullen, 1997; Roese, 1997). Such thoughts, in turn, can strongly affect our judgments about these events or situations. However, the nature of such thinking seems to shift over time, from a focus on what we *did do* to a focus on what we *didn't do*. Whatever the focus of such thoughts, one point seems clear: We seem to torture ourselves with thoughts of possible outcomes as well as with thoughts about actual ones.

Why a Cognitive Miser Strategy Sometimes Pays Off

Have you ever had the experience of thinking about some problem or decision so long and so hard that, ultimately, you found yourself becoming more and more confused? If so, you are aware of the fact that even where rational thought is concerned, there can sometimes be too much of a good thing.

Surprising as this conclusion may be, it has been confirmed by many studies conducted by social psychologists (e.g., T. D. Wilson & Brekke, 1994; Yost & Weary, 1996). For example, Wilson and Schooler (1991) asked college students to sample and rate several strawberry jams. Half of the participants were simply asked to taste the jams and rate them; the others were asked to analyze their reactions to the jams—to indicate why they felt the way they did about each product. Wilson and Schooler (1991) reasoned that when individuals engage in such careful introspection, the reasons they bring to mind may simply be the ones that are most prominent and accessible—the easiest to remember or put into words. However, they may *not* be the most important factors in their judgments. As a result, people may actually be misled by the reasons they report, and this may cause them to make less accurate judgments.

Wilson and Schooler (1991) obtained similar findings in a follow-up study in which they asked students to read course descriptions and student evaluations of college courses, and then to indicate the likelihood that they would take these courses themselves. Some students merely rated the courses (the control condition), while those in two other conditions were asked either (1) to analyze the reasons they might want or not want to take each course, or (2) to stop and think about each piece of information as they read it and to rate the extent to which it made them more or less likely to take the course. Results indicated that those in the two "think deeply" conditions were less likely to make effective decisions—to preregister for and actually enroll in the most popular courses.

In sum, it appears that on some occasions, thinking too much can get us into serious cognitive trouble. Yes, attempting to think systematically and rationally about important matters is important; such high-effort activities do often yield better decisions or judgments than shoot-from-the-hip modes of thought. But careful thought, like anything else, can be overdone; and when it is, the result may be increased confusion and frustration rather than better and more accurate conclusions.

Rational versus Intuitive Processing

Imagine the following situation: You are shown two bowls containing red jelly beans and white jelly beans. One holds a single red bean and nine white ones, the other holds ten red beans and ninety white ones. Further, imagine that you will win money each time you select (blindfolded) a red bean. From which bowl would you prefer to draw? Rationally, it makes no difference: the chances of winning are exactly 10 percent in both cases. But if you are like most people, you'd prefer the bowl with one-hundred beans. In fact, in several studies, more than two-thirds of the participants given this choice preferred the bowl with the larger number of jelly beans; and—even more surprisingly—*they were willing to pay money to guarantee this choice* (Kirkpatrick & Epstein, 1992). In a sense, it's hard to imagine a clearer illustration of the fact that our thinking is far from perfectly rational in many situations.

What accounts for this and related findings? According to one model, known as **cognitive–experiential self-theory** (CEST for short), our efforts to understand the world around us proceed in two distinct ways. One of these is deliberate, rational thinking, which follows basic rules of logic. The other is a more *intuitive* system, which operates in a more automatic, holistic manner—a kind of "fly-by-the-seat-of-our-pants" approach, in which we make quick decisions according to simple heuristics we've developed through experience (e.g., Donovan & Epstein, 1997; Epstein, Pacini, Denes-Raj, & Heier, 1996). CEST theory suggests that we tend to use these contrasting styles of thought in different kinds of situations. Rational thinking is used in situations involving analytical thought—for example, solving mathematical problems. Intuitive thinking is used in many other situations, including most social ones. In other words, when we try to understand others' behavior, we often revert to intuitive, gut-level thinking. So why do we tend to prefer the larger bowl of jelly beans? Because in situations like this, the intuitive system is dominant. We *know*, rationally, that the odds of winning are the same in both cases; but we *feel* that we have a better chance of winning when there are ten red jelly beans rather than only one. Denes-Raj and Epstein (1994) suggest that this is because information in the experiential system is encoded primarily in the form of concrete representations. In other words, we can visualize one red jelly bean and nine white ones more easily than ten red and ninety white ones, so we choose the larger bowl for this reason: It seems to hold out a greater chance of winning.

The powerful effects of intuitive thought are dramatically illustrated in a recent study conducted by Denes-Raj and Epstein (1994). These researchers allowed participants to choose between two bowls of jelly beans under conditions where, if they were successful in drawing red beans from the bowl they chose, participants could win actual money. In one condition, the proportion of red beans was identical in both bowls (10 percent). In other conditions, however, the proportion of red beans in the larger bowl was actually *lower* than 10 percent: it ranged from 5 to 9 percent. In other words, there were only 5 red beans and 95 white ones (5 percent), 6 red beans and 94 white ones (6 percent), and

so on. What would participants do? Rationally, they should certainly choose the small bowl, since it always contained 1 red bean (10 percent). As you can see from Figure 3.5, however, this was definitely *not* the case. Substantial proportions of persons chose the larger bowl *even when the odds of winning were lower*. Similar results were obtained in a follow-up study where the amount of money at stake was larger—participants could win as much as $35 by drawing red jelly beans. Even under these conditions, however, fully 85 percent of the participants made nonoptimal choices: They preferred to draw from the larger bowl. Interestingly, participants were well aware of the conflict between rational and intuitive modes of thought. Many reported that they *knew* the chances of winning were better with the small bowl, but went with the big one because they "felt" they had more chances of winning when there were more red beans.

These findings, and the results of related research (e.g., S. T. Fiske & Taylor, 1991) provide convincing evidence for the conclusion we offered at the start of this section: Often, we *don't* process information in a totally rational manner. On the contrary, under many conditions—especially, it appears, when we are experiencing strong emotional arousal and when we are in social situations involving other persons—we fall back on a more intuitive mode of thought. Such thought is certainly comfortable, quick, and familiar; but as you can readily see, it doesn't always provide us with the best or most accurate answers to the puzzles of everyday life!

Social Cognition: A Word of Optimism

The planning fallacy, automatic vigilance, the costs of thinking too much, counterfactual thinking—having read our discussions of these and other sources of error in social thought, you may be ready to despair: Can we ever get it right? The answer, we believe, is *absolutely*. No, we're not perfect information-processing machines. We have limited cognitive capacities, and we can't—unfortunately—increase these by buying pop-in memory upgrades. And yes, we are somewhat lazy: We generally do the least amount of cogni-

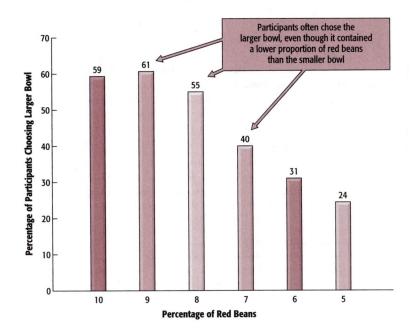

Participants often chose the larger bowl, even though it contained a lower proportion of red beans than the smaller bowl

FIGURE 3.5 The Power of Intuitive Thought.

When asked whether they wanted to draw jelly beans from a bowl containing one red bean and nine white ones or from a bowl containing larger numbers of red and white beans, individuals often chose the latter—*even though the odds of drawing a winning red bean were actually lower!* These findings indicate that, often, we don't process information in a completely rational manner. Rather, we go with our "intuitions," even if we know these are likely to be wrong.

(*Source:* Based on data from Denes-Raj & Epstein, 1994.)

tive work possible in any situation. Despite these limitations, however, we frequently do an impressive job in thinking about others. Despite being flooded by truly enormous amounts of social information, we manage to sort, store, remember, and use a significant portion of this input in an intelligent and efficient manner. Certainly, we're not perfect; but we do manage to get the job done in a manner that permits us to introduce a surprising degree of order and predictability into our lives, and into our constructions of the social world around us. So, while we can imagine being better at these tasks than we are, there's no reason to be disheartened. On the contrary, it's not unreasonable to take some pride in the fact that we do accomplish quite a lot with the limited tools at our disposal. For more information on the cultural basis of these tools of social cognition, see the Social Diversity box on pages 68–69.

Integrating Principles

1. We are *not* perfect information processors. On the contrary, our social thought is subject to many different sources of potential error, ranging from the tendency to be extremely sensitive to negative information (automatic vigilance), to the planning fallacy, to magical thinking.

2. These tendencies sometimes cause us to make errors in our inferences or judgments about others. Such errors are related to many aspects of social behavior, including first impressions of others (Chapter 2), persuasion (Chapter 5), and even judgments about others' innocence or guilt (Chapter 11).

The Interplay of Affect and Cognition

Look at the cartoon in Figure 3.6. What happened to Cathy? She was all set to be logical and assertive but then . . . she saw the chocolate candy. So long, good intentions! Her affective reactions quickly changed her cognitive processes. This cartoon actually illustrates an important area of research in social psychology: efforts to investigate the interplay between *affect*—our current moods or feelings—and *cognition*—the ways in which we process, store, remember, and use social information (Forgas, 1995; Isen & Baron, 1991). We say *interplay* because research on this topic indicates that in fact the relationship is very much a two-way street: Our feelings and moods exert strong effects on several aspects of cognition, and cognition, in turn, exerts strong effects on our feelings and moods (e.g., Seta, Hayes, & Seta, 1994). In this section we'll describe many of these effects. Before turning to these, however, we'll

pause briefly to examine several contrasting views concerning the nature of emotion (e.g., Ekman, 1992; Izard, 1991). *Emotions* are complex reactions involving physiological responses, subjective cognitive states, and expressive behaviors. In general, emotions are viewed as being more intense than *affective states*, our relatively mild feelings and moods (Forgas, 1995). However, the dividing line between *emotion* and *affect* (or *mood*) is uncertain, so it is both useful and informative to take a quick look at what modern psychology has to say about the nature of emotions.

FIGURE 3.6   How Affect Influences Cognition: A Humorous Example.

When Cathy saw the chocolate candy and experienced positive affect, her thinking changed drastically. Growing evidence points to the conclusion that our affective states *do* often exert strong effects on many aspects of our cognition.

(*Source:* CATHY copyright 1996 Cathy Guisewite. Reprinted with permission of UNIVERSAL PRESS. All rights reserved.)

1. A large body of research evidence indicates that affect and cognition are intimately—and complexly—linked. Our feelings influence many aspects of our cognition, and cognition, in turn, can strongly shape our moods and feelings.
2. These connections rest on several basic mechanisms, including *priming* of affect-related associations and memories and our tendency to use our moods as a quick basis for formulating social judgments.
3. Links between affect and cognition play an important role in many forms of social behavior, including attitudes (Chapter 5), prejudice (Chapter 6), attraction (Chapter 7), helping (Chapter 9), and important practical situations such as job interviews (Chapter 11).

The Nature of Emotion: Contrasting Views and Recent Advances

Feelings, and rapid changes in them, are a central part of everyday life; so over the centuries, scholars have developed many different views about the nature of emotions. Indeed, even today there is a continuing debate over whether emotions precede cognitions, cognitions precede emotions, or even whether emotions and cognitions reflect fundamentally different systems in the brain (e.g., Izard, 1993; Lazarus, 1993; LeDoux, 1995). Some theorists argue that our emotional reactions to events come first, followed by our thoughts about the emotions or about what caused them. Others argue that our thoughts appear first, followed by our feelings.

One perspective that has gained many adherents proposes that emotions represent a brain system that evolved earlier than did higher cognitive functions (e.g., LeDoux, 1995). According to this **neuropsychological** view, the emotional systems in the brain evolved as a survival mechanism (e.g., limbic systems such as the amygdala or thalamus), which helped organisms to recognize good versus bad situations—things that might harm and things that might help. In humans, at least, this emotional system remains, but is more primitive than the cognitive system (e.g., cerebral cortex). Emotions continue to function as a sort of early warning system that allows people to react quickly to threatening situations. However, the cognitive system, which is more conscious than the affective system, moderates these quick impulses with more deliberate responses.

Despite these debates, what is clear is that emotions and thoughts do often work together, closely and quickly. Within the field of social psychology, one widely accepted perspective is Schachter's (1964) **two-factor theory of emotion,** which suggests that any form of arousal, whatever its source, initiates a search for the causes of these feelings. The causes we then identify play a key role in determining the label we place on our arousal, and so in the emotion experience. Thus, if we feel aroused in the presence of an attractive person, we may label our arousal as "love" or "attraction." If we feel aroused after a near miss in traffic, we label our feelings as "fear" or perhaps "anger" toward the other driver who was—of course!—clearly at fault. In short, as Figure 3.7 shows, we perceive ourselves to be experiencing the emotion that external cues suggest we *should* be feeling. As we'll see in Chapter 9, the results of many studies offer support for the view proposed by Schachter, so it is clear that cognitive and situational factors do play a role in our subjective emotional reactions.

Other social psychological evidence seems to support the conclusion that we experience emotions in part because of our awareness of psychological reactions to various stimuli or situations. First, studies conducted with highly sophisticated equipment indicate that different emotions are indeed associated with different patterns of physiological activity (Levenson, 1992). Not only do various emotions *feel* different, but also it appears that they are reflected in somewhat different patterns of bodily changes, including brain and muscle activity (Ekman, Davidson, & Friesen, 1990; Izard, 1991). Second, changes in our facial expressions sometimes *produce* changes in out emotional experiences rather than merely reflecting them, which is known as the **facial feedback hypothesis** (Zajonc, Murphy, & Inglehart, 1989). Briefly, this theory suggests that there is a close association

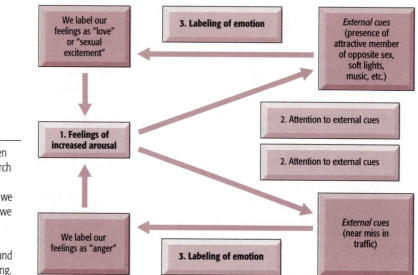

FIGURE 3.7 Schachter's Two-Factor Theory of Emotion.

According to Schachter's theory, when we experience arousal, we often search the external world around us for the source of such feelings. The sources we identify strongly influence the labels we then attach to our arousal. In other words, we often label our feelings in accordance with what the world around us suggests we *should* be experiencing.

between the facial expressions we show and our internal feelings, and that in this relationship the facial expressions may themselves yield information that feeds back into our brains and influences our subjective experiences of emotion. In other words, we do not only smile because we feel happy; sometimes, when we smile, we feel happier *because* we have smiled. Thus, mere physiological activity *can* produce emotional responses. Subjective emotional experiences do often arise directly in relation to specific external stimuli.

Connections between Affect and Cognition: Some Intriguing Effects

Earlier, we noted that the links between affect and cognition operate in both directions: Our current moods or feelings influence the way we think, and our thoughts can influence our feelings. As we'll see in this section, the influence of affect on cognition can be intriguing—and dramatic. Suppose that you have just received some very good news—you did much better on an important exam than you expected—and are feeling great. Now, you run into one of your friends in the student union and she introduces you to someone you don't know. You chat with this per-

son for a while and then leave for another class. Will your first impression of the stranger be influenced by the fact that you are feeling so good? Your own experience probably suggests that it will. As one old song puts it, when we are in a good mood we tend to "see the world through rose-colored glasses"—everything takes on a positive tinge. Evidence that such effects actually do occur—that our feelings do influence the way we think and our social judgments—is provided by the findings of many different studies (e.g., Clore, Schwarz, & Conway, 1994).

The results of these studies point to a general fact about the influence of affect on cognition: In general, there is a *mood-congruent judgment effect*. That is, there is often a good match between our mood and our thoughts. When we are feeling happy, we tend to think happy thoughts and retrieve happy ideas and experiences from memory; when we are in a negative mood, we tend to think *unhappy* thoughts and to retrieve negative information from memory (Mayer & Hanson, 1995; Seta, Hayes, & Seta, 1994). This mood-congruent judgment effect has important practical implications. For example, it has been found that when interviewers are in a good mood, they tend to assign higher ratings to job applicants (R. A. Baron, 1993b). In this way, temporary fluctuations in mood can sometimes influence the course of individuals' careers.

These are not the only ways in which affect influences cognition, however. Other findings indicate, for example, that being in a happy mood can sometimes increase creativity—perhaps because being in a happy mood activates a wider range of ideas or associations, and creativity involves combining these into new patterns. A study conducted with practicing physicians by Estrada, Isen, and Young (1995) clearly illustrates such effects. These researchers gave one group of participants some candy—a small, unexpected gift designed to give them a small "mood boost," whereas the other physicians did not receive this small gift. Those who received the candy answered more questions correctly than those who did not. Since accurately diagnosing complex medical problems often involves recognizing links between test results and symptoms that do not at first appear to be related, these findings suggest that physicians' affective states may play some role in their success at this crucial task. Obviously, to the extent this is so, there are important implications for the quality of medical treatment.

The Affect Infusion Model: How Affect Influences Cognition

Before concluding this discussion of the relationship between affect and cognition, let's address one final issue: *How*, precisely, does affect influence cognition? Through what mechanisms do our feelings influence our thought? A theory proposed by Forgas (1995), known as the **affect infusion model (AIM),** offers some intriguing answers. According to this model, affect influences social thought and, ultimately, social judgments through two major mechanisms. First, affect serves to *prime* (i.e., trigger) similar or related cognitive categories. In other words, when we are in a good mood, these feelings serve to prime positive associations and memories; when we are in a negative mood, in contrast, these feelings tend to prime predominantly negative associations and memories (e.g., T. D. Wilson &

Klaaren, 1992). In addition, affective states may influence attention and encoding so that we pay more attention to information congruent with our current mood, and invest more time and effort in entering mood-congruent information into memory.

Second, affect may influence cognition by acting as a *heuristic cue*—a quick way for inferring our reactions to a specific person, event, or stimulus. According to this *affect-as-information* mechanism (Clore et al., 1994), when asked to make a judgment about something in the social world, we examine our feelings and then respond accordingly. If we are in a good mood, we conclude: "I like it" or "I'm favorable toward it." If we are in a bad mood, in contrast, we conclude: "I don't like it" or "I'm unfavorable toward it." In other words, we ask ourselves, "How do I feel about it?" and use our current affective states to answer this question—*even if they are unrelated to the object, person, or event itself.*

When do such effects occur? Forgas (1995) suggests that affective states influence cognition through the first mechanism, priming, in situations that require *substantive* thought—where we attempt to interpret new information and relate it to existing knowledge. In contrast, affective states influence cognition primarily through the second mechanism, affect-as-information, in situations where we think *heuristically*—situations where we can get away with minimal cognitive effort. Evidence from many studies offers support for these suggestions (e.g., Clore et al., 1994). Consider an ingenious field study conducted recently by Forgas (1994).

In this investigation, people were approached on the street either immediately after seeing a sad or happy film, or (in the control group) *before* seeing one of these films. They were asked to complete a questionnaire dealing with six trivial and six serious conflicts in their personal relationships. (Examples of trivial conflicts: which TV channel to watch, what music to play. Examples of serious conflicts: jealous behavior, amount of time spent with partner.) For each conflict, participants rated the extent to which they and their partner were responsible for the conflict. Forgas (1994) predicted that because

Social Diversity: A Critical Analysis

Trust As a Cognitive Bias: A Cross-National Study

Quick: Who do you think are more trusting—Japanese or Americans? Given media reports of much lower crime rates in Japan and the emphasis in Japanese culture on stable, long-term relationships (in business as well as personal life), it is tempting to conclude, "Japanese, of course." But in fact, several studies have reported precisely the opposite result: Americans turn out to be more trusting than Japanese (M. Yamagishi & Yamagishi, 1989).

How can this be so? According to two Japanese researchers (T. Yamagishi & Yamagishi, 1994), the answer lies in the definition of *trust* and in the distinction between *trust* and *assurance*. Trust, they contend, can be viewed as another tendency or bias in social cognition: A tendency to infer more benign intentions on the part of others than may actually be justified by the incomplete social information at our disposal. In other words, when we trust someone else, we may overestimate the extent to which their actions stem from desirable traits and positive intentions, and therefore tend to overestimate, too, the predictability of their future actions: the likelihood that they'll continue to behave in a benign and trustworthy manner. In contrast, *assurance* relates only to the belief that others will continue to act in a predictable manner because of incentives that make it worth their while to do so. There is no assumption that their intentions are good—or that they should be trusted.

Going farther, Yamagishi and Yamagishi (1994) propose that what is often mistaken for a high level of trust in Japanese society is really a high level of assurance: Because long-term relationships are a central part of Japanese culture, and acting in accordance with them is highly valued, individuals know that others will continue to honor these relationships. At the same time, though, Japanese individuals do not attribute such predictability to others' good intentions or positive traits. On the contrary, they recognize that these outcomes stem mainly from the structure of the relationships rather than from personal characteristics such as being honest or trustworthy. In the United States, in contrast, long-term relationships are less prevalent, so predictability tends to stem, instead, from personal trust. Thus, Americans will actually be more trusting than Japanese—they will be more subject than Japanese to this particular form of cognitive bias.

To test these intriguing predictions, Yamagishi and Yamagishi (1994) had hundreds of individuals in the United States and Japan complete a questionnaire designed to measure trust, assurance, and related concepts such as the importance of personal reputations. Results obtained with this questionnaire were very revealing. First, as predicted, Americans were indeed higher in general trust than Japanese—they more strongly agreed with such statements as "Most people are basically honest" and "Most people are basically good and kind." Moreover, this was the case whether the other persons involved were strangers or personal acquaintances. Second, Japanese reported perceiving more value in dealing with others through personal relations than did Americans. Third, Americans rated one's personal reputation as more important than did Japanese. Finally, and perhaps most surprising of all, Americans rated themselves as honest and fair more than did the Japanese participants (see Figure 3.8).

In sum, results offered support for the view that what are often mistaken for high levels of *trust* in Japanese society are really high levels of mutual *assurance*—the perception that others will act in predictable ways because they are involved with the perceiver in long-term,

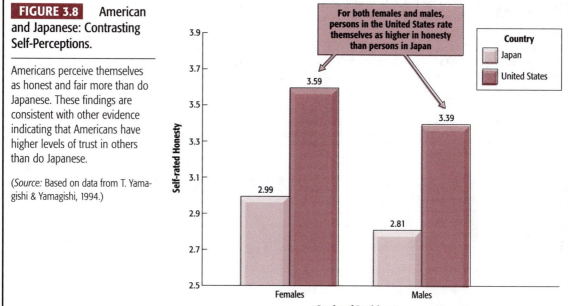

FIGURE 3.8 American and Japanese: Contrasting Self-Perceptions.

Americans perceive themselves as honest and fair more than do Japanese. These findings are consistent with other evidence indicating that Americans have higher levels of trust in others than do Japanese.

(*Source:* Based on data from T. Yamagishi & Yamagishi, 1994.)

stable relationships. Outside of the context of such relationships, Americans are actually more trusting than Japanese; they assume that other persons, strangers as well as friends, are likely to behave in an honest manner and out of good intentions.

Is the tendency to trust others really a form of bias in social cognition? It is, but only to the extent that levels of trust exceed those that reflect reality. In any case, it is our view that too much trust—too much faith in others' motives and intentions—may be a far less serious social error than the opposite tendency, to perceive malevolence in others' motives and behavior when none actually exists. We'll have more to say about this phenomenon in Chapter 9.

individuals would be more likely to engage in substantive processing about serious conflicts, the effects of mood would be stronger for such conflicts than for trivial conflicts because priming effects would be stronger for serious conflicts. As you can see from Figure 3.9, results offered support for these predictions. Persons in a sad mood were much more likely to blame themselves for serious conflicts than those who were in a happy mood. However, such effects were much weaker with respect to the trivial conflicts, about which, presumably, individuals thought less carefully.

These and other findings provide evidence for the affect infusion model and help us to understand precisely *how* our current moods or feelings can influence our thoughts and judgments. Apparently, several different mechanisms can underlie the important links between affect and cognition, and which is most important in a given situation depends on the kind of social thought in which we engage—substantive or heuristic—plus several additional factors. Contrary to what our everyday experience suggests, therefore, there is considerably more to the interplay between feelings and thought than at first meets the eye.

FIGURE 3.9   Evidence for the AIM Model: How Affect Influences
Our Interpretations of Interpersonal Conflicts.

As predicted by the *affect infusion model* (AIM), individuals in a sad mood (who had just seen a sad movie) blamed themselves for serious conflicts to a greater extent than persons who were in a happy mood (who had just seen a happy movie). These effects were much weaker in the case of trivial conflicts.

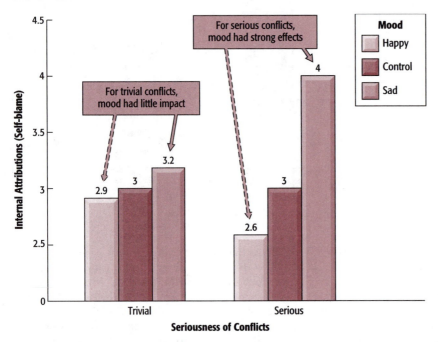

(*Source:* Based on data from Forgas, 1994.)

Connections   Integrating Social Psychology

In this chapter, you read about . . .

- schemas and prototypes

- potential sources of error in social cognition

- the interplay between affect and cognition

In other chapters, you will find related discussions of . . .

- the effects of schemas and prototypes on other aspects of social behavior, such as attitudes (Chapter 5) and prejudice (Chapter 6)
- the role of these errors in first impressions (Chapter 2) and persuasion (Chapter 5)
- the role of such interplay in many forms of social behavior, including prejudice (Chapter 6), attraction (Chapter 7), helping (Chapter 9), and effects of the physical environment on social behavior (Chapter 11)

Thinking about Connections

1. As we noted in this chapter, we possess cognitive frameworks known as *schemas* that help us interpret many social situations. Do you think such frameworks play a role in intimate relationships? (See Chapter 7.) Do you believe that we possess relatively clear frameworks suggesting, for instance, that relationships should change in various ways over time, and even *when* such changes should occur? If so, what are these frameworks like?

2. Suppose that one day, you met someone who seemed to be the boldest, most adventurous person you had ever encountered; no risk seemed to be too great for this person, and she was truly ready for "action" of every conceivable kind. Then, much to your surprise, you learned that this individual was a professor of English literature. Drawing on what you now know about social cognition, how would you handle this information? Would it influence your first impression of this new acquaintance? (See Chapter 2.)

3. Suppose that you help another person in need of assistance (see Chapter 9), and by doing to, you improve your own mood. Would this "soft glow of kindness" now influence your impression of this person? What about your future behavior toward her or him?

Summary and Review

Schemas and Their Effects

Social cognition involves the processes through which we notice, interpret, remember, and later use information about the social world. *Schemas* are mental frameworks containing information relevant to specific traits, situations, or events. They are formed through experience and, once developed, exert strong effects on many aspects of social cognition, including attention, encoding, and retrieval of social information. *Prototypes* are mental models of the typical qualities of members of some group or category. They, too, exert strong effects on social cognition once formed.

Heuristics: Mental Shortcuts

Because we have limited capacity to process social information, we often use mental shortcuts. *Heuristics* are mental rules of thumb that permit us to make rapid decisions or judgments about complex social stimuli. According to the *representativeness heuristic*, the more similar an individual is to typical members of a given group, the more likely she or he is to belong to that group. Another important heuristic is *availability*, according to which the more readily information can be brought to mind, the more important or frequent it is judged to be. *The false consensus effect*—our tendency to assume that others are more similar to us than they actually are—also stems in part from the availability heuristic. *Priming* involves procedures that increase the availability of specific information in consciousness. External conditions can serve as primes, but in many cases we seem to generate our own primes on the basis of our inferences about others' traits.

Potential Sources of Error

We are not perfect information-processing mechanisms. On the contrary, social cognition is subject to several tendencies and biases that can reduce its accuracy. We often engage in *intuitive* rather than *rational* thought. We tend to pay more attention to information that is inconsistent with our expectations than to information consistent with them. We also tend to notice and emphasize negative social information—the *automatic vigilance* effect. Thinking too much about a particular problem or decision can sometimes prove counterproductive and lead to reduced rather than increased accuracy. Finally, we often engage in *counterfactual thinking,* imagining "what might have been," which can affect our judgments about events that actually did take place. In addition, we tend to experience greater regrets over actions we didn't take than over ones we did take that yielded negative outcomes.

The Interplay of Affect and Cognition

Sharply contrasting views of the nature of emotions have been proposed. A *neuropsychological view* suggests that emotions stem from an evolutionarily primitive brain system that functions as a sort of early warning system that allows people to react quickly to threatening situations. Schachter's *two-factor theory* proposes that it is the cognitive label we attach to physiological arousal that is crucial.

Affective states have been found to influence memory, creativity, and many forms of social judgment, including evaluations of job applicants. Recent evidence indicates that changes in mood are often reflected in changes in social judgments. Also, cognition often influences affect. The emotions we experience are determined, at least in part, by the labels we attach to arousing events, and our emotional reactions to provocative actions by others depend in part on our interpretation of the causes behind these actions. If we expect to like or dislike some stimulus or event, our affective reactions to it will usually be consistent with such expectations.

The *affect infusion model* explains how our affective states influence cognition. According to this model, such effects occur because affect primes related associations, memories, and thoughts, and because we use our affective states as a basis for inferring our judgments about social stimuli. The model also predicts that affect will have a stronger impact upon cognition at times when we engage in careful, substantive thought.

Social Diversity: Trust As a Cognitive Bias

Trust can be viewed as a form of bias in social cognition—a tendency to attribute benign intentions and motives to others to a greater extent than may be justified by available information. Recent evidence indicates that, contrary to popular belief, Americans are actually more trusting than Japanese. This phenomenon seems to stem from the fact that in Japanese culture, predictability in social interactions derives primarily from confidence that people will behave in accordance with the requirements of long-term, committed social relationships. Such relationships are less common in American culture, resulting in greater cultural emphasis on trust.

 # Key Terms

Affect (p. 51)

Affect Infusion Model (p. 69)

Attention (p. 53)

Automatic Priming (p. 56)

Automatic Vigilance (p. 58)

Availability Heuristic (p. 55)

Base Rate Fallacy (p. 54)

Cognitive–Experiential Self-Theory (p. 61)

Counterfactual Thinking (p. 59)

Encoding (p. 53)

Facial Feedback Hypothesis (p. 65)

False Consensus Effect (p. 55)

False Uniqueness Effect (p. 55)

Heuristics (p. 54)

Information Overload (p. 53)

Law of Cognitive Structure Activation (p. 56)

Neuropsychological (p. 65)

Pluralistic Ignorance (p. 55)

Priming (p. 56)

Prototypes (p. 51)

Representativeness Heuristic (p. 54)

Retrieval (p. 53)

Schemas (p. 51)

Social Cognition (p. 50)

Two-Factor Theory of Emotion (p. 65)

For More Information

Fiske, S. T., & Taylor, S. E. (1991). *Social cognition* (2nd ed.). New York: McGraw-Hill.

A clear and thorough review of research on social cognition. Many basic aspects of our thinking about others (e.g., attribution, memory for social information) are examined in an insightful manner.

LeDoux, J. (1996) *The emotional brain: The mysterious underpinnings of emotional life.* New York: Simon & Schuster.

Written by a noted neuroscientist, this book is one of the first to examine our emotions from a biological rather than psychological perspective, arguing that our conscious feelings are irrelevant to the way the emotional brain works. A provocative account of what our emotions are, how they operate in the brain, and how they influence our lives.

Ross, L., & Nisbett, R. N. (1991). *The person and the situation: Perspectives of social psychology.* New York: McGraw-Hill.

An integrative view of social behavior that draws on attributional and social cognitive perspectives in social psychology. The book considers many personal, interpersonal, and cross-cultural phenomena.

chapter 4

The Self

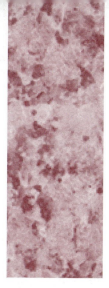

Who are you? If you suddenly found yourself in radio contact with beings on another planet, and that question were asked, what would you say in the next thirty seconds? Who are you?

Think about a very pleasant experience that you have had. Maybe the day you first fell in love, the day you received an unexpected A on a test, the day you bought your first car, or whatever. How did you feel about yourself? How did you react to the people you met? Were you optimistic about the future? Now think about a very unpleasant experience that you have had and consider the same questions about your feelings, reactions, and optimism. Assuming that you reacted differently to the two experiences—why?

Can you remember how old you were when you first realized that people were divided into boys and girls, men and women? Even if you can't precisely recall having such a realization, what did you think about the other gender when you were little, and what do you think now? How different are men and women?

Very early in our lives, each of us begins learning who we are. We develop a **social identity,** or a self-definition, that includes how we conceptualize ourselves, including how we evaluate ourselves (e.g., Higgins, 1996). For each person, this identity includes unique aspects such as one's name and self-concept, and aspects shared with others. Familiar categories include one's gender and relationships (such as woman, man, daughter, son, divorced person); vocation or avocation (such as student, musician, psychologist, salesperson, athlete); political or ideological affiliation (feminist, environmentalist, Democrat, Republican); attributes that at least some people dislike (such as being homeless, overweight, homosexual, a drug user); and ethnicity or religion (such as Catholic, Southerner, Hispanic, Jewish, African American; see M. B. Brewer & Gardner, 1996; Deaux et al., 1995).

These various categories are closely tied to our interpersonal world, and they indicate ways in which we are like and unlike other individuals. Note that when a person's social context changes, this places a strain on his or her social identity that requires some degree of coping. For example, when Hispanic students enter a primarily Anglo university, one response is to become increasingly involved in Hispanic activities and groups, thus strengthening identification with this aspect

of themselves. The opposite reaction—becoming less identified with Hispanics and seeking other ties—is also a familiar way to deal with the new situation (Ethier & Deaux, 1994).

In this chapter, we will concentrate on just two of the major components of social identity. First, we describe some of the crucial elements of the *self,* including self-concept, self-esteem, self-focusing, self-monitoring, and self-efficacy. Second, we examine *gender,* especially the social determinants of gender identity, gender roles, and the way behavior is influenced by these attributes.

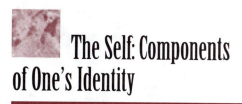

The Self: Components of One's Identity

We humans spend a lot of time and effort thinking about *ourselves.* Indeed, it may even be that selves are something that we humans have evolved as a survival mechanism in response to environmental pressures (Sedikides & Skowronski, 1997). Perhaps it's logical, therefore, that to some extent, we are literally self-centered. That is, the self is the center of each person's social universe. Your self-identity, or *self-concept*, is acquired primarily through social interactions that begin with your immediate family and continue with the other people you meet throughout life. The **self-concept** is often defined as an organized collection of beliefs and feelings about oneself—in other words, it is a schema that functions like other schemas as discussed in Chapter 3. Thus, the self-concept is a special framework that influences how we process information about the social world around us along with information about ourselves—such as our motives, emotional states, self-evaluations, abilities, and much else besides (Baumeister, in press). As in Figure 4.1, even possessions are often perceived as part of oneself; have you ever spoken of "my dog," "my clock," "my room" and so forth?

FIGURE 4.1　The Self-Concept Includes All Self-Relevant Information.

The schema that is the self-concept includes all of the information and feelings relevant to our past, present, and future selves. Even possessions can be viewed as part of the self, as this photograph suggests.

Self-Concept: The Central Schema

At the beginning of this chapter, we asked, "Who are you?" Beginning with William James (1890) more than a century ago, several variations of this question (such as "Who am I?") have been used to measure self-concept (e.g., Ziller, 1990). These studies point to the conclusion that each person possesses a unique self-concept with *specific content*, but that the *overall structure* of the self-content is the same for all individuals (e.g., Rentsch & Heffner, 1994). Thus, for example, each person has an *interpersonal* dimension as a component of his or her identity, but each person has different attributes within that dimension (e.g., being a student; being a truck driver; being a psychology major).

The Cognitive and Affective Effects of a Person's Self-Schema. Self-schemas are probably much more complex than the responses to "Who am I?" would suggest. Beyond the overall framework, such a schema would also reflect all of your relevant past experiences, all of your memories about what happened in your past, your knowledge about what you are like now, and your beliefs about what you will be like in the future. In other words, a self-schema is the sum of everything a person knows and can imagine about herself or himself. Because a person's knowledge and ability to imagine is always changing, so also must the self-concept change.

　　Because the self is the center of each person's social world and because self-schemas are very well developed, it follows that we are able to do a better job of processing self-relevant information than any other kind of information—the **self-reference effect.** For example, because my last name is Byrne, I can easily remember that Gabriel Byrne is an Irish actor, Jane Byrne was mayor of Chicago, and Brendan Byrne was governor of New Jersey—even though I've never seen any of these individuals in person. In a similar way, if you participate in an experiment, are shown a series of words, and are asked, "Does this word describe you?" after each one, you will be able to recall the words better than if you are shown the same words and asked after each, "Is this word printed in big letters?" Self-relevant information is most likely to catch your attention, to be retained in memory, and to be recalled easily, as shown in a recent research synthesis of the numerous studies on this effect (Symons & Johnson, 1997). The self-reference effect is one example of the self's cognitive effects.

Other research shows how focusing on the self can have affective, as well as cognitive implications. First, consider that at any given moment, a person's attention can be directed inward toward the self or outward toward the environment. **Self-focusing** is defined as the extent to which attention is directed toward oneself. Recall of relevant past events and processing of relevant current information is required for self-focusing to occur. Self-focus affects the accuracy of biographical recall (retrieving factual information about yourself) and the complexity of self-descriptive judgments (Dixon & Baumeister, 1991; Klein, Loftus, & Burton, 1989). A question such as "Where were you born?" directs you toward the retrieval process. A question such as "How would you describe your relationship with your parents?" can elicit relatively simple or relatively complex judgments about yourself.

Self-focusing increases between childhood and adolescence (Ullman, 1987), and some adults consistently self-focus more than others. Nevertheless, situational influences have a great effect, and self-focusing is easily induced by simple instructions (Right now, please think about the most positive aspects of yourself!) or by environmental cues such as the presence of a video camera or a mirror (Fenigstein & Abrams, 1993).

To some extent, a brief period of self-focusing improves self-insight. When research participants are instructed to spend a few minutes thinking about themselves, they are more accurate in judging social feedback than other participants who are not asked to self-focus (Hixon & Swan, 1993). However, we saw in Chapter 3 that thinking too much about the *reasons* for our feelings can have disruptive effects, such as making a person less accurate about why they like something. Similarly, on a long-term basis, self-

focused attention (among depressed individuals, for example) may simply reflect a continuing *attempt* to understand oneself rather than increased awareness (Conway et al., 1993).

One's self-concept is complex and contains a great many discrete elements. As a result, the focusing process involves only a small fraction of the total at any given time—much like a flashlight pointed at various objects in a very large, dark room. Where one's focus is directed is determined in part by the *framing* of the question (see Chapter 3). Focus affects not only retrieval but what specifically is retrieved (Kunda et al., 1993). For example, if your knowledge about your social life contains both positive and negative elements, you might give a positive response to the question, "Are you happy with your social life?" and a negative response to the question, "Are you unhappy with your social life?"

We are not always aware of exactly when we pay attention to ourselves (Epstein, 1983); but self-focusing is more likely in a familiar, comfortable situation than in an unfamiliar, threatening one. For example, if you are driving in daylight along a road you know well, you may well begin thinking about yourself. In contrast, you tend to focus on the environment when driving on an unfamiliar road on a stormy night.

Storing Positive and Negative Information about Self in Memory. It appears that many people file positive and negative aspects of themselves separately in memory (Showers, 1992). A person's mood, in turn, is affected by whether the focus is on positive or negative elements. This interrelationship between affect and cognition was also discussed in Chapter 3. If you think about only the negative aspects of yourself, you can easily become unhappy. Not only does self-focusing influence mood (Sedikides, 1992); but also mood affects self-focusing. As a result, any external event that affects mood also tends to direct self-focusing (Kernis & Waschull, 1995; Leith & Baumeister, 1996). For example, if you are unhappy following an argument with a close friend, you are more likely to focus on and recall negative things about yourself and to be pessimistic about the future. Figure 4.2 outlines these interconnections. When you are confronted by extremely stressful negative events, it is better to have some clearly differentiated (compartmentalized) aspects of the self that are *very positive* and *very important*. The presence of separate, positive elements of the self on which you can fall back is a protection against becoming depressed when stress occurs (Showers & Ryff, 1993).

One Self-Concept or Many? People ordinarily speak of themselves as though the self were a stable and unchanging entity. Even so, we are aware that we can and do change over time. You are not the same person you were ten years ago, and you are

---

FIGURE 4.2   The Interrelationship of External Events, Mood, Self-Focusing, and Expectancies.

Many people store positive and negative self-information separately in memory. When attention is focused on positive information, this results in a positive mood and optimistic expectancies. Positive external events also can lead to positive mood, self-focusing on positive information, and optimism. In just the same way, negative external events, a negative mood, self-focusing on negative information, and pessimistic expectancies are also interrelated.

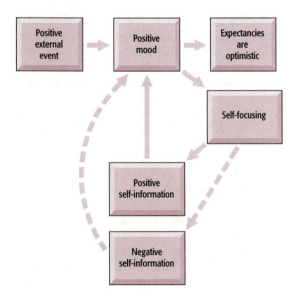

not likely to be the same person ten years from now that you are today. Sometimes you may imagine what your life will be like after college—entering the job market, getting married, having children, earning more money, living somewhere else. In effect, you have a self-concept, but you are also aware of other **possible selves,** as well (Niedenthal & Beike, 1997).

Markus and Nurius (1986) suggest that a self-concept at any given time is actually just a **working self-concept,** one that is open to change in response to new experiences, new feedback, and new self-relevant information. The existence of alternative possible selves affects us in several ways. The image of a future self may have an effect on one's *motivation,* as when a decision is made to spend more time studying or to stop smoking. Though you may have a clear image of your future self, others tend to perceive only your present self, and the *discrepancy* can be a source of discomfort. Even more upsetting is a discrepancy between the person we are and the person we want to be (Higgins, 1996).

In addition to optimistic and pessimistic conceptions of a future self, people also differ in whether they imagine many possible alternatives or only a very limited number. Research by Niedenthal, Setterlund, and Wherry (1992) indicated that people who have a very limited number of possible future selves are emotionally vulnerable to relevant feedback. For example, if you are considering twenty different possible future careers, information that you don't have the necessary ability for one of them is of relatively limited importance—there are nineteen other possibilities. If you have only one career goal, however, information indicating a lack of ability may be devastating. For example, the more strongly and the more exclusively a person identifies with the role of athlete, the more emotionally upsetting is an athletic injury (B. W. Brewer, 1993). More broadly, research indicates that adjustment following various sorts of traumatic events is best for those who can envision many different positive selves (Morgan & Janoff-Bulman, 1994). Further, self-complexity actually serves as a cognitive buffer against depression and stress-related illness (Linville, 1987). Finally, learning to imagine additional possible selves appears to have helpful benefits (Day et al., 1994). Thus, it seems that having a complex view of one's possible selves (assuming that they are realistically grounded) is more emotionally beneficial than having a very simple view.

Changes in Self-Concept. We have suggested that the self-concept slowly changes over time, as we grow older. Other factors, however, can change our beliefs about who we are in a very short period of time. One example is the negative effects on a person's self-concept when he or she loses a job and suddenly has a new social identity—*unemployed* (Sheeran & Abraham, 1994). The opposite experience—entering a new occupation—also leads to changes in the self-concept; for example, new police officers are found to develop new views of themselves (Stradling, Crowe, & Tuohy, 1993). Even greater changes occur when an individual joins the armed forces and is thrust into combat. This experience can lead to many self-relevant problems, including confusion about "Who am I? ("Am I a civilian or a military person?"), confusion about time perspective ("I was too young to feel so old"), interpersonal and work-related problems, and the development of a negative self-identity (Silverstein, 1994).

It appears, then, that the self-concept is far from a fixed aspect of a person, and that external events can bring about changes. Recent studies have shown that these shifts happen almost automatically when we encounter various group identities that may be relevant to ourselves (e.g., E. R. Smith & Henry, 1996). Realizing that words such as "we" and "us" seem to have automatic positive associations (e.g., Purdue, Dovidio, Gurtman, & Tyler, 1990), Brewer and Gardner (1996) used a word-choice task to make the identity of either "we" or "they" salient. In three experiments, their college student participants then made judgments about whether various statements were similar or dissimilar to their own views. Brewer and Gardner theorized that being primed by "we" should make a collective identity salient that would make the stu-

dents *faster* when they were judging similar statements than when they judged dissimilar statements. They expected the reverse pattern when the students were primed by "they." As Figure 4.3 illustrates, this is exactly what happened. These results again point to the conclusion that we accommodate group identities quite rapidly; when we meet other people, different group identities become instantly salient and affect how we view ourselves.

A different way of viewing such findings is to take the view of William James (1890) that while we have a central core self ("set like plaster" by age thirty), we also have many different *social selves* that we express to different people in different social interactions. To pursue this conception, Roberts and Donahue (1994) studied a sample of middle-aged women and assessed their *role-specific self-concepts* as well as their *general self-concepts*. The role-specific concepts for each individual were worker, wife, friend, and daughter. The women were asked to describe themselves in these different roles with respect to positive affect, competence, and dependability. As hypothesized, each participant's self-conceptions differed across roles; but there was also a high degree of consistency for individuals from role to role. For example, two women could each describe affect as a function of social role (both might indicate more positive feelings in the role of friend than in the role of daughter), thus indicating role-*specific* self-concepts. But the two women could also differ from each other in that one experienced more positive affect in both situations than the other. Because this difference between them is consistent across roles, it indicates the operation of a *general* self-concept.

Self-Esteem: Evaluating Oneself

Perhaps the most important schema each person holds is his or her attitude (see Chapter 5) about self, an evaluation that we label **self-esteem.** A person with high self-esteem perceives himself or herself as better, more capable, and of greater worth than does someone with low self-esteem. Self-evaluations are based in part on the opin-

FIGURE 4.3   Judgments Can Be Automatically Affected by What Identity Is Salient.

Three experiments by Brewer and Gardner suggest that priming the positive concept of "we" helps judgments of similarity but impairs judgments of dissimilarity. Likewise, having the relatively negative concept of "they" salient hastens judgments of dissimilarity but impairs judgments of similarity. The graph shows that study participants were faster to make similarity judgments when "we" was primed than when "they" was primed. Similarly, participants were faster to make dissimilarity judgments when "they" was primed than when "we" was primed.

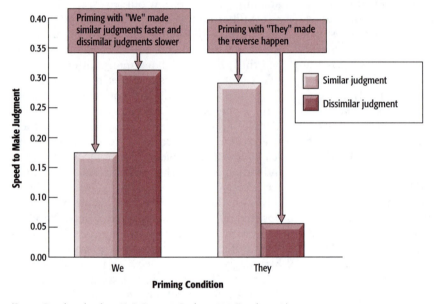

(*Source:* Based on data from M. B. Brewer & Gardner, 1996, Experiment 2.)

ions of others and in part on how we perceive specific experiences. Interestingly, negative self-perceptions lead to more predictable behavior than positive self-perceptions, possibly because negative self-views involve more tightly organized schemas than positive ones (Malle & Horowitz, 1995). As a result, someone with generally high self-esteem can interpret a success in a variety of ways, but someone with low self-esteem tends to overgeneralize the implications of a failure (Brown & Dutton, 1995).

Though most of the research on self-esteem is focused on a global indication of self-evaluation, it is also clear that people subdivide aspects of their self. For example, I might rate myself very high on being able to make delicious pizza and very low on being able to speak French. Because of such subdividing, you can have very positive attitudes about some aspects of yourself and very negative attitudes about other aspects. Your overall, global self-esteem can be conceptualized as the combination of the relative number and relative intensity of these positive and negative self-evaluations (Marsh, 1993).

A slightly different approach to assessing self-esteem is to compare a person's self-concept with his or her conception of an ideal self. The greater the discrepancy, the lower the self-esteem. That is, the more you perceive that your characteristics fail to measure up to what you feel they should be, the more negative your attitude about yourself. Credible feedback indicating that one has some of the characteristics of his or her ideal self is a positive experience, while feedback indicating the presence of undesired characteristics is negative (Eisenstadt & Leippe, 1994). It also matters whether one's "good" and "bad" qualities are common or rare. The lowest level of self-esteem is found among those who perceive their liked characteristics to be quite common and their unliked characteristics to be relatively rare (Ditto & Griffin, 1993).

Self-Esteem and Social Comparison. As we'll see in Chapter 7, we tend to make self-evaluations by comparing ourselves to others. These comparisons are a major determinant of how we evaluate ourselves (Brown et al., 1992). This fact explains some research findings that might otherwise seem surprising. For example, given the very real problems of racism and sexism (see Chapter 6), you might expect women and minority group members to be low in self-esteem. Instead, women and minorities appear to express somewhat *higher* self-esteem than white males (Crocker & Major, 1989). Clearly, social comparisons must differ for these different groups of people.

Depending on your comparison group, specific successes and failures may contribute to high or low self-evaluations or be completely irrelevant. For example, Osborne (1995) points out that despite better academic performance among whites than among African Americans in U.S. schools, global self-esteem is significantly higher for the latter group. Apparently, among Whites academic success and failure are related to self-evaluation more than they are among African Americans. In the earliest grades, both racial groups indicate a connection between grades and self-esteem; but by the tenth grade, the relationship tends to drop dramatically for African Americans, especially males (Steele, 1997). For them, the comparison groups affecting self-esteem seem to involve not classmates engaging in academic activities, but other people and different activities.

Several lines of research help clarify some of the ways in which these complex social comparisons operate. When you compare yourself to others, your esteem goes up when you perceive some inadequacy in them—a *contrast effect*. This kind of comparison with someone who is worse off (a downward comparison) arouses positive feelings and raises your self-esteem (T. J. Reis, Gerrard, & Gibbons, 1993). When, however, the comparison is with someone to whom you feel close, your esteem goes up when you perceive something very good about them—an *assimilation effect* (Brown et al., 1992). In a similar way, a person who compares unfavorably with ingroup members experiences lower self-esteem and increased depression much more than if the unfavorable comparison is with outgroup members (Major, Sciacchitano, & Crocker, 1993). In effect, social comparison with others in the ingroup is the most self-relevant comparison. It follows that doing well within one's own, relatively unsuccessful group—like a big frog in a little pond—can be a much bigger boost to self-esteem than performing equally well in a larger and more successful group—like a little frog in a big pond (McFarland & Buehler, 1995).

Why Do We Engage in Self-Evaluation? Sedikides (1993; Sedikides & Strube, in press) suggests three motives for evaluating oneself: **self-assessment** (seeking accurate self-knowledge, whether positive or negative), **self-enhancement** (seeking favorable self-knowledge), and **self-verification** (seeking fairly obvious self-knowledge that is probably true). When research participants are given the opportunity to select questions whose answers would provide various kinds of knowledge about themselves, self-enhancement is most often sought, while self-assessment is the least popular type of knowledge. Despite what they may believe to be true, most people do not really want to know more about themselves; rather, they want either positive information or information that simply confirms what they already know.

If we want only positive information about ourselves, it follows that self-esteem can readily be enhanced by external events. For example, any experience that creates a positive mood tends to raise self-esteem—we feel good and so feel good about ourselves (Esses, 1989). Even dressing in clothes you like can increase self-esteem (Kwon, 1994). For this reason, self-esteem can be raised quite easily in an experimental setting; for example, when research participants are given fake feedback that they did well on a personality test, their self-esteem goes up (J. Greenberg et al., 1992).

People with very low self-esteem are most apt to focus on self-protection (J. V. Wood et al., 1994). They, too, want positive information and self-enhancement, but only when it is not risky to seek such information. That is, they seek social comparison only after they have already received feedback indicating success on a task. People with high self-esteem seek social comparison even after receiving failure feedback, possibly to determine how to perform better in the future, but also to make themselves feel better by concentrating on the negative performance of others (Crocker, 1993). In other words, one coping strategy to maintain a positive view of oneself is to focus on the shortcomings of others.

A contrasting perspective on why we self-evaluate comes from **terror management theory** (e.g., J. Greenberg, Solomon, & Pyszczynski,

in press; Simon et al., in press), which suggests that high self-esteem calms deep-seated concerns about death. According to this theory, our primary motive in life is the avoidance of death—and the implications that death might bring (e.g., the end of existence)—and maintenance of high self-esteem is a primary means that we have developed to perform this function. Consistent with this theory, Harmon-Jones and her colleagues (1997) found in three experiments that individuals with high self-esteem were unaffected by concerns about death, whereas individuals with moderate self-esteem were affected. Pyszczynski and colleagues (1996) conducted two provocative experiments that support terror management theory's view that death is an important psychological variable. Pedestrians were approached and asked to complete an opinion survey. In one condition, they were in front of a funeral parlor, so the concept of death should be primed; in two control conditions, the pedestrians had not reached the parlor or had just passed it. As Figure 4.4 shows, pedestrians who were in front of a funeral parlor were more likely to believe that others shared their views about an issue (e.g., about whether Christian values should be taught in public schools). (See the discussion of

FIGURE 4.4   Death-Related Thoughts Can Affect Judgments.

Pedestrians on a street were approached before reaching, in front of, or after passing a funeral parlor and asked to complete a survey. Consistent with the idea that death-related ideas affect judgments, participants were more likely to believe that others supported their views (known as the false consensus effect) when they were in front of the funeral parlor (and death was salient) than either before or after passing the parlor. Other research suggests that such effects are weaker or disappear for individuals who have high self-esteem.

(*Source:* Based on data from J. Greenberg and colleagues, 1996, Experiment 2.)

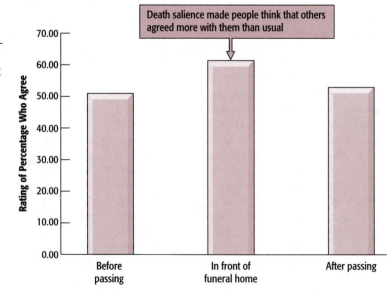

the false consensus effect in Chapter 3.) Together, these results suggest that we self-evaluate as a way to protect ourselves against negative events, including the ultimate negative event, death.

The Consequences of Positive versus Negative Self-Evaluations. Research consistently indicates that high self-esteem is beneficial while low self-esteem has many negative consequences. For example, a negative self-evaluation is associated with less adequate social skills (Olmstead et al., 1991); depression, especially among women (Jex, Cvetanovski, & Allen, 1994); and adverse reactions to job insecurity (Orpen, 1994). It has even been suggested that *unrealistically* positive self-evaluations and *unrealistic* optimism are associated with good mental health (Taylor & Brown, 1988); but more recent research suggests that in the long run, accurate self-evaluation seems to be essential to healthy mental functioning (Colvin, Block, & Funder, 1995).

There is evidence of specific physiological correlates of self-esteem. For example, experimental procedures that induce a negative self-evaluation (and associated negative emotions) lead to a weakening of the immune system and, presumably, greater susceptibility to disease (Strauman, Lemieux, & Coe, 1993). More complex associations are also being discovered. *Serotonin* is a biochemical contained in various fruits and nuts as well as in the venom of wasps and scorpions. In mammals, serotonin is found in blood serum, the brain, and the stomach. It is involved in constricting blood vessels, stimulating the smooth muscles, and transmitting impulses between nerve cells. Studies of male monkeys indicate that social success (high dominant status and affiliative interactions with females) is associated with higher levels of serotonin; low serotonin levels, in turn, are associated with impulsivity and aggressiveness (Raleigh et al., 1991). Though still quite speculative, the intriguing possibility has been raised that in humans, as self-esteem goes up, so does the level of serotonin (Wright, 1995). This further suggests that any factor that influences self-esteem may also have biochemical effects *and* that biochemicals might be used to raise self-esteem and decrease aggressiveness.

Self-Monitoring and Self-Efficacy

Though self-concept and self-esteem have been the central concerns of research on the self, several other aspects of self-functioning are also of interest. We will now examine two of these: *self-monitoring,* and *self-efficacy.*

Self-Monitoring of Internal versus External Cues

One person I (Donn Byrne) know fairly well behaves in exactly the same friendly and jolly way in every setting in which I've observed him—with his employees, with fellow professionals, with his wife, with close friends at a party, with strangers at a restaurant, and so on. At the opposite extreme, I also know someone else whom I've seen acting in an authoritative way with employees, conducting herself as a serious and concerned colleague at work, exchanging teasing insults with her husband, being a bubbly flirt at parties, and remaining totally distant and silent with strangers. The first individual is solidly predictable, while the second could be described as a "social chameleon."

First developed by Snyder (1974), **self-monitoring** refers to the relative tendency of individuals to regulate their behavior on the basis of external events such as the reactions of others (high self-monitoring) or on the basis of internal factors such as their own beliefs, attitudes, and interests (low self-monitoring). Low self-monitors tend to respond more consistently across differing situations than do high self-monitors (e.g., John, Cheek, & Klohnen, 1996). Hoyle and Sowards (1993) have further described self-monitoring in terms of differences in responses to social situations. High self-monitors analyze a social situation by referring to the public self, compare this self to social standards of behavior, and strive to alter the public self to match the situation. In contrast, low self-monitors analyze a social situation by referring to the private self, compare this self to their personal standards of behavior, then strive to alter the situation to match their private self.

Snyder proposed that high self-monitors engage in role-playing because they are striving to receive positive evaluations from other people. In other words, they mold their behavior to fit their audience—a useful characteristic for politicians, salespeople, and actors. The description of Lieutenant General George S. Patton in the April 9, 1945, issue of *Time* magazine seems appropriate to this concept:

> *Patton the General is also Patton the Actor. Showmanship is instinctive in him. Like all practiced actors he can manage a deft touch of corn or a flight of oratory. He fits his act to his audience's mood.*

Differences between High and Low Self-Monitors. Many behaviors differ for high versus low self-monitors. For example, Ickes, Reidhead, and Patterson (1986) found that high self-monitors, when they speak, more often use the third person (he, she, his, her, their, etc.) while low self-monitors use the first person (I, me, my, mine, etc.). DeBono and Packer (1991) found that highs respond best to advertising that is image-based ("Heineken—you're moving up") and lows to quality-based ads ("Heineken—you can taste the difference"). Because people who are confident about their deci-

sions tend to be liked and respected, Cutler and Wolfe (1989) correctly predicted that the higher the self-monitoring tendency, the greater the confidence in one's decisions, regardless of whether a decision was right or wrong.

High self-monitors make interpersonal choices on the basis of their external qualities (for example, selecting a tennis partner on the basis of how well he or she plays), while low self-monitors make choices based on how much they like the other person (M. Snyder, Gangestad, & Simpson, 1983). Even in romantic relationships, low self-monitors are more committed to the other individual (and so have fewer and longer-lasting relationships), while high self-monitors are attuned to the situation and to a variety of partners (M. Snyder & Simpson, 1984).

Such findings led Jones (1993) to investigate motivational differences in the dating behavior of high and low self-monitors. She administered a test that assesses dating motivation to undergraduate men and women. Intrinsic motives for dating are indicated by such items as "We share the same interests and concerns" and "We have the same attitudes and values." Intrinsic motivation means that an individual enjoys being with the partner. Extrinsic motives are indicated by such items as "He (she) has the right connections" and "His (her) friends and relatives could be of benefit to my career and future aspirations." Extrinsic motivation means that the partner is selected on the basis of expected rewards beyond the relationship (see Figure 4.5). Low self-monitors tended to emphasize intrinsic dating motivation more than highs, while high self-monitors stressed extrinsic dating motives more than lows. Once again, low self-monitors appear to be oriented toward the other person, while high self-monitors are oriented toward satisfying their own broader needs.

In thinking about the differences that have been found between high and low self-monitors, you may have concluded that lows are better adjusted than highs. That is, lows are consistent, honest in expressing their actual beliefs, and committed to their romantic partners, while highs are inconsistent, eager to please others, and happy with multiple relationships.

FIGURE 4.5 Intrinsic versus Extrinsic Dating Motives: Low versus High Self-Monitors.

When asked about their motivation in selecting a dating partner, low self-monitors tend to stress intrinsic motives (such as similarity) more than high self-monitors do, while high self-monitors stress extrinsic motives (such as the helpfulness of the partner's connections) more than low self-monitors do.

(*Source:* Based on data from M. Jones, 1993.)

Yet the same findings, of course, could be described as showing that lows are self-centered, closed-minded, insensitive to the opinions of others, and lacking in social skills, while highs are sensitive to the feelings of others, open-minded, and socially skillful. In fact, greater maladjustment (neuroticism) is more characteristic of individuals falling at both extremes of the dimension than of those who score in the middle (M. L. Miller & Thayer, 1989).

Self-Efficacy: "I Think I Can, I Think I Can . . ."

Self-efficacy refers to a person's evaluation of his or her ability or competency to perform a task, reach a goal, or overcome an obstacle (Bandura, 1977). Can you succeed in a calculus course? Can you learn to drive a car? Can you overcome your fear of heights? Your answer may differ from question to question because feelings of self-efficacy vary as a function of the task. I (Donn Byrne) am confident that I can eventually put together any toy or piece of furniture for which "some assembly is required," and equally confident that I cannot fill out my tax forms correctly each year. Research confirms such differ-

ences in feelings of efficacy—after the severe 1989 earthquake in California, college students there expressed low self-efficacy about their ability to cope with natural disasters; but in unrelated aspects of their lives (such as school performance), self-efficacy was unaffected (Burger & Palmer, 1992).

Self-Efficacy and Performance. Performance in both physical and academic tasks is enhanced by the appropriate type of self-efficacy. For example, those high in athletic self-efficacy are able to continue longer at exercise requiring physical endurance than those low in such self-efficacy (Gould & Weiss, 1981). One reason for this ability is that feelings of high self-efficacy for physical tasks stimulates the body to produce *endogenous opioids*, and these function as natural painkillers that make it possible for a person to continue a physical task (Bandura et al., 1988).

In academics, self-efficacy is equally beneficial. When college students were given the task of writing test questions for a class, questions written by those high in self-efficacy were rated as better than those written by low self-efficacy individuals (Tuckman & Sexton, 1990).

These same research participants were also asked to estimate how well they would do at this task. The high-self-efficacy students did better than they expected, and those who were low failed to meet their expectancies. In related research, Sanna and Pusecker (1994) found that when students expect to perform well, they also expect a positive self-evaluation, and the result is improved performance. Expectations of a poor performance are associated with expectations of a negative self-evaluation and impaired performance.

Increasing a Person's Feelings of Self-Efficacy. Self-efficacy is by no means fixed and unchanging. When a person receives positive feedback about his or her skills (even false feedback), self-efficacy is likely to rise (Bandura, 1986). In a pioneering experiment, Bandura and Adams (1977) were able to show that a phobia such as fear of snakes can be interpreted in cognitive terms as a reaction based on low self-efficacy—on a lack of confidence in one's ability to cope with a snake. In a program of behavioral therapy (*systematic desensitization*), snake-phobic individuals learned to relax while viewing a snake photograph, then a toy snake, then a small snake in a glass cage, and so on, over a period of time. Eventually, they could deal comfortably with a large, uncaged snake. As the phobia decreased, physiological arousal to a snake stimulus decreased, and self-efficacy increased.

More recently, Riskind and Maddux (1993) have examined additional elements of a frightening situation and the ways in which external cues and self-efficacy interact in determining the strength of fear. These investigators point out that two models of fear have been proposed. The *harm-looming model* describes fear as a function of the closeness of the feared object to the individual and whether it is moving. You have probably seen many horror movies in which you become increasingly uncomfortable as some dreaded creature comes closer and closer to the potential victim. The *self-efficacy model* focuses on the individual's perception that he or she has the ability to prevent harm. An ex-

perimental test suggested that both models are correct and that they can be integrated. Male and female undergraduates looked at video presentations in which tarantulas either moved toward the camera, moved backward, or were still. Before viewing the tarantulas, the research participants either were asked to imagine one of two situations: In one situation, they see a large spider in the room and can choose to smash it with a magazine or leave the room (inducing feelings of high self-efficacy); in the other situation, they are helpless, strapped to a chair in a locked soundproofed room with a large spider (inducing feelings of low self-efficacy). As shown in Figure 4.6, both the "looming" object and the level of self-efficacy influenced fear. The still or retreating tarantula was less frightening, regardless of self-efficacy. The advancing tarantula aroused more fear, but only for those low in self-efficacy.

Integrating Principles

1. Self-functioning is associated with many specific aspects of cognition, affect, and overt physical behavior. For example, one's attention can be focused on positive or on negative elements of oneself—or of the external world. As discussed in Chapter 3, the result is an interaction of cognitive and affective factors.

2. Attentional focus is also involved in individual differences in monitoring of overt behavior—whether to conform to fixed internal standards or to adapt to the situationally specific reactions of other people in order to gain popularity and acceptance (Chapter 7). As a result of differences in such monitoring behavior, some people behave in the same, unchanging way in quite different social situations, while others are social chameleons.

3. A third important type of self-functioning involves the relative strength of feelings of efficacy about one's ability to perform a task or to cope with a particular stressful event. Feelings of high self-efficacy affect not only task performance but also such broad realms as interpersonal behavior (Chapter 7) and the body's ability to maintain good health through effective coping responses (Chapter 11).

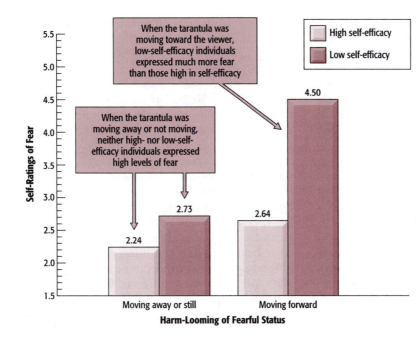

When the tarantula was moving toward the viewer, low-self-efficacy individuals expressed much more fear than those high in self-efficacy

When the tarantula was moving away or not moving, neither high- nor low-self-efficacy individuals expressed high levels of fear

High self-efficacy
Low self-efficacy

FIGURE 4.6 Effects of a Harm-Looming Stimulus and Self-Efficacy on Fear.

Feelings of high or low self-efficacy in responding to spiders were induced in research participants, and they were then shown video presentations of a tarantula that was harm-looming (moving toward the viewer) or not (standing still or moving away). The importance of harm-looming was shown by the fact that little fear was aroused by a still or retreating tarantula. The importance of self-efficacy was shown by the greater fear among low- than high-self-efficacy individuals when the tarantula was moving toward them.

(*Source:* Based on data from Riskind & Maddux, 1993.)

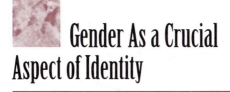

Gender As a Crucial Aspect of Identity

Perhaps the most pervasive element of personal identity is that portion of social identity in which each of us is assigned to one of two categories: male or female.

The terms *sex* and *gender* are often used to mean the same thing. In our discussion, however, we follow the lead of others (e.g., Beckwith, 1994) and define **sex** in biological terms—in terms of the anatomical and physiological differences that develop on the basis of genes present at conception. **Gender** refers to everything else associated with one's sex, including the roles, behaviors, preferences, and other attributes that define what it means to be a male or a female in a given culture. Until research provides unambiguous answers, we can simply assume that many of these attributes are probably learned while oth-

ers may very well be based in whole or in part on biological determinants. An example of the interaction of genetics and learning occurs when physical attributes are interpreted as indications of masculinity or femininity. Presumably as the result of learned stereotypes, a muscular build and a deep voice are perceived as attributes of masculinity while long hair and a high voice are perceived as feminine (Aube, Norcliffe, & Koestner, 1995).

Please note that the specific definitions used here are not universally accepted by those actively working in this field (e.g., Gentile, 1993; Unger & Crawford, 1993).

Gender Identity and Stereotypes

Each of us has a **gender identity;** that is, we label ourselves as male or female. Except in relatively rare instances, a person's biological sex and gender identity correspond.

The Origin of Gender Identity. Though all observed differences in the behavior of men and women were long assumed to be biological givens, it seems increasingly likely that many "typical" masculine and feminine characteristics are in fact acquired. *Gender schema theory* (Bem, 1974, 1984) suggests that children have a "generalized readiness" to organize information about the self in a way that is based on cultural definitions of what is appropriate behavior for each sex. Once a young child learns to apply the label "girl" or "boy" to herself or himself, the stage is set for the child to learn the "appropriate" roles that accompany these labels (see Figure 4.7). As childhood progresses, **sex typing** occurs when children learn in detail the stereotypes associated with maleness or femaleness in their culture. Though recent studies provide some evidence of widely held stereotypes (for example, compared to men, women are perceived as more sociable and happier), such effects are often small and often different for male and female observers (Feingold, 1995). In contrast to gender schema theory, multifactorial gender identity theory (Spence, 1993) suggests that the gender-relevant aspects of self are composed of many factors rather than a simple division into male and female.

Part of what children learn about gender is based on observing their parents and trying to be like them. Generally, children are rewarded for engaging in gender-appropriate behavior and discouraged (or ridiculed) when they engage in gender-inappropriate behavior. Consider, for example, the probable response to a little girl who requests a doll for Christmas versus the response to a little boy who makes the same request. In an analogous way, do you think parents respond differently to a little boy who wants boxing gloves and a punching bag for his birthday versus a little girl who expresses the same desire?

In countless ways, a culture's gender stereotypes are learned. Girls can cry and boys can fight. Boys can play football and girls can play jacks. Boys and girls are given different clothes to wear, have their hair cut differently, are assigned different chores around the house, are encouraged to identify with different fictional characters, and so on.

As the years pass, the lessons are well learned, and by the time they reach the sixth grade, the overwhelming majority of children in the United States have learned the prevailing gender stereotypes (Carter & McCloskey, 1984), even if they do not personally agree with them. They know what is considered suitable for each gender and what constitutes out-of-role behavior.

FIGURE 4.7   Gender Identity.

Gender identity refers to the sex that a person identifies as his or her own—a subjective self-perception as being a male or a female that usually corresponds to the person's biological sex. Though social psychologists are not totally sure of how this self-perception originates, the conscious process suggested in this cartoon is, of course, only a joke.

(*Source:* Drawing by Mankoff; © 1995 The New Yorker Magazine, Inc.)

"We don't believe in pressuring the children. When the time is right, they'll choose the appropriate gender."

The Content of Gender Identity

The specific content of these stereotypes about masculinity and femininity was something first addressed by Bem (1974), who pointed out that up until the 1970s, psychologists and people in general tended to think of masculinity and femininity as being opposite characteristics. In other words, there was no way for a person to be *both* masculine and feminine, or *neither* masculine and feminine. Bem theorized that masculinity and femininity were separate dimensions; in this way, a person might actually be high on characteristics associated with both genders (for example, both competitive and sensitive to the needs of others), which is psychological **androgyny.** An androgynous person is one who combines traditional masculine and traditional feminine characteristics.

The various terms used by those studying sex and gender can become confusing, and it may be helpful to keep in mind Beckwith's (1994) differentiation of *sex* (biological maleness or femaleness), *gender* (social categorization as female or male), *gender identity* (one's self-perception as male or female), and **gender-stereotype identification** (self-reported masculinity or femininity).

Gender-Role Behavior and the Reactions of Others

Once people acquire a specific pattern of gender-relevant characteristics, they tend to behave in ways that are consistent with their assumptions about appropriateness (Chatterjee & McCarrey, 1991). That is, they behave in ways identified as masculine, feminine, androgynous, or none of the above.

Androgynous versus Gender-Typed Behavior. Many past studies were consistent with the proposition that "androgyny is good." For example, compared to gender-typed individuals, androgynous men and women were found to be better liked (Major, Carnevale, & Deaux, 1981); better adjusted (D. E. Williams & D'Alessandro, 1994); more flexible in coping with stress (McCall & Struthers, 1994); more comfortable with their

sexuality (Garcia, 1982); more satisfied interpersonally (Rosenzweig & Daley, 1989); and, in an elderly sample, more satisfied with their lives (Dean-Church & Gilroy, 1993). Spouses report happier marriages when both partners are androgynous than is true for any other combination of roles (Zammichieli, Gilroy, & Sherman, 1988). Further, sexual satisfaction is greater if one or both partners is androgynous than if both are sex-typed (Safir et al., 1982).

In contrast, strong adherence to traditional gender roles is often found to be associated with problems. For example, men who identify with the extreme masculine role behave more violently and aggressively than men who perceive themselves as having some feminine characteristics (Finn, 1986). Among adolescent males, high masculinity is associated with having multiple sexual partners, viewing men and women as adversaries, low condom use, and the belief that getting a partner pregnant is a positive indication of one's masculinity (Pleck, Sonenstein, & Ku, 1993). Both men and women who endorse a purely feminine role are lower in self-esteem than either masculine or androgynous individuals (Lau, 1989). In interpersonal situations, high femininity is associated with feeling depressed after failing at an interpersonal task (Sayers, Baucom, & Tierney, 1993). Most of these findings suggest that some gender roles are better than others.

Aube and her colleagues (1995) point out the importance of studying not just the self-reports of research participants in gender-role studies but also the way these individuals are viewed by others. For example, in one study men high in masculinity described their relationships with roommates and romantic partners as more positive than did those low in masculinity; but this association was not confirmed when the roommates and partners were asked for their views about the relationship.

The Effects of Gender Roles on Behavior at Home and in the Workplace. Keep in mind that there is consensus about which characteristics are preferred for each gender and that these stereotypes influence interpersonal behavior in many ways. Gender roles still influence what men and women do within the home (Major, 1993). Even when both partners are employed in demanding and high-paying jobs, work around the house is most often divided along traditional gender lines (see Chapter 7). That is, men often take out the garbage, make repairs, and do the yard work, while women clean the house, cook, and engage in child care. Altogether, women spend more time doing housework than men, whether they personally are gender-typed or androgynous (Gunter & Gunter, 1991). When it comes time to clean the bathroom or paint the garage, the culturally prescribed gender roles seem to be more powerful than one's self-description of masculinity or femininity.

In the workplace, gender and gender roles also remain of central importance. For example, when women are chosen to do a task and then told that gender constituted the primary reason for their selection, they evaluate their performance as being less adequate than women told that the assignment was based on merit (Turner, Pratkanis, & Hardaway, 1991). Men might well react the same way, but research has not been conducted to find out how men react to being chosen primarily because of their gender.

Despite a vast increase in the percentage of women in the workforce (Uchitelle, 1994) and federal laws against discrimination based on gender, gender-related occupational restrictions still operate in the labor market (K. Kelley & Streeter, 1992). In academia, for example, U.S. women remain at a disadvantage compared to men with respect to doctorates granted, salaries, and professorships (Callaci, 1993). One reason is that women are more likely than men to believe that they *deserve* to earn a lower salary than others (D. Moore, 1994), presumably because they have been taught to evaluate themselves in a less egotistical way.

Though sexism and gender stereotypes may well play a major role in differential male–female success, Tannen (1994) stresses the additional importance of gender differences in communication styles. For example, women are not as likely as men to brag about their accomplishments, and one result is a failure to receive the appropriate credit when their work is exceptionally good. Women are expected to express positive emotions about the successes of others but not about their own accomplishments (Stoppard & Gruchy, 1993). Tannen (1994) also points out that the promotion of women to management positions is hindered because the men in charge of deciding who gets promoted misinterpret female communication styles as indicating "indecisiveness, inability to assume authority and even incompetence." Managers need to know that modest self-descriptions versus bragging self-descriptions represent an aspect of interpersonal style rather than actual worth.

What happens when women catch up to men in a given occupation? A common reaction is, "There goes the neighborhood." That is, when barriers are overcome in a specific job and a higher and higher percentage of women engage in that occupation, the job is then viewed as less prestigious (Eagly, 1987). It is as if negative reactions to the feminine role are so pervasive that the only way to explain newfound female success in an occupation is to devalue the work itself. We'll return to the topic of gender discrimination in Chapter 6.

Why Do Traditional Gender Roles Remain Powerful? The concept of male–female differences and of male superiority has a long history. In the Judeo-Christian tradition, men were originally identified as the owners of their families (N. Wolf, 1992). In the Jewish Talmud, categories of property included cattle, women, and slaves. In the New Testament, Ephesians (5.22–24) instructs Christian women as follows: "Wives, be subject to your husbands as you are to the Lord. For the husband is the head of the wife just as Christ is the head of the Church."

Despite the passage of many centuries, gender differences still have strong cultural support. For example, in children's books and stories, stereotypes of boys and girls and of men and women have been generally accepted until fairly recently (McArthur & Eisen, 1976; Weitzman et al., 1972). That is, men and boys tended to play active, initiating roles while women and girls either tagged along as followers or needed to be rescued when they found themselves in danger. As the artificiality of these stereotypes became increasingly obvious in the 1970s, different books came along. In 1974, *He Bear, She Bear* told readers that fatherhood is reserved for boy bears and motherhood for girl bears, but that otherwise gender isn't tied to activities or occupations—"There's *nothing* that we cannot try. We can do all these things you see, whether we are he OR she."

Despite this new consciousness, the old stories still remain popular. Lurie (1993) points out that traditional fairy tales were deliberately designed to teach children various moral and behavioral lessons. A familiar story line is that a rule is given to a child, the child disobeys, and negative consequences then occur; for example, Little Red Riding Hood should have followed her mother's advice about how best to get to grandma's house. The threatened punishment was provided by the hungry wolf. Luckily, a male with an ax was able to save her from the consequences of her reckless independence.

The story is not much different with computer software. Most students in the sixth, seventh, and eighth grades react with stress to stereotypical opposite-gender computer software (Cooper, Hall, & Huff, 1990). Possibly because most educational software is based on male stereotypes, boys greatly outnumber girls in computer courses, use of computer labs, enrollment in computer camps, and expressed interest in the field of computer science.

The evolutionary social psychology explanation of this history of male dominance over females is that the roles once served an evolutionary function, were perpetuated genetically and continue even now (e.g., Archer, 1996; Buss, 1996). Thus, for example, a behavior whereby males were dominant over females might have once been a valuable reproductive strategy (see Chapter 7), with the consequences that dominant males were more likely to pass their genes to future generations, and so on. As we will discuss below, males continue today to differ from females in several ways.

Moving beyond Gender Stereotyping: Signs of Progress.
There is still hope for a gradual move away from gender stereotypes in our culture. For one thing,

despite assumptions that most individuals personally hold these stereotypes, research participants are, in fact, much more likely to think nonstereotypically or to underestimate gender differences than to overestimate them (Swim, 1994); under threatening conditions, however, stereotypes and gender differences become accentuated (Grant, 1993). Also, some stories are now published in which brave and intelligent heroines fight when necessary, rescue male victims, and otherwise engage in nontraditional feminine behavior (Phelps, 1981).

As shown in Figure 4.8, even advertising has begun occasionally to present men and women in nontraditional ways (Kilbourne, 1994). Do such role models matter? Keep in mind that when small children are exposed to stories in which the traditional male and female roles are reversed, their expectancies about possible female accomplishments rise (Scott & Feldman-Summers, 1979). Perhaps exposure to "Ellen," *Mrs. Doubtfire,* and the equal-opportunity-for-violence Mighty Morphin Power Rangers will have some positive lasting effects.

FIGURE 4.8   Depicting Nontraditional Gender Roles in Advertisements.

Though ads are one of the many places where traditional gender stereotypes are regularly presented, an increasing percentage are now attracting attention by reversing male and female roles. Here, a man is depicted as a sex object.

Social Diversity:
A Critical Analysis

Cultural Differences in Concern about Weight

We described the greater concern among women than among men about appearance, including a special dissatisfaction with weight. Because this is a strong gender difference, a cross-cultural comparison of weight concern should be helpful in showing the possible power of societal influences in shaping differential male–female reactions.

One consequence of wanting to be thinner is to take dieting to an extreme; sometimes the result is death. Wardle and her colleagues (1993) point out that eating disorders are much less common in developing nations than in Western society. Also, within the United Kingdom and North America, African American and Asian women have fewer eating disorders than Caucasian women. Similar ethnic comparisons indicate that Caucasian women are the most

likely to judge themselves as being overweight and to evaluate their bodies negatively.

To examine these cultural differences more precisely, Wardle and her colleagues studied white and Asian schoolgirls (aged fourteen to fifteen) and female college students (aged nineteen to twenty-two) in London. The first question was whether racial differences were associated with differential concern about weight. A higher percentage of white than of Asian females at each of the two age levels wanted to lose weight and were actively trying to do so. The summary data are shown in Figure 4.9. Also, among those with access to scales, Asians reported weighing themselves significantly less often than whites. Clearly, female concern with weight seems to be different for whites and Asians.

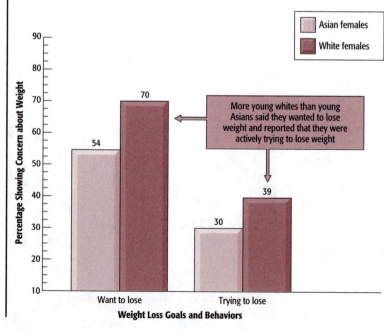

FIGURE 4.9 Female Concern about Weight: Young Asians versus Young Whites.

Young women enrolled in various schools in London were asked about their desire to lose weight and about their active attempts to do so. A higher percentage of white females than of Asians wanted to lose weight and were trying to lose weight. These and other findings suggest the role of cultural factors in specific gender differences in body image and appearance anxiety, but the mechanisms are far from clear.

(*Source:* Based on data from Wardle et al., 1993.)

Unexpectedly, however, the difference was not based on racial differences in concepts of ideal body weight. Both groups agreed that it was best to be thin and that men prefer a woman who is slim.

Alternatively, it seemed possible that differences in actual body characteristics accounted for the findings. The investigators noted that, compared to the white research participants, the Asians were shorter and lighter, and had a smaller body mass. When these differences are taken into account statistically, however, whites still reported feeling larger than Asians, even when their size was the same. Among those who were the thinnest, more white than Asian females said they felt "fat."

Altogether, then, cultural differences in female concern about weight were confirmed, but the underlying reason is still not known. One hypothesis is that white men reject overweight women to a greater extent than is true among Asian men. Further research will be required to explain what it is about these two cultures that creates the difference.

What Explains Differences between Males and Females?

Studies of gender identity clearly show that social factors determine the ways in which maleness and femaleness are defined. Cross-cultural research also provides evidence that the characteristics associated with each gender differ when cultural influences differ. Such findings do not, however, rule out the possibility of some built-in, genetically linked differences between the sexes in personality, ability, response tendencies, or something else (Wright, 1994). *Some* behavioral differences between men and women are important; but the question is whether the differences are based on biology, learning, or some combination of the two (Archer, 1996). How this question is answered sometimes involves a clash between scientific data and a feminist political agenda, according to Eagly (1995); but others argue that there is *no* uniform feminist agenda (Hyde & Plant, 1995). Interestingly, among undergraduates both men and women believe that social and biological factors each play a role, but that socialization is the more important determinant (Martin & Parker, 1995).

Interpersonal Behavior. In interacting with other people, women are more likely than men to share rewards (Major & Deaux, 1982) or to deprive themselves in order to help someone else (Leventhal & Anderson, 1970). Many investigators assume that these male–female differences are based on learned expectancies associated with gender roles (Major & Adams, 1983). It should come as no surprise that women whose lives have been spent experiencing social pressure to accept second place in assertive and aggressive situations may deal with people in a way different from men (Nadkarni, Lundgren, & Burlew, 1991). Perhaps women have better social skills than men because they *have* to.

Other investigators stress the importance of biochemical differences. The male hormone—*testosterone*—has a limited effect on sexual behavior, but it strongly affects the tendency to dominate and control others. Presumably, among our distant ancestors those males who produced the most testosterone were combative and dominant, thus enabling them to subdue rival males, obtain mates, and so pass on their high testosterone genes. Modern men have higher testosterone levels than women and behave in more aggressive and dominant ways (Berman, Gladue, & Taylor, 1993), especially with male strangers (Moskowitz, 1993) and when provoked (Bettancourt & Miller, 1996). Perhaps men are more likely than women to initiate sexual contact because they tend to behave dominantly rather than because of differences in sexual needs (P. B. Anderson & Aymami, 1993).

Also, those males with the highest testosterone levels tend to choose dominant and controlling occupations such as trial lawyer, actor, politician, or criminal (Dabbs, 1992). Hormone level is also affected by the situation, such as participating in competitive athletics or even just watching from the sidelines. Dabbs (1993) reported that before a basketball game, testosterone rises for those on the team and for male fans, and the levels go even higher if one's team wins.

Given these investigations of how testosterone affects behavior, you might wonder about the behavioral effects of the female hormone—*estrogen*. Strangely enough, research on estrogen effects has tended to concentrate on physical consequences, such as skin tone, vaginal lubrication, and the risk of cancer.

Self-Perception. Gender differences in self-perception are commonly found. Compared to men, women are much more likely to be concerned about their body image (Pliner, Chaiken, & Flett, 1990), to express dissatisfaction about their bodies (Heinberg & Thompson, 1992) and about physical appearance in general (Hagborg, 1993), to develop eating disorders (Forston & Stanton, 1992), and to become depressed (Strickland, 1992). Obesity is a special issue for women. When males blame them for being overweight ("It's your own fault"), women are likely to accept this evaluation. When an overweight woman is viewed as an unacceptable date by a male, instead of being mad at him and attributing the problem to his prejudice, she is more likely to blame herself (Crocker, Cornwell, & Major, 1993). Even though obese women tend to attribute rejection in the workplace as caused by unfair biases, romantic rejection is perceived to be justified (Crocker & Major, 1993). The Social Diversity box on pages 92–93 considers the cultural bases of obesity.

Why is appearance a major problem for women? Possibly because from infancy on, others respond to appearance differently on the basis of gender. College women report a high frequency of childhood experiences in which they were teased by peers and by brothers about such characteristics as facial appearance and weight (Cash, 1995). Even parents discriminate against overweight daughters (but not overweight sons) with respect to providing financial support for college (Crandall, 1995). Figure 4.10 only mildly

exaggerates male–female differences in concerns about body image. To the extent that young men express any appearance anxiety, it is a relatively mild dissatisfaction about not measuring up to the body-builder muscular ideal of male attractiveness (C. Davis, Brewer, & Weinstein, 1993).

Consider for a moment the day-to-day negative effects of the special emphasis our society places on the physical attractiveness of women in general and on specific anatomical details such as breast size (J. K. Thompson & Tantleff, 1992). One consequence is that women often are vulnerable and easily upset when their appearance becomes an issue (Mori & Morey, 1991). For example, after looking at magazine pictures showing ultrathin models, undergraduate women respond with feeling of depression, stress, guilt, shame, insecurity, and dissatisfaction with their own bodies (Stice & Shaw, 1994). As they age, women are perceived as increasingly less feminine, though men are not viewed as becoming less masculine with age (F. M. Deutsch, Zalenski, & Clark, 1986).

Beyond appearance, other self-perceptions also differ for men and women. On self-report measures, women describe themselves as more anxious, gregarious, trusting, and nurturing than men, while men describe themselves as more assertive and dominant than women (Feingold, 1994; W. Wood, Christiansen, Hebl, & Rothgerber, in press). Compared to men, women respond with greater emotional intensity, as indicated by self-reports and by physiological assessment (Grossman & Wood, 1993). Some evidence suggests that the explanation for such gender differences rests on differences in the specific areas of the brain used by men and women in thinking and responding to emotional cues (Gur et al., 1995).

At this time, no one can sensibly reach a grand conclusion about the reason for differences between men and women. We understand that you probably feel frustrated when we say that, but such uncertainty reflects the reality of current scientific research. It is easy enough to find certainty among people who rely on their opinions rather than on objective data. Some probably still agree with Queen Victoria (1881) who was convinced that "God created men and

FIGURE 4.10   Female versus Male Concern with Body Image.

Presumably because of societal pressures, women are much more concerned with body image than men, especially with respect to weight. This cartoon ridicules the gender stereotypes that result in insensitivity among egocentric men and oversensitivity and self-depreciation among women. Interestingly, some reviewers perceived this particular strip as a sexist attack on women, whereas cartoonist Cathy Guisewite had exactly the opposite intention.

(*Source:* CATHY copyright 1991 Cathy Guisewite. Reprinted with permission of UNIVERSAL PRESS SYNDICATE. All rights reserved.)

women different" and that any attempt to change things and speak of women's rights was a "mad, wicked folly." Happily, more than a hundred years have passed since such views were common. Today, many of us are convinced that men and women differ primarily because they have learned to differ. The final answer will almost certainly lie in the specifics as to which differences are biologically based, which are acquired, and which reflect both kinds of influence.

Integrating Principles

1. An extremely important aspect of one's personal identity includes a complex gender schema that is the result of being categorized from infancy on as either a male or a female. Beyond biological differences, we acquire attitudes, beliefs, emotions, and prejudices (Chapters 2, 3, 5, and 6) that are associated with gender—both our own and that of others.

2. Once we learn the gender-role behavior "appropriate" for our culture, much of our behavior and many of our reactions to others are guided by our conceptions of masculinity and femininity. Male–female differences are influenced in part by the prevailing beliefs of parents and others and are reinforced by images provided by the media. The effects of these gender roles extend to interpersonal relationships (Chapter 7) and the workplace (Chapter 11).

Connections   Integrating Social Psychology

In this chapter you read about . . .

- self-schemas

- self-esteem

- self-efficacy

- gender stereotypes

In other chapters, you will find related discussions of . . .

- schemas and information processing (Chapter 3); attitudes as schemas (Chapter 5); and stereotypes as schemas (Chapter 6)
- effects of self-esteem in persuasion (Chapter 5); self-esteem after receiving help (Chapter 9)
- effects of self-efficacy on health (Chapter 11)
- prejudice and stereotypes (Chapter 6)

Thinking about Connections

1. In this chapter we discuss attitudes about self (self-esteem) as one aspect of self-schemas. In Chapter 5, we present a more general discussion of attitudes as schemas. Consider some widely known situation, such as the O. J. Simpson trials, and try to determine whether your attitudes about race, spouse abuse, gender, or whatever else influenced the way you processed information about the trials as they progressed. Did such schemas influence who you liked and believed among the attorneys on each side and among the witnesses? Do you think you were best at remembering information and events that fit your schemas?

2. Can you think of any situations in which your feelings of self-esteem influenced what you did, or situations in which your self-esteem was affected by what hap-

pened? You might consider incidents in which someone tried to persuade you—or vice versa (Chapter 5); in which you met someone for the first time (Chapter 7); in which you were in a relationship that ended (Chapter 7); in which someone asked you to do something (Chapter 9) or to help them (Chapter 9); or in work situations (Chapter 11) or when you became ill (Chapter 11).

3. We each have different degrees of self-efficacy in different situations. Think about yourself with respect to various tasks or goals and whether you felt confident and sure of your ability or felt a lack of confidence and unsureness. Why the difference? What did you do in these situations? When you lacked self-efficacy, was there any possible way to change your self-perception?

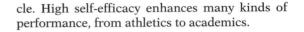

Summary and Review

Social identity refers to the way we conceptualize ourselves. Two of the major components of social identity are self and gender.

The Self: Components of One's Identity

Each person's self-identity, or *self-concept,* is acquired through interaction with others. The self operates as a schema that determines how we process information about the world around us and about ourselves. The *self-reference effect* implies that we process information about ourselves better than any other kind of information. *Self-focusing* refers to directing one's attention toward self as opposed to the external world. Self-focusing (on positive versus negative memories), mood, external events, and expectancies about future success and failure are interconnected. The self-concept is not a fixed entity. We are aware of other *possible selves* that we could become; self-concept changes with age and in response to situational changes. The evaluation of oneself is known as *self-esteem.* In general, high self-esteem is preferable to low self-esteem, and self-esteem can increase in response to positive experiences.

Self-Monitoring and Self-Efficacy

Self-monitoring behavior refers to whether a person's behavior is guided by external or internal factors. High and low self-monitors respond differently in many situations, and those who are extremely high or extremely low in self-monitoring tend to be less well adjusted than those whose self-monitoring is intermediate. *Self-efficacy* refers to a person's evaluation of his or her ability to perform a task, reach a goal, or overcome an obsta-cle. High self-efficacy enhances many kinds of performance, from athletics to academics.

Gender As a Crucial Aspect of Identity

Sex refers to anatomical and physiological differences based on genetic determinants, and *gender* refers to all of the attributes associated with being a male or a female, whether determined by biology or by culture. In the developmental process, we acquire *gender identity* when we learn to label ourselves as female or male and include this as part of our self-concept. Gender characteristics can involve stereotypic masculine or feminine qualities, some combination of the two (*androgyny*), or neither. The gender role that we adopt affects what we do and the way that other people respond to us. Gender stereotypes tend to be supported by many aspects of the culture, but these currently seem to be weakening in our culture. A central question in the study of gender differences is whether such differences are based on physiology, learning, or a combination of factors.

Social Diversity: Cultural Differences in Concern about Weight

For reasons that are not clear, Western societies are characterized by female concerns about appearance in general and body weight in particular more than other societies. A comparison of young Asian and Caucasian females indicates differential concern about weight, but this concern is not based on different images of ideal weight. More white than Asian females feel fat, desire to lose weight, and actively try to lose weight, though both groups agree that a thin body is ideal.

Key Terms

Androgyny (p. 89)
Gender (p. 85)
Gender Identity (p. 85)

Gender-Stereotype Identification (p. 89)
Possible Selves (p. 78)
Self-Assessment (p. 81)

For More Information

Ashmore, R. D., & Jussim, L. (1997). *Self and identity: Fundamental issues*. New York: Oxford University Press.

A collection of insightful essays by scholars in the burgeoning area of self and identity. This volume presents a critical analysis of fundamental issues in the scientific study of self and identity, highlighting new and contrasting perspectives on topics including the personal versus social nature of self and identity, multiplicity of selves versus unity of identity, and the societal, cultural, and historical formation and expression of selves.

Swann, W. B., Jr. (1996). *Self-traps: The elusive quest for higher self-esteem*. New York: W. H. Freeman.

A compelling book that proposes that self-esteem is multidimensional, shows how self-esteem plays out in relationships, and explains how social norms can interfere with self-esteem and make it difficult to improve low self-esteem. The author also offers several ways to improve self-esteem.

Osborne, R. E. (1996). *Self: An eclectic approach*. Boston, MA: Allyn & Bacon.

A concise yet comprehensive treatment of the gargantuan subject of the self. The author argues that a complete understanding of the self hinges on taking an eclectic view that shows how different aspects of the self interrelate.

Attitudes: Evaluating the Social World

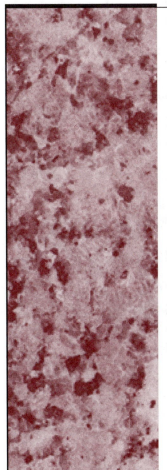

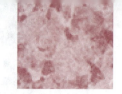

What are your views about abortion? Affirmative action? Capital punishment? Welfare? How do you feel about Newt Gingrich, O. J. Simpson, Bill Clinton (see Figure 5.1)? We doubt that you are neutral toward all of these issues and people. In fact, the chances are good that you have strong views and reactions to at least some of them. You may be passionately against—or for—abortion; you may believe that affirmative action is mainly beneficial—or harmful—in its effects. You may have strong positive or negative feelings and beliefs about Newt Gingrich, O. J. Simpson, and Bill Clinton. The fact that you have such reactions is hardly surprising. As human beings, we are usually not neutral toward important aspects of the social world that affect us in some manner. And of course, all the issues and people named here do have an impact upon many of us. (If you don't live in the United States, just insert the issues and names that are most important in your own society; the basic principle remains the same.)

Social psychologists have long been interested in such reactions, which they term **attitudes.** There are many definitions of this term,

but most center in the fact that we tend to evaluate many aspects of the social world. Thus, a good working definition of attitudes is as follows: *Attitudes are evaluations of virtually any aspect of the social world* (Eagly & Chaiken, 1993; Tesser & Martin, 1996). Thus, attitudes refer to how positive or negative we are about some object or entity. Another way to think about attitudes is that they are evaluative associations stored in memory (e.g., Fazio & Roskos-Ewoldsen, 1994). For example, if you have a positive attitude toward pizza, then you have many positive associations with pizza stored in memory. You might remember the excellent deep-dish pizza you had with your friends last weekend and many other positive experiences like it, all having to do with pizza.

Why are attitudes important? For two basic reasons. First, they strongly influence social thought—the way we think about and process social information. Attitudes often function as *schemas*—cognitive frameworks that hold and organize information about specific concepts, situations, or events (Wyer & Srull, 1994). As we saw in Chapter 3, these "mental scaffolds"

FIGURE 5.1   What Are Your Reactions
to This Person?

You may have strong feelings about this person.
Social psychologists call such reactions *attitudes*.

strongly influence the way we process social information—what we notice, enter into memory, and later remember. To the extent that attitudes operate as schemas, they, too, exert such effects. For example, imagine two people who hold very different attitudes about capital punishment: one is strongly in favor of the death penalty for convicted criminals, the other is just as passionately against it. Both now read a newspaper article describing a recent study indicating that murder rates are no lower in countries that have the death penalty than in ones that do not. Will the two people interpret this information differently? The chances are good that they will. The person who is against the death penalty may reason: "See, it's just what I thought all along. Executing people is useless; it doesn't deter others from committing similar crimes." In contrast, the person in favor of capital punishment may think: "So what? The death penalty isn't designed to deter other criminals; its main function is eliminating dangerous people so they won't hurt other victims." In this and many other ways, attitudes can strongly influence our social thought and the conclusions and inferences we reach.

That's not the only reason social psychologists have been interested in attitudes since the 1920s, however. Attitudes have also been a focus of research because, it has been assumed, they often influence behavior. Do you believe that abortion is wrong and should be outlawed? Then you may take part in a demonstration against it. Do you hold a negative attitude about your representative? Then you may vote against him or her in the next election. If attitudes influence behavior, then knowing something about them can help us to predict people's behavior in a wide range of contexts. As we'll see in Chapters 7 and 8, we also hold attitudes toward specific persons and groups—for example, we like them or dislike them. Clearly, such attitudes can play a key role in our relations with these persons.

For these and other reasons, attitudes have been a central concept—and a major focus of research—in social psychology since its earliest days (e.g., F. H. Allport & Hartman, 1925). In this chapter, we'll provide you with an overview of what social psychologists have discovered about

these evaluations of the social world and their effects. Beginning at what is, logically, the beginning, we'll first consider the ways in which attitudes are *formed* or developed. Obviously, attitudes don't come from nowhere, but be ready for some surprises: Many factors seem to play a role in attitude formation. Next, we'll consider a basic and crucial question: *Do attitudes actually influence behavior?* As we'll soon see, they do; but this link is much more complex than you might at first assume, and the correct question is not "Do attitudes influence behavior?" but "When and how do they exert such effects?" Third, we'll turn to the question of how, sometimes, attitudes are changed—the process of *persuasion.* Please emphasize the word "sometimes," because as we'll discover, changing attitudes is trickier than advertisers, politicians, salespersons, and many others seem to assume. Fourth, we'll examine some of the reasons why attitudes are usually difficult to change—why people are often so resistant to persuasion. Finally, we'll consider the intriguing fact that on some occasions, our actions shape our attitudes rather than vice versa. The process that underlies such effects is known as *cognitive dissonance,* and it has fascinating and unexpected implications for many aspects of social behavior.

Forming Attitudes: How We Develop the Views We Hold

Are you born with the attitudes you have now? Few persons would answer yes. On the contrary, most would agree that these and many other attitudes are acquired through experience. In a word, as Figure 5.2 shows, most attitudes are *learned.* Social psychologists, too, accept this position. But please take note: We would be remiss if we did not mention the fact that a small but growing body of evidence suggests that attitudes may be influenced by genetic factors, too. We'll describe some of the evidence pointing to this surprising conclusion after we examine the major ways in which attitudes are learned.

FIGURE 5.2 Attitudes: Born or Made?

Social psychologists believe that attitudes are usually acquired in life through learning and related processes. As the lectures implied in this cartoon suggest, over time, learned attitudes can become quite powerful!

THE FAR SIDE   By GARY LARSON

Eventually, Billy came to dread his father's lectures over all other forms of punishment.

(*Source: The Far Side* © 1992 FarWorks Inc. Used by permission of Universal Press Syndicate. All rights reserved.)

Social Learning: Acquiring Attitudes from Others

One source of our attitudes is obvious: We acquire them from other persons through the process of **social learning.** In other words, many of our views are acquired when we interact with others or merely observe their behavior. Such social learning occurs through several processes.

Classical Conditioning: Learning Based on Association. It is a basic principle of psychology that when

one stimulus regularly precedes another, the one that occurs first may soon become a signal for the one that occurs second. Thus, when the first stimulus is presented, individuals expect that the second will follow. As a result, they may gradually acquire the same kind of reactions to the first stimulus as they show to the second stimulus, especially if the second is one that induces fairly strong and automatic reactions. Consider, for example, a woman whose shower emits a low hum just before the hot water runs out and turns into an icy stream. At first, she may show little reaction to the hum. After it is followed by freezing water on several occasions, though, she may well experience strong emotional arousal (fear!) when it occurs. After all, it is a signal for what will soon follow—something that is quite unpleasant.

What does this process—known as **classical conditioning**—have to do with attitude formation? Potentially, quite a bit. Many studies indicate that when initially neutral words are paired with stimuli that elicit strong negative reactions—for instance, electric shocks or loud sounds—the neutral words acquire the capacity to elicit favorable or unfavorable reactions (e.g., Berkowitz & Devine, 1995). Since evaluative reactions lie at the very core of attitudes, these findings suggest that attitudes toward initially neutral stimuli can be acquired through classical conditioning. To see how this process might work under real-life conditions, imagine the following situation. A young child sees her mother frown and show other signs of displeasure each time the mother encounters members of a particular racial group. At first, the child is quite neutral toward members of this group and their visible characteristics (skin color, style of dress, accent). After these visible characteristics are paired (associated) with the mother's negative emotional reactions, however, classical conditioning occurs; gradually, the child comes to react negatively to these stimuli, and so to members of this racial group (see Figure 5.3). We'll consider such *racial prejudice* in detail in Chapter 6.

Interestingly, studies indicate that classical conditioning can occur below the level of conscious awareness—even when people are not aware of the stimuli that serve as the basis for this kind of conditioning. For example, in one study (Krosnick et al., 1992) students saw photos of a stranger engaged in routine daily activities such as shopping in a grocery store or walking into her apartment. While these photos were shown, other photos, known to induce either positive or negative feelings, were exposed for very brief periods of time—so brief that participants in the study were not aware of their presence. One group of participants was exposed to photos that induced positive feelings (e.g., a bridal couple, people playing cards and laughing) while another was exposed to photos that induced negative feelings (open-heart surgery, a werewolf). Later, both groups expressed their attitudes toward the stranger. Results indicated that even though participants were unaware of the photos, these stimuli significantly affected their attitudes toward the stranger. Those exposed to the positive photos reported more favorable attitudes toward this person than those exposed to the negative photos. These findings suggest that attitudes can be influenced by **subliminal conditioning**—classical conditioning that occurs in the absence of conscious awareness of the stimuli involved.

Muscle Movements and Attitude Formation. If you found our brief description of subliminal conditioning of attitudes surprising, hold onto your seat: Other studies indicate an even more surprising mechanism for the conditioning—and hence formation—of attitudes. This mechanism involves the movement of certain muscles and appears to involve a very basic fact: We draw things we like toward ourselves by flexing our arm muscles, but push things we don't like away by extending our arm muscles. Apparently, the association between these muscle movements and positive and negative feelings can serve as the basis for attitude conditioning (Cacioppo,

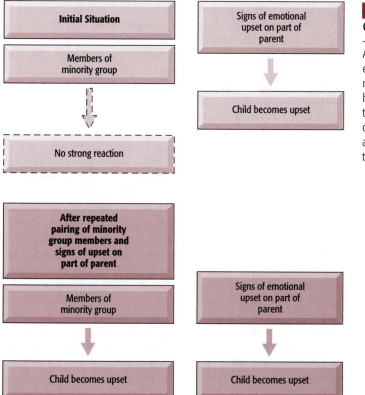

FIGURE 5.3 Classical Conditioning of Attitudes.

A young child sees her mother show signs of emotional discomfort when she encounters members of a minority group. Initially, the child has little or no emotional reaction to the characteristics of these people. After repeated pairings of her mother's emotional upset with these characteristics, however, she acquires negative emotional reactions to the characteristics herself.

Priester, and Berntson, 1993). You'll notice that this arm flexion effect is quite similar to the *facial feedback hypothesis* that we discussed in Chapter 3. Our attitudes, like our moods, can indeed be shaped by subtle processes of which we are largely unaware and therefore can't describe verbally.

Instrumental Conditioning: Learning to State the "Right" Views. Have you ever heard a three-year-old state, with great conviction, that she is a Republican or a Democrat? Or that Fords (or Hondas) are superior to Chevrolets (or Toyotas)? Children of this age have little understanding of what these statements mean. Yet they make them all the same. Why? The answer is obvious: They have been praised or rewarded in various ways by their parents for stating such views. As we're sure you know, behaviors that are followed by positive outcomes are strengthened and tend to be repeated. In contrast, behaviors that are followed by negative outcomes are weakened, or at least suppressed. Thus, another way in which attitudes are acquired from others is through the process of **instrumental conditioning.** By rewarding children with smiles, approval, or hugs for stating the "right" views—the ones they themselves favor—parents and other adults play an active role in shaping youngsters' attitudes. It is for this reason that until they reach their teen years, most children express political, religious, and social views highly similar to those held by their families. Given the power of positive reinforcement to influence behavior, it would be surprising if they did not.

Modeling: Learning by Example. Still another process through which attitudes are formed can operate even when parents have no desire to transmit specific views to their children. This process is **modeling,** in which individuals acquire new forms of behavior merely through observing the actions of others. And where attitude formation is concerned, modeling appears to play an important role. In many cases children hear their parents say things not intended for their ears, or observe their parents engaging in actions the parents tell them not to perform. For example,

parents who smoke often warn their children against smoking, even as they light up a cigarette. What message do children acquire from such instances? The evidence is clear: They learn to do as their parents *do,* not as they *say.*

Social Comparison and Attitude Formation

While many attitudes are formed through social learning, this is not the only way in which they are acquired. Another mechanism involves **social comparison**—our tendency to compare ourselves with others in order to determine whether our view of social reality is or is not correct (Festinger, 1954). To the extent our views agree with those of others, we conclude that our ideas and attitudes are accurate; after all, if others hold the same views, the views *must* be right! Because of the operation of this process, we often change our attitudes so as to hold views closer to those of others. On some occasions, moreover, the process of social comparison may contribute to the formation of new attitudes, ones we didn't previously hold. For instance, imagine that you heard others you know, like, and respect expressing positive views about some product you've never tried. Do you think you'd acquire a positive attitude toward it, and be more likely to try it yourself? Probably you would. In this case, you've acquired an attitude, or at least an *incipient* attitude, from social information and social comparison. The same processes may operate with respect to attitudes directed toward various social groups. For example, imagine that you heard individuals you like and respect expressing negative views toward a group with whom you've had no contact. Would this influence your views? While it's tempting to say, "Of course not! I wouldn't form any opinions without seeing for myself!" research findings indicate that hearing others state negative views might actually influence you to adopt similar attitudes—without ever meeting a member of the group in question (e.g., Maio, Esses, & Bell, 1994). Thus, often our attitudes are shaped by social information, coupled with our own desire to hold the "right" views—those held by people we admire or respect.

Genetic Factors: Some Surprising Recent Findings

Can we inherit our attitudes, or at least a tendency to develop certain attitudes about various topics or issues? At first glance, most people—and most social psychologists—would answer *no*. While we readily accept the fact that genetic factors can influence our height, eye color, and other physical characteristics, the idea that they might also play a role in our thinking seems strange, to say the least. Yet if we remember that thought occurs within the brain and that brain structure, like every other part of our physical being, is certainly affected by genetic factors, the idea of genetic influences on attitudes becomes, perhaps, a little easier to imagine. In fact, a small but growing body of empirical evidence indicates that genetic factors may play some small role in attitudes (e.g., Keller et al., 1992; Tesser, 1993).

Most of this evidence involves comparisons between identical (monozygotic) and nonidentical (dizygotic) twins. Because identical twins share the same genetic inheritance while nonidentical twins do not, higher correlations between the attitudes of the identical twins would suggest that genetic factors play a role in shaping such attitudes. This is precisely what has been found: The attitudes of identical twins *do* correlate more highly than those of nonidentical twins (e.g, Waller et al., 1990). Of course, such findings are open to an important criticism: Perhaps the environments of identical twins are more similar than those of nonidentical twins—for example, perhaps people treat them more similarly. Thus, the finding that identical twins hold more similar attitudes than nonidentical twins may stem from environmental factors. To deal with such complexities, other studies have focused on identical and nonidentical twins separated very early in life (see Figure 5.4). Even though these twin pairs were raised in very different environments, identical twins' attitudes still correlate more highly than those of nonidentical twins, and more highly than the attitudes of unrelated persons (Waller et al., 1990).

FIGURE 5.4 Identical Twins Separated Very Early in Life: Often, Their Attitudes Are Very Similar.

The attitudes of identical twins separated very early in life correlate more highly than those of nonidentical twins or unrelated persons. This finding provides support for the view that attitudes are influenced by genetic factors, at least to some extent.

Moreover, these findings hold true for several kinds of attitudes, ranging from interest in religious occupations and activities through job satisfaction (Bouchard et al., 1992).

In contrast to this research suggesting that attitudes are always passed through the genes of our ancestors, some dimensions, such as opinions about straitjackets, have been shown to have a smaller genetic component than other dimensions, such as appreciation for jazz music (Tesser, 1993). Thus, some attitudes are more *heritable* than others. However, we shouldn't let this research mislead us into thinking that genetic influences on attitudes are trivial. For example, we make judgments faster for attitude dimensions that are highly heritable than for attitude dimensions that are less heritable. Similarly, heritable attitude dimensions are difficult to influence compared to less heritable dimensions (Tesser, 1993). Finally, highly heritable attitude dimensions are more powerful reinforcers than dimensions that are acquired (Crelia & Tesser, in press). For example, we're more attracted to strangers who possess similar attitudes on heritable dimensions than to strangers who possess similar attitudes on less heritable dimensions (Tesser, 1993). Thus, heritable attitudes appear to be strong attitudes. (We'll consider other dimensions of attitude strength below.)

But how, we can almost hear you asking, can such effects occur—how can genetic factors influence attitudes? One possibility is that genetic factors influence more general dispositions, such as the tendency to experience positive or negative affect—to be in a positive or negative mood much of the time (George, 1990). Such tendencies, in turn, could then influence evaluations of many aspects of the social world. For instance, an individual who tends to be in a positive mood much of the time might tend to express a high level of job satisfaction, no matter where the person works; in contrast, someone who tends to be in a negative mood might tend to express more negative attitudes in the same settings. Only time, and further research, will allow us to determine whether, and how, genetic factors influence attitudes. But at present, social psychologists are giving this possibility serious consideration, so an answer seems likely to emerge very soon.

Integrating Principles

1. Attitudes are acquired from other persons through *social learning*—a process that plays a role in many aspects of social behavior, such as helping and aggression (Chapter 9).
2. Attitudes are also shaped by *social comparison*—a basic process that influences many aspects of social behavior, including attraction (Chapter 7), relationships (Chapter 7), and perceptions of fairness (Chapter 11).
3. Genetic factors, too, may influence some kinds of attitudes, and other aspects of social behavior, such as mate selection (Chapters 1 and 7) and aggression (Chapter 9).

When and *How* Do Attitudes Influence Behavior?

Do our attitudes influence our behavior? Your first reaction is probably to say, "Of course!"

However, we're willing to bet that you have had plenty of opportunities to observe a sizable gap between your attitudes and your behavior. To the extent that such a gap exists, of course, social psychologists find themselves facing a disturbing question: Have they been wasting their time studying attitudes for so many years? That an attitude–behavior gap *does* sometimes exist is clear. The fact that attitudes do not always predict behavior was uncovered in some of the earliest research in our field (LaPiere, 1934) and was repeatedly confirmed during the 1960s and 1970s (e.g., Wicker, 1969). But it is equally clear that attitudes often do exert important effects on behavior. So our conclusion is: *No*, social psychologists have definitely *not* wasted their time by studying attitudes. The key question, however, is not "Do attitudes influence behavior?" but rather "When and how do they exert such effects?" These issues have been very central to modern research on the attitude–behavior link, so we'll focus on them in this discussion.

When Do Attitudes Influence Behavior?

Research on the question of *when* attitudes influence behavior has uncovered several different factors that serve as what social psychologists term *moderators*—they influence the extent to which attitudes affect behavior. While many of these moderators exist, most seem to be related to aspects of the *situation*, aspects of *attitudes* themselves, and aspects of *individuals* (Fazio & Roskos-Ewoldsen, 1994).

Aspects of the Situation. Dress on campuses is very casual these days, so I (Bob Baron) don't usually pay much attention to the way students in my classes are dressed. Once in a while, though, someone comes to class looking so dirty and sloppy that I can't help but notice. I'd like to say something about it, because I do feel that college is important and that it's worth maintaining some minimal standards of appearance. But I never say a word. Why? Because I realize that the *norms* in this situation are dead set against me. *Norms,* as we'll see in Chapter 8, are rules indicating how people are supposed to behave in a given situation; and for faculty, the norm is clearly "How students dress is *not* your concern." This kind of incident illustrates one important factor that moderates (influences) the relationship between attitudes and behavior: *situational constraints.* Sometimes, people can't express their attitudes because doing so would be contrary to the norms in a given social situation. Much research provides support for this view (e.g., Fazio & Roskos-Ewoldsen, 1994), so it is clear that gaps between attitudes and behavior often involve such factors.

Another aspect of situations that influences the attitude–behavior link is *time pressure.* Attitudes, as we noted, often function as cognitive frameworks for processing social information. When individuals are under time pressure and have to decide to act very quickly, they tend to fall back upon their attitudes as quick-and-easy guides. Thus, in situations in which time pressure is great, the attitude–behavior link tends to be stronger than in situations in which such pressures are lacking, and in which individuals have the time to consider available information more carefully (Jamieson & Zanna, 1989).

Situational factors can influence the link between attitudes and behavior in one additional way. Think for a moment: Whom are you likely to find at a rally against abortion—people in favor of personal choice where abortion is concerned, or people in favor of outlawing abortion? The answer is obvious: Except perhaps for a few hecklers, most people attending such a meeting will be opponents of abortion. The same principle holds for many other situations, and this points to an important fact: In general, we tend to prefer situations that allow us to maintain a close match between our attitudes and our be-

havior. In other words, we often choose to enter and spend time in situations in which what we say and what we do can coincide (M. Snyder & Ickes, 1985). Indeed, because individuals tend to choose situations where they can engage in behaviors consistent with their attitudes, the attitudes themselves are strengthened and so become better predictors of behavior (DeBono & Snyder, 1995).

These findings indicate that the relationship between attitudes and situations may be a two-way street. Situational pressures shape the extent to which attitudes are expressed in overt actions; but in addition, attitudes determine whether individuals choose to enter various situations. So, in order to understand the link between attitudes and behavior, we must take careful account of both sets of factors.

Aspects of Attitudes Themselves. Years ago, I witnessed a very dramatic scene. A large timber company had signed a contract with the government allowing the company to cut trees in a national forest. Some of the trees scheduled to become backyard fences and patios were ancient giants, hundreds of feet tall. A group of conservationists objected strongly to plans to cut these magnificent trees, and they quickly put their money where their mouths were. They joined hands and formed a human ring around each of the largest trees, thus preventing the chain saw–wielding workers from cutting them. The tactic worked: There was so much publicity that soon the contract was revoked, and the trees were saved.

Why did these people take such drastic action? The answer is obvious: They were passionately committed to saving the trees. In other words, they held powerful attitudes that strongly affected their behavior. Incidents like this one are far from rare. For example, persons who are passionately against abortion demonstrate outside abortion clinics—and even physically assault doctors who perform abortions. And in 1995, one or more persons who held strong anti-government attitudes blew up a federal building in Oklahoma City, killing hundreds of innocent persons through this violent expression of their views (see Figure 5.5). Incidents like these call attention to the fact that the link between attitudes and behavior is strongly moderated by several aspects of attitudes themselves. Let's consider several of these factors.

Attitude Origins. One has to do with how attitudes were formed in the first place. Considerable evidence indicates that attitudes formed on the basis of direct experience often exert stronger effects on behavior than ones formed indirectly through hearsay (e.g., Regan & Fazio, 1977; refer to our earlier discussion of attitude formation). Apparently, attitudes formed on the basis of direct experience are easier to bring to mind, and this magnifies their impact on behavior.

Attitude Strength. Another factor—and obviously one of the most important—involves what is typ-

ically termed the *strength* of the attitudes in question. The stronger attitudes are, the greater their impact on behavior (Petkova, Ajzen, & Driver, 1995). By the term *strength,* social psychologists mean several things: the extremity or intensity of an attitude (how strong is the emotional reaction provoked by the attitude object?); its *importance* (the extent to which an individual cares deeply about and is personally affected by the attitude); *knowledge* (how much an individual knows about the attitude object); and *accessibility* (how easily the attitude comes to mind in various situations). Recent findings indicate that all these components play a role in attitude strength, but that, as you can probably guess, they are all related (Krosnick et al., 1993). Not only do strong attitudes exert a greater impact on behavior, they are also more resistant to change, are more stable over time, and have a greater impact on several aspects of social cognition. Thus, attitude strength is truly an important factor in the attitude–behavior link—so important that it's worth taking a closer look at some of the components that influence it (Kraus, 1995).

Let's start with attitude *importance*—the extent to which an individual cares about the attitude (Krosnick, 1988). Growing evidence indicates that the greater the importance of various attitudes, the greater individuals' tendency to make use of such attitudes in processing information; making decisions; and, of course, taking specific actions (Kraus, 1995). What factors influence attitude importance—in other words, why are some attitudes so important to specific persons? Research conducted by Boninger, Krosnick, and Berent (1995) provides some important clues.

These researchers reasoned that three factors may play a key role in determining attitude importance. One is *self-interest*—the greater the impact on an individual's self-interest, the more important the attitude. Another is *social identification*—the greater the extent to which an attitude is held by groups with which an individual identifies, the greater its importance. Finally, attitude importance also stems from *value relevance*—the more closely an attitude is connected to an individual's personal values, the greater its importance. To test this reasoning,

---

FIGURE 5.5   Strong Attitudes in Action: A Tragic Example.

When individuals hold certain attitudes passionately, they often express these in relatively extreme forms of behavior. In 1995, one or more persons holding powerful antigovernment attitudes blew up this building to express their views, killing hundreds of innocent victims in the process.

Boninger and his colleagues (1995) called persons chosen randomly from the telephone book of a large city, and asked them to express their views about one current issue in the United States—gun control. Participants were asked to indicate how much the issue affected their lives (self-interest), how much it affected members of the social group to which they felt most similar and close (social identification), and how much their opinions on gun control were related to their own personal values (value relevance). Consistent with predictions, results indicated that all of these factors played an important role in overall attitude importance (Figure 5.6). So, in sum, it appears that what makes an attitude important is its relationship to basic social and individual needs and values. It should come as no surprise, therefore, that our important attitudes wind up being difficult to change, as we'll see later in this chapter.

Attitude Specificity. Finally, we should mention *attitude specificity*—the extent to which attitudes are focused on specific objects or situations rather than general ones. For example, you may have a general attitude about religion (e.g., it is important for everyone to have some religious convictions) but much more specific attitudes about the importance of attending services every week (it's important—or unimportant—to go every week)

or about wearing a religious symbol (it's something I like to do—or don't want to do). Research findings indicate that the attitude–behavior link is stronger when attitudes and behaviors are measured at the same level of specificity. For instance, we'd probably be more accurate in predicting whether you'll go to services *this* week from your attitude about weekly attendance than from your attitude about religion generally. On the other hand, we'd probably be more accurate in predicting your willingness to take action to protect religious freedoms from your general attitude toward religion than from your attitude about wearing religious jewelry (Fazio & Roskos-Ewoldsen, 1994). So attitude specificity, too, is an important factor in the attitude–behavior link.

We could go on to describe many other studies, because social psychologists have focused a great deal of attention on attitude strength and related concepts. The basic conclusion of this research, however, is straightforward: The stronger attitudes are, the greater the impact on overt behavior.

Aspects of Individuals: Is the Attitude–Behavior Link Stronger for Some Persons Than for Others? So far, we've discussed the attitude–behavior link in general terms—as it exists for all individuals. In other words, we've ignored individual differences in

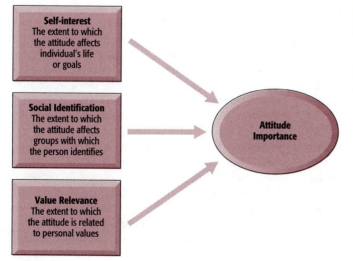

FIGURE 5.6 Major Components of Attitude Importance.

As shown here, attitude importance appears to stem from three major factors: self-interest, social identification, and value relevance.

(*Source:* Based on suggestions by Boninger, Krosnick, & Berent, 1995.)

this respect—the possibility that the link between attitudes and behavior is stronger for some persons than for others. Is this the case? Growing evidence suggests that it is. Specifically, it appears that attitudes are indeed a better predictor of behavior for low self-monitors—people who use their attitudes as important guides to behavior (see Chapter 4). In contrast, this link is weaker for high self-monitors (e.g., DeBono & Snyder, 1995).

How Do Attitudes Influence Behavior?

Understanding *when* attitudes influence behavior is an important topic. But as we noted in Chapter 1, social psychologists are interested not only in the *when* of social thought and social behavior, but in the *why* and *how* as well. So it should come as no surprise that researchers have also tried to understand *how* attitudes influence behavior. Work on this issue points to the conclusion that in fact, there may be two basic mechanisms through which attitudes shape behavior.

Attitudes, Reasoned Thought, and Behavior. The first of these mechanisms seems to operate in situations where we give careful, deliberate thought to our attitudes and their implications for our behavior. For example, in his **theory of planned behavior,** Ajzen (1987) suggests that the best predictor of how we will act in a given situation is the strength of our intentions with respect to that situation. Perhaps a specific example will help illustrate the eminently reasonable nature of this assertion. Suppose a student is considering body piercing—for instance, wearing a nose ornament. Will he actually engage in body piercing? According to Ajzen, the answer depends on his intentions; and these, in turn, are strongly influenced by three key factors. The first factor is the person's attitudes toward the behavior in question. If the student really dislikes pain and resists the idea of someone sticking a needle through his nose, his intention to engage in such behavior may be weak. The second factor relates to the person's beliefs about how others will evaluate this behavior (this factor is known as *subjective norms*). If the student thinks that others will approve of body piercing, his intention to

perform it may be strengthened. If he believes that others will disapprove of it, his intention may be weakened. Finally, intentions are also affected by *perceived behavioral control*—the extent to which a person perceives a behavior as hard or easy to accomplish. If it is viewed as difficult, intentions are weaker than if it is viewed as easy to perform. Together, these factors influence *intentions;* and these, in turn, are the best single predictor of the individual's behavior.

Attitudes and Immediate Behavioral Reactions. The model described above seems to be quite accurate in situations when we have the time and opportunity to reflect carefully on various actions (e.g., Terry & Hogg, 1996; Trafimow & Finlay, 1996). That is, intentions appear to affect behavior very well for *deliberate* actions (Dovidio et al., 1996). But what about situations in which we have to act quickly—for example, when a panhandler approaches on a busy street? In such situations, attitudes seem to influence behavior in a more direct and seemingly automatic manner. According to one theory—Fazio's **attitude-to-behavior process model** (Fazio, 1989; Fazio & Roskos-Ewoldsen, 1994)—the process goes something like this: Some event activates an attitude; the attitude, once activated, influences our perceptions of the attitude object. At the same time, our knowledge about what's appropriate in a given situation (our knowledge of various social norms) is also activated. Together, the attitude and this stored information about what's appropriate or expected shape our definition of the event; and this definition or perception, in turn, influences our behavior. Let's consider a concrete example.

Imagine that a panhandler does approach you on the street. What happens? This event triggers your attitudes toward panhandlers and also your understanding about how people are expected to behave on public streets. Together, these factors influence your definition of the event, which might be "Oh no, another one of those worthless bums!" or "Gee, these homeless people really have it rough!" Your definition of the event then shapes your behavior (refer to Figure 5.7). Several studies provide support for this model, so it seems to offer a reasonable descrip-

FIGURE 5.7   Fazio's Attitude-to-Behavior Process Model.

According to one recent model, in situations where we don't have time to engage in careful, reasoned thought, attitudes guide behavior in the manner shown here.

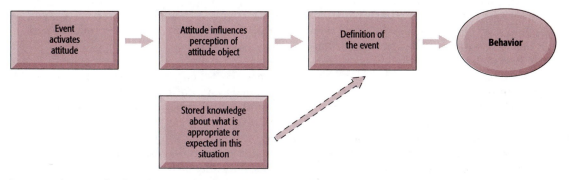

(*Source:* Based on suggestions by Fazio, 1989, and Fazio & Roskos-Ewoldsen, 1994.)

tion of how attitudes influence behavior in some situations.

In short, it appears that attitudes affect our behavior through at least two mechanisms, and that these operate under somewhat contrasting conditions. When we have time to engage in careful, reasoned thought, we can weigh all the alternatives and decide, quite deliberately, how to act. Under the hectic conditions of everyday social life, however, we often don't have time for this kind of deliberate weighing of alternatives; in such cases, our attitudes seem to spontaneously shape our perceptions of various events, and hence our immediate behavioral reactions to them (Bargh, 1997; Dovidio et al., 1996).

To recap: Contrary to what early research suggested, attitudes are related to behavior. Indeed, in many cases—when they are strong and important, were acquired through direct experience, influence individuals' self-interest, and come readily to mind—attitudes can exert strong effects on behavior (Kraus, 1995). So social psychologists have definitely *not* wasted their time by studying attitudes, because these evaluations of the social world turn out to be an important determinant of social behavior in many contexts. In the Social Diversity box on pages 119–120 we discuss how attitudes affect a very important area of social concern: economic growth.

Integrating Principles

1. Contrary to early findings, recent evidence indicates that attitudes do indeed influence behavior and that they can affect behavior in either a deliberate or a spontaneous fashion. Such effects are readily apparent with respect to several forms of social behavior, including prejudice (Chapter 6), attraction (Chapter 7), and helping (Chapter 9).

2. The strength of the attitude-to-behavior link, however, is moderated by several factors relating to the situation in which attitudes are activated, aspects of attitudes themselves (such as their strength), personal characteristics of the individuals who hold them.

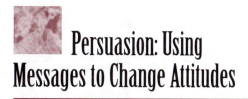

Persuasion: Using Messages to Change Attitudes

How many times during the past day has someone, or some organization, tried to change your attitudes? If you stop and think for a moment, you may be surprised at the answer, for it is clear that each day we are literally bombarded with many efforts of this type (see Figure 5.8). Newspaper and magazine ads, radio and television commercials, political speeches, appeals from charities—the list seems almost endless. To what extent are such attempts at **persuasion**—efforts to change our attitudes—successful? And what factors determine whether they succeed or fail?

It is just such considerations that have led social psychologists and other social scientists to conduct countless studies on persuasion (e.g., Eagly, Wood, & Chaiken, 1996; Hovland, Janis, & Kelley, 1953). Unfortunately, it was not until the 1980s that compelling general theories of message-based persuasion emerged (see Eagly, 1992). This new **cognitive perspective** on persuasion (Eagly et al., 1996; Petty et al., 1994) focuses on the cognitive processes that determine how individuals are actually persuaded. In other words, this newer perspective focuses on what many researchers term a **cognitive response analysis**—efforts to understand (1) what people think about when they are exposed to persuasive messages, and (2) how these thoughts and basic cognitive processes determine whether, and to what extent, people experience attitude change.

Processes Involved in Persuasion

Most cognitive perspectives on persuasion assume that two main processes underlie persuasion (e.g., Chaiken, Liberman, & Eagly, 1989; Eagly & Chaiken, 1993, in press; Petty & Cacioppo, 1986; Petty et al., 1994). One process may be called **systematic processing,** which refers to careful consideration of message content. When this process happens, message recipients examine the message in a thoughtful manner, evaluating the strength or rationality of the arguments it contains. If the message recipient's thoughts—or cognitive responses—are positive, then their attitudes and other existing cognitive structures may be changed and persuasion occurs. If their cognitive responses are negative, then the message recipient may resist persuasion or oppose the position the message takes (Killeya & Johnson, in press).

The second process may be called **heuristic processing,** which refers to our use of heuristics—

FIGURE 5.8

Bombarded by Promotions and Advertisements?

Such appeals seem to be a fact of our information-packed modern life: Every day you probably are exposed to hundreds, if not thousands, of advertisements and other appeals. *How* do these appeals influence you? *When* do they influence you?

learned short-cuts—to decide whether to agree with the message (see Chapter 3). In this form of processing, a message recipient bases his or her attitude on cues present in the situation. If these cues are positive, then the attitude may shift to be more positive; if the cues are negative, then the attitude may shift to be more negative. For example, because we have deeply internalized the *if . . . then* heuristic that if an expert says it, it must be true, we tend to believe experts and are persuaded by them (e.g., Chaiken & Maheswaran, 1994; Petty et al., 1994). We have internalized many other heuristics relevant to the communicators of messages, including such dimensions as attractiveness, status, and prestige. Similarly, we may use heuristics based on the sheer beauty of the illustrations in an advertisement; in such cases, it's as though we are thinking, "If it's beautiful, it must be good." Needless to say, advertisers, politicians, salespersons, and others wishing to change our attitudes are well aware of such heuristic cues and rely heavily on them in their efforts to persuade us.

The Role of Ability and Motivation to Process Messages.
Cognitive perspectives on persuasion place a heavy emphasis on the role of ability and motivation to process message. According to these perspectives, if a recipient is unable to process the message, perhaps because he or she is distracted, or because he or she does not understand what the message is saying, then there is little chance that systematic processing of the message will occur. Instead, these circumstances make it much more likely that heuristic processing will affect our reactions to a message. In contrast, when we *are* motivated and able to process the content of the message, systematic processing will occur. Many studies now support these basic patterns (Eagly & Chaiken, in press).

Multiple Motives for Processing Messages

Some cognitive perspectives on persuasion suggest that when we are motivated to process the message, this motivation may take one of three forms: accuracy, defense, or impression. In some

instances, we may try to form *accurate* judgments about what our attitudes should be (*accuracy motivation*); in other instances, we might be moved to defend the attitudes we already have (*defense motivation*); in still other instances, we may be most concerned with using our opinions to make the best impression on another person (*impression motivation*). We'll consider each of these motives in turn.

Accuracy Motivation. In many circumstances, we may try to form *accurate* judgments about what our attitudes should be because it is very important for us to do so. For example, if you knew that your college was planning to institute a new requirement for you to graduate, you might be very concerned with deciding whether the college is taking the right action. Let's say your school wants to require that every senior has to pass a comprehensive examination in order to graduate; this exam would test essential concepts within each student's declared major and would commence with the current academic year. Because the policy change would have strong implications for your future, you will probably want to learn more about the policy and decide whether you agree with the idea. Thus, if a college official delivers a message proposing such a policy, you will probably pay extremely close attention to the merits of the exam. If the arguments are compelling—perhaps they say that the exams will increase the prestige of the college's graduates and therefore increase your earning potential—then you should have positive cognitive responses and you will be persuaded the exams are a good idea. If the arguments are weak or silly—perhaps the administrator says that instituting the exams will allow your school to maintain an ancient Greek tradition—then you will have negative cognitive responses and you will decide that the exams are a bad idea. Many studies have explored exactly the scenario we have described here and their results support the conclusion that accuracy motivation causes our attitudes to align with the presented information (e.g., B. T. Johnson, 1994; Killeya & Johnson, in press; Petty & Cacioppo, 1986).

Defense Motivation. However, in other instances, we have **defense motivation**—the desire to maintain our own attitudes even in the face of otherwise strong arguments. As Chaiken, Giner-Sorolla, and Chen (1996) suggest, there are many reasons we may have defense motivation, of which we summarize several here:

- When someone has directly challenged an important group with which we identify, such as our families or gender (e.g., Garst & Bodenhausen, 1996; Wood et al., 1996)
- When a message challenges an attitude that serves a self-identity or self-expression function, or reflects central values (e.g., Johnson & Eagly, 1989; Johnson et al., 1995)
- When others challenge or threaten our personal freedom and *reactance* results (e.g., Rhodewalt & Davison, 1983)
- When others challenge our personal wishes, hopes and desires (e.g., W. J. McGuire, 1990)
- When people have personality traits such as a high need for closure (Kruglanski & Webster, 1996), high dogmatism (e.g., a tendency to be stubborn) or a low openness to experience (McCrae, 1996).

As you'll recall, we addressed several of these dimensions in our chapter on the self (Chapter 4).

Regardless of the cause of defense motivation, Giner-Sorolla and Chaiken (1997) theorize that when we do have this motive, we will deploy either heuristic or systematic processing, or both, to defend the attitude, rather than to adopt the message's opposing view. To test these ideas, these researchers examined how college students reacted to a proposal to require only essay exams in high-level courses. These researchers reasoned that students who tended to perform poorly on essay exams relative to multiple-choice examinations would have a vested interest, and therefore would be motivated, to defend their views using heuristic and systematic processing. Giner-Sorolla and Chaiken first asked the students to fill out a questionnaire that assessed how well they did on essay exams. Then, half of the participants received a heuristic cue hostile to the proposal—

a poll that showed a strong majority (68 percent) of the student body *opposed* it; the other half of the participants received a heuristic cue bolstering the proposal—a poll that showed a strong majority (68 percent) of the student body *supported* essay exams. As you can probably imagine, the heuristic cue at work here is that the majority is right. The students then received a series of handwritten comments supposedly written by other students; these messages were evenly split between comments that supported or opposed the essays exams. After the messages were processed, attitudes and other reactions were assessed. Giner-Sorolla and Chaiken's analyses revealed that students with a vested interest tended to process the messages in a biased way, producing negative cognitive responses; they heavily relied on the heuristic cue in deciding whether to agree with the proposal to mandate essay exams. For example, students who opposed the essay exams but who were told that the student body supported them tended to conclude that the poll was biased.

These results and those of many other studies (e.g., B. T. Johnson et al., 1995; Zuwerink & Devine, 1996) suggest that when our prized views are threatened, we use whatever defenses are at our disposal to maintain them, no matter how much evidence to the contrary we're shown.

Impression Motivation. Just as there are many causes of defense motivation, there are many possible causes of impression motivation, but all are focused on the context of interpersonal interactions. Thus, **impression motivation** occurs when we realize that our attitudes might express some aspect of our self to others (Chaiken et al., 1996; Johnson & Eagly, 1989). In such cases, Chen, Schechter, and Chaiken (1996, Study 2) predicted that we'll use any combination of heuristic and systematic processing in order to present a socially optimal opinion. To test this prediction, these researchers conducted a clever experiment in which accuracy motivation was compared to impression motivation. Undergraduate students expected to discuss an issue with another student. Prior to these discussions, however, the students were first asked to perform an unrelated task, to read through and respond to some short "imagine-yourself-in-this-situation" scenarios. In the accuracy motive–condition, the scenarios primed the need to be precise. For example, the participants were asked to imagine that they were reporters trying to get the facts on an issue. The choices listed for the scenario included such options as "I would go to the library to look up statistics." In the impression motive–condition, the scenarios primed the need to "get along" in the social situation. For example, the participants were asked to imagine they were on a blind date with a close friend's cousin who they did not find attractive. The choices listed for the scenario included such options as "I would make the best of it."

Following these scenarios, which established either accuracy- or impression-motivation by use of the priming technique, participants were told that they would be discussing the issue of whether the media should disclose presidential election results before all the polls close. Then participants were given a page of information about their discussion partner, including the per-

son's name ("Steven Read"), some demographic details, and a comment about his position on the issue. (Of course, Steven Read was a fictitious person, created for the purposes of the study; no discussions actually took place.) In one condition, the partner wrote that he strongly supported the idea of media disclosure of results prior to all polls closing; in the other condition, the partner wrote that he strongly opposed the idea. After reading this partner position, participants were asked to read an essay on whether the media should disclose the presidential results prior to all the polls closing. Finally, participants completed some measures meant to be given to the discussion partner. Chen and her colleagues predicted that the position of the partner would be extremely important to the participants who had impression motivation and would not be important to participants who had accuracy motivation. As Figure 5.9 shows, these are exactly the results that occurred: Impression-motivated participants expressed attitudes that closely matched their partner's views. In contrast, the partner's position on the issue had no impact on accuracy-motivated participants.

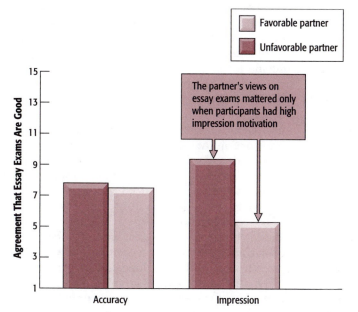

Favorable partner

Unfavorable partner

The partner's views on essay exams mattered only when participants had high impression motivation

Agreement That Essay Exams Are Good

Accuracy

Impression

FIGURE 5.9 Social Motives in Persuasion.

When making a good impression is our primary concern, we tend to pick up and use information that will help us do just that. To make this good impression, Chen and her colleagues predicted that we will use either heuristic processing, systematic processing, or both. In this study, information about another person's opinion proved valuable to impression-motivated participants, but not to accuracy-motivated participants.

(*Source:* Based on data presented by Chen, Shechter, & Chaiken, 1996, Study 2.)

Other research also supports the finding that impression motivation can be a powerful factor in persuasion. Consider the principle that where social behavior is concerned, *reciprocity* is quite important. With few exceptions, we like others who like us, cooperate with others who cooperate with us, help others who help us, and aggress against others who treat us harshly. Given the strength and generality of this principle, it seems possible that reciprocity might play a role in persuasion, too; and recent evidence suggests that it does. In other words, we tend to change our attitudes—or at least our public expression of them—in response to persuasion from others who have previously changed *their* views in response to our own efforts at persuasion. This principle has been supported by the findings of careful research (e.g., Cialdini, Green, & Rusch, 1992), so it seems that reciprocity does indeed play an important role in at least some instances of attitude change.

In summary, a great deal of evidence supports these and other predictions made by the HSM. We do seem to be driven by accuracy, defense, or impression motives, and these motives can affect how we think about issues that concern us.

Forewarning: Prior Knowledge of Persuasive Intent

When we watch television, we fully expect commercials to interrupt most programs (unless we are watching public television). We know full well that these messages are designed to change our views—to get us to buy various products, for instance. Similarly, we know, when we listen to a political speech, that the politician delivering it has an ulterior motive: She or he wants our vote. Does the fact that we know in advance about the persuasive intent behind such messages help us to resist them? Research evidence on such advance knowledge—known as **forewarning**—indicates that it does (e.g., Cialdini & Petty, 1979; B. T. Johnson, 1994). When we know that a speech, taped message, or written appeal is designed to alter our views, we are often less likely to be affected by it than if we do not pos-

sess such knowledge. Why is this the case? Because forewarning influences several cognitive processes that play a role in persuasion. First, forewarning provides us with a greater opportunity to formulate *counterarguments* that can lessen the message's impact. In addition, forewarning also provides us with more time in which to recall relevant facts and information—information that may prove useful in refuting a persuasive message (W. Wood, 1982). The benefits of forewarning are more likely to occur with respect to attitudes we consider important (Krosnick, 1989), but they seem to occur to a smaller degree even for attitudes we view as fairly insignificant. In many cases, then, it appears that to be forewarned is indeed to be forearmed where persuasion is concerned.

Selective Avoidance

Still another way in which we resist attempts at persuasion is through **selective avoidance,** a tendency to direct our attention away from information that challenges our existing attitudes. As we explained in Chapter 3, selective avoidance is one of the ways in which schemas guide the processing of social information, and attitudes often operate as schemas. A clear illustration of the effects of selective avoidance is provided by television viewing. People do not simply sit in front of the tube and absorb whatever the media decide to dish out. Instead, they channel surf, mute the commercials, engage in many other activities, or cognitively tune out when confronted with information contrary to their views. The opposite effect occurs as well. When we encounter information that *supports* our views, we tend to give it our full attention. These tendencies to ignore or avoid information that contradicts our attitudes while actively seeking information consistent with them constitute the two sides of what social psychologists term *selective exposure*, and such selectivity in what we make the focus of our attention helps ensure that our attitudes remain largely intact for long periods of time. Incidentally, these tendencies play a role in our preference for friends who share our attitudes—a topic we'll examine in detail in Chapter 7.

Integrating Principles

1. Persuasion is a form of social influence Chapter 8). A primary factor in persuasion is whether the message recipient can and will try to be accurate about the information that the message contains. In such cases, persuasion depends on what the message recipient actively *thinks* about the message content. Thus, persuasion is closely linked to basic aspects of social cognition (Chapter 3).

2. When there is not sufficient motivation or ability to be accurate about the message, other, peripheral factors such as communicator attractiveness become more important in affecting persuasion. Thus, persuasion is closely linked to basic aspects of social perception (Chapter 3).

3. Message recipients will often process information in a way biased to support their own views (defense motivation) or to look good to others (impressive motivation). Prior knowledge of message content and selective exposure help to ensure that the countless messages to which people are exposed every day usually do not succeed in persuading us.

Cognitive Dissonance: When Our Behavior Affects Our Attitudes

I (Bob Baron) pride myself on being pro-environmental. Last year our village had a "paint collection day," a Saturday when everyone who had old oil-based paint was supposed to bring it to a collection point so it could be safely destroyed. My wife and I had some old paint, so we took it to the designated spot at the designated time, even though we had to wait in line for two hours. Two weeks later, the village announced another paint-collection day, this time for latex-based paint. I had three cans of this type of paint in my basement, so I put them aside with the intention of taking them to the collection point. But then I began to think about that long line, and another ruined Saturday. Guess what I did? Shame on me, but I left the cans where they were and conveniently "forgot" all about the col-

lection day. So much for my pro-environment attitudes!

That's bad enough, but I have a confession: After a while, I got so tired of looking at those half-filled cans of paint and thinking to myself "I should have gotten rid of them," that I *did* get rid of them—I put them in with our regular trash. That's not strictly forbidden in our town, but I certainly looked around to be sure my neighbors didn't see me the day I did it! In fact, I still feel a little uncomfortable about it now, more than six months later. Why? Because in this situation, my behavior was clearly inconsistent with my attitudes. Social psychologists term the kind of discomfort I experienced **cognitive dissonance**—an unpleasant state that occurs when we notice that various attitudes we hold, or our attitudes and our behavior, are somehow inconsistent (Festinger, 1957).

Unfortunately, cognitive dissonance is an all-too-common experience. Any time you say things you don't really believe, make a tough decision, or discover that something you've purchased isn't as good as you expected, you may well experience dissonance. In all these situations, there is a gap between your actions and your attitudes, and it tends to make us quite uncomfortable (Elliot & Devine, 1994). Most important from the present perspective, cognitive dissonance can sometimes lead us to change our attitudes—to shift them so that they are consistent with other attitudes we hold or with our overt behavior. Put another way, because of cognitive dissonance and its effects, *we sometimes change our own attitudes*, without any outside pressure to do so. Let's take a closer look at the theory of cognitive dissonance, which has been one of the most influential views in the history of social psychology, and at the role of cognitive dissonance in the process of attitude change.

Cognitive Dissonance: What It Is and How It's Reduced

Dissonance theory, we've already noted, begins with a very reasonable idea: People don't like inconsistency, and are uncomfortable when it occurs. In other words, when we notice that two or more of our attitudes are inconsistent with each other ("I'm against prejudice" but "I don't want minority people living in my neighborhood"), or that our attitudes and behavior are inconsistent ("I'm on a diet because I want to be slim" but "I'm sitting here eating a huge, rich dessert"), we experience an uncomfortable state known as *cognitive dissonance.* When we do, the theory continues, we experience motivation to reduce that unpleasant state. In short, we are motivated to reduce dissonance. How can we accomplish this goal? The theory focuses on three basic mechanisms.

First, we can change our attitudes or behavior so that these are more consistent with each other. For instance, in the first example above, the person in question can become more favorable toward having minority persons as neighbors. In the second example, in contrast, the individual can actually push the dessert away before finishing it, thus reducing the inconsistency between present behavior and his underlying attitudes. Second, we can acquire new information that supports our attitude or our behavior. For instance, persons who smoke may search for evidence suggesting that the harmful effects of this

habit are minimal or far from conclusive. Third, we can decide that the inconsistency actually doesn't matter; in other words, we can engage in **trivialization**—concluding that the attitudes or behaviors in question are not important ones, so any inconsistency between them is insignificant (Simon, Greenberg, & Brehm, 1995; see Figure 5.10).

Which of these various modes of dissonance reduction do we use? In general, the one requiring least effort. As we saw in Chapter 3, this seems to be a guiding principle for many aspects of human behavior, including social thought. In other words, as with other situations, we are pragmatic where dissonance reduction is concerned; we take whatever steps will reduce this unpleasant state and at the same time require the least effort. When we experience dissonance, something has to give, and this something is generally the cognitive element that is easiest or most open to change. Moreover, once individuals choose the easiest or most convenient form of dissonance reduction, they tend to ignore all others (Simon et al., 1995). In short, not only do we choose the path of least resistance; once we head down it, we don't bother to glance, cognitively, at the alternatives.

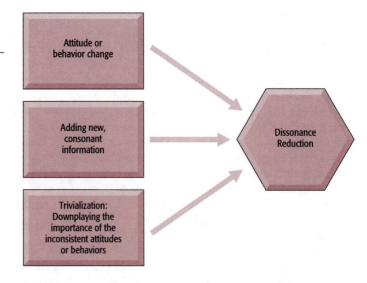

FIGURE 5.10   Major Ways of Reducing Cognitive Dissonance.

Individuals experiencing cognitive dissonance can reduce it in several different ways. The three mechanisms shown here are the most important of these.

Attitude or behavior change

Adding new, consonant information

Trivialization: Downplaying the importance of the inconsistent attitudes or behaviors

Dissonance Reduction

Social Diversity:
A Critical Analysis

Attitudes and Economic Growth: A Cross-National Study

That the economic fortunes of nations rise and fall with the passage of time is obvious. When I (Bob Baron) took high school economics in the late 1950s, our teacher showed us many graphs suggesting that the United States was truly the dominant economic power: This nation accounted for a majority of the world's output of steel, automobiles, and electricity, to name just a few important items. Today, of course, such graphs tell a very different story. The United States no longer accounts for most of the world's production in these areas; and in recent years, its rate of growth has been much lower than that of several Asian countries. What factors contribute to such trends? Most persons (including trained economists) would quickly list such variables as the price and availability of natural resources, labor costs, and government policies that encourage or discourage growth. To this list we'd add another, and uniquely social psychological, factor: *attitudes*. Growing evidence indicates that people in different countries do indeed hold sharply contrasting attitudes about the importance of work, achievement, competitiveness, saving, and the importance of personal wealth (Furnham, 1990). And these attitudes, it appears, play a role in the economic fortunes of their countries.

Direct evidence for such links between attitudes and economic trends has been reported in several studies. Perhaps the most comprehensive of these, however, is a massive study conducted by Furnham, Kirkcaldy, and Lynn (1994) involving more than 12,000 participants in forty-one different countries. These researchers examined the relationship between a wide range of attitudes and two economic indicators: gross domestic product (the amount of annual income per person in the country), and growth rate (rate of increase in

economic output from year to year). Included were attitudes toward work, achievement, competitiveness, money, and saving.

When scores on measures of these attitudes were related to the two economic indicators, significant relationships emerged. First, the researchers found that across all countries, attitudes toward competitiveness were a significant predictor of economic growth: The stronger these attitudes were, the greater the rate of growth. Second, attitudes about the importance of money or personal wealth were a significant predictor of gross domestic product: The stronger these attitudes were, the greater the wealth in the countries studied. In addition, interesting differences emerged among the countries with respect to economic attitudes. Participants from countries in North and South America scored highest on belief in the work ethic, mastery, and savings. On the other hand, Asian/Eastern countries (Bangladesh, China, Hong Kong, India, Iraq, Israel, Japan, Jordan, Korea, Singapore, Syria, Taiwan, Turkey, United Arab Emirates) scored highest on competitiveness and money beliefs (favorable attitudes toward the importance of personal wealth). Interestingly, persons from European countries scored lowest on most of the dimensions studied.

What do these findings mean? One possible interpretation is as follows: Certain attitudes are related to economic growth because they lead individuals to behave in ways that contribute to their countries' wealth. For instance, note that persons from Asian and Eastern countries scored highest on competitiveness and money beliefs—attitudes that were found to be significant predictors of economic growth. Of course, it is a large leap from attitudes held by individuals to the economic well-being of entire nations. Yet it should be noted that in the final analysis, economic trends reflect actions by large numbers of individuals. To the extent this is so, it is not really very surprising that attitudes relevant to economic activity may well play a role in shaping the destiny of national economies. The economic whole, after all, is indeed the sum of its parts—and these parts consist of thinking, feeling, behaving human beings.

The Effects of Induced Compliance

There are many occasions in everyday life when we must say or do things inconsistent with our real attitudes. For example, your friend buys a new car and proudly asks you how you like it. You have just read an article indicating that this model is such a lemon that the manufacturer puts a free ten-pound bag of sugar in the trunk. But what do you say? Probably something like "Nice, really nice." Social psychologists refer to such situations as ones involving **induced compliance**— situations in which we are constrained to say or do something contrary to our real views. And by now you can probably guess what social psychologists predict will happen in such situations: often, when we can't change our behavior, we'll change the attitudes that are inconsistent with it (Murphy & Miller, 1997). You may conclude that your friend's car must be better than the article says. In short, dissonance theory suggests that sometimes we really do change our own attitudes in order to bring them into closer alignment with our overt actions. And, of course, we are especially likely to do this when other techniques for reducing dissonance require greater effort.

Dissonance and the Less-Leads-to-More Effect. So far, so good. Predictions derived from dissonance theory seem straightforward and make good sense. But now consider this question: Will the reasons why you engaged in behavior inconsistent with your attitudes matter? Obviously, we can engage in attitude-discrepant behavior for many reasons, and some of these are stronger or more compelling than others. For instance, if you expect your friend with the new car to give you a lift to school every day, you have strong reasons for concealing your true reactions to it. But if your friend is about to move to another town, your reasons for saying that you like it when you think it's a lemon are somewhat weaker. Now for the key question: When will dissonance be stronger— when we have many good reasons for engaging in attitude-discrepant behavior, or when we have few such reasons? The answer is surprising: Dissonance will be stronger when we have few reasons for engaging in attitude-discrepant behavior. This is so because under these conditions, we can't explain away our actions to ourselves; we performed them even though there was no compelling reason for doing so. The result: Dissonance looms large in our consciousness.

In other words, as shown in Figure 5.11, predictions derived from dissonance theory suggest that it may be easier to change individuals' attitudes by getting them to engage in attitude-discrepant behavior under conditions where they have just barely enough reasons to engage in such behavior. Social psychologists sometimes refer to this surprising prediction as the **less-leads-to-more effect**—less reason leads to more attitude change—and it has been confirmed in many different studies. For example, in the first and most famous of these experiments (Festinger & Carlsmith, 1959), participants were offered either a small reward ($1) or a large one ($20) for telling another person that some dull tasks they had just performed were very interesting. One of these tasks consisted of placing spools on a tray, dumping them out, and repeating the process over and over again. After engaging in the attitude-discrepant behavior— telling another person that the dull tasks were interesting—participants were asked to indicate their own liking for these tasks. As predicted by the less-leads-to-more effect, those given the small reward for misleading a stranger actually

FIGURE 5.11   Why Less (Smaller Inducement) Often Leads to More (Greater Attitude Change) after Attitude-Discrepant Behavior.

When individuals have strong reasons for engaging in attitude-discrepant behavior, they experience relatively small amounts of dissonance and relatively weak pressure to change their attitudes. However, when individuals have weak reasons for engaging in attitude-discrepant behavior, they experience larger amounts of dissonance and stronger pressure to change their attitudes. The result: Less (smaller reward) leads to more (greater amount of attitude change).

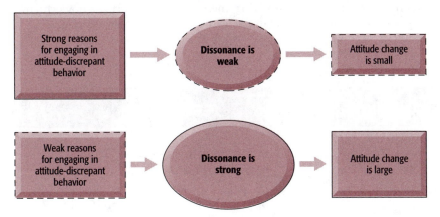

reported liking the tasks to a greater extent than those given the large reward.

While this effect has been confirmed in many studies, we should note that it does not occur under all conditions. Rather, it seems to happen only when several circumstances exist (Cooper & Scher, 1994). First, the less-leads-to-more effect occurs only in situations in which people believe that they have a choice as to whether or not to perform the attitude-discrepant behavior. Second, small rewards lead to greater attitude change only when people believe that they were personally responsible for both the chosen course of action and any negative effects it produced (Goethals, Cooper, & Naficy, 1979). And third, the less-leads-to-more effect does not occur when people view the payment they receive as a bribe rather than as a well-deserved payment for services rendered. These and related findings indicate that there are definite limits on the impact of induced compliance: It doesn't lead to attitude change on all occasions. Still, the conditions just outlined often do exist—often people do have (or think they have) freedom of action; they accept responsibility for

their own behavior and its consequences; and they tend to view inducements they receive as well-earned rewards. As a result, the strategy of offering others just barely enough to induce them to say or do things contrary to their true attitudes can often be an effective technique for inducing attitude change—and self-generated change at that.

Dissonance and Healthy Behavior

Using condoms is a highly reliable method of preventing the spread of HIV, the virus that causes AIDS. Although almost everyone knows this fact (Carey, Morrison-Beedy, & Johnson, 1997), some individuals nonetheless engage in unprotected sexual behavior even though it could kill them if they contract HIV (e.g., Mac-Donald, Zanna, & Fong, 1996; Thompson et al., 1996). This dramatic inconsistency led Aronson and his colleagues to investigate how dissonance could be used to promote safer sex and other beneficial changes in social behavior (Aronson, Fried, & Stone, 1991; Stone et al., 1997). Specifically, they suggest that this can be accomplished through the use of a procedure that points out *hypocrisy*—(1) inducing individuals to make a public commitment to some course of action (e.g., use of condoms), and (2) reminding them that sometimes they have failed to behave in accordance with this commitment. Under these conditions, individuals are made to recognize their hypocrisy: the inconsistency between their public commitment (and the attitudes underlying this) and their actual behavior. The result is

a high degree of dissonance and subsequent change in the relevant behaviors. Thus, dissonance *can* produce safer sexual behavior. Similar effects have been obtained for health behaviors such as smoking (Gibbons, Eggleston, & Benthin, 1997; G. E. Smith, Gerrard, & Gibbons, 1997). If dissonance can motivate the change of behaviors, even those as highly addictive as smoking, then dissonance is truly a powerful motivator of attitude and behavior change.

Connections   Integrating Social Psychology

In this chapter, you read about . . .

- the role of social learning in attitude formation

- persuasion

- cognitive dissonance

In other chapters, you will find related discussions of . . .

- the role of social learning in several forms of social behavior—attraction (Chapter 7), helping (Chapter 9), and aggression (Chapter 9)
- other techniques for changing attitudes and behavior and why they are effective or ineffective (Chapter 8); the use of persuasive techniques in health-related messages (Chapter 11)
- the role of cognitive dissonance in various attitudes and forms of social behavior; for example, in job satisfaction (Chapter 11)

Thinking about Connections

1. Suppose that you wanted to launch a campaign to prevent teenagers from starting to smoke (a major threat to their future health; see Chapter 11). What specific features would you build into this program in order to maximize its effectiveness?
2. Suppose that shortly after graduation, you receive two job offers. After a lot of painful thought, you choose one and reject the other. Do you think that your satisfaction with the job you chose (i.e., your job satisfaction [see Chapter 11]) will be greater

because the decision was so difficult? Would your job satisfaction be lower if the decision were an easy one?
3. If attitudes are indeed learned, this implies that important aspects of social behavior that involve attitudes—for instance prejudice (see Chapter 6)—are open to change. Drawing on our discussion of attitude change in this chapter, what steps could a society that wishes to reduce prejudice take in order to reach this important goal?

Summary and Review

Forming Attitudes

Attitudes are enduring evaluations of various aspects of the social world—evaluations that are stored in memory. Attitudes are acquired through experience or from other persons through *social learning*. This involves three basic forms of learning: classical conditioning, instrumental conditioning, and modeling. Recent evidence indicates that *subliminal conditioning* of attitudes is also possible and may play a role in their development. Attitudes can also be formed through *social comparison*, a process in which we compare ourselves with others. Recent evidence indicates that genetic factors, too, may play a role in the formation of attitudes.

Do Attitudes Influence Behavior?

Contrary to early findings, growing evidence indicates that attitudes do indeed influence behavior. However, this relationship is far from simple. Numerous factors influence (moderate) the strength of the attitude-to-behavior link. These include aspects of the situation, such as the operation of social norms and time pressure; aspects of attitudes themselves, such as their strength, importance, and accessibility; and aspects of individuals, such as *self-monitoring*.

Attitudes seem to guide behavior through two distinct processes. If we have enough time to engage in careful thought about our attitudes and our behavior, then attitudes guide behavior primarily by affecting our intentions. When we do not have the opportunity to engage in such reasoned thought, in contrast, attitudes seem to influence behavior in a more automatic manner involving our perceptions of the attitude object and our knowledge about what is appropriate or expected in a given situation.

Persuasion

Persuasion is the process of changing attitudes. The first compelling models of persuasion focus on the cognitive processes that underlie attitude change, including especially *systematic processing* of message content and *heuristic processing* of cues in and around the message. Message recipients are particularly likely to process heuristically when they have little ability or motivation to pay close attention to a message. Under *accuracy motivation*—the desire to hold the correct attitude—however, messages containing strong arguments will persuade, whereas weak arguments will not. *Impression motivation* may induce a message recipient to express attitudes that they may not privately adopt, in the service of social goals. Numerous other factors can thwart the persuasion process, including *defense motivation*—the goal of maintaining our attitudes, *forewarning* of the persuasive intent, and *selective avoidance* of information inconsistent with our attitudes.

Cognitive Dissonance

When individuals notice inconsistency between attitudes they hold or between their attitudes and their behavior, they experience *cognitive dissonance*. Dissonance motivates persons experiencing it to attempt to reduce it. They can accomplish this in several ways: by changing the attitudes in question, by acquiring information to support the behavior, or by means of *trivialization*—downplaying the importance of the attitudes or the behavior. Recent evidence indicates that dissonance is indeed an unpleasant state. The fewer good reasons people have for engaging in attitude-discrepant behavior, the greater the dissonance and the stronger the pressure for attitude change, which is known as the *less-leads-to-more effect*. Individuals also experience dissonance when they experience *hypocrisy*—when they recognize that they have not lived up to attitudes that they have stated publicly. Recognition of hypocrisy can induce individuals to change their behavior in order to match their attitudes. Recent findings indicate that it can even be effective in encouraging individuals to engage in safe sex, thereby helping prevent the spread of AIDS.

Social Diversity: Attitudes and Economic Growth

Growing evidence indicates that attitudes held by individuals in various countries are related to the wealth and economic growth of these nations. For example, it appears that individuals in many Asian countries that have recently had very high rates of economic growth have more favorable attitudes toward competitiveness and toward acquiring personal wealth than persons in many Western countries.

Key Terms

Accuracy Motivation (p. 113)
Attitude-to-Behavior Process Model (p. 110)
Attitudes (p. 100)
Classical Conditioning (p. 102)
Cognitive Dissonance (p. 117)
Cognitive Perspective (on persuasion) (p. 112)
Cognitive Response Analysis (p. 112)
Defense Motivation (p. 114)
Forewarning (p. 116)
Heuristic Processing (p. 112)
Impression Motivation (p. 114)
Induced Compliance (p. 120)

Instrumental Conditioning (p. 104)
Less-Leads-to-More Effect (p. 120)
Modeling (p. 104)
Persuasion (p. 112)
Selective Avoidance (p. 116)
Social Comparison (p. 104)
Social Learning (p. 102)
Subliminal Conditioning (of attitudes) (p. 103)
Systematic Processing (p. 112)
Theory of Planned Behavior (p. 110)
Trivialization (p. 118)

For More Information

Eagly, A. H., & Chaiken, S. (1993). *The psychology of attitudes.* San Diego, CA: Harcourt Brace & Jovanovich.

A comprehensive review of the vast existing literature on attitudes. The book is written by two expert researchers and contains much valuable information about the nature of attitudes, how they can be changed, and their effects on behavior.

Gollwitzer, P. M., & Bargh, J. A. (1996). *The psychology of action: Linking motivation and cognition in behavior.* New York: Guilford.

A collection of state-of-the-art essays relevant to the general theme of understanding how and why people behave the way they do.

Shavitt, S., & Brock, T. C. (1994). *Persuasion: Psychological insights and perspectives.* Boston: Allyn & Bacon.

Explores all aspects of persuasion. The chapters on when and how attitudes influence behavior, cognitive dissonance, and the cognitive perspective on persuasion are all outstanding. The book is written in an interesting style that undergraduates should find easy to understand

Prejudice and Discrimination

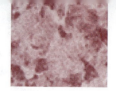

People who know me well (Bob Baron) say that I'm usually in a hurry. Where getting my career started was concerned, that was definitely the case. I worked hard to complete my Ph.D. by June so I could get right to work teaching that summer. Although I grew up in the northern U.S., my first job was at a large Southern university; and like all new professors, I wanted very badly to succeed. I was pleased, therefore, when most of the ratings and comments I received from my students were favorable. Mixed in among these, though, were a few that literally sent me reeling. The words varied, but all said something to this effect: *"What makes you think you're better than we are? We're proud of our heritage, too."* I was truly floored; what had I said or done to give a few of my students the impression that I was prejudiced against them—that I held negative views about their Southern culture? I racked my brain, but at first I couldn't figure it out: I wasn't aware of any negative views or feelings about the South. Gradually though, a glimmer of light began to emerge. Social psychologists often have assistants who help them with their research by pretending to be one of the participants; and often, social psychologists refer to these people as . . . *confederates!* That was it! The word *confederate* had a special meaning for some students in my classes, and I had totally missed this connection. So, unaware of what I was doing, I had spouted this word repeatedly while describing various studies. Some of my students must have perceived my use of a word with sensitive connotations for them as careless at best, or—even worse—as a deliberate effort to be condescending. No wonder they were annoyed at me. Right then and there, I made a vow never to refer to experimental assistants as *confederates* again, either in class or in anything I wrote. (You won't see that word in *this* book again!) This change did the trick: I never received another one of those angry comments from my students.

Why do we start with this incident? Mainly, to call a key fact to your attention: *At some time or other in our lives, virtually every one of us comes face to face with prejudice.* It may not be the malignant form that leads to dangerous riots, crimes of violence, or horrible atrocities such as Nazi death camps and "ethnic cleansing," but meet it we do. And even when prejudice takes relatively subtle or mild forms, its effects can be very damaging both to the victims of prejudice and to the persons who hold it. To mention just one example, recent findings indicate that many persons harbor prejudice toward overweight individuals (Zebrowitz, 1996). For example, overweight persons receive lower ratings in job interviews than persons of normal weight (Pingitore et al., 1994). And nurses report feeling less empathy toward overweight patients, and greater reluctance to care for them (Maroney & Golub, 1992; Figure 6.1). Certainly, no one would equate these mild aversions toward overweight persons with the strong racial or ethnic bigotry that has caused so much suffering throughout human history. Yet even these mild forms of prejudice can have important consequences for the persons toward whom they are directed.

Social psychologists have long recognized the pervasive impact of prejudice on human behavior and human societies. Thus, they have used the impressive tools of their field to study this topic for several decades. In this chapter, we'll review the major findings of their research efforts. We'll start by examining the nature of *prejudice* and *discrimination,* two words that are often used as synonyms but which in fact refer to very different concepts. Second, we'll consider the causes of prejudice and discrimination—why they occur and what makes them so intense and persistent. Third, we'll explore various strategies for reducing prejudice and discrimination. Finally, because it has been the subject of an especially large amount of research and because it influences the lives of more than half of all human beings, we will focus on the nature and effects of *sexism*—prejudice based on gender.

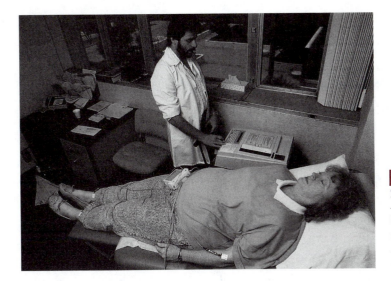

FIGURE 6.1   Prejudice: Even Subtle Forms Can Be Harmful.

Recent findings indicate that many nurses hold mild prejudice toward overweight persons: They are more reluctant to care for them than for persons of normal weight.

The Nature of Prejudice and Discrimination

In everyday speech, the terms *prejudice* and *discrimination* are often used interchangeably. Are they really the same? Most social psychologists draw a clear distinction between them. *Prejudice* refers to a special type of *attitude*—generally, a negative one—toward the members of some social group. In contrast, *discrimination* refers to negative *actions* toward those individuals—attitudes translated into actions, if you will. This is an important distinction, so let's consider it more closely.

Prejudice: Choosing Whom to Hate

We'll begin with a more precise definition: **Prejudice** is *an attitude (usually negative) toward the members of some group, based solely on their membership in that group.* In other words, a person who is prejudiced toward some social group tends to evaluate its members in a specific manner (usually negatively) merely because they belong to that group. Their individual traits or behaviors play little role; they are disliked (or, in a few cases, liked), simply because they belong to a specific social group. When prejudice is defined as a special type of attitude, two important implications follow. First, as we saw in Chapters 3 and 5, attitudes often function as *schemas*—cognitive frameworks for organizing, interpreting, and recalling information (e.g., S. T. Fiske & Taylor, 1991). Thus, individuals who are prejudiced toward particular groups tend to process information about these groups differently from the way they process information about other groups. For example, information that is consistent with their prejudiced views often receives more attention, is rehearsed more frequently, and as a result tends to be remembered more accurately than information that is not consistent with these views (e.g., S. T. Fiske & Neuberg, 1990; Judd, Ryan, & Park, 1991). Thus, prejudice often becomes a kind of closed cognitive loop and, in the absence of events or experiences that shatter this self-confirming effect, can only grow stronger over time.

Second, if prejudice is a special kind of attitude, then it may involve more than negative evaluations of the groups toward whom it is directed: it may also include negative feelings or emotions on the part of prejudiced persons when they are in the presence of, or merely think about, members of the groups they dislike (Bodenhausen, Kramer, & Susser, 1994; Dovidio et al., 1996). Prejudice may also involve beliefs and expectations about members of these groups—specifically, *stereotypes* suggesting that all members of these groups demonstrate certain characteristics and behave in certain ways. As we'll soon discuss, stereotypes—which can be defined, most generally, as people's beliefs about the members of some social group (e.g., Jussim et al., 1995)—play a central role in many aspects of prejudice. Finally, prejudice may involve tendencies to act in negative ways toward those who are the object of prejudice.

One additional—and central—point: When people think about prejudice, they tend to focus on its emotional or evaluative aspects. They emphasize the strong negative feelings and irrational hatreds that so often characterize racial, religious, or ethnic prejudice. Such reactions are important; and as we'll see in a later section, there are important links between the affective (feeling) and cognitive components of prejudice, just as there are important links between affect and cognition generally (see our discussion of this topic in Chapter 3). Yet it is crucial to note that prejudice is also related to, and involves, certain aspects of *social cognition*—the ways in which we notice, store, recall, and later use information about others in various ways, for example, in making judgments about them. Because we have only limited capacity to perform these tasks, we often adopt various cognitive shortcuts in our efforts to make sense out of the social world (Gilbert & Hixon, 1991). We are especially likely to do this at times when our capacity for handling social information is pushed to the limits; it is at such times that we are most likely to fall back on *stereotypes* as mental shortcuts for understanding others or making judgments about them (e.g., Macrae, Hewstone, & Griffiths, 1993). As Gilbert and Hixon (1991) put it, stereotypes are tools that "jump out" of our cognitive toolbox when we realize that we are being exposed to more information than we can readily handle.

We'll return to a detailed examination of stereotypes and their role in prejudice in a later section. Here, however, we want to note that there is a large and growing amount of evidence pointing to the conclusion that the tendency to stereotype others, and to think about them in terms of stereotypes, does indeed stem—at least in part—from the fact that this strategy saves us cognitive effort. Strong support for this view is provided by research conducted recently by Macrae, Milne, and Bodenhausen (1994).

In the first of a series of carefully executed studies, the researchers asked participants to perform simultaneously two unrelated tasks: (1) an impression formation task, in which participants were to form impressions of fictitious persons whose names were paired on a computer screen with adjectives describing their supposed traits, and (2) an unrelated listening task, in which they heard a tape describing the geography and economy of Indonesia. After these tasks were completed, participants were asked to remember as many of the traits of each person shown as possible, and also to answer a series of questions about the information on the tape about Indonesia. Macrae, Milne, and Bodenhausen reasoned as follows: If stereotypes serve as mental shortcuts, freeing up cognitive resources for other tasks, then persons in whom stereotypes were activated during the impression formation task would do better on both tasks. This would be so because the stereotypes, once activated, would free resources for use in both simultaneous tasks. But how could stereotypes be activated? Macrae and his colleagues accomplished this by showing not only the strangers' names but also labels about them (e.g., doctor, artist) to half of the participants; the remainder did not see these labels. If labels evoke stereotypes and stereotypes free up cognitive resources, then participants exposed to them should do better on both tasks than those not exposed to these labels. As you can see from Figure 6.2, this is precisely what happened.

In an ingenious follow-up study, Macrae, Milne, and Bodenhausen (1994) presented the labels so quickly that participants could not even recognize them or report their presence. Despite

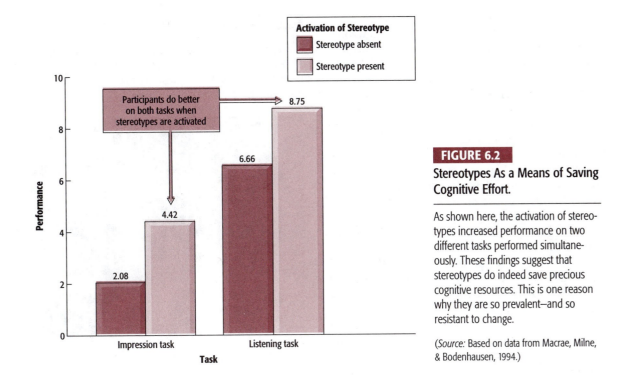

FIGURE 6.2
Stereotypes As a Means of Saving
Cognitive Effort.

As shown here, the activation of stereotypes increased performance on two
different tasks performed simultaneously. These findings suggest that
stereotypes do indeed save precious
cognitive resources. This is one reason
why they are so prevalent—and so
resistant to change.

(*Source:* Based on data from Macrae, Milne,
& Bodenhausen, 1994.)

this fact, however, performance was still better in
the group who were exposed to these stereotype-
inducing labels than in the control condition.
These findings suggest that stereotypes can serve
as an "energy-saving tactic" where cognition is
concerned, even when people are not aware of
their presence Combined with the findings of related studies (e.g., Bodenhausen, 1993), the findings also suggest that one reason stereotypes are
so pervasive, and so resistant to change, is that,
in one sense, they "work": They do succeed in saving cognitive resources for the persons who use
them. Of course, such stretching of cognitive resources comes at the cost of reduced accuracy—
a kind of trade-off in life with which all of us are
very familiar.

Integrating Principles

1. Prejudice can be viewed as a special type of attitude (see
   Chapter 5)—usually a negative attitude toward the mem-

bers of specific social groups, based solely on their membership in these groups.
2. As an attitude, prejudice usually involves not only negative evaluations but beliefs about others which are often
   reflected in *stereotypes.* Stereotypes, in turn, influence the
   processing of social information in ways that make them
   self-confirming (see Chapter 3).
3. Stereotypes also serve as mental shortcuts, reducing the
   cognitive effort we must exert to understand others, form
   impressions of them (Chapter 2), or make judgments
   about them (see Chapter 3).

Discrimination: Prejudice in Action

Attitudes, we noted in Chapter 5, are not always
reflected in overt actions, and prejudice is definitely no exception to this rule. In many cases,
persons holding negative attitudes toward the
members of various groups cannot express
these views directly. Laws, social pressure, fear
of retaliation—all serve to deter people from
putting their prejudiced views into open practice.

In addition, many persons who hold prejudiced views do feel that overt discrimination is wrong, and perceive such actions on their own part as a violation of personal standards. When such individuals observe that they *have* shown discrimination, they experience considerable discomfort, in the form of guilt and related feelings (Devine & Monteith, 1993). This, in turn, may reduce their tendency to behave in similar ways again. Unfortunately, people don't always notice such inconsistencies between how they behave and how they feel they *should* behave, but when they do, overt discrimination may indeed be reduced (Monteith, 1996a).

For several reasons, blatant forms of **discrimination**—negative actions toward the objects of racial, ethnic, or religious prejudices—have decreased in recent years in the United States and many other countries (e.g., Dovidio et al., 1996; Swim et al., 1995). Such actions as restricting members of various groups to certain seats on buses or in movie theaters, or barring them from public restaurants, schools, or neighborhoods—all common practices in the past (see Figure 6.3)—have now largely vanished in many countries. Of course, they have not disappeared completely: Anyone who watches the evening news well knows that open expressions of prejudice, and violent confrontations stemming from them, still occur throughout the world with disturbing frequency. For the most part, though, the expression of prejudice in social behavior has become increasingly subtle in recent decades. What are these *subtle* or *disguised* forms of discrimination like? Research by social psychologists points to several interesting conclusions.

The New Racism: More Subtle, But Just As Deadly. At one time, many people felt no qualms about expressing openly racist beliefs. They would state that they were against school desegregation, that they viewed members of minority groups as inferior in various ways, and that they would consider moving away if persons belonging to these groups took up residence in their neighborhoods (Plous & Williams, 1995; Sears, 1988). Now, of course, very few persons would openly state

FIGURE 6.3   Discrimination in the Past.

In the past, members of various minority groups (especially African Americans) were barred from many public places in the United States. Fortunately, such open forms of discrimination have now totally vanished.

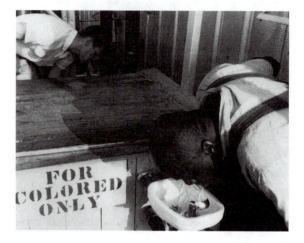

such views. Does this mean that racism, a particularly virulent form of discrimination, has disappeared? While many social psychologists would argue that this is the case (e.g., Martin & Parker, 1995), others would contend that in fact, all that has happened is that "old-fashioned" racism (read "blatant" for "old-fashioned") has been replaced by more subtle forms, which these researchers often term *modern racism* (Dovidio et al., 1996). What is such racism like? Swim and her colleagues (Swim et al., 1995) have recently gathered data indicating that this new variety of racism focuses on three major components: (1) denial that there is continuing discrimination against minorities (e.g., "Discrimination against African Americans is no longer a problem in the United States"); (2) antagonism to the demands of minorities for equal treatment (e.g., "African Americans are getting too demanding in their push for equal rights"); and (3) resentment about special favors for minority groups (e.g., "Over the past few years, the government and news media have shown more respect to African Americans than they deserve"). As you can readily see, such views are certainly different from those involved in "old-fashioned" racism, but they can still be very damaging to the victims. For example, as noted by Swim et al. (1995), modern racism may influence the likelihood of voting for a minority candidate to an even stronger extent than "old-fashioned" racism.

Similarly, research has shown that individuals who sincerely desire not to be prejudiced about various stigmatized groups must still somehow control the negative stereotypes they hold about these groups. In one study, Devine (1989) showed that even low-prejudiced individuals have knowledge of stereotypes about African Americans (e.g., "poor," "criminal," "uneducated"), knowledge that closely matched that of high-prejudiced individuals. According to this research (Devine et al., 1991; Zuwerink, Devine, & Monteith, 1996), low-prejudiced individuals actively and consciously suppress such stereotypes so that their behavior will remain unbiased. Low-prejudiced individuals even feel guilty when they realize they are having stereotypic reactions to events (Devine et al., 1991; Monteith, 1996).

So—and we want to emphasize this point strongly—despite the fact that blatant forms of racism have all but vanished from public life in the United States and many other countries, this especially repulsive and damaging form of prejudice is still very much alive and represents a serious problem in many societies (Dovidio et al., in press-b; Hopkins, Reicher, & Levine, 1997).

The Origins of Prejudice: Contrasting Perspectives

Why does prejudice exist? Why, even today, do so many people hold negative views about the members of specific social groups—attitudes that sometimes lead to tragic results? Many different answers to these questions have been offered. Here, we will consider several perspectives on prejudice that have proved influential.

Competition As a Source of Prejudice

It is sad but true that the things people want and value most—good jobs, nice homes, high status—are always in short supply. This fact serves as the foundation for what is perhaps the oldest explanation of prejudice—**realistic conflict theory** (e.g., Bobo, 1983). According to this view, prejudice stems from competition among social groups over valued commodities or opportunities. In short, prejudice develops out of the struggle over jobs, adequate housing, good schools, and other desirable outcomes. The theory further suggests that as such competition continues, the members of the groups involved come to view each other in increasingly negative terms (Hepworth & West, 1988). They label each other as "enemies," view their own group as morally superior, and draw the boundaries between themselves and their opponents more and more firmly. The result is that what starts out as simple competition relatively free from hatred gradually develops into full scale, emotion-laden prejudice.

Evidence from several different studies confirms the occurrence of this process. As competition persists, individuals come to perceive each other in increasingly negative ways. Even worse, such competition often leads to direct, and sometimes violent, conflict. A very dramatic demonstration of this principle in operation is provided by a well-known field study conducted by Muzafer Sherif and his colleagues (Sherif et al., 1961).

For this unusual study, the researchers sent eleven-year-old boys to a special summer camp in a remote area where, free from external influences, the nature of conflict and its role in prejudice could be carefully studied. When the boys arrived at the camp (named *The Robber's Cave* in honor of a nearby cave that was once, supposedly, used by robbers), they were divided into two separate groups and assigned to cabins located quite far apart. For one week, the campers in each group lived and played together, engaging in such enjoyable activities as hiking, swimming, and other sports. During this initial phase, the boys quickly developed strong attachments to their own groups. They chose names for their teams (*Rattlers* and *Eagles*), stenciled them onto their shirts, and made up flags with their groups' symbols on them.

In the next phase, the boys in both groups were told that they would now engage in a series of competitions. The winning team would receive a trophy, and its members would earn prizes (pocket knives and medals). Since these were prizes the boys strongly desired, the stage was set for intense competition. As the boys competed, the tension between the groups rose. At first it was limited to verbal taunts and name-calling, but soon it escalated into more direct acts—for example, the Eagles burned the Rattlers' flag. The next day the Rattlers struck back by attacking the rival group's cabin, overturning beds, tearing out mosquito netting, and seizing personal property. Such actions continued until the researchers intervened to prevent serious trouble. At the same time, the two groups voiced increasingly negative views of each other. They labeled their opponents "bums" and "cowards," while heaping praise on their own group at every turn. In short, after only two weeks of conflict, the groups showed all the key components of strong prejudice toward each other.

As you can see, this study offers a chilling picture of how what begins as rational competition over scarce resources can quickly escalate into full-scale conflict, which then in turn fosters the accompanying negative attitudes toward opponents that form the core of prejudice.

Fortunately, the story had a happy ending. In the study's final phase, Sherif and his colleagues attempted to reduce the negative reactions described above. Merely increasing the amount of contact between the groups failed to accomplish this goal; indeed, it seemed to fan the flames of anger. But when conditions were altered so that the groups found it necessary to work together to reach *superordinate goals*—ones they both desired—dramatic changes occurred. After the boys worked together to restore their water supply (previously sabotaged by the researchers), pooled their funds to rent a movie, and jointly repaired a broken-down truck, tensions between the groups largely vanished. In fact, after six days of such experiences the

boundaries between the groups virtually dissolved, and many cross-group friendships were established.

The Role of Social Learning

A second explanation for the origins of prejudice is straightforward: It suggests that prejudice is *learned* and that it develops in much the same manner, and through the same basic mechanisms, as other attitudes (see Chapter 5). According to this **social learning view,** children acquire negative attitudes toward various social groups because they hear such views expressed by parents, friends, teachers, and others, and because they are directly rewarded (with love, praise, and approval) for adopting these views. In addition to direct observation of others, *social norms*—rules within a given group suggesting what actions or attitudes are appropriate—are also important (Pettigrew, 1969). As we will see in Chapter 8, most persons choose to conform to most social norms of groups to which they belong. The development and expression of prejudice toward others often stems from this tendency. "If the members of my group dislike them," many children seem to reason, "then I should too!"

The mass media also play a role in the development of prejudice. Until recently, members of various racial and ethnic minorities were shown infrequently in movies or on television. And when they did appear, they were often cast in low-status or comic roles. Given repeated exposure to such materials for years or even decades, it is not surprising that many children came to believe that the members of these groups must be inferior. After all, why else would they be shown in this manner?

Fortunately, this situation has changed greatly in recent years in the United States and elsewhere. Members of various racial and ethnic minorities now appear more frequently and are shown in a more favorable manner than was true in the past. Such changes are clearly documented by a recent study conducted by Weigel, Kim, and Frost (1995). These researchers systematically examined prime-time television programming and prime-time product commercials appearing during 1989 in order to determine whether African Americans were shown more frequently, and in different ways, than was true in 1978, when another major survey of this kind was conducted (Weigel, Loomis, & Soja, 1980). (See Figure 6.4.) Results indicated that in terms of appearance in actual programs, there had indeed been significant change. African Americans appeared more frequently in regular programming in 1989 than was true in 1978, and the percentage of cross-racial interaction time in these shows also increased significantly. The programming picture was not entirely rosy, however. While the frequency with which African Americans was shown did increase, further analyses indicated that cross-racial interactions in these television programs showed a lower level of intimacy and were rated as less intense and multifaceted than within-race interactions. So, while there was considerable change during the period studied, there were still differences in the treatment of whites and African Americans in television programs even in 1989. Of course, it seems possible that an analysis of current programming might indicate even more progress toward comparable presentation of all ethnic and racial groups in popular shows. Until such treatment is equal, the possibility remains that the mass media are contributing, to some degree, to the persistence of various forms of prejudice.

Us versus Them and the "Ultimate" Attribution Error

A third perspective on the origins of prejudice begins with a basic fact: People generally divide the social world into two distinct categories—*us* and *them*. In short, they view other persons as belonging either to their own group (usually termed the **ingroup**) or to another group (the **outgroup**). Such distinctions are based on many dimensions, including race, religion, gender, age, ethnic background, occupation, and income, to name just a few.

If the process of dividing the social world into "us" and "them"—**social categorization**—stopped there, it would have little bearing on prejudice. Unfortunately, however, it does not. Sharply contrasting feelings and beliefs are usually attached to members of one's ingroup and members of various outgroups. Persons in the former ("us") category are viewed in favorable terms, while those in the latter ("them") category are perceived more negatively. Outgroup members are assumed to possess more undesirable traits, are perceived as being more alike (i.e., more homogeneous) than members of the

FIGURE 6.4 The Changing Image of African Americans on American Television.

During the 1980s the presence of African Americans in many popular television programs increased substantially, although their representation in product commercials did not show a similar increase.

ingroup, and are often disliked (Judd, Ryan, & Parke, 1991; Linville & Fischer, 1993). The ingroup–outgroup distinction also affects *attribution*—the ways in which we explain the actions of persons belonging to these two categories. Specifically, we tend to attribute desirable behaviors by members of our ingroup to stable, internal causes (e.g., their admirable traits), but attribute desirable behaviors by members of outgroups to transitory factors or to external causes. For example, when students in Hong Kong were asked to explain why students from one university tend to receive better starting jobs than those from another university, those at the favored school attributed their success to better preparation. Those at the school whose graduates received less desirable jobs, however, attributed this outcome to better personal connections on the part of the students at the other school (Hewstone, Bond, & Wan, 1983). This tendency to make more favorable and flattering attributions about members of one's own group than about members of other groups is sometimes described as the **ultimate attribution error,** since it carries the correspondence bias we described in Chapter 2 into the area of intergroup relations—with potentially devastating effects.

That strong tendencies exist to divide the social world into "us" and "them" has been demonstrated in many studies (e.g., Tajfel, 1982). But how, precisely, does this tendency translate into prejudice? Why do we view others in biased and negative ways once we define them as being different from ourselves? An intriguing answer has been provided by Tajfel and his colleagues (e.g., Tajfel, 1982). These researchers suggest that individuals seek to enhance their self-esteem by identifying with specific social groups. This tactic can succeed, however, only to the extent that the persons involved perceive these groups as somehow superior to other, competing groups. Since all individuals are subject to the same tendencies, the final result is inevitable: Each group seeks to view itself as somehow better than its rivals, and prejudice rises out of this clash of social perceptions. Support for the accuracy of these suggestions has been obtained in several experiments (e.g.,

Meindl & Lerner, 1984). Thus, it appears that our tendency to divide the social world into two opposing camps often plays a role in the development of important forms of prejudice.

Cognitive Sources of Prejudice: Stereotypes

Next, we come to sources of prejudice that are, in some ways, the most unsettling of all. These involve the possibility that prejudice stems, at least in part, from basic aspects of *social cognition*— the ways in which we think about other persons, integrate information about them, and then use this information to make social judgments or decisions. Because this has clearly been the focus of most recent research on prejudice in social psychology, we'll divide our discussion of this topic into two parts. First we'll examine what appears to be the central cognitive component in prejudice—*stereotypes*. Then we'll examine other cognitive mechanisms that also play a role in the occurrence of prejudice.

Stereotypes: What They Are and How They Operate. Consider the following groups: Korean Americans, homosexuals, Jews, Cuban Americans, African Americans. Suppose you were asked to list the traits most characteristic of each. Would you find this to be a difficult task? Probably you would not. You would be able to construct a list for each group—and, moreover, you could probably do so *even for groups with whom you have had limited personal contact*. Why? The reason involves the existence and operation of **stereotypes**—cognitive frameworks consisting of knowledge and beliefs about specific social groups. As noted by Judd and his colleagues (1991), stereotypes involve generalizations about the typical or "modal" characteristics of members of various social groups. In other words, they suggest that all members of such groups possess certain traits, at least to a degree. Once a stereotype is activated, these traits come readily to mind; and it is this fact that explains the ease with which you can probably construct lists like the ones mentioned above. You may not have had much direct experience with Korean Americans, Cuban Americans, or Jews, for instance; but you *do* have stereotypes for them, so you can readily list their supposed traits.

Like other cognitive frameworks we have considered, stereotypes exert strong effects on how we process social information. For example, information relevant to an activated stereotype is processed more quickly than information unrelated to it (e.g., Dovidio et al., in press-a; Fazio et al., 1995; Zárate & Sandoval, 1995). Similarly, stereotypes lead persons holding them to pay attention to specific types of information—usually, information consistent with the stereotypes (Steele, 1997). And when information *inconsistent* with stereotypes does manage to enter consciousness, it may be actively refuted or even simply denied (Monteith, 1993). For example, recent evidence indicates that when individuals encounter persons who behave in ways contrary to stereotypes they hold, they often perceive these persons as a new "subtype," rather than changing their stereotype (Kunda & Oleson, 1995). In sum, stereotypes exert powerful effects on our thinking about others.

Given the potential errors that can occur as a result of stereotype-driven thinking, what accounts for the persistence of these cognitive frameworks? As we noted earlier, part of the answer lies in the fact that stereotypes operate as a labor-saving device where social cognition is concerned (Macrae et al., 1994). When activated, stereotypes allow us to make quick-and-dirty judgments about others without engaging in complex, and more effortful, thought. Of course, the conclusions we reach on the basis of stereotypes are often wrong; but the saving of cognitive effort is so great that we tend to rely on stereotypes in many different contexts.

As you can probably already see, stereotypes are closely related to prejudice. Once an individual has acquired a stereotype about some social group, she or he tends to notice information that fits readily into this cognitive framework and to remember "facts" that are consistent with it more readily than "facts" that are inconsistent. As a result, the stereotype becomes, to a large degree, self-confirming. Even exceptions to it

make it stronger, for they simply induce the person in question to bring more supporting information to mind. Evidence for the role of stereotypes in social thought have been reported in many different studies (e.g., Dovidio et al., 1996; Monteith, 1993). Moreover, additional findings indicate that stereotypes are activated quite readily in most social situations. Doing so requires cognitive resources (Gilbert & Hixon, 1991); but again, once they are activated, stereotypes seem to provide such handy mental shortcuts that they are an integral part of everyday social thought. We'll have more to say about the profound effects of stereotypes not only on social thought, but on personal health as well, in the Social Diversity box on page 146. Now, however, we'll turn to another intriguing question regarding stereotypes: the relationship of *affective states* (moods, positive and negative feelings) to stereotypes and their role in prejudice.

The Role of Affect in Stereotypic Thinking: The Interface between Feelings and Thought Revisited. Do you remember our discussion of the relationship between affect and cognition in Chapter 3? If so, you may recall our key conclusion: Feelings (for example, our current moods) often exert strong effects upon cognitive processes; and cognitive processes, in turn, often exert powerful effects upon our feelings. Here, we will return to this important issue as it relates to stereotypes and their role in prejudice.

Let's begin with a very basic question: Do stereotypes operate in a purely cognitive manner, or do they also involve an emotional component? We know that they strongly influence our thinking about others and our judgments of them, but do they exert such effects solely because they provide mental shortcuts—rapid ways of perceiving the complex social world? Until quite recently, most social psychologists would have replied *yes*. Stereotypes were viewed primarily as cognitive mechanisms or structures, and most research attention was focused on just how they functioned and on their relationship to other aspects of social cognition, such as schemas, expectations, and *base rates*—our estimates of the frequency of occurrence of various traits or outcomes (e.g., Jussim, 1991).

Now, however, a growing number of social psychologists are investigating the possibility that stereotypes also contain an affective component or, at least, are influenced by affective states to an important extent (e.g., Jussim et al., 1995; Pettigrew, 1997, in press). Research in this area is very new, but convincing evidence for the role of affect in stereotypic thinking has already been reported. Studies of this sort measure feelings, thoughts, and social judgments about social group members and examine whether these judgments are more closely related to feelings or thoughts. Some studies have even shown that feelings have a stronger association with stereotyping than cognitive factors (e.g., Hamberger & Hewstone, 1997; Jussim et al., 1995).

Other Cognitive Mechanisms in Prejudice

Consider the following set of information: (1) There are one thousand members of Group A but only one hundred members of Group B; (2) one-hundred members of Group A were arrested by the police last year, and ten members of Group B were arrested. Suppose you were asked to evaluate the criminal tendencies of these two groups. Would your ratings of them differ? Your first answer is probably "Of course not—why should they? The rate of criminal behavior is 10 percent in both groups, so why rate them differently?" Surprisingly, though, a large body of evidence suggests that you might actually assign a less favorable rating to Group B (e.g., E. E. Henderson-King & Nisbett, 1996; Mullen & Johnson, 1990). Social psychologists refer to this tendency to overestimate the rate of negative behaviors in relatively small groups as **illusory correlation.** This term makes a great deal of sense, because such effects involve perceiving links between variables that aren't really there—in this case, links between being a member of a Group B and the tendency to engage in criminal behavior.

As you can readily see, illusory correlations, to the extent they occur, have important implications for prejudice. In particular, they help explain

why negative behaviors and tendencies are often attributed by majority group members to the members of various minority groups (see Figure 6.5). For example, some social psychologists have suggested that illusory correlation effects help explain why many white persons in the United States overestimate crime rates among African American males (D. L. Hamilton & Sherman, 1989). For many reasons, young African American men are, in fact, arrested for various crimes at higher rates than young white men or men of Asian descent (U.S. Department of Justice, 1994). But white Americans tend to *overestimate*

FIGURE 6.5 Negative Behaviors by Minority Members Receive More Attention.

Even if members of the majority group are as likely as members of a minority group to commit a particular negative behavior, such as depicted in this picture, the behavior of the minority group member will receive more attention. The consequence of this, in turn, is that members of this group are liked less. This *illusory correlation* has important implications for many social phenomena, such as our perceptions of crimes and who is most likely to commit them.

the size of this difference, and this can be interpreted as an instance of illusory correlation. Why do such effects occur? One explanation is based on the *distinctiveness* of infrequent events or stimuli. According to this view, infrequent events are distinctive—readily noticed. As such, they are encoded more extensively than other items when they are encountered, and so become more accessible in memory. When we make judgments about the groups involved at later times, therefore, the distinctive events come readily to mind and lead us to overinterpret their importance.

A large number of studies offer support for this *distinctiveness-based interpretation* of illusory correlation (e.g., Mullen & Johnson, 1995). However, recent findings indicate that this theory should be modified in at least one important respect. Apparently, it is not crucial that information be distinctive when it is first encountered; rather, information can *become* distinctive at later times and thus produce illusory correlations (McConnell, Sherman, & Hamilton, 1994). Put in practical terms, even if individuals don't extensively encode negative information about minority group members when they first receive it, they may go back and do so in the light of new, and perhaps even more attention-getting, news coverage of violent crimes. Then such information may produce an illusory correlation: the tendency to overestimate the rate of such behaviors among minority groups. In this respect, it is interesting to speculate about the consequences of the massive news coverage of the O. J. Simpson trials. Did this coverage serve to make negative information about African Americans more distinctive in the minds of other Americans? Only research can provide an answer, but even the question itself is quite unsettling.

Ingroup Differentiation, Outgroup Homogeneity: "They're All the Same"–Or Are They?

Persons who hold strong prejudice toward some social group often make remarks like these: "You know what *they're* like; they're all the same," or "If you've met one, you've met them all." What such comments imply is that the members of an outgroup are much more similar to one another (are more *ho-*

mogeneous) than the members of one's own group. This tendency to perceive persons belonging to groups other than one's own as all alike is known as the **illusion of outgroup homogeneity** (Linville et al., 1989). The mirror image of this tendency is known as **ingroup differentiation**—the tendency to perceive members of our own group as showing much larger differences from one another (as being more heterogeneous) than those of other groups.

Existence of the illusion of outgroup homogeneity has been demonstrated in many different contexts. For example, individuals tend to perceive persons older or younger than themselves as more similar to one another in terms of personal traits than persons in their own age group—an intriguing type of "generation gap" (Linville et al., 1989). Perhaps the most disturbing example of the illusion of outgroup homogeneity, however, appears in the context of *cross-racial facial identification*—the tendency for persons belonging to one racial group to be more accurate in recognizing differences among the faces of strangers in their own group than in another racial group. In the United States, this tendency has been observed among both African Americans and whites, although it appears to be somewhat stronger among whites (Anthony, Copper, & Mullen, 1992).

What accounts for the tendency to perceive members of other groups to be more homogeneous than members of our own group? One explanation involves the fact that we have a great deal of experience with members of our own group, and so are exposed to a wider range of individual variation within that group. In contrast, we generally have much less experience with members of other groups, and hence less exposure to *their* individual variations (e.g., Linville et al., 1989). As noted recently by Lee and Ottati (1993, 1995), however, several other factors may play a role as well.

First, it is possible that some groups *are* actually more homogeneous than others. For example, as Lee and Ottati (1993) note, Americans *are* less homogeneous than Chinese in terms of several physical characteristics (e.g., hair color, eye color). Thus, if an American perceives greater heterogeneity among Americans than among Chinese, this perception may be related to reality, at least to a degree. Second, it is possible that perceptions of outgroup homogeneity may be related to more basic tendencies to evaluate other groups in an evaluatively consistent manner. Americans, for example, tend to value individuality. Thus, to the extent that they dislike another group, they would tend to perceive its members as homogeneous, which would be consistent with their overall negative evaluation of the group. If, instead, they *liked* another group, they might tend to perceive its members as relatively heterogeneous; in this case, perceiving heterogeneity (individuality) in the group would be consistent with positive feelings toward it.

Thus, in some instances the tendency to perceive other groups as more homogeneous than our own may stem from sources other than prejudice—factors such as actual differences along this dimension and our tendency to evaluate outgroups in a consistent manner. However, it is equally clear that on many other occasions the illusion of outgroup homogeneity *is* an illusion: We tend to perceive members of outgroups as more homogeneous than they really are. This perception saves us a great deal of cognitive effort, but once we conclude that "they're all alike," there is little reason to seek contact with members of various outgroups. This, in turn, lessens the probability that we will ever learn that they really *do* differ. For this reason alone, the illusion of outgroup homogeneity is another cognitive source of prejudice we should make every effort to avoid.

Integrating Principles

1. Prejudice seems to derive, in part, from basic aspects of social thought. Once they are established, *stereotypes* strongly affect important aspects of social thought (Chapter 3). Stereotypes involve beliefs about various social groups, but are also influenced by affective states and reactions (Chapters 3, 5). Thus, the effects reflect the complex interaction between affect and cognition discussed at several points in this book (e.g., Chapter 3).

2. Illusory correlations—the tendency to overestimate the rate of negative behaviors in small groups—seem to stem primarily from the fact that both minority group members and negative behaviors are high in distinctiveness and thus more accessible in memory (Chapters 2, 3).

3. We tend to perceive greater heterogeneity among members of our own group than among members of various outgroups. These effects reflect the fact that we have less experience with members of other groups than with members of our own group, but may also reflect actual differences in heterogeneity across groups. Several aspects of group functioning are examined in Chapter 10.

Striking Back against Prejudice: Techniques That Can Help

Given that prejudice is common in all human societies and exerts damaging effects both on its victims and on those who hold such views, the next question is obvious: What steps can be taken to reduce the impact of prejudice? In this section, we'll summarize the major findings of social psychological research with respect to this issue.

On Learning *Not* to Hate

Few persons would argue that children are born with prejudices firmly in place. Rather, most would contend that bigots are *made*, not born. Social psychologists share this perspective: They believe that children acquire prejudice from their parents, other adults, their peers, and—as we noted earlier—the mass media. Given this fact, one useful technique for reducing prejudice follows logically: Somehow, we must discourage parents and other adults who serve as models for children from providing training in bigotry.

Having stated this principle, we must now admit that putting it into practice is far from simple. How can we induce parents who are prejudiced to encourage unbiased views among their children (see Figure 6.6). One possibility involves calling parents' attention to their own prejudiced

FIGURE 6.6 Eliminating Prejudice Using Intergroup Contact, Re-Drawing Group Boundaries.

Researchers have discovered many ways to erase prejudice, not the least of which are intergroup contact and changing the groups of "us" and "them" into "we." This cartoon offers a similarly optimistic view on prejudice.

For Better or For Worse®   by Lynn Johnston

(*Source: For Better or For Worse* © 1996 Lynn Johnston Prod., Inc. Reprinted with permission of Universal Press Syndicate. All rights reserved.)

views. Few persons are willing to describe themselves as prejudiced; instead, they view their own negative attitudes toward various groups as entirely justified. A key initial step, therefore, is somehow convincing parents that the problem exists. Once they see their own prejudices, many people do seem willing to modify their words and behavior so as to encourage lower levels of prejudice among their children. True, some extreme fanatics actually *want* to turn their children into hate-filled copies of themselves. Most people, however, recognize that we live in a world of increasing diversity and that this environment calls for a higher degree of tolerance than ever before.

Another argument that can be used to shift parents in the direction of teaching their children tolerance rather than prejudice lies in the fact that prejudice harms not only those who are its victims, but those who hold such views as well (Dovidio & Gaertner, 1993; J. M. Jones, 1997). Persons who are prejudiced, it appears, live in a world filled with needless fears, anxieties, and

anger. They fear attack from presumably dangerous social groups; they worry about health risks stemming from contact with such groups; and they experience anger and emotional turmoil over what they view as unjustified incursions by these groups into *their* neighborhoods, schools, or offices. In other words, their enjoyment of everyday activities and life itself is reduced by their own prejudice. Since most parents want to do everything in their power to further their children's well-being, calling these costs to parents' attention may help discourage them from transmitting prejudiced views to their offspring.

Direct Intergroup Contact

At the present time many American cities resemble a doughnut in one respect: A disintegrating and crime-ridden core inhabited primarily by minority groups is surrounded by a ring of relatively affluent suburbs inhabited mainly by whites and minority group members who have succeeded economically. Needless to say, contact between the people living in these different regions is minimal.

This state of affairs raises an intriguing question: Can communities reduce prejudice by somehow increasing the degree of contact between different groups? This idea is known as the **contact hypothesis,** and there are several good reasons for predicting that such a strategy might prove effective (J. M. Jones, 1997; Pettigrew, 1997). First, increased contact between persons from different groups can lead to a growing recognition of similarities between them. As we will see in Chapter 7, perceived similarity can enhance mutual attraction. Second, while stereotypes are resistant to change, they *can* be altered when sufficient information inconsistent with them is encountered, or when individuals meet a sufficient number of "exceptions" to their stereotypes (Hamberger & Hewstone, 1997). Third, increased contact may help counter the illusion of outgroup homogeneity described earlier. For these reasons, it seems possible that direct intergroup contact may be one effective means of combating prejudice. Is it? Existing evidence suggests that it is, but only when the following conditions are met:

The groups interacting must be roughly equal in social, economic, or task-related status.

The contact situation must involve cooperation and interdependence so that the groups work toward shared goals (as in the Robber's Cave experiment described earlier).

Contact between the groups must be informal so that they can get to know one another as individuals.

Contact must occur in a setting in which existing norms favor group equality.

The groups must interact in ways that permit disconfirmation of negative stereotyped beliefs about one another.

The persons involved must view one another as typical of their respective groups.

When contact between initially hostile groups occurs under these conditions—which are, unfortunately, quite rare—prejudice between them does seem to decrease (Cook, 1985). Such effects have been observed in the United States, where increased contact between African Americans and whites has been found to reduce prejudice between them and in many other nations as well (Pettigrew, 1997). For example, increased school contact between Jews of Middle Eastern origin and Jews of European or American origin tends to reduce intergroup bias among Israeli soldiers (Schwarzwald, Amir, & Crain, 1992). Similarly, individuals who have contact with people diagnosed with mental illness tend to develop more positive attitudes toward members of this stigmatized group, especially when the contact is of a voluntary nature (Kolodziej & Johnson, 1996).

In sum, when used with care, direct intergroup contact *can* be an effective tool for combating cross-group prejudice. When people get to know one another, it seems, many of the anxieties, stereotypes, and false perceptions that have previously kept them apart can melt in the face of new information and the warmth of new friendships.

Recategorization: Changing Who Is "Us" and "Them"

Think back to your high school days. Imagine that your school's basketball team was playing an important game against a rival high school from a nearby town or neighborhood. In this case, you would certainly view your own school as "us" and the other school as "them." But now imagine that the other school's team won, and went on to play against a team from another state or province in a national tournament. Now how would you view them? The chances are good that under these conditions, you would view the other school's team as "us"; after all, it represents your area. And of course, if a team from a state or province other than your own was playing against teams from other countries, you might now view it as "us" relative to those foreigners.

Situations like this, in which we shift the boundary between "us" and "them," are quite common in everyday life, and they raise an interesting question: Can such shifts—or **recategorizations,** as they are termed by social psychologists—be used to reduce prejudice? A theory proposed by Gaertner, Dovidio, and their colleagues (1989, 1993) suggests that it can. This theory, known as the **common ingroup identity model,** suggests that when individuals belonging to different social groups come to view themselves as members of a *single social entity,* their attitudes toward each other—toward former outgroup members—become more positive. These favorable attitudes then promote increased positive contacts between members of the previously separate groups, which in turn reduces intergroup bias still further. In short, weakening or eliminating initial us–them boundaries starts a process that carries the persons involved toward major reductions in prejudice and hostility (see Figure 6.7).

How can this process be launched? In other words, how can we induce people belonging to different groups to perceive each other as members of a single group? Gaertner and his colleagues (1990) suggest that one crucial factor in this process is the experience of working together cooperatively. When individuals belonging to initially distinct groups work together toward shared goals, they come to perceive themselves as a single social entity. Then feelings of bias or hostility toward the former outgroup—toward "them"—seem to fade away, taking prejudice with them. Such effects have been demonstrated in several laboratory studies (e.g., Gaertner et al., 1989, 1990; Dovidio et al., in press-a) and in a field study carried out by Gaertner, Dovidio, and their associates (1993).

Another way that the recategorization shift can occur is suggested by our reactions to movies such as *The Elephant Man, The Color Purple, One Flew Over the Cuckoo's Nest, Rain Man,* and *Philadelphia.* Think back to your experiences with these films: How did you react to their leading characters and their plights? We're willing to bet you felt empathy for these individuals. People who saw *Rain Man* often reported feeling empathy for autistic individuals such as the savant

---

FIGURE 6.7   The Common Ingroup Identity Model.

The common ingroup identity model suggests that when individuals belonging to different groups come to perceive themselves as members of a single group, their attitudes toward each other become more positive. This increases contact between members of the groups, which reduces intergroup bias still further.

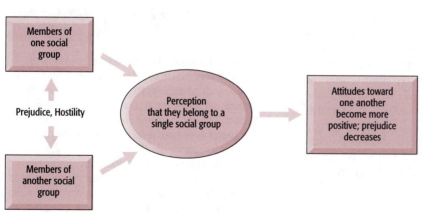

(*Source:* Based on suggestions by Gaertner, Dovidio et al., 1990, 1993.)

played by Dustin Hoffman. Those who saw *Philadelphia* often reported empathy for persons with AIDS, such as the young lawyer played by Tom Hanks. The results of a series of studies by Batson and his colleagues (1997) supports the view that empathy for a single member of a stigmatized group will result in more positive views about the stigmatized group.

In the first of their three experiments, Batson and his colleagues asked their participants, female college students, to help evaluate a new radio program including a taped interview that was going to air soon. The interview concerned a young woman named Julie who was experiencing the personal tragedy of AIDS. In the low-empathy condition, participants were asked to be objective about what they were to hear; in the high-empathy condition, they were asked to imagine how the woman feels about her condition and the ways it affected her life. All participants then heard a tape in which Julie vividly described how AIDS had been such a horrible nightmare to her. Then, half of the participants heard Julie describe how she had contracted the AIDS virus through a contaminated blood transfusion following an accident; in this way, Julie could not be held personally responsible for her condition. The other participants heard Julie describe how she had contracted the AIDS virus through unprotected sexual intercourse.

Batson and his colleagues reasoned that empathy should generally improve attitudes toward the stigmatized group, in this case persons with AIDS. However, they also reasoned that the circumstances of the individual with AIDS could undercut the effect of empathy. That is, if the person was responsible for her plight, such as the Julie who had unprotected intercourse, then empathy could have less of an effect. In fact, this is exactly the pattern of effects that emerged from this study, as Figure 6.8 shows. Participants reacted more positively and were empathetic to people with AIDS when the victim was not responsible for acquiring HIV, the virus that causes AIDS. However, when the victim had acquired HIV through her own careless behavior, the participants' empathy was sharply reduced. In two further studies, Batson and colleagues

found highly similar results with target individuals from two other stigmatized groups, the homeless, and murderers. Importantly, in the last of their studies these researchers showed that the empathy-induced attitude change was not limited to the laboratory setting. In fact, the attitudes were still more positive two weeks later. Apparently, when we feel empathy for a member of a stigmatized group, we begin to see the world as they do—to include ourselves in that group—and the result is that our attitudes become more positive for the entire group. Findings such as these suggest that efforts to induce persons belonging to different groups to engage in *recategorization*—to shift the boundary between "us" and "them" so as to include persons previously excluded—can be an important step toward the reduction of many forms of prejudice. We should hasten to add, however, that broadening the "us" category to include groups that were previously excluded does *not* eliminate the human tendency to enhance our own self-identity by cognitively boosting our own group while belittling others (Jetten, Spears, & Manstead, 1996). This seems to be a basic tendency that cannot be entirely eliminated. However, recategorization can certainly reduce prejudice in some contexts, and any reduction in such blanket negative reactions is a definite plus in ongoing social life.

Integrating Principles

1. Techniques for reducing prejudice have been derived from basic principles of social psychology. Efforts to reshape prejudiced attitudes through altered socialization practices and persuasion (Chapter 5) can sometimes be effective. Similarly, increased contact often enhances liking (Chapter 7) and can reduce prejudice if the contact occurs under appropriate conditions.

2. Breaking down the us–them boundary by inducing individuals to perceive themselves and others as belonging to a single group is also successful in reducing prejudice and intergroup conflict (Chapter 10). Promoting empathy for stigmatized individuals can play a strong role in this process.

FIGURE 6.8   Feeling Empathy Can Reduce Prejudice toward a Group.

When we see the world through the eyes of a member of a stigmatized group, the result is that our attitudes toward that group grow more positive. In a series of three experiments, Batson and colleagues (1997) found that empathy generally improves attitudes toward stigmatized group members, especially when the group member was not personally responsible for joining the stigmatized group.

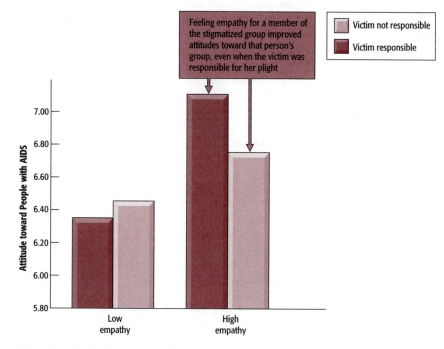

Feeling empathy for a member of the stigmatized group improved attitudes toward that person's group, even when the victim was responsible for her plight

Victim not responsible
Victim responsible

(*Source:* Based on data from Batson et al., 1997, Experiment 1)

Prejudice Based on Gender: Its Nature and Effects

Although women are a majority numerically, in many cultures females have been treated like a minority group (see Figure 6.9). They have been excluded from economic and political power; they have been the subject of strong negative stereotypes; and they have faced overt discrimination in many areas of life—work settings, higher education, government (Heilman, Block, & Lucas, 1992). In the late 1990s, this situation is changing, at least in some countries and to some degree. Overt discriminatory practices have been banned by laws in many nations, and there has been at least some weakening of negative gender-based stereotypes. Yet such progress has been spotty at best, and **sexism**—prejudice based on gender—continues to exert harmful effects upon females in many countries (e.g., Kanekar, Kolsawalla, & Nazareth, 1988). Between 1970 and 1992, the proportion of managers who are female rose from 16 percent to more than 42 percent (U.S. Department of Labor, 1992). Yet the proportion of top executives who are women increased only from 3 percent to 5 percent (A. B. Fisher, 1992). These facts have led many authors to suggest the existence of a

FIGURE 6.9	Are Women Treated Fairly?

Despite that fact that there are more women than men worldwide, women often experience discrimination similar to members of other minority groups.

glass ceiling—a final barrier that prevents females, as a group, from reaching the top positions in many companies. More formally, the U.S. Department of Labor has defined the glass ceiling as "those artificial barriers based on attitudinal or organizational bias that prevent qualified individuals from advancing upward in their organization" (U.S. Department of Labor, 1992). Because prejudice based on gender affects more individuals than any other single kind (more than half the human race) and produces negative outcomes for males as well as females, we will consider it here in detail.

Gender Stereotypes: The Cognitive Core of Sexism

Females have often been the object of strong, persistent stereotypes. To an extent, so have males: They too are perceived as being "all alike" with respect to certain traits—and in many cultures, woe to the male who fails to live up to these stereotypes (Aube & Koestner, 1992). By and large, how-

ever, stereotypes about females are usually more negative in content than those about males. For example, in many cultures, males are assumed to have such desirable traits as *decisiveness, forcefulness, confidence, ambition,* and *rationality.* In contrast, the corresponding assumptions about females include less desirable traits such as *passivity, submissiveness, indecisiveness, emotionality,* and *dependence* (e.g., Unger, 1994).

Are such **gender stereotypes** accurate? Do men and women really differ in the ways these stereotypes suggest? This question is complex, for differences between the sexes, even if observed, may be more a reflection of the impact of stereotypes and their self-confirming nature than of basic differences between females and males (Jussim, McCauley, & Lee, 1995). Existing evidence, however, points to these conclusions: (1) There are indeed some differences between females and males with respect to several aspects of social behavior—the ability to send and "read" nonverbal cues (DePaulo, 1992), aggression (Bettencourt & Miller, 1996), and the nature of same-sex friendships (Elkins & Peterson, 1993), to name just a few; *but* (and this is an important *but*) (2) the magnitude and scope of these differences are smaller than gender stereotypes suggest (Feingold, 1992). Unfortunately, though, the fact that gender stereotypes are quite inaccurate does not prevent them from exerting harmful effects—for example, from preventing women from obtaining some jobs, some promotions, and equal pay for the jobs they do obtain (e.g., Lander, 1992). How do the stereotypes exert these negative effects? This is the question to which we turn next.

Discrimination against Women

In the late 1990s, overt discrimination on the basis of gender is illegal in many countries. Despite this fact, females continue to occupy a relatively disadvantaged position in many societies in certain respects. They are concentrated in low-paying, low-status jobs, and their average salary remains lower than that for males, even in the same occupations. Why is this the case? One possibility is that sufficient time has not passed for women to realize the full benefits of the changes that occurred during the 1970s and 1980s. Another possibility—one supported by a large body of research evidence—is that while overt barriers to female advancement have largely disappeared, other, more subtle forces continue to operate against women in many contexts. We'll now review several of these.

The Role of Expectations. One factor impeding women's progress involves their own expectations. In general, women seem to hold lower expectations about their careers than men. They expect to receive lower starting and peak salaries (Jackson, Gardner, & Sullivan, 1992). And they view lower salaries for females as being somehow fair (Jackson & Grabski, 1988). Why do women hold these lower expectations? Research findings indicate that several factors play a role.

First, females expect to take more time out from work (for example, to spend with their children), which tends to lower their expectations for peak career salaries. Second, many women place somewhat less importance on job outcomes generally, including salary, than men do and thus may find lower pay relatively acceptable. Third, women realize that females do generally earn less than males. Thus, their lower expectations may simply reflect their recognition of current reality and its likely impact on their own salaries. Fourth, as we noted earlier, women tend to perceive relatively low levels of pay as fairer than males do (Desmarais & Curtis, 1997). Fifth, women may rate their own ability as being lower than that of men, even when they actually have the same level of ability (Beyer & Bowden, 1997). Finally, and perhaps most important, women tend to compare themselves with other women, and since women earn less than men in many instances, this leads them to conclude that they aren't doing too badly after all (Major, 1989). Whatever the specific basis for women's lower salary expectations, it is a fact of life that, in general, people tend to get what they expect or what they request. Thus, females' lower expectations with respect to such outcomes may be one important factor operating against them in many organizations.

The Role of Self-Confidence. Confidence, it is often said, is the single best predictor of success. People who expect to succeed often do; those who expect to fail find *that* prediction confirmed. Unfortunately, women tend to express lower self-confidence than men in many achievement-related situations (Beyer & Bowden, 1997). This may be one reason why almost 10 percent of the executives who responded to a survey in *Business Week* reported believing that females are not as aggressive or determined to succeed as males (Lander, 1992). In short, women are less self-confident than men in at least some situations, and people notice these differences. This, in turn, may contribute to the fact that women have not yet attained full equality with men in many work settings.

Negative Reactions to Female Leaders. In the late 1990s, most people agree that females can definitely be effective leaders. Women have been elected to major offices (prime minister, senator); have been appointed as senior judges (e.g., to the Supreme Court of the United States); hold high ranks in the military, and—in a few cases—head major companies and organizations. But how do people react to female leaders? Do they hold them in equally high regard and evaluate them as favorably as men? The answer to both questions appears to be no. First, although subordinates often *say* much the same things to female and male leaders, research findings indicate that they actually demonstrate more negative *nonverbal behaviors* toward female leaders (Butler & Geis, 1990). Moreover, such differences occur even when individuals strongly deny any bias against females. Apparently, many persons still find women in leadership roles to be somewhat disturbing, perhaps because leadership on the part of women runs counter to prevailing gender stereotypes.

Perhaps even more disturbing, however, is the fact that when they do serve as leaders, females tend to receive lower ratings from subordinates than males do. In a meta-analysis of existing evidence on this issue, Eagly, Makhijani, and Klonsky (1992) found that overall, female leaders received slightly lower evaluations than male leaders, especially when males rather than

Social Diversity: A Critical Analysis

How Memory Loss in Our Later Years Is Influenced by Cultural Age Stereotypes

Throughout this chapter, we've emphasized the importance of stereotypes in prejudice. These mental frameworks exert powerful effects on social thought, and so on our reactions to, and judgments about, persons belonging to various social groups. But now get ready for a surprise: Recent findings indicate that stereotypes can do more than shape social thought—they can actually affect our physical well-being as well. Dramatic evidence for this conclusion has been reported by Levy and Langer (1994) in a study concerned with the effects of aging on memory.

Do you think that your own memory will decline with age? Many Americans believe that this is so. In fact, the stereotype of "the elderly" in the United States is largely negative (Kite & Johnson, 1988): It suggests that aging is associated with unavoidable declines in appearance, health, and mental abilities. Growing old, in other words, is viewed as no fun. Other cultures, however, have a very different view of older persons. In China, for example, older persons are revered for their wisdom and accumulated knowledge; moreover, Chinese culture does *not* assume that older persons will lose their memories or show other declines in cognitive functions. Similar views are held among deaf persons in the United States; they, too, have relatively positive views of older persons, and do not assume that they will experience reduced cognitive capacities as they age. In short, stereotypes about older persons differ sharply in different cultures.

But how, you are probably wondering, can stereotypes influence physical well-being? Levy and Langer (1994) suggest that they can exert such effects through premature *cognitive commitments*—beliefs that people accept unconditionally. Once such beliefs are formed, they are never reexamined; on the contrary, they are accepted in a largely unconscious manner and often remain unchanged throughout life. Levy and Langer (1994) argue that such beliefs can be incorporated into stereo-

types and then, since they are strong and unchanging, can contribute to the powerful self-fulfilling effects that stereotypes so often exert. In other words, if, in a given culture, the prevailing stereotype of older people suggests that they will show a decline in cognitive abilities, then older people probably will. If, in contrast, such declines are not part of prevailing stereotypes, then they will occur to a lesser degree.

To test these intriguing predictions, Levy and Langer (1994) studied three groups of subjects: American deaf individuals, American persons who were not deaf, and Chinese. In each group, half of the participants were young (in their twenties) while the remainder were older adults (from their late fifties to their nineties). All participants then performed several tasks designed to measure their memory—for example, reproducing patterns of dots shown on a computer screen for ten seconds, or remembering which sentences accompanied photos of eight different strangers. The young persons from the three different groups did not differ significantly in their performance. Among the older participants, however, those from the Chinese and American deaf groups performed significantly better than those from the normal hearing group. Additional findings indicated that culture did indeed affect participants' stereotypes about aging—these were more favorable among Chinese and American deaf participants than among the American participants with normal hearing. Further, the more positive these views, the better participants' performance on the memory tasks.

These results provide dramatic evidence for the powerful self-confirming impact of stereotypes. Not only do they act as filters for new social information; they can also influence our performance on various tasks and our physical well-being. It is difficult to think of a more convincing illustration of the crucial interface between social thought and social behavior that is one of the major themes of modern social psychology—and of this book.

females made the evaluations. Similarly, the tendency to down-rate female leaders was considerably stronger when the female leaders adopted a style of leadership viewed as stereotypically masculine (autocratic, directive), when the persons who evaluated them were males, and when the females occupied leadership roles in fields where most leaders were males. Together, these findings and those of other studies (e.g., Kent & Moss, 1994) suggest that females continue to face subtle disadvantages even when they do manage to obtain positions of leadership and authority.

The Role of Social Dominance Orientation and Occupation Choice. With these gender differences in career expectations and evaluations as a background, it should come as no surprise that men and women also consciously pick different occupations. Thus, one explanation for the gender gap in achieving high-level positions is simply that men, more than women, choose positions that allow them to achieve career advancement, power, and prestige. Growing evidence indicates that men's and women's career choices may unwittingly—and indirectly—preserve the status quo of men holding prestigious positions relative to women (e.g., Pratto et al., 1997). For example, many studies have shown that men value status, prestige, and high incomes more than women do (e.g., Perron & St.-Onge, 1991). Pratto and her colleagues (e.g., Pratto, 1996; Pratto et al., 1997) reasoned that these value differences might be related to **social dominance orientation,** which is how much an individual supports group inequalities. For example, someone who is high on this dimension endorses keeping inferior groups in their place and opposes treating all people equally, which these researchers labeled *hierarchy-enhancing;* someone low on this dimension endorses equality and opposes getting ahead in life by almost any means, which was labeled *hierarchy-attenuating.*

In a first study, Pratto and her colleagues (1997) confirmed in a sample of college undergraduates that men had higher social dominance orientation scores than women. As predicted, these researchers also found that social dominance orientation was strongly related to work values. For example, those who were socially dominant valued having a high income, gaining personal prestige, leadership opportunities, and being famous; whereas, those who were not socially dominant valued helping the underprivileged, serving the community, and helping others. In a second study, Pratto and colleagues asked individuals who scored either very low or very high on social dominance orientation to indicate their personal preferences of a list of jobs. Results confirmed that those high in social dominance orientation tended to select hierarchy-enhancing jobs such as public relations director for a major oil company; those low in social dominance orientation tended to select hierarchy-attenuating jobs like public relations director for a public service organization (such as United Way). As Pratto (1996) notes, this pattern parallels a tendency for women to be more communal (caring, interpersonally oriented) than men, which we discussed in Chapter 4. Thus, these first two studies provided evidence that individuals use their levels of social dominance as a basis for career selection. Women, with their lower levels of social dominance orientation, tend to select careers such as philanthropic fundraiser, whereas men tend to select careers such as corporate attorney.

Thus, it appears that social dominance orientation to some extent guides our decisions of what careers to pursue (see Figure 6.10). However, these studies do not address the question of whether employers desire candidates who are lower or higher in social dominance orientation. In two additional studies, Pratto and colleagues (1997) examined just this question. The researchers asked their study participants, who were placed in the role of a prospective employer, to select the best candidate for a variety of jobs, such as advertising, investments, and librarianship. Four different résumés were provided for each job that varied systematically in terms of gender and social dominance orientation. Experiences listed on each résumé permitted the employers to determine each candidate's social dominance orientation. For example, one applicant had started a free enterprise club (high social dominance), whereas another applicant had

Social Dominance Orientation—and Gender—Affect Hiring Decisions.

As this figure shows, when people have high social dominance scores—and these are usually men—they tend to value prestige, leadership opportunities, and fame, and these hierarchy-supporting values lead to career choices that facilitate the attainment of these goals. When instead people have low dominance scores—and these are usually women—they value service to the community and helping underprivileged groups, and these hierarchy-attenuating values lead to matching career choices.

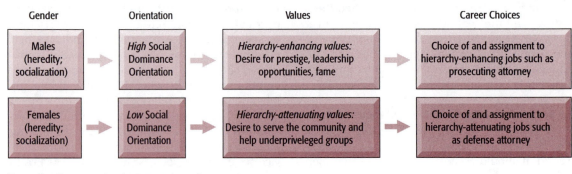

(*Source:* Based on suggestions by Pratto et al., 1997.)

started a club for saving lives (low social dominance). By altering the first names of the individuals listed on each résumé, Pratto and colleagues were able to adjust the gender of the applicant without altering his or her qualifications in any way. Some employers received a male version of a résumé and others received the comparable female version. Thus, across the applicants in the studies, the male and female applicants for the positions were equal on both qualifications and social dominance orientation. The results confirmed the predictions of Pratto and colleagues: Prospective employers matched applicants with high social dominance to hierarchy-maintaining roles (such as paralegal working for a corporation filing suits against injured laborers). In contrast, they matched applicants with low social dominance to hierarchy-attenuating roles (such as paralegal helping low-status groups of the poor, immigrants, and children). More interestingly, the raters were more likely to place male applicants in hierarchy-maintaining roles and female applicants in hierarchy-attenuating roles, even when the men and women were evenly matched in terms of their qualifications. This finding implies that employers use gender as a heuristic for an applicant's social dominance orientation. Sug-

gesting that these patterns are widespread, the same results emerged with samples of college undergraduates (Study 3) and for professionals who were in actual positions to hire others (Study 4). However, and this is somewhat disturbing, the tendency to prefer males and those of high social dominance for hierarchy-enhancing roles was even more pronounced among the group of professionals than for the students.

The results of these studies and many others (e.g., Pratto, 1996; Sidanius, Pratto, & Brief, 1995) point to a two-part explanation of why women have not attained high status positions in business: (1) Women have lower social dominance orientations than men, and therefore tend to select roles for themselves that are hierarchy-attenuating rather than hierarchy-enhancing. Put differently, even before entering the employment arena on a full-time basis, men are more predisposed to seek roles that favor privileged groups, whereas women are predisposed to seek roles that favor oppressed groups. These differences may derive from socialization and other factors, such as those addressed in Chapter 4; (2) Employers exacerbate the self-selection bias by choosing individuals who are high on social-dominance orientation for privileged, high-status positions; and these individuals are more often men than women. Indeed, even when women have high social dominance orientations, they are often passed over in favor of men who also have high social dominance orientations (Pratto et al., 1997). These factors suggest that it may be difficult for women to achieve full equality in the workplace in the near future because some societies have built-in biases against women, both within the home (such as child-rearing practices that make boys more socially dominant), and in businesses (because

those doing hiring favor high social dominance individuals for high prestige positions).

Finally, it is important to note that not all high-status individuals are high social dominance individuals. Many of these people (e.g., Andrew Carnegie) establish charitable foundations that help underprivileged people. Similarly, other research has shown that successful, generative older people often try to assist the younger generation (e.g., Mansfield & McAdams, 1996; McAdams, Hoffman, Mansfield, & Day, in press).

Connections   Integrating Social Psychology

In this chapter, you read about . . .

- stereotypes as mental shortcuts—one means of saving cognitive effort
- the tendency to divide the social world into "us" and "them" and its effects
- social domination orientation differing between men and women
- sexual discrimination in work settings

In other chapters, you will find related discussions of . . .

- heuristics and other mental shortcuts (Chapter 3)
- other effects of group membership (Chapter 10)
- gender differences in femininity, masculinity, and other dimensions (Chapter 4)
- other aspects of social behavior in work settings (Chapter 11)

Thinking about Connections

1. Some observers suggest that as open forms of discrimination have decreased, more subtle forms have increased. Do you agree? And if so, do you think these new forms of discrimination are condoned or accepted by various groups (Chapter 10), and by more widespread social norms (Chapter 8)?
2. Stereotypes, it appears, save us considerable cognitive effort. And we've noted repeatedly in this book, as human beings, we usually seek to hold such effort to a minimum (Chapters 2, 3). Given this fact, do you think that the tendency to think about others in terms of stereotypes can really be

reduced? And if not, are we doomed to continuing cycles of prejudice, discrimination, and violence (Chapter 9)?
3. The fact that relatively few women have made it to the top in the world of business may indicate the existence of prejudice against them—for example the glass ceiling. However, it may also reflect other factors, such as different career orientations on the part of women and men, contrasting approaches to intimate relationships (Chapter 7), or persisting gender stereotypes. What factors do *you* think are the most important in this situation? Can they be changed or overcome?

Summary and Review

Prejudice and Discrimination

Prejudice is a negative attitude toward the members of some social group that is based solely on their membership in that group. *Discrimination* refers to harmful actions directed toward the persons or groups who are the targets of prejudice. Because overt discrimination is now illegal in many countries, such behavior now frequently takes more subtle forms. These include attitudes described as *the "new" racism and sexism*. Unfortunately, these newer and more subtle forms of prejudice—especially disguised forms of racism—are still present, and continue to exert extremely harmful effects on the persons and groups who are their targets.

The Origins of Prejudice

Prejudice stems from a number of different sources. According to *realistic conflict theory,* it derives from competition between social groups for scarce resources. The *social learning view* suggests that children acquire prejudice from parents, teachers, friends, and mass media. *Social categorization* suggests that prejudice stems from our strong tendencies to divide the social world into "us" and "them."

Much recent evidence supports the view that prejudice stems from certain aspects of *social cognition*—the ways in which we think about others and make judgments about them. *Stereotypes,* cognitive frameworks involving beliefs about the typical characteristics of members of social groups, play an especially important role in this regard. Once stereotypes are activated, they exert profound effects on social thought. Stereotypes serve as mental shortcuts, reducing cognitive effort; for this reason, they are very difficult to change. Recent findings indicate that stereotypes contain an affective component, and that persons in a good mood are more likely to engage in stereotypic thinking than those in a more neutral mood. Other aspects of social cognition that play a role in prejudice include *illusory correlations*—perceptions of stronger relationships between distinctive events than actually exist; and the illusion of *outgroup homogeneity,* which involves the tendency to perceive lower variability among outgroup members than among ingroup members.

Striking Back against Prejudice

One way to reduce prejudice is to encourage parents and others to transmit tolerant rather than prejudiced attitudes to children. *Direct intergroup contact* can be helpful, provided that the contact occurs under appropriate conditions. Another useful technique involves *recategorization*—somehow inducing individuals to shift the boundary between "us" and "them" so that outgroup members are now included as part of the ingroup. Inducing *empathy* appears to help individuals view stigmatized persons as part of the ingroup.

Prejudice Based on Gender

Sexism, prejudice based on gender, involves acceptance of *gender stereotypes* suggesting that males and females possess sharply different traits. In fact, gender differences are usually smaller than these stereotypes suggest. Overt discrimination against females is now illegal in many countries, but several subtle forces continue to operate against female achievement. These include lower expectations and low self-confidence on the part of females, negative reactions to and evaluations of female leaders, preference for *hierarchy-attenuating* career positions that do not permit great upward mobility, and the lack of relevant experiences instrumental to being promoted to key positions. These factors result in a *glass ceiling* that frequently prevents women from attaining the highest-level jobs in an organization.

Social Diversity: Physical Effects of Stereotypes

Recent evidence indicates that stereotypes can influence not only social thought but also important aspects of physical well-being. Declines in mental abilities such as memory are greater in cultures that possess negative stereotypes about "the elderly" than is true in cultures that possess more positive stereotypes of the elderly. These findings suggest that the self-confirming nature of stereotypes can extend to task performance and physical well-being.

Key Terms

Common Ingroup Identity Model (p. 141)
Contact Hypothesis (p. 140)
Discrimination (p. 130)
Gender Stereotypes (p. 144)
Glass Ceiling (p. 144)
Illusion of Outgroup Homogeneity (p. 137)
Illusory Correlation (p. 136)
Ingroup (p. 133)
Ingroup Differentiation (p. 137)
Outgroup (p. 133)

Prejudice (p. 127)
Realistic Conflict Theory (p. 131)
Recategorization (p. 141)
Sexism (p. 143)
Social Categorization (p. 133)
Social Dominance Orientation (p. 147)
Social Learning View (of prejudice) (p. 132)
Stereotypes (p. 134)
Ultimate Attribution Error (p. 134)

For More Information

Jones, J. M. (1997). *Prejudice and racism* (2nd ed.). New York: McGraw-Hill.

An updated version of the classic first edition, this volume surveys the burgeoning field of race-related prejudice and discrimination and provides hopeful solutions. If you want a thorough treatment of race relations, this is the book for you.

Macrae, C. N., Stangor, C., & Hewstone, M. (1996). *Stereotypes & stereotyping.* New York: Guilford.

A collection of essays written by contemporary scholars in the area of stereotyping, focusing on the development of stereotypes, their functions and uses, and methods to undermine stereotypes.

Lee, Y., Jussim, L. J., & McCauley, C. R. (1995). *Stereotype accuracy: Toward appreciating group differences.* Washington, DC: American Psychological Association.

A collection of essays pointing toward a more positive view of stereotypes—that they can sometimes be accurate and that sometimes perceiving group differences should be applauded rather than rebuked.

chapter **7**

Interpersonal Attraction: Friendship, Love, and Relationships

Some time in your life, you probably moved into a new neighborhood, apartment complex, or dormitory where you didn't know anyone. During the first several days, however, some of the people you passed on the sidewalk, in the hallway, or wherever began to seem familiar. You didn't know them, but you recognized them. Eventually, you probably became acquainted with some of these former strangers. Why? On what basis did a few of them become acquaintances while others remained strangers?

Falling in love is one of the most intense experiences that anyone can have, and the topic seems to have an endless fascination for us—in real life, in songs, on television, and in movies and books. What do we mean by love? When you are strongly attracted to another person, how can you know whether the feelings are genuine or based in part on fiction and on what you have learned to expect about love and romance?

For most people, marriage is the ultimate goal of close interpersonal relationships. A husband and wife can be emotionally and physically close, raise sons and daughters, and face the good and the bad aspects of life as a close-knit unit. The dark side of the picture is that marriages all too often lead to unhappiness, bickering (or worse), and a deteriorating relationship that culminates in a broken family. What goes wrong, and what can people do to avoid an unhappy ending?

All through our lives, we make judgments about people, objects, and events. Recent laboratory experiments provide evidence that we instantly evaluate every word, sound, picture, and person as soon as the perception registers, and this occurs before we are actually conscious of having perceived anything (Bargh, 1997). Some things we like, some we dislike, but we seldom if ever have a neutral reaction. We instantly evaluate even nonsense words—for example, English-speaking research participants tend to like "juvalamu" and to dislike "chakaka" (Goleman, 1995). With respect to how we feel about other people, is it possible that our selection of friends, romantic partners, and spouses is also based on relatively automatic processes that are predictable and understandable? Many social psychologists strongly believe that the answer is *yes*. In the pages to follow, we will describe some of the reasons for this answer.

The very human tendency to evaluate almost everything and everyone was discussed in Chapter 5; we form *attitudes* about the people, objects, and events that we encounter. As we encounter other individuals at school, at work, or in our neighborhoods, we develop attitudes about each of them.

These interpersonal evaluations fall along a dimension ranging from like to dislike, from positive to negative. Our attitudes about other people are the specific target of investigation in research on **interpersonal attraction.** Attraction research consists of identifying in detail the factors responsible for interpersonal evaluations.

In this chapter, we will first describe what is known about the initial attraction process, evaluating strangers, which requires physical proximity and involves emotional states. We will then explore how factors of physical attractiveness, similarity, and reciprocity influence the attraction process. We'll then describe the factors that are involved in falling in love and examine the outcomes—both good and bad—that may result.

Initial Factors
in the Attraction Process

Although we each have about six billion potential friends and acquaintances on this planet, we are likely to interact with only a very small percentage of them. Among those, some become acquaintances and some remain strangers. Why? Our physical surroundings exert a critical influence on who we are (or are not) likely to meet. Simply stated, two people will most probably become acquainted if they are brought into regular contact through physical **proximity** (closeness; sometimes labeled *propinquity*) and if each of them is experiencing positive rather than negative *affect* (feelings or mood) at the time.

Repeated Contact Leads to Attraction

When two strangers regularly pass one another in the corridor of a dormitory, sit in adjoining classroom seats each day, or wait together every morning at the bus stop, these casual and unplanned contacts soon lead to mutual recognition. Next, they may well begin exchanging a brief greeting when they meet ("Hi") and maybe a word or two about the weather or some newsworthy event. In other words, a familiar face evokes positive feelings. Even infants tend to smile at a photograph of someone they have seen before, but not at a photograph of someone they are seeing for the first time (Brooks-Gunn & Lewis, 1981). On a college campus, employees are better able to identify buildings close to the one in which they work than more distant buildings; they also express a preference for nearby buildings (A. B. Johnson & Byrne, 1996). How can such responses be explained?

Why Does Repeated Contact Increase Interpersonal Attraction? In a monograph that initiated a large body of research, Zajonc (1968) proposed that **repeated exposure** to a new stimulus—frequent contact with that stimulus—leads to a more and more positive evaluation of the stimulus. Whether that stimulus is a drawing, a word in an unknown foreign language, a new product being advertised, a political candidate, or a stranger in a classroom, the more frequent the exposure, the more positive the response (Moreland & Zajonc, 1982). The general idea is that we often respond with at least mild discomfort to anything or anyone new. With repeated exposure, the feelings of

anxiety decrease, and the *new* something or someone gradually becomes *familiar*. That is, you begin to feel friendly toward the stranger sitting next to you in class because you see that individual over and over again. In the same class, you are much less likely to see someone sitting three rows back on the other side of the room, so familiarity and friendliness don't develop.

To illustrate this process, Moreland and Beach (1992) asked one female research assistant to attend a college class fifteen times during the semester, another to attend ten times, another five times, and one not to attend at all. Then, at the end of the semester, all four individuals came to the classroom, and the experimenters asked the students to indicate how much they liked each one on a rating scale. The assistants were fairly similar in appearance, and none interacted with any of the class members during the semester. Nevertheless, attraction increased as the number of classroom exposures increased—see Figure 7.1. Clearly, repeated exposure affected liking.

Other research has shown that repeated exposure operates even when we are not consciously aware that a stimulus has been presented (S. T. Murphy, Monahan, & Zajonc, 1995). Indeed, this effect appears to be even stronger when the stimuli are presented subliminally rather than consciously. The repeated exposure effect is thus a powerful influence on our liking for practically anything, including our attraction to others.

In real-life settings, repeated contact is consistently linked to the development of friendships. For example, in college dormitories, students rarely get to know those living more than one floor away and even dating choices among undergraduates in part depend on the amount of distance between the partners' college residences (Whitbeck & Hoyt, 1994). Similar findings have been obtained in adults living in suburban areas (e.g., Ebbesen, Kjos, & Konecni, 1976) and in natural experiments (e.g., Segal, 1974). For example, people who see each other often because they are co-workers in an organization are more likely to become romantic partners than people outside of that organization

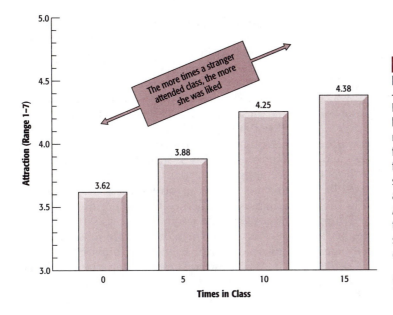

Attraction (Range 1–7)

The more times a stranger attended class, the more she was liked

3.62 3.88 4.25 4.38

Times in Class

FIGURE 7.1 Classroom Contacts Lead to Attraction.

Four female research assistants pretended to be students in a large college class. One did not attend class at all, another attended class five times, a third attended ten times, and a fourth, fifteen times; those who came to class sat quietly in the classroom and did not interact with the professor or with fellow students. At the end of the semester, the attraction of the students toward all four assistants was assessed. Attraction increased as the number of exposures to the strangers increased.

(*Source:* Based on data from Moreland & Beach, 1992.)

(Pierce & Aguinis, in press), although many other factors are involved (Pierce, 1997; Pierce, Byrne, & Aguinis, 1996).

Attraction Hinges on Affect

We experience and express emotions throughout our daily lives, and our emotional state at any given moment influences perception, cognition, motivation, decision making, *and* interpersonal judgments (Erber, 1991; Forgas, 1993). As you may remember from Chapter 3, psychologists often use the term *affect* when referring to emotions or feelings. The two most important characteristics of affect consist of *intensity* (the weakness or strength of the emotion) and *direction* (whether the emotion is positive or negative). Positive emotions such as excitement and happiness were once thought to fall at one end of a continuum with negative emotions such as anxiety and depression falling at the opposite end. It now appears, however, that positive and negative emotions involve two separate and independent dimensions (Smeaton & Byrne, 1988). For example, when emotions are measured before and after students receive feedback indicating that they did well on an exam, positive

affect is aroused by the good news but negative affect remains unchanged; also, receiving feedback that they did badly on an exam arouses negative affect but has no influence on positive feelings (M. D. Goldstein & Strube, 1994).

Experiments consistently indicate that positive feelings lead to positive evaluations of other people—liking—while negative feelings lead to negative evaluations—disliking (Dovidio et al., 1995). Affect can influence attraction in two ways. First, another person can do something to make you feel good or bad; you tend to like people or events that make you feel good and to dislike them if they make you feel bad (Downey & Damhave, 1991). It is obvious that you will prefer someone who brightens your day by giving you a sincere compliment to someone who brings you down with an unfair criticism. Something similar happens when someone initiates a conversation with a stranger. (See our discussion of impression formation in Chapter 2.) What are the affective and evaluative consequences of different kinds of "opening lines"?

Kleinke, Meeker, and Staneski (1986) investigated the kinds of things people say when they try to interact with someone they don't know. Many people—especially men—attempt to be amusing by saying something cute or flippant, presumably hoping to elicit positive affect and to be liked. One example from Kleinke and colleagues' research is, "Hi. I'm easy, are you?" As you might expect, the most common emotional response to such attempted cleverness was negative, the opposite of what was intended. In contrast, a positive affective response is much more common when the opening line is either innocuous ("Where are you from?") or direct ("Hi. I'm a little embarrassed about this, but I'd like to get to know you"). Some additional liked and disliked opening lines from this research appear in Table 7.1. Expanding this research to a real-life setting, research assistants were sent to a singles bar to use these different kinds of openers on strangers to determine their effects, and the same results were obtained in a bar as in the laboratory (Cunningham, 1989). Apparently, those who try to be too cute manage to turn other people off.

The Affect-Centered Model of Attraction. The proposal that attraction is based on affective responses is known as the **affect-centered model of attraction** (Byrne, 1992; Pierce et al., 1996). The emphasis on affect does not mean, however,

that cognitive processes are irrelevant, as shown in Figure 7.2. The top row of boxes illustrates what we have just been discussing. An individual's affective state—whether or not the target person is the direct cause of the affect—has a direct effect on evaluative responses such as attraction and on subsequent interpersonal behavior. In addition, any available information about the target person must be processed, and this information can be affectively arousing, thus contributing to the evaluative response. This cognitive pathway to emotions is involved when the perceiver's schemas include positive or negative information relevant to another person's attitudes, gender, race, clothing style, sexual orientation, or any other information about him or her.

When you consider the importance of affect and the ease with which it is conditioned to previously neutral targets, you can see that interpersonal behavior is often quite predictable, even though it is not always entirely reasonable. For example, Rozin, Millman, and Nemeroff (1986) point out that even a brief contact between a neutral object and something that arouses affect can transfer the emotional response to the neutral object. In one study of this

TABLE 7.1 ■ Opening Lines: Making a Good (or Bad) First Impression

In a social situation, how one initiates a conversation with a stranger of the opposite sex can be crucial in creating a favorable first impression. Research indicates that the best strategy is to avoid cute or flippant openers. Women are especially negative in evaluating men's attempts to be amusing.

SETTING	MOST PREFERRED OPENING LINE	LEAST PREFERRED OPENING LINE
General	Hi.	Your place or mine?
Bar	Do you want to dance?	Bet I can outdrink you.
Restaurant	I haven't been here before. What's good on the menu?	I bet the cherry pie jubilee isn't as sweet as you are.
Supermarket	Can I help you to the car with those things?	Do you really eat that junk?
Laundromat	Want to go have a beer or a cup of coffee while we're waiting?	Those are some nice undies you have there.
Beach	Want to play frisbee?	Let me see your strap marks.

(*Source:* Based on data from Kleinke, Meeker, & Staneski, 1986.)

FIGURE 7.2 The Affect-Centered Model of Attraction.

In this theoretical model of attraction, affective responses play a central role in determining who is liked or disliked. Positive and negative affect can be aroused directly by the acts of another person (and by that person being associated with some other source of affect), or by that person's words or observable characteristics. In the latter instance, the words or characteristics must be cognitively processed before resulting in an affective response. The cumulative affective response leads to an evaluation of the other person and/or to relevant overt acts.

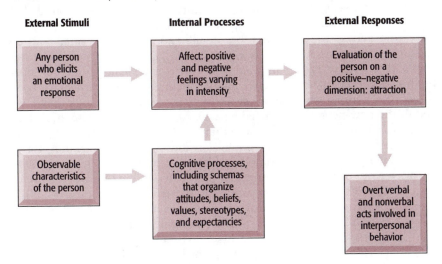

(*Source:* Based on concepts from Byrne, 1992.)

process, a laundered shirt that had been worn by a disliked person was rated as less desirable than a laundered shirt that had been worn by a liked person. Though the shirts did not actually differ, one elicited a positive response and the other a negative response on the basis of learned associations.

If negative emotions lead us to dislike other people, and if affect is easily associated with any given person, do we also transfer our negative feelings about person A to person B just because we observe them at the same time? For example, if I very much dislike John and see him talking to Bill—someone I barely know—do I then dislike Bill as a consequence? The answer seems to be yes. In this example, my response may be at least partly reasonable. That is, if Bill is friendly with someone as unpleasant as John, we probably wouldn't like each other anyway. But—what if my dislike for John was based on prejudice?

What would you think then about my subsequent transfer of negative affect to Bill?

Research on *stigmas* indicates that just such negative associations occur as easily as positive ones. A **stigma** is any characteristic of a person that some observers perceive negatively—race, age, a foreign accent, physical disability, or whatever. As is true of prejudice in general (see Chapter 6), a person perceived as having a stigma tends to elicit a negative stereotype (Frable, 1993). The stigmatized person may even arouse fear or disgust; but at the very least such an individual tends to be disliked and avoided. Even if a stigma is overcome, research suggests that the negative affect associated with a past stigma does not necessarily go away (Rodin & Price, 1995). You might receive credit for having improved yourself, but you are nevertheless perceived as less acceptable socially. "Once-damaged goods" are less valued than never-damaged goods. A possible implication of such research is that a person who wants to be liked, to be hired for a job, or to win an election would do well *not* to reveal past stigmas. Honesty may be the best policy, but not necessarily the best interpersonal strategy.

Responding to Observable Features

When we like—or dislike—someone at first sight, it probably means that our response is based on something we observe about that person that may or may not provide accurate information about him or her. For example, if a stranger resembles someone we have known, the positive or negative characteristics of the person we know tend to be transferred to the new person (Andersen & Baum, 1994). However different the new person may be from the one in our past, our evaluations are strongly affected by this association. Similarly, we very often react to other people on the basis of incorrect beliefs stemming from their superficial characteristics. The characteristic most studied has been physical attractiveness.

Physical Attractiveness: A Major Determinant of Liking.
Despite much cultural wisdom telling us that "beauty is only skin deep" and "you can't judge a book by its cover," people respond strongly to the **physical attractiveness,** or aesthetically appealing outward appearance, of others (eg., M. A. Collins & Zebrowitz, 1995); this is especially true when a person tries to judge someone's desirability as a date (Sprecher & Duck, 1994). Sometimes attractiveness can outweigh other considerations. For example, in one experiment, undergraduate men were sufficiently eager to be liked by an attractive female stranger that they tried to ingratiate themselves by expressing false attitudes in order to agree with her; in response to an unattractive woman, they did the opposite and expressed false disagreements (Plesser-Storr, 1995). Men and women differ to some degree; men are affected more by female attractiveness than women are by male attractiveness (Pierce, 1992).

Why should physical attractiveness lead to attraction? According to the affect-centered model described earlier, good-looking individuals arouse positive affect (Kenrick et al., 1993), and we have seen that affect is an all-important determinant of attraction. Evolutionary theory provides a possible explanation as to why men overemphasize female attractiveness. In responding to the opposite sex, men have been reproductively successful most often when they have favored females whose appearance was associated with youth and fertility. More specifically, Singh (1993) found that men respond to a woman's waist-to-hip ratio: The lower a woman's ratio (the more small-waisted she is, in other words), the more men prefer her and rate her as attractive, healthy, and reproductively valuable. Women, in contrast, have been more reproductively successful when they have reacted positively to a male's character and abilities more than to his looks; because such a mate can provide resources and protection for a woman and her offspring (Kenrick et al., 1994). However, Singh (1995) found that women prefer men to have *both* high financial status—ability to provide—*and* attractiveness, defined as a man with normal weight and hips that roughly equaled his waist. Men who had low incomes, were under- or over-weight, and had more woman-like hip-to-waist ratios were least attractive. Based both on her research and on biological studies showing that human fat distribution on the body is regulated by sex hormones (testosterone for men and estrogen for women; see Björntorp, 1991), Singh concluded that in *both* genders the distribution of fat provides visible cues regarding reproductive capacity: In women, smaller waists indicate fertility; in men, waists equal to hips indicate fertility. Of course, these findings do not explain how these features become associated with physical attractiveness in the first place.

Reactions to various observable characteristics are based on learned stereotypes, and attractiveness is no exception (Calvert, 1988). Research findings show that people tend to believe that attractive men and women are also more poised, interesting, sociable, independent, dominant, exciting, sexy, well adjusted, socially skilled, and successful than those who are unattractive (Moore, Graziano, & Miller, 1987). Handsome men are perceived as more masculine and beautiful women as more feminine than their less attractive counterparts (Gillen, 1981). Attractiveness even affects judgments about a stranger who is HIV-positive; attractive individuals are assumed to have contracted the infection in a heterosexual relationship, while unattractive ones are assumed to have acquired the virus in a homosexual relationship or through sharing a needle (Agnew & Thompson, 1994). Essays identified as the work of attractive students are evaluated more positively than those whose authors were identified as unattractive (Cash & Trimer, 1984). Altogether, as social psychologists discovered more than two decades ago, people assume that "what is beautiful is good" (Dion, Berscheid, & Hatfield, 1972).

Despite the strength of these stereotypes based on appearance, most of them are quite wrong (Feingold, 1992; Kenealy et al., 1991). The only characteristics actually associated with attractiveness are those related to popularity (e.g., Reis, Nezlek, & Wheeler, 1989) and good interpersonal skills (O'Grady, 1989). Further, the more positive a person's self-rating of attractiveness, the stronger his or her feelings of subjective well-being (Diener, Wolsic, & Fujita, 1995). Presumably, these differences based on appearance develop primarily because attractive individuals are liked and treated nicely by others from their earliest years, while those who are unattractive receive less-favorable treatment.

Though most of the attractiveness studies have concentrated on adolescents and young adults in the context of dating, elderly men respond to the attractiveness of young women just as young men do (Singh, 1993). And attractive babies are assumed to have more positive characteristics (such as sociability and competence) than unattractive ones (Karraker & Stern, 1990). More surprising than adult reactions to attractive infants is the fact that infants respond to the attractiveness of adults, regardless of the adult's gender, race, or age (Langlois et al., 1991). Even when the stimulus is a doll, children spend more play time with attractive than with unattractive ones.

Despite the overwhelmingly positive effects of being attractive, a few negative attributes are also associated with good looks. For example,

beautiful women are often perceived as vain and materialistic (Cash & Duncan, 1984). Though attractive male political candidates receive more votes than unattractive ones, beauty is not helpful to female candidates (Sigelman et al., 1986), possibly because an elected official who is "too feminine" is assumed to be ineffective.

The Search for Physical Details That Constitute Attractiveness. Research shows that people tend to agree extremely well about who is or is not attractive, even across racial and ethnic lines and with respect to targets whose race or ethnicity matches or does not match the participants' own (Cunningham et al., 1995). Nevertheless, it is difficult to identify the precise cues that determine judgments of relative attractiveness.

One approach is to identify individuals who are perceived by others as attractive and then determine what these attractive people have in common. For example, Cunningham (1986) asked male college students to look at photographs of young women and rate their attractiveness. The "most attractive" pictures were of women who had either childlike features (large, widely spaced eyes and a small nose and chin) or "mature" features (prominent cheekbones, narrow cheeks, high eyebrows, large pupils, and a big smile), as shown in Figure 7.3. These same two facial types were perceived as equally attractive among white, African American, and Asian women. Another finding is that women with the childlike features are stereotyped as "cute" (McKelvie, 1993).

Langlois and Roggman (1990) took a very different approach to determine what is meant by attractiveness. They began with photographs of faces, then produced computer-generated pictures that combined several faces into one. That is, the image in each photo was transformed into a series of numbers representing shades of gray, the numbers were averaged across the group of pictures, and the result was translated back into a photo. For both men and women, a composite face was rated as more attractive than most of the individual faces that went into making it. Further, the more faces that were used to make the composite, the more attractive the result.

FIGURE 7.3   Women's Faces Rated Most Attractive by Men.

When male undergraduates examined pictures of young women and rated their attractiveness, two distinct types were identified. Women with "childlike" or "mature" features were the ones rated most attractive.

These investigators concluded that, for most people, an attractive face is simply one whose components represent the arithmetic mean of the details of many faces (Langlois, Roggman, & Musselman, 1994; Rhodes & Tremewan, 1996). Why? Because the average of multiple individual faces is perceived as more *familiar* than any of the actual faces, the investigators assume that they are *representative* of the total sample of faces. Even though we don't ordinarily see a truly average face (or an average apple or an average anything), our experiences lead us to define what we mean by "face" by using an informal averaging process; that is, we construct a mental prototype from our many experiences with faces. This cognitive construction—a schema for the concept of face—makes it possible to process a face easily and readily whenever we encounter one. The computer-average faces presented in the experiment resemble one's own cognitive schema for what is meant by "face," and that is why they are familiar. And, as in the proximity studies, that which is familiar elicits a positive response.

Other Observable Cues That Influence Attraction. In addition to general attractiveness, several other observable cues elicit stereotypes and emotional responses, which can result in instant likes and dislikes based on superficial factors. Here are the main conclusions that a huge amount of research has generated about these cues:

1. As we alluded above, *physique* tends to be a big concern to both men and women. Beginning in childhood (Brylinsky & Moore, 1994), and continuing to adulthood, people in some societies have negative reactions to chubby body builds (Crandall & Martinez, 1996; C. T. Miller et al., 1990). Despite this powerful stereotype, obese individuals have no more social anxiety, no less social competence, and no smaller social networks than non-obese individuals (C. T. Miller et al., 1995).

2. *Age* also is a factor, with adults who look or sound very young perceived in stereotypic ways (Kite & Johnson, 1988). Those who look or act older—even in terms of walking style or posture—receive more negative reactions, being judged as weak, naïve, and incompetent, but warm and honest (Berry & Brownlow, 1989).

3. Individuals who act in prosocial or extraverted ways seem to make the best first impressions (Jensen-Campbell, Graziano, & West, 1995).

4. Predictably positive reactions appear to result from other outward cues such as stylish clothing (Cahoon & Edmonds, 1989),

good grooming (Mack & Rainey, 1990), taller height (Pierce, 1996), the absence of disabilities (Fichten & Amsel, 1986), the absence of eyeglasses (Hasart & Hutchinson, 1993), healthy eating habits (Stein & Nemeroff, 1995), and even cheerful-sounding first names such as Scott or Brittany (compared to Willard or Agatha; see Mehrabian & Piercy, 1993).

Similarity and Attraction

More than two thousand years ago, Aristotle wrote about the characteristics of friendship. Among other things, he hypothesized that people who agree with one another become friends, while those who disagree do not. Throughout the twentieth century, social psychological research has consistently confirmed this ancient prediction. A friendly relationship is often based on the discovery of **attitude similarity.** As we will show shortly, the importance of similarity to attraction goes far beyond attitudes. In the words of New York radio "shock jock" Howard Stern, "If you're not like me, I hate you" (Zoglin, 1993).

Attraction and Attitude Similarity. The proposed association between attitude similarity and attraction has been documented in numerous correlational and experimental studies that help to explain why the attitude-similarity effect occurs. When people interact, various topics are likely to come up (school, work, music, television, politics, or whatever), and each person is very likely to express his or her likes and dislikes (Hatfield & Rapson, 1992). The effects of these expressions of attitude are surprisingly precise. Each person in the interaction evaluates the other on the basis of the **proportion of similar attitudes** that are expressed, regardless of the total number of topics (e.g., Smeaton, Byrne, & Murnen, 1989). To determine proportion, simply divide the number of topics on which two people express similar views by the total number of topics about which they exchange information. Attraction is the same if two people agree on three out of four issues ($3 \div 4 = .75$) or on 75 out of 100

($75 \div 100 = .75$). The higher the proportion of similar attitudes, the greater the liking. This cause-and-effect relationship can be expressed in mathematical terms as a linear (straight-line) function. The wide-ranging generality of the similarity–attraction relationship has been shown in studies of people across different age groups, different socioeconomic levels, and different cultures (Pilkington & Lydon, 1997). Even on the information superhighway, it has been noted that those using e-mail exchange lists are most likely to seek out others who share their views and to exclude those who disagree (Schwartz, 1994).

As we learned in Chapter 3, we tend to believe that others agree with our positions on various issues, a phenomenon known as the *false consensus effect*. An implication of assuming a false consensus is that agreement is expected while disagreement is surprising (R. Singh & Tan, 1992). Disagreement can have a greater effect, because this negative information "stands out" (remember the automatic vigilance effect discussed in Chapter 3?). Consistent with these factors, research does indicate a slightly greater effect for dissimilar attitudes than for similar ones, in part because most people assume that a stranger, especially an attractive one, holds attitudes similar to their own (Miyake & Zuckerman, 1993). Of course, the effect here is the reverse of the attitude-similarity effect: Dissimilar attitudes create *dis*liking.

Why Do Similar and Dissimilar Attitudes Influence Attraction? The simplest explanation for the effect of attitudes on attraction is that similar attitudes arouse positive affect while dissimilar attitudes arouse negative affect, and we have already described how affect leads to attraction. As accurate as that may be, it is still not entirely clear *why* the attitudes of another person are emotionally pleasing or displeasing.

The oldest explanation, described by Newcomb and also by Fritz Heider among others, is **balance theory**. The proposal is that people naturally organize their likes and dislikes in a symmetrical way. **Balance,** a pleasant emotional state, exists when two people like each other and agree about some topic (Newcomb, 1961). When people like each other but disagree, an unpleasant state occurs because of **imbalance** (Orive, 1988). In response, each person strives to restore balance by changing his or her attitudes in order to reach agreement, convincing the other person to change attitudes for the same reason, minimizing the disagreement through misperception, or deciding to dislike rather than like the other person (Monsour, Betty, & Kurzweil, 1993). Research suggests that we seek balanced states so routinely that this process is nearly automatic (Andersen, Reznik, & Manzella, 1996). When two people dislike each other, they are in a state of **nonbalance,** and each is indifferent about the other's attitudes.

Though balance theory appears to be accurate, it doesn't really explain why attitudinal information matters in the first place. One answer is provided by Festinger's (1954) social comparison theory: In effect, you turn to other people to obtain **consensual validation** of your opinions; agreement provides "evidence" that you are correct. It is pleasing to discover that your judgment is sound, your intelligence is high, and so forth. Disagreement suggests the reverse, and it is uncomfortable to find that you have poor judgment, low intelligence, and so on. This formulation suggests that we are interested in the views of other people

not because we are seeking accuracy, but only because we want to verify what we already believe.

The Matching Hypothesis: Liking Others Who Are Like Yourself. Attraction is affected by many types of interpersonal similarity. Though it is commonly believed that "opposites attract," research overwhelmingly indicates that similarity is the rule, as Figure 7.4 suggests.

Sir Francis Galton first determined that "like marries like" in 1870, but the **matching hypothesis** became a matter of interest to social psychologists in the context of research on physical attractiveness (Berscheid et al., 1971). The idea is that romantic partners tend to pair off on the basis of being *similar* in physical attractiveness. Not only are dating couples similar in attractiveness, but married couples are, also (Zajonc et al., 1987). Observers usually react negatively when they perceive couples who are "mismatched." The dissimilar couples are rated as having less ability, being less likable, and having a less satisfactory relationship than couples who are similar in attractiveness (Forgas, 1993).

Numerous studies have reported that similarity and perceived similarity on a wide variety of specific characteristics are associated with attrac-

FIGURE 7.4 Birds of a Feather Flock Together: Similarity Attracts.

People who are similar show a marked tendency to affiliate. The similarity can be in terms of attitudes, personality traits, habits, needs, and demographic features such as race, as this photograph shows.

tion (Hogg, Cooper-Shaw, & Holzworth, 1993). For example, college students who choose their roommates do so in part because the two individuals are similar in sociability (Joiner, 1994). Among other similarity findings are the positive effects on attraction of being alike in expressing emotions (Alliger & Williams, 1991); smoking marijuana (Eisenman, 1985); belonging to a given religion (Kandel, 1978); having similar self-concepts (LaPrelle et al., 1990); smoking, drinking, and engaging in premarital sex (Rodgers, Billy, & Udry, 1984); accepting traditional gender roles (E. R. Smith, Byrne, & Fielding, 1995); being morning versus evening people (Watts, 1982); and agreement as to what is a funny joke (Cann, Calhoun, & Banks, 1997).

Opposites may not attract, but birds of a feather most certainly do flock together.

Reciprocity: Mutual Liking

Once two individuals discover enough areas of similarity to move toward friendship, one additional step is all-important. Each individual must somehow indicate that the other person is liked and evaluated positively (e.g., Condon & Crano, 1988). Almost everyone is extremely happy to receive such positive feedback and is quite displeased to be evaluated negatively (Coleman, Jussim, & Abraham, 1987). It is not unusual for even an inaccurate positive evaluation (Swann et al., 1987) or an obvious attempt at flattery (Drachman, DeCarufel, & Insko, 1978) to be well received, even from a total stranger. One exception is that individuals with negative self-concepts (see Chapter 4) sometimes respond well to accurate negative evaluations (Swann, Stein-Seroussi, & Giesler, 1992), presumably because such evaluations are consistent with their self-schemas.

A positive or negative evaluation affects attraction, and interpersonal behavior as well. Curtis and Miller (1986) led some research participants to believe that a stranger liked them and others to believe that they were disliked by a stranger. Participants interacted with a fellow participant who was falsely identified as the stranger who had made the evaluation, and their behavior was strongly influenced by whether they believed the other person had given a positive or a negative evaluation. Those who believed they had been evaluated positively were more self-disclosing, expressed more positive attitudes, made more eye contact, and spoke in a warmer tone than those who believed the other person gave negative evaluations. Expecting to be liked leads to positive interpersonal behavior; when two students each received the false information about positive evaluations from the other, greater reciprocal liking was expressed afterward.

Although mutual liking is often expressed in words, the first signs of attraction may be nonverbal cues (discussed in Chapter 2). For example, when a woman maintains eye contact while conversing with a man and leans toward him, these acts tend to be interpreted (sometimes incorrectly) to mean that she likes him; his response is then attraction toward her (Gold, Ryckman, & Mosley, 1984).

In brief, we like those who like us or who we believe like us.

Integrating Principles

1. Repeated contacts between any two strangers are facilitated by the arrangement of their physical surroundings, and the repeated exposure that occurs in these contacts most often results in positive affect and thus in positive evaluations (Chapter 3).

2. Attraction (as well as other evaluations) is influenced by affect, whether the positive and negative emotions are directly aroused by the target person or simply associated with the target. Affect also is a crucial factor in attitude formation (Chapter 5), prejudice (Chapter 6), love (this chapter), and decisions made in the courtroom (Chapter 11).

3. First impressions of others are determined in part by stereotypes that are associated with observable characteristics (see Chapters 2 and 6). These stereotypes elicit positive or negative affect and hence result in liking or in dislike.

4. Similarity on a wide variety of verbal and nonverbal attributes leads to attraction. We like people who like us and evaluate us positively and dislike people who dislike us and evaluate us negatively. Indicating a positive reaction to others is important in close relationships and in the workplace (Chapter 11).

Close Relationships: Friends and Romantic Partners

At one extreme, initial feelings of attraction can blossom into lifelong close friendships or even into highly intimate romantic relationships such as marriages. At the other extreme, the initial feelings of attraction might be thwarted so that no relationship at all develops. In this section, we will consider the factors that result in each of these outcomes.

Friendships and Loneliness

Friendships. Beginning in childhood, most of us establish casual friendships with several others of about the same age who share common interests, and also form a close friendship with just one person. In adolescence and young adulthood, friendships tend to be more intimate than in childhood, and women report having more close friends than men do (Fredrickson, 1995). Being involved in an intimate friendship most often has positive effects on the two individuals forming the pair (Berndt, 1992). For example, having a good friend where one works is associated with greater job satisfaction (Winstead et al., 1995). Close friends frequently interact, and they become increasingly accurate in describing the characteristics of one another (Paulhus & Bruce, 1992) and in inferring what the other person is thinking and feeling (Stinson & Ickes, 1992). When events such as college graduation interrupt close friendships, they pose an emotional threat to which the friends must adapt (Fredrickson, 1995). As a result, graduating seniors (compared to students not approaching a time of separation) reported more intense emotional involvement in their contacts with close friends.

Among friends of the same or of the opposite sex, an "intimate relationship" means that the two individuals feel free to engage in self-disclosing behavior, express their emotions, provide support and receive it, experience trust, engage

in physical contact, and generally relax with one another (Planalp & Benson, 1992).

Bartholomew and her associates (Bartholomew, 1990; Bartholomew & Horowitz, 1991) have proposed that there are four attachment patterns based on two underlying dimensions: positive versus negative evaluation of self and positive versus negative evaluation of other people (Griffin & Bartholomew, 1994a, 1994b). These two evaluative dimensions consist of a person's sense of self-worth and the person's perception of others as trustworthy or unreliable, as shown in Figure 7.5.

A person with a positive self-image tends to assume that others will respond positively; the individual expects to be liked and treated well and for that reason should ordinarily feel comfortable in close relationships. A negative self-image is associated with the expectation that others will be rejecting, and therefore close relationships tend to arouse feelings of anxiety, unworthiness, and dependency. Individuals with a positive image of other people expect them to be available and supportive, so close relationships tend to be sought; but people with a negative image of others are motivated to avoid close relationships because they expect others to be unavailable and nonsupportive. It is possible to fall on the positive or negative end of each dimension, so four basic patterns of adult attachment are possible—as shown in the figure. Two of the patterns are very clear: Those who are self-positive and other-positive (*secure*) seek closeness with others, while those who are self-negative and other-negative (*avoidant* or *fearful*) avoid rejection by avoiding closeness. That is, they regulate the possible threat of a close relationship by simply staying away (Brennan & Morris, 1997; Tidwell, Reis, & Shaver, 1996). Relationships are also potentially threatening to those falling into the other two patterns. Each involves emotional conflict, and they represent two aspects of what we have previously labeled as the *ambivalent* attachment style. A *preoccupied* person has a negative self-view along with the belief that other people will be loving and accepting; as a result, the individual seeks closeness in relationships (sometimes excessive closeness) but experiences

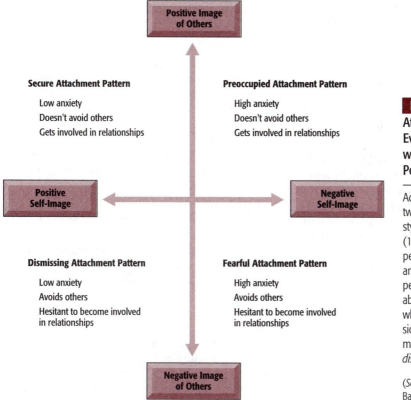

Positive Image
of Others

Secure Attachment Pattern

Low anxiety
Doesn't avoid others
Gets involved in relationships

Preoccupied Attachment Pattern

High anxiety
Doesn't avoid others
Gets involved in relationships

Positive
Self-Image

Negative
Self-Image

Dismissing Attachment Pattern

Low anxiety
Avoids others
Hesitant to become involved
in relationships

Fearful Attachment Pattern

High anxiety
Avoids others
Hesitant to become involved
in relationships

Negative Image
of Others

FIGURE 7.5   Four Adult Attachment Patterns Based on Evaluations and Expectancies with Respect to Self and Other People.

According to Bartholomew's analysis, two dimensions underlie attachment style, the extent to which an individual (1) has a positive self-image and expects others to respond accordingly, and (2) has a positive image of other people and expects others to be available and supportive. Depending on where one falls on these two dimensions, the result is one of four attachment patterns: *secure, preoccupied, dismissing,* or *fearful.*

(*Source:* Based on information from Griffin & Bartholomew, 1994a, 1994b.)

distress whenever emotional needs are not met. *Dismissing* individuals avoid genuine closeness because they expect the worst from others, but they maintain a positive self-image, stress their independence, and perceive the world through egocentric glasses.

Loneliness. Most people place a high value on establishing relationships, but many have difficulty in achieving that goal. The outcome is likely to be **loneliness**—the feeling a person has whenever the quantity and quality of desired relationships is higher than the quantity and quality of actual relationships (Archibald, Bartholomew, & Marx, 1995; Peplau & Perlman, 1982). Loneliness is associated with negative emotions such as depression, anxiety, unhappiness, dissatisfaction, and shyness (e.g., Neto, 1992). Those who know lonely individuals tend to evaluate them as maladjusted

(Lau & Gruen, 1992; Rotenberg & Kmill, 1992). Note, however, that many people prefer solitude; they may be alone, but not lonely (Burger, 1995). The question of why some people desire relationships but are unable to establish them has been answered in more than one way. For example, Duggan and Brennan (1994) trace the problem to Bartholomew's attachment patterns, noting that both "dismissing" and "fearful" individuals are hesitant to become involved in relationships.

Others propose that loneliness begins in childhood; if a child fails to develop appropriate social skills—for whatever reason, he or she simply doesn't know how to interact successfully with other children (Braza et al., 1993). For example, a child who is either withdrawn or aggressive is very likely to be rejected as a playmate (J. C. Johnson, Poteat, & Ironsmith, 1991). Unless something is done to change the inappropriate behavior, interpersonal difficulties typically continue through childhood and into adolescence and adulthood—they don't just go away (Asendorpf, 1992).

These patterns of socially skilled versus unskilled behavior are associated with different sorts of cognitions. Langston and Cantor (1989) studied the interpersonal successes and failures of college students for several months. These investigators found that students who were socially successful perceived interpersonal tasks differently from those who failed. Consistent with other research, the two groups of students also were found to use different strategies in interacting with others. Specifically, unskilled students appraise a social situation negatively and react with *social anxiety*. Given this negative perception of the situation, the socially unskilled person develops a restrained and conservative social strategy, attempting to avoid the risk of being rejected. This tendency to hold back and "play it safe" interpersonally makes a negative impression on others. In contrast, a socially successful student is more likely to perceive a new social situation as an interesting challenge and an opportunity to make new friends. The resulting strategy is to be open and informative, with the result that other people respond positively.

Romantic Relationships

Some degree of physical intimacy is one of the defining characteristics of romantic relationships, as suggested by Figure 7.6. Intimacy may involve simply kissing, holding hands, or embracing, or it may also involve a variety of interpersonal sexual acts. Rapid cultural changes over the past several decades have made it difficult to know precisely what is implied by terms such as "hanging out together," "dating," "going steady," "living together," and "becoming engaged"; but each suggests romantic attraction, possible feelings of love, the strong likelihood of sexual interest, and marriage as something that may occur at some future date.

Similarities between Romantic Relationships and Close Friendships. In some respects the attraction between a male and a female is much like other close relationships. For example, similarity influences who is likely to date whom (Whitbeck & Hoyt, 1994). *Attachment style* is once again an important aspect of interpersonal behavior. In a four-month study of heterosexual relationships among Canadian undergraduates, Keelan, Dion, and Dion (1994) found that those with a secure attachment style expressed more satisfaction with and greater commitment to the relation-

FIGURE 7.6 Physical Intimacy: One Indicator of a Romantic Relationship.

One of the differences between a friendship and a romantic relationship is that romance usually includes some degree of physical intimacy. Cultural influences define what kind of contact is suitable.

ship, and that they trusted the partner more, than students whose attachment styles were avoidant or ambivalent. Among undergraduates involved in a romantic relationship, there is a also a weak but significant tendency to be attracted to someone with an attachment style like one's own (Brennan & Shaver, 1995). Thus, some aspects of interpersonal style that can be traced to infant experiences continue to be reflected in adult romantic interactions.

Differences between Romantic Relationships and Close Friendships. Some aspects of a romantic interaction differ from other relationships. For example, Swann, De La Ronde, and Hixon (1994) indicate that among friends, college roommates, and even married couples, the preference is for a partner who can validate one's self-concept. That is, we generally want to be with someone who knows us well enough to understand our best and our worst characteristics. Dating, however, is different. Early in such a relationship, at least, two people are not committed to one another and aren't looking for self-validation. Rather, they are looking for acceptance and want to like and to be liked, hoping most of all for compliments and praise. In effect, people go out to have fun, and they are on their best behavior. We "test drive" potentially acceptable models—but our judgments are often unrealistic because of this search for uncomplicated *positivity feedback.*

Consistent with the general conceptualization of romantic relationships as built in part on fantasy are findings in both the United States and the Netherlands that couples judge their own relationships to be better (more positive) than the relationships that other people have (Van Lange & Rusbult, 1995). The hidden (and sometimes not so hidden) agenda of sexual motivation also differentiates romantic relationships from other types. Simpson and Gangestad (1992) have found that people differ in whether their primary motivation in seeking a romantic partner is sex or closeness. This difference falls along a personality dimension labeled **sociosexuality.** At one extreme are individuals who have an *unrestricted sociosexual orientation;* they are willing to engage in sexual interactions with partners in the ab-

sence of either closeness, commitment, or emotional bonding. At the other extreme are people who have a *restricted sociosexual orientation*; they believe that a sexual relationship *must* be based on closeness, commitment, and emotional bonding. In addition, restrictive sociosexuality is associated with having a secure attachment style (Brennan & Shaver, 1995).

An unrestricted orientation is more characteristic of men than of women, but either gender can be restricted or unrestricted. Compared to those who are restricted, unrestricted people engage in sex earlier in a relationship, are less interested in love, and are more likely to be involved with two or more partners at the same time. Sociosexual orientation is not related to sex drive, sexual satisfaction, or sex guilt, but it *is* related to the kind of romantic partner that the person finds attractive.

How Do You Love Me?

Love is one of the most common themes in our songs, movies, and everyday lives, as suggested by the woman in Figure 7.7. Data support the proposition that most people perceive love as a very common experience. A 1993 poll of 1,000 American adults revealed that almost three out of four say that they are currently "in love." What do they mean when they say that? One possibility is that a friendship between a man and a woman is redefined as a loving relationship when the two people begin to perceive themselves as potential sexual partners. As we shall see in the following section, a quarter century of social psychological research and theory indicates that love is more complex and much less straightforward than that.

Passionate Love Is Not Like Friendship. Aron and colleagues (1989) point out that many people fall in love, but no one ever reports "falling in friendship." We discussed many factors—from propinquity to similarity—that gradually facilitate the establishment of a friendship. In contrast, **passionate love** (an intense and often unrealistic emotional reaction to a potential romantic partner) seems to occur suddenly and to depend

In our songs and movies, and in our lives (past, present, and
future), love seems to be one of the most common and most
popular of themes.

FAIR GAME   Stephanie Piro

"Right now, my future boyfriend is
walking around down there, pathetically
unaware of my existence. He's just a
matter of time before we meet,
fall in love and move in together.
And you know, somehow, I think
this relationship is going to last!"

primarily on specific observable cues provided
by the other person, as well as on what one believes and expects about love. McClelland (1986)
suggests that a person can talk about (and write
about) love or friendship as a logical process
when using the left brain, but the often illogical
experience of falling in love occurs only when a
person is using the right brain.

The person you love may not even love you;
unrequited love refers to this one-way flow of affection. Both the one who loves and the one who
does not love feel distressed—one is rejected and
undergoes a loss of self-esteem, while the other

feels guilty about hurting the would-be lover
(Baumeister, Wotman, & Stillwell, 1993). Sur-
veying more than four hundred respondents,
Bringle and Winnick (1992) found that most (60
percent) said they had experienced unrequited
love at least once in the past two years.

Most social psychological research dealing
with love has focused on the more common situation, in which two people fall in love with each
other. What have we learned so far?

Why and How Do People "Fall in Love"?   When people say they are in love, they tend to mean passionate love (Hatfield, 1988); but love also can
take several other forms—and we will discuss
these variations shortly. Passionate love usually
begins as a sudden, overwhelming, all-consum-
ing reaction to another person—something that
feels as if it's beyond your control, an unpre-
dictable accident—"falling head over heels." A
person experiencing such love is preoccupied
with the loved one—who has no faults or imper-
fections ("love is blind"). It is even possible to
convince yourself that your lover's faults are really virtues (Murray & Holmes, 1994).

Passionate love seems to be a mixture of sexual attraction, physiological arousal, the desire to
be physically close, an intense need to be loved as
much as you love, and the constant fear that the
relationship might end. A measure of this emotional state, the *Passionate Love Scale,* includes
items such as "I would feel deep despair if _____
left me" and "For me, _____ is the perfect romantic partner" (Hatfield & Sprecher, 1986).
These emotions are sufficiently intense that simply thinking about a past experience of falling in
love creates a positive mood, while thinking
about a failed love affair in one's past has the opposite effect (L. F. Clark & Collins, 1993).

More often than you might think, passionate
love can arise without warning—literally, love at
first sight (Averill & Boothroyd, 1977). In Chapter 3, we described how facial feedback influences your emotional response (smile and you
feel happier, etc.). Somewhat surprisingly, an
emotion such as love can also be aroused by what
you are doing. When two opposite-sex strangers
are simply asked to gaze into each other's eyes for
two minutes, each is then more likely to express

affectionate feelings toward the other (Kellerman, Lewis, & Laird, 1989). The positive effect of physical acts such as gazing at and holding hands with an opposite-sex stranger is most likely for research participants who strongly believe in romantic ideals: love at first sight, love conquers all, and love as the major foundation for relationships (G. P. Williams & Kleinke, 1993).

How is it that something as basic as passionate love can be generated so easily? Increasingly, many psychologists, anthropologists, and others believe that love is a universal phenomenon (Hatfield & Rapson, 1993a), though its specific meaning can vary greatly from culture to culture and in different eras (Beall & Sternberg, 1995). One popular explanation of passionate love's universal presence is based on evolutionary theory (Buss & Schmitt, 1993; D. P. Schmidt & Buss, 1996). About four or five million years ago, our ancestors began to walk in an upright position and forage for whatever food could be carried back to a safe shelter. The survival of our species depended on reproductive success—on men and women (1) engaging in sexual intercourse and (2) investing the time and effort required to feed and protect their offspring until the young ones, in turn, were old enough to seek partners and reproduce. These two different but equally crucial aspects of reproductive success—lust and commitment—were enhanced among those humans whose biochemistry led them to seek and enjoy not only sexual satisfaction but also male–female bonding and parent–child bonding.

With emotional attachments motivated by physiological underpinnings, early human male–female pairs became more than just sex partners—they also liked and trusted one another and divided up the necessary tasks into hunting and gathering food versus caring for the children. Humans who behaved in this fashion were more likely to pass on their genes than humans who were not motivated to seek intercourse *and* also to establish strong interpersonal bonds. As a result, today's humans have been genetically primed to seek sex, fall in love, and care for their children (Trivers, 1972). While it is difficult—if not impossible—to provide a definitive test of this kind of theoretical formulation, evolutionary pressures nevertheless provide a convincing explanation of some of our interpersonal behavior. If you are deeply in love with someone at this moment, you may not want to think of yourself as driven by genetics and biochemistry; but it seems quite possible that such factors could help explain why you feel the way you do.

Nevertheless, even if the evolutionary scenario just described turns out to be totally accurate, cultural influences can still overcome these tendencies, guide them into quite specific forms, or even add to them, by way of the stories we tell our children (and ourselves), our religious practices, and the laws we enact.

Given the widespread cultural support of love, marriage, and parenthood, Hatfield and Walster (1981) have proposed that for most individuals, passionate love is easily aroused if three simple conditions are present. *First*, you must be exposed to romantic images and role models that lead you to expect that you will someday find the right person and fall in love. Consider how, since childhood, each of us has repeatedly learned that life includes love, marriage, and living happily ever after from fairy tales (*Snow White, Cinderella, Sleeping Beauty*, and hundreds of others) not to mention unlimited later exposure to love songs and love stories.

Second, you must come in contact with an appropriate person to love. Who you believe is "appropriate" is likely to be strongly influenced by what you have learned from your culture—for example, the potential love object should be of the opposite sex, physically attractive, unmarried, a member of the same religious faith, and on and on. Besides these criteria based on cultural rules, evolutionary psychologists suggest that we are also strongly influenced by unconscious factors that direct us toward a love object who is able to reproduce and to take care of our future offspring (Buss, 1988). Because men can reproduce daily from puberty until they die, while a woman's reproductive capability is more limited; and because pregnancy and child care create longer pauses during her fertile years, and thus interfere with a woman's ability to seek food and other necessities, the sexes differ in the attributes they seek in a partner. A man is attracted to women younger than himself (making them more likely to be capable of reproducing), whereas a woman is often attracted to older men who offer the material resources and character she and her offspring will need (e.g., Kenrick et al., 1993; Sprecher, Sullivan, & Hatfield, 1994; see also the discussion in Chapter 1). These male–female differences appear in Figure 7.8. Evolutionary psychologists further propose that physical similarity (skin color, etc.) is preferred (Bailey & Czuchry, 1994), because mating with a similar partner increases the odds that your kind of genes will be passed on to future generations (Rushton, 1990; Rushton & Nicholson, 1988). As convincing as evolutionary principles may be, they are seemingly difficult to apply in some situations, including those of homosexual couples

(Metz, Rosser, & Strapko, 1994), heterosexual couples who decide never to have children, or couples who mate in later life. In such circumstances, do men and women employ similar strategies? If so, do genetics play *any* role?

The *third* condition for experiencing passionate love is strong emotional arousal. Schachter's two-factor theory (see Chapter 3) states that we interpret an aroused state on the basis of whatever cues are present. If you expect to fall in love and if you perceive an appropriate love object, you may well interpret arousal of any kind as indicating love. Research consistently shows that arousal based on emotions as different as fear (Dutton & Aron, 1974), frustration and anger

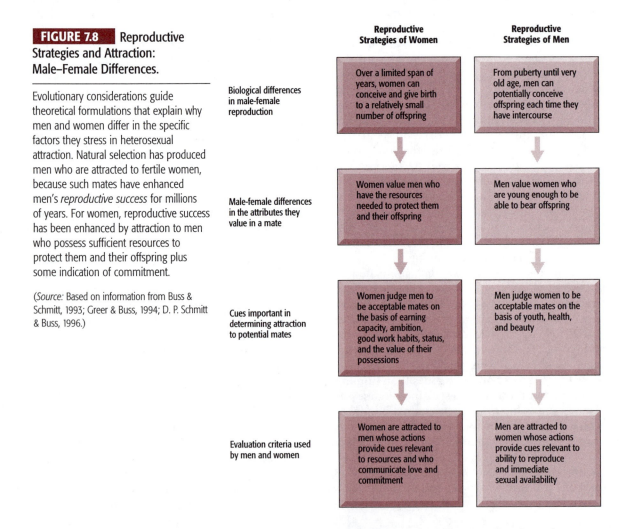

FIGURE 7.8 Reproductive Strategies and Attraction: Male–Female Differences.

Evolutionary considerations guide theoretical formulations that explain why men and women differ in the specific factors they stress in heterosexual attraction. Natural selection has produced men who are attracted to fertile women, because such mates have enhanced men's *reproductive success* for millions of years. For women, reproductive success has been enhanced by attraction to men who possess sufficient resources to protect them and their offspring plus some indication of commitment.

(*Source:* Based on information from Buss & Schmitt, 1993; Greer & Buss, 1994; D. P. Schmitt & Buss, 1996.)

Biological differences in male-female reproduction

Male-female differences in the attributes they value in a mate

Cues important in determining attraction to potential mates

Evaluation criteria used by men and women

Reproductive Strategies of Women

Over a limited span of years, women can conceive and give birth to a relatively small number of offspring

Women value men who have the resources needed to protect them and their offspring

Women judge men to be acceptable mates on the basis of earning capacity, ambition, good work habits, status, and the value of their possessions

Women are attracted to men whose actions provide cues relevant to resources and who communicate love and commitment

Reproductive Strategies of Men

From puberty until very old age, men can potentially conceive offspring each time they have intercourse

Men value women who are young enough to be able to bear offspring

Men judge women to be acceptable mates on the basis of youth, health, and beauty

Men are attracted to women whose actions provide cues relevant to ability to reproduce and immediate sexual availability

(Driscoll, Davis, & Lipetz, 1972), or sexual excitement (Istvan, Griffitt, & Weidner, 1983) can easily be attributed to "love." Altogether, these factors based on culture, genetics, and emotional attributions make it very easy for most people to experience the often irrational and overpowering feelings of passionate love.

Love Can Take Many Forms. Passionate love occurs frequently, but it is too intense to be maintained indefinitely. Emotion-based love is sufficiently fragile that simply being asked to think about one's relationship or to answer questions about it can change relationship-relevant attitudes (T. D. Wilson & Kraft, 1993). Passionate love may thrive best when our fantasies are not interrupted by close, rational inspection.

There are, however, other kinds of love that *can* be long-lasting and thoughtful. Hatfield (1988, p. 205) describes **companionate love** as "the affection we feel for those with whom our lives are deeply entwined." Unlike passionate love, companionate love represents a very close friendship in which two people are attracted, have a great deal in common, care about one another's well-being, and express mutual liking and respect (Caspi & Herbener, 1990). This is a kind of love that can sustain a relationship over time—even though it does not lend itself to emotionally stirring songs and movies.

Several other formulations of love and relationships have also been developed (for example, by Hecht, Marston, & Larkey, 1994; Rusbult, Onizuka, & Lipkus, 1993; Snell & Finney, 1993). Most of this research has maintained passionate and companionate love and added other "love styles" (Borrello & Thompson, 1990; Hendrick & Hendrick, 1986; Lasswell & Lobsenz, 1980). One major conceptualization is Sternberg's (1988) **triangular model of love.** This model suggests that—instead of different styles—each love relationship contains three basic components that are present in varying degrees for different couples. One component is **intimacy**—the closeness two people feel and the strength of the bond holding them together. Partners high in intimacy are concerned with each other's welfare and happiness, and they value, like, count on, and understand one another. The second component, **passion,** is

based on romance, physical attraction, and sexual intimacy. **Decision/commitment** is the third component, representing cognitive factors such as the decision that you love the other person and are committed to maintaining the relationship. Couples who have all three components tend to have lasting relationships (Whitley, 1993). We discuss the cultural basis of love in the Social Diversity box on pages 176–177.

Premarital Sexuality

Despite centuries of religious and legal sanctions against premarital sex in many parts of the world, dramatic changes in sexual attitudes and behavior have occurred during the second half of the twentieth century. Increasingly, sexual interactions have become a common and widely accepted part of romantic relationships.

Patterns of Sexual Behavior. The United States, Western Europe, Australia, and Canada have witnessed the greatest sexual changes. Surveys taken before and after World War II provide evidence of a steady and consistent shift toward more permissive sexual expression. By the 1960s, these changes had been labeled as the beginning of a "sexual revolution." To take one example, oral sex was considered to be a perversion in the first half of this century. By the 1990s, most American adults said they liked to give and to receive oral sex (Michael et al., 1994).

Similar changes did not even begin to occur in China until about 1988—and that nation's response has been to ban all written, audio, and visual material describing sexual behavior; to arrest those who produce it; and to execute those who sell it (Pan, 1993). The power of culture to influence sexuality is demonstrated by studies of Chinese American students, whose attitudes about premarital sex as well as their actual practices are much more permissive than is true for students in China; the more acculturated they are, the more their sexuality is like that of other American students (Huang & Uba, 1992).

With a few exceptions, such as Northern Ireland (Sneddon & Kremer, 1992), by the early 1980s, women in the Western world were as likely as men to engage in premarital intercourse

(Breakwell & Fife-Schaw, 1992; Weinberg, Lottes, & Shaver, 1995), though men still play a traditional role in initiating sexual activity (O'Sullivan & Byers, 1992). Both male and female undergraduates say they offer token resistence when sexual activity is suggested by the partner; the reasons given by both genders include maintaining their image, teasing and game playing, trying to gain control in the relationship, and wanting to slow things down (O'Sullivan & Allgeier, 1994). In serious relationships, sexuality has become expected and widely accepted. Among young adults in the United States, only 5 percent of the women and 2 percent of the men have intercourse for the first time on their wedding night (Laumann et al., 1994; Michael et al., 1994).

Some gender differences are still found. College men and women differ in how long they believe they must know the other person before it's acceptable to consent to intercourse. As shown in Figure 7.9, men more than women say that sex with a relative stranger is something they would do, while women say that they prefer to know the other person for a longer period of time (Buss & Schmitt, 1993). Of course, it is possible that both genders are trying to impress the investigators—men want to appear macho, and women want to appear selective. Perhaps people's verbal responses to a survey do not reflect their real attitudes, behavioral intentions, or actions. Another gender difference has continued in this new sexual era—male adolescents want and actually have more sexual partners than female adolescents (Buss & Schmitt, 1993; Traeen, Lewin, & Sundet, 1992). Also, in an ongoing relationship, women want their partners to express more love and intimacy, while men want more arousing and more varied sexual activity (Hatfield et al., 1989). Many of these findings could be based on gender differences in sociosexuality.

Teenage pregnancies and incurable diseases such as HIV/AIDS might be expected to result in decreases in premarital sexual activity, and some changes have in fact been reported, though not as

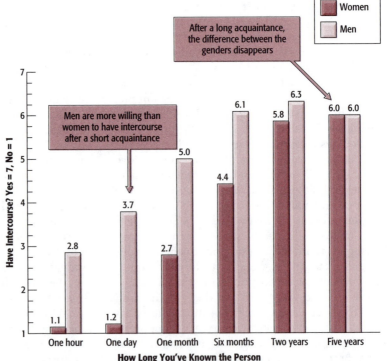

FIGURE 7.9 How Long Should You Know a Person before Having Sex? Men and Women Differ.

College students were asked, "If the conditions were right, would you consider having sexual intercourse with someone you viewed as desirable if you had known that person for one hour? One day?" (etc. up to five years). The students answered on a seven-point scale ranging from "definitely not" to "definitely yes." While both men and women were more likely to say yes as the time period increased, men were more inclined than women to agree to sex at every acquaintance level through two years. Once the person had been known for five years, gender differences disappeared.

(*Source:* Based on data from Buss & Schmitt, 1993.)

much as you might guess. In the mid-1990s, the U.S. Centers for Disease Control and Prevention reported that the number of sexually active teenagers has leveled off at about 53 percent, and that more than half of these individuals regularly use condoms; as a result, there has been a slight decrease in the teenage birth rate and in the incidence of gonorrhea (Number of sexually . . . , 1995). The greatest behavioral changes (safer sexual practices and fewer partners) have, however, been confined to those individuals most at risk for HIV infections—gays and prostitutes (Ehrhardt, Yingling, & Warne, 1991). For example, Australian undergraduates report little behavioral change and little concern about HIV/AIDS, in part because they don't perceive such infections as relevant to themselves (Rosenthal & Shepherd, 1993).

Integrating Principles

1. Romantic relationships are based in part on similarity and, like friendships, are influenced by attachment style. Unlike friendships, they are based in part on sexual desire and sometimes on unrealistic expectations and fantasies.
2. Much of what we call love refers to passionate love, which combines cultural influences, the need to find a suitable mate, and misattribution of physiological arousal (Chapter 3). Several other types of love have been identified, but companionate love—a close, caring friendship—is perhaps the most important.
3. Since the mid-twentieth century, most of the Western world has witnessed changes in sexual attitudes (see Chapter 5) and behaviors, with premarital sex becoming the norm for romantic relationships. In recent years, fear of AIDS has resulted in a slightly more cautious approach to sexual experimentation.

Marital Relationships

Before, during, and after the high point of the sexual revolution, marriage remained the primary interpersonal goal of most young people. More than 90 percent of eighteen-year-olds consistently say that they expect to get married, and

more than 90 percent of fifty-year-olds are (or have been) married (Thornton & Freedman, 1982). And, despite the realities of death, separation, and divorce, two-parent families are still much more common than one-parent families; more than three-fourths of U.S. households with children also contain both a father and a mother (Burrell, 1995). Still, there are millions of families that are blended (remarried parents with a child or children from another marriage), single-parent families, children being raised by grandparents, and so on. We will now describe some of the research that deals with what it means to live as husband and wife, including what is known about maintaining (or failing to maintain) a satisfying relationship.

Marital Sex, Parenthood, and General Satisfaction

American surveys of married partners consistently indicate that sexual interactions become less frequent over time, and the most rapid decline occurs during the first four years of marriage (Udry, 1980). Nevertheless, 41 percent of all married couples have sex twice a week or more often, while only 23 percent of single individuals have sex that frequently. Cohabiting singles are the most sexually active of all, however, in that 56 percent have sex at least twice a week (Michael et al., 1994).

It is not surprising that passionate love tends to decrease over the years, but Aron and Henkemeyer (1995) found that women who still felt passionate love after the passage of several years were more satisfied with their marriages than women who no longer had these feelings. Male satisfaction with the marriage was unrelated to feelings of passionate love. For both men and women, satisfaction is related to behavior that suggests companionate love—sharing activities, exchanging ideas, laughing together, and working together on projects. It appears that companionate love is a key to a satisfying marriage, but that women are happier if they also continue to feel sparks of passionate love.

Further, while people who are married consistently report being happier and healthier than those who are single (Steinhauer, 1995), the gap is not as great as it used to be—because unmarried men are happier now than in the past, while married women are not as happy (Glenn & Weaver, 1988). A possible explanation for these changes may lie in the availability of sexual relationships for unmarried men (D. Reed & Weinberg, 1984) and the conflicts women face in pursuing a career while simultaneously having the role of mother (Batista & Berte, 1992). A Norwegian study also indicates that married individuals are better off than those who are unmarried—a lower suicide rate and higher self-reported feelings of well-being—up until age thirty-five to forty, but that after that, the advantages of being married rapidly decline (Mastekaasa, 1995).

A major task for both spouses is discovering how best to adjust to the demands of a two-career family (Helson & Roberts, 1992). For one thing, as discussed in Chapter 4, even when they have an active career, women still do much more than 50 percent of the housework (Hochschild, 1989). In fact, compared to heterosexual and gay couples, only lesbian pairs seem able to share household labor in a fair manner (Kurdek, 1993).

Factors in Troubled Relationships

Each year, about 2.4 million American couples marry and another 1.2 million get divorced, most often after two to six years of marriage (Glick, 1983). More than one-third of the children in the United States have had to go through the painful experience of their parents' divorce (Bumpass, 1984). Among the consequences for these children are negative long-term effects on their health and their lifespans (Friedman et al., 1995). To some extent, risk for divorce appears to be built into our genes; one study found that between 30 and 42 percent of divorce risk could be attributed to genetic factors related to personality (Jockin, McGue, & Lykken, 1996). But troubled relationships result from many other factors.

What happens to turn a loving, romantic relationship into one characterized by unhappiness, dissatisfaction, and—often—hate? At times, even an originally positive attribute of the other person becomes a primary reason for dislike (Felmlee, 1995). Some problems are universal in

that being in an intimate relationship involves some degree of compromise. For example, two people have to decide what to have for dinner, what show to watch on TV, what to do in bed; and hundreds of other major and minor decisions must continually be made. Neither individual can do exactly what she or he wants, and a conflict between the desire for independence and the need for closeness is inevitable (Baxter, 1990). Other problems are specific, and some can be avoided. We will describe a sample of the common difficulties that arise in marriage and the painful effects of relationship failure.

Problems: General and Specific. Because any partner (including oneself) is less than perfect, spouses who initially believe they are ideally suited for one another inevitably come to realize that there are negative elements in the relationship. Only 1.2 percent of married couples say that they *never* have any disagreements, and most report that conflicts arise monthly or more often (McGonagle, Kessler, & Schilling, 1992). Because spouses greatly overestimate how much they agree about most matters (Byrne & Blaylock, 1963), they often don't realize that their views differ even when they believe they are communicating (Sillars et al., 1994). Financial woes are another source of relationship strain. Vinokur, Price, and Caplan (1996) studied 815 recently unemployed people and their partners. Financial strain made both individuals more depressed and led them to withdraw socially and to undermine their significant others.

Partners who are similar in the way they cope with stress are more satisfied with their relationship than those whose coping strategies differ (Ptacek & Dodge, 1995), and men more than women tend to believe that avoiding a conflict is a legitimate way to deal with it (Oggins, Veroff, & Leber, 1993). One of the greatest problems is the tendency to respond to the negative words or deeds of one's partner in an equally negative and destructive way; when people have time to consider the long-term consequences for the relationship, a constructive response is more likely to occur (Yovetich & Rusbult, 1994).

Individual differences in characteristics such as hostility, defensiveness, and depression are important determinants of how partners interact (Newton et al., 1995). In general, those who are best able to express their emotions are happiest in their marriages (King, 1993). Gender roles (see Chapter 4) also matter (Bradbury, Campbell, & Fincham, 1995; Peplau, Hill, & Rubin, 1993). Women who describe themselves as feminine or expressive are most likely to report marital satisfaction, as are men who describe themselves as instrumental or expressive (Langis et al., 1994).

Buss (1989) proposes that many difficulties arise because of built-in differences between men and women. Remember the differences in the qualities sought by each gender in a mate? Look back at Figure 7.9—these same qualities in reverse can cause conflict between partners. That is, a woman becomes upset by any indication that her partner is not loving and protective, while a man becomes upset if his partner rejects him sexually. Jealousy is also a common problem in relationships (Buunk, 1995; DeSteno & Salovey, 1996; Sharpsteen, 1995). Presumably because of our evolutionary history, a man becomes most jealous when his partner is sexually unfaithful, but a woman becomes most jealous when her partner becomes emotionally committed to someone else (Buss et al., 1992; Shackelford & Buss, 1996).

Considering the importance of affect in relationships, it is not surprising that sexual satisfaction is closely associated with the perception of marital well-being for both women and men (Henderson-King & Veroff, 1994). Sex is obviously not the only source of positive or negative affect, however. Negative emotions aroused on the job can spill over to one's home life, and vice versa (Geller & Hobfoll, 1994). Interestingly, mothers feel more positively when they are away from the home (including on the job), while fathers are happier at home than elsewhere (R. W. Larson, Richards, & Perry-Jenkins, 1994).

Further, negative affect caused by conflicts and disagreements can add greatly to the couple's dissatisfaction (Margolin, John, & O'Brien, 1989). Instead of trying to solve a given problem, unhappy partners may simply express their mutually negative evaluations as they blame one another and express their anger (Kubany et al., 1995). Miller (1991, p. 63) observes that some of

the "most hateful, caustic, and abusive interactions take place with those we say we love." Videotaped interactions of satisfied and dissatisfied couples reveal much more negative verbal and nonverbal behavior between partners whose relationship is deteriorating than between satisfied partners (Halford & Sanders, 1990). Unhappy couples express less positive affect and more negative affect than those who are satisfied (Levenson, Carstensen, & Gottman, 1994). All expressions of positive affect—including nicknames such as "sweet pea" and "pussycat"—are more common in satisfied than in dissatisfied marriages (Bruess & Pearson, 1993).

Though much of the research focuses on problems, it should be remembered that as many marriages succeed as fail. One secret seems to involve placing an emphasis on friendship, commitment, similarity, and efforts to create positive affect and general satisfaction (Bui, Peplau, & Hill, 1996). Older couples who remain married express more positive affect than younger and middle-aged couples (Levenson, Carstensen, & Gottman, 1994), perhaps because people get smarter and mellower about relationships as they grow older (M. Locke, 1995).

Relationship Failure: When Dissatisfaction Leads to Dissolution. Though it is possible for friends simply to drift apart with no strong affect, the partners in an intimate relationship are more likely to feel intense distress and anger when the relationship fails (Fischman, 1986), in part because they have invested a great amount of time, exchanged powerful rewards, and expressed a lasting commitment to one another (Simpson, 1987). Men and women differ in how they cope with a failed relationship: Women tend to confide in their friends, whereas men tend to start a new relationship as quickly as possible (Sorenson et al., 1993).

Rusbult and Zembrodt (1983) point out that people respond either actively or passively to an unhappy partnership. An active response can involve ending the relationship (*exit*—"I talked to a lawyer, and I'm filing for divorce") or working to improve it (*voice*—"I believe we should give marital counseling a try"). Passively, one can simply wait for improvement (*loyalty*—"I'll stand by my man until things get better") or simply wait for

Social Diversity: A Critical Analysis

Love and Intimacy: Cultural Differences

Much of the cross-cultural research in social psychology is based on the differences between individualistic societies—most Western nations—and collectivistic societies—most Eastern nations (Triandis, 1995). Simply put, individualism places central importance on personal goals, while collectivism stresses group goals. These orientations can be applied at the level of individuals or at the cultural level (Dion & Dion, 1991). Psychological individualism and collectivism can occur anywhere, and societal individualism or collectivism refers to a situation in which one of these value orientations is characteristic of most of a society's citizens.

Dion and Dion (1993) suggest that these different orientations strongly affect how people conceptualize love and intimacy. These researchers offer three specific propositions, supported by relevant data from two individualistic societies (Canada and the United States) and three collectivistic societies (China, India, and Japan).

(1) Romantic love is more likely to be considered an important basis for marriage in individualistic societies than in collectivistic ones.

For North Americans, it seems natural and even self-evident to say that two people meet, fall in love, decide to get married (or live together), and hope to live happily ever after. Marriage provides an opportunity for two individuals to explore and share their real selves, and to experience personal growth through the relationship. In contrast, in many Asian societies the person getting married is supposed to take into account the wishes of others, especially of parents and other family members. It is not unusual for marriages to be arranged by the respective families on the basis of such factors as occupation and status, not on the basis of love and the lovers' free choice. The intense feelings of passionate love

and the self-absorption of two lovers would be disruptive to the functioning of the group.

(2) Psychological intimacy in marriage is more basic to marital satisfaction and personal well-being in individualistic than in collectivistic societies.

In Canada and the United States, for example, much of the research on marriage deals with how the partners evaluate one another, how well they know one another, and how satisfied each person feels in the relationship. In China, India, and Japan, there is less concern about this kind of marital happiness or satisfaction—because the primary ties of intimacy and the source of well-being are rooted in family relationships with parents, siblings, and other relatives. One example of the difference is that marital satisfaction in the United States is based on the couple's interaction; in Japan, socioeconomic factors determine satisfaction (Kamo, 1993). At a more general level, those in individualistic societies express more unrealistic optimism than those in collectivistic ones (Heine & Lehman, 1995). So, when expectations are not fulfilled, Westerners react with surprise and disappointment.

(3) Although individualism values romantic love as the basis for marriage, some aspects of psychological individualism make it difficult to develop and maintain intimacy.

Earlier, we pointed out the problems faced by married partners who must make compromises in their everyday interactions. This issue is all-important in individualistic societies, which emphasize the value of autonomy, personal control, and independence. It is clearly difficult to strive simultaneously for intimacy and for independence, and Dion and Dion suggest that this conflict may account for the high divorce rate in the United States and Canada—a relationship simply ends when either partner feels sufficiently dissatisfied. The strongly individualistic person finds it difficult to care for, need, and trust his or her partner. In collectivistic societies, in contrast, dependency on others is not something to be avoided but a highly valued aspect of relationships.

Given these societal differences, what can we conclude? It seems that individualistic societies place us in an unavoidable conflict between wanting freedom and independence and striving for love and intimacy. One result

is unhappiness in relationships, a booming business in marital advice and marital counseling, and a high divorce rate. No one can foresee the future, but changes seem to indicate that North Americans are becoming even more individualistic than previously and that collectivistic societies are slowly shifting toward an individualistic orientation (Dion & Dion, 1993). If so, the future prospects for relationship satisfaction do not seem especially good.

---

the inevitable breakup (*neglect*—"I know things are bad, but I won't do anything until she becomes totally impossible"). These alternatives appear in Figure 7.10. If the goal is to maintain a relationship, *exit* and *neglect* are clearly the least constructive and *voice* the most constructive choice. *Loyalty* tends to go unnoticed or to be misinterpreted; people report themselves as having responded with loyalty but not their partners (Drigotas, Whitney, & Rusbult, 1995).

Among quite different kinds of couples (college students, older couples, gays, and lesbians), men and women with high self-esteem respond to relationship failure by exiting, while low self-esteem is associated with passive neglect (Rusbult, Morrow, & Johnson, 1990). It is very difficult to reverse a deteriorating relationship, but sometimes problems can be solved and the couple can reconcile if (1) the partnership satisfies the needs of each individual, (2) each remains committed to staying together, and (3) alternative, relatively attractive, lovers are not available (Bui et al., 1996; Rusbult, 1983). The more dependent a person is on the relationship, the less he or she is motivated to dissolve it (Drigotas & Rusbult, 1992), even in response to physical abuse (Rusbult & Martz, 1995).

It is interesting to note that most divorced persons remarry, especially men; in the United States, more than two million people have been married three or more times (G. H. Brody, Neubaum, & Forehand, 1988). The desire for love and happiness in a relationship seems to have a greater influence on behavior than negative past experiences.

Returning to the concept of attachment styles, only those in the secure category seem to be able to form long-lasting, committed, satisfying relationships. In Bartholomew's model (see Figure 7.5), verbal and physical abuse were least likely for those with a secure attachment style, most likely for those with a fearful style, and less so for those with a preoccupied style; a dismissing style was unrelated to abusiveness (Dutton et al., 1994). Without a warm, secure, consistent relationship with one's parents early in life, future relationships are very likely to suffer (Radecki-Bush, Farrell, & Bush, 1993).

Integrating Principles

1. As with other types of interpersonal relationships, marriage is most likely between two relatively similar individuals. Married couples face an array of potential conflicts, challenges, and compromises as they interact in areas as diverse as sexual intimacy, the division of household chores, dealing with two careers, and raising children. Marital satisfaction depends in part on how well couples deal with such interactions.

2. In the United States, about half of all marriages fail. Among the reasons are the discovery or development of dissimilarities, boredom, differences in ways of coping with stress (Chapter 11), attachment style, gender roles and gender differences in perceiving threat (Chapter 4), and a shift from positive to negative affect in the couple's interactions. Unfortunately, we know more about why relationships fail than about how to prevent the emotional trauma of a breakup.

FIGURE 7.10 Four Alternative Responses to a Troubled Relationship.

When a relationship is beginning to fail, the partners can respond in either an *active* or a *passive* way. Within each of these alternatives, the response can be *positive* or *negative.* The decision to end the relationship is an active–negative response ("exit"), and the decision to work on improving the relationship is an active–positive response ("voice"). Simply waiting for the problems to get worse is a passive–negative response ("neglect"), and simply waiting for improvement to occur is a passive–positive response ("loyalty").

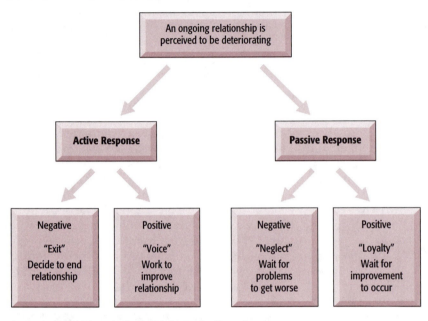

(*Source:* Based on information from Rusbult & Zembrodt, 1983.)

Connections Integrating Social Psychology

In this chapter, you read about . . .

- the role of associated affect in determining attraction and love
- social comparison theory

- stereotypes based on observable characteristics
- effects of your behavior on feelings of love

- love based on emotional attributions

In other chapters, you will find related discussions of . . .

- the roles of affect in attitude formation (Chapter 5) and prejudice (Chapter 6)
- social comparison as a factor in social influence (Chapter 8), in emergency situations (Chapter 9)
- stereotypes as they operate in prejudice (Chapter 6)
- the effect of facial feedback on emotional responses (Chapter 3)
- Schachter's two-factor theory of emotions (Chapter 3)

Thinking about Connections

1. In the past week, try to recall an instance in which you reacted to someone you didn't know (in real life, on TV, or wherever) on the basis of their appearance, their accent, or something about their behavior. What did you assume about this person, what feelings were aroused, and what kind of evaluation did you make? What are some of the stereotypes you hold about specific observable characteristics of others, and how much do they influence you?
2. Think about yourself in a close romantic relationship—either in the past, in the present, or in an imaginary romance. Is your partner at all like your ideal? How did the two of you meet, and what attracted you to this individual? Are there aspects of this person that you would like to change? Are there things about you that he or she

would like to change? Would you say that you love this person? What do you mean by "love"? Is it possible that feelings of love—at least at the beginning—were based on misattributed emotions, genetically related reproductive strategies, or expectancies based on stories about love? In other words, does the research and theory dealing with relationships and emotions connect at all with your own life?
3. Have you gone through the experience of a romance that breaks up or a divorce—your own or your parents'? If so, why do you think it happened, and what were the aftereffects? Could anything have prevented the breakup? Current research focuses on attachment styles; can you apply attachment concepts to your own experience?

Summary and Review

Our attitudes about other people range from strong liking to strong dislike, and research on *interpersonal attraction* deals with the factors that determine such interpersonal attitudes.

Proximity and Emotions

Attraction between two strangers often begins with unplanned encounters that depend on the physical details of their shared environment. When dormitory assignments, classroom seating arrangements, neighborhood layouts, or the structure of the workplace bring two people into repeated contact, they are likely to become acquainted. Research in many settings over a long period indicates that *proximity* leads to repeated interpersonal contact and hence repeated exposure to specific individuals. The result is familiarity and the increased likelihood of a friendly interaction.

The central determinant of attraction is *affect*—a person's emotional state during an interpersonal interaction. Positive affect leads to liking, while

negative affect causes dislike. Such effects occur whether the other person is responsible for the emotion or is simply present at the same time as the emotional arousal. Through simple conditioning, we associate our positive or negative emotional state with anyone (or anything) we encounter while aroused.

Needing to Affiliate and Responding to Observable Characteristics

A positive relationship is most likely to form between two people if they each are high in *need for affiliation*. This motivation differs from person to person as a dispositional variable, and there are specific motives (emotional support, attention, etc.) that underlie affiliation. In addition, the need to affiliate can be aroused by an exciting or confusing situation that brings people together—in part because they are seeking *social comparison*, as a way to verify their opinions and perceptions.

Initial attraction or avoidance is often based on stereotypes about the *observable characteristics* of others—race, sex, age, height, physique, clothing, and so on. Social psychologists have focused a great of research on the effects of *physical attractiveness*. For both males and females, it is generally beneficial to be physically attractive. Judgments of this attribute are influenced not only by a person's physical appearance but also by situational and interpersonal factors.

Similarity and Reciprocal Positive Evaluations

Observers have long noted the importance of *attitude similarity* in determining interpersonal likes and dislikes. In this century, correlational studies supported the observations. In the last fifty years, both longitudinal field research and laboratory experimentation have established the causal effect of similarity on attraction. Theoretical explanations of the response to attitudes include balance theory, the need for consensual validation, and the sociobiological importance of genetic similarity. Though attitudinal similarity and dissimilarity have been investigated extensively, many other types of similarity (physical attractiveness, personality, intelligence, age, etc.) also influence who likes whom.

In order to move beyond being acquaintances or casual friends toward a closer relationship, two individuals need to express mutual liking and other mutual positive evaluations (reciprocity) either in words or overt acts.

Romantic Relationships, Love, and Physical Intimacy

Some degree of physical intimacy is a defining characteristics of an *intimate relationship*. Romantic relationships are like close friendships with respect to the importance of similarity and attachment style, but different in other respects—the desire for positive feedback and for sexual contact. *Love* is a common experience and a common theme in songs and stories. It is manifested in multiple forms, including *passionate love*, which is based on cultural influence, genetics, and emotional misattributions. *Companionate love* is the other major variety, much like a close, caring friendship. Widespread changes in sexual attitudes and behaviors in Western nations have resulted in premarital intercourse becoming normative behavior in romantic relationships. The new-found sexual freedom has also led to many problems, including unwanted pregnancies and the spread of sexually transmissible diseases.

Marital Relationships

Most people seek marriage as a major life goal. People tend to select a marriage partner on the basis of some of the same factors (such as similarity) that determine friendships. Spouses must work out how best to interact while dealing with daily decisions about such diverse issues as household tasks, careers, leisure time, sex, and parenthood. The challenge of this task is shown by the fact that about half of the marriages in the United States and Canada end in divorce. Dissatisfaction is common because of such factors as stress, dissimilarities, boredom, and the presence of more negative than positive affect. Relationship failure is a frequent, though emotionally traumatic, occurrence.

Social Diversity: Love and Intimacy

A comparison of intimate relationships in individualistic and collectivistic societies suggests that, compared with collectivism, individualism results in romantic love being seen as a more important basis for marriage and psychological intimacy as a more important determinant of marital satisfaction; a built-in conflict between independence and intimacy often leads to relationship failure.

 # Key Terms

---

For More Information

Buss, D. M., & Malamuth, N. (1996). *Sex, power, and conflict.* New York: Oxford University Press.

The chapters of this book are written by active investigators, who examine research and theory relevant to most of the topics you've read about here—including close relationships, attachment, love, commitment, sexuality, jealousy, and the need to cope with relationship dissolution.

Duck, S. (1994). *Meaningful relationships: Talking, sense, and relating.* Thousand Oaks, CA: Sage.

A leading investigator and theorist in the field of interpersonal behavior, Professor Duck describes how relationships are a continual challenge because of the need to think about and to respond to what the other person says and does. Relationships are never a "done deal," but rather require constant effort to maintain.

Gottman, J. M. (1993). *What predicts divorce? The relationship between marital processes and marital outcomes.* Hillsdale, NJ: Erlbaum.

This book covers research on marriage and divorce from that of Terman to current studies. The emphasis is on predicting marital success and failure, but the author also presents a theory of marital stability and recommendations about how to achieve a stable marriage.

Social Influence: Changing Others' Behavior

How many times each day does someone try to influence you—to get you to think, feel, or act in ways that they want? If your life is like mine (Bob Baron), the answer is probably "Who can keep count?!" Thus most of us are on the receiving end of a large number of attempts at **social influence** every day—efforts by others to change our attitudes, beliefs, perceptions, or behaviors. Consider the number of radio and television commercials, magazine and newspaper ads, and billboards you encounter each day: All involve efforts to influence you in some manner (see Figure 8.1). Now add to this the number of direct requests you receive from people you know—friends, relatives, co-workers, and even total strangers such as panhandlers, salespersons, or politicians. When you do, you'll quickly realize that social influence is a basic fact of social life.

But we are not merely the passive targets or recipients of such influence: We also seek to exert it on others. Consider my own day. Often, it begins with gentle efforts on my part to wake my wife and get her out of bed; she truly hates getting up in the morning, so I have to start applying my knowledge of social influence early on. As the hours pass, I usually find myself engaging in conversations where I make various requests to try to persuade other people do something I'd like them to do: I ask the waiter in the restaurant to hold the mayonnaise on my sandwich; I try to convince the clerk at the dry cleaners' to get my coat back by Tuesday instead of Thursday; I ask one of my colleagues if she'll take over my class on a day when I have to be out of town; I plead with my daughter to drive carefully when she goes to visit her boyfriend . . . and so it goes, throughout the day. In short, like you, I definitely get my turns at bat where social influence is concerned.

From the standpoint of sheer frequency, then, social influence is clearly an important part of social interaction. Its importance doesn't rest on frequency alone, however; social influence is also important because it plays a key role in many forms of social interaction, including *leadership* (Chapter 11), *aggression* (Chapter 9), *prejudice* (Chapter 6), and *helping* (Chapter 9). Indeed, in one sense we began the discussion of social influence back in Chapter 5, where we examined the nature of *persuasion*. Because of its role in many forms of social behavior, social influence has long been the subject of careful study by social psychologists. This research has added greatly to our knowledge of this process, and we'll summarize much of this information for

FIGURE 8.1 Social Influence: A Fact of Daily Life.

Each day, we are exposed to many different forms of social influence—efforts by others to change our attitudes, beliefs, perceptions, or behaviors.

you in the remainder of this chapter. We'll begin by focusing on **conformity**—pressures to go along with the crowd, to behave in the same manner as other persons in one's group or society. Next, we'll turn to **compliance**—efforts to get others to say "yes" to direct requests. As we'll soon see, a wide range of tactics, many of them quite ingenious, are used to induce compliance—to increase the likelihood that others really will say "yes." Finally, we'll examine **obedience**—a form of social influence in which one person simply orders one or more others to do what they want. Usually, the persons who issue commands have some means of enforcing submission to them—they have *power* over those on the receiving end. Research findings indicate, however, that direct orders can often be effective in inducing obedience even in situations where the persons who issue these commands have little or no means for backing them up.

Conformity: Group Influence in Action

Have you ever found yourself in a situation in which you felt that you stuck out like the proverbial sore thumb? If so, you have already had direct experience with pressures toward *conformity*. In such situations, you probably experienced a strong desire to fit in with the other people around you. Such pressures toward conformity stem from the fact that in many contexts, there are explicit or unspoken rules indicating how we *should* or *ought to* behave. These rules are known as **social norms.** In some instances, social norms are both detailed and precise. For example, governments generally function through constitutions and written laws, athletic contests are usually regulated by written rules, and signs in many public places (e.g., along highways, in parks, at airports) frequently describe expected behavior in considerable detail.

In contrast, other norms are unspoken or implicit. Most of us obey such unwritten rules as

"Don't stand too close to strangers on elevators if you can help it" and "Don't arrive at parties exactly on time." Similarly, we are often influenced by current and rapidly changing standards of dress, speech, and personal grooming. Regardless of whether social norms are explicit or implicit, one fact is clear: *Most people obey them most of the time.* For example, few persons visit restaurants without leaving a tip for their server. And virtually everyone, regardless of personal political beliefs, stands when the national anthem of their country is played at sports events or other public gatherings.

At first glance, this strong tendency toward conformity—toward going along with society's expectations about how we should behave in various situations—may strike you as objectionable. After all, it does place restrictions on personal freedom, which is an important value in Western societies like the United States (e.g., R. Bond & Smith, 1996). Actually, though, there is a strong basis for the existence of so much conformity: Without it, we would quickly find ourselves facing social chaos. Imagine what would happen outside movie theaters or voting booths or at supermarket checkout counters if people did *not* obey the norm "Form a line and wait your turn." And consider the danger to both drivers and pedestrians if there were not clear and widely followed traffic regulations. In many situations, then, conformity serves a useful function, but this in no way implies that it is always helpful. Some norms governing individual behavior appear to have no obvious purpose; they simply exist. For example, although dress codes have weakened or vanished in recent years, they still prevail in some settings—especially in the business world, where many companies still require that their male employees wear neckties and that their female employees wear skirts or dresses. While such clothing can be attractive, it is often unrelated to performance of various jobs and may be a cause of personal discomfort when temperatures are very high (neckties) or very low (short skirts).

Given that strong pressures toward conformity exist in many social settings, it is surprising to learn that conformity, as a social process, received relatively little attention from social psychologists until the 1950s. At that time Solomon Asch (1951) carried out a series of experiments with dramatic results.

Asch's Line-Judgment Conformity Studies

In his research, Asch asked participants to respond to a series of simple perceptual problems such as the one in Figure 8.2. On each problem they indicated which of three comparison lines matched a standard line in length. Several other persons (usually six to eight) were also present during the session; but, unknown to the real participant, all were accomplices of the experimenter. On certain occasions known as critical trials (twelve out of the eighteen problems) the accomplices offered answers that were clearly wrong: They unanimously chose the wrong line as a match for the standard line. Moreover, they stated their answers before the participant responded. Thus, on these critical trials, the participants faced the type of dilemma described above. Should they go along with the other persons present or stick to their own judgments? A large majority of the participants in Asch's research opted for conformity. Indeed, in several different studies, fully 76 percent of those tested went along with the group's false answers at least once; in fact, they voiced their agreement with these errors about 37 percent of the time. In contrast, only 5 percent of the subjects in a control group, who responded to the same problems in the absence of any accomplices, made such errors.

Of course, there were large individual differences in this respect. Almost 25 percent of the participants *never* yielded to the group pressure. At the other extreme were persons who went along with the majority nearly all the time. When Asch questioned them, some of these persons stated "I am wrong, they are right"; they had little confidence in their own judgment. Others, however, said they felt that the other persons present were the victims of some sort of optical illusion, or were merely sheep following the responses of the first person. Nevertheless, when it was their turn to speak, these participants still went along with the group.

In further studies, Asch (1951, 1956) investigated the effects of shattering the group's unanimity by having one of the accomplices break with the others. In one study, this person gave the correct answer, becoming an "ally" of the real participant; in another, he chose an answer in between the one given by the group and the correct one; and in a third, he chose an answer that was even more incorrect than that chosen by the majority. In the latter two conditions, in other words, he broke from the group but still disagreed with the real participant. Results indicated that conformity was reduced under all three conditions. However, somewhat surprisingly, this reduction was greatest when the dissenting accomplice expressed views even more extreme (and wrong) than the majority. Together, these findings suggest that it is the unanimity of the group that is crucial: It is much easier to resist group pressure when such unanimity is lacking.

There's one more aspect of Asch's research that is important to mention. In later studies, he repeated his basic procedure, but with one important

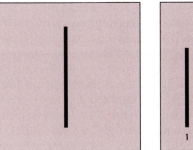

Standard Line

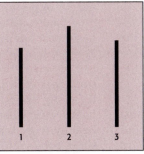

Comparison Lines

FIGURE 8.2 Asch's Line Judgment Task: An Example.

Participants in Asch's research were asked to report their judgments on problems such as this one. On each problem, they indicated which of the comparison lines (1, 2, or 3) best matched the standard line in length.

change: Instead of stating their answers out loud, participants wrote them down on a piece of paper. As you might guess, conformity dropped sharply. This finding points to the importance of distinguishing between *public conformity*—doing or saying what others around us say or do—and *private acceptance*—actually coming to feel or think as others do. Often, it appears, we follow social norms overtly, but don't actually change our private views (Maass & Clark, 1984). This distinction between public conformity and private acceptance is an important one, and we'll have reason to comment on it at several points in this book.

Asch's research was the catalyst for a flurry of activity in social psychology, as many other researchers rushed to investigate the nature of conformity, to identify factors that influence its impact, and to establish its limits (e.g., Crutchfield, 1955; M. Deutsch & Gerard, 1955). Indeed, such research is still continuing today, and is still adding to our understanding of this crucial form of social influence (e.g., Arrow, 1997; W. Wood et al., 1996). We will next discuss what is known about factors that affect the degree of conformity.

Major Factors Affecting Conformity

Asch's research demonstrated the existence of powerful pressures toward conformity. Even a moment's reflection indicates, however, that conformity does not occur to the same degree in all settings. This fact raises an intriguing question: What factors determine the extent to which individuals yield to conformity pressure or resist it? Many variables play a role, but here we'll focus on four that have proven very important: (1) *cohesiveness*—the target person's degree of attraction to the group exerting influence, (2) *group size*—the number of persons exerting social influence, (3) the *need to be accurate*, and (4) the degree to which a person *values individuality*. We consider a fifth possible factor—gender—in the Social Diversity box on pages 202–203.

Cohesiveness and Conformity: Accepting Influence from Those We Like.
Consider the following situation: You move in with a new group of roommates. You knew them slightly before, and liked them—that's

why you accepted their offer to move into their apartment. After you are there for a few weeks, you begin to realize that they hold political views considerably more conservative than your own. They repeatedly state their opposition to various government programs and criticize judges who, in their view, are too lenient toward criminals. Will your own views change as a function of living with these new friends? Perhaps. You may find yourself agreeing with them more and more as time passes.

Now, in contrast, imagine that you have signed up for an evening course in personal self-defense. During these sessions, you hear other members of the class express conservative views about law and order, the right to own guns, and punishment of criminals. Will you be influenced by these statements? Probably not; you may refrain from disagreeing with them openly in order to avoid trouble, but it is unlikely that your private views will change. Why do you react differently in these two contexts—why are your views more likely to be influenced by your roommates than by the strangers in your evening class? One answer involves what social psychologists term **cohesiveness**—your degree of attraction to a group. Clearly, you like your roommates and want to gain their approval and acceptance, but you are more neutral toward the people in your self-defense class. A classic finding of social psychology is that when cohesiveness (attraction) is high, pressures toward conformity are magnified. After all, if you want to be liked and accepted by others, it is best to share their views—or at least to express acceptance of these (that distinction between private acceptance and public conformity again). This is a basic reason why most persons are more willing to accept social influence from friends or persons they admire than from others.

Finally, research has demonstrated that cohesiveness has a powerful impact on compliance. For example, in Chapter 7 we saw that similarity is a powerful force in creating cohesiveness (attraction) in the first place. So strong is the desire to belong that friends tend to adopt each others' habits, even when the habit is undesirable or unhealthy (e.g., binge eating, Crandall, 1988). In short, conformity makes it easier to blend in with our friends (Latané & L'Herrou, 1996).

Need for Accuracy: Using the Group as a Clue to the Nature of Reality. One reason that people conform to groups is that they provide important clues about the nature of reality, especially when the nature of reality is vague. However, the group does not always provide accurate information, as studies using the Asch line-judgment task amply demonstrate. Robert S. Baron (not the Bob Baron whose name appears on the cover of this book), Vandello, and Brunsman (1996) theorized that participants would ignore a group's false judgment when the right answer is clear (e.g., for easy tasks), but go along with a group's judgment when the right answer is difficult (e.g., for complex tasks). However, these researchers further theorized that these patterns would be especially the case when participants had a high need to be accurate about their task. In a clever modification of the Asch line-judgment task, these researchers used a series of eyewitness identification tasks: They showed participants a line-drawing of a person for either a very short period of time (.5 seconds), which made the task difficult, or else for a longer period of time (5 seconds), which made the task easier. Then they presented several persons and asked participants to choose the correct individual from the line-up. This task was then repeated. Two experimental accomplices were trained to give the wrong responses at crucial times, always in agreement. Finally, prior to the study, half of the participants were given a reason to think that the results of the study were not very important; they told the participants that it was a pilot study, and the only reactions of interest were in finding out the optimal conditions to present the slides. This set of instructions resulted in *low task importance* and low need to be accurate. The other half of the participants were asked to try hard to do their accurate best; this set of instructions resulted in *high task importance*.

Results from two studies using these procedures showed the same pattern: As Figure 8.3 shows, participants were much more likely to go along with the group's false judgments when the task was difficult (short viewing time) than when the task was easy (long viewing time), but this pattern held true only when the task was important. These results suggest that the need to be accurate can override erroneous group judgments, but only

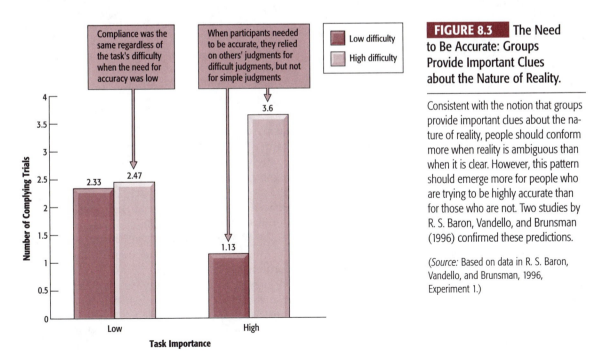

Compliance was the same regardless of the task's difficulty when the need for accuracy was low

When participants needed to be accurate, they relied on others' judgments for difficult judgments, but not for simple judgments

Low difficulty
High difficulty

FIGURE 8.3 The Need to Be Accurate: Groups Provide Important Clues about the Nature of Reality.

Consistent with the notion that groups provide important clues about the nature of reality, people should conform more when reality is ambiguous than when it is clear. However, this pattern should emerge more for people who are trying to be highly accurate than for those who are not. Two studies by R. S. Baron, Vandello, and Brunsman (1996) confirmed these predictions.

(*Source:* Based on data in R. S. Baron, Vandello, and Brunsman, 1996, Experiment 1.)

for easy tasks; for difficult or ambiguous tasks, group influence is powerful indeed. It is under these circumstances that group influence provides powerful clues about the nature of reality.

Conformity and Group Size: Why More Is Better with Respect to Social Influence. In general, the greater the number of individuals who comprise the group trying to influence a person, the more likely it is that the person will go along with the group. Initially, Asch (1956) thought that group influence levels off after about three or four group members, presumably because study participants begin to suspect collusion. However, Bond and Smith (1996) conducted a systematic research synthesis of these studies and found no conformity dip whatsoever for large groups (e.g., 8 or more members); instead, influence increased along with group size. This finding again suggests that the group-based information is a powerful influence on social judgments.

The Degree to Which One Values Individuality. These demonstrations of social influence might lead you to the impression that pressures toward conformity are all but impossible to resist. But take heart: If you recall Asch's research, most of the participants yielded to social pressure, but *only part of the time.* On many occasions they stuck to their own judgments, even in the face of a unanimous disagreeing majority. What accounts for this ability to resist even powerful pressures toward conformity? Research findings point to two key factors.

First, as you probably already realize, most of us have a strong desire to maintain our uniqueness or individuality. We want to be like others, but not to the extent that we lose our personal identity. In other words, along with the needs to be right and to be liked, most of us possess a desire for **individuation**—for being distinguished from others in some respects (e.g., Maslach, Santee, & Wade, 1987). The result is that most people want to be similar to others *generally,* but don't want to be *exactly* like the people around them. In short, they want to hold on to at least a pinch of individuality (e.g., C. R. Snyder & Fromkin, 1980). It is partly because of this mo-

tive that individuals sometimes choose to disagree with others or to act in unusual or even bizarre ways. They realize that such behavior may be costly in terms of gaining the approval or acceptance of others, but their desire to maintain a unique identity is simply stronger than various inducements to conformity.

A second reason why individuals often choose to resist group pressure involves their desire to *maintain control* over the events in their lives (e.g., Burger, 1992; Daubman, 1993). Most persons want to believe that they can determine what happens to them, and yielding to social pressure sometimes runs counter to this desire. After all, going along with a group implies behaving in ways one might not ordinarily choose, which can be interpreted as a restriction of personal freedom and control.

Thus, individuality appears to reduce conformity to others. Intriguingly, this pattern even applies when viewed cross-culturally. Because research on compliance has been conducted since the earliest days of social psychology, there are literally hundreds of studies on compliance. In fact, the research synthesis conducted by Bond and Smith (1996) located 133 studies, from seventeen countries, that used the Asch line-judgment task alone. Because compliance has been examined in such a uniform way across so many different countries and across such a long span of time, Bond and Smith could examine some interesting questions. One question is whether compliance, as gauged by conformity in the line-judgment task (see Figure 8.3), has reduced across time within the United States, perhaps because of changing cultural factors within this country (e.g., social activism in the 1960s, growing emphasis on "being your own person"). Indeed, Bond and Smith discovered that conformity *has* diminished since the 1950s.

A second question that Bond and Smith (1996) addressed is whether conformity varies according to the individualism or collectivism of the country in which the study was conducted. As we discussed in Chapter 7, individualistic societies—most Western nations—place central importance on personal goals. Collectivistic societies—most Asian and African nations—stress group goals.

Bond and Smith obtained judgments of the degree to which the seventeen countries had either individualistic or collectivist orientation. Based on the perspective that members of collectivist societies should place greater value on getting along with others than do members of individualistic societies, Bond and Smith predicted greater conformity in collectivistic countries. As shown in Figure 8.4, their prediction was confirmed. Finally, as the Figure also shows, this pattern held up even in smaller groups, when conformity pressure was lower. Thus, the values that societies induce in their members appear to play an important role in conformity. Other studies have confirmed this pattern using alternative compliance techniques (e.g., V. L. Hamilton & Sanders, 1995). (We will consider another variable that was once assumed to strongly influence conformity—*gender*—in the *Social Diversity* section later in this chapter.)

Why We Often "Go Along"— and What Happens after We Do

As we have just seen, several factors determine whether and to what extent conformity occurs.

Yet the essential point remains: Conformity is a basic fact of social life. Most people conform to the norms of their groups or societies much, if not most, of the time. Why is this so? Why do people often choose to go along with these social rules or expectations instead of resisting them? The answer seems to center primarily on two powerful needs possessed by all human beings— the desire to be liked or accepted by others and the desire to be right (M. Deutsch & Gerard, 1955; Insko, 1984)—plus cognitive processes that lead us to view conformity as fully justified after it has occurred (e.g., Griffin & Buehler, 1993).

The Desire to Be Liked: Normative Social Influence. How can we get others to like us? This is one of the eternal puzzles of social life. As we saw in Chapter 7, many tactics can prove effective in this regard. One of the most successful of these is to appear to be as similar to others as possible. From our earliest days, we learn that agreeing with the persons around us, and behaving as they do, causes them to like us. Parents, teachers, friends, and others often heap praise and approval on us

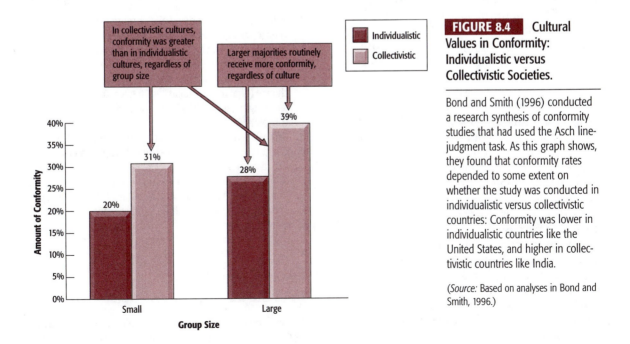

FIGURE 8.4   Cultural Values in Conformity: Individualistic versus Collectivistic Societies.

Bond and Smith (1996) conducted a research synthesis of conformity studies that had used the Asch line-judgment task. As this graph shows, they found that conformity rates depended to some extent on whether the study was conducted in individualistic versus collectivistic countries: Conformity was lower in individualistic countries like the United States, and higher in collectivistic countries like India.

(*Source:* Based on analyses in Bond and Smith, 1996.)

for demonstrating such similarity (see our discussion of attitude formation in Chapter 4). One important reason we conform, therefore, is simple: We have learned that doing so can yield the approval and acceptance we crave. This source of social influence—and especially of conformity—is known as **normative social influence,** since it involves altering our behavior to meet others' expectations.

The Desire to Be Right: Informational Social Influence.
If you want to know your weight, you can step onto a scale. If you want to know the dimensions of a room, you can measure them directly. But how can you establish the accuracy of your own political or social views or decide which hairstyle suits you best? There are no simple physical tests or measuring devices for answering these questions. Yet most of us have just as strong a desire to be correct about such matters as about questions relating to the physical world. The solution is obvious: To answer these questions, we must turn to other people. We use *their* opinions and their actions as guides for our own. Obviously, such reliance on others can be another source of conformity, for in an important sense, other people's actions and opinions define social reality for us. This source of social influence is known as **informational social influence,** since it is based on our tendency to depend upon others as a source of information about many aspects of the social world.

Justifying Conformity: The Cognitive Consequences of Going Along with the Group.
Asch reported that some people who conform do so without any reservations: They conclude that they are wrong and the others are right. For these people, conforming poses only a very temporary dilemma, at most. But for many persons, the decision to yield to group pressure and do as others do is more complex. Such persons feel that their own judgment is correct, but at the same time they don't want to be different; so they behave in ways that are inconsistent with their private beliefs. What are the effects of conformity on such persons? Recent findings (e.g., Griffin & Buehler, 1993; Buehler & Griffin, 1994) suggest that one may involve a tendency to alter their perceptions

of the situation so that conformity appears, in fact, to be justified. As John Kenneth Galbraith stated, "Faced with the choice between changing one's mind and proving that there is no need to do so, almost everyone gets busy on the proof!" (cited in Buehler & Griffin, 1994, p. 993).

Several studies suggest that the decision to conform may be followed by changes in perceptions of the facts—changes that tend to justify conformity (Griffin & Buehler, 1993; Buehler & Griffin, 1994). It is interesting to speculate on whether this pattern would be equally true in all cultures. In cultures such as that of the United States, which value individual choice backed by rational analysis, it is not surprising that such effects occur: People feel the need to explain why they conformed. In cultures that place greater value on group judgments and on avoiding actions that rock the social boat, however, the pressure toward such cognitive justification may be weaker (R. Bond & Smith, 1996). As noted by Buehler and Griffin (1994), this is an intriguing issue for further study.

Integrating Principles

1. Social influence—efforts by one or more persons to change the attitudes, behaviors, or perceptions of one or more others—is a very common and important form of social behavior. As such, it plays a key role in many other forms of social behavior, including attitude formation and change (Chapter 5), prejudice (Chapter 6), helping (Chapter 9), aggression (Chapter 9), and group decision making (Chapter 10).
2. Our willingness to conform stems from several basic social motives, including the desire to be right and the desire to be liked. These motives play a role in other forms of social behavior, too. For example, the desire to be liked is important in many relationships (Chapter 7) and underlies at least some efforts at impression management (Chapter 2).

Minority Influence: Does the Majority Always Rule?

As we have just noted, individuals can—and often do—resist group pressure. Lone dissenters or small minorities can dig in their heels and refuse to go along. Yet there is more to the story; in addition, there are cases in which such persons or groups can turn the tables on the majority and exert rather than merely receive social influence. History provides numerous examples of such events. Many giants of the scientific world—Galileo, Pasteur, Freud—faced virtually unanimous majorities who rejected their views in harsh terms. Yet over time, they won growing numbers of colleagues to their side, until ultimately their views prevailed. More recent examples of minorities influencing majorities are provided by the successes of environmentalists. Initially, such persons were viewed as wild-eyed radicals operating at the fringes of society. Over time, however, they have succeeded in changing strongly held attitudes and laws so that society itself has been altered through their efforts.

When do minorities succeed in exerting social influence on majorities? Research findings suggest that they are most likely to succeed under certain conditions (Moscovici, 1985). First, the members of such groups must be *consistent* in their opposition to majority opinions. If they waffle or show signs of yielding to the majority view, their impact is reduced. Second, members of the minority must avoid appearing to be rigid and dogmatic (Mugny, 1975). A minority that merely repeats the same position over and over again is less persuasive than one that demonstrates a degree of flexibility. Third, the general social context in which a minority operates is important. If a minority argues for a position that is consistent with current social trends (e.g., conservative views at a time of growing conservatism), its chances of influencing the majority are greater than if it argues for a position that is out of step with such trends.

Of course, even when minorities are consistent, flexible, and in line with current social trends, they face a tough uphill struggle. The power of majorities is great, partly because, in ambiguous or complex social situations, people view majorities as providing more information about correctness—in other words, majorities function as an important source of both informational and normative social influence (W. Wood et al., 1996). Why, then, are minorities sometimes able to get their message across?

One possibility is that when people are confronted with a minority stating views they don't initially accept, they are puzzled, and exert cognitive effort to understand why these people hold these views and why they are willing to depart so visibly from widely accepted views (Nemeth, 1995; Vonk & van Knippenburg, 1995). Similarly, individuals exposed to minority views may devote more, or more careful, scrutiny to the minority's ideas, a conclusion that studies have consistently supported (e.g., C. M. Smith, Tindale, & Dugoni, 1996; W. Wood et al., 1996).

A study by Zdaniuk and Levine (1996) provides some intriguing evidence about the nature of minority influence. These investigators led their college participants to believe that they were members of either a majority or minority faction in a group that was given the task of reaching a consensus on a controversial issue: Whether their university should require their graduating seniors to pass a comprehensive examination in their major area of concentration. After participants gave their initial opinions about this proposal (and, of course, most were solidly opposed to it!), Zdaniuk and Levine gave each participant information about the five other individuals with whom they would try to reach consensus. Some individuals were told that four of the five agreed with their perspective; in this case, the participant was part of a strong majority. Others were told that three of the five agreed, two of the five, or only one of the five agreed. In this last case, the participant was part of a distinct minority. The researchers then asked each study participant to rate how much pressure they would face in their group discussion, how likely they thought the proposal was to be adopted, and to write down their initial thoughts about the proposal. This latter task allowed the researchers to determine how the individuals prepared themselves to discuss the issue with others.

Zdaniuk and Levine predicted that group pressure would be greatest when there were more opposing members and that this pressure would increase the number of thoughts that participants would generate opposing the proposal—in preparation for a fierce debate, no doubt. As Figure 8.5 shows, these are exactly the patterns that emerged. Participants who were in majority factions tended to perceive very little pressure and very few opposing thoughts. Participants who were in the minority factions tended to develop more thoughts opposing the proposal. Moreover, participants in majority factions were very likely to think that the proposal would be adopted by the university. Note that these results occurred in the absence of any actual group discussions. Thus, these findings suggest that the *mere anticipation* of having to exert minority influence is sufficient to increase the creativity of thinking.

During actual group debates, it is possible that minorities lead individuals to consider ideas and alternatives they would otherwise have ig-

nored. Would large numbers of people have paid any attention to the hole in the ozone layer or the possibility of the greenhouse effect during the 1980s and 1990s if vocal minorities had not started them thinking about environmental issues during preceding decades? It seems unlikely. So, in sum, even when minorities fail to sway majorities initially, they may initiate processes that lead to eventual social change, which numerous studies have supported (e.g., Alvaro & Crano, 1996). In this sense, as well as in several others, there is much truth to Franklin Roosevelt's remark that "No democracy can long survive which does not accept as fundamental to its very existence the recognition of the rights of minorities" (June 15, 1938).

FIGURE 8.5   How Minority Group Members Prepare Themselves to Influence Others.

When people expect that they will have to defend a position with which the majority disagrees, they anticipate a great deal of pressure from the other group members (left-hand graph) and therefore are more likely to develop arguments that oppose the majority's position (right-hand graph).

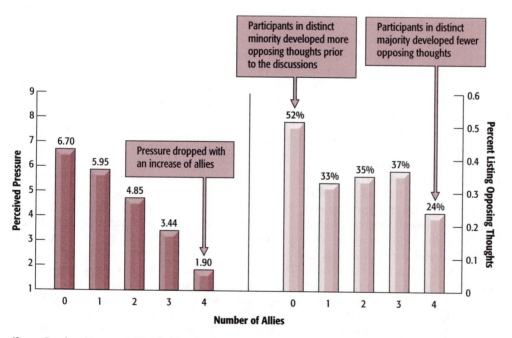

(*Source:* Based on data presented by Zdaniuk and Levine, 1996.)

Compliance: To Ask— Sometimes—Is to Receive

Suppose that you wanted someone to do something for you: How would you go about getting them to do it? If you think about this question for a moment, you'll quickly realize that you—like me!—have quite a few tricks up your sleeve for gaining *compliance*—for inducing others to say yes to your requests. What are these techniques like? Which ones work best—and when? These are among the basic questions studied by social psychologists in their efforts to understand this, the most frequent form of social influence. In the discussion that follows, we'll examine a number of different tactics for gaining compliance. Before turning to these, however, let's briefly examine one basic framework for understanding all of these procedures.

Compliance: The Underlying Principles

Some years ago, Robert Cialdini, a well-known social psychologist, decided that the best way to find out about compliance was to study what he termed *compliance professionals*—people whose success (financial or otherwise) depends on their ability to get others to say yes. Who are such persons? They include salespeople, advertisers, political lobbyists, fund-raisers, con artists and—one might argue—trial attorneys, professional negotiators, and politicians. Cialdini's technique for learning from these people was straightforward: He temporarily concealed his true identity and took jobs in various settings where seeking compliance is a way of life. In other words, he worked in advertising, direct (door-to-door) sales, fund-raising organizations, and other settings. On the basis of these firsthand experiences, he concluded that although techniques for gaining compliance take many different forms, they all rest to some degree on six basic principles (Cialdini, 1994):

Friendship/Liking: In general, we are more willing to comply with requests from friends or from people we like than with requests from strangers or people we don't like.

Commitment/Consistency: Once we have committed ourselves to a position or action, we are more willing to comply with requests for behaviors that are consistent with that position. We generally want to behave in a consistent manner, so once we are committed to a position or view, we try to say or do things that fit with it in various ways.

Scarcity: In general, we value, and try to secure, opportunities that are scarce or decreasing. As a result, we are more likely to comply with requests that focus on "disappearing opportunities" than on ones that make no reference to such changes.

Reciprocity: We are generally more willing to comply with a request from someone who has previously provided a favor or concession to *us* than to someone who has not. In other words, we feel obligated to pay people back in some way for what they have done for us.

Social Validation: We are generally more willing to comply with a request for some action if this action is consistent with what we believe persons similar to ourselves are doing (or thinking). We want to be correct, and one way to do so is to act and think like others.

Authority: We value authority, so we are usually more willing to comply with requests from someone who is a legitimate authority—or simply looks like one.

According to Cialdini (1994), these basic principles underlie many techniques professionals use for gaining compliance. We'll now examine specific techniques based on these principles, plus a few others as well.

Tactics Based on Friendship or Liking

We've already considered several techniques for increasing compliance through liking in our discussion of *impression management* (Chapter 2). As you may recall, impression management involves various procedures for making a good impression on others. While this can be an end in itself, impression management techniques are often used for purposes of **ingratiation:** getting others to like us so that they will be more willing to agree to our requests (E. E. Jones, 1964).

What ingratiation techniques are effective? Virtually all of the ones we described in Chapter 2. Under the heading of *self-enhancing tactics* are such procedures as improving one's appearance, emitting many positive nonverbal cues (e.g., smiling, a high level of eye contact), and associating oneself with positive events or people the target person already likes. In contrast, *other-enhancing tactics* include flattery, agreeing with target persons, showing interest in them, and providing them small gifts or favors. Research findings indicate that all of these tactics can be successful, at least to a degree, in increasing others' liking for us (e.g., Gordon, 1996; Wayne & Liden, 1995). And increased liking, in turn, can lead to greater compliance.

Tactics Based on Commitment or Consistency

As observed by Cialdini (1994), experts in compliance—salespersons, advertisers, fundraisers—often start their campaigns for gaining compliance with a trivial request. For example, a salesperson may ask potential customers to accept a free sample or to answer a few questions about products they use. Only after these small requests are granted do the experts move on to the requests they really want—ones that can prove quite costly to the target persons. In all such instances, the basic strategy is much the same: Somehow induce another person to comply with a small initial request and thereby increase the chances that he or she will agree to a much larger one. What is the basic idea behind this technique—which is often known as the **foot-in-the-door technique**? The desire to be *consistent*. Once the target person agrees to the small request, it is more difficult for that person to disagree to a larger, subsequent request, because doing so would be somewhat inconsistent

with the first response. It's almost as if by saying "yes" to the small request, the target has indicated that "I'm a helpful person who does try to help others." Refusing the second request is inconsistent with this flattering self-perception, so the pressure is on to agree to the second, larger request.

The results of many studies indicate both that the foot-in-the-door technique really works (e.g., Beaman et al., 1983) and that its effectiveness stems, at least in part, from the operation of the consistency principle. Additional evidence suggests that the technique may work because people wish to gain social approval (to look good by complying with the second request), or to do what we think everyone else is doing (Gorassini & Olson, 1995).

Another technique based on the consistency/commitment principle is the **lowball procedure.** In this technique, which is often used by automobile salespersons, a great deal is offered to a customer. After the customer accepts, however, something happens that makes it necessary for the salesperson to change the deal and make it less advantageous for the customer—for example, an "error" in price calculations is found, or the sales manager rejects the deal. The totally rational reaction for customers, of course, is to walk away. Yet often they agree to the changes and accept the less desirable arrangement.

Such informal observations have been confirmed by carefully conducted studies. In one, for example, students first agreed to participate in a psychology experiment (Cialdini et al., 1978). Only after making this commitment did they learn that it started at 7:00 A.M. Despite the inconvenience of this early hour, however, almost all persons in this *lowball* condition appeared for their appointments. As you can probably guess, a much lower proportion of students who learned in advance about the 7:00 A.M. starting time agreed to take part in the study. In instances such as this, an initial commitment seems to make it more difficult for individuals to say no, even though the conditions under which they said yes are now changed.

In sum, these tactics for gaining compliance take full advantage of our desire to be consistent and to stick to initial commitments. So beware of situations in which you are asked to do something trivial, or are asked to make a commitment to a course of action early on: In such cases, the persons with whom you are dealing may be laying the groundwork for something entirely different.

Tactics Based on Reciprocity

Reciprocity is a basic rule of social life. When someone does something for us, we generally feel an obligation to do something for them in return. While these feelings make a great deal of sense and are viewed by most persons as being only fair and just, the principle of reciprocity also serves as the basis for several important techniques for gaining compliance. One of these is, on the face of it, the opposite of the foot-in-the-door technique: Instead of beginning with a small request and then escalating to a larger one, persons seeking compliance sometimes start with a very large request and then, after this is rejected, shift to a smaller request—the one they wanted all along (see Figure 8.6). This tactic is known as the **door-in-the-face technique** (because the first refusal seems to slam the door in the face of the requester), and several studies indicate that it can be quite effective. For example, in one well-known experiment, Cialdini and his colleagues (1975) stopped college students on the street and presented a huge request: Would the students serve as unpaid counselors for juvenile delinquents two hours a week for the next *two years*? As you can guess, none agreed. When the experimenters then scaled down their request to a much smaller one—would the same students take a group of delinquents on a two-hour trip to the zoo—fully 50 percent agreed. In contrast, less than 17 percent of those in a control group agreed to this smaller request when it was presented cold, rather than after the larger request.

The same tactic is often used by negotiators, who may begin with a position that is extremely advantageous to themselves but then back down to a position much closer to the one they really hope to obtain. Similarly, sellers often begin with a price they know that buyers will reject, and then lower the price to a more reasonable one—but one that is still quite favorable to themselves. In all these cases, the persons using the door-in-the-face tactic appear to make a concession after their first request or proposal is rejected; then target persons feel obligated to make a matching concession in return—a concession that may end up giving the requester what she or he wanted all along.

A related procedure is known as the **that's-not-all technique.** Here, an initial request is followed, before the target person can make up

---

FIGURE 8.6   The Door in the Face: An Example.

Mr. Dithers is using the door-in-the-face technique: He starts with relatively large requests and, when these are rejected, moves to the one he wanted all along. But Dagwood is aware of what he's doing, and this may reduce this tactic's effectiveness.

(*Source:* Reprinted with special permission of King Features Syndicate.)

her or his mind to say yes or no, by something that sweetens the deal—a small extra incentive from the person using this tactic. For example, auto dealers sometimes decide to throw in a small additional option to the car in the hope that this will help them close the deal; and often, it really does! Persons on the receiving end of the that's-not-all technique view this small extra as a concession on the part of the other person, and so feel obligated to make a concession themselves. Several studies indicate that this technique, too, really works: Throwing in a small "extra" before people can say no does indeed increase the likelihood that they will say yes (e.g., Burger, 1986).

Tactics Based on Scarcity

It's a general rule of life that things that are scarce, rare, or difficult to possess are viewed as being more valuable than those that are easy to obtain. Thus, we are often willing to expend more effort, or go to greater expense, to obtain items or outcomes that are scarce than to obtain ones that are common. This principle, too, serves as the basis for several techniques for gaining compliance. One of the most intriguing of these is **playing hard to get.**

Many people know that this can be an effective tactic in the area of personal romance: By suggesting that it is difficult to win their affections or that there are many competitors for their love, they can greatly increase their desirability (e.g., Walster, Walster, Piliavin, & Schmidt, 1973). This tactic is not restricted to interpersonal attraction, however; research findings indicate that it is also sometimes used by job candidates to increase their attractiveness to potential employers, and hence to increase the likelihood that the employers will offer them a job. For example, the hard-to-get job candidates are rated more favorably than the easy-to-get candidates, especially when they are also highly qualified (Williams et al., 1993).

A related technique based on the same "what's-scarce-is-valuable" principle is one frequently used by retailers. Ads using this **deadline technique** state a specific time limit during which an item can be purchased for a specific

price. After the deadline runs out, the ads suggest, the price will go up. Of course, in many cases the sale is not a real one, and the time limit is bogus. Yet many persons reading such ads believe them and hurry down to the store in order to avoid missing out on a great opportunity. I encountered this recently myself, when ads proclaiming "Closeout of Winter Merchandise" in several major department stores appeared in our local newspaper. When I questioned salesclerks, they confirmed the claims in the ads: winter merchandise would be removed from the stores to make way for spring fashions when the sale ended. However, a week after the proclaimed deadline, the sale was still going on in several of the stores that ran these ads. So when you encounter an offer that suggests that "the clock is ticking," be cautious: it may be based more on good sales techniques than on reality.

Mindlessness and the Pique Technique

The techniques described by Cialdini (1994) seem to work optimally under certain conditions. To illustrate, quick: What's your typical reaction to panhandlers, or even to people soliciting funds for charitable organizations? If you are like most individuals, you probably look away, avoid eye contact with these persons, and don't even think about responding favorably to their requests. Is this because you are hard-hearted and callous? Not at all. Many social psychologists would offer a kinder interpretation of your actions in such situations: You ignore these requesters because you are operating on "automatic pilot"—you are following an automatic refusal script. This interpretation relates to a basic fact about social thought we mentioned in Chapter 3: In general, people follow the path of least resistance in social cognition, just as they do in many other areas of life. And where compliance is concerned, we are faced with so many requests each day that we tend to react to such requests—especially when they come from strangers—in a non-thinking, automatic manner. We reject such requests in an automatic manner because we don't want to bother thinking about them. Social psychologists refer to our actions in such cases as "mindless," to reflect the fact that we are proceeding with a minimum of cognitive effort or thought (Langer, Blank, & Chanowitz, 1978).

If our tendency to ignore many requests from strangers is indeed due to such "mindlessness" (or to automatic refusal scripts that we follow), then anything that shocks people out of this "mindless" state and gets them to think about a request, might increase compliance with it. This reasoning is the basis for the **pique technique**—a procedure for increasing compliance based on *piquing* (stimulating) target persons' interest. Evidence that the *pique technique* really works is provided by several studies (e.g., Langer et al., 1978). Recently, for example, Santos, Leve, and Pratkanis (1994) conducted an experiment in which female accomplices played the role of panhandlers and asked passersby for money. In two standard conditions not expected to pique interest, they asked, "Can you spare any change?" or "Can you spare a quarter?" In two other pique conditions, in contrast, they made unusual requests: "Can you spare 17 cents?" or "Can you spare 37 cents?" As you can see from Figure 8.7, the pique technique was quite effective: A higher proportion of passersby donated in the pique conditions than in the nonpique control groups.

Integrating Principles

1. There are many different techniques for increasing the likelihood that others will comply. Many of these tactics are based on fundamental principles of social behavior, such as *reciprocity, the desire to be consistent,* and *liking* or *friendship.*
2. These principles also play an important role in other forms of social behavior. For example, we tend to like persons who like us (Chapter 7) and to aggress against others who have aggressed against us (Chapter 9). Similarly, we sometimes change our own attitudes because we want them to be consistent with other attitudes we hold or with our overt behavior (Chapter 5).

Obedience: Social Influence by Demand

In discussing compliance, we noted that often, we are more willing to agree to requests from persons with *authority*—persons whose position in an organization or social system seems to

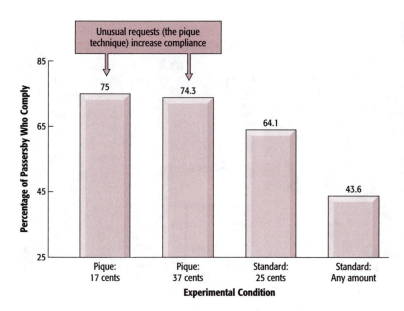

FIGURE 8.7   The Pique Technique in Operation.

Passersby were more likely to give money to a panhandler when she asked for an unusual amount of money (17 cents or 37 cents) than when she made a more standard appeal for funds. This happened because the unusual nature of the request prevented potential donors from refusing the request in an automatic "mindless" manner.

(*Source:* Based on data from Santos, Leve, & Pratkanis, 1994.)

Figure content:

Unusual requests (the pique technique) increase compliance

Percentage of Passersby Who Comply

- Pique: 17 cents — 75
- Pique: 37 cents — 74.3
- Standard: 25 cents — 64.1
- Standard: Any amount — 43.6

Experimental Condition

give them the right to make such requests—than to requests from persons lacking in authority. This principle also underlies another major form of social influence: obedience. Obedience occurs when people obey commands or orders from others to do something. Obedience is less frequent than conformity or compliance, because even persons who possess authority and power generally prefer to exert it through the *velvet glove*—through requests rather than direct orders (e.g., Yukl & Falbe, 1991). Still, obedience is far from rare. Business executives sometimes issue orders to their subordinates; military officers shout commands that they expect to be followed without question; and parents, police officers, and sports coaches, to name just a few, seek to influence others in the same manner. Obedience to the commands of persons who possess authority is far from surprising; they usually have some means of enforcing their orders. More surprising is the fact that often, persons lacking in such power can also induce high levels of submission from others. The clearest and most dramatic evidence for the occurrence of such effects was reported by Stanley Milgram in a series of famous—and controversial—studies (Milgram, 1974).

Milgram's Obedience Studies

In his research, Milgram wished to learn whether individuals would obey commands from a relatively powerless stranger requiring them to inflict what seemed to be considerable pain on another person—a totally innocent stranger. Milgram's interest in this topic derived from the occurrence of tragic events in which seemingly normal, law-abiding persons actually obeyed such directives. For example, during World War II, troops in the German army frequently obeyed commands to torture and murder unarmed civilians—millions of them. In fact, the Nazis established horrible but highly efficient death camps designed to eradicate Jews, Gypsies, and other groups they felt were inferior or a threat to their own racial purity (see Figure 8.8). In the United States these events—known as the *holocaust*—are depicted in a new

---

FIGURE 8.8   The Holocaust: Destructive Obedience Carried to the Extreme.

During World War Two, the Nazis established death camps where soldiers and even prisoners obeyed commands to systematically murder millions of innocent victims. These tragic events are the focus of a new museum in Washington, D.C.

museum that is part of the famous Smithsonian Institution.

In an effort to gain insights into the nature of such events, Milgram designed an ingenious, if unsettling, laboratory simulation. The experimenter informed participants in the study (all males) that they were taking part in an investigation of the effects of punishment on learning. Of each pair of participants, one would serve as a "learner," and would try to perform a simple task in which the learner would supply the second word in pairs of words after hearing the first. The other, the "teacher," would read these words and would punish errors by means of electric shock, delivered by the device shown in Figure 8.9. This apparatus contained thirty numbered switches, with the first labeled "15 volts," the second "30 volts," and so on, up to 450 volts. The two persons present—a real participant and an accomplice— then drew slips of paper from a hat to determine who would play each role; as you can probably guess, the drawing was fixed so that the real participant always became the teacher. The teacher was then instructed to deliver a shock to the learner each time he made an error on the task. Moreover—and this is crucial—teachers were instructed to *increase the strength of the shock each time the learner made an error*. This meant that a learner who made many errors would receive strong jolts of electricity. It's important to note that this was bogus information: In reality, the accomplice (the learner) *never received any shocks* during the experiment. The only real shock ever used was a mild demonstration pulse from button number three to convince participants that the equipment was real.

During the session, the learner (following prearranged instructions) made many errors. Thus, participants soon found themselves facing a dilemma: Should they continue punishing this person with what seemed to be increasingly painful shocks? Or should they refuse to go on? If they hesitated, the experimenter pressured them to continue with a series of graded prods presented one after the other: "Please continue"; "The experiment requires that you continue"; "It is absolutely essential that you continue"; "You have no other choice; you *must* go on."

FIGURE 8.9   Studying Obedience in the Laboratory.

The left-hand photo shows the apparatus Stanley Milgram used in his famous experiments on obedience. (It has recently been displayed in a special exhibit at the Smithsonian Institution in Washington, D.C.) The right photo shows the experimenter (right front) and a participant (rear) attaching electrodes to the learner's (accomplice's) wrist.

(*Source:* From the film *Obedience,* distributed by the New York University Film Library, Copyright 1965 by Stanley Milgram. Reprinted by permission of the copyright holder.)

Since participants were all volunteers and were paid in advance, you might predict that most would quickly refuse the experimenter's orders. In reality, though, fully *65 percent showed total obedience*—they proceeded through the entire series to the final 450-volt level. In contrast, persons in a control group who were not given such commands generally used only very mild shocks during the session. Many participants, of course, protested and asked that the session be ended. When ordered to proceed, however, a majority yielded to the experimenter's influence and continued to obey. Indeed, they continued doing so even when the victim pounded on the wall as if in protest against the painful shocks (at the 300-volt level), and then *no longer responded*. The experimenter told participants to treat failures to answer as errors; so from this point on, "teachers" believed that they were actually delivering dangerous shocks to someone who might, perhaps, be unconscious!

In further experiments, Milgram (1974) found that similar results could be obtained even under conditions that might be expected to reduce such obedience. When the study was moved from its original location on the campus of Yale University to a run-down office building in a nearby city, participants' level of obedience remained virtually unchanged. Similarly, a large proportion continued to obey even when the accomplice complained about the painfulness of the shocks and begged to be released. Most surprising of all, many (about 30 percent) obeyed even when they were required to grasp the victim's hand and force it down upon a metal shock plate! That these chilling results are not restricted to a single culture is indicated by the fact that similar findings were soon reported in studies conducted in several different countries (e.g., Jordan, Germany, Australia) and with children as well as adults (e.g., Kilham & Mann, 1974; Shanab & Yahya, 1977). Thus, Milgram's findings seemed to be alarmingly general in scope.

I (Bob Baron) went to high school with Milgram's niece, and I can remember the shock with which students in my class reacted when she told us about her uncle's findings, several years before they were published. Yet I was dis-

mayed again when, as a college student, I read the actual report of his study. Psychologists, too, found Milgram's findings highly unsettling (Elms, 1995). On the one hand, many wondered whether it was appropriate to conduct such research; many participants experienced extreme stress when confronted with the dilemma of either harming an innocent stranger or disobeying an authority figure. Milgram conducted a complete and thorough debriefing after each session; but still, important ethical issues remained that could not be readily dismissed. On the other hand, psychologists were shaken by the actual results: Milgram's studies seemed to suggest that ordinary people are willing, albeit with some reluctance, to harm an innocent stranger if ordered to do so by someone in authority. An important question remained: Why does such destructive obedience occur?

Destructive Obedience: Its Social Psychological Basis

One reason why the results reported by Milgram are so disturbing is that they seem to parallel many real-life events involving atrocities against innocent victims (for example, the willingness of Chinese troops to fire on unarmed civilians during the Tiananmen Square demonstrations in 1989; the willingness of Saddam Hussein's troops to murder unarmed citizens of their own country). Why does such *destructive obedience* occur? Why were subjects in these experiments—and many persons in tragic situations outside the laboratory—so willing to yield to this powerful form of social influence? Several factors appear to play a role.

First, in many situations, the persons in authority relieve those who obey of the responsibility for their own actions. "I was only carrying out orders" is the defense many offer after obeying harsh or cruel directions. In life situations this transfer of responsibility may be implicit. In Milgram's experiments, in contrast, it was explicit. Participants were told at the start that the experimenter (the authority figure), not they, would be responsible for the learner's well-being.

In view of this fact, it is not surprising that many tended to obey; after all, they were completely off the hook (Darley, 1995; Meeus & Raaijmakers, 1995).

Second, persons in authority often possess visible badges or signs of their status. These consist of special uniforms, insignia, titles, and similar symbols. Faced with such obvious reminders of who's in charge, most people find it difficult to resist (e.g., Bushman, 1988; Darley, 1995).

A third reason for obedience in many situations where the targets of such influence might resist involves the gradual escalation of the authority figure's orders. Initial commands call for relatively innocuous actions. Only later do directives increase in scope and come to require behavior that is dangerous or objectionable. For example, police or military personnel may at first be ordered to question, threaten, or arrest potential victims. Gradually, demands are increased to the point where these personnel are commanded to beat, torture, or even kill unarmed civilians. In a similar manner, participants in the laboratory research on obedience were first required to deliver only mild and harmless shocks to the victim. Only as this person continued to make errors on the learning task did the intensity of punishments rise to harmful levels.

Finally, events in many situations involving destructive obedience move very quickly: Demonstrations become riots, or arrests become mass beatings—or murder—suddenly. The fast pace of such events gives participants little time for reflection: People are ordered to obey and—almost automatically—they do so. Such conditions prevailed in Milgram's research; within a few minutes of entering the laboratory, participants were faced with commands to deliver strong electric shocks to the learner. This fast pace, too, operates to increase obedience.

In sum, several factors contribute to the high levels of obedience witnessed in laboratory studies and in a wide range of real-life contexts. Together, these pressures merge into a powerful force—one that many persons find difficult to resist. Unfortunately, the consequences of this compelling form of social influence can be disastrous for innocent and largely defenseless victims.

Resisting Destructive Obedience

Now that we have considered some of the factors responsible for the strong tendency to obey sources of authority, we will turn to a related question: How can this type of social influence be resisted? Several strategies seem to help to reduce tendencies to obey.

First, individuals exposed to commands from authority figures can be reminded that they—not the authorities—are responsible for any harm produced. Under these conditions sharp reductions in the tendency to obey have been observed (e.g., G. V. Hamilton, 1978; Kilham & Mann, 1974).

Second, individuals can be provided with a clear indication that beyond some point, total submission to destructive commands is inappropriate. One procedure that is highly effective in this regard involves exposing individuals to the actions of *disobedient models*—persons who refuse to obey an authority figure's commands. Research findings indicate that such models can greatly reduce unquestioning obedience (e.g., Rochat & Modigliani, 1995).

Third, individuals may find it easier to resist influence from authority figures if they question the expertise and motives of these figures (Modigliani & Rochat, 1995). Are authority figures really in a better position to judge what is appropriate and what is not? What motives lie behind their commands—socially beneficial goals or selfish gains? By asking such questions, persons who might otherwise obey may find support for independence rather than submission.

Finally, simply knowing about the power of authority figures to command blind obedience may be helpful in itself. Some research findings (e.g., S. J. Sherman, 1980) suggest that when individuals learn about the results of social psychological research, they sometimes change their behavior to take account of this new knowledge. With respect to destructive obedience, there is some hope that knowing about this process can enhance individuals' ability to resist. To the extent this is so, then even exposure to findings as disturbing as those reported by Milgram can have positive social value. As they become widely known, they may produce desirable shifts within society.

Social Diversity: A Critical Analysis

Gender Differences in Social Influence: More Apparent Than Real

Suppose that you approached one hundred people at random in some public place (e.g., a large shopping mall) and asked them the following question: "Do women and men differ in their tendencies to conform or accept social influence from others?" What would you find? Even today, the chances are good that a majority of individuals would suggest that females are higher in conformity than males. In support of this supposed difference, such persons might note that women are more likely than men to follow changing fashions, and that women are more concerned with being liked or being pleasing to others. In short, they would call attention to contrasting gender-role stereotypes for females and males.

Are such views accurate? Are women really more susceptible to conformity pressure or to other forms of social influence than men? Early studies on this issue seemed to indicate that they are (e.g., Crutchfield, 1955). The results of these investigations indicated that women yielded more to social pressure than men. More recent studies, however, point to very different conclusions (e.g., Eagly & Carli, 1981). They suggest that, in fact, there are no significant differences between males and females in this respect, at least in most situations. Why did the findings of these two groups of studies differ so sharply? Several factors may have played a role.

One of these involves the nature of the tasks and materials used in the early experiments (those conducted in the 1950s and 1960s). In many of these studies, the tasks employed were ones more familiar to males than to females. Since individuals of both genders yield more readily to social influence when they are uncertain about how to behave than when they are more confident, it is hardly surprising that females demonstrated higher levels of conformity. After all, the dice were strongly loaded against them.

Another reason for the disagreement between early and more recent studies involves major shifts in gender roles and gender-role stereotypes during the 1970s and 1980s (Steffen & Eagly, 1985). An ever increasing number of women have moved into jobs and fields once occupied solely by men; and stereotypes suggesting that women are less ambitious, less competent, and less independent than males have weakened. It seems reasonable to suggest that one result of such changes has been a fading of any tendency for females either to be, or simply to be perceived as being, more susceptible to social influence than males (Maupin & Fisher, 1989).

A Possible Exception to the "No Difference" Rule: Judgments of Physical Attractiveness

While females and males do not appear to differ in overall susceptibility to social influence, this does not mean that they may not differ in this respect in some situations. In fact, research findings indicate that modest gender differences in susceptibility to social influence may exist with respect to one specific kind of judgment—ratings of others' physical attractiveness. For example, in a series of studies on this issue, Graziano and his colleagues (1993), asked male and female students to rate the attractiveness of opposite-sex strangers shown in photographs. The strangers had previously been rated as being average in attractiveness; but before making their own ratings, participants in the study received information suggesting that other students had rated the persons in some of the photos as attractive and other as unattractive. For other photos no ratings were provided, so these served as no–social influence (control) stimuli. Results indicated that males' judgments of the attractiveness of female strangers were not significantly affected by the ratings supposedly provided by other persons. In contrast, females' ratings of males were influenced by information indicating that these persons had been rated as unattractive by other women (see Figure 8.10). Similar results were found in additional studies, so these results appeared to be quite stable.

What accounts for this difference? Graziano and his colleagues (1993) suggest that it may stem, at least to some degree, from the fact that men base their judgments of attractiveness largely on observable physical characteristics while women base such judgments on such characteristics *plus* information about behavioral dispositions, especially ones relevant to a man's being a cooperative, responsible parent and provider (Jensen-Campbell et al, 1995). Since such traits are hard to see in a photo, there would be good reason for females to pay attention to—and be influenced by—the judgments of other women

with respect to males' attractiveness. As you can see, this reasoning is related to the *evolutionary perspective* we discussed in previous chapters, which contends that in the realm of mate selection, females tend to place greater emphasis on such various traits or characteristics (for example, *dominance* and *status*), while males place greater emphasis on physical traits such youth and physical beauty (Kenrick et al., 1994). Regardless of the precise basis for the findings reported by Graziano and his colleagues, however, they call attention to the fact that while males and females do not differ in susceptibility to social influence across many situations, such differences may exist in a few restricted instances. Overall, however, our basic conclusion remains the same: With few if any exceptions, there are no important differences between females and males in terms of susceptibility to social influence.

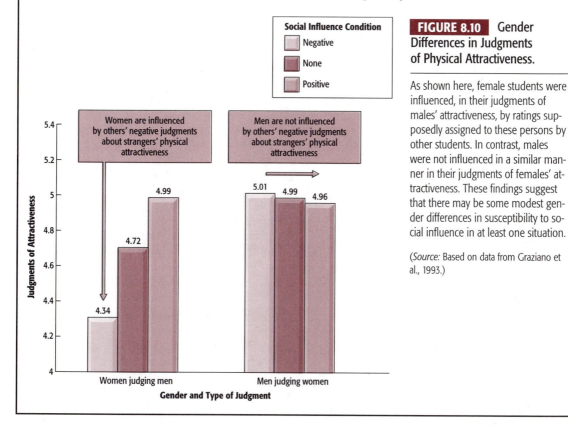

Social Influence Condition
- Negative
- None
- Positive

FIGURE 8.10 Gender Differences in Judgments of Physical Attractiveness.

As shown here, female students were influenced, in their judgments of males' attractiveness, by ratings supposedly assigned to these persons by other students. In contrast, males were not influenced in a similar manner in their judgments of females' attractiveness. These findings suggest that there may be some modest gender differences in susceptibility to social influence in at least one situation.

(*Source:* Based on data from Graziano et al., 1993.)

Women are influenced by others' negative judgments about strangers' physical attractiveness

Men are not influenced by others' negative judgments about strangers' physical attractiveness

4.99
4.72
4.34

5.01 4.99 4.96

Judgments of Attractiveness

Women judging men   Men judging women

Gender and Type of Judgment

To conclude: The power of authority figures to command obedience is certainly great, but it is definitely *not* irresistible. Under appropriate conditions, it *can* be countered or reduced. As in many other areas of life, there *is* a choice. Deciding to resist the commands of persons in authority can, of course, be highly dangerous. Those holding power have tremendous advantages in terms of weapons and other resources. Yet, as events in Russia, Eastern Europe, and elsewhere in the late 1980s and 1990s indicate, the outcome is by no means certain when committed groups of citizens choose to resist. Ultimately, victory may go to those on the side of freedom and decency rather than to those who possess the guns and tanks and who wish to control and repress their fellow citizens.

Connections   Integrating Social Psychology

In this chapter, you read about . . .

- the role of social norms in conformity

- the basic principles underlying many different techniques for gaining compliance

- obedience to the commands of authority figures

In other chapters, you will find related discussions of . . .

- the role of social norms in attraction (Chapter 7), helping (Chapter 9), aggression (Chapter 9), and group decision making (Chapter 10)
- the role of these principles in other aspects of social behavior:

  . . . the role of reciprocity in attraction (Chapter 7), aggression (Chapter 9), and cooperation (Chapter 9)

  . . . the role of the desire to be consistent in attitude change (Chapter 5), the self-concept (Chapter 4), and helping (Chapter 9)

  . . . the role of liking or friendship in social perception (Chapter 2), social relationships (Chapter 7), leadership (Chapter 10)
- the role of power and conflict in racial prejudice (Chapter 6), in various forms of social groups (Chapter 10), and in charismatic leadership (Chapter 10)

Thinking about Connections

1. Some observers have suggested that a "culture of violence" has developed in the United States (see Chapter 9). By this, they mean that the norms governing aggression have changed in recent decades, becoming more permissive about such behavior. While assaults against others were once strongly censured, they are now viewed as more appropriate and acceptable by many persons. Do you agree? If so, what factors do you think may have been responsible for this shift in social norms?

2. In many situations, we can tell when another person is trying to influence us. What may be harder to determine, at least

sometimes, are the reasons why they wish to influence us (see our discussion of persuasion in Chapter 5). Are they engaging in such tactics for selfish reasons, purely for their own benefit? Or do they have our best interests at heart, too? On the basis of our discussion of attribution in Chapter 2, how do you think we try to determine oth-

ers' motives in such situations? And how successful do you think we are at this important task?

3. It has sometimes been argued that social influence is the most basic and important aspect of social behavior. Do you agree? Can you think of any forms of social behavior in which influence does *not* play a role?

Summary and Review

Conformity

Conformity occurs when individuals change their attitudes or behavior to comply with *social norms*—rules or expectations about how they should behave in various situations. Conformity increases with *cohesiveness*—liking for the sources of such influence—and with the number of persons exerting pressure, but only up to a point. Conformity is reduced in the presence of *social support*—one or more persons who share the target person's views, or who depart from the majority's position in some manner.

We tend to conform because of two basic social motives: the need to be liked and the need to be right. The first motive leads us to accept influence from others so that we will be liked by others whose acceptance we desire (*normative social influence*), while the second leads us to accept social influence so that we can be correct in our judgments or actions (*informational social influence*). In addition, recent evidence indicates that after we decide to conform or resist such pressure, we change our perceptions of the situation so as to justify our previous behavior.

While there are strong tendencies to conform, individuals often resist social pressure. One reason for this is that they wish to maintain their unique identity as individuals. Minorities can sometimes influence larger majorities, especially when they appear to be deeply committed to the views they support. We do not automatically pay more attention to information from majorities or minorities; rather, we tend to pay special attention to information that is *imbalanced*—for example,

when majorities support disagreeable positions or minorities support agreeable ones.

Compliance

Compliance involves efforts by one or more individual to change the behavior of others. Many techniques can be used to gain compliance, but most of these seem to rest on six basic principles: *friendship/liking, commitment/consistency, scarcity, reciprocity, social validation,* and *authority*. Ingratiation is one major technique based on friendship and liking. Techniques based on commitment or consistency include the *foot in the door* and the *lowball*. Some tactics are based on reciprocity, including the *door in the face,* and the *"that's-not-all"* approach. Techniques based on scarcity include *playing hard to get* and the *fast-approaching deadline* technique. Additional procedures for gaining compliance involve the *pique technique,* which relies on presenting surprising requests.

Obedience

The most direct form of social influence is *obedience*—yielding to direct orders from another person. Research findings indicate that we often obey commands from authority figures even when such persons have little power to enforce their orders. These tendencies toward obedience stem from several causes (e.g., authority figures gradually escalate the scope of their orders; they have visible signs of power; there is little time for target persons to consider their actions in detail). Several procedures can help individuals resist obedience. These include reminding target persons that they, not the authority figures, will be responsible for any harmful outcomes and exposing target persons to disobedient models.

Social Diversity: Gender Differences in Social Influence

Early investigations suggested that females are more susceptible to conformity pressures and other forms of social influence than males. More recent investigations, however, have called these conclusions into question. It now appears that early studies used materials and tasks more familiar to males than to females and so placed females at a disadvantage in terms of susceptibility to conformity pressure. In addition, other findings suggest that many persons continue to believe that females are more conforming than males, because females generally occupy lower-status positions in society, and low-status persons tend to conform to a greater degree than high-status persons. But, there appear to be no overall gender differences in susceptibility to social influence among equal-status persons. However, recent evidence indicates that females and males may differ in this respect in a few situations; for example, females appear to be influenced to a greater degree than males by others' judgments concerning the attractiveness of opposite-sex strangers.

 ## Key Terms

Cohesiveness (p. 186)
Compliance (p. 184)
Conformity (p. 184)
Deadline Technique (p. 196)
Door-in-the-Face Technique (p. 195)
Foot-in-the-Door Technique (p. 194)
Individuation (p. 188)
Informational Social Influence (p. 190)
Ingratiation (p. 194)

Lowball Procedure (p. 194)
Normative Social Influence (p. 190)
Obedience (p. 184)
Pique Technique (p. 197)
Playing Hard to Get (p. 196)
Social Influence (p. 183)
Social Norms (p. 184)
That's-Not-All Technique (p. 195)

 ## For More Information

Cialdini, R. B. (1993). *Influence: Science and practice* (3rd ed.). New York: HarperCollins.

An insightful account of the major techniques people use to influence others. The book draws both on the findings of systematic research and on informal observations made by the author in a wide range of practical settings (e.g., sales, public relations, fund-raising agencies, organizations). This is the most readable and informative account of knowledge about influence currently available.

Milgram, S. (1974). *Obedience to authority.* New York: Harper & Row.

More than twenty years after it was written, this book remains the definitive work on obedience as a social psychological process. The untimely death of its author only adds to its value as a lasting contribution to our field.

chapter 9

Helping and Hurting: The Nature of Prosocial Behavior and Aggression

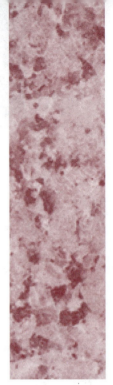

On the news, you watch a segment about a civil war taking place on the other side of the world. You see unbelievably thin men, women, and children in a refugee camp, staring blankly at the TV camera. The voice-over says there is an immediate need for donations to provide food and medicine for these refugees before the death toll rises. Do you feel sorry for them? Will you do anything?

Each year, more than 1.8 million wives are beaten by their husbands (Straus & Gelles, 1988); many incidents involving abuse of husbands by their wives also occur, although such actions appear to be much less likely to result in serious injury to the victim (e.g., Holtzworth-Munroe & Stuart, 1994).

Homicide is the leading cause of death among African American males ages 15–34 in the United States (Butterfield, 1992).

In a grocery store, you notice a small child sitting in a shopping cart, crying. A woman, probably his mother, slaps him in the face and yells, "Stop crying or you'll get worse than that!" You feel sorry for the child, but will you just make things worse if you say something?

In the United States there were 6,621,140 crimes of violence in one recent year (1992; U.S. Department of Justice, 1994).

In that same year, there were 140,930 forcible rapes and 657,550 assaults that resulted in injury to the victim (U.S. Department of Justice, 1994)—more than one rape every 5 minutes and one assault every 28 seconds.

These examples highlight the importance of two phenomena that have long been of central concern to the field of social psychology: helping and hurting, or **prosocial behavior** and **aggression,** as they are known within the field. Psychologists wish to understand and predict prosocial behavior—actions that provide benefit to others but that have no obvious benefits for the person who carries them out—and aggression—the intentional infliction of some form of harm on others.

On the surface, these two forms of behavior may seem like two sides of a coin: After all, as Figure 9.1 suggests, isn't helping the opposite of hurting? When someone hurts another person, aren't they doing the opposite of helping? Isn't helping *good* and hurting *bad*? to these questions we answer a qualified *yes:* The qualification is that, as we'll see in this chapter, the causes of prosocial behavior and aggression are often quite different and the mechanisms that underlie these forms of behavior also differ. Thus, while common sense may suggest that they are opposites, helping and hurting are perhaps best viewed as different forms of behavior. In this chapter, therefore, we'll first discuss what is known about prosocial behavior, and then address the topic of aggression.

The Nature of Prosocial Behavior

Prosocial behavior first became a topic of major interest to social psychologists in the 1960s. As we will describe, a widely publicized event helped motivate a number of social psychologists to create theories and design experiments to explain why bystanders sometimes do and sometimes do not *respond to an emergency.* We'll see how this initial work led to a large body of research that expanded far beyond the concerns of the initial investigations. In a variety of situations, research has dealt with *external factors that influence prosocial behavior.* We will also explore *additional theoretical explanations of prosocial motivation.*

FIGURE 9.1   Hurting and Helping: Is One the Opposite of the Other?

Victims of harm-doers often need help, people sometimes help others who are hurt, and sometimes people harm by not helping. Yet, because aggression and prosocial behaviors appear to be caused by different factors, they cannot be considered direct opposites of each other.

Explaining Bystander Apathy

The event that launched research on the prosocial behavior occurred in the early morning hours of March 13, 1964, in New York. Catherine (Kitty) Genovese was returning home from her job as the manager of a bar. As she crossed the street from her car to her apartment building, a man with a knife approached. She ran; he chased, caught, and stabbed her. Genovese screamed for help, and lights came on in the windows of several apartments overlooking the street. The attacker retreated briefly, and then came back to his bleeding victim. She screamed again, but he continued stabbing her until she died. It was later determined that this horrifying forty-five-minute interaction was viewed by thirty-eight bystanders, but no one came to Kitty Genovese's rescue or even called the police (Rosenthal, 1964).

Following the news stories about this *bystander effect*, there was widespread debate about why no one helped. Were people apathetic, cold, indifferent to the problems of others? Was something wrong with our society? Did urban life make people callous? When one is sitting in a comfortable chair and reading about emergencies, there is no ambiguity about what should be done. The witnesses to Genovese's murder should have shouted at the attacker and called the police. Things are different, however, when *you* are ac-

tually confronted by such situations; it is not that easy to do the right thing. Latané and Darley (1970) outlined a series of five choices that a bystander must make (often unconsciously) before help can occur. Notice that at each point, the simplest choice is the path of least resistance—doing nothing, and thus failing to provide help.

Step 1. The Bystander Must Perceive the Emergency. We don't spend our lives standing idly around, waiting for an emergency to occur. Instead, we tend to be engaged in some activity and thinking about our own concerns when an emergency event intrudes. To take the first step toward helping, we must shift our attention away from personal matters and toward the unexpected happening. Much of the time we screen out passing sights and sounds because they are personally irrelevant. As a result, it is easy to ignore an emergency.

Darley and Batson (1973) investigated how preoccupation can inhibit prosocial acts. The experimenters gave seminary students the task of going to a nearby building to present a talk about the Bible's parable of the Good Samaritan or about jobs. To manipulate preoccupation, the investigators created different degrees of time pressure for different research participants. They told some that they were ahead of schedule and had plenty of time to get to their talk, others that they were right on schedule, and a third group that they were already late for the speaking engagement. Presumably, the first group would be the least preoccupied and the third group the most preoccupied. On the way to the building where the talk was to be given, each seminary student encountered a research assistant who was slumped in a doorway, coughing and groaning. Would they notice this seemingly sick or hurt individual and help him? Though the topic of the upcoming talk (jobs or the Good Samaritan) had no effect on the seminarians' behavior, preoccupation (time pressure) did. Sixty-three percent of those with plenty of time provided help. Helping dropped to just 45 percent among those who were on time, and even lower (only 10 percent) among those in a hurry. Many of the most preoccupied seminarians simply stepped over the victim and rushed along to their appointment. Clearly, if you don't notice the problem, you won't help.

Step 2. Correctly Interpreting the Situation As an Emergency. In our daily contact with passing strangers, we usually don't know what they are doing or why. If we wonder why a man is running past us down the sidewalk, it is much easier to imagine a routine, everyday explanation than a highly unusual and unlikely one (Macrae & Milne, 1992). That is, he might be hurrying to catch a bus, to find his dog, to get some exercise, or—least likely—to grab a thief who has just robbed him. Surely a dramatic chase following a daylight robbery is not the first possibility that would occur to you. The difficulty with interpreting an ordinary event as an extraordinary emergency is that you can look foolish. Unless you conclude that you are really witnessing an emergency, you won't help, because there is no reason to help and you want to avoid making stupid mistakes.

When there is any ambiguity about what is going on, potential helpers hold back and wait for more information. If the signals are mixed—some indicating that everything is OK and others indicating that a serious problem exists—people are inclined to give more weight to the information indicating that nothing need be done (J. P. Wilson & Petruska, 1984). When the situation is unclear, you will probably engage in social comparison (see Chapter 7) to validate your impressions by finding out what the other people say and do. This isn't a problem when the bystanders are friends, because they are likely to communicate with one another, greatly reducing the bystander effect (Rutkowski, Gruder, & Romer, 1983). If, however, fellow bystanders are strangers and the others fail to react, the inhibition against helping is very strong. A victim should not expect help from a group of uninformed bystanders who incorrectly interpret the situation and also hold back to avoid being embarrassed by losing their cool.

This group reaction, called **pluralistic ignorance** (see Chapter 3), was documented in an experiment involving a smoke emergency (Latané & Darley, 1968). The research participants were each given a questionnaire to fill out. Some did so in a room by themselves, while others were in a room with two other participants. After a few minutes, the experimenters pumped smoke into the room through a vent. Do you think the number of bystanders would affect whether students would react to the smoke as indicating an emergency? Among other possibilities, their building might be on fire! Of those who were alone in the room, 75 percent left to tell someone about the smoke, half of them in the first two minutes. In contrast, with three people in the room, only 38 percent reacted, while 62 percent did absolutely nothing—even when the smoke became so thick that it was hard to see. And, of the minority who responded, only one did so in the first *four* minutes. It seems that an unreactive group can be a powerful inhibiting force.

Step 3. Assuming Responsibility to Act. At the third choice point in the model, the bystander either does or does not assume responsibility for doing something. In many situations, responsibility is clear: If a house is burning, help is the responsibility of firefighters. If a store is being robbed, help is the responsibility of police officers. If someone is injured, medical personnel take responsibility. When, however, responsibility is less clear, we tend to assume that someone in a leadership role is the one to act (Baumeister et al.,

1988). That is, a professor should deal with an emergency in a classroom, a bus driver is responsible for dealing with an emergency on his vehicle, and an adult assumes responsibility among a group of children.

One of the reasons that a lone bystander is most likely to act is that there is no one else who *could* take responsibility. Thus, **diffusion of responsibility** is one explanation for why bystanders sometimes fail to respond. These psychologists hypothesized that when one person sees someone in need of help, the bystander's responsibility is clear; but with multiple witnesses to an emergency, as in Kitty Genovese's murder, any one of the 38 individuals *could* have acted. In effect, each had only 1/38 of the total responsibility, and that was not enough to motivate any one of them to act. The general hypothesis, then, is that as the number of bystanders increases, the likelihood of prosocial behavior decreases. Moreover, much research has confirmed this hypothesis. For example, when Darley and Latané (1968) created a scenario in which unsuspecting study participants encountered another participant having an epileptic seizure, actual participants were much

less likely to help when there were five bystanders than when they were alone. Moreover, among those who *did* help, those in the larger group were *slower* to help, as Figure 9.2 illustrates. Even with just two bystanders, helping becomes less likely unless one of them (for whatever reason) *feels personally responsible* for providing help.

Step 4. Knowing What to Do. At the fourth choice point, the bystander must ponder whether he or she knows *how* to be helpful. Some emergencies are simple. If you see someone slip on an icy sidewalk, you help the person up. If you see two rough-looking men trying to break into a parked car, you pick up the phone and call 911. Other emergencies require special knowledge and skills. In one of the news stories cited earlier, the motorists who stopped to help the driver of the delivery truck had previously been trained to administer cardiopulmonary resuscitation. In a similar way, if you don't know how to swim, you are unable to provide immediate help to someone who is drowning.

Whenever a bystander possesses the necessary knowledge, experience, or skills, he or she tends to

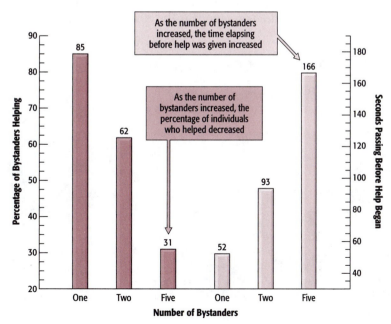

FIGURE 9.2 The Bystander Effect: More Bystanders = Less Help.

In the initial experiment designed to explore the *bystander effect,* students heard what seemed to be a fellow student having a seizure. The research participant was supposedly either the only bystander to this emergency, one of two bystanders, or one of five. As the number of bystanders increased, the percentage of individuals who tried to help the "victim" decreased. In addition, among those who *did* help, as the number of bystanders increased, the more time passed before help began.

(*Source:* Based on data from Darley & Latané, 1968.)

assume responsibility and to provide help whether or not other bystanders are present. For example, with two bystanders present at an accident, registered nurses offer help more than nonnurses; with only one bystander, nurses and nonnurses are equally helpful (Cramer et al., 1988).

Step 5. Making the Final Decision to Help. Even when a bystander has passed through each of the first four choice points with a yes, helping behavior still may not occur: Helping may be inhibited by fears about negative consequences. If you try to help a person who slipped on the ice, you may fall down yourself. If you help a person who is coughing and groaning on the sidewalk, your clothes may get dirty or you may catch a disease. And most serious of all, others may erroneously conclude that you caused the mishap in the first place. Altogether, unless one is especially motivated to provide help, helping may not occur because the potential costs simply appear too great (A. M. McGuire, 1994).

Who *Gives* Help?

The research described so far has emphasized aspects of the *situation* that increase or decrease the probability of prosocial acts. We have also indicated that individuals are more likely to help if they possess the necessary knowledge and skills to help (e.g., in a medical emergency). That some *people* are more or less helpful is dramatically illustrated with the two photographs in Figure 9.3. Some individuals are deeply concerned about any distress experienced by others; others seem totally indifferent to and unaffected by the distress of others. Research has related many factors to helpfulness. For example, people who have a strong *need for approval* are more likely to help others, presumably because they are especially gratified when they receive appreciation and praise. Their helpfulness is most apparent if they have previously been rewarded for such behavior (F. M. Deutsch & Lamberti, 1986). If you are the one in need of help, of course, you may not quibble about the possibly selfish motives of the person who provides you with assistance.

The broadest attempt to identify the *altruistic personality* was undertaken by Bierhoff, Klein, and Kramp (1991). They obtained several personality variables identified in previous prosocial research and compared the scores of people at the scene of an accident who had and had not administered first aid before the ambulance arrived. These two groups were matched with respect to sex, age, and social class, and then were compared on the personality measures. Results revealed five components of the **altruistic personality**:

FIGURE 9.3   Individual Differences in Helpfulness.

The capacity for helpfulness appears to play a crucial role in differentiating those who engage in prosocial behavior and those who do not. Clearly, human beings span a wide range in this characteristic.

1. Among those who helped, *empathy* was an important part of the self-concept. Helpers also described themselves as responsible and socialized, and as having self-control, wanting to make a good impression, and being conforming and tolerant.
2. Those who provided first aid expressed a strong *belief in a just world*. They assume that giving first aid is the right thing to do and that the person who helps will benefit from doing so. Altogether, they perceive the world as a fair and predictable place in which good behavior is rewarded and bad behavior punished—people get what they deserve.
3. *Social responsibility* also differentiated the helpers from the nonhelpers. A person high on this dimension believes that we should all do our best to help others.
4. Altruistic individuals were characterized as assuming an *internal locus of control*. This is the belief that one can behave in such a way as to maximize good outcomes and minimize bad ones—that the individual can make a difference and is not helplessly at the mercy of luck, fate, and other uncontrollable forces.
5. The helpers were lower than the nonhelpers on the measure of *egocentrism*. Those who failed to help tended to be self-absorbed and competitive.

Interestingly, these same five dispositional variables were found to be characteristic of people throughout Europe who were active during the 1940s in rescuing Jews from Nazi persecution (Oliner & Oliner, 1988).

Who *Receives* Help?

You are walking down the sidewalk in a large city and see a man lying unconscious next to the curb. Would you be more likely to stop and help (a) if a wine bottle were clutched in his hand and his clothes were stained and torn or (b) if he were neatly dressed and had a bruise on his forehead? The odds are that you would be more

strongly motivated to help the second man than the first. Why? Victim characteristics are important determinants of helping: we are inclined to help those we *like*, including those who are most *similar* to ourselves (Chapter 7), and those who are *not responsible* for their plight.

Helping a Liked Victim. On the basis of the discussion in Chapter 7 about the effect of attraction on our evaluations of other people, you might assume that the more we like a person, the stronger our tendency to provide needed assistance. You would be right (M. S. Clark, 1987). Whatever factors increase attraction also increase prosocial responses. For example, a physically attractive victim receives more help than an unattractive one (Benson, Karabenick, & Lerner, 1976).

Also discussed in Chapter 7 was the fact that many people see homosexuality as a stigma. Given this widespread prejudice based on a person's sexual orientation, Shaw, Borough, and Fink (1994) predicted that a homosexual stranger in need would receive less help than a comparable heterosexual stranger. To test this proposal, they used the "wrong number technique." A research assistant dials a random telephone number and, if an adult answers, says that he was trying to call for assistance from a pay phone using his last quarter but made a mistake in dialing; he then asks the stranger to make the call for him. The number given is actually that of the assistant, who can thus determine whether the stranger in fact dials the number as requested.

To suggest a heterosexual relationship, the caller ("Mike") asked to speak to his girlfriend, Lisa. In the homosexual condition, he asked to speak to his boyfriend, Rick. In both conditions, finding that he had the "wrong number," Mike apologized for his mistake, then explained that he had a flat tire and would be late for the first-anniversary celebration with his opposite-sex or same-sex companion. Because Mike had no more change, he asked the stranger to please call Lisa or Rick for him. Help by the stranger consisted of actually making the phone call within the next three minutes. Nonhelp consisted of hanging up on the caller, refusal to write down

Lisa's or Rick's number, refusal to make the call, or failure to call within the next three minutes. As shown in Figure 9.4, slightly more than half of the forty men and forty women Mike called helped by making the requested call, but such help was given much less frequently to the homosexual stranger than to the heterosexual one.

Because similarity generally has a positive effect on attraction, it is reasonable to expect people to help those who are like themselves. This is often the case, and the response to homosexual versus heterosexual phone requests may in part reflect greater helpfulness of heterosexual respondents toward a similar stranger (that is, by chance the great majority of the random calls would have been to heterosexuals). There are additional factors at work in some situations, however. For example, in some situa-

---

FIGURE 9.4   Helping a Heterosexual versus a Homosexual Stranger.

Using the "wrong number technique," a male experimental assistant called a telephone number at random and asked for his girlfriend or his boyfriend by name. Discovering that he had the "wrong number," he apologized, said that he had a flat tire and would be late for their anniversary celebration but had no more change for the pay phone, and asked the stranger please to call Lisa or Rick to explain. When the caller was identified as heterosexual, most people helped out by making the requested telephone call. When the caller was identified as homosexual, most people did not help. It seems clear that a negative attitude about the person in need can inhibit prosocial behavior.

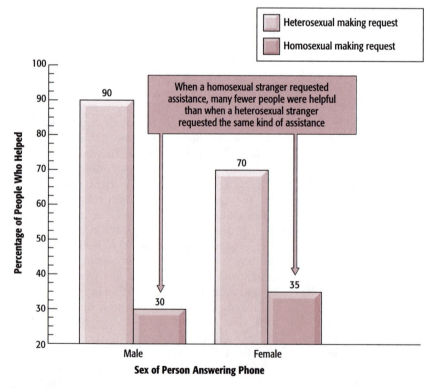

(*Source:* Based on data from Shaw, Borough, & Fink, 1994.)

tions similarity seems to be irrelevant. Born-stein's (1994) meta-analysis of twenty-three in-vestigations showed that the more the victim is dependent on others for help, the greater the likelihood that others actually *will* help. With a very dependent victim, similarity or lack of sim-ilarity to the person providing assistance ceases to matter.

Integrating Principles

1. Prosocial behavior can be inhibited by preoccupation, fail-ure to interpret an ambiguous situation as an emergency, lack of clarity about who should take responsibility, absence of appropriate knowledge and skills, and fear of potential consequences. Among the processes involved are the inter-pretation of nonverbal cues and attributions (Chapter 2), cognition (Chapter 3), and social comparison (Chapter 7).
2. Prosocial behavior is facilitated by the presence of rele-vant dispositional variables, of which, the most crucial is empathy, which is also associated with a secure attach-ment style (Chapter 7). Also playing a role are self-con-cept (Chapter 4) and locus of control (Chapter 11).
3. Victims are most likely to receive help if the bystander likes them, for any of the reasons described in Chapter 7. Similarity between the victim and the bystander tends to promote helpfulness, but too much similarity can some-times be threatening and cause potential helpers to blame the victim.

Why Does Prosocial Behavior Occur?

Thus far in this chapter, we've examined evi-dence concerning several factors that influence prosocial behavior—preoccupation with matters other than helping, fear of negative effects, sim-ilarity between the potential helper and the per-son needing help, and so on. At this point, you may be wondering: *Why* does prosocial behavior occur? What psychological mechanisms lead in-dividuals to help others, even when they expect nothing in return? Some theories have focused on the role of affective states, assuming that there is an interaction between the potential helper's emotional state and specific aspects of

the emergency situation. The most general as-sumption is that people respond so as to maxi-mize positive affect and minimize negative affect. For example, Baron (1997) found that helping was more likely near a pleasant smelling business (a bakery) than near a relatively odor-less business (clothing store); pleasant smells tend to elicit positive moods, which in turn often elicit greater helping. Presumably, the greater the amount of positive affect relative to the amount of negative affect, the more likely an in-dividual is to behave in a prosocial way.

In a slightly oversimplified summary, a by-stander will help a victim if the helpful act is perceived as leading to a *more positive* or to a *less negative* emotional outcome for the by-stander. The theoretical explanations of *why* one might provide help for a stranger in distress tend to stress either selfish or selfless motives for altruism (D. T. Campbell & Specht, 1985). As you might guess, people tend to attribute their own helpful behavior to selfless motives ("It was the right thing to do") while observers are equally likely to attribute selfless or selfish mo-tives ("He wanted to make a good impression") when someone else helps (Doherty, Weigold, & Schlenker, 1990).

Figure 9.5 depicts four somewhat different but influential theoretical proposals relative to the motives underlying prosocial behavior. In this section we'll examine each of these theories in turn.

Unselfish Motivation: Empathy Leads to Helpfulness. We discussed empathy earlier as the tendency to ex-perience the other person's emotional state, to feel sympathy for him or her, and to perceive the situation from that person's perspective. Based on this conception, Batson and his colleagues (1981) proposed the **empathy–altruism hypoth-esis,** which is that at least some prosocial behav-ior is motivated entirely by the unselfish desire to help someone who needs help. This motivation to help someone in need can even be at the expense of oneself and of the group as a whole. That is, feelings of compassion may outweigh such con-siderations as fairness and justice (Batson, Klein,

FIGURE 9.5   Four Alternative Proposals to Explain Why People Help.

Four somewhat different explanations have been proposed to explain the motivation underlying prosocial behavior. The *empathy–altruism hypothesis* suggests that people help because someone needs help and because
it is satisfying to provide help. The *negative state relief model* suggests that people help in order to reduce their
negative affect. The *empathetic joy hypothesis* suggests that people help in order to have a successful influence
on the person in need. The *genetic determinism model* suggests that people help others like themselves because of an unconscious desire to maximize the odds that their common genes will survive in subsequent generations. Supporting data have been generated for each proposal, and it is possible that each is correct. That is,
helping may be based on more than one motive, depending on the situation and the individual who helps.

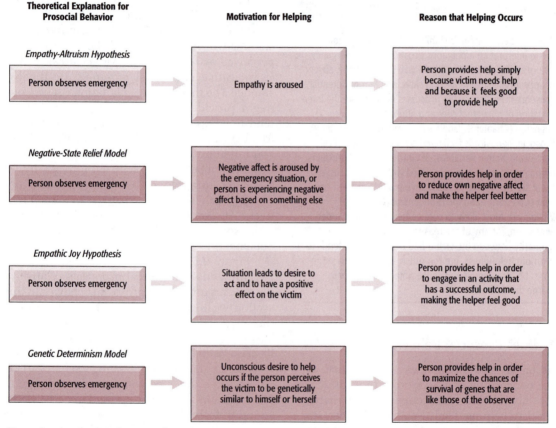

(*Source:* Based on data from Forgas, 1994.)

et al., 1995; Batson & Weeks, 1996). A cognitive
component enhances the emotional effect—the
experience of empathy provides information that
one *values* the other person's welfare and therefore must want to provide help; this effect is most
likely to occur when one has experienced the
same plight (Batson et al., 1996).

To test this altruistic view of helping behavior, Batson and colleagues devised an experimental procedure to manipulate a bystander's
empathy and provide an opportunity for that individual to be helpful (Batson et al., 1983; Toi &
Batson, 1982). Each participant served as the
"observer" as another student performed a task

while (supposedly) receiving random electric shocks. The female student being shocked was actually an accomplice recorded on videotape. After the task began, she indicated she was in pain and confided that, as a child, she had had a traumatic experience with electricity. Though she said she was able to continue, the experimenter asked whether the participant was willing to trade places. Empathy was manipulated by means of information indicating that the person being shocked was quite similar to (high empathy) or dissimilar from (low empathy) the participant. When empathy was low and it was easy to get out of the experiment, participants tended to leave rather than engage in a prosocial act. When empathy was high, the participants volunteered to take the victim's place and receive the shocks, whether or not it was easy to leave. Batson and his colleagues concluded that this altruism was motivated by empathy.

Notice that people will gladly leave such a situation if empathy is not high. After all, the cost of helping is high—the observers believe they will receive electric shocks. What would happen if a person had a choice about whether to feel empathy? Shaw, Batson, and Todd (1994) asked college students to take part in a new program to help a homeless man—a program with either a low cost (spending an hour preparing letters to solicit contributions) or a high cost (meeting with the homeless person on three occasions for an hour and a half or two hours each time). The students then had a choice of getting additional information involving either an unemotional, factual description of the homeless man or an emotional, empathy-arousing message about what he is going through and how it affects his life. When the cost of helping was low, most students wanted to hear the emotional message. When the cost of helping was high, most wanted to hear the informational message. In other words, they engaged in *empathy avoidance* so they would not be motivated to engage in high-cost helping.

Selfish Motivation: Helping in Order to Feel Better. People sometimes act in a prosocial way simply in order to make themselves feel better. In a more general form, this idea is known as the **negative state relief model** (Cialdini, Baumann, & Kenrick, 1981). This model assumes that prosocial behavior is motivated primarily by the desire to improve one's own emotional state.

Note that it doesn't matter whether the negative emotions are already present when the emergency is encountered or if they are aroused by the emergency itself. You may have unpleasant feelings because you argued with a friend earlier in the day or because you are upset about seeing a stranger on crutches trip and fall. Either way, you engage in a prosocial act because you want to make yourself feel better (Fultz, Schaller, & Cialdini, 1988).

According to this theoretical model, the only role of empathy is as an additional source of negative affect. For example, Cialdini and his colleagues (1987) found that when empathy for a victim is aroused, one of the accompanying emotions is sadness. When the experimenters were able to separate empathic feelings from sad ones, they found that sadness alone leads to increased helping but that empathy alone does not.

Selfish Motivation: Helping Because It Feels Good to Have an Impact. Another interpretation of the role of empathy has been offered by K. D. Smith, Keating, and Stotland (1989). According to the **empathic joy hypothesis,** empathy leads to helping because the helper anticipates feeling good about accomplishing something.

What difference does it make whether you feel good because you helped or because you know your helping has an impact on the victim? Smith and his colleagues (1989) point out that with purely empathic motivation, the helper would not need feedback about the success of his or her actions. The empathic joy hypothesis predicts that empathy alone is not enough; altruism must be followed by information about one's success—an egoistic reward. These investigators designed an experiment in which the research participants saw a videotape of a female student who expressed feelings of isolation and stress and said she was considering withdrawing from college. The viewers had the opportunity to offer advice. Some were told they would get feedback about the effectiveness of their advice, and others were told that they would receive no further information about the woman. Participants' empathy was aroused by means of information about the woman's similarity to themselves; non-empathy was created by dissimilarity information. Under these conditions, empathy led to helping (the giving of advice) only when the research participants thought they would receive feedback about the effect of their advice. In other words, empathy alone was not enough to produce prosocial behavior; rather, knowledge of one's impact was necessary so that empathic joy could be felt.

It is possible, of course, to label any act of altruism as selfish simply because it feels good to help someone in need (e.g. Williamson & Clark, 1989). The positive emotion that accompanies prosocial behavior is known as *helper's high*—a feeling of calmness, self-worth, and warmth (Luks, 1988). In fact, it sometimes feels so good to be helpful that if a victim refuses help when it is offered, the frustrated prosocial person becomes angry (Cheuk & Rosen, 1992). Similarly, refusing to help someone in need causes positive affect to deteriorate (Williamson, Clark, Pegalis, & Behan, 1996).

Selfish Motivation: Helping Similar Others to Preserve Your Common Genes. Whereas the previous explanations of prosocial motivation are based on the role of emotions, the **genetic determinism model** is based on a more general theory of human behavior. Rushton (1989) and other evolutionary psychologists stress that we are not conscious of why we respond to genetic influences; but they hypothesize we do so in many situations. Any behavior that increases an individual's ability to reproduce successfully (known as *fitness*) will be represented in subsequent generations more frequently than a behavior that is irrelevant to reproductive success or that interferes with reproduction (Archer, 1991).

Studies of other species indicate that the greater the genetic similarity between two animals, the more likely it is that one will help the other when help is needed (Ridley & Dawkins, 1981). Such behavior is said to be the result of the "selfish gene"; because when one helps a genetically similar other, genes like one's own are more

likely to survive and be passed on—even if the helper dies in the process (Rushton, Russell, & Wells, 1984). The assumption is that each individual is unconsciously motivated not only to live long enough to reproduce his or her own individual genes but also to enhance the reproductive odds of anyone else who shares those genes (Browne, 1992). By helping people like ourselves, therefore we are actually behaving so as to preserve whatever genes we are likely to have in common (Burnstein, Crandall, & Kitayama, 1994).

In reviewing the literature on altruism, Buck and Ginsburg (1991) conclude that there is no evidence of a gene that determines prosocial behavior. Among humans, however, there *are* genetically based capacities to communicate one's emotional state and to form social bonds. These inherited aspects of social behavior make it likely that we will help one another when the need arises. In other words, people are inherently sociable, and when they interact in social relationships, "they are always prosocial, usually helpful, and often altruistic" (A. P. Fiske, 1991, p. 209).

You would probably find it more satisfying if we were able to declare one of these explanations entirely correct and the other three totally wrong, but that is not the case. In fact, it seems quite possible that prosocial behavior is based on a variety of motives; and it seems that little is gained by labeling some of them as selfless and others selfish. Regardless of the underlying reason for being helpful, it is good to help and good to receive help when you need it.

Integrating Principles

1. Most theoretical explanations of the motivation for prosocial behavior involve the emotional state of the potential helper and the emotional effect of engaging in helping behavior.
2. Though there are debates about the ultimate selflessness or selfishness of the resulting behavior, it is generally agreed that altruistic reactions occur because they enhance positive affect and/or decrease negative affect. Affect is given an equally important emphasis in the study of cognition (Chapter 3), attitudes (Chapter 5), prejudice (Chapter 6), attraction and relationships (Chapter 7), and aggression.

The Nature of Aggression

Why do human beings aggress against others? What makes them turn, with brutality unmatched by even the fiercest of predators, against their fellow human beings? (See Figure 9.6.) Scientists and scholars from many different fields have pondered these questions for centuries and have proposed many contrasting explanations for the paradox of human violence.

Contrasting Theories of Aggression

One of the earliest explanations of aggression suggested that people aggress because it is in their nature to do so. For example, Sigmund Freud held that aggression stems mainly from a powerful *death wish* or instinct (thanatos) possessed by all persons. Similarly, Konrad Lorenz (1974), a Nobel Prize–winning scientist, proposed that aggression springs mainly from an inherited *fighting instinct* that human beings share with many other species. However, social psychologists have tended to reject these views that aggression stems from inborn tendencies because of studies showing that at least some forms of aggression vary tremendously from country to country. For example, many developed countries have lower rates of violent crimes than the United States; in many developing countries, rates are even higher (Osterman et al., 1994). Thus, even if aggression stems in part from innate tendencies, these are literally overwhelmed by social and cultural factors. In this section, we discuss some other theories that have greater currency among social psychologists.

Biological Theories. While social psychologists overwhelmingly reject instinct views of aggression, this does not imply that they also reject *any* role of biological factors in such behavior. On the contrary, there is increasing recognition by social psychologists of the importance of biological factors in many forms of social behavior (e.g., Buss, 1996; Nisbett, 1990), and aggression is no exception to this general pattern. Indeed, growing evidence points to the conclusion that biological factors do predispose some individuals toward aggression (e.g., Gladue, 1991). For example, research has shown that people who are aggressive and those who have attempted suicide have higher levels of *serotonin* than normal; presumably, the higher levels of this important neurotransmitter in the nervous system made it difficult for highly aggressive persons and for those attempting suicide to control their aggressive impulses (Marazzitti et al., 1993).

Perhaps even more dramatic evidence in this regard is provided by a recent investigation

FIGURE 9.6 Violence: A Worldwide Problem.

As this scene from war-ravaged Somalia indicates, the costs of aggression in terms of human suffering are often very high.

conducted with female transsexuals: People who decided to change their gender from female to male (Van Goozen, Frijda, & de Poll, 1994). As part of their medical treatment, these individuals received regular, large doses of male sex hormones (testosterone) either by injection or orally. During the study, these transsexuals completed questionnaires designed to assess their level of overt aggression and their tendency to become angry in various situations (anger-proneness); these measures were completed both before the women began receiving male sex hormones and three months later. Although there was little change in reports of overt aggression, participants did report higher tendencies to become angry after receiving these hormones.

These findings, and many others, point to the conclusion that biological factors may indeed play a role in aggressive behavior. It's important to note, however, that none of this evidence indicates that aggressive tendencies are inherited in a simple or direct manner or that biological factors are overwhelmingly important as determinants of human aggression. On the contrary, existing evidence suggests that biological processes exert their effect against a rich backdrop of social and cognitive factors. So, just as human beings are not pushed to harm others by irresistible aggressive instincts, they are not driven to engage in such behavior by all-powerful biological forces. Where human aggression is concerned, biology may be important, but it is definitely *not* destiny.

Social Learning Theory: Aggression As Learned Social Behavior. Another, and sharply contrasting, perspective on aggression is known as the **social learning view.** This approach emphasizes the idea that aggression, like other complex forms of social behavior, is largely *learned* (Bandura, 1973, 1986; R. A. Baron & Richardson, 1994). Human beings, this perspective contends, are *not* born with a large array of aggressive responses at their disposal. Rather, they must acquire these in much the same way that they acquire other complex forms of social behavior: through direct experience or by observing the actions of others.

Thus, depending on their past experience, people in different cultures learn to attack others in contrasting ways—by means of kung fu, blowguns, machetes, guns—or in more subtle ways. Through direct and vicarious experience, even as early as 6 years of age (Huesmann & Guerra, 1997), individuals also learn (1) which persons or groups are appropriate targets for aggression, (2) what actions by others either justify or actually require aggressive retaliation, and (3) what situations or contexts are ones in which aggression is appropriate or inappropriate.

In short, the social learning perspective suggests that whether a specific person will aggress in a given situation depends on a vast array of factors, including that person's past experience, the current reinforcements (rewards) associated with aggression, and many variables that shape the person's thoughts and perceptions concerning the appropriateness and potential effects of such behavior. Because most if not all of these factors are open to change, the social learning approach is quite promising with respect to the possibility of preventing or controlling overt aggression. Needless to say, this makes it an appealing theory for social psychologists.

Cognitive Theories of Aggression: The Roles of Scripts, Appraisals, and Affect. Imagine that you are in a busy supermarket when suddenly another shopper rams you with her cart. How do you react? Certainly, with surprise and pain. But do you retaliate in kind, shoving your cart into *her*? Or do you swallow your annoyance and proceed with your shopping? Obviously, this depends on many different factors: the size and apparent ferocity of the shopper, who else is present on the scene, and so on. According to several modern theories of aggression, though, *cognitive factors* play a crucial role in determining how you will react (e.g., C. A. Anderson, Anderson, & Deuser, 1995; Berkowitz, 1989; Huesmann, 1988, 1994). One of these involves what social psychologists term *scripts*—cognitive "programs" for the events that are supposed to happen in a given setting. Since your script for visiting a supermarket doesn't include getting into a battle with another shopper, this factor would probably operate *against* retaliation on your part in this setting.

Another cognitive factor that will influence your behavior is your interpretation of the situation—your *appraisal* of *why* the other shopper bumped you. Did she do it on purpose? Was it totally an accident? You will do a quick assessment of available information (for instance, is the other shopper smiling in glee or apologizing profusely?) and then, very quickly, decide whether there was malice on the other person's part or not (C. A. Anderson, Anderson, & Deuser, 1996; Ohbuchi, Chiba, & Fukushima, 1996). This initial appraisal may then be followed by *reappraisal,* in which you take a little more time to consider the situation and assess such factors as what may happen if you act in various ways. If you ram the other shopper, you may get momentary satisfaction but may not be able to finish your shopping. She may retaliate, and ultimately you may both be thrown out of the store. Thoughts such as these clearly influence aggression in situations where people take the time to consider their actions and the possible results these will produce.

Finally, it's important to consider your current mood. Aversive (unpleasant) experiences, such as being rammed by another shopper, produce *negative affect.* As we noted in Chapter 3, our current moods exert strong effects on our cognitive processes. Thus, as suggested by Berkowitz (1989, 1994), the pain you experience may lead you to experience not only immediate tendencies to either retaliate or withdraw ("fight or flight") but also thoughts and memories related to other painful or annoying experiences. These, in turn, could trigger an aggressive reaction.

In sum, **cognitive theories** of aggression suggest that such behavior stems from a complex interplay between our current moods and experiences, the thoughts and memories these elicit, and our cognitive appraisals of the current situation (see Figure 9.7; R. A. Baron, in press-a). Clearly, this kind of framework for understanding the roots of aggression is more complex than the early ones offered by Freud and Lorenz. But as you can readily see, it is much more likely to be accurate and useful than these earlier frameworks.

Social Determinants of Aggression

Think back to the last time you lost your temper. What made you lose your cool? The chances are quite good that your anger stemmed from the actions of another person. In fact, when asked to describe situations that made them angry, most people refer to something another person said or did (Harris, 1993; Torestad, 1990). They are much

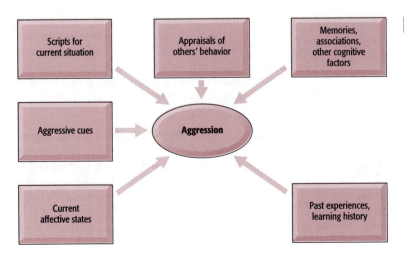

FIGURE 9.7   Cognitive Theories of Aggression.

Modern theories suggest that aggressive behavior is influenced by complex interactions between cognitive factors (scripts, appraisals of others' behavior, memories and associations elicited by aggressive cues) and our current affective states.

(*Source:* Based on suggestions by C. A. Anderson, Anderson, & Deuser, 1996; Berkowitz, 1989; Zillmann, 1994; and others.)

Scripts for current situation

Appraisals of others' behavior

Memories, associations, other cognitive factors

Aggressive cues

Aggression

Current affective states

Past experiences, learning history

less likely to mention purely physical events such as a flat tire, bad weather, or the like. In short, aggression often stems from various *social* conditions that either initiate its occurrence or increase its intensity. In this section we'll examine some of the most important of these factors.

Frustration: Why Not Getting What You Want (or What You Expect) Can Sometimes Lead to Aggression. Suppose that you asked twenty people you know to name the single most important cause of aggression. What would they say? The chances are good that most would reply frustration. And if you asked them to define frustration, many would state, "The way I feel when something—or someone—prevents me from getting what I want or expect to get in some situation." This widespread belief in the importance of frustration as a cause of aggression stems, at least in part, from the famous frustration–aggression hypothesis first proposed by Dollard and his colleagues on the eve of World War II (Dollard et al., 1939). In its original form, this hypothesis made the following sweeping assertions: (1) Frustration always leads to some form of aggression, and (2) aggression always stems from frustration. In short, the theory held that frustrated persons always engage in some type of aggression and that all acts of aggression, in turn, result from frustration. Although this bold statement is appealing, existing evidence suggests that both portions of the frustration–aggression hypothesis go too far with respect to the importance they assign to frustration.

First, it is clear that frustrated individuals do not always respond with aggressive thoughts, words, or deeds. On the contrary, they show many different reactions to frustration, ranging from despair or depression on the one hand, to direct attempts to overcome the source of their frustration on the other. Second, it is equally clear that not all aggression results from frustration. People aggress for many different reasons and in response to many different factors. For example, professional boxers hit their opponents because they wish to win valued prizes—not be-

cause of frustration. Similarly, during wars, air force pilots report that flying their planes is a source of pleasure, and that they bomb enemy targets while feeling elated, not frustrated. In these and many other cases, aggression definitely stems from factors other than frustration. We'll consider many of these other causes of aggression below.

In view of these considerations, few social psychologists now accept the idea that frustration is the only, or even the most important, cause of aggression. Instead, most believe that it is simply one of many factors that can potentially lead to aggression. Along these lines, Berkowitz (1989) has proposed a revised version of the frustration–aggression hypothesis that seems consistent with a large amount of evidence about the effects of frustration. According to this view, frustration is an aversive, unpleasant experience, and frustration leads to aggression because of this fact. In short, frustration sometimes produces aggression because of a basic relationship between negative affect and aggressive behavior—a relationship that has been confirmed in many different studies (e.g., da Gloria, Pahlavan, Duda, & Bonnet, 1994). These suggestions help explain why *unexpected* frustration and frustration that is viewed as *illegitimate* or unjustified produce stronger aggression than frustration that is expected or legitimate. Presumably, unexpected or illegitimate frustration generates greater amounts of negative affect than frustration that is expected or viewed as legitimate.

In sum, while it appears that frustration can, indeed, be one potential cause of aggression, it is definitely not the only factor leading to such behavior, and does not play the very central role in human aggression that many people believe.

Direct Provocation: When Aggression Breeds Aggression. Remember the shopping cart episode described above? Suppose that when you looked at the shopper who rammed her cart into you, she gave you a dirty look and muttered "That'll teach you to get in my way!" How would you react? Probably with anger, and perhaps with some kind of retaliation. You might make a biting remark, such as "Who do you think *you* are?" or "What's wrong with you—are you crazy?" Alternatively, you might, if you were angry enough, push *your* cart into hers, or even aim at her directly.

This incident illustrates an important point about aggression: Often, it is the result of physical or verbal **provocation** from others. That is, when we are the victims of some form of aggression from others, we rarely turn the other cheek, at least not if we can help it. Instead, we tend to reciprocate, returning as much aggression as we have received—or perhaps even slightly more, especially if, as in this incident, we are quite certain that the other person *meant* to harm us in some way (Ohbuchi et al., 1996; Quigley & Tedeschi, 1996). This latter finding—that we often return a bit more aggression than we have received—helps explain why aggression often spirals upward from mild taunts to stronger insults, and from pushing or shoving to kicks, blows, or worse (e.g., Harris, 1993). As we will see in the Social Diversity box on pages 230–231, cultural factors also play a role in such responses.

Exposure to Media Violence: The Effects of Witnessing Aggression. List several films you have seen in recent months. Now, answer the following question: How much aggression or violence did each of these contain? How often did characters in these movies, hit, shoot at, or otherwise attempt to harm others? Unless your moviegoing habits are somewhat unusual, you probably recognize that many popular films contain a great deal of violence—much more than you are ever likely to see in real life (see Figure 9.8). Careful analyses of the contents of television programs, films, and televised sports events indicate that all contain a great deal of violence (Reiss & Roth, 1993; Waters et al., 1993). Indeed, one recent study that analyzed the content of commercials for food products—for example, milk, soups, and cereals—found that even *these* often contained themes of violence (Rajecki et al., 1994).

These findings have lead many social psychologists to pose the following question: Does

FIGURE 9.8   The Prevalence of Media Violence.

Many popular films contain large amounts of violence—more violence, and in more graphic forms, than was true in the past. Does exposure to such materials increase the likelihood of aggression by persons who are exposed to them? This important question has received a great deal of attention in ongoing research by social psychologists.

exposure to such materials increase aggression among children or adults? This is an important issue, so it is not surprising that it has been the subject of literally hundreds of research projects (e.g., Huesmann & Miller, 1994). The findings of these studies have not been entirely consistent, but taken together, they point to the following conclusion: *Exposure to media violence may indeed be one factor contributing to high and rising levels of violence in the United States and elsewhere.*

Perhaps the most convincing evidence for an important link between exposure to media violence and aggression, however, is provided by *long-term (longitudinal) research* in which participants have been studied for many years (e.g., Huesmann & Eron, 1986). For example, in one of the best-known of these investigations, all third-graders in one county of upstate New York were questioned about their favorite television programs. In addition, ratings of the children's aggression were obtained from their classmates. Results indicated that there was a link between these variables, at least among boys: The more violence these eight-year-olds watched, the higher the ratings of their aggression by other children. Ten years later, the same participants were studied again, and this relationship was confirmed: The more violence they had watched as children, the higher their level of aggression as teenagers. Finally, the same persons were studied once more when they were about thirty years old. Again, the amount of aggression viewed by participants as children predicted their level of aggression—both their self-ratings of such behavior and state records of arrests for aggressive actions. These dramatic results have been replicated in several other long-term studies conducted in many different countries—for example, Australia, Finland, Israel, Poland, and South Africa (Botha, 1990; Huesmann & Eron, 1986). In all these studies, too, the greater the amount of violent television watched by participants, the greater their subsequent levels of aggression. Moreover, in these later studies, these findings have been obtained for females as well as for males.

While these studies are impressive, and have been very carefully conducted, it's important to remember that they are still only correlational in nature. As we pointed out in Chapter 1, the fact that two variables are correlated does *not* imply that one necessarily causes the other. Further, as we noted earlier, not all studies on the potential effects of media violence have yielded consistent findings. Still, when all types of research evidence are considered, and when the findings of all these studies are subjected to meta-analysis (Comstock & Paik, 1991; Wood, Wong, & Chachere, 1991), results do point to the conclusion we stated at the outset: Exposure to media violence can contribute, along with many other factors, to the occurrence of overt aggression. A similar conclusion has been reached in research on exposure to *violent pornography* in which women are generally the victims and they are shown being raped, tortured, and brutalized in many ways (e.g., Linz, Donnerstein, & Penrod, 1988; Zillmann & Bryant, 1984). Exposure to such materials can increase males' willingness to engage in such behavior themselves (e.g., Kutchinsky, 1991; Linz et al., 1988).

Heightened Arousal: Emotion, Cognition, and Aggression. Suppose that you are driving to the airport to meet a friend. Just before you get there, another driver cuts in front of you so suddenly that you almost have a collision. Your heart pounds wildly and you feel your blood pressure shoot through the roof; but fortunately, no accident occurs. Now you arrive at the airport. You park and rush inside, because it's almost time for your friend's flight to arrive. When you get to the security check, there's an elderly man in front of you. As he walks through, the buzzer sounds and he becomes confused. The security guard can't make him understand that he must empty his pockets and walk through again. In fact, you feel yourself growing extremely angry. "What's wrong with him?" you think to yourself. "Hasn't he ever been to an airport before?" As the delay continues, you feel yourself sorely tempted to shout at the elderly man or even to push your way by him.

Now for the key question: Do you think that your recent near miss in traffic may have played any role in your sudden surge of anger? In short, could the emotional arousal from that incident have somehow transferred to the totally unrelated situation at the security gate? Indeed, under some conditions, heightened arousal—whatever its original source—*can* enhance aggression in response to frustration or provocation. In fact, in various experiments arousal stemming from such diverse sources as participation in competitive games (Christy, Gelfand, & Hartmann, 1971), vigorous exercise (Zillmann 1979), and even some types of music (Rogers & Ketcher, 1979) has been found to facilitate subsequent aggression. Why is this the case? A compelling explanation is offered by **excitation transfer theory** (Zillmann, 1994).

Excitation transfer theory begins by noting that physiological arousal, however produced, tends to dissipate slowly over time. As a result, some portion of such arousal may persist as a person moves from one situation to another. In the example above, some portion of the arousal you experienced as a result of a near miss in traffic, which is known as **residual arousal,** may still be present as you approach the security gate in the airport. Now, when you encounter minor annoyances, the residual arousal intensifies your emotional reactions to the annoyance. The result: You become enraged rather than just mildly irritated. Excitation theory further suggests that

such effects are most likely to occur when the persons involved are relatively unaware of the presence of residual arousal—a common occurrence, since small elevations in arousal are difficult to notice (Zillmann, 1994). Excitation transfer theory also suggests that such effects are likely to occur when the persons involved recognize their residual arousal but attribute it to events occurring in the present situation (Taylor et al., 1991). In the incident we have been describing, for instance, your anger would be intensified if you recognized your feelings of arousal but attributed them to the elderly man's actions (see Figure 9.9). We'll return to the role of cognition in aggression in our later discussion of the prevention and control of aggression; as we'll see then, reestablishing cognitive control over behavior can be highly effective in reducing the likelihood of interpersonal violence (Zillmann, 1993).

FIGURE 9.9   Excitation Transfer Theory: An Overview.

Excitation transfer theory suggests that arousal occurring in one situation can persist and intensify emotional reactions in later, unrelated situations. Thus, the arousal generated by a near miss in traffic can intensify feelings of annoyance or frustration produced by delays at an airport security gate.

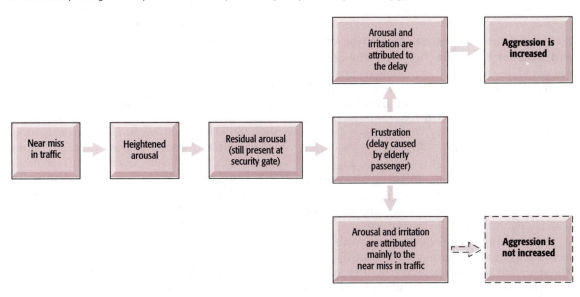

(*Source:* Based on suggestions by Zillmann, 1988, 1994.)

Integrating Principles

1. Contrary to earlier beliefs, human aggression does not stem from a single, all-important cause such as frustration. In fact, it is influenced by many different social factors, including provocations from others, exposure to aggressive models, and heightened arousal.

2. Several of these factors play important roles in other forms of social behavior as well as in aggression. For example, modeling influences prosocial behavior (this chapter); heightened arousal affects many aspects of social behavior, such as attraction (Chapter 7); and aggression, in the form of sexual jealousy, influences many relationships (Chapter 7).

Who Aggresses?

Are some persons "primed" for aggression by their personal characteristics? Informal observation suggests that this is so. While some individuals rarely lose their tempers or engage in aggressive actions, others seem to be forever blowing their tops, often with serious consequences. In this section, we will consider several personal traits or characteristics that seem to play an important role in aggression.

The Type A Behavior Pattern: Why the *A* in Type A Could Well Stand for *Aggression.* Do you know anyone you could describe as (1) extremely competitive, (2) always in a hurry, and (3) especially irritable and aggressive? If so, this person shows the characteristics of what psychologists term the **Type A behavior pattern** (Glass, 1977; Strube, 1989). At the opposite end of the continuum are persons who do not show these characteristics—individuals who are not highly competitive, who are not always fighting the clock, and who do not readily lose their temper; such persons are described as showing the **Type B behavior pattern.**

Given the characteristics mentioned above, it seems only reasonable to expect that Type As would tend to be more aggressive than Type Bs in many situations. In fact, the results of several experiments indicate that this is actually the case (R. A. Baron, Russell, & Arms, 1985). For exam-

ple, consider a study by Berman, Gladue, and Taylor (1993). These researchers exposed young men known to be Type A or Type B to increasing provocation from a stranger: This person set increasingly strong shocks for them in a competitive reaction time task where the slower-to-respond person (the loser on each trial) received the shock set for him by his opponent, which is a method for studying aggression.

The researchers also measured participants' testosterone level by taking samples of participants' saliva before the start of the reaction time task. Results indicated that during the competitive task, Type As who also had a high level of testosterone set the highest level of shocks for their opponent. In addition, Type As with high testosterone levels were much more likely than other participants to use the highest shock setting available. These findings indicate that two different personal characteristics—the Type A behavior pattern and testosterone level—both play a role in determining aggressive behavior.

Additional findings indicate that Type As are truly hostile people: They don't merely aggress against others because this is a useful means for reaching other goals, such as winning athletic contests or furthering their own careers. Rather, they are more likely than Type Bs to engage in what is known as **hostile aggression**—aggression in which the prime objective is inflicting some kind of harm on the victim (Strube et al., 1984). In view of this fact, it is not surprising to learn that Type As are more likely than Type Bs to engage in such actions as child abuse or spouse abuse (Strube et al., 1984). Moreover, such individuals appear to *spontaneously* judge other people in terms of hostility (Zelli, Huesmann, & Cervone, 1995). In contrast, Type As are *not* more likely to engage in **instrumental aggression**—aggression a person performs not primarily to harm the victim but to attain other goals, such as control of valued resources or praise from others for behaving in a "tough" manner.

Irritability, Rumination, and the "Big Five" Dimensions of Personality. In recent years, research on personality has converged on a startling conclusion: While people differ in a very large number of

TABLE 9.1 ■ The "Big Five" Dimensions of Personality

A growing body of research findings indicate that the dimensions shown here are very basic ones with respect to human personality.

DIMENSION	DESCRIPTION
Extraversion	A dimension ranging from sociable, talkative, fun-loving, affectionate, adventurous at one end to retiring, sober, reserved, silent, and cautious at the other.
Agreeableness (Related to Aggression)	A dimension ranging from good-natured, gentle, cooperative, trusting, and helpful at one end to irritable, ruthless, suspicious, uncooperative, and headstrong at the other.
Conscientiousness	A dimension ranging from well-organized, careful, self-disciplined, responsible, and scrupulous at one end to disorganized, careless, weak-willed, and unscrupulous at the other.
Emotional Stability (Related to Aggression)	A dimension ranging from poised, calm, composed, and not hypochondriacal at one end to nervous, anxious, excitable, and hypochondriacal at the other.
Openness to Experience	A dimension ranging from imaginative, sensitive, intellectual, and polished at one end to down-to-earth, insensitive, crude, and simple at the other.

ways, many of these are related only to the five underlying basic dimensions, shown in Table 9.1 (McCrae & Costa, 1997; Funder & Sneed, 1993). Many studies indicate that they are, indeed, very basic dimensions of personality. For example, where individuals stand on several of these dimensions is readily apparent to strangers meeting them for the first time (Funder & Colvin, 1991; Watson, 1989). And standing on several of the "Big Five" dimensions is closely linked to satisfaction in and performance of many different jobs (Barrick & Mount, 1993). Are these dimensions also related to aggression? Research carried out by Caprara and his colleagues (e.g., Caprara et al., 1994) indicates that they are.

In these studies—most of which were conducted in European countries such as Italy—Caprara (e.g., 1986, 1987) found that several traits, including *irritability* (the tendency to react impulsively or rudely to even slight provocations), *emotional reactivity* (the tendency to overreact emotionally to frustration), and *rumination* (the tendency to think about provocations and seek revenge for them), are all related to aggression. These characteristics, in turn, have been found to be closely linked to two aspects of the "Big Five" dimensions of personality: *agreeable-*

ness and *emotional stability*. In other words, persons who are high in irritability and emotional reactivity tend to fall toward the hostile end of the agreeableness–hostility "Big Five" dimension, while those who are high in rumination tend to fall toward the unstable end of the emotional stability dimension. Similarly, other research supports the view that agreeableness—in the form of *sensitivity to others' needs*—reduces sexual aggression (Dean & Malamuth, 1997). So, in short, highly aggressive persons often are disagreeable, suspicious, and hostile, as well as emotionally overreactive and unstable.

Gender Differences in Aggression: Are They Real? Are males more aggressive than females? Folklore suggests that they are, and research findings suggest that in this case, such informal observation is correct: When asked whether they have ever engaged in any of a wide range of aggressive actions, males report a higher incidence of many aggressive behaviors than do females (Harris, 1994, in press; see Figure 9.10). On closer examination, however, the picture regarding gender differences in aggression becomes more complex. On the one hand, males are generally more likely both to perform aggressive actions and to

Research evidence indicates that, as shown here, males are more likely to engage in *physical* aggression than females. However, females are more likely than males to engage in other forms of aggression, especially verbal and *indirect* forms.

(*Source:* Reprinted with special permission of King Features Syndicate.)

serve as the target for such behavior (Bogard, 1990; Harris, 1992, 1994)—although incidents involving sexual jealousy appear to represent an important exception to this rule (de Weerth & Kalma, 1993; Harris, 1994; Malamuth et al., 1995). On the other hand, however, the size of these differences appears to vary greatly across situations.

First, gender differences in aggression are much larger in the absence of provocation than in its presence. In other words, males are significantly more likely than females to aggress against others when these persons have *not* provoked them in any manner (Bettencourt & Miller, 1996). In situations where provocation *is* present, in contrast, gender differences in aggression tend to shrink or even disappear. Further, the size—and even the direction—of gender differences in aggression seems to vary greatly with the *type* of aggression in question. While males are more likely than females to engage in various forms of *physical* aggression—hitting, punching, kicking, use of weapons—the opposite seems to be true with respect to verbal aggression and various *indirect* forms of aggression. Females actually seem to be more likely to engage in forms of aggression that

make it difficult for victims to identify who aggressed, or even to realize that they have been the target of aggressive behavior (Archer & Haigh, 1996; Bjorkqvist, Lagerspetz, & Kaukiainen, 1992). Among children, such indirect forms of aggression include telling lies or spreading rumors behind the target's back, replacing the person as a friend with a rival, and ignoring the target person. Research findings indicate that these gender differences are present among children as young as eight and increase through age fifteen (Bjorkqvist et al., 1992), persisting into adulthood (A. Campbell, Sapochnik, & Muncer, 1996). In fact, recent findings (Bjorkqvist, Osterman, & Hjelt-Back, 1994) can be interpreted as suggesting that although males show increased use of indirect forms of aggression as they mature, females continue to "outshine" them in this respect.

In sum, there do appear to be some differences between females and males with respect to aggression, but these differences are often more subtle and complex than informal observation might suggest. Eagly and her colleagues (Eagly, 1987; Eagly & Wood, 1991) offer a *social-role interpretation* for gender differences in aggression. According to this view, many societies expect males to be more assertive and masterful—and aggressive—than females, but also expect females to be more nurturant, more emotional, and more concerned for the well-being of others than males. It is these contrasting expectations, these researchers argue, that account for gender differences in aggression. While such arguments are compelling and are supported by the findings of many studies (e.g., Coats & Feldman, 1996; Eagly & Steffen, 1986), some evidence points to the conclusion that biological or genetic factors also play a role in the greater tendency of males to engage in at least some forms of aggression. Perhaps most convincing in this regard is the evidence suggesting that among males, the higher the level of testosterone, the higher the level of aggression either reported or shown by research participants (e.g., Berman, Gladue, & Taylor, 1993; Gladue, 1991).

Taken together, these findings and those of several other studies (e.g., Olweus, 1986) suggest that social and biological factors influence gender differences in aggression. It's important to realize, however, that even if hormonal factors play some role in gender differences in aggression, this in no way implies that males *must* show higher levels of aggression than females. On the contrary, it seems clear that gender differences in aggression, like other gender differences we have considered, stem from a complex interplay of many different factors and are definitely *not* an unchangeable given where social behavior is concerned.

Integrating Principles

1. Several personal characteristics influence aggression. These include the Type A behavior pattern, the hostile attributional bias, and two traits from the "Big Five" dimensions of personality.
2. These same characteristics also influence many other aspects of social behavior. For example, the Type A behavior pattern plays a role in behavior in work settings (Chapter 11), while the "Big Five" dimensions of personality are related to self-perceptions (Chapter 4) and behavior in groups (Chapter 10).

Preventing Aggression

If there is one idea in this chapter we hope you'll remember in the years ahead, it is this: Aggression is *not* an inevitable or unmodifiable form of behavior. On the contrary, because it stems from a complex interplay between external events, cognitions, and personal characteristics, it *can* be prevented or reduced. In this final section, we consider several procedures that, when used appropriately, can be effective in this regard.

Punishment: Effective Deterrent to Violence? Do you support *capital punishment*—the death penalty for certain crimes of violence? Some politicians think that it acts as a *deterrent* to criminals who engage in aggressive acts, but other politicians doubt this logic. Other politicians argue that capital punishment makes society a safer place by permanently removing violent criminals. As we explain below, this is a complex issue, and evidence relating to it is mixed. Thus, we can't hope to resolve it here (R. A. Baron & Richardson, 1994). What we *can* do, however, is point out a few pertinent facts about the use of **punishment**—delivery of aversive consequences in order to decrease some behavior—as a technique for reducing overt aggression.

First, we should note that existing evidence points to the conclusion that punishment *can* succeed in deterring individuals from engaging in many forms of behavior: However, such effects are neither automatic nor certain. Unless punishment is administered in accordance with basic principles, it can be totally *ineffective* in this respect. What conditions must be met for punishment to succeed? First, it must be prompt—it must follow aggressive actions as quickly as possible. Second, it must be *certain*—the probability that punishment will follow aggression must be 100 percent. Third, it must be *strong*—it must be of sufficient magnitude to be highly unpleasant to potential recipients. Finally, it must be seen as *justified;* if, in contrast, it is perceived by recipients as random or unrelated to their past actions, its deterrent effects will be greatly reduced.

Unfortunately, as you can readily see, these conditions are often *not* present in the criminal justice systems of many nations. In many societies,

Social Diversity: A Critical Analysis

U.S. Geographical Differences in "The Culture of Honor"

Within the United States, the South has long been regarded as somewhat more violent than the North, possibly because of its higher temperatures, its higher poverty rates, or perhaps because of its history of slavery. Cohen, Nisbett, Bowdle, and Schwarz (1996) investigated a contrasting hypothesis, that Southerners possess differing social norms about aggression. However, it is not that Southerners favor being aggressive; instead, Southern men are more likely than Northern men to possess a *culture of honor,* a deeply held belief in the honor of one's self and one's family (D. Cohen & Nisbett, 1994; Nisbett, 1993). For men raised in the South, these norms imply being honest, taking pride in one's courage, strength, and virtue. From this perspective, insults are perceived as lowering a man's reputation so that it is necessary to restore status through the use of aggressive or violent behavior.

According to Cohen and his colleagues, the culture of honor persisted for generations of Southerners and persists even today in laws and policies that favor greater aggression relative to those in the North (D. Cohen, 1996; Nisbett, 1993; Nisbett & Cohen, 1996). Thus, even for a southern man in the 1990s, a provocation may threaten his social standing and require aggressive retribution in order to regain his esteem. You'll recall reading in this chapter how provocations often lead to aggression; the "culture of honor" hypothesis suggests that for Southerners the provocation effect is even more exaggerated because these men have internalized beliefs that support aggressive reactions in response to such threats.

To test these expectations, Cohen and his colleagues conducted an intriguing series of experiments at the University of Michigan. The researchers recruited the participants using the telephone and offered them $5 to take part in the study supposedly about response time and human judgments. The men, who participated individually, had no idea that the study actually concerned regional differences in aggression. After a short introduction to the study, the men completed a demographic questionnaire and then were directed by the experimenter to place it on a table which was down a narrow corridor immediately adjacent to the laboratory area.

Just as the experimenter finished giving these instructions, an experimental accomplice (whom we'll call "Biff") entered the hallway and opened a file drawer, appearing to work on something. Because the hallway was so narrow, Biff had to close the file drawer in order for the participant to pass; Biff then reopened the drawer. When the participant returned a moment later, Biff had to close the drawer again; this time he *slammed* the file shut, bumped into the participant with his shoulder, and insulted him, calling him an a–hole as he stomped into an adjacent room. As you can see, this insult was quite a provocation! Confirming the hypothesis, Southern men reacted with more anger than Northern men. Similarly, Southerners were more likely to respond with aggressive reactions when asked to imagine that another man was making passes at their fiancée.

Cohen and his colleagues used the insult procedure in two further studies. Their second study showed that the insult actually raised the Southerners', but not the Northerners', testosterone levels. Thus, this study showed physiological evidence of *preparedness* for aggression, but not actual aggression. In the third study, showed that Southern men who had been insulted were more daring than other men who had not been insulted and compared to Northerners.

These results suggest that in the United States, a "culture of honor" characterizes Southern men relative to Northern men, in which insults diminish a man's reputation and attempts are made to regain status by using aggressive behavior. Given the intriguing nature of this research, it is important to highlight several points about these studies, some of which Cohen and his colleagues emphasized. First, even Northern men reacted with greater aggression in response to a provocation; the Southern men reacted somewhat more strongly. Second, results concerning regional differences such as these are *correlational*—they do not allow a researcher to determine whether a variable such as the culture of honor actually *caused* the pattern of results. Third, these studies examined only one side of the culture of honor—if helpfulness or politeness were examined instead of aggression, reversed results might well emerge. Finally, as we discussed in this chapter, aggressive behavior results from the interplay of social learning, situational variables such as provocation, and biological variables such as testosterone. The mere fact that someone is from the North or the South of a country is unlikely to be a good clue about whether that person is likely to aggress against you!

the delivery of punishment for aggressive actions is delayed for months or even years; many criminals avoid arrest and conviction; the magnitude of punishment itself varies from one courtroom or jurisdiction to another; and punishment *is* often perceived as unjustified or unfair by those who receive it. In view of these facts, it is hardly surprising that punishment often seems to fail as a deterrent to violent crime. The dice, so to speak, are heavily loaded against it. Would punishment prove effective as a deterrent to violence if it were used more effectively? While we can't say for certain, existing evidence does suggest that it could, potentially, exert such effects, but only if it were used in accordance with the principles noted above.

Cognitive Interventions: Apologies and Overcoming Cognitive Deficits. Let's return once again to our shopping cart example. This time, imagine that immediately after ramming you, the other shopper apologizes profusely. "Excuse me!" she says, obviously upset. "Are you hurt? I'm so sorry!" Will you get angry? Probably not. Her apology—an admission of wrongdoing plus a request for forgiveness—will go a long way toward defusing your emotional reaction. Of course, your reactions will depend strongly on the nature of her excuses—and on the apparent sincerity of her apologies. Research findings suggest that excuses that make reference to causes beyond the excuse-giver's control are much more effective than ones that refer to events within this person's

control (Weiner et al., 1987). And we are much less likely to get angry when apologies seem to be sincere than when they appear to be an attempt to conceal true malicious intent (R. A. Baron, 1989b; Ohbuchi, Kameda, & Agarie, 1989b). So both excuses and apologies can be effective as cognitive strategies for reducing aggression.

Other cognitive techniques are related to the concept of *cognitive deficit,* which refers to the fact that when we experience strong anger, our ability to evaluate the consequences of our own actions may be reduced. As a result, the effectiveness of restraints that normally serve to hold aggression in check (e.g., fear of retaliation) may be reduced. Any procedures that serve to overcome this cognitive deficit, then, may help reduce overt aggression (Zillmann, 1993). One such technique involves *preattribution*—attributing annoying actions by others to *unintentional* causes before the provocation actually occurs. For example, before meeting with someone you know can be irritating, you could remind yourself that she or he doesn't mean to make you angry—it's just the result of an unfortunate personal style. Another technique involves preventing yourself—or others—from ruminating about previous real or imagined wrongs (Zillmann, 1993). One way to do so is by participating in pleasant, absorbing activities that have no connection to anger and aggression—anything from watching a funny movie or television program to solving interesting puzzles. Such activities allow for a cooling-off period during which anger can dissipate, and also help to reestablish cognitive controls over behavior—controls that play a key role in inhibiting overt aggression.

Training in Social Skills: Learning to Get Along with Others. One reason why many persons become involved in aggressive encounters is that they are sorely lacking in basic social skills. They don't know how to respond to provocations from others in a way that will soothe these persons rather than inflame them. Similarly, they don't know how to make their wishes known to others, and they grow increasingly frustrated when people don't take account of these wishes. Persons lacking in basic social skills seem to account for a high proportion of violence in many societies (Toch, 1985). Thus, equipping these individuals with the social skills they lack may go a long way toward reducing the incidence of aggression.

Fortunately, systematic procedures for teaching individuals such skills do exist, and they are not very complex. For example, both adults and children can rapidly acquire improved social skills from watching *social models*—people who demonstrate both effective and ineffective behaviors (Schneider, 1991). Moreover, such gains can be obtained through just a few hours of treatment (Bienert & Schneider, 1993). These findings serve to underscore the following points: (1) Highly aggressive persons—children and adults—are not necessarily "bad" individuals who attack others because of uncontrollable hostile impulses; (2) their aggression often stems from deficits in basic social skills; and (3) such deficits can readily be overcome.

Integrating Principles

1. Several different techniques useful in preventing or reducing human aggression are suggested by basic principles of social psychology. Punishment can be effective, but only under favorable conditions.
2. These include inducing individuals to attribute provocative actions to causes other than personal malice (attributions; see Chapter 2), and equipping them with improved social skills (modeling; see Chapter 6).

Connections   Integrating Social Psychology

In this chapter, you read about . . .	In other chapters, you will find related discussions of . . .
▪ bystanders' response to the nonverbal cues provided by other bystanders	▪ interpretation of nonverbal cues (Chapter 2)
▪ genetics and helping	▪ the roles of genetics in prejudice (Chapter 6), attraction (Chapter 7), mate selection (Chapter 8), and aggression (Chapter 9)
▪ the role of affect in helping and aggression	▪ the roles of affect in attitudes (Chapter 5), prejudice (Chapter 6), and relationships (Chapter 7)
▪ social comparison among bystanders in emergency situations	▪ social comparison as a factor in affiliative behavior (Chapter 7) and as a factor in social influence (Chapter 8)
▪ attribution processes in perceptions of emergency situations and of others' aggressive actions	▪ theories of attribution (Chapter 2)
▪ cognitive theories of aggression and helping	▪ cognitive theories relating to other forms of social behavior: attitude change (Chapter 5), prejudice (Chapter 6)

Thinking about Connections

1. Attorneys sometimes defend individuals who commit violent acts—including murder—by suggesting that these persons were "overwhelmed" by emotions beyond their control. In view of our discussions in other chapters (e.g., Chapter 3, Chapter 10) of the effects of emotions on social thought and social behavior, what are your reactions to such defenses? And do you think that such reactions, if they occur, excuse the persons who commit such acts from personal responsibility for them?

2. You are hurrying toward a movie theater in a busy mall a few minutes before your film is scheduled to begin when a woman in front of you slips and drops several small packages that she is carrying. Make of list of all the factors that might deter-

mine whether you stop and help or continue toward the movie.

3. You have probably observed a stranger who possibly needed help. For example, on our campus a letter to the student newspaper described a scene near the student union late one cold Saturday evening. A student lay on a bench—apparently unconscious. Many students walked past him as they left the building. If you were one of them, how would you react? Make a list of the nonverbal cues possibly provided by other bystanders. How would social comparison processes operate in this instance? What possible attributions would you make about the stranger who might (or might not) need help? How would these nonverbal cues, social comparisons, and attributions influence your behavior?

Summary and Review

Prosocial behavior refers to acts of helping others that have no obvious benefits for the person who helps.

Responding to an Emergency

Latané and Darley proposed that a bystander responds or fails to respond to an emergency as a function of choices made (often unconsciously) in a series of five steps. A prosocial act will not occur unless the bystander pays attention to the situation, interprets it as an emergency, assumes responsibility for taking action, knows what must be done to provide help, and decides to engage in the helping behavior. In addition to various aspects of the situation that encourage or discourage helping, dispositional factors are also involved, and a combination of traits make up the *altruistic personality.*

Additional Factors That Influence Prosocial Behavior

Helping behavior is enhanced by the presence of helpful models, including exposure to such mod-

els in the media. A victim is most likely to receive help if he or she is liked by the bystander and is similar to that person. When similarity is too great, however, the situation can be threatening, because it suggests to the bystander that "this could happen to you." One way to control this threat is to attribute responsibility to the victim, blaming the victim for the problem. Not all helping involves emergencies, and long-term volunteering is motivated by both selfless and selfish needs. A victim who asks for help is most likely to receive it, though the need for help can constitute a stigma. Receiving help is often uncomfortable and threatening to one's self-esteem, especially when the helper is a sibling or otherwise similar to oneself.

Theoretical Explanations of Prosocial Motivation

Most explanations of helpfulness assume that the final motivation to act is based on whether the perceived outcome for the bystander is increased positive affect or decreased negative affect. The more specific proposals include the idea that at least some prosocial behavior is based on *empathy* and the unselfish desire to be helpful, that helping is based on *relieving a negative emotional state*, and that helping is done to make the helper *feel good*. From an evolutionary perspective, we have inherited the tendency to help those most like ourselves because their survival increases the odds that our shared genes will be passed on to future generations.

Theoretical Perspectives on Aggression

Aggression—the intentional infliction of harm on others—has been attributed to many different causes. *Instinct theories,* such as the ones proposed by Freud and Lorenz, suggest that aggression stems from innate urges. *Biological theories* suggest that aggression is influenced, at least to some degree, by biological factors such as sex hormones and various neural disorders. *Drive theories* suggest that aggression stems from externally generated motives. The *social learning view,* in contrast, emphasizes the role of learning, calling attention to the fact that human beings learn how to aggress against others through both direct and vicarious experience. Finally, *cognitive theories* of aggression suggest that aggression stems from a complex interplay among cognitive factors, past experiences, and current moods.

Social Determinants of Aggression

Many acts of aggression are triggered by the words or deeds of persons with whom the aggressor interacts, or by social conditions generally. *Frustration*—interference with goal-directed behavior—can facilitate aggression, perhaps because of the negative feelings it generates; but frustration is *not* the only or the strongest determinant of aggression. *Direct provocations* from others are important causes of aggression, especially when such actions appear to stem from malevolent intent. Exposure to *media violence* (in films or television shows) can increase aggression on the part of viewers.

Heightened arousal can increase aggression. However, the impact of arousal on aggression depends on the complex interplay between emotions and cognitions. Cognitions—for example, our interpretations of the motives behind others' behavior—can strongly influence our emotional reactions to provocation. Similarly, strong emotions can interfere with our ability to formulate rational plans or to assess the likely results of our behavior—an effect known as *cognitive deficit.*

Personal Causes of Aggression

Persons showing the *Type A behavior pattern* are more aggressive in many situations than persons showing the *Type B behavior pattern.* Individuals who perceive hostile intent behind others' actions, even when this does not really exist, are more aggressive than those who do not show this *hostile attributional bias.* Recent findings indicate that several traits related to aggression—for example, *irritability* and *rumination* (the tendency to think about real or imagined provocations)—are closely related to the "Big Five" dimensions of personality. Specifically, aggression-related traits appear to be linked to the dimensions of *agreeableness* and *emotional stability.*

Males are more aggressive overall than females. However, these differences occur primarily in situations where provocation is lacking; when provoked, males and females do not differ appreciably in level of aggression. In addition, while males tend to show higher levels of physical aggression than females, females demonstrate higher levels of *indirect* aggression than males. Both cultural and biological factors may be involved in these gender differences in aggression.

The Prevention and Control of Aggression

Several techniques are effective in reducing aggression. *Punishment* can be effective if it is delivered swiftly and surely, is intense, and is perceived as justified. Direct *apologies* can sometimes deter aggression. In addition, several techniques help to overcome the *cognitive deficits* produced by intense anger. These include *preattribution*—attributing provocative actions by others to causes other than malice *before* these provocations occur—and participation in activities that divert attention away from anger-producing events or situations. Another technique for reducing aggression is the induction of *incompatible responses*—reactions incompatible with anger or overt aggression.

Social Diversity: Aggression and the Culture of Honor

Within the United States, Southern men may be more likely than Northern men to adopt and internalize the *culture of honor,* a social norm in which personal insults, or provocations, should be met with aggression in order to restore esteem. Research suggests that Southerners respond to

these insults in many ways, including raised testosterone levels, perceiving that others view them as having low masculinity, and aggressive behavior.

Key Terms

Aggression (p. 208)
Altruistic Personality (p. 212)
Bystander Effect (p. 209)
Cognitive Theories (of aggression) (p. 221)
Diffusion of Responsibility (p. 211)
Empathic Joy Hypothesis (p. 217)
Empathy–Altruism Hypothesis (p. 216)
Excitation Transfer Theory (p. 225)
Frustration–Aggression Hypothesis (p. 222)
Genetic Determinism Model (p. 218)
Hostile Aggression (p. 226)

Instrumental Aggression (p. 226)
Negative State Relief Model (p. 217)
Pluralistic Ignorance (p. 210)
Prosocial Behavior (p. 208)
Provocation (p. 223)
Punishment (p. 229)
Residual Arousal (p. 225)
Social Learning View (p. 220)
Type A Behavior Pattern (p. 226)
Type B Behavior Pattern (p. 226)

For More Information

Baron, R. A., & Richardson, D. R. (1994). *Human aggression,* (2nd ed.). New York: Plenum.

This book provides a broad introduction to current knowledge about human aggression. Separate chapters focus on the biological, social, environmental, and personal determinants of aggression. Additional chapters examine the development of aggression and the incidence of aggression in many natural settings.

Huesmann, L. R. (Ed.). (1994). *Aggressive behavior: Current perspectives.* New York: Plenum.

A collection of chapters by well-known researchers, dealing with many different aspects of aggression. The chapters on gender differences, the long-term effects of exposure to media violence, and delin-

quent gangs are especially interesting, and expand on topics covered in this book.

Schroeder, D. A., Penner, L. A., Dovidio, J. F., & Piliavin, J. A. (1995). *The social psychology of helping and altruism: Problems and puzzles.* New York: McGraw-Hill.

The first text entirely devoted to the topic of prosocial behavior. The authors cover much of the material contained in this chapter, plus such topics as the developmental aspects of helping, cooperation, and collective helping. Their concluding chapter is designed to integrate the research material into an affective and cognitive model and to suggest future research.

chapter **10**

Groups and Individuals: The Consequences of Belonging

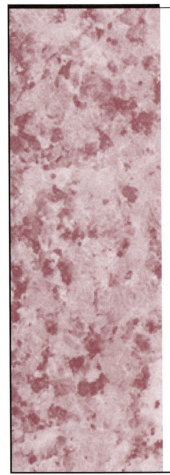

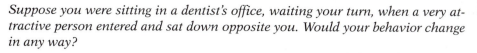

*Suppose you were sitting in a dentist's office, waiting your turn, when a very at-
tractive person entered and sat down opposite you. Would your behavior change
in any way?*

*Imagine that you were part of a group that had to make an important decision. Sup-
pose that later, after making it, your group learned that its decision had been a bad
one. Would you and the other members feel any pressure to stick with it anyway?*

*Have you ever had to perform in public? Give a solo musical recital? Rush to meet
a deadline while others watched? How did you do?*

*Quick: Can you name any current leaders (political, spiritual, military, or other-
wise) that you consider to be truly great?*

These are intriguing questions, and although they seem diverse, social psychologists would argue that they are actually related: All refer to various aspects of *group influence*—the effects of being part of (or belonging to) social groups. As you'll soon see, group influence is a pervasive and powerful force. All of us belong to many different social groups, and the effects of such member-ship can be profound. To provide you with an overview of the scope and impact of group influ-ence, we'll focus in this chapter on five important topics. First, we'll consider the basic nature of groups: What they are and how they exert their ef-fects on individuals. Second, we'll examine the impact of groups on *task performance*—how our performance on various tasks can be affected by working with others, or merely by their presence on the scene (as in the first question above). Third, we'll examine *decision making* in groups, focusing on the ways in which groups can affect, and sometimes distort, this important process. Finally, we'll conclude with a discussion of *leadership*—why certain individuals become lead-ers and how they influence other group members.

Groups: Their Nature and Function

Look at the photos in Figure 10.1. Which show social groups? Probably you would identify the one on the left as involving groups, but the one on the right as showing a mere collection of per-

sons. Why? Because implicitly, you already ac-cept a definition of the term **group** close to the one adopted by social psychologists: *A group con-sists of two or more interacting persons who share common goals, have a stable relationship, are somehow interdependent, and perceive that they are in fact part of a group* (Paulus, 1989). Let's ex-amine this definition more closely.

First, the definition suggests that to be part of a group, individuals must usually *interact* with each other, either directly or indirectly. Second, they must be *interdependent* in some manner—what happens to one must affect what happens to the others. Third, their relationship must be relatively *stable;* it must persist over appreciable periods of time (days, weeks, months, or even years). Fourth, the individuals involved must share at least some goals that they all seek to at-tain. Fifth, their interactions must be *structured* in some manner so that, for instance, each group member performs the same or similar functions each time they meet. Finally, the persons involved must recognize that they are part of a group.

Are all these conditions really necessary be-fore we can describe several persons as belong-ing to a group? While all are important, it's crucial to note that there are varying degrees of "groupness". At the high end, for instance, are groups consisting of persons who have worked together for many years. Clearly, they meet all re-quirements of the definition. At the low end are persons who have only a fleeting relationship with one another—for example, the passengers on an airplane. They are interdependent to a de-gree: If one blocks the aisle, others can't pass. They share certain basic goals, such as getting

---

FIGURE 10.1   What Makes a Group a Group?

In order for two or more persons to be termed a *group,* several criteria must be met. The left photo shows an actual social group; the right photo shows a mere collection of individuals who are *not* part of a group.

safely to their destination. But they don't expect to interact in the future and usually don't perceive themselves as part of a group—unless there is an emergency in flight, which could change this picture radically. Between these extremes are many social entities that we might be more or less inclined to describe as *groups.* So, in brief, deciding whether a collection of persons constitutes a true group is a complex matter, one of degree, rather than a simple yes/no decision. Having said this, we should note that many social psychologists feel that the key issue is whether the persons involved perceive themselves as part of a group. Only to the extent they do does it make sense to talk about a social group (Kosmitzki, 1996; Phinney, 1996).

Why Do People Join Groups?

Think about all the groups to which you belong at present: clubs, student associations, religious groups, informal groups consisting of the people with whom you hang out. Why did you join them in the first place? Social psychologists who have studied this issue have reached the conclusion that people join social groups for several different reasons (Paulus, 1989). First, groups help us satisfy important psychological or social needs, such as those for giving and receiving attention and affection, or for attaining a sense of belonging. These are subtle, but very real needs: Imagine what it would be like to live in total social isolation. You might not mind it much at first, but after a while, you'd probably get very lonely. Second, groups help us achieve goals that we could not attain as individuals. By working with others, we can often perform tasks we could not perform alone. Third, group membership often provides us with knowledge and information that would otherwise not be available to us. Fourth, groups help meet our need for security; in many cases there is safety in numbers, and belonging to various groups can provide protection against common enemies (see Figure 10.2). Finally, group membership also contributes to establishment of a positive *social identity*—it becomes part of our self-concept (see Chapter 4). And the greater the number of prestigious, restrictive groups to which an individual is admitted, the more her or his self-concept is bolstered (Tajfel, 1982). Groucho Marx—a famous comedian of the 1930s, '40s, and '50s—once remarked: "I wouldn't want to belong to any club that would accept me." As you can see, he was well aware of the value of joining prestigious groups—ones that would *not* accept someone such as himself!

FIGURE 10.2   Mutual Defense: One Reason Why People Join Groups.

Young people join gangs for many reasons. One of these is to gain protection against real or imagined enemies.

How Groups Function

That groups often exert powerful effects upon their members is obvious and is a basic theme of this entire chapter. Before turning to such group influence, however, we should address a basic issue: How, precisely, do groups affect their members? A complete answer to this question involves many processes we have examined in previous chapters (e.g., conformity, persuasion, attraction). In addition, though, four aspects of groups themselves play a key role in this regard: *roles*, *status*, *norms*, and *cohesiveness*.

Roles: Differentiation of Function within Groups. Think of a group to which you belong or have belonged—anything from the scouts to a professional association relating to your career. Now consider the following question: Did everyone in the group act in the same way or perform the same functions? Your answer is probably *no*. Dif-

ferent persons performed different tasks and were expected to accomplish different things for the group. In short they fulfilled different **roles.** Sometimes roles are assigned in a formal manner; for instance, a group may choose an individual to serve as its leader, secretary, or bouncer. In other cases, individuals gradually acquire certain roles without being formally assigned to them. In whatever fashion people acquire roles, they often *internalize* them, linking their roles to key aspects of their self-concept and self-perceptions (see Chapters 2 and 4). In this fashion, a role may exert profound effects on a person's behavior, even at times when the individual interacts with others who are not part of the group (Kollock, Blumstein, & Schwartz, 1994). For example, a high-powered attorney may find herself behaving toward her children in the same confrontational "Oh yeah?" manner she adopts in the courtroom.

Roles help to clarify the responsibilities and obligations of the persons belonging to a group. In addition, they provide one important way in which groups shape the behavior and thoughts of their members. They do have a potential downside, however: Group members sometimes experience *role conflict*—stress stemming from the fact that two roles they play are somehow incompatible. A very common example of role conflict involves the pressures experienced by new mothers and fathers who find the obligations of one role—*parent*—inconsistent with the obligations of the role of *student* or *employee*. Recent findings indicate that this kind of role conflict can be extremely stressful (K. J. Williams et al., 1991). So, while roles serve an important function in the effective functioning of groups, they can sometimes exert negative as well as positive effects.

Status: The Prestige of Various Roles. Have you ever met someone like the character in Figure 10.3? If so, you know that **status**—social standing or rank within a group—is a serious matter for many persons. In fact, status may play a key role in our perceptions of whether we are being treated fairly by others (Greenberg, 1993b; Tyler, 1994). If we feel we are getting treatment that is appropriate to our status, we feel that we are being treated fairly, and all is fine (Greenberg &

FIGURE 10.3   Status: An Important Feature of Groups.

Like the person shown here, most of us are deeply concerned with our *status* in the groups to which we belong.

Scott, 1996). This condition is known as equity (Greenberg, 1993a). If our treatment falls short of what we feel we deserve in this respect, however, we may take strong steps to rectify the situation (George & Brief, 1992).

In any case, status is another important factor in the functioning of groups. Different roles or positions in a group are associated with different levels of status, and people are often exquisitely sensitive to this fact. Moreover, since status is linked to a wide range of desirable outcomes—everything from one's salary to perks such as the size of one's office or the use of a reserved parking spot—it is something individuals frequently seek. Thus, groups often confer or withhold status as a means of influencing the behavior of their members. And as you know from your own experience, such tactics can be highly effective.

Norms: The Rules of the Game. A third factor responsible for the powerful impact of groups upon their members is one we considered in Chapter 8: **norms.** Norms are rules, implicit or explicit, established by groups to regulate the behavior of their members. They tell group members how to behave (*prescriptive norms*) or how *not* to behave (*proscriptive norms*) in various situations. Most groups insist upon adherence to

their norms as a basic requirement for membership. Thus, it is not surprising that individuals wishing to join or remain in specific groups generally follow these rules of the game quite closely. If they do not, they may soon find themselves on the outside looking in.

Cohesiveness: The Glue That Binds. Consider two groups. In the first, members like one another very much, strongly desire the goals their group is seeking, and feel that they could not possibly find another group that would better satisfy their needs. In the second, the opposite is true: Members don't like one another, they do not share common goals, and they are actively seeking other groups that might offer them a better deal. Which group would exert stronger effects upon its members? The answer is obvious: the first. The reason for this difference involves **cohesiveness,** which has traditionally been defined in social psychology as all the forces (factors) that cause members to remain in the group such as liking for the other members and the desire to maintain or increase one's status by belonging to a high-status group (Festinger et al., 1950). At first glance, it might seem that cohesiveness involves primarily liking or attraction between group members. However, recent analyses of cohesiveness suggest that it involves what has been termed *depersonalized attraction*—liking for other group members stemming from the fact that they belong to the group and embody or represent its key features. The individual characteristics of the group members play little role in such attraction (Hogg & Hains, 1996).

In the past, cohesiveness was viewed as a unitary dimension ranging from low to high. Now, however, it is often viewed in *multidimensional terms*—in other words, it actually involves several factors, and these can vary independently of one another (Zaccaro & McCoy, 1988). For example, Cota and his colleagues (1995) suggest that cohesiveness involves two primary dimensions: *task–social* and *individual–group*. The task–social dimension relates to the extent to which individuals are interested in the goals of the group (task) or in social relationships within it (social). The individual–group dimension has to do with the extent to which members are committed to the group or to other members. In addition, Cota and his colleagues (1995) suggest that group cohesiveness involves *secondary dimensions* as well—dimensions relating to particular kinds of groups. For example, in military groups, cohesiveness may relate to status (ranks), with higher-ranking persons having higher cohesiveness than lower-ranking ones. In sports teams, the roles individuals play may be more important in determining cohesiveness.

Additional factors that influence cohesiveness include (1) the amount of effort required to gain entry into the group—the greater the costs of joining the group in the first place, the higher members' attraction to it (see our discussion of dissonance theory in Chapter 5); (2) external threats or severe competition (see Chapter 6); and (3) size—small groups tend to be more cohesive than large ones (Mullen & Copper, 1994).

In sum, several aspects of groups—roles, status, norms, and cohesiveness—determine the extent to which groups can, and do, influence their members. Since these factors play an important role in group influence, keep them in mind as we consider some of the specific ways in which groups shape the behavior and thought of their members. You'll certainly see them in operation at several points.

Groups and Task Performance

Some activities, such as reading, solving complex mathematical problems, or writing love letters, are best carried out alone. Most tasks we perform, however, are done in cooperation with others, or at least in their presence. This fact raises an intriguing question: What impact, if any, do groups exert upon task performance? In order to answer this question, we'll consider two separate but related issues: (1) What are the effects on performance of the presence of others, even if we are not actively coordinating our efforts with them, and (2) do individuals exert more effort or less when working with others in a group?

Performance in the Presence of Others

Imagine that you are a young athlete—an ice-skater, for example—and that you are preparing for your first important competition. You practice your routines alone for several hours each day, month after month. Finally, the big day arrives, and you skate out onto the ice in a huge arena filled with the biggest crowd you've ever seen. How will you do? Better or worse than was true when you practiced alone, or in front of your coach? Floyd Allport (1920, 1924) conducted an ingenious series of studies on this topic, which soon came to be known as **social facilitation,** defined as effects on performance resulting from the presence of others.

In one study, for example, Allport asked participants to write down as many associations as they could think of for words printed at the top of an otherwise blank sheet of paper (e.g., "building," "laboratory"). Results were clear: Ninety-three percent of the participants produced more associations when working in the presence of others than when working alone. But still Allport was not satisfied: He wondered whether the same effect would be found with a more complex task—one requiring high levels of thought. To find out, he asked participants to read short passages from ancient Roman authors, and then to write down all the arguments they could think of that would tend to *disprove* the points made in these passages. Once more, they performed this task while alone and while in the presence of several other persons. Once more, results indicated that performance was increased when individuals worked in groups. Not only did they come up with more arguments, but also the quality of their ideas was better.

The Presence of Others: Is It Always Facilitating? Allport's research, and that conducted by other early social psychologists (e.g., Triplett, 1898), seemed to indicate that the presence of others is a definite plus—it improves performance on many different tasks. As the volume of research on this topic increased, however, puzzling findings began to appear: Sometimes the presence of others, as audience or as coactors, facilitated performance; but sometimes it produced the opposite effect (Pessin, 1933). So social facilitating was not always *facilitating;* indeed, it appeared as though this term was somewhat misleading. But *why* was this the case? Why did the presence of others sometimes enhance and sometimes impair performance? Believe it or not, this question remained unresolved until the mid-1960s, when a famous social psychologist, Robert Zajonc, offered an insightful answer. Let's take a closer look at his ideas.

The Drive Theory of Social Facilitation: Other Persons As a Source of Arousal. The basic idea behind Zajonc's **drive theory of social facilitation** is simple: The presence of others produces increments in arousal. As you can readily see, this suggestion agrees with our informal experience: The presence of other persons, especially when they are paying close attention to our performance as an interested audience, does seem to generate feelings of increased arousal. But how do such increments in arousal then affect our performance? Zajonc suggested that the answer involves two facts. First, it is a basic principle of psychology that increments in arousal increase the occurrence of *dominant responses*—the responses an individual is most likely to make in a given situation. Thus, when arousal increases, the tendency to make dominant responses, too, increases. Second, such dominant responses can be either correct or incorrect for any given task.

When these two facts are combined with the suggestion that the presence of others is arousing, two predictions follow: (1) The presence of others will facilitate performance when an individual's dominant responses are the correct ones in a given situation; but (2) the presence of others will impair performance when a person's dominant responses are incorrect in a given situation. (Figure 10.4 summarizes these points.) Another implication of Zajonc's reasoning is that the presence of others will facilitate performance when individuals are highly skilled in performing the task in question; under these conditions, their dominant responses are correct ones. In contrast, the presence of others will impair performance when individuals are not highly skilled—for example, when they are learning to perform a new task. Here, their dominant responses are likely to be errors.

Initial studies designed to test Zajonc's predictions generally yielded positive results (e.g., Matlin & Zajonc, 1968; Zajonc & Sales, 1966). Individuals were more likely to emit dominant responses in the presence of others than when alone, and performance on various tasks was either enhanced or impaired depending on whether these responses were correct or incorrect in each situation (Geen, 1989; Geen & Gange, 1977).

The Drive Theory of Social Facilitation.

According to the *drive theory of social facilitation* (Zajonc, 1965), the presence of others increases
arousal, and arousal in turn increases the tendency to perform dominant responses. If these are correct in a given situation, performance is enhanced; if they are incorrect, performance is impaired.

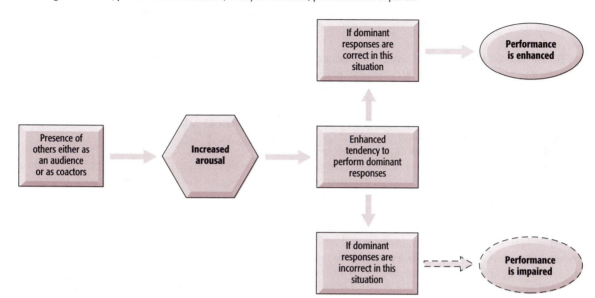

Additional research, however, soon raised an
important question: Does social facilitation stem
from the mere physical presence of others? Or do
other factors, such as concern over others' evaluations, also play a role? Support for the latter
possibility was provided by the results of several
ingenious studies indicating that social facilitation occurred only when individuals believed
that their performance could be observed and
evaluated by others (e.g., C. F. Bond, 1982). Such
findings led some social psychologists to propose
that social facilitation actually stems either from
evaluation apprehension—concern over being
judged by others (which is often arousing), or
from related concerns over *self-presentation*—
looking good in front of others (see our discussion of this topic in Chapter 2). Thus, it may be
these factors, not the mere physical presence of
others, that are crucial in determining the impact
of an audience or coactors on task performance.

These conclusions make good sense; after all,
would your performance be affected by the pres-

ence of someone who was sleeping soundly while
you worked on a task? Probably not. But we must
note that other evidence points to the conclusion
that sometimes social facilitation effects occur
even when concern over looking good to others,
or over evaluations of our work, do *not* seem to
play a role. For example, it has een found that
animals—even insects—perform simple tasks
better in the presence of same-species audience
than when alone (Zajonc, Heingartner, & Herman, 1969). Since it is difficult to assume that insects are concerned about the impressions they
make on other insects, these findings raise serious
questions about an interpretation of social facilitation based solely on evaluation apprehension.
Corresponding effects have also been found in
studies with human participants. For instance,
Schmitt and his colleagues (1986) found that performance on a simple task (typing one's own
name) was improved by the presence of others
who wore blindfolds and earphones, and so could
not possibly observe participant's performance.

However, when the audience did not wear blindfolds and earphones, performance was increased even more. These findings suggest that the mere presence of others is arousing and influences performance, but that the possibility of being evaluated by others increases arousal even more, and produces even stronger social facilitation effects.

The Distraction–Conflict Theory of Social Facilitation. An alternate model of social facilitation has been proposed by Robert S. Baron—not the Bob Baron whose name appears on the cover of this book—and his colleagues (e.g., R. S. Baron, 1986; Sanders, 1983). Like other explanations of social facilitation, this theory—known as **distraction–conflict theory**—assumes that audiences and coactors increase arousal. In contrast to earlier views, however, distraction–conflict theory suggests that such arousal stems from conflict between two tendencies: (1) the tendency to pay attention to the task being performed, and (2) the tendency to direct attention to an audience or coactors. Such conflict is arousing, and such arousal, in turn, enhances the tendency to perform dominant responses. If these are correct in a given situation, performance is enhanced; if they are incorrect, performance is impaired.

Several findings offer support for this theory. For example, audiences produce social facilitation effects only when directing attention to them conflicts in some way with task demands (Groff, R. S. Baron, & Moore, 1983). When paying attention to an audience does not conflict with task performance, social facilitation fails to occur. Similarly, individuals experience greater distraction when they perform various tasks in front of an audience than when they perform them alone (R. S. Baron, Moore, & Sanders, 1978). Finally, when individuals have little reason to pay attention to others present on the scene (e.g., when these persons are performing a different task), social facilitation fails to occur; when they have strong reasons for paying attention to others, social facilitation occurs (Sanders, 1983).

One major advantage of distraction–conflict theory is that it can explain why animals, as well as people, are affected by the presence of an audience. Briefly, since animals can experience conflicting response tendencies of the kind described above, it is not surprising that they are susceptible to social facilitation. Obviously, any theory that can explain similar patterns of behavior among organisms ranging from the lowly cockroach through human beings is powerful indeed, and worthy of very careful attention. So, while distraction–conflict theory may not provide a final answer to the persistent puzzle of social facilitation, it has certainly added substantially to our understanding of this process.

Letting Others Do the Work in Group Tasks

Suppose that you and several other people are helping a friend to move. In order to lift the heaviest pieces of furniture, you all pitch in. Will all of the people helping exert equal effort? Probably not. Some will take as much of the load as possible, while others will simply hang on, appearing to help more than they really do.

This pattern is quite common in situations where groups of person perform what are known as **additive tasks**—ones in which the contributions of each member are combined into a single group product. On such tasks, some persons work hard while others goof off, doing less than their share, and less than they might do if they were working alone (see Figure 10.5). Social psychologists refer to such effects as **social loafing**—reductions in motivation and effort when individuals work collectively in a group compared to when they work individually or as independent coactors (Karau & Williams, 1993, 1995).

That social loafing occurs has been demonstrated in many experiments. For example, in one of the first of these studies, Latané, Williams, and Harkins (1979) asked groups of male students to clap or cheer as loudly as possible at specific times, supposedly so that the experimenter could determine how much noise people make in social settings. Participants engaged in clapping and cheering either alone or in groups of two, four, or six persons. Results were clear: The magnitude of the sounds made by each person decreased sharply as group size rose. In other words, each participant put out less and less effort as the num-

FIGURE 10.5 Social Loafing: A Fact of Social Life.

When individuals work together with others on some task, they often experience reductions in motivation, make less effort, and do less (as individuals) than they would when working alone. Such effects are known as *social loafing*.

ber of other group members increased. And this was *not* due merely to increasing lack of coordination between group members; on the contrary, it stemmed from actual reductions in effort in the group condition. Additional research suggests that such social loafing is quite general in scope. It occurs among both males and females; among children as well as adults (K. D. Williams & Karau, 1991); in several different cultures—although it is stronger in Western than in Asian cultures (Yamaguchi, Okamoto, & Oka, 1985); under a wide variety of work conditions (e.g., Brickner, Harkins, & Ostrom, 1986; Harkins, 1987); and for cognitive tasks as well as ones involving physical effort (Weldon & Mustari, 1988; K. D. Williams & Karau, 1991). In short, social loafing appears to be a basic fact of social life. As noted by Karau and Williams (1993), social loafing has important im-

plications because many crucial tasks can only be accomplished in groups—sports teams, committees, juries, and government task forces, to mention just a few (e.g., G. W. Russell, 1993). The prevalence of social loafing has lead social psychologists to focus their attention on two important issues: *Why* do such effects occur? And what steps can be taken to reduce social loafing?

The Collective Effort Model: An Expectancy Theory of Social Loafing. Many different explanations for the occurrence of social loafing have been proposed. For example, one view—*social impact theory*—has related social loafing to a topic we examined in Chapter 9, *diffusion of responsibility* (Latané, 1981). According to social impact theory, as group size increases, each member feels less and less responsible for the task being performed. The result: Each person exerts decreasing effort on it. In contrast, other theories have focused on the fact that in groups, members' motivation decreases because they realize that their contributions can't be evaluated on an individual basis—so why work hard? (Harkins & Szymanski, 1989). Perhaps the most comprehensive explanation of social loafing offered to date, however, is the **collective effort model** proposed by Karau and Williams (1993, 1995).

These researchers suggest that we can understand social loafing by extending a basic theory of individual motivation—*expectancy–valence theory*—to group performance. Expectancy–valence theory suggests that individuals will work hard on a given task only to the extent that the following conditions exist: (1) They believe that working hard will lead to better performance (*expectancy*); (2) they believe that better performance will be recognized and rewarded (*instrumentality*); and (3) the rewards available are ones they value and desire (*valence*). In other words, individuals working alone will exert effort only to the extent that they believe that doing so will yield the outcomes they want.

According to Karau and Williams (1993, 1995), these links are often weaker when individuals work together in groups than when they work alone. First, consider *expectancy*—the perception that increased effort will lead to better performance. This may be high when individuals work alone, but lower when they work together in groups, because people realize that other factors aside from their own effort will determine the group's performance, such as the amount of effort exerted by other members. Similarly, *instrumentality*—the belief that good performance will be recognized and rewarded—may also be weaker when people work together in groups. They realize that valued outcomes are divided among all group members, and that as a result, they may not get their fair share, given their level of effort. Therefore, social loafing occurs; and within the framework of the collective effort model, this is not surprising. After all, when individuals work together with others, the relationship between their own effort and performance and rewards is more uncertain than when they work alone. See Figure 10.6 for a summary of the collective effort model, or CEM for short.

Is the collective effort model accurate? To find out, Karau and Williams performed a meta-analysis of dozens of studies of social loafing. The CEM makes several predictions concerning the conditions under which social loafing should be most and least likely to occur. For example, it predicts that social loafing will be weakest when (1) individuals work in small rather than large groups; (2) they work on tasks that are intrinsically interesting or important to them; (3) they work with respected others (friends, teammates, etc.); (4) they perceive that their contributions to the group product are unique rather than redundant; (5) they expect their coworkers to perform poorly; and (6) they come from cultures that emphasize individual effort and outcomes rather than group outcomes (Western versus Asian cultures, for instance). The results of the meta-analysis offered support for all the CEM's predictions. In other words, social loafing was weakest and strongest under conditions predicted by the theory. In addition, the meta-analysis confirmed that social loafing was a very reliable and pervasive effect: It occurred across many different studies conducted with many different kinds of participants and many different kinds of tasks.

On the basis of these findings, Karau and Williams (1993) concluded that the CEM provides a useful framework for understanding social loafing. Moreover, they also noted that the

---

FIGURE 10.6 The Collective Effort Model.

According to the *collective effort model* (Karau & Williams, 1993), social loafing occurs because when individuals work together with others, the links (1) between their effort and the group's performance and (2) between the group's performance and their own rewards are weaker than when individuals work alone.

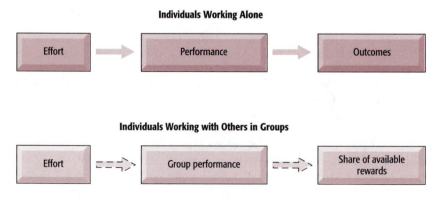

(*Source:* Based on suggestions by Karau & Williams, 1993.)

results of their meta-analysis indicate that social loafing is a potentially serious problem: It is most likely to occur under conditions in which individuals' contributions can't be evaluated, when people work on tasks they find boring or uninspiring, and when they work with others they don't greatly respect or don't know very well. Unfortunately, precisely these conditions exist in many settings where groups of persons work together—for instance, in many manufacturing plants and government offices.

If social loafing poses a threat to performance in many settings, the next question is obvious: What steps can be taken to reduce it? The most obvious tactic involves making the output or effort of each participant readily identifiable (e.g., K. D. Williams, Harkins, & Latané, 1981). Under these conditions, people can't sit back and let others do their work, so social loafing is in fact reduced (e.g., Aiello & Kolb, 1995). Second, groups can reduce social loafing by increasing group members' commitment to successful task performance (Brickner et al., 1986). Pressures toward working hard will then serve to offset temptations to engage in social loafing. Third, social loafing can be reduced by increasing the apparent importance or value of a task (Karau & Williams, 1993). Fourth, social loafing is reduced when individuals view their contributions to the task as unique rather than merely redundant with those of others (Weldon & Mustari, 1988). And finally, social loafing can be reduced by strengthening group cohesiveness, which increases the extent to which members care about the group's outcomes, and hence their level of individual effort.

Together, these steps can sharply reduce the magnitude of social loafing in many situations. Social loafing, it appears, is *not* an unavoidable feature of task-performing groups. It can be reduced if appropriate safeguards are built into the situation. When they are, individuals will perceive strong links between their effort, the group's performance, and their own outcomes. And then the tendency to goof off at the expense of others may be greatly reduced. Further research suggests that the degree of social loafing varies significantly across cultures, as we will see in the Social Diversity box on pages 256–257.

 # Decision Making by Groups

Groups are called upon to perform a wide range of tasks—everything from conducting surgical operations through harvesting the world's crops. One of the most important activities they perform, however, is **decision making**—combining and integrating available information in order to choose one out of several possible courses of action. Governments, large corporations, military units, sports teams—virtually all social entities entrust key decisions to groups. As a result, most of the laws, policies, and business practices that affect our daily lives are determined by committees and other groups. There are several reasons for this fact, but perhaps the most important is this: Most people believe that groups, by pooling the expertise and knowledge of their members and by avoiding extreme courses of action, usually reach better decisions than individuals.

Are such beliefs accurate? Do groups actually make better or more accurate decisions than individuals? In their efforts to answer this practical question, social psychologists have focused on three major topics: (1) How do groups actually go about moving toward consensus? (2) Do decisions reached by groups differ in any way from those reached by individuals? And (3) what accounts for the fact that groups sometimes make truly disastrous decisions—ones so bad that they are, in retrospect, hard to explain?

Attaining Consensus In Groups

When groups first begin to discuss any issue, their members rarely voice unanimous agreement. Rather, they support a wide range of views and favor competing courses of action. After some period of discussion, however, they usually reach a decision. This does not always happen—juries, for instance, sometimes become hung, and other decision-making groups, too, may deadlock. In most cases, though, some decision is reached. Is there any way of predicting the final outcome from information about the views initially held by a group's members? Growing evidence suggests that there is.

Social Decision Schemes: Blueprints for Decisions. To summarize briefly some very complex findings, it appears that the final decisions reached by groups can often be predicted quite accurately by relatively simple rules known as **social decision schemes.** These rules relate the initial distribution of members' views or preferences to the group's final decisions. For example, one scheme—the *majority-wins rule*—suggests that in many cases the group will opt for whatever position is initially supported by most of its members. According to this rule, discussion serves mainly to confirm or strengthen the most popular view; it rarely reverses it, no matter how strongly the minority argues for its position. In contrast, a second decision scheme—the *truth-wins rule*—indicates that the correct solution or decision will ultimately emerge as its correctness is recognized by a growing number of members. A third decision scheme, adopted by many juries, is the *two-thirds majority rule.* Here, juries tend to convict defendants if two-thirds of the jurors initially favor this decision. Finally, some groups seem to follow a *first-shift rule.* They tend, ultimately, to adopt a decision consistent with the direction of the first shift in opinion shown by any members.

Surprising as it may seem, the results of many studies indicate that these straightforward rules are quite successful in predicting even complex group decisions. Indeed, they have been found to be accurate up to 80 percent of the time (e.g., Stasser, Taylor, & Hanna, 1989). Of course, different rules seem to be more successful under some conditions than under others. The majority-wins scheme, for instance, predicts decisions best in *judgmental tasks*—ones that are largely a matter of opinion. In contrast, the truth-wins rule seems best in predicting group decisions on *intellective tasks*—ones for which there *is* a correct answer (Kirchler & Davis, 1986).

Procedural Processes: When Decisions Are Influenced by the Procedures Used to Reach Them. While the

decisions reached by groups can often be predicted from knowledge of members' initial positions, it is clear that many other factors play a role in this complex process. Among the most important of these are several aspects of the group's *procedures*—the rules it follows in addressing its agenda, managing interactions among members, and so on. One procedure adopted by many decision-making groups is the **straw poll,** in which members indicate their present positions or preferences in a nonbinding vote. While straw polls are nonbinding and thus allow group members to shift to other positions, research findings indicate that these informal votes often exert strong effects on members. Apparently, simply learning about the current distribution of opinions within a group—or about the opinions of especially influential members (see Figure 10.7)—may cause some persons to join the majority, thus tilting the decision in this direction (Davis et al., 1993; MacCoun & Kerr, 1988). Research on the effects of straw polls and several other procedures adopted by groups indicate that such procedures can strongly influence the decisions they reach, quite apart from information relating to these decisions.

Are Group Decisions Too Extreme?

Truly important decisions are rarely left to individuals. Instead, they are usually assigned to groups—and highly qualified groups at that. Even kings, queens, and dictators usually consult with groups of skilled advisers before taking major actions. As we mentioned earlier, the major reason behind this strategy is the belief that groups are far less likely than individuals to make serious errors—to rush blindly over the edge. Is this really true? Research on this issue has yielded surprising findings. Contrary to popular beliefs, a large body of evidence indicates that groups are actually *more* likely to adopt extreme positions than individuals making decisions alone. In fact, across many different kinds of decisions and in many different contexts, groups show a pronounced tendency to shift toward views more extreme than the ones with which they initially began (Burnstein, 1983; Lamm & Myers, 1978). This is known

YEA   YEA   YEA   NAY   THE NAYS HAVE IT

as **group polarization,** and its major effects can be summarized as follows: Whatever the initial leaning or preference of a group prior to its discussions, it is strengthened during the group's deliberations. Not only does the *group* shift toward more extreme views—*individual* members, too, often show such a shift. (Please note: The term *group polarization* does not refer to a tendency of groups to split apart into two opposing camps or poles; on the contrary, it refers to a strengthening of the group's initial preferences.)

Why does this effect occur? Research findings have helped provide an answer. Apparently, two major factors are involved. First, it appears that *social comparison*—a process we examined in Chapter 7—plays an important role. Everyone, it seems, wants to be "above average," as we discussed in Chapter 3. Where opinions are concerned, this desire implies holding views that are "better" than those of most other persons, and, especially, better than those of other group members. What does "better" mean? It depends on the specific group. Among a group of liberals, "better" would mean "more liberal." Among a group of conservatives, it would mean "more conservative." Among a group of racists, it would mean "even more bigoted." In any case, during group discussions, at least some members discover—to their shock!—that their views are *not* "better" than those of most other members. The result: After comparing themselves with these persons, they shift to even more extreme views, and the group polarization effect is off and running (e.g, Zuber, Crott, & Werner, 1992).

A second factor involves the fact that during group discussion, most arguments presented are ones favoring the group's initial leaning or preference. As a result of hearing such arguments, persuasion occurs, and members shift increasingly toward the majority view. This, of course, increases the proportion of arguments favoring this view, and ultimately members convince themselves that this is the "right" view and shift toward it with increasing strength. Similarly, repeated attitude expression—such as happens when each person in the group repeats the same viewpoint—also makes our judgments more extreme, as we discussed in Chapter 7 (Brauer, Judd, & Gliner, 1995; Fiedler, 1996).

Regardless of the precise basis for group polarization, it definitely has important implications. The occurrence of polarization may lead many decision-making groups to adopt positions that are increasingly extreme, and therefore increasingly dangerous. In this context, it is chilling to speculate about the potential role of such shifts in disastrous decisions by political, military, or business groups who should by all accounts have known better—for example, the decision by the hard-liners in the now dissolved Soviet Union to stage a coup to restore firm communist rule. This backfired so badly that the government fell within a matter of days. Did group polarization influence this and other disastrous decisions—the decision by President Johnson to escalate the Vietnam war, the decision by IBM to refuse to buy a new operating system created by a struggling young technician named Bill Gates (now president of Microsoft, Inc.)? It is impossible to say for sure. But the findings of many experiments on group polarization suggest that this is a real possibility.

Potential Dangers of Group Decision Making

The drift of many decision-making groups toward polarization is a serious problem—one that can interfere with their ability to make accurate decisions. Unfortunately, this is not the only process that can exert such negative effects. Several others, too, seem to emerge out of group discussions and can lead groups to make costly, even disastrous, decisions (Hinsz, 1995). Among the most important of these are (1) groupthink, and (2) groups' seeming inability to share and use information held by some, but not all, of their members.

Groupthink: When Too Much Cohesiveness Is a Dangerous Thing. Earlier, we suggested that tendencies toward group polarization may be one reason why decision-making groups sometimes go off the deep end—with catastrophic results. However, another, even more disturbing factor may also contribute to such outcomes. This is a process known as **groupthink**—a strong tendency for decision-making groups to close ranks, cognitively, around a decision, assuming that the group *can't* be wrong, that all members must support the decision strongly, and that any information contrary to it should be rejected (Neck & Moorhead, 1995). Once this collective state of mind develops, groups become unwilling—and perhaps *unable*—to change their course of action, even if external events suggest very strongly that their original decision was a poor one. In fact, according to Janis (1982), the social psychologist who originated the concept of *groupthink*, norms soon emerge in the group that actively prevent its members from considering alternative courses of action. The group is viewed as being incapable of making an error, and anyone with lingering doubts is quickly silenced, both by group pressure and by their own desire to conform.

Why does groupthink occur? Research findings (e.g., Kameda & Sugimori, 1993; Tetlock et al.,1992) suggest that two factors may be crucial. The first is a very high level of *cohesiveness* among group members. Decision-making groups that fall victim to groupthink tend to consist of persons who share the same background and ideology. The second factor is the kind of *emergent group norms* mentioned above—norms suggesting that the group is infallible and morally superior, and that therefore there should be no further discussion of the issues at hand: The decision has been made, and the only task now is to support it as strongly as possible. Once groupthink takes hold in a decision-making group, Janis (1982) argues, pressure toward maintaining high levels of group consensus—*concurrence seeking* is his term for it—overrides the motivation to evaluate all potential courses of action as accurately as possible. Such groups shift from focusing on making the best decisions possible to focusing on maintaining a high level of consensus and the belief that the group is right, no matter what.

Research on groupthink indicates that it is real, and that it does play an important role in at least some disastrous decisions (e.g., Mullen et al., 1994; Tetlock et al., 1992). For example, groupthink may be closely linked to another important pitfall in group decision making—one known as **collective entrapment** (Kameda & Sugimori, 1993). This is the tendency for groups to cling stubbornly to unsuccessful decisions or policies even in the face of overwhelming evidence that the decisions are bad ones. Entrapment (sometimes known as *sunk costs* or *escalation of commitment*) also occurs at the individual level (Bobocel & Meyer, 1994; Brockner, 1992; Mikolic, Parker, & Pruit, 1997).

Collective entrapment involves similar tendencies on the part of decision-making groups; they, too, find it difficult to admit that they made a mistake. To test this reasoning, Kameda and Sugimori (1993) conducted a study in which Japanese students were asked to decide which of two job applicants to hire for their companies. The participants worked in three-person groups, and were, in two different conditions, to make this decision by reaching either a unanimous consensus or a simple majority. The groups were formulated so that in some, initial opinions about promoting the employee were split, while in others, all members agreed. After making their decisions, all the groups learned that the person they hired had done very poorly during a probationary period. They were then asked whether to fire this person or to promote her to full employee status. In making this second decision—the crucial one for purposes of the study—participants were told to reach a unanimous decision.

Kameda and Sugimori (1993) reasoned that the greater the effort groups had to expend in reaching their initial decision, the more strongly they would stick to it, and thus the more likely they would be to promote the poorly performing employee. When would effort be greatest? When the groups were told to make the initial decision unanimously and when opinions were split in the group; under these conditions, the groups would have to work hard to resolve differences between members. The researchers reasoned that as a result, cohesiveness would be high and emergent norms supporting the group's decision would be strong—in other words, key elements of groupthink would emerge. Thus, the groups would be

most likely to stick to their poor decision under these conditions. As you can see from Figure 10.8, groups in which opinion was initially split and which originally reached a unanimous decision about whom to hire *were* much more likely to promote the employee than those in the other conditions. These findings indicate that groupthink is indeed closely related to collective entrapment: Similar factors play a role in both processes.

When it develops, groupthink can be a powerful force serving to lock decision-making groups into bad choices or policies. Can anything be done to prevent its occurrence? Several procedures seem useful. First, groups wishing to avoid groupthink should promote open inquiry and *skepticism* among their members. Group leaders should encourage careful questioning of each alternative or policy and should, if necessary, play the role of devil's advocate, intentionally finding faults with various options. Second, once a decision is reached, *second-chance* meetings, in which group members are asked to express any lingering doubts, can be extremely valuable. Third, it is often helpful to ask different groups of

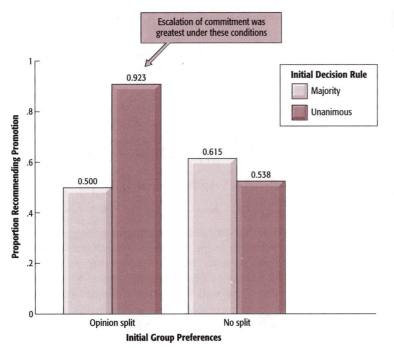

FIGURE 10.8 Groupthink and Collective Entrapment.

Groups in which opinion was initially split and which originally had to reach a unanimous decision about whom to hire showed the strongest tendencies toward escalation of commitment—promoting the employee even though she had performed very poorly. These findings indicate that groupthink is indeed closely related to collective entrapment: Similar factors play a role in both processes.

(*Source:* Based on data from Kameda & Sugimori, 1993.)

persons than those who made the initial decision to decide whether to continue with it. Since the second group did not make the initial decision, it does not experience strong pressures to justify the original choice; in this way, pressures toward collective entrapment are reduced, and one important ingredient in groupthink may be eliminated. In sum, while groupthink is a real danger faced by decision-making groups, several steps can reduce the likelihood of its occurrence—and hence the risk that groups will adopt, and stick to, failing courses of action.

Why Groups Often Fail to Pool Their Resources: Information Sampling and the Common Knowledge Effect. One reason why many key decisions are entrusted to groups is the belief that members will pool their resources—share information and ideas unique to each individual. In this way, the decisions they reach will be better, it is reasoned, than those that would be reached by individuals working in isolation. Is this actually the case? Do groups really share the knowledge and expertise brought to them by their individual members? Research on this issue (Gigone & Hastie, 1993; Stasser & Stewart, 1992) suggests that in fact, such pooling of resources may occur less often than common sense predicts. Fortunately, at least one technique does seem effective in countering this tendency to discuss shared information over and over again. When group members are told that there is a correct solution or decision and that their task is to find it, the tendency to discuss *unshared* information increases (Stasser & Stewart, 1992). In most cases, however, group discussions tend to focus on information already known to most members.

This is not the only problem that gets in the way of the hoped-for pooling of resources in decision-making groups. Research findings indicate the existence of a **common knowledge effect**—the tendency for information held by most members to exert a stronger impact on the group's final decision than information that is not held by most members (Gigone & Hastie, 1993). This seems to occur because such information shapes members' views prior to the group discussion, and also because such information *is*

discussed more often than unshared information. So not only does shared information tend to gain the floor during group discussions, but also it is more influential in determining the group's decision. Additional findings indicate that as groups continue to work together, they may come to recognize what information most members share and what information is unique. Then the likelihood of a pooling of resources may tend to increase. However, taken as a whole, existing evidence indicates that decision-making groups do not automatically benefit from the fact that various individual members have unique knowledge and skills.

1. Contrary to popular belief, groups tend to make more extreme decisions than individuals, in part because of social comparison and persuasion (see Chapters 7 and 5).
2. Groups are sometimes subject to *groupthink,* a strong tendency to assume that the group *can't* be wrong and to ignore information inconsistent with the group's decisions. Groupthink stems, in part, from strong pressures toward conformity with the group's norms (Chapter 8).
3. One pitfall of group decision making is that they often fail to pool the resources of their members: They discuss information already known by most members rather than information held by only one or a few members.

Leadership: Patterns of Influence within Groups

Try this simple demonstration with your friends. Ask each one to rate themselves, on a seven-point scale ranging from 1 (very low) to 7 (very high), in terms of *leadership potential.* What do you think you will find? Probably, that most people rate themselves as average or above on this characteristic, reflecting the fact that people view leadership in very favorable terms. But what, precisely, *is* **leadership?** Social psychologists define it as *the process through which one member of a group (its leader) influences other group members toward the attainment of specific group goals* (Yukl, 1994). In other words, leadership has to do with *influence*—who influences whom in various groups. The assumption, of course, is that leaders do most of the influencing; but as we'll soon see, leadership, like all social relationships, is reciprocal in nature—leaders are influenced by, as well as exert influence over, their followers.

Research on leadership has been a part of social psychology since its very earliest days; and in recent decades, this research has spilled outside social psychology to the closely related fields of *industrial/organizational psychology* and *organizational behavior* (Fiedler, 1994; Greenberg & Baron, 1995). In this discussion, we'll provide you with an overview of what social psychologists and others have discovered about leadership. We'll start by examining the question of *who* becomes a leader. We'll turn next to the various *styles* of leadership—how leaders exert their influence over others. And we will conclude with some comments on what is perhaps the most dramatic form of leadership—*charismatic* or *transformational* leadership.

Who Becomes a Leader?

Are some people born to lead? Common sense suggests they are. Eminent leaders of the past such as Alexander the Great, Queen Elizabeth I, and Abraham Lincoln seem to differ from ordinary human beings in several respects. Such observations led early researchers to formulate a view of leadership known as the **great person theory.** According to this theory, great leaders possess certain traits that set them apart from most human beings. Further, the theory suggests that these traits remain stable over time and across different cultures so that *all* great leaders, no matter when or where they lived, resemble one another in certain respects.

Despite the allure of the great person theory, researchers had great difficulty formulating a short, agreed-upon list of the key traits shared by all leaders (Geier, 1969; Yukl, 1981). In recent years, however, many researchers have concluded that leaders *do* indeed differ from other persons in several important respects (Kirkpatrick & Locke, 1991). What, then, are the key traits of leaders—the characteristics that suit them for this important role? The findings of research on this topic are summarized in Table 10.1. As you

TABLE 10.1 ■ The Characteristics of Successful Leaders

Research findings indicate that successful leaders show the traits listed here to a greater extent than other persons.	
TRAIT	**DESCRIPTION**
Drive	Desire for achievement; ambition; high energy; tenacity; initiative
Honesty and Integrity	Trustworthiness; reliability; openness
Leadership Motivation	Desire to exercise influence over others to reach shared goals
Self-Confidence	Trust in own abilities
Cognitive Ability	Intelligence; ability to integrate and interpret large amounts of information
Creativity	Originality
Flexibility	Ability to adapt to needs of followers and to changing situational requirements
Expertise	Knowledge of the group's activities; knowledge of relevant technical matters

(*Source:* Based on suggestions by Kirkpatrick & Locke, 1991.)

can see from this table, leaders appear to be higher than other persons in terms of characteristics such as *drive*—the desire for achievement coupled with high energy and resolution; *self-confidence; creativity;* and *leadership motivation*—the desire to be in charge and exercise authority over others. Perhaps the most important single characteristic of leaders, however, is a high level of *flexibility:* the ability to recognize what actions or approaches are required in a given situation, and then to act accordingly (Zaccaro, Foti, & Kenny, 1991). You'll notice that flexibility is very similar to being a *high self-monitor*, a personality dimension that we discussed in Chapter 4.

While certain traits do seem to be related to leadership, however, it is also clear that leaders do *not* operate in a social vacuum. On the contrary, different groups, facing different tasks and problems, seem to require different types of leaders—or at least, leaders who demonstrate different styles. This basic fact is recognized in all modern theories of leadership, which take careful note of the fact that leadership is a complex role, involving not only influence but many other kinds of interaction between leaders and followers as well (Bass, 1990; House & Podsakoff, 1994; E. A. Locke, 1991). So *yes,* traits do matter where leadership is concerned, but they are only part of the total picture. Leadership, like all forms of social behavior, can be understood only in terms of complex interactions between social situations and individual characteristics. For example, Kirkpatrick and Locke (1996) found that leaders who embodied features such as those in Table 10.1 *did* improve group performance, but group attitudes toward the tasks improved even more. Thus, the effects of "good leaders" may *seem* greater than they really are. Approaches that focus entirely on one of these aspects are appealing in their simplicity, but decades of research indicate that they are also inaccurate.

How Leaders Operate: Contrasting Styles and Approaches

All leaders are definitely *not* alike. On the contrary, a very large volume of research indicates that they differ greatly in terms of personal *style* or approach to leadership (e.g., George, 1995). In fact, there are actually several key dimensions along which leaders differ in terms of their style. One of these is the *autocratic–democratic* dimension (Lewin et al., 1939); autocratic leaders make decisions unilaterally, while democratic leaders invite input and participation in decision making from their followers. Another important dimension, however, is one involving the extent to which leaders dictate how followers should carry out their assigned tasks versus giving them the freedom to work in any way they wish. This aspect is referred to as the *directive–permissive* dimension, and it crosscuts the autocratic–democratic dimension; thus, leaders tend to show one of the four different patterns summarized in Figure 10.9 (Muczyk & Reimann, 1987).

Finally, leaders' styles also differ along two other important dimensions, sometimes known as *task orientation* and *person orientation.* Task orientation refers to the extent to which a given leader focuses on getting the task done—whatever it happens to be (Kenney, Schwartz-Kenney, & Blascovich, 1996). Person orientation, in contrast, refers to leaders' interest in maintaining good, friendly relations with their followers. Leaders can be high or low on each of these dimensions; for instance, a given leader can be high on both, low on both, high on one and low on the other, or moderate on both. These dimensions of leader style appear to be very basic ones: They have been observed among thousands of different leaders in many different contexts (e.g., business groups, military groups, and sports teams), and in several different countries (Bass, 1990). Interestingly, no single style seems to be best; rather, which one is most effective depends on the specific circumstances. For example, when leaders are high on person orientation, they often have friendly relations with their followers—who may then be reluctant to give them any bad news. Such leaders may get into serious trouble because they are not receiving vital feedback from followers. In contrast, leaders high in task orientation often do wring high

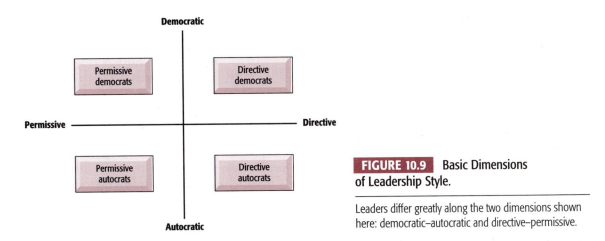

FIGURE 10.9 Basic Dimensions of Leadership Style.

Leaders differ greatly along the two dimensions shown here: democratic–autocratic and directive–permissive.

levels of performance out of their followers. These people may feel that the leader has no interest in them, though, and this may weaken their commitment to the group.

In sum, leaders do appear to differ greatly with respect to personal style—how they go about fulfilling the role of leader—and these differences have important effects on their groups. However, because many factors influence leadership, it would be misleading to suggest that one leadership style is always—or even usually—best.

Gender Differences in Leadership

Do male and female leaders differ in their styles of leadership? While there is a widespread belief that they do, systematic research on this issue suggests that in general, they actually do not (Powell, 1990). Eagly and Johnson (1990) examined the results of more than 150 studies in order to determine whether female and male leaders actually differ in terms of leadership style. Gender-role stereotypes suggest that female leaders might show more concern with persons than male leaders and might make decisions in a more democratic manner. However, results offered support only for differences with respect to the autocratic–democratic dimension. Female leaders were slightly more likely to adopt a democratic style than male leaders. They were not,

however, more person-oriented than male leaders. This conclusion has been supported in other recent investigations (e.g., N. Brewer, Socha, & Potter, 1996).

In a follow-up investigation, Eagly and her colleagues (Eagly, Makhijani, & Klonsky, 1992) focused on a related issue: Are female and male leaders evaluated differently by others? Because serving as a leader is in some respects contrary to the gender stereotype for females, the researchers predicted that female leaders might receive lower ratings than male leaders, even when their performance was identical. Moreover, Eagly and her colleagues also expected that such down-rating of female leaders would be greater among male evaluators than among female evaluators, and that it would be more likely to occur in fields dominated by males, and in situations in which the female leaders adopted a directive, autocratic style of leadership—a traditionally "masculine" leadership approach. Results provided support for all of these predictions. There was a small, but significant, tendency for female leaders to be rated lower than male leaders. However, this down-rating of female leaders was stronger when they adopted a style of leadership viewed as stereotypically masculine (autocratic, directive), when the evaluators were male, and when the female leaders were working in fields dominated by males.

Social Diversity:
A Critical Analysis

Social Loafing: An International Perspective

In our earlier discussion of social loafing, we noted that the collective effort model proposed by Karau and Williams (1993) predicts that such behavior will be less prevalent in cultures that value group outcomes more than individual outcomes. In fact, many such cultures exist. They are typically described as *collectivistic* in orientation, because they place a high value on shared responsibility and the collective good of all, such as we described in Chapter 8. In such cultures, it is often viewed as bad form to stand out from the group by exceeding others in terms of performance. Rather, it is group performance that is important. In *individualistic* cultures such as those in many Western countries, in contrast, the emphasis is on individual accomplishments and success (R. Bond & Smith, 1996).

Is social loafing actually less frequent in collectivistic cultures? To find out, Earley (1993) asked individuals from the United States, Israel, and the People's Republic of China to complete a task that simulated the daily activities of managers—for example, writing memos, filling out forms, and rating job applicants. They were asked to perform these tasks for one hour either alone or as part of a group of ten persons. In the *alone* condition, participants simply wrote their names on

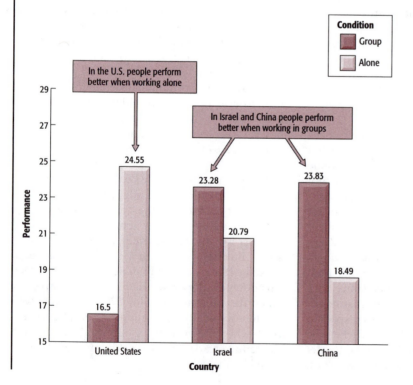

FIGURE 10.10 Social Loafing in Three Different Countries.

As shown here, Americans performed far better on a task when they worked alone than when they worked with others. In contrast, persons from Israel and China performed better when they worked as part of a group. These findings are consistent with the prediction that social loafing will be greater in *individualistic* cultures such as the United States than in *collectivistic* cultures such as Israel and China.

(*Source:* Based on data from Earley, 1993.

each item as they completed it and turned it in. In the *group* condition, however, participants were told that their group's overall performance would be assessed at the end of the session.

Earley (1993) predicted that for persons from the United States, performance would be lower in the group than in the alone condition; in other words, social loafing would occur. In contrast, for persons from Israel and China—two cultures that are more collectivistic than the United States—performance would be better in the group than in the alone condition. In other words, social loafing would not occur; on the contrary, participants would actually work *harder* when part of a group. As you can see from Figure 10.10, results offered clear support for these predictions.

These results indicate that culture plays an important role in shaping individuals' willingness to engage in social loafing. In societies that place high value on individual accomplishment, people seem to experience reduced motivation when they feel that their performance will not be evaluated on an individual basis. The result: They engage in social loafing. In societies that place high value on group outcomes, working together with others does not lead to reductions in motivation. On the contrary, people may actually work harder when they are part of a group. The moral is clear: Social loafing, like many other aspects of social behavior, occurs against a background of complex cultural factors. Thus, taking careful account of these can add significantly to our understanding of many social processes.

In sum, it appears that female leaders continue to face disadvantages in many settings. While their behavior or style differs from that of male leaders in only a few relatively minor respects, female leaders continue to receive lower ratings than their male counterparts. We can only hope that this situation will change in the years ahead, as gender stereotypes weaken and as the number of females in leadership positions continues to increase.

Leadership through Vision and Charisma

Have you ever seen films of John F. Kennedy? Franklin D. Roosevelt? Martin Luther King Jr.? If so, you may have noticed that there seemed to be something special about these leaders. As you listened to their speeches, you may have found yourself being moved by their words and stirred by the vigor with which they delivered their messages. If so, you are not alone: These leaders exerted such effects on many millions of persons and, by doing so, changed their society—and perhaps even the entire world. Leaders who accomplish such feats are often termed **transformational** or **charismatic leaders,** and the

terms (which are used interchangeably) seem fitting. Such persons do indeed transform social, political, or economic reality; and they do seem to possess special skills that equip them for this task. What personal characteristics make certain leaders charismatic? And how do such leaders exert their dramatic influence on large numbers of followers? Systematic research on this issue has begun to yield some intriguing answers.

The Basic Nature of Charisma: Traits or Relationships?
At first glance, it is tempting to assume that transformational leaders are special because they possess certain traits; in other words, that such leadership can be understood in terms of the *great person theory* described earlier. While traits may play a role in transformational leadership, there is growing consensus that it makes more sense to understand such leadership as involving a special type of *relationship* between leaders and their followers (House, 1977). Charismatic leadership, it appears, rests more on specific types of reactions by followers than on traits possessed by charismatic leaders (Conger & Kanungo, 1994). Such reactions include: (1) high levels of devotion, loyalty, and reverence toward the leader;

(2) enthusiasm for the leader and the leader's ideas; (3) a willingness by followers to sacrifice their own personal interests for the sake of a larger group goal; and (4) levels of performance beyond those that would normally be expected. In short, transformational or charismatic leadership involves a special kind of leader–follower relationship, one in which the leader can, in the words of one author, "make ordinary people do extraordinary things in the face of adversity" (Conger, 1991).

The Behavior of Transformational Leaders. But what, precisely, do transformational leaders do to generate this kind of relationship with followers? Studies designed to answer this question point to the fact that such leaders cultivate a *vision* (Howell & Frost, 1989). They describe, usually in vivid, emotion-provoking terms, an image of what their nation or group can—and should—become. Consider the following words, spoken by Martin Luther King Jr. in his famous "I Have a Dream" speech:

> So I say to you, my friends, that even though we must face the difficulties of today and tomorrow, I still have a dream. It is a dream deeply rooted in the American dream that one day this nation will rise up and live out the true meaning of its creed—we hold these truths to be self-evident, that all men are created equal. This will be the day when all of God's children will be able to sing with new meaning "My country, tis of thee, sweet land of liberty."

But transformational leaders do more than merely describe a dream or vision; in addition, they offer a route for attaining it. They tell their followers, in straightforward terms, how to get from here to there. This, too, seems to be crucial, for a vision that seems perpetually out of reach is unlikely to motivate people to try to attain it. Transformational leaders engage in what Conger (1991) terms *framing*: They define the purpose of their movement or organization in a way that gives meaning and purpose to whatever actions they are requesting from followers. Perhaps the nature of framing is best illustrated

by the well-known story of two stonecutters working on a cathedral in the Middle Ages. When asked what they were doing, one replied, "Why cutting this stone, of course." The other answered, "Building the world's most beautiful temple to the glory of God." Which person would be more likely to expend great effort on his task? The answer is obvious.

Other tactics shown by transformational leaders include high levels of self-confidence and confidence in their followers, a high degree of concern for their followers' needs, excellent communication skills, and a stirring personal style (House, Spangler, & Woycke, 1991). Finally, transformational leaders are often masters of *impression management*, engaging in many actions designed to enhance their appeal to others (see Chapters 2 and 7). When these forms of behavior are added to the exciting visions they promote, the tremendous impact of transformational leaders loses most of its apparent mystery. In fact, it rests firmly on principles and processes well understood by social psychologists.

The Effects of Transformational Leaders: A Very Mixed Bag. Are transformational or charismatic leaders always a plus for their groups or societies? As you probably already realize, definitely not. Many charismatic leaders use their skills for what they perceive to be the good of their group or society—people like Martin Luther King Jr., Franklin D. Roosevelt, and Indira Gandhi, to name just a few. But others use this leadership style for purely selfish ends (Howell & Avolio, 1992; O'Connor et al., 1995). For example, Michael Milken, former head of the brokerage firm Drexel Burnham Lambert, was described by followers as being extremely charismatic. Yet he used the trust and loyalty he inspired for illegal ends: stock fraud that cost innocent investors millions of dollars.

In short, charismatic or transformational leadership is definitely a two-edged sword. It can be used to promote beneficial social change consistent with the highest principles and ethical standards; or it can be used for selfish, illegal, and immoral purposes. The difference lies in the personal conscience and moral code of the persons who wield it.

Integrating Principles

1. Leadership involves the exercise of influence by one group member over other members. In exerting such influence, leaders use many different tactics (see Chapter 9).

2. Leaders appear to differ from followers in terms of several traits, but not all leaders are alike. On the contrary, they adopt very different styles.

3. Transformational or charismatic leaders are masters of impression management (Chapter 2) and use techniques such as framing (see Chapter 3) and a vision to exert profound effects upon their followers.

Connections Integrating Social Psychology

In this chapter, you read about . . .

- the role of norms in the functioning of groups
- individuals' concern with others' evaluations of their performance

- the role of persuasion and other forms of social influence in group decision making
- the role of personal characteristics in leadership

- gender and leadership

In other chapters, you will find related discussions of . . .

- the nature of norms and their role in social influence (Chapter 8)
- the effects of others' evaluations on our self-concept (Chapter 4) and on our liking for others (Chapter 7)
- the nature of persuasion (Chapter 5) and various forms of social influence (Chapter 8)
- the role of personal characteristics in many other forms of social behavior, such as helping (Chapter 9) and aggression (Chapter 9)
- the role of gender in many other aspects of social behavior: persuasion and conformity (Chapters 4, 8), attraction and close relationships (Chapters 7), helping (Chapter 9), and aggression (Chapter 9)

Thinking about Connections

1. Suppose that despite high wages and access to excellent equipment, a work team in a large company is performing far below expectations. Do you think that social norms (see Chapter 8) might be playing a role in this surprising outcome? How could this be so?

2. As we noted in this chapter, some group members do less than their fair share with respect to the group's work—they engage in *social loafing*. Drawing on what you know about the impact of norms (Chapter 8), interpersonal attraction (Chapter 7), and long-term relationships (Chapter 7), what steps could a group take to minimize such "goofing off" among its members?

3. Some leaders, such as those of religious cults, exert incredibly powerful effects on their followers. Drawing on what you know about social influence (see Chapter 8), what are your views on how these leaders attain such power? In other words, what tactics or procedures do they use to gain an amazing degree of control over their follower?

Summary and Review

Groups: Their Nature and Function

A *group* consists of two or more persons who share common goals, whose fates are interdependent, who have a stable relationship, and who recognize that they belong to a group. Groups influence their members through *roles*—members' assigned functions in the group; *status*—their relative standing in the group; *norms*—rules concerning appropriate behavior for members; and *cohesiveness*—all the factors that cause members to remain in the group.

Groups and Task Performance

Individuals' performance of various tasks is often affected by the presence of others or by the potential evaluation of their work by these persons. Such effects are known as *social facilitation*, although they can involve reduced as well as enhanced task performance. According to *distraction–conflict theory*, social facilitation effects stem from the arousal induced by conflict between two incompatible tendencies—paying careful attention to others, and paying careful attention to a task.

When individuals work on a task with others, they may show *social loafing*—reduced motivation and effort. Social loafing appears to be influenced by several different factors. The *collective effort model* suggests that when individuals work with others in a group, social loafing occurs because relationships between their effort and their outcomes become less certain. Several techniques are effective in reducing social loafing. These include making the output or effort of each group member readily identifiable, increasing members' commitment to successful performance, increasing the apparent importance of the task being performed, and strengthening group cohesiveness.

Decision Making by Groups

Many important decisions are entrusted to groups. Group decisions can sometimes be predicted by *social decision schemes*—simple rules relating the initial views held by members to the group's final decision. Procedures such as *straw polls* can influence group decisions. Group discussions often result in a shift toward more extreme positions—the *group polarization effect*. Thus, contrary to popular belief, groups may tend to make more extreme decisions than individuals. Decision-making groups also face other potential pitfalls. One of these is *groupthink,* tendencies for a group to assume that it is infallible coupled with refusal to examine relevant information. Recent evidence indicates that groupthink may be related to *collective entrapment*—the tendency to stick to bad decisions even in the face of increasing evidence that they are wrong. Another important problem faced by decision-making groups is their apparent inability to pool the resources of members. Groups tend to discuss information shared by all members rather than information held by only one or a few members. Moreover, such shared information exerts stronger effects on group decisions than other information, which is known as the *common knowledge effect*.

Leadership

Leadership involves the exercise of influence by one group member over other group members. According to the *great person theory,* all great leaders share similar traits. Recent evidence indicates that in fact, leaders do seem to differ from followers with respect to several characteristics. However, successful leadership involves a complex interplay between these characteristics, many aspects of the situation faced by the group, and leaders' relations with group members. Leaders differ greatly in terms of personal style. Important dimensions of leadership style include the autocratic–democratic and directive–permissive dimensions, and two dimensions relating to leaders' degree of emphasis on task performance or personal relationships with followers. Male and female leaders do not differ in most respects. However, female leaders appear to adopt a more democratic leadership style than males.

Transformational or *charismatic* leaders exert profound effects on their followers. They do this by establishing a special kind of relationships with followers, by proposing an inspiring vision, and by the expert use of many tactics of influence.

Social Diversity: Social Loafing

The *collective effort model* predicts that social loafing will be less common in collectivistic cultures—ones that emphasize the importance of group performance and outcomes—than in individualistic cultures—ones that emphasize the importance of individual performance and success. Research findings have confirmed this prediction, indicating that social loafing is more common in the United States than in Israel and China.

Key Terms

Additive Tasks (p. 244)
Charismatic Leaders (p. 257)
Cohesiveness (p. 240)
Collective Effort Model (p. 245)
Collective Entrapment (p. 250)
Common Knowledge Effect (p. 252)
Decision Making (p. 247)
Distraction–Conflict Theory (p. 244)
Drive Theory of Social Facilitation (p. 242)
Evaluation Apprehension (p. 243)
Great Person Theory (of leadership) (p. 253)
Group (p. 237)

Group Polarization (p. 249)
Groupthink (p. 250)
Leadership (p. 253)
Norms (p. 240)
Roles (p. 239)
Social Decision Schemes (p. 248)
Social Facilitation (p. 242)
Social Loafing (p. 244)
Status (p. 239)
Straw Poll (p. 248)
Transformational Leaders (p. 257)

For More Information

Castellan, N. J. Jr. (Ed.). (1993). *Individual and group decision making: Current issues.* Hillsdale, NJ: Erlbaum.

This book contains chapters prepared by many experts on the topic of decision making by both individuals and groups. It is an excellent source to consult if you want to learn more about this fascinating topic.

Simonton, D. K. (1994). *Greatness: Who makes history and why?* New York: Guilford Press.

A social psychologist who has conducted extensive research on leadership offers his perspective on why certain persons become great leaders and on how these leaders exert powerful effects on large numbers of people. A must if you are interested in transformational or charismatic leadership.

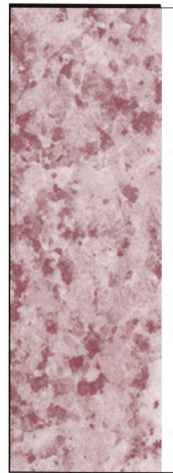

chapter **11**

Applying Social Psychology to Law, Work, and Health

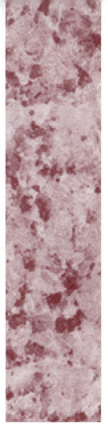

In recent years the U.S. public has discovered the courtroom as a source of seemingly endless fascination. Have you watched any portion of the trials involving Lorena Bobbitt (accused of severing her husband's penis with a knife), the Menendez brothers (accused of murdering their parents), several Los Angeles policemen (accused of using excessive violence against Rodney King), or O. J. Simpson (accused of murdering his former wife and one of her friends)? If so, did you observe anything in the proceedings that reminded you of the social psychological research you read about in this book?

Have you ever held a job that you hated, or one that you truly enjoyed? What are some of the factors that created these different experiences? Was your performance on the job affected by your feelings and attitudes? If you owned a business, which reaction would you prefer among your employees, and what could you do to increase the likelihood of such an outcome?

On the morning news you hear a story about a new finding related to health. Someone conducted a survey and reported that people who eat food high in beta carotene have a lower risk of several kinds of cancer than people who do not eat such food. You don't particularly like any of the vegetables that the newscaster mentions as being high in this substance. She also mentions that it is possible to take beta carotene in pill form. Are the pills as effective as the vegetables? Because you want to avoid cancer, what do you do with this information? Would it be best to change your diet, buy some pills, consult your doctor, wait to see if other studies confirm the findings or contradict them, or just ignore the whole thing? You probably won't develop cancer anyway. Right?

When social psychologists apply their theories and research skills in real-life settings such as the legal system and the organizations in which we work, the relevance of our field to societal concerns becomes crystal clear. In the following pages, we first describe the way in which social psychology has been applied to numerous aspects of the *legal system,* one of the original applied interests of the early social psychologists. Cognitive and emotional processes are crucial at each step in the legal process, from police interrogations and pretrial publicity to the behavior of the participants in the courtroom. We then examine applications of social psychology to business, focusing on several areas of research that rest directly on basic principles of our field: *work-related attitudes* (job satisfaction and organizational commitment), social aspects of *job interviews, organizational politics,* and *conflict* in work settings. Finally, we discuss *health psychology* and how emotions, cognitions, and behavior are relevant to many aspects of human health, from the way we

process relevant information to our ability to cope with medical treatment.

Applying Social Psychology to the Legal System

If the real world lived up to our ideals, the judicial process would provide an elaborate and totally fair set of procedures to reach objective, unbiased decisions about violations of criminal and civil laws. (See Figure 11.1.) In fact, the legal system is neither as perfect as our ideal nor as terrible as our nightmares. Research in **forensic psychology** (the psychological study of legal issues) repeatedly indicates that the human participants in the judicial process usually try their best to do what is right but are inevitably affected by many factors other than objectivity and the unbiased search for truth and justice. As you know from the previous chapters, social psychological research shows clearly that our perceptions, attributions, recollections, and interpersonal behaviors are influenced by cognitions and emotions. Among the many consequences are biased judgments, reliance on stereotypes, faulty memories, and incorrect or unfair decisions. Those same influences operate as strongly in the courtroom as in the laboratory, and the consequences clearly affect the outcome of legal proceedings, as we shall see.

The Media and Perceptions about Crime

In newspapers, on television and radio, and in other media sources, we are routinely exposed to

information about crimes and criminals. Crime information is so pervasive that people easily develop a distorted view of this aspect of our world. On a daily basis, the media suggest to us that crime is a widespread problem that threatens each of us, and the availability heuristic clearly applies (see Chapter 3) when we make assumptions about the crime rate and its dangers. For example, polls show that U.S. citizens believe criminal activity has reached epidemic proportions. Polls also indicate that crime is ranked as one of the two or three greatest problems faced by U.S. society (Blonston, 1993).

In fact, record highs for violent crime in the United States, including homicide and burglary, were set in the early 1980s and have been dropping ever since. According to the U.S. Bureau of Justice Statistics, the total number of crimes dropped from 41.2 million in 1981 to 34.4 million in 1991. FBI statistics indicate that the rates of seven major offenses (including violent crime) continued to drop in 1994—for the third consecutive year. One explanation is that most violent crimes are committed by young males, and the baby boomer generation (including violent boomers) is now reaching middle age. The bad news—and one reason that we perceive more rather than less violence—is that the rate of gun murders by teenage boys rapidly increased (Crime rate down . . . , 1995). In fact, the number of juvenile murderers has tripled over the last decade (Number of young . . . , 1996). Who are these young people shooting? The U.S. Bureau of Justice Statistics indicates that youngsters aged 12 to 15 have a 1 in 8 chance of being a crime victim in the 1990s, whereas the chance is only 1 in 179 for those 65 and older (Teens top . . . , 1995). Thus, the facts about crime are complicated. Altogether, violent crime is decreasing while teenage crime (especially against other teenagers) is increasing; but our perceptions tend to simplify the issue by leaving out specific details. It is easier to take what information is easily available and believe that criminal violence is worse than ever. The point is that we magnify the overall problem on the basis of the amount of media attention devoted to each tragic crime. We find such stories easy to re-

FIGURE 11.1   The Legal System: Loaded with Social Psychological Aspects.

Because the legal system involves many interpersonal interactions, understanding it fully would be difficult without social psychology.

member, and it becomes easy to believe that similar events are everyday occurrences.

Pretrial Publicity and Perceptions of a Specific Crime and a Specific Suspect. If distortions about the general incidence of crime are common, what happens when a specific case is widely publicized? With events as traumatic as the bombing of the federal office building in Oklahoma City, there is detailed coverage of the event and background news about the victims and their families. When a suspect is arrested, we are provided information about that individual, most dramatically in the form of a photo or videotape of the suspect in handcuffs surrounded by law enforcement officials. We each form an impression of the suspect, and primacy effects (see Chapter 2) are likely to create an impression of guilt (Imrich, Mullin, & Linz, 1995). Because most people are horrified by the crime and eager to convict whoever committed it, the guilt of the arrested suspect is immediately assumed by most of the general public: "Why else would the police have arrested him and put him in handcuffs?" Think of the reactions to Lee Harvey Oswald being led through the Dallas police station after President Kennedy was shot and to O. J. Simpson being led to a squad car after the murder of Nicole Simpson and Ron Goldman. (See Figure 11.2.) Remember—these

assumptions are created *before* we know anything about the evidence or the legal basis of the suspect's defense. Because all subsequent information is influenced by this first impression, wouldn't you guess that such publicity would have a major effect?

Using actual criminal investigations in Florida, Moran and Cutler (1991) surveyed potential jurors and found that exposure to news about a crime and about the accused criminal was associated with potential jurors' reaching the pretrial conclusion that the defendants were in fact guilty. Other research also indicates that the greater the publicity about a crime, the more prone are jurors to convict whoever has been accused of committing it (Linz & Penrod, 1992; Otto, Penrod, & Dexter, 1994).

Among the reasons for the power of the media's effects on our perception of crime and criminals is the very strong tendency for people to believe what they have read in print, heard on the radio, or viewed on television; if we can comprehend whatever assertions are made, we are also very likely to believe them (Gilbert, Tafarodi, & Malone, 1993). It's almost as if we automatically assume that "They wouldn't have put it on television if it weren't true."

Still another reason for the impact of crime news is that when we make morality judgments

FIGURE 11.2 Pretrial Publicity about a Crime and about a Subject: First Impression = Guilty.

There is abundant evidence that pretrial publicity about a crime generates interest and a general desire to punish the perpetrator. When a subject is identified, the information tends to focus on his or her arrest, the presence of handcuffs, and other details that suggest guilt. Because of primacy effects, the general public often concludes that the accused individual is guilty long before the trial even begins. In the case of O. J. Simpson, the guilty verdict of his civil trial suggests that those first impressions were correct.

(good versus bad, innocent versus guilty), negative information has a greater impact than positive information (Skowronski & Carlston, 1989). We discussed this "automatic vigilance" in Chapter 3. To learn that Congressman X is a good legislator and a devoted family man makes only a minor impression. The vivid news that the congressman is accused of ties to organized crime and has been engaged in an intimate relationship with his secretary affects our evaluation of him in a much stronger and more lasting way.

In the United States many of us are exposed to publicity not only before a trial but also *during* a trial. Canadian law, in contrast, imposes restrictions designed to insure a fair trial and to avoid "polluting" the jury. One Canadian reporter summed up the difference as follows: "In the States, we sequester the jury; in Canada we sequester the public" (Farnsworth, 1995, p. E-8). Similarly, neither pretrial publicity nor live broadcasts of trials is permitted in the United Kingdom. Citizens of Great Britain were thus intrigued by the extraordinary U.S. coverage of O. J. Simpson, beginning with the murder and the travels of the white Bronco and continuing through very popular nightly satellite presentations of the first sensational trials (Lyall, 1995).

Is Eyewitness Testimony Accurate?

Anyone who witnesses a crime or who has observed something relevant to the case may be asked to testify about what was seen or heard. Each year witnesses provide crucial evidence relevant to 75,000 suspects in U.S. courtrooms (Goldstein, Chance, & Schneller, 1989). These witnesses frequently make mistakes, in part because intense emotions caused by the situation can interfere with information processing (see Chapter 3). A related factor is Zillmann's (1994) "cognitive deficit" hypothesis (Chapter 9). Despite the danger of errors, eyewitness testimony has a major impact on jurors (S. Wolf & Bugaj, 1990). Studies of wrongful convictions indicate that inaccurate eyewitness identification is the single most important reason that innocent defendants are convicted (Loftus, 1992; Wells, Luus, & Windschitl, 1994).

Eyewitness Accuracy and Inaccuracy. After many decades of research, it is now very clear that even the most honest, intelligent, and well-meaning witnesses of an event very often make mistakes. As Loftus (1992) has pointed out, a major obstacle to accuracy in a great many instances is that an extended time period passes between the event that was witnessed and the task of presenting testimony in court. During this interval, numerous potential sources of *misleading postevent information* (including police questions, media stories, and statements made by others) are responsible for additions to memory that tend to be incorporated as subjective "truth," thus reducing accuracy. It becomes difficult to distinguish what one remembers of the original event from what has subsequently been learned about it. A variety of other factors interfere with witness accuracy (Wells & Luus, 1990; Youille & Tollestrup, 1990). For example, accuracy decreases if the suspect is holding a weapon (Tooley et al., 1987), if the suspect and the witness belong to different racial or ethnic groups (Platz & Hosch, 1988), and if misleading suggestions are offered to the witness (Ryan & Geiselman, 1991).

What influences members of the jury to believe or not to believe a given witness? The more certain the witness appears and the more details he or she can provide, the greater the impact on the jury (B. E. Bell & Loftus, 1988; Whitley & Greenberg, 1986). A special problem arises when children are the witnesses, as in cases of alleged sexual abuse. As you might expect, the credibility of children on the witness stand is lower than that of adults (Leippe & Romanczyk, 1987). Nevertheless, when observers view the actual testimony of children—in their own words—this bias can be erased (Luus, Wells, & Turtle, 1995).

Attempts to Increase Eyewitness Accuracy. Police often ask eyewitnesses to pick the offender from a lineup of other innocent individuals. Wells and Luus (1990) suggest that the lineup is analogous to a social psychological experiment. For example, the officer conducting the lineup is the *experimenter*, the eyewitnesses are the *research participants*, the suspect is a *stimulus*, and the other people in the lineup and the placement of the suspect constitute the *design*. Consider also that the police have a *hypothesis* as to the guilt of the suspect; the identification made by a witness provides the *data* that may be evaluated by the police, prosecutor, judge, and jury; and in both experiments and testimony the data are stated in terms of *probability*, because neither procedure provides absolute certainty.

In Chapter 1 you read about factors that can interfere with researchers' obtaining accurate results, such as demand characteristics, experimenter bias, or the absence of a control group. Therefore, it should not surprise you that the same factors can interfere with the accuracy of a witness examining a lineup. For example, do you see anything wrong with a lineup in which the suspect is a tall, fat man while the nonsuspects in the lineup are all short and thin?

Using the same analogy, police can improve the validity of lineups by using common experimental procedures such as a *control group*. One procedure is the **blank-lineup control**—witnesses are first shown a lineup in which each "suspect" is really an innocent volunteer (Wells, 1984). No matter who is identified, the witness is wrong. (Or if the witness identifies no one, confidence in that witness's accuracy is increased.) This control experience tends to induce caution and increase later accuracy, especially when information is then provided about the serious consequences of making a mistake.

Another technique to improve witnesses' memory is to "reinstate the context" just before the identification is made (Cutler, Penrod, & Martens, 1987). That is, the witness is first shown pictures of the crime scene and of the victim before seeing the suspects. Accuracy is also increased if a witness looks at one suspect at a time rather than at a lineup of several suspects (Leary, 1988).

A different approach is to identify accurate and inaccurate witnesses and then to look for ways in which they differ. Dunning and Stern (1994) presented research participants with a videotape of a staged crime and then asked them to identify the criminal from a photo lineup. Accurate witnesses said that their judgments were "automatic"—"His face just 'popped out' at me."

In contrast, inaccurate witnesses went through an elimination process, comparing photos to each other and narrowing the choices. Why the difference? These researchers suggest that faces are stored in memory in a visual pattern rather than in words. Witnesses who make an instant and accurate identification are using a nonverbal process and often do not know exactly what influenced the decision. When people are informed that giving a first impression is a better strategy than going through an elimination process, they can change their approach. As a result, accuracy increases.

How Attorneys and Judges Can Affect Verdicts

The outcome of a trial is in part influenced by what is said and done by the opposing attorneys and by the judge. We will describe some of the ways that this influence has been documented.

Attorneys: Adversaries with Opposite Goals. Lawyers obviously play a major role in the courtroom, but their effect is not limited to matters of evidence and legal technicalities. For example, the prosecutor in the first O. J. Simpson trial, Marcia Clark, was advised to change her behavioral style, her wardrobe, and her hair because research with mock jurors revealed that she needed to be "warmer, fuzzier, and more juror-friendly" (Margolick, 1994). The first problem faced by attorneys, however, is not their image but jury selection. Who does and does not serve on the jury can be critical (Hans & Vidmar, 1982). Jurors are selected (and rejected) during a pretrial procedure known as **voir dire,** in which attorneys for each side (as well as the judge) can "see and speak" with potential jurors to determine which individuals are most and least suitable to serve.

Despite the stated goal of choosing the most competent citizens to serve on the panel, the goal of the opposing attorneys differs. They, of course, try very hard to select those jurors they perceive as being most likely to favor their side, and to eliminate jurors most likely to favor the other side. To facilitate this process, the opposing sides may each use a certain number of *peremptory challenges*, which permit a potential juror to be dismissed without the attorney having to state any reason for the dismissal. Abramson (1994) suggests that jury trials have become a game in which each side attempts to load the jury with members who will show bias in a given direction. Studies suggest that even experienced attorneys select jurors who match positive stereotypes (e.g., based on such factors as occupation, age, appearance, gender, race). However, these expectations appear to have little bearing on behavior, as we reviewed in Chapter 6. For example, Olczak, Kaplan, and Penrod (1991) found that attorneys were no better than (untrained) introductory psychology students at guessing whether actual jurors would favor the prosecution or the defense.

The Judge: Bias from the Bench. Though the ideal judge in a trial is totally objective, judges are actually human beings who sometimes make mistakes or hold biases. These mistakes and biases are likely to determine how jurors respond. For example, when a judge allows the jury to hear evidence that is later ruled inadmissible (Cox & Tanford, 1989) or when the judge attacks the credibility of a witness (Cavoukian & Doob, 1980), the final verdict is affected. Many of the cognitive processes described in Chapter 3 (such as priming) obviously apply to how the judge's statements influence the jurors.

In a trial, the judge instructs the jury to form impressions about guilt and innocence, but to refrain from making a final decision about the verdict until the trial ends and the panel can deliberate as a group (Hastie, 1993). Despite this goal of suspending judgment, the judge often forms his or her own private impression and concludes what the verdict is likely to be. These expectations, in turn, influence the judge's verbal and nonverbal behavior, and thus the final decision of the jurors—however unintentional the influence may be (Blanck et al., 1990).

Hart (1995) studied the effect of a judge's unstated opinions about the defendant in an experiment using citizens who had been summoned for jury duty. These prospective jurors were shown videotapes of judges made while the judges were reading the identical standard instructions to ju-

ries in various trials. Before reading the instructions, each judge had privately indicated to those conducting the research whether he or she expected a verdict of guilty or not guilty. The individuals taking part in the research were shown the tape of a single trial (not one involving any of the taped judges). Then they were shown a tape of judicial instructions (falsely described as coming from the trial they had just viewed). As summarized in Figure 11.3, these research participants were significantly more likely to give a "verdict" of guilty when the judge expected a guilty vote than when the judge expected the outcome to be not guilty. It seems that beliefs about guilt and innocence must have influenced the judge's nonverbal behavior (Chapter 2), and this in turn influenced the decisions of these mock jurors.

Many people believe that some judges are soft on crime and biased toward protecting the rights of criminals while others ("hanging judges") give maximum sentences. Carroll and colleagues (1987) found that it *is* in fact possible to classify judges into one of two categories. Judges tend either to emphasize the social and economic causes of crime and therefore stress rehabilitation, or to blame the criminal for breaking the law and therefore stress punishment and retribution. Public support for "hard" or "soft" judges depends, in turn, on what each individual believes about the causes of crime. Among university students, for example, relatively liberal social science majors blame society, while relatively conservative business and engineering majors blame the criminal (Guimond & Palmer, 1990).

How Defendant Characteristics Affect Verdicts

Social psychological research on prejudice (Chapter 6) and interpersonal attraction (Chapter 7) indicates that people respond to one another on the basis of such characteristics as race, gender, and physical attractiveness. Similarly, the courtroom, a defendant's likability is an important determinant of how much he or she is blamed for causing harm (Alicke, 1994). Stereotypes and liking should of course be irrelevant in a trial, but they nevertheless *do* influence the out-

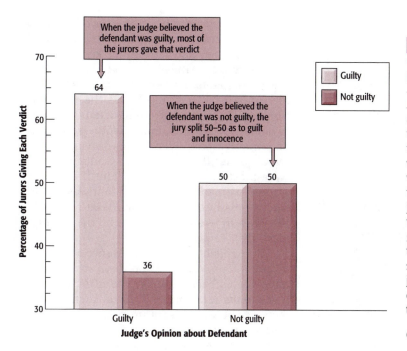

When the judge believed the defendant was guilty, most of the jurors gave that verdict

When the judge believed the defendant was not guilty, the jury split 50–50 as to guilt and innocence

Guilty

Not guilty

Percentage of Jurors Giving Each Verdict

64

36

50

50

Guilty

Not guilty

Judge's Opinion about Defendant

FIGURE 11.3 Judge's Opinion about Guilt and Innocence and Jury's Verdict.

Jurors were shown videotapes of a trial and of a judge giving standard instructions to the jury. The tape showing the instructions was actually from a different trial, in which the judge had privately given the investigators his or her opinion that the defendant was guilty or not guilty. When the judge believed the defendant to be guilty, the jurors overwhelmingly returned a guilty verdict. When the judge believed the defendant to be not guilty, the jurors split 50–50 in their verdict. Evidently the judge's opinion (apparently communicated through nonverbal cues) influenced the jurors' decision.

(*Source:* Based on data from Hart, 1995.)

come of both real and simulated trials (Dane, 1992). For most crimes, it is to the defendant's advantage to be physically attractive, a female, and of high rather than low socioeconomic status (Mazzella & Feingold, 1994).

Each of these positive attributes can, however, have negative effects under some circumstances. For example, attractiveness is a disadvantage if it appears to have helped the suspect commit the crime—such as when a swindler is attractive (Sigall & Ostrove, 1975). In an assault case, a female defendant is more likely than a male defendant to be found guilty (Cruse & Leigh, 1987), presumably because an assaultive woman is engaging in unacceptable gender-role behavior (see Chapter 5), while an assaultive man is not. Also, high status becomes a liability if the crime is related to the defendant's profession; an example would be a therapist who rapes a client (Skolnick & Shaw, 1994).

Are All Defendants Equal under the Law? Attractive defendants are consistently at an advantage compared to unattractive ones with respect to being

acquitted, receiving a light sentence, and gaining the sympathy of the jurors (Esses & Webster, 1988; Stewart, 1980; Wuensch, Castellow, & Moore, 1991; see Figure 11.4). This attractiveness effect is strongest with serious but nonfatal crimes such as burglary, and with female defendants (Quigley, Johnson, & Byrne, 1995). Because attorneys are well aware of the importance of the bias toward attractiveness, they usually advise a client to do everything possible to enhance his or her appearance before entering the courtroom.

You might assume that even if the attractiveness of a defendant could influence the responses of a juror, judges surely would be unaffected by how a defendant looks. In fact, as Downs and Lyons (1991) discovered, judges are as susceptible to the effects of appearance as the rest of us. These investigators collected data on the dollar amounts assigned by forty judges for bail and for fines in more than 1,500 court cases involving misdemeanors. The attractiveness of each defendant was rated by police officers who were not involved in the arrest and who did not know the purpose of the study. The results clearly

FIGURE 11.4   What Is Beautiful Is Good Revisited: Effect of Defendant's Physical Attractiveness on Judicial Decisions.

Though the physical appearance of a defendant is obviously unrelated to his or her guilt, a great many studies indicate a general tendency for jurors to respond more favorably to an attractive than to an unattractive defendant.

indicated that the more attractive a defendant, the lower the amount of bail or the fine set by the judge. The seriousness of the crime also influenced the amount of the bails and fines (the more serious, the higher the dollar amount), but the attractiveness effect was evident at each level of seriousness. A similar analysis of still more serious cases—felonies—revealed that attractiveness becomes irrelevant when extremely serious crimes are involved, and other research supports this finding (McKelvie & Coley, 1993).

Does the *victim's* attractiveness have any effect on judgments about the *defendant?* The answer is, sometimes. When, for example, the case is one of alleged sexual harassment, the attractiveness of *both* the plaintiff and the defendant influence decisions about guilt and innocence (Castellow, Wuensch, & Moore, 1990). In a test of these effects, research participants read the trial summary of a case in which a young secretary/

receptionist accused her employer of repeatedly making suggestive remarks, attempting to kiss and fondle her, and letting her know in detail what sexual activities he would enjoy with her. The participants saw two photographs that were identified as the plaintiff and the defendant. Some saw two attractive individuals, some saw two unattractive ones, and still others saw either an attractive male defendant and an unattractive female plaintiff or the reverse. Guilty judgments were most likely when the plaintiff was an attractive woman and the defendant was an unattractive man (83 percent) and least likely when the plaintiff was unattractive and the defendant attractive (41 percent).

Subsequent research by Moore and his colleagues (1994) revealed that these attractiveness effects occur because jurors use attractiveness as a cue to judge *character*. Thus, attractiveness effects disappeared when jurors had direct information about the character of the defendant and plaintiff. It seems quite possible, then, that the attractiveness effect in legal decisions is real but that it operates only because of its effect on assumptions about character.

In the United States, African American defendants have generally been found to be at a disadvantage. For example, they are more likely than whites to be convicted of homicide and to receive the death penalty (Sniffen, 1991). Of the prisoners awaiting execution at any given time, about 40 percent are black, a much higher figure than the proportion of blacks in the total population (about 11 percent). The explanation for this overrepresentation on death row is not a simple one. The most obvious—but not necessarily correct—hypothesis is that white judges and jurors tend to be racially biased. The reason may not be that straightforward. We noted earlier that young males tend to commit a high proportion of crimes of violence; and a higher proportion of blacks than of whites are involved in such offenses. The suggested reasons for black overrepresentation include the pervasive effects of poverty and unemployment on young black males, and the influence of a subculture in which violent social models are readily available to these young men. Still another explanation is that white defendants have an economic advantage and can afford more skillful attorneys. Racism, however, seems the most likely explanation for another black–white finding: A study of U.S. trials revealed that regardless of a criminal's race, 11.1 percent who kill a white victim receive a death sentence, but only 4.5 percent of those killing a black victim are sentenced to die (Henderson & Taylor, 1985).

In addition to attractiveness and race, what a defendant says in court can also influence judgments. When defendants deny guilt, this has little effect on whether observers believe the statement to be true. When, however, defendants deny accusations that have not been made ("I am not a crook"), they are perceived as being less trustworthy, more nervous, more responsible for what happened, and more likely to be guilty (Holtgraves & Grayer, 1994). When defendants do not speak English, and the testimony must be translated, they are more likely to be found guilty than if precisely the same testimony is simply given in English (Stephan & Stephan, 1986).

Integrating Principles

1. Pretrial publicity in the media can shape public opinion, including the opinions of those who will eventually serve as jurors, negative media coverage yields negative first impressions of the suspect, and these effects tend to persist as a function of primacy (Chapter 2).
2. In providing accurate eyewitness testimony, an individual must retrieve material from memory, but the efficiency of such cognitive processing (Chapter 3) can be subject to interference from both internal and external factors.
3. In our legal system, attorneys act as adversaries who seek to influence the attitudes and judgments (Chapter 5) of the jury by selecting individuals they believe to be biased toward their position. Lawyers on each side attempt to manipulate the affective responses (Chapter 7) of those who must reach a verdict.
4. Jury members reach conclusions about a given defendant on the basis of processes familiar to social psychologists such as social cognition (Chapter 3); attitudes about specific crimes and their causes (Chapter 5); prejudices based on race and gender (Chapter 4 and 6); and interpersonal attraction and therefore numerous characteristics that should be irrelevant to judgments about guilt and innocence (Chapter 7).

 # Applying Social Psychology to Business

What single activity fills more of most persons' time than any other? The answer is simple: work. Unless we are fortunate enough to be born with or to acquire vast wealth, most of us spend a majority of our waking hours doing some type of job. And we don't work alone; on the contrary, most of us work together with other persons in what, from the point of view of social psychology, are certainly social situations. It's not surprising, then, that the principles and findings of social psychology have often been applied to the task of understanding what goes on in work settings—mainly with an eye toward making this central part of life more satisfying and productive. In many cases, social psychologists themselves have used the knowledge of their field to address important questions and to solve practical problems relating to work. In other cases, however, the findings and principles of social psychology have been put to use by **industrial/organizational psychologists**—psychologists who specialize in studying all aspects of behavior in work settings (Murnighan, 1993). Regardless of who has applied social psychology in this manner, the results have been rewarding: Social psychology *does* provide many insights into the complex world of work. In this section, we'll examine three major topics: *work-related attitudes*—employees' attitudes toward their jobs and their organizations; the role of impression management in *job interviews*—how job applicants attempt to look good to interviewers; and the nature and causes of interpersonal *conflict* in work settings.

Work-Related Attitudes

As we saw in Chapter 5, we are rarely neutral to the social world around us: On the contrary, we hold strong *attitudes* about many aspects of it. Jobs are no exception to this general rule. In fact, if asked, most persons can readily report their attitudes toward their work and also toward their organization. Attitudes concerning one's own job or work are generally referred to by the term **job satisfaction.** Don't let this term confuse you: Not everyone likes their job. So *job satisfaction* actually refers to a dimension of reactions ranging from very positive (high job satisfaction) to very negative (low job satisfaction or high job *dis*satisfaction; Hulin, 1991).

In contrast, attitudes toward one's company are known as **organizational commitment.** This term refers to the extent to which an individual identifies with his or her company and is unwilling to leave it (e.g., Hackett, Bycio, & Hausdorf, 1994). Let's take a closer look at the factors that influence both kinds of work-related attitudes.

Factors Affecting Job Satisfaction. Despite the fact that many jobs are repetitive and boring in nature, large-scale surveys of employees' attitudes toward their jobs indicate that for most, job satisfaction is quite high (e.g., Page & Wiseman, 1993). In part, high job satisfaction may reflect the operation of *cognitive dissonance,* a process we discussed in Chapter 5. Briefly, since most persons know that they have to go on working and that there is often considerable effort—and risk—involved in changing jobs, stating that they are not satisfied with their current jobs tends to generate dissonance. To avoid or reduce such reactions, then, many persons report relatively high levels of job satisfaction—and may actually come to believe their own ratings in this respect (e.g., J. A. Greenberg & Baron, 1995).

Individuals do report a wide range of job satisfaction, though, so the question remains: What factors influence such attitudes? Research on this issue indicates that two major groups of factors are important: *Organizational factors*—ones related to a company's practices or the working conditions it provides—and *personal factors*—ones related to the traits of individual employees.

Among organizational factors, a very important one is the company's *reward system*—the way in which raises, promotions, and other rewards are distributed. *Fairness* is an extremely important value for most persons, and this value comes into full operation with respect to job-related rewards. Job satisfaction is higher when individuals believe that rewards are distributed fairly and impartially

than when they believe they are distributed unfairly (Konovsky & Organ, 1996; Miceli & Lane, 1991). Moreover, this is true in countries around the world (e.g., Steiner & Gilliland, 1996). Another organizational factor that plays an important role in job satisfaction is the *perceived quality of supervision*—the extent to which employees believe that their bosses are competent, have employees' best interests at heart, and treat them with respect. A third factor influencing job satisfaction is the extent to which individuals feel that they can participate in decisions that affect them. The greater such participation, the higher the reported job satisfaction (Callan, 1993). Finally, as you can readily guess, the nature of jobs themselves plays an important role in job satisfaction. Individuals who must perform boring, repetitive jobs report much lower levels of job satisfaction than ones whose jobs provide a degree of variety (C. D. Fisher, 1993). In fact, recent findings indicate that not only do boring, monotonous jobs reduce job satisfaction—but also they may undermine psychological and even physical health. A study conducted by Melamed and his colleagues (1995) provides important insights into this relationship.

These researchers reasoned that repetitive work, and work that exposes individuals to *underload*—jobs that do not give people enough to do or that are beneath their capacities—would cause strong feelings of monotony, and that these, in turn, would produce low job satisfaction, psychological distress, and even physical illness. Melamed as his associates (1995) further reasoned that repetitive jobs that are also *hectic*—jobs requiring individuals to repeat the same task over and over again very quickly—would have especially negative effects. To test these predictions, they analyzed the work performed by almost 1,300 blue-collar workers working in manufacturing plants to see how monotonous and hectic the jobs were. Then they asked these individuals to complete questionnaires designed to measure their subjective feelings of monotony, their job satisfaction, and their psychological distress (feelings of depression, anxiety, irritability). Finally, they obtained records of sickness-related absences for these employees. Results offered support for the key predictions. The more monotonous the jobs were, the lower employees' job satisfaction, the higher their psychological distress, and the greater their absences from work (although the last of these findings was stronger for women than for men). And these negative effects were especially pronounced for jobs classified as *hectic* in nature.

Turning to personal factors that influence job satisfaction, several interesting findings have been uncovered. Job satisfaction is related to several personal traits, such as the Type A behavior pattern, which we discussed in Chapter 9 (D. V. Day & Bedian, 1991): Type A's satisfaction is higher than Type B's, despite their greater overall irritability. Job satisfaction is also related to *status* and *seniority*. The higher a person's position within a company, the greater his or her reported satisfaction. Also, the longer an individual has been on the job, the greater his or her job satisfaction (Zeitz, 1990). Fourth, the greater the extent to which jobs are *congruent* with people's interests, the greater their satisfaction (Fricko & Beehr, 1992). Indeed, very low levels of satisfaction are often reported by persons working in fields that do

not interest them. Finally, job satisfaction is related to people's *general life satisfaction*. The more individuals are satisfied with aspects of their lives outside work, the higher the levels of job satisfaction they report (Judge & Watanabe, 1993), although what is causing this pattern remains unclear (Cramer, 1995). In sum, many different factors seem to influence job satisfaction.

Organizational Commitment: Attitudes toward One's Company. Do you know anyone who constantly knocks your college or university, criticizing it constantly and harshly? What about the opposite: Do you know anyone who frequently praises your college, telling others what a great place it is and how nice all the professors are? Our own experience tells us that the second pattern is much more rare than the first one; but in any case, you probably do know people with contrasting reactions to their school or the organization in which they work. This range of reactions indicates that people hold attitudes not only toward their jobs, but also toward their companies (see Figure 11.5).

FIGURE 11.5   Organizational Commitment and Employee Morale.

Organizational commitment stems, in part, from the attitudes that employees have toward their organization. Many companies have orientation seminars in which their new employees learn about the organization. As this comic strip suggests, supervisors have a large impact on employee morale—and therefore commitment—whether they intend to have this impact or not. This comic strip also highlights the fact that companies have an impact on their employees' health, not only in the options they offer for health insurance, but also in terms of the demands that they place on their employees!

(*Source:* Washington Post Writers Group.)

Such attitudes are known as organizational commitment, because they refer to the extent to which individuals identify with, are involved with, and are unwilling to leave their organizations—whether these are universities, small businesses, or giant corporations (Meyer & Allen, 1991; Dunham, Grube, & Castaneda, 1994). High organizational commitment tends to reduce absenteeism and voluntary turnover (T. M. Lee, 1992), and to increase **organizational citizenship behavior** (e.g., Konovsky & Pugh, 1994; Van Dyne, Graham, & Dienesch, 1994). In other words, individuals with high organizational commitment tend to be more willing to do what's good for the company even at some cost to themselves. Clearly, organizational commitment is an important variable to understand.

A model proposed by Allen and Meyer (1990) suggests that organizational commitment involves three different components. First, there is what Meyer and Allen (1991) term the *affective component*. This involves emotional attachment to and identification with the organization. A person high on this component feels good about her or his company and has made working for it a part of her of his self-concept. "I'm an IBM person," or "I'm a Marine!" such a person might state with pride. Second, there is what Allen and Meyer describe as the *continuance component*. This relates to the potential costs involved in leaving the company. For example, after working for a company for several years, an individual may have a considerable sum built up in its pension fund; if the employee leaves, a part (or even all) of these funds many be lost. Similarly, an individual may realize that it will be difficult to find another comparable job. Third, there is what Meyer and Allen describe as a *normative component*. This refers to feelings of obligation to stay with the company—mainly because of norms and values indicating that loyalty is desirable, that it's wrong to jump from job to job, or that the individual owes the company allegiance. According to Meyer and Allen (1991), these three components combine to generate an individual's level of organizational commitment.

This model has been tested in many recent studies (e.g., Dunham et al., 1994; Hackett, Bycio, & Hausford, 1994), and in general results have supported its accuracy. Thus, it appears that organizational commitment does involve the three components we've described. What factors influence such commitment? Recent findings suggest that somewhat different conditions play a role in each of the three components (e.g., Dunham et al., 1994). For example, with respect to affective commitment, the following variables seem to be important: quality of supervisory feedback, autonomy (freedom to structure one's own work), task identity (being able to complete a whole piece of work from beginning to end), and skill variety (working on a job that requires a number of different activities). Tenure (length of time with the company) also plays a role; the longer the tenure, the higher affective commitment tends to be. Tenure plays an even more important role with respect to continuance commitment: The longer people have been with a given company, the more they have to lose, in many cases, if they leave. Finally, normative commitment is influenced by such factors as commitment on the part of one's coworkers and the extent to which individuals are allowed to participate in decisions relating to their jobs: Being able to participate in decisions creates a sense of obligation to stay with a company that has treated the individual fairly and with respect. Moreover, these patterns have been obtained in countries around the world (e.g., Sommer, Bae, & Luthans, 1996). In short, many different factors influence organizational commitment, and these seem to differ for each of the components of such commitment.

Job Interviews: Impression Management Revisited

Do you remember our discussion of *impression management* in Chapter 2? At that time, we pointed out the importance of first impressions and described some of the tactics individuals employ to look good to others they are meeting for the first time (Wayne & Liden, 1995). One important context where such tactics are often used is during **job interviews**—interviews organizations conduct with applicants for various jobs in order to choose the best candidates. Think about it: Wouldn't *you* try your best to make a good first impression on an interviewer if you were applying for a job? Actually, you've probably already had experience in doing just this—in trying to look your best during an interview. Taking a cue from research on first impressions and impression management conducted by social psychologists, industrial/organizational psychologists have studied these processes as they occur during interviews. The results of this research are somewhat unsettling; for it has been found that interviewers' ratings of job applicants are influenced by a wide range of factors that, most persons would agree, should *not* play a role in the selection of employees (e.g., Dipboye, 1992). These factors include (1) applicants' physical appearance, which we discussed earlier in this chapter in connection with jurors' reactions to defendants; (2) the mood of interviewers (R. A. Baron, 1993a); and (3) many tactics of impression management that can be used, with varying success, by applicants (Wayne & Liden, 1995). Since job interviews remain one of the most widely used procedures for choosing employees (McDaniel et al., 1994), these findings have important implications. Let's take a closer look at some of the social factors that can influence the judgments of even experienced interviewers who are trying hard to choose the best applicants.

Applicants' Appearance. Almost without exception, people preparing for job interviews dress and groom themselves as carefully as possible. After all, everyone "knows" that appearance really matters where first impressions are concerned. Systematic research suggests that such beliefs are well-founded: Interviewers' ratings of job applicants are indeed sometimes influenced by the applicants' appearance and factors relating to this. For example, attractive persons often have an edge over less attractive ones, and persons who dress for interviews in a manner considered appropriate by interviewers—a manner consistent with the style of dress adopted in their companies—often receive higher ratings than persons who dress in a less appropriate manner (Forsythe, Drake, & Cox, 1985). Similarly, inter-

viewers often assign higher ratings to applicants who emit positive nonverbal cues—persons who smile, nod, and lean forward frequently during an interview (Riggio & Throckmorton, 1988).

In short, the outcome of interviews is often influenced by aspects of applicants' appearance over which they exert direct control. Perhaps even more unsettling is evidence indicating that such effects also occur for variables over which individuals have relatively little control, such as gender (Heilman, Martell, & Simon, 1988) and being overweight (Klesges et al., 1990). The strong impact of this latter factor is clearly illustrated in a study by Pingitore and her colleagues (1994).

These researchers prepared eight different videotapes of simulated job interviews in which three factors were systematically varied: (1) nature of the job (either sales—a job for which personal appearance is relevant—or systems analysis, for which it is not relevant); (2) gender of the applicants (male or female); and (3) weight of the applicants (normal-weight or considerably overweight). Professional actors were hired to play the roles of job applicants in the videotapes, and these persons wore special makeup and padding under their clothes to make themselves appear overweight or of normal weight in the appropriate conditions. After watching one of the eight tapes, participants rated the extent to which they would hire the job applicant they saw. In addition, they reported on their own level of satisfaction with their own bodies and weight. It was predicted that participants would assign lower ratings to the applicants when they appeared to be overweight, and that this tendency might be stronger for female than for male applicants. As you can see from Figure 11.6, the overweight applicants did receive significantly lower ratings, and this effect was indeed stronger for female applicants than for male applicants. Interestingly, the nature of the job made no difference: Overweight applicants received lower ratings even for the systems analyst job, one for which appearance is largely irrelevant. Finally, individuals who were themselves pleased with their own bodies and weight—especially women—were somewhat harsher in their evaluations of

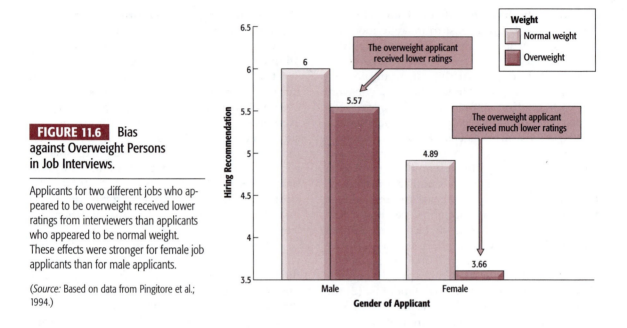

FIGURE 11.6 Bias against Overweight Persons in Job Interviews.

Applicants for two different jobs who appeared to be overweight received lower ratings from interviewers than applicants who appeared to be normal weight. These effects were stronger for female job applicants than for male applicants.

(*Source:* Based on data from Pingitore et al.; 1994.)

the overweight applicants. It was as though they reasoned, "If I'm so slim, why aren't you?"

In sum, the findings reported by Pingitore and her colleagues (1994), as well as other researchers (e.g., Larwood, 1995), indicate that there is indeed a bias against overweight job applicants and that such bias is especially strong for females. Clearly, these are unsettling findings, which serve to underscore a point we made in Chapter 3: As human beings, we are definitely *not* perfectly rational information-processing machines. On the contrary, we are often influenced, in our social judgments, by factors that, we would be quick to agree, should not play a role in such decisions.

Conflict in Work Settings

In several important respects, all persons working in the same organization are *interdependent*. Their individual fates are linked, to some degree, at least while they remain in that organization. If the enterprise prospers, they can all share in a growing pie. If it fails, their individual outcomes may be sharply reduced or may even come to an end. Given these basic facts, it seems reasonable

to assume that *cooperation*—working together to attain various benefits—would be the dominant mode of interaction in work settings. In fact, however, this is often not the case. Instead of working together in a coordinated fashion, individuals and groups often engage in **conflict**—they work against each other and attempt to block one another's interests. Unfortunately, conflict is far from rare in many work settings. In surveys, managers in a wide range of companies have reported that they spend more than 20 percent of their time dealing with conflict and its effects (e.g., R. A. Baron, 1988; Kilmann & Thomas, 1977). Moreover, it is clear that grudges, the desire for revenge, and other ill effects of intense conflicts can persist for months or even years, exacting a toll both on individuals and on their companies. As you can readily see, such conflicts are clearly related to *aggression,* a topic we examined in detail in Chapter 9. But the two concepts are not identical. While aggression refers to intentional efforts to harm one or more persons, conflict is defined as behavior resulting from two perceptions: (1) One's own and another person's interests are incompatible; and (2) the other person is about to interfere—or already has interfered—with the perceiver's interests (e.g., van de Vliert & Euwema, 1994). As you can readily see, these perceptions may sometimes lead to aggressive acts; but in other situations, they may lead to actions that are definitely not aggressive in nature—for example, trying to resolve the conflict through negotiation (see below). What are the causes of conflict? How do people actually behave in conflict situations? And what steps can be taken to reduce the potentially harmful effects of conflict? These are the questions on which we'll now focus.

The Causes of Conflict at Work: Organizational and Interpersonal. Suppose that you asked a large number of people to describe the factors that contribute to conflict in their work settings. How would they answer? The chances are good that most would refer to what have been described as *organizational causes* of conflict (R. A. Baron, 1993b). That is, they would describe factors such as those shown on the left side of Figure 11.7—

causes relating to the structure and functioning of their companies, such as *competition over scarce resources,* or *ambiguity over responsibility* (who's in charge here, anyway?). Such answers reflect a traditional approach to organizational conflict—one that dominated the study of this topic in the past.

More recently, however, another perspective—one deriving directly from social psychology—has emerged. According to this point of view, conflict in work settings, like conflict in many other contexts, stems, at least in part, from *interpersonal factors*—factors related to individuals, their social relationships, and the ways in which they think about others (e.g., R. A. Baron, 1990; Hammock & Richardson, 1992; Kabanoff, 1991). As shown on the right side of Figure 11.7, such factors include stereotypes, prejudice, faulty styles of interpersonal communication, grudges stemming from loss of face and other factors, and faulty attributions—assuming that others

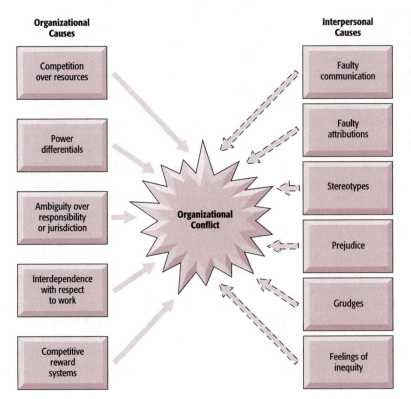

FIGURE 11.7 Causes of Conflict in Work Settings.

As shown here, conflict in work settings stems from both organizational causes (e.g., competition over scarce resources, ambiguity over responsibility) and interpersonal causes (grudges, stereotypes, faulty attributions).

are out to get us even if they are not (see Chapter 9). A growing body of evidence offers support for this perspective (e.g., R. A. Baron, 1988; 1990; Bies, Shapiro & Cummings, 1988; Ohbuchi & Takahashi, 1994), so it appears to be a useful one for understanding the causes of conflict.

Strategies for Dealing with Conflict: Contrasting Patterns, Underlying Dimensions. When I (Bob Baron) was the chair of my department, I often faced a conflict situation like this one. At a meeting of department chairs, the dean would announce that he had some funds he could distribute to individual departments. We would then discuss the division of these funds—often in a very heated manner. As you can see, this was basically a "win–lose" situation: If one department received some funds, the others could not. So it was clearly a conflict situation. I soon observed that different chairpersons reacted differently in this situation. Most, as you can guess, were quite competitive: They tried to convince the dean and the rest of us that they needed the money most. I must admit that I usually behaved in this manner myself. In contrast, a few chairpersons recommended dividing the money equally—equal shares for all. Surprisingly, there was one chair who often made comments to this effect: "My department needs the money, but let's give it to [another department], because I'm convinced that they need it more; and our real goal is to strengthen the entire school, right?"

These actions represent very different modes of responding to conflict. In fact, a large amount of research on conflict indicates that most people tend to adopt one of five distinct patterns: *competition*—get as much as possible for oneself or one's group; *compromise*—split everything down the middle or equally; *accommodation*—give up and let the others take all the benefits; *avoidance*—avoid conflict in any way possible, including withdrawal from the situation; and *collaboration*—attempt to maximize everyone's gains. As you can see, most department chairs (me included) chose competition; a few selected compromise; and one actually pushed for collaboration. (No one could avoid this situation; the dean expected us all to be at the meeting.)

If you think about these contrasting patterns—which have been confirmed in many studies (e.g., Graziano, Jensen-Campbell, & Hair, 1996; Putnam, 1990)—you may quickly realize that they seem to relate to two basic dimensions: concern for one's own outcomes and concern for others' outcomes. Competition is high on concern for one's own outcomes and low on concern for others' outcomes, while accommodation (surrender) is high on concern for others' outcomes but low on concern for one's own outcomes. Compromise, of course, is in the middle on both dimensions. Interestingly, large individual differences seem to exist with respect to preferences among these patterns (e.g., Rahim, 1983). In other words, across many situations, some individuals tend to prefer confrontation (competition), while others tend to prefer less confrontational modes of resolving conflicts (compromise, collaboration, avoidance). Figure 11.8 shows the placement of all five patterns on these two dimensions.

Are any of the various modes for handling conflict we have discussed most effective? As you can see, this is a complex question, because what works in one situation may be inappropriate in another. Collaboration, which focuses on maximizing the outcomes of both sides, is often very useful. However, if one is faced with an opponent who sticks rigidly to competition, collaboration can't be used. Similarly, there are some conflicts that are best avoided—ones in which there is virtually no chance of obtaining an acceptable outcome or in which the conflict seems likely to escalate to ever more intense levels. Recent evidence suggests that *competition* tends to escalate conflicts, whereas *cooperation* reduces it; moreover, many individuals combine more than one mode to resolve a conflict (van de Vliert, Euwema, & Huismans, 1995).

Techniques for Reducing the Harmful Effects of Conflict. As we noted earlier, conflict is often a costly process for both individuals and organizations. The effects are not always negative—conflict sometimes encourages both sides to examine the issues more carefully and, as a result, to formulate more creative solutions or decisions (e.g., Amason, 1996). This is especially true in cases

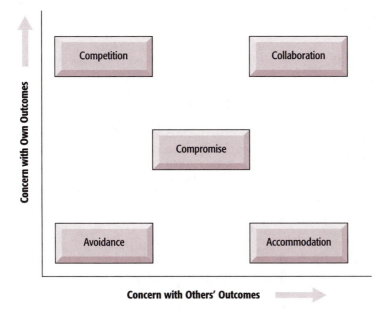

Concern with Own Outcomes

Competition

Collaboration

Compromise

Avoidance

Accommodation

Concern with Others' Outcomes

FIGURE 11.8 Reactions to Conflict: Five Basic Patterns.

When faced with conflict situations, individuals often adopt one of the five patterns shown here: competition, compromise, accommodation, avoidance, collaboration. These reactions, in turn, are related to two underlying dimensions: concerns with one's own outcomes and concern with others' outcomes.

where participants focus on issues and ideas, and emotions such as anger do not rise to high levels (R. A. Baron, in press). In many instances, however, conflict *is* disruptive, and generates negative outcomes. For this reason, it seems important to develop practical techniques for reducing its negative effects. Many different procedures for attaining this goal have been developed, and several of them rest firmly on the principles and findings of social psychology.

By far the most widely used procedure for resolving conflicts, and therefore for heading off their adverse effects, is **negotiation** or bargaining (e.g., R. A. Johnson, 1993; Sheppard, Bazerman, & Lewicki, 1990). In this process, the opposing sides exchange offers, counteroffers, and concessions, either directly or through representatives. If the process is successful, a solution acceptable to both sides is attained and the conflict is resolved. If, instead, bargaining is unsuccessful, a costly deadlock may result, intensifying the conflict. What factors tip the balance toward favorable or unfavorable outcomes? Research findings offer some intriguing answers.

One group of factors that strongly affect the outcomes of negotiation involves the tactics adopted by each side. Many of these are designed to lower opponents' aspirations—to convince opponents that they have little chance of reaching their goals. One of the specific strategies used for this purpose is the suggestion by one side that it has an "out" (another potential partner with whom to make a deal). Another is the *big lie* technique—claims that one's break-even point is much higher or lower than it really is. A third tactic often used by negotiators involves making "tough" or extreme initial offers. Relatively extreme offers seem to put strong pressure on opponents to make concessions, often to their own detriment.

A second group of factors that determine the nature and outcomes of bargaining involves the perceptions of the persons involved in the process. Studies by Thompson and her colleagues reveal that negotiators often enter negotiations with important misperceptions about the situation (L. Thompson, 1990). In particular, they seem to begin with the view that their own interests and those of the other side are totally incompatible—the **incompatibility error.** In turn, they overlook interests that are actually compatible. Research findings indicate that this incompatibility error stems from the tendency of negotiators to perceive (falsely) that the quantity of available outcomes is fixed and that they must seize the largest possible share of this amount (L. Thompson, 1993).

A second important technique for resolving conflicts, aside from bargaining, rests firmly on social psychological foundations. It involves the induction of the kind of **superordinate goals** we discussed in Chapter 6—goals that are shared by both sides. Do you remember our discussion of the Robber's Cave experiment? If so, you already know that when opposing sides recognize the fact that they share certain goals, conflicts between them may be greatly reduced. In fact, this technique underlies several practical programs for resolving costly conflicts (e.g., Blake & Mouton, 1984; Kolb & Bartunek, 1992).

Finally, we should note that one technique useful in reducing aggression, the incompatible response strategy, has also been found to be useful in reducing interpersonal conflicts (R. A. Baron, 1984, 1993c). Since intense conflicts often generate strong anger, and since strong emotions, in turn, interfere with cognitive efficiency (Zillmann, 1994), getting people to lower the volume by exposing them to events or stimuli that induce feelings incompatible with anger can be a useful means for getting negotiations back on track, and hence for resolving serious conflicts.

In sum, the findings, principles, and theories of social psychology serve as the basis for several techniques for reducing or resolving conflicts. In this respect, as in many others, our field has made valuable contributions to understanding human behavior in work settings and to making such environments more pleasant and productive for large numbers of persons.

Integrating Principles

1. Work-related attitudes influence several aspects of behavior in work settings (e.g., job performance, voluntary turnover), although this relationship is not a very strong one. This illustrates, once again, the complexities in the attitude–overt behavior link (see Chapter 5).
2. Even professional job interviewers are influenced by such factors as the appearance of applicants, tactics of impression management used by applicants, and even the inter-

viewers' moods (see Chapter 2). These findings illustrate a basic principle of social thought to which we've referred many times throughout this book: Human beings are definitely not perfect information processors (see Chapter 3).
3. Conflicts often stem from the fact that opposing sides have incompatible interests. However, they are also influenced by many social factors—stereotypes, grudges, attributions, and so on. This fact underscores the import of social factors and processes in business settings; see discussions of social cognition (Chapter 3), prejudice (Chapter 6), attraction (Chapter 7), and aggression (Chapter 9).

Applying Social Psychology to Health

When we speak of good health or of illness, we are clearly referring to a person's physical state. And whether a person is well or sick might seem to involve purely medical issues unrelated to the concerns of psychologists. Over the years, however, it has become very clear that psychological factors affect all aspects of our physical well-being (Salovey, Rothman, & Rodin, in press). Work on these problems is labeled **health psychology**—the research specialty focusing on the psychological processes that affect the development, prevention, and treatment of physical illness (Glass, 1989). How are psychological and physiological processes interconnected?

Dealing with Health-Related Information

One obstacle to taking the necessary steps that help prevent physical disorders is our understandable confusion in processing the large quantity of relevant information that bombards us daily (D. Thompson, 1992)—see Figure 11.9 for an example. For an actual example, consider a recent article in *The British Medical Journal:* A Danish study over a twelve-year period reported a lower death rate among those who drank three to five glasses of wine each day than among those who drank beer, liquor, or no alcoholic beverages.

FIGURE 11.9 Processing Health-Related Information.

We frequently are overwhelmed by information about how to maximize health and prevent illness. Even when the scientific facts are clear (and they sometimes are not), product advertising can be misleading.

One explanation for the finding that alcohol has a positive effect on longevity is its tendency to raise the blood level of "good" HDL cholesterol—a substance that reduces the risk of death from cardiovascular disease. Does that mean you should stock up on wine and drink it often to prolong your life? Wait. Almost immediately, other researchers issued cautions about consuming any alcohol, including wine, because the Danish results might have been based on special genetic factors among Danes, high-quality medical care in that country, the possibility that the extremely straight roads in Denmark decrease the accident rate among drunk drivers, or the fact that wine drinkers tend to be more health-conscious than most other individuals. Whatever the explanation, Dr. Charles Hennekens of Harvard Medical School concluded that "People shouldn't change their habits on the basis of one study" (Brody, 1995). Meanwhile, while ordinary citizens wait for competing explanations to be sorted out, they must decide whether to avoid alcohol altogether, drink only wine, or move to Denmark. In relation to this and many other relevant research findings, a final answer is simply not yet available.

A second obstacle, even when all of the research data are in and experts agree as to precisely which information is valid, is our extreme reluctance to alter major aspects of our behavior. For example, there is little doubt that cigarette smoking is harmful and that exercise is beneficial; but many smokers resist giving up the habit, and many couch potatoes resist strenuous physical activity.

What Information Is Most Available? Previously, we described the discrepancy between what people believe about crime and the actual crime rate. Similar discrepancies are found with respect to health. When news reports inform us about the AIDS epidemic, a drug-resistant strain of tuberculosis, Lyme disease, and outbreaks of "flesh-eating bacteria," you might reasonably conclude that health problems are overwhelming us. It may come as a surprise to learn from the U.S. Centers for Disease Control and Prevention that people are living longer than ever before (the average is 76 years), that the annual death rate is at a record low (504.5 deaths per 100,000 people in 1992), and that the death rates for the six leading causes of death (heart disease, cancer, stroke, lung disease, accidents, and pneumonia–influenza) all are dropping. As in overestimating the seriousness of crime, people also overestimate threats to health on the basis of the *availability heuristic* that was discussed in

Chapter 3 (Eisenman, 1993). In any event, things are better than they seem.

What Information Do We Accept? A basic question facing those who provide information about health to the general public is whether to emphasize factual details or to make an emotional appeal. The emotion most commonly manipulated is fear—the consequences of engaging in certain behavior (for example, smoking) or not engaging in certain behavior (for example, not going to the dentist) are often described in horrifying detail. Though the results are not entirely consistent across studies, there is evidence that when fear is induced, people actually process a health message more carefully than when fear is absent (R. S. Baron et al., 1994).

Whatever the message, it might seem obvious to predict that people would be most receptive to information personally relevant to them. This is not, however, always true—we often defend ourselves against threat, and this defensiveness can be maladaptive, as we discussed in Chapter 5. For this reason, Liberman and Chai-

ken (1992) proposed that the more relevant a health threat is to an individual, the less likely that person is to accept the truth of a message about the threat. These experimenters created a fictitious article, supposedly from the *New England Journal of Medicine,* that described a link between amount of caffeine consumed and fibrocystic breast disease. The reported study was either highly threatening (follow-up studies supposedly confirmed the original finding) or low in threat (follow-up studies were described as yielding inconsistent results). The personal relevance of this information to the female research participants differed in that some did not drink coffee (low relevance) while some drank two to seven cups a day (high relevance). Regardless of how threatening the message was, it was believed *less* by those for whom it was highly relevant than by those for whom it had little relevance, as shown in Figure 11.10. Clearly, a common response to a message about a self-relevant health problem is to reduce anxiety by rejecting the information. A person feels better if the information is processed as "untrue." A sec-

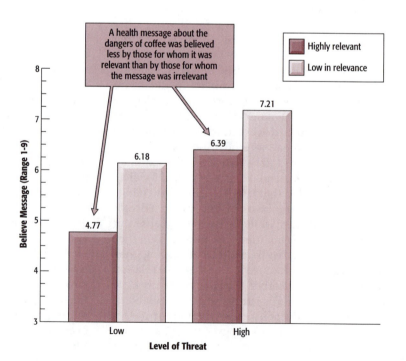

FIGURE 11.10 A Threatening Health Message: If It's Relevant, Don't Believe It.

Information about possible health threats can arouse fear and anxiety, and the more relevant such messages are to oneself, the greater the tendency to reduce the threat by not believing the message. In an experiment, women received either a low-threat or a high-threat message about the health dangers of coffee. The high-threat message was more believable, but at both levels of threat, the coffee drinkers (high relevance) were less likely to believe the message than those who did not drink coffee (low relevance).

(*Source:* Based on data from Liberman & Chaiken, 1992.)

ond "benefit" of rejecting the information is that there is no need to alter one's current behavior.

The general point of this research is that the effectiveness of a health message depends on message content, the way an individual characteristically defends himself or herself against threat, and how attention is focused at the time the message is received.

Stress and Illness

At least since World War II, psychologists have been interested in *stress* and its effects on human behavior (Lazarus, 1993). The original focus of research and theory was on the physical causes of stress (Selye, 1956), but interest soon broadened to include psychological factors (Lazarus, 1966). We now use the word **stress** to indicate negative responses to physical or psychological events that are perceived by the individual to cause physical harm or emotional distress. When confronted by perceived danger, the individual feels threatened and tries to cope with the situation (Bar-Tal & Spitzer, 1994). Such **coping** behavior is considered successful if it reduces or eliminates the threat (Taylor, Buunk, & Aspinwall, 1990). Of special interest has been the connection between stress and physical illness.

Illness As a Consequence of Stress. Research consistently indicates that as stress increases, illness becomes more likely. And we encounter a great many sources of stress. For example, work-related stress is commonly found, and both depression and health complaints increase with continued stress. These effects have been demonstrated among auto workers, medical residents working in emergency rooms, hospital staff, social workers, psychiatric health-care staff, railroad workers, and steel pipe mill workers. College students encounter their own array of stress-inducing events, such as low grades, unwanted pregnancies, and parents who get divorced; again, the greater the stress a person experiences, the more likely that physical illness will occur (Brody, 1989). For each of us, everyday hassles such as interacting with a rude or indifferent spouse (Hendrix, Steel, & Schultz, 1987) or driving an automobile in heavy traffic on a regular basis (Weinberger, Hiner, & Tierney, 1987) can increase the probability of catching a cold or developing the flu. With a more serious problem such as the death of a loved one, the likelihood of becoming ill is even greater (Schleifer et al., 1983). When several negative events occur in the same general time period, they have a cumulative effect (J. J. Seta, Seta, & Wang, 1991); that is, as the total number of stressful experiences increases, the probability of illness increases (S. Cohen, Tyrrell, & Smith, 1993).

How could stress cause physical illness? Two factors are involved. First, in times of stress, the resulting depression (Whisman & Kwon, 1993), worry, and anxiety can interfere with health-related behaviors such as eating a balanced diet, exercising, and getting enough sleep (Wiebe & McCallum, 1986). Second, and more directly, the body's immune system functions less well when stress is high (Stone et al., 1987). Work on *psychoneuroimmunology* examines the interrelationships among stress, emotional and behavioral reactions, and the immune system (Ader & Cohen, 1993). For example, it is frequently reported that college students show an increase in upper respiratory infections when exams are approaching (Dorian et al., 1982). To understand just how this might occur, Jemmott and Magloire (1988) obtained samples of students' saliva over several weeks in order to assess the presence of *secretory immunoglobulin A—* the body's primary defense against infections. The level of this substance dropped during final exams and then returned to normal levels when the exams were over. Thus, the psychological stress of finals brought about a change in body chemistry, and this in turn increased susceptibility to disease.

Individual Differences in Vulnerability to Stress. When exposed to the same objectively stressful conditions, some people experience a high level of stress and become ill, while other people experience much less stress and remain well. For example, men who are perfectionists ("I feel that I must do things perfectly, or not do them at all") are more depressed than nonperfectionists when stress is high (Joiner & Schmidt, 1995).

Though genetic factors explain some of the differences in the effects of stress (Kessler et al., 1992), Friedman, Hawley, and Tucker (1994) present evidence from a large number of studies indicating a difference between **disease-prone personalities** and **self-healing personalities.** People who are disease-prone respond to stressful situations with negative emotions and unhealthy behavior patterns, resulting in illness and a shorter life span. At the opposite extreme are self-healing individuals, who deal effectively with stress and resist illness. They are found to be enthusiastic about life, emotionally balanced, alert, responsive, energetic, curious, secure, and constructive—"people one likes to be around." Research on *subjective well-being* indicates the many benefits of interpreting daily life in positive terms, being engaged in your work and in leisure activities, feeling a sense of purpose, and hoping for positive future outcomes (Myers & Diener, 1995; Diener & Diener, 1996). What specific personality characteristics differentiate disease-prone versus self-healing individuals?

People with disease-prone personalities are often characterized as neurotic (Booth-Kewley & Vickers, 1994), maladjusted (Bernard & Belinsky, 1993), pessimistic (Scheier & Carver, 1987), and having low self-esteem (J. D. Campbell, Chew, & Scratchley, 1991) and an external locus of control (Birkimer, Lucas, & Birkimer, 1991). In contrast, self-healing individuals are described as hardy (Priel, Gonik, & Rabinowitz, 1993), optimistic (Scheier & Carver, 1993), extraverted (Amirkhan, Risinger, & Swickert, 1995), conscientious (Friedman et al., 1993, 1995), and as having an internal locus of control (Quadrel & Lau, 1989) and believing in a just world (Tomaka & Blascovich, 1994).

Other factors also differentiate those most and least vulnerable to stress. Perceived control is very important (S. C. Thompson, Nanni, & Levine, 1994). Stressful events have negative effects in part because they make us realize that sometimes we cannot control such unpleasant occurrences as accidents, bad grades, and failed love affairs. Other research suggests that our reactions to stressful health events rest on our *causal attributions* for them (Chapter 2). Research on HIV, the virus that causes AIDS, has suggested that if HIV-positive individuals internalize blame for acquiring a disease, it hastens the onset of full-blown AIDS, with all of its negative consequences from reduced immunity (e.g., Reed, Kemeny, Taylor, & Visscher, in press).

For example, Segerstrom and her colleagues (1996) tracked eighty-six HIV-positive individuals over an eighteen-month period to determine the health consequences of attributions about the disease. At the beginning of this period, the participants completed an inventory in which they described various attributions about their HIV status. Of crucial importance were items that assessed the extent to which participants attributed various negative events to their selves—for example, losing friends because they were HIV-positive, feeling that a loss of immunological functions was inevitable, and feeling as though they had no control over the course of the disease. Consistent with the predictions of Segerstrom and her colleagues, over the eighteen-month period, individuals who had negative beliefs on such dimensions—who essentially blamed themselves for their condition—lost immunological functioning more rapidly than individuals who had positive beliefs. This conclusion has been supported by many other studies (e.g., Kemeny & Dean, 1995; Reed et al., in press; Strauman et al., 1993). Thus, improving our optimism and avoiding pessimism about the course of a disease should improve coping with the disease.

Individuals who are highly sensitive to social rejection also seem to have more difficulty coping with diseases like HIV. Specifically, Cole, Kemeny, and Taylor (1997) studied seventy-two homosexual men and assessed *rejection sensitivity*, which is generally the sensitivity to being rejected by others; in this case, however, the researchers specifically assessed homosexual rejection sensitivity because many of the men had never revealed they were gay. Cole and his colleagues reasoned that if a person identifies him- or herself as homosexual, there are predictable negative consequences—even verbal and physical abuse—resulting from people's stereotypes about gay men (see Chapter 6). The researchers reasoned that individuals who are highly sensitive to rejection would be more likely to remain "in the closet" about their homosexual status, and would limit their public expression of feelings, thoughts, and behaviors—factors that have been found to relate to decrements in health (e.g., Pennebaker, 1988, 1993). However, men who have disclosed they are gay have most likely experienced many of the negative reactions from others; Cole and his colleagues reasoned that these negative events would have stronger consequences for men who are more sensitive to rejection than others. The researchers were able to track these gay men across a nine-year period, determining when AIDS developed and examining whether rejection sensitivity played a role. Sensitivity to social rejection *was* related to the development of AIDS in the manner that the researchers predicted, as Figure 11.11 shows. Thus, for men who had identified as gay, the onset of AIDS was faster when they were sensitive to rejection by others and slower when the men were less sensitive to rejection. Rejection sensitivity had no apparent relation to AIDS onset for gay men who were still "in the closet." These findings suggest that social dis-

closure is helpful, but only for individuals who are less sensitive to rejection.

In Chapter 4, one of the characteristics of high efficacy is an increase in physical endurance because of the body's production of a natural painkiller. As you might expect, then, self-efficacy also is a key factor in how well we deal with stress. Bandura (1997) has described several kinds of research that are relevant to health. A relatively basic finding involves how a person's perceived self-efficacy in coping with stressors affects bodily reactions that are essential to maintaining health. Volunteer research participants are subjected to physical stress until they reach a point that is beyond their ability to cope. For example, a familiar procedure is to place the participant's hand in a bowl containing water and ice until the pain becomes too great for the participant to continue. This experience causes a series of negative physiological reactions, including activation of the autonomic nervous system. In ordinary life, when such bodily reactions continue over time, the immune system is weakened and the body is less able to defend itself

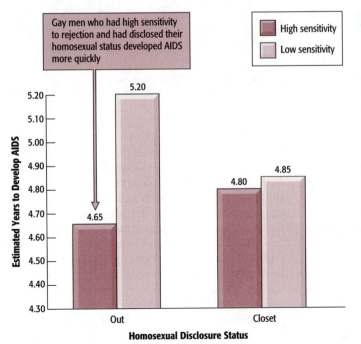

FIGURE 11.11 Rejection Sensitivity and the Onset of AIDS.

In research conducted by Cole and his colleagues (1997), sensitivity rejection was a very important factor for HIV-positive gay men who had disclosed that they were homosexuals. For men who had identified as gay, the onset of AIDS was faster when they were sensitive to rejection by others and slower when the men were less sensitive to rejection. Rejection sensitivity had no apparent relation to AIDS onset for gay men who had not disclosed that they were gay and were still "in the closet."

(*Source:* Based on data presented by Cole, Kemeny, & Taylor, 1997.)

against disease. In the experiments with the ice-cold water, the participants are given a guided procedure that increases their confidence in being able to cope—thus raising their perceived self-efficacy. When self-efficacy is at a maximum, they are again subjected to the stressful experience; the stressors that had previously been biologically disruptive now cause very little physiological activation. Simply stated, uncontrollable stressors impair the immune system, but controllable stressors do not.

Taking Active Steps to Cope with Stress

Because some stress is almost inevitable in our lives and because not everyone is blessed with a self-healing personality, what can we do to cope with stress and/or to ward off its negative effect on health? Three strategies have been identified: (1) becoming physically fit; (2) increasing positive affect by altering our cognitions, behaviors, and environmental surroundings; and (3) seeking social support.

Increasing Physical Fitness. Perhaps the simplest coping strategy is to stay as healthy as possible through a sensible pattern of diet, sleep, and regular physical exercise (see Figure 11.12). The result is increased *fitness*—the maintenance of a good physical condition as indicated by one's endurance and strength. For example, just thirty-five minutes of aerobic dancing has immediate positive effects, with increased feelings of well-being and decreased feelings of distress (Lox & Rudolph, 1994). Together, studies provide much evidence that physical fitness lowers vulnerability to the negative health effects of stress (e.g., Brown, 1991). Keep in mind that the personality dispositional variables discussed previously are equally important. A combination of fitness and hardiness provides the greatest protection against illness (Roth et al., 1989).

Creating Positive Affect. A second strategy for dealing with stress and maintaining good health is to discover how to create more positive affect for oneself. By its very nature, however, stress creates negative affect; and negative affect, in turn,

FIGURE 11.12 Exercise As a Strategy to Cope with Stress and Prevent Illness.

Research indicates that *fitness* (endurance and strength) is an important element in resisting the negative effects of stress. Regular exercise results in fitness, and people who are fit are less likely to become ill in response to stress than those who are not fit.

interferes with the body's immune system. One way to overcome stress, in turn, is to engage in acts that will generate positive affect. Research by A. A. Stone and his colleagues (1994) indicates that positive events (such as a family celebration or getting together with friends) enhance the immune system over a longer time period more than a negative event (such as being criticized) weakens it. We have already described how an increase in negative events leads to illness, but Stone's research found that a *decrease* in positive events had an even greater adverse effect on health.

What are some of the other things you can do to promote positive feelings? An ideal activity is to engage in work that is enjoyable (Csikszent-mihalyi, 1993). Positive cognitions also help; women diagnosed as having breast cancer reported less distress if they accepted the situation and used humor as a coping device than if they denied the problem and thus attempted to avoid the threat (Carver et al., 1993).

Environmental factors influence affect, and we can utilize this knowledge to make ourselves feel happier. For example, in Chapter 9 we described the beneficial effects of pleasant fragrances on positive affect (and on prosocial responding as well). In a similar way, when research participants are working on a stressful task in a laboratory setting, the introduction of such fragrances results in a more positive emotional state *and* improved performance on the task (R. A. Baron & Bronfen, 1994). It is quite possible that we could each alleviate the negative effects of stress by manipulating our own surroundings to include pleasant music, fragrances, lighting, art, and anything else that helps improve our mood.

Seeking Social Support. The third important coping strategy is to seek **social support**—physical and psychological comfort provided by friends and family (Sarason, Sarason, & Pierce, 1994). Even among monkeys, stress leads to an increase in affiliative behavior, and affiliation in turn enhances the immune system (Cohen et al., 1992). Among humans, people who interact closely with others are generally better able to avoid illness than those who remain isolated from interpersonal contact. When illness does occur, people who receive social support recover more quickly than those who do not. The negative effects of stressors in a work setting can be lessened if the employee receives support from coworkers and from the organization itself (Shinn et al., 1993). Studies of real-life stress in Israel—during combat training for the military and during Iraqi missile attacks on civilians in the Gulf War—indicate that people who differ in attachment style (Chapter 7) also differ in their ability to seek and thus benefit from social support (Mikulincer & Florian, 1995; Mikulincer, Florian, & Weller, 1993). Individuals whose attachment pattern is secure are more likely to cope effectively with stress through

support seeking than are those with ambivalent or avoidant attachment patterns (Cole et al., 1997).

The utilization of social support is also associated with fewer sports injuries among young people (R. E. Smith, Smoll, & Ptacek, 1990), less postpartum depression (and higher-birth-weight babies) among women (N. L. Collins, 1993), decreased risk of heart disease among the elderly (Uchino, Kiecolt-Glaser, & Cacioppo, 1992), and less chance of contracting the common cold (Cohen et al., 1997).

One of the reasons for the positive effects of interpersonal support is that talking to someone else (especially about ways to solve one's problems) reduces stress and the incidence of both major and minor health problems (L. F. Clark, 1993; Costanza, Derlega, & Winstead, 1988; Pennebaker, Hughes, & O'Heron, 1987). Interestingly enough, there are also positive emotional, physiological, and health benefits associated with simply writing about one's negative experiences (e.g., M. A. Greenberg & Stone, 1992; Hughes, Uhlmann, & Pennebaker, 1994) instead of talking about them (Mendolin & Kleck, 1993). The more an individual is secretive and conceals from others any personal information that is negative or distressing, the greater the feelings of anxiety and depression and the more likely the development of physical symptoms (Larson & Chastain, 1990). It appears that "confession" is good not only for the soul but also for the body.

Coping with Medical Care

Illnesses often require medical care, and this is another context in which social psychology has been brought to bear.

Dealing with Diagnosis and Treatment. Medical procedures designed to reveal the source of a patient's symptoms and to treat the underlying problem are often intrusive, sometimes painful, and occasionally dangerous. Diagnostic tests and medical treatment are thus stressful, and patients must somehow cope with this very specific type of stress. What can be done by medical personnel and what can be done by the patient to reduce this kind of medical threat?

Social Diversity: A Critical Analysis

Asian and American Responses to Illness

Attitudes and beliefs about illness and health care constitute one of the clearest examples of the effects of cultural differences on our attitudes and behavior. Physicians often stress the difficulty they have in assessing, understanding, and treating a patient whose cultural background differs from their own.

Research interest in this question arose for Nilchaikovit, Hill, and Holland (1993) when two of these individuals (one Asian and the other American) were each involved in assessing the depression of a twenty-four-year-old Korean woman who was a leukemia patient at a New York hospital. After examining her independently, the two professionals had very different perceptions of this woman and recommended very different ways to help her. The American believed that the patient's mother and father were overinvolved with their daughter, and that the young woman needed to distance herself from her family in order to gain independence and control. The Asian disagreed, indicating that the patient wanted even *more* involvement with her family; indeed, it was suggested that her depressed symptoms developed because the hospital staff failed to understand what was involved in effective health care in a culture unlike their own. The attempts of these two practitioners to understand why their perceptions and recommendations differed led them to explore cultural differences in (1) aspects of the self-concept, (2) the effects of self-concept on communication and interpersonal behavior, and (3) how very different worldviews affect how an individual responds to illness and to medical care.

Nilchaikovit, Hill, and Holland (1993) suggest that Eastern and Western concepts of self constitute the basic reasons for different responses to a medical setting. Each of us acquires our self-concept within the context of our family, and our culture plays a central role in determining how the self is defined. As described in several earlier discussions of cross-cultural comparisons, the central contrast is between a society's emphasis on collectivism versus individualism. In Asian countries, for example, the self tends to be conceived as interdependent and centered on family so that the individual is part of an interconnected group. In many Western nations, such as the United States, the self is usually conceived as independent, and there is a sharp distinction between "I" or "me" and other people. Americans and Asians typically differ in the way they conceptualize family and the individual's role in that group. Americans tend to define family in terms of those now living, and the husband and wife constitute the core relationship. This small unit is financially independent, the family is oriented toward feelings, and the overall goal is individual happiness. In contrast, Asians tend to define family in terms of past, present, and future generations, and the core relationship is parent–child. In addition, people have an economic obligation to all of their relatives, they are task-oriented, and the overall goal is the welfare of the family.

Nilchaikovit and his colleagues (1993) also point out specific ways in which Asian–American differences influence health-related behavior. One example is suicide. An American may take his or her own life, but the decision is made by the individual. On this topic, an Asian woman expressed her collective sense of the self:

Your life is not yours as many people like to think. You cannot grow up without the help of others, your family, your friends, the society, and many others. You owe your life to others and you cannot take it away without affecting and hurting other people. Thus you have no right to take your own life without the consent of the others involved. (p. 42)

The most general conclusion to be drawn from this type of research is that a physician must understand how a patient views herself or himself, what the patient is communicating, how the individual conceptualizes illness, and what kind of patient–physician relationship is considered appropriate. Such understanding and sensitivity are extremely important in diverse cultures—such as Canada and the United States—where patient and physician very often come from different cultural backgrounds.

Early in an illness episode, it is important to notice symptoms and to make accurate attributions about their cause. At that point, coping mechanisms such as avoidance and denial can be very dangerous. When, however, you are undergoing a medical examination or treatment, those same defenses can be quite beneficial (Suls & Fletcher, 1985): You will experience less stress if you can mentally avoid and deny what is being done to you. The next time you are in a dentist's office having your teeth cleaned or a cavity drilled, try concentrating on something else—past experiences, future plans, a movie you liked. To a surprising extent, these incompatible thoughts actually prevent or at least greatly reduce pain and discomfort.

Mood also is important. For example, Stalling (1992) found that inducing a positive mood leads to a decrease in self-reports of pain. In related research Zillmann et al. (1993) found, as expected, that exposure to humorous videotapes such as stand-up comedy (*A Night at the Improv*) or a situation comedy (*Married with Children*) reduced physical discomfort compared to a control tape involving cooking instructions (*The Frugal Gourmet*). Unexpectedly, however, tragic material in which a dying mother says good-bye to her three small children (from *Terms of Endearment*) had the same effect. It appears that either positive or negative material buffers the effects of a painful stimulus, presumably because it is helpful to become emotionally involved with something other than your immediate situation.

These various effects all seem to involve *distraction*—thinking about something else. You can make a painful experimental task (leaving your hand in ice-cold water as long as possible) less painful by engaging in distracting thoughts such as thinking about your room at home (Cioffi & Holloway, 1993). Less obviously, the opposite strategy—paying careful attention to the painful sensations—also can have a beneficial effect. When receiving a shot or having blood withdrawn for a test, some people look away and think about something else, while others watch the needle very closely. Both approaches are more effective as coping strategies than trying to deal with pain by suppressing awareness ("Just empty your mind").

The Role of Perceived Control in Coping with Treatment. Earlier, in discussing how people cope with stress, we noted the importance of *perceived control*. Perceived control is also of crucial importance when you are dealing with the stress of medical care (Affleck et al., 1987). As a simple example, it is much less stressful to remove a splinter from your own finger than to have another person remove it. In situations that are not actually controllable, it is still helpful to *believe* that you can determine the outcome. Studies of patients with heart disease, cancer, and AIDS indicate that those who believe themselves able to control symptoms, health care, and treatment make a much better adjustment than do patients who believe that what happens is totally beyond their control (Taylor et al., 1991; Thompson et al., 1993). When one's beliefs about control are entirely fictional, the benefits cannot continue indefinitely. Optimal medical adjustment occurs when threat is high and the perception of control has at least *some basis in reality* (Helgeson, 1992).

A different kind of control has been introduced in some medical settings by means of an interactive laser-disc player, a touch-screen terminal, and a keyboard (Freudenheim, 1992). The process works as follows. A physician informs a patient that, for example, he has an enlarged prostate gland and surgery is one of his options. At this point, the patient becomes directly involved in the decision process. Using the laser-disc player, he enters his own health data (age, weight, symptoms, etc.) and then requests information about the pros and cons of having the surgery, being treated with drugs, or simply doing nothing at present and waiting to see whether the condition improves or worsens. After he considers the pluses and minuses of each option, it's up to the patient to make a final decision.

Still another type of control is provided by accurate information about what is happening to you and what is going to happen next (Jay et al., 1983). Knowledge—even knowledge about unpleasant procedures—is less stressful than ignorance and the resulting fear of the unknown (Suls & Wan, 1989). For a patient hospitalized for surgery, it helps to have a roommate who has already undergone the same kind of operation. Kulik and Mahler (1987) found that patients with a postoperative roommate (compared to those whose roommate had not yet had the operation) were less unhappy and anxious, needed less medication for their pain, and were able to be discharged from the hospital more quickly. Information provides a kind of cognitive road map

that keeps the patient knowledgeable and thus able to avoid fearful surprises.

Note that perceived control has little benefit for patients who don't *want* to have control of the situation (R. S. Baron & Logan, 1993; Law, Logan, & Baron, 1994). For those of us who prefer control, however, it is all-important. Note also that our responses to illness and our strategies for coping with it vary significantly across cultures, as we saw in the Social Diversity box on pages 288–289.

Integrating Principles

1. Psychological factors affect each aspect of one's physical well-being. When we process information dealing with health risks, preventive measures to help maintain good health, or medical procedures, the cognitive functions described in Chapters 2, 3, and 10 (including the availability heuristic, priming, and attributional processes), are clearly relevant. Information designed to improve our health-related behaviors relies on knowledge what is known about attitude change and persuasion (Chapter 5).

2. A central concept in health psychology is the effect of stress (and our ability to cope with stress) on our risk of developing major and minor illnesses. Stress both interferes with health-promoting activities and, at the physiological level, decreases the efficiency of the immune system. Coping with stress (both in everyday life and in medical settings once an illness develops) is based on such psychological characteristics as possessing feelings of self-efficacy (Chapter 4), having a secure attachment style (Chapter 7), being physically fit, and increasing positive affect (Chapter 7).

Connections   Integrating Social Psychology

In this chapter, you read about . . .
- forming attitudes about a suspect based on pretrial publicity
- accuracy of eyewitness testimony

In other chapters, you will find related discussions of . . .
- first impressions (Chapter 2); attitude formation (Chapter 5)
- information processing and retrieving information from memory (Chapter 3)

- the similarity of police lineups and experiments
- nonverbal communication from judge to jury
- attraction toward and evaluation of defendants
- stereotypes and prejudice in judgments about defendants
- work-related attitudes

- effects of impression management on job interviews

- processing health-related information

- self-efficacy in responding to stress

- self-healing personality

- the negative affect caused by thinking about alternatives to stressful events
- seeking social support as a coping strategy
- attachment style as a determinant of social support behavior

- designing experiments to maximize objectivity of results (Chapter 1)
- basic channels of nonverbal communication (Chapter 2)
- factors influencing interpersonal attraction (Chapter 7)
- stereotypes and prejudice based on race and gender (Chapter 6)
- attitudes as a basic aspect of social thought (Chapter 5)
- impression management as a basic aspect of social perception (Chapter 2) and attraction (Chapter 7)
- use of the availability heuristic and the resulting distortions (Chapter 3) and persuasive appeals (Chapter 5)
- the general effects of self-efficacy (Chapter 4)
- the altruistic personality, which has many similar characteristics (Chapter 9)
- counterfactual thinking (Chapter 3)

- the importance of affiliation (Chapter 7)
- attachment style in interpersonal relationships (Chapter 7)

Thinking about Connections

1. Sometime in the past few months a major crime has probably captured the attention of the media either nationally or in the community in which you live. Try to remember what information about the crime you obtained from the newspaper, radio, and television. Once a suspect was arrested, what is your memory of the images that were published or broadcast? What impressions did you form about the suspect (Chapter 2), and what were your attitudes (Chapter 5) about the crime and the person accused of committing it? To what extent do you believe you were influenced by the media presentations?

2. Suppose that a manager discovered that job satisfaction among the employees working under her supervision was low. Drawing on what you know about attitudes (Chapter 5) and social influence (Chapter 8), what steps could she take to improve these attitudes?

3. In the past few years you have probably experienced at least one stressful situation. How did you respond? Did you seek social support from anyone, or did you feel that you would rather handle the problem by yourself? List any parallels you see between your use (or nonuse) of social support and how you see yourself with respect to affiliation need (Chapter 7) and your opinion about your attachment style (Chapter 7).

Summary and Review

The findings and principles of social psychology have been applied to many phenomena, including the legal system, business-related behavior, and the promotion and maintenance of health.

Applying Social Psychology to the Legal System

Forensic psychology has produced extensive evidence that the reality of our legal system often fails to live up to its stated ideals. For example, judgments about the defendant by the general public and by potential jurors are influenced by pretrial publicity in the media. Eyewitness testimony may be inaccurate, but can be improved using *blank-lineup controls* and when the witnessing context is reinstated. The behavior (both deliberate and accidental) of attorneys and judges can influence verdicts. Jurors respond in part on the basis of emotional biases for and against specific defendants, as well as on the basis of their own general attitudes, cognitive processing skills, and assumptions about various physical and behavioral attributes of the person on trial.

Applying Social Psychology to Business

The principles of social psychology have been applied to the understanding of behavior in work settings, especially within the field of industrial/organizational psychology. *Work-related attitudes* include employees' evaluations of their jobs (*job satisfaction*) and of their organizations (*organizational commitment*). Many factors influence such work-related attitudes, and these attitudes, in turn, have been found to play a role in important aspects of work-related behavior, such as performance and turnover. Organizations frequently use job interviews to choose employees. Because these interviews involve social interactions between applicants and interviewers, they are influenced by many social factors. Applicants' appearance—including whether they are overweight—and their use of nonverbal cues influence the ratings they receive.

A common problem in organizations is *conflict*, which results from perceptions of incompatible interests between groups or individuals. Conflict stems from organizational causes, such as competition over scarce resources, and from interpersonal causes, such as stereotypes, prejudices, grudges, and ineffective communication styles. Individuals react to conflict in several different ways; among the most common patterns are competition, compromise, accommodation, avoidance, and collaboration. These contrasting patterns reflect underlying dimensions: concern with one's own outcomes versus concern with others' outcomes. Conflicts can be reduced or resolved by several techniques based on social psychological principles and findings, including negotiation, superordinate goals, and the induction of responses incompatible with anger and conflict.

Applying Social Psychology to Health

Health psychology is concerned with the effect of emotions, cognitions, and behavior on preventing physical illness, maintaining good health, and responding to medical problems. An important topic is how we process relevant health information—and sometimes reject it because it is perceived as threatening. A great deal of research has dealt with the effects of *stress* on susceptibility to illness and with the personality factors that make some individuals better than others at *coping* with physical and psychological threats. Beyond dispositional variables, coping with stress is aided by being physically fit, maintaining high levels of *positive affect*, and receiving *social support*. When a health problem arises, the individual must make a series of critical choices and decisions—noticing and interpreting the symptoms, deciding what action to take, and coping with medical procedures.

Social Diversity: Asian and American Responses to Illness

Differences between Asian and American patients in medical settings led to an examination of the way self-concept is shaped by cultural factors. In Asian countries, the self-concept is tied to other people and centered on one's extended family. In the United States and other Western societies, the self-concept is individualistic and independent. Among the consequences are very different ways of expressing emotions and communicating with others, and doctor–patient relationships differ as a result. Another difference is the American belief that life should involve happiness and be controllable; illness and death constitute failure and must be fought. In contrast, a typical Asian belief is that life involves suffering and is beyond one's control; illness and death are the normal result of bad luck or of your past deeds, and they must be accepted.

Key Terms

Blank-Lineup Control (p. 267)
Conflict (p. 276)
Coping (p. 283)
Disease-Prone Personality (p. 284)
Forensic Psychology (p. 263)
Health Psychology (p. 280)
Incompatibility Error (p. 279)
Industrial/Organizational Psychologists (p. 271)
Job Interviews (p. 274)

Job Satisfaction (p. 272)
Negotiation (p. 279)
Organizational Citizenship Behavior (p. 274)
Organizational Commitment (p. 272)
Self-Healing Personality (p. 284)
Social Support (p. 287)
Stress (p. 283)
Superordinate Goals (p. 280)
Voir Dire (p. 267)

For More Information

Greenberg, J., & Baron, R. A. (1995). *Behavior in organizations* (5th ed.). Englewood Cliffs, NJ: Prentice-Hall.

A broad introduction to what research by psychologists and others tells us about behavior in work settings. The chapters on work-related attitudes, conflict, and perception are closely related to topics covered in this book.

Loftus, E. F. (1992). *Witness for the defense.* New York: St. Martin's Press.

A comprehensive summary of a great deal of research in forensic psychology by one of the leading researchers in this field.

Wilson, D. K., Rodrigue, J. R., & Taylor, W. C. (1997). *Health-promoting and health-compromising behaviors among minority adolescents.* Washington, DC: American Psychological Association.

A collection of essays written by experts in the field, addressing the topic of minority adolescent health. Many health problems begin in youth and these essays consider many solutions to these problems.

# References

Abramson, J. (1994). *We, the jury.* New York: Basic Books.

Ader, R., & Cohen, N. (1993). Psychoneuroimmunology: Conditioning and stress. *Annual Review of Psychology, 44,* 53–85.

Affleck, G., Tennen, H., Pfeiffer, C., & Fifield, J. (1987). Appraisals of control and predictability in adapting to a chronic disease. *Journal of Personality and Social Psychology, 53,* 273–279.

Agnew, C. R., & Thompson, V. D. (1994). Causal inferences and responsibility attributions concerning an HIV-positive target: The double-edged sword of physical attractiveness. *Journal of Social Behavior and Personality, 9,* 181–190.

Aiello, J. R., & Kolb, K. J. (1995). Electronic performance monitoring and social context: Impact on productivity and stress. *Journal of Applied Psychology, 80,* 339–353.

Ajzen, I. (1987). Attitudes, traits, and actions: Dispositional prediction of behavior in personality and social psychology. In L. Berkowitz (Ed.), *Advances in experimental social psychology* (Vol. 20, pp. 1–63). San Diego: Academic Press.

Alicke, M. D. (1994). Evidential and extra-evidential evaluations of social conduct. *Journal of Social Behavior and Personality, 9,* 591–615.

Allen, N. J., & Meyer, J. P. (1990). The measurement and antecedents of affective, continuance and normative commitment to the organization. *Journal of Occupational Psychology, 63,* 1–18.

Alliger, G. M., & Williams, K. J. (1991). Affective congruence and the employment interview. *Advances in Information Processing in Organizations, 4,* 31–43.

Allport, F. H. (1920). The influence of the group upon association and thought. *Journal of Experimental Psychology, 3,* 159–182.

Allport, F. H. (1924). *Social psychology.* Boston: Houghton Mifflin.

Allport, F. H., & Hartman, D. A. (1925). The measurement and motivation of atypical opinion in a certain group. *American Political Science Review, 19,* 735–760.

Allport, G. W. (1985) The historical background of social psychology. In G. Lindzey & E. Aronson (Eds.), *Handbook of social psychology.* New York: Random House.

Alvaro, E. M., & Crano, W. D. (1996). Cognitive responses to minority- or majority-based communications: Factors that underlie minority influence. *British Journal of Social Psychology, 35,* 105–121.

Amason, A. C. (1996). Distinguishing the effects for functional and dysfunctional conflict on strategic decision making: Resolving a paradox for top management teams. *Academy of Management Journal, 39,* 123–148.

Amirkhan, J. H., Risinger, R. T., & Swickert, R. J. (1995). Extraversion: A "hidden" personality factor in coping? *Journal of Personality, 63,* 189–212.

Andersen, S. M., & Baum, A. (1994). Transference in interpersonal relations: Inferences and affect based on significant-other representations. *Journal of Personality, 62,* 459–497.

Andersen, S. M., Reznik, I., & Manzella, L. M. (1996). Eliciting facial affect, motivation, and expectancies in transference: Significant-other representations in social relations. *Journal of Personality and Social Psychology, 71,* 1108–1129.

Anderson, C. A., Anderson, K. B., & Deuser, W. E. (1996) Examining an affective aggression framework: Weapon and temperature effects on aggressive thoughts, affect, and attitudes. *Personality and Social Psychology Bulletin, 22,* 366–376.

Anderson, C. A., Deuser, W. E., & DeNeve K. M. (1995). Hot temperatures, hostile affect, hostile cognition, and arousal: Tests of a general model of affective aggression. *Personality and Social Psychology Bulletin, 21,* 434–448.

Anderson, N. H. (1981). *Foundations of information integration theory.* New York: Academic Press.

Anderson, P. B., & Aymami, R. (1993). Reports of female initiation of sexual contact: Male and female differences. *Archives of Sexual Behavior, 22,* 335–343.

Anthony, T., Copper, C., & Mullen, B. (1992). Cross-racial identification: A social cognitive integration. *Personality and Social Psychology Bulletin, 18,* 296–301.

Archer, J. (1991). Human sociobiology: Basic concepts and limitations. *Journal of Social Issues, 47*(3), 11–26.

Archer, J. (1996). Sex differences in social behavior: Are the social role and evolutionary perspectives compatible? *American Psychologist, 51,* 909–917.

Archer, J., & Haigh, A. M. (1997). Do beliefs about aggressive feelings and actions predict reported levels of aggression? *British Journal of Social Psychology, 36,* 83–105.

Archibald, F. S., Bartholomew, K., & Marx, R. (1995). Loneliness in early adolescence: A test of the cognitive discrepancy model of loneliness. *Personality and Social Psychology Bulletin, 21,* 296–301.

Aron, A., Dutton, D. G., Aron, E. N., & Iverson, A. (1989). Experiences of falling in love. *Journal of Social and Personal Relationships, 6,* 243–257.

Aron, A., & Henkemeyer, L. (1995). Marital satisfaction and passionate love. *Journal of Social and Personal Relationships, 12,* 139–146.

Aronoff, J., Woike, B. A., & Hyman, L. M. (1992). Which are the stimuli in facial displays of anger and happiness? Configurational bases of emotion recognition. *Journal of Personality and Social Psychology, 62,* 1050–1066.

Aronson, E., Fried, C., & Stone, J. (1991) Overcoming denial: Increasing the intention to use condoms through the induction of hypocrisy. *American Journal of Public Health, 18,* 1636–1640.

Arrow, H. (1997). Stability, bistability, and instability in small group influence patterns. *Journal of Personality and Social Psychology, 72,* 75–85.

Asch, S. E. (1946). Forming impressions of personality. *Journal of Abnormal Psychology, 41,* 258–290.

Asch, S. E. (1951). Effects of group pressure upon the modification and distortion of judgment. In H. Guetzkow (Ed.), *Groups, leadership, and men.* Pittsburgh: Carnegie.

Asch, S. E. (1956). Studies of independence and conformity: A minority of one against unanimous majority. *Psychological Monographs, 70* (Whole No. 416).

Asendorpf, J. B. (1992). A Brunswickean approach to trait continuity: Application to shyness. *Journal of Personality, 60,* 55–77.

Aube, J., & Koestner, R. (1992). Gender characteristics and adjustment: A longitudinal study. *Journal of Personality and Social Psychology, 63,* 485–493.

Aube, J., Norcliffe, H., & Koestner, R. (1995). Physical characteristics and the multifactorial approach to the study of gender characteristics. *Social Behavior and Personality, 23,* 69–82.

Averill, J. R., & Boothroyd, P. (1977). On falling in love: Conformance with romantic ideal. *Motivation and Emotion, 1,* 235–247.

Bailey, R. C., & Czuchry, M. (1994). Psychological kinship fulfillment and dating attraction. *Social Behavior and Personality, 22,* 157–162.

Bandura, A. (1973). *Aggression: A social learning analysis.* Englewood Cliffs, NJ: Prentice-Hall.

Bandura, A. (1977). Self-efficacy: Toward a unifying theory of behavior change. *Psychological Review, 84,* 191–215.

Bandura, A. (1986). *Social foundations of thought and action: A social cognitive view.* Englewood Cliffs, NJ: Prentice-Hall.

Bandura, A. (1997). *Self-Efficacy: The Exercise of Control.* W. H. Freeman & Co.

Bandura, A., & Adams, N. E. (1977). Analysis of self-efficacy theory of behavioral change. *Cognitive Therapy and Research, 1,* 287–310.

Bandura, A., Cioffi, D., Taylor, C. B., & Brouillard, M. E. (1988). Perceived self-efficacy in coping with cognitive stressors and opioid activation. *Journal of Personality and Social Psychology, 55,* 479–488.

Bargh, J. A. (1997). Automaticity in everyday life. In R. S. Wyer (Ed.), *Advances in social cognition* (Vol. 10). Mahwah, N.J.: Erlbaum.

Bargh, J. A., Chen, M., & Burrows, L. (1996). Automaticity of social behavior: Direct effects of trait constructs and stereotype activation on action. *Journal of Personality and Social Psychology, 71,* 230–244.

Bargh, J. A., & Pietromonaco, P. (1982). Automatic information processing and social perception: The influence of trait information presented outside of conscious awareness on impression formation. *Journal of Personality and Social Psychology, 43,* 437–449.

Barkow, J. H. (1989). *Darwin, sex, and status.* Toronto: University of Toronto Press.

Baron, R. A. (1981). The "costs of deception" revisited: An openly optimistic rejoinder. *IRB: A Review of Human Subjects Research, 3,* 8–10.

Baron, R. A. (1984). Reducing organizational conflict: An incompatible response approach. *Journal of Applied Psychology, 69,* 272–279.

Baron, R. A. (1988). Attributions and organizational conflict: The mediating role of apparent sincerity. *Organizational Behavior and Human Decision Processes, 41,* 111–127.

Baron, R. A. (1989a). Applicant strategies during job interviews. In G. R. Ferris & R. W. Eder (Eds.), *The employment interview: Theory, research, and practice* (pp. 204–216). Newbury Park, CA: Sage.

Baron, R. A. (1989b). Personality and organizational conflict: The Type A behavior pattern and self-monitoring. *Organizational Behavior and Human Decision Processes, 44,* 281–297.

Baron, R. A. (1990). Attributions and organizational conflict. In S. Graha & V. Folkes (Eds.), *Attribution theory: Applications to achievement, mental health, and interpersonal conflict* (pp. 185–204). Hillsdale, NJ: Erlbaum.

Baron, R. A. (1993a). Criticism (informal negative feedback) as a source of perceived unfairness in organizations: Effects, mechanisms, and countermeasures. In R. Cropanzano (Ed.), *Justice in the workplace: Approaching fairness in human resource management* (pp. 155–170). Hillsdale, NJ: Erlbaum.

Baron, R. A. (1993b). Effects of interviewers' moods and applicant qualifications on ratings of job applicants. *Journal of Applied Social Psychology, 23,* 254–271.

Baron, R. A. (1993c). Reducing aggression and conflict: The incompatible response approach, or why people who feel good usually won't be bad. In G. C. Brannigan & M. R. Merrens (Eds.), *The undaunted psychologist* (pp. 203–218). Philadelphia: Temple University Press.

Baron, R. A. (1994). The physical environment of work settings: Effects of task performance, interpersonal relations, and job satisfaction. In M. Staw & L. L. Cummings (Eds.), *Research in organizational behavior* (Vol. 16, pp. 1–46). Greenwich, CT: JAI Press.

Baron, R. A. (1997). The sweet smell of . . . helping: Effects of pleasant ambient fragrance on prosocial behavior in shopping malls. *Personality and Social Psychology Bulletin, 23,* 498–503.

Baron, R. A. (in press). Positive effects of conflict: A cognitive perspective. In C. K. W. deDreu & V. de-Vliert (Eds.), *Conflict escalation and organization performance.* Thousand Oaks, CA: Sage.

Baron, R. A., & Bronfen, M. I. (1994). A whiff of reality: Empirical evidence concerning the effects of pleasant fragrances on work-related behavior. *Journal of Applied Social Psychology, 23,* 1179–1203.

Baron, R. A., & Richardson, D. R. (1994) *Human aggression* (2nd ed.). New York: Plenum.

Baron, R. A., Russell, G. W., & Arms, R. L. (1985). Negative ions and behavior: Impact on mood, memory, and aggression among Type A and Type B persons. *Journal of Personality and Social Psychology, 48,* 746–754.

Baron, R. S. (1986). Distraction–conflict theory: Progress and problems. In L. Berkowitz (Ed.), *Advances in experimental social psychology* (Vol. 20). New York: Academic Press.

Baron, R. S., & Logan, H. (1993). Desired control, felt control, and dental pain: Recent findings and remaining issues. *Motivation and Emotion, 17,* 181–204.

Baron, R. S., Logan, H., Lilly, J., Inman, M., & Brennan, M. (1994). Negative emotion and message processing. *Journal of Experimental Social Psychology, 30,* 181–201.

Baron, R. S., Moore, D., & Sanders, G. S. (1978). Distraction as a source of drive in social facilitation research. *Journal of Personality and Social Psychology, 36,* 816–824.

Baron, R. S., Vandello, J. A., & Brunsman, B. (1996). The forgotten variable in conformity research: Impact of task importance on social influence. *Journal of Personality and Social Psychology, 71,* 915–927.

Barrick, M. R., & Mount, K. (1993). Autonomy as a moderator of the relationships between the Big Five personality dimensions and job performance. *Journal of Applied Psychology, 78,* 111–118.

Bartholomew, K. (1990). Avoidance of intimacy: An attachment perspective. *Journal of Social and Personal Relationships, 7,* 147–178.

Bartholomew, K., & Horowitz, L. M. (1991). Attachment styles among young adults: A test of a four category model. *Journal of Personality and Social Psychology, 61,* 226–244.

Bar-Tal, Y., & Spitzer, A. (1994). Coping use versus effectiveness as moderating the stress-strain relationship. *Journal of Community and Applied Social Psychology, 4,* 91–100.

Bass, B. M. (1990). *Bass and Stogdill's handbook of leadership* (3rd ed.). New York: Free Press.

Batista, S. M., & Berte, R. (1992). Maternal behavior and feminine work: Study with Belgian mothers with infants. *Interamerican Journal of Psychology, 26*, 143–157.

Batson, C. D., Duncan, B. D., Ackerman, P., Buckley, T., & Birch, K. (1981). Is empathic emotion a source of altruistic motivation? *Journal of Personality and Social Psychology, 40*, 290–302.

Batson, C. D., Klein, T. R., Highberger, L., & Shaw, L. L. (1995). Immorality from empathy-induced altruism: When compassion and justice conflict. *Journal of Personality and Social Psychology, 68*, 1042–1054.

Batson, C. D., O'Quin, K., Fultz, J., Vanderplas, M., & Isen, A. M. (1983). Influence of self-reported distress and empathy on egoistic versus altruistic motivation to help. *Journal of Personality and Social Psychology, 45*, 706–718.

Batson, C. D., Polycarpou, M. P., Harmon-Jones, E., Imhoff, H. J., Mitchener, E. C., & Bednar, L. L. (1997). Empathy and attitudes: Can feeling for a member of a stigmatized group improve feelings toward the group? *Journal of Personality and Social Psychology, 72*, 105–118.

Batson, C. D., Sympson, S. C., Hindman, J. L., Decruz, P., Todd, R. M., Weeks, J. L., Jennings, G., & Burris, C. T. (1996). "I've been there, too": Effect on empathy of prior experience with a need. *Personality and Social Psychology Bulletin, 22*, 474–482.

Batson, C. D., & Weeks, J. L. (1996). Mood effects of unsuccessful helping: Another test of the empathy-altruism hypothesis. *Personality and Social Psychology Bulletin, 22*, 148–157.

Baumeister, R. F. (in press). The Self. In G. Lindzey, S. T. Fiske, & D. T. Gilbert (Eds.), *Handbook of social psychology.* New York: Oxford University Press and McGraw-Hill.

Baumeister, R. F. (in press). The self. In D. T. Gilbert, S. T. Fiske, & G. Lindzey (Eds.), *Handbook of social psychology* (4th ed.). New York: McGraw-Hill.

Baumeister, R. F., Chesner, S. P., Sanders, P. S., & Tice, D. M. (1988). Who's in charge here? Group leaders do lend help in emergencies. *Personality and Social Psychology Bulletin, 14*, 17–22.

Baumeister, R. F., Stillwell, A., & Wotman, S. R. (1990). Victim and perpetrator accounts of interpersonal conflict: Autobiographical narratives about anger. *Journal of Personality and Social Psychology, 59*, 994–1003.

Baumeister, R. F., Wotman, S. R., & Stillwell, A. M. (1993). Unrequited love: On heartbreak, anger, guilt, scriptlessness, and humiliation. *Journal of Personality and Social Psychology, 64*, 377–394.

Baumrind, D. (1979). The costs of deception. *IRB: A Review of Human Subjects Research, 6*, 1–4.

Baumrind, D. (1985). Research using intentional deception: Ethical issues revisited. *American Psychologist, 40*, 165–174.

Baxter, L. A. (1990). Dialectical contradictions in relationship development. *Journal of Social and Personal Relationships, 7*, 69–88.

Beall, A. E., & Sternberg, R. J. (1995). The social construction of love. *Journal of Social and Personal Relationships, 12*, 417–438.

Beaman, A. L., Cole, M., Preston, M., Klentz, B., & Steblay, N. M. (1983). Fifteen years of the foot-in-the-door research: A meta-analysis. *Personality and Social Psychology Bulletin, 9*, 181–186.

Beckwith, J. B. (1994). Terminology and social relevance in psychological research on gender. *Social Behavior and Personality, 22*, 329–336.

Bell, B. E., & Loftus, E. F. (1988). Degree of detail of eyewitness testimony and mock juror judgments. *Journal of Applied Social Psychology, 18*, 1171–1192.

Bell, P. A., Baum, A., Green, T. E. F., & Fisher, J. D. (1995). *Environmental psychology* (4th ed.). New York: Holt, Rinehart & Winston.

Bell, S. T., Kuriloff, P. J., & Lottes, I. (1994). Understanding attributions of blame in stranger rape and date rape situations: An examination of gender, race, identification, and students' social perceptions of rape victims. *Journal of Applied Social Psychology, 24*, 1719–1734.

Bem, S. L. (1974). The measurement of psychological androgyny. *Journal of Consulting and Clinical Psychology, 42*, 155–162.

Bem, S. L. (1984). Androgyny and gender-schema theory: A conceptual and empirical integration. *Nebraska Symposium on Motivation: Psychology and Gender, 32*, 179–226.

Benson, P. L., Karabenick, S. A., & Lerner, R. M. (1976). Pretty pleases: The effects of physical attractiveness, race, and sex on receiving help. *Journal of Experimental Social Psychology, 12*, 409–415.

Berkowitz, L. (1989). Frustration-aggression hypothesis: Examination and reformulation. *Psychological Bulletin, 106*, 59–73.

Berkowitz, L. (1994). Is something missing? Some observations prompted by the cognitive-neoassociationist view of anger and emotional aggression. In L. R. Huesmann (Ed.), *Aggressive behavior: Current perspectives* (pp. 35–57). New York: Plenum.

Berkowitz, L., & Devine, P. G. (1995). Has social psychology always been cognitive? What is "cognitive" anyhow? *Personality and Social Psychology Bulletin, 21,* 696–703.

Berman, M., Gladue, B., & Taylor, S. (1993). The effects of hormones, Type A behavior pattern and provocation on aggression in men. *Motivation and Emotion, 17,* 125–138, 182–199.

Bernard, L. C., & Belinsky, D. (1993). Hardiness, stress, and maladjustment: Effects on self-reported retrospective health problems and prospective health center visits. *Journal of Social Behavior and Personality, 8,* 97–110.

Berndt, T. J. (1992). Friendship and friends' influence in adolescence. *Current Directions in Psychological Science, 1,* 156–159.

Berry, D. S., & Brownlow, S. (1989). Were the physiognomists right? Personality correlates of facial babyishness. *Personality and Social Psychology Bulletin, 15,* 266–279.

Berscheid, E., Dion, K. K., Hatfield (Walster), E., & Walster, G. W. (1971). Physical attractiveness and dating choice: A test of the matching hypothesis. *Journal of Experimental Social Psychology, 7,* 173–189.

Bettencourt, B. A., & Miller, N. (1996). Gender differences in aggression as a function of provocation: A meta-analysis. *Psychological Bulletin, 119,* 422–447.

Beyer, S., & Bowden, E. M. (1997). Gender differences in self-perceptions: Convergent evidence from three measures of accuracy and bias. *Personality and Social Psychology Bulletin, 23,* 157–172.

Bienert, H., & Schneider, B. H. (1993). Diagnosis-specific social skills training with peer-nominated aggressive–disruptive and sensitive–isolated preadolescents. *Journal of Applied Developmental Psychology, 26,* 182–199.

Bierhoff, H. W., Klein, R., & Kramp, P. (1991). Evidence for the altruistic personality from data on accident research. *Journal of Personality, 59,* 263–280.

Bies, R. J., Shapiro, D. L., & Cummings, L. L. (1988). Causal accounts and managing organizational conflict: Is it enough to say it's not my fault? *Communication Research, 15,* 381–399.

Birkimer, J. C., Lucas, M., & Birkimer, S. J. (1991). Health locus of control and status of cardiac rehabilitation graduates. *Journal of Social Behavior and Personality, 6,* 629–640.

Björntorp, P. (1991). Adipose tissue distribution and functions. *International Journal of Obesity, 15,* 67–87.

Bjorkqvist, K., Lagerspetz, K. M. J., & Kaukiainen, A. (1992). Do girls manipulate and boys fight? Developmental trends in regard to direct and indirect aggression. *Aggressive Behavior, 18,* 117–127.

Bjorkqvist, K., Osterman, K., & Hjelt-Back, M. (1994). Aggression among university employees. *Aggressive Behavior, 20,* 173–184.

Blake, R. R., & Mouton, J. S. (1984). *Solving costly organizational conflicts.* San Francisco: Jossey-Bass.

Blanck, P. D., Rosenthal, R., Hart, A. J., & Bernieri, F. (1990). The measure of the judge: An empirically-based framework for exploring trial judges' behavior. *Iowa Law Review, 75,* 653–684.

Blonston, G. (1993, October 21). New crime wave? Not necessarily so: Statistics don't match America's fears. *Albany Times Union,* pp. A-1, A-9.

Bobo, L. (1983). Whites' opposition to busing: Symbolic racism or realistic group conflict? *Journal of Personality and Social Psychology, 45,* 1196–1210.

Bobocel, D. R., & Meyer, J. P. (1994). Escalating commitment to a failing course of action: Separating the role of choice and justification. *Journal of Applied Psychology, 79,* 360–363.

Bodenhausen, G. V. (1993). Emotion, arousal, and stereotypic judgment: A heuristic model of affect and stereotyping. In D. Mackie & D. Hamilton (Eds.), *Affect, cognition, and stereotyping: Intergroup processes in intergroup perception* (pp. 13–37). San Diego, CA: Academic Press.

Bodenhausen, G. V., Kramer, G. P., & Susser, K. (1994). Happiness and stereotypic thinking in social judgment. *Journal of Personality and Social Psychology, 66,* 621–632.

Bogard, M. (1990). Why we need gender to understand human violence. *Journal of Interpersonal Violence, 5,* 132–135.

Bond, C. F. (1982). Social facilitation: A self-presentational view. *Journal of Personality and Social Psychology, 42,* 1042–1050.

Bond, R., & Smith, P. B. (1996). Culture and conformity: A meta-analysis of studies using Asch's [1952b, 1956] line judgment task. *Psychological Bulletin, 119,* 111–137.

Boninger, D. S., Krosnick, J. A., & Berent, M. K. (1995). Origins of attitude importance: Self-interest, social identification, and value relevance. *Journal of Personality and Social Psychology, 68,* 61–80.

Booth-Kewley, S., & Vickers, R. R. Jr. (1994). Associations between major domains of personality and health behavior. *Journal of Personality, 62,* 281–298.

Bornstein, R. F. (1994). Dependency as a social cue: A meta-analytic review of research on the dependency–helping relationship. *Journal of Research in Personality, 28,* 182–213.

Borrello, G. M., & Thompson, B. (1990). An hierarchical analysis of the Hendrick–Hendrick measure of Lee's typology of love. *Journal of Social Behavior and Personality, 5,* 327–342.

Bosveld, W., Koomen, W., van der Pligt, J., & Plaisier, J. W. (1995). Differential construal as an explanation for false consensus and false uniqueness effects. *Journal of Experimental Social Psychology, 31,* 518–532

Botha, M. (1990). Television exposure and aggression among adolescents: A follow-up study over 5 years. *Aggressive Behavior, 16,* 361–380.

Bouchard, T. J., Jr., Arvey, R. D., Keller, L. M., & Segal, N. L. (1992). Genetic influences on job satisfaction: A reply to Cropanzano and Hames. *Journal of Applied Psychology, 77,* 89–93.

Bradbury, T. N., Campbell, S. M., & Fincham, F. D. (1995). Longitudinal and behavioral analysis of masculinity and femininity in marriage. *Journal of Personality and Social Psychology, 68,* 328–341.

Brauer, M., Judd, C. M., & Gliner, M. D. (1995). The effects of repeated expressions on attitude polarization during group discussions. *Journal of Personality and Social Psychology, 68,* 1014–1029.

Braza, P., Braza, F., Carreras, M. R., & Munoz, J. M. (1993). Measuring the social ability of preschool children. *Social Behavior and Personality, 21,* 145–158.

Breakwell, G. M., & Fife-Schaw, C. (1992). Sexual activities and preferences in a United Kingdom sample of 16- to 20-year-olds. *Archives of Sexual Behavior, 21,* 271–293.

Brennan, K. A., & Morris, K. A. (1997). Attachment styles, self-esteem, and patterns of seeking feedback from romantic partners. *Personality and Social Psychology Bulletin, 23,* 23–31.

Brennan, K. A., & Shaver, P. R. (1995). Dimensions of adult attachment, affect regulation, and romantic relationship functioning. *Personality and Social Psychology Bulletin, 21,* 267–283.

Brewer, B. W. (1993). Self-identity and specific vulnerability to depressed mood. *Journal of Personality, 61,* 343–364.

Brewer, M. B., & Gardner, W. (1996). Who is this "we"? Levels of collective identity and self representations. *Journal of Personality and Social Psychology, 71,* 83–93.

Brewer, N., Socha, L., & Potter, R. (1996). Gender differences in supervisors' use of performance feedback. *Journal of Applied Social Psychology, 26,* 786–803.

Brickner, M., Harkins, S., & Ostrom, T. (1986). Personal involvement: Thought provoking implications for social loafing. *Journal of Personality and Social Psychology, 51,* 763–769.

Bringle, R. G., & Winnick, T. A. (1992, October). *The nature of unrequited love.* Paper presented at the first Asian Conference in Psychology, Singapore.

Brockner, J. (1992). The escalation of commitment to a failing course of action: Toward theoretical progress. *Academy of Management Review, 17,* 39–61.

Brody, G. H., Neubaum, E., & Forehand, R. (1988). Serial marriage: A heuristic analysis of an emerging family form. *Psychological Bulletin, 103,* 211–222.

Brody, J. E. (1989, August 24). Boning up on possible mental and physical health needs of children who are bound for college. *The New York Times,* p. B12.

Brody, J. E. (1995, May 5). Danish study shows wine aiding longevity. *The New York Times,* p. A18.

Brooks-Gunn, J., & Lewis, M. (1981). Infant social perception: Responses to pictures of parents and strangers. *Developmental Psychology, 17,* 647–649.

Brown, J. D. (1991). Staying fit and staying well: Physical fitness as a moderator of life stress. *Journal of Personality and Social Psychology, 60,* 555–561.

Brown, J. D., & Dutton, K A. (1995). The thrill of victory, the complexity of defeat: Self-esteem and people's emotional reactions to success and failure. *Journal of Personality and Social Psychology, 68,* 712–722.

Brown, J. D., Novick, N. J., Lord, K. A., & Richards, J. M. (1992). When Gulliver travels: Social context, psychological closeness, and self-appraisals. *Journal of Personality and Social Psychology, 62,* 717–727.

Brown, J. D., & Rogers, R. J. (1991). Self-serving attributions: The role of physiological arousal. *Personality and Social Psychology Bulletin, 17,* 501–506.

Browne, M. W. (1992, April 14). Biologists tally generosity's rewards. *The New York Times,* pp. C1, C8.

Bruess, C. J. S., & Pearson, J. C. (1993). "Sweet pea" and "pussy cat": An examination of idiom use and marital satisfaction over the life cycle. *Journal of Social and Personal Relationships, 10,* 609–615.

Brylinsky, J. A., & Moore, J. C. (1994). The identification of body build stereotypes in young children. *Journal of Research in Personality, 28,* 170–181.

Buck, R., & Ginsburg, B. (1991). Spontaneous communication and altruism: The communicative gene hypothesis. In M. S. Clark (Ed.), *Prosocial behavior* (pp. 149–175). Newbury Park, CA: Sage.

Buehler, R., & Griffin, D. (1994). Change-of-meaning effects in conformity and dissent: Observing construal processes over time. *Journal of Personality and Social Psychology, 67,* 984–996.

Bui, K. T., Peplau, L. A., & Hill, C. T. (1996). Testing the Rusbult model of relationship commitment and stability in a 15-year study of heterosexual couples. *Personality and Social Psychology Bulletin, 22,* 1244–1257.

Bumpass, L. (1984). Children and marital disruption: A replication and update. *Demography, 21,* 71–82.

Burger, J. M. (1986). Increasing compliance by improving the deal: The that's-not-all technique. *Journal of Personality and Social Psychology, 51,* 277–283.

Burger, J. M. (1991). Changes in attributions over time: The ephemeral fundamental attribution error. *Social Cognition, 9,* 182–193.

Burger, J. M. (1992). *Desire for control: Personality, social, and clinical perspectives.* New York: Plenum.

Burger, J. M. (1995). Individual differences in preference for solitude. *Journal of Research in Personality, 29,* 85–108.

Burger, J. M., & Palmer, M. L. (1992). Changes in and generalization of unrealistic optimism following experiences with stressful events: Reactions to the 1989 California earthquake. *Personality and Social Psychology Bulletin, 18,* 39–43.

Burger, J. M., & Pavelich, J. L. (1993). Attributions for presidential elections: The situational shift over time. Unpublished manuscript, Santa Clara University.

Burnstein, E. (1983). Persuasion as argument processing. In M. Brandstatter, J. H. Davis, & G. Stocker-Kriechgauer (Eds.), *Group decision processes.* London: Academic Press.

Burnstein, E., Crandall, C., & Kitayama, S. (1994). Some neo-Darwinian rules for altruism: Weighing cues for inclusive fitness as a function of the biological importance of the decision. *Journal of Personality and Social Psychology, 67,* 773–789.

Burrell, C. (1995, April 24). Number of fatherless children in U.S. quadruples in 45 years. *Albany Times Union,* p. A-8.

Bushman, B. J. (1988). The effects of apparel on compliance: A field experiment with a female authority figure. *Personality and Social Psychology Bulletin, 14,* 459–467.

Buss, D. M. (1988). Love acts: The evolutionary biology of love. In R. J. Sternberg & M. L. Barnes (Eds.), *The psychology of love* (pp. 100–118). New Haven, CT: Yale University Press.

Buss, D. M. (1989). Conflict between the sexes: Strategic interference and the evocation of anger and upset. *Journal of Personality and Social Psychology, 56,* 735–747.

Buss, D. M. (1990). Evolutionary social psychology: Prospects and pitfalls. *Motivation and Emotion, 14,* 265–286.

Buss, D. M. (1996). The evolutionary psychology of human social strategies. In E. T. Higgins & A. W. Kruglanski (Eds.), *Social psychology: Handbook of basic principles* (pp. 3–38). New York: Guilford.

Buss, D. M. (in press). Human social motivation in evolutionary perspective: Grounding terror management theory. *Psychological Inquiry.*

Buss, D. M., Larsen, R. J., Westen, D., & Semmelroth, J. (1992). Sex differences in jealousy: Evolution, physiology, and psychology. *Psychological Science, 3,* 251–255.

Buss, D. M., & Schmitt, D. P. (1993). Sexual strategies theory: An evolutionary perspective on human mating. *Psychological Review, 100,* 204–232.

Butler, D., & Geis, F. L. (1990). Nonverbal affect responses to male and female leaders: Implications for leadership evaluations. *Journal of Personality and Social Psychology, 58,* 48–59.

Butterfield, F. (1992, October 23). Dispute threatens U.S. plan on violence. *The New York Times,* p. A8.

Buunk, B. P. (1995). Sex, self-esteem, dependency and extradyadic sexual experience as related to jealousy responses. *Journal of Social and Personal Relationships, 12,* 147–153.

Byrne, D. (1992). The transition from controlled laboratory experimentation to less controlled settings: Surprise! Additional variables are operative. *Communication Monographs, 59,* 190–198.

Byrne, D., & Blaylock, B. (1963). Similarity and assumed similarity of attitudes among husbands and wives. *Journal of Abnormal and Social Psychology, 67,* 636–640.

Cacioppo, J. T., Martzke, J. S., Petty, R. E., & Tassinary, L. G. (1988). Specific forms of facial EMG response index emotions during an interview: From Darwin to the continuous flow hypothesis of affect-laden information processing. *Journal of Personality and Social Psychology, 54*, 592–604.

Cacioppo, J. T., Priester, J. R., & Berntson, G. G. (1993). Rudimentary determinants of attitudes: II. Arm flexion and extension have differential effects on attitudes. *Journal of Personality and Social Psychology, 65*, 5–17.

Cahoon, D. D., & Edmonds, E. M. (1989). Male-female estimates of opposite-sex first impressions concerning females' clothing styles. *Bulletin of the Psychonomic Society, 27*, 280–281.

Callaci, D. (1993, March 3). The glass is half full. *New York Teacher*, 9–11.

Callan, V. J. (1993). Subordinate manager communication in different sex-dyads: Consequences for job satisfaction. *Journal of Occupational and Organizational Psychology, 66*, 13–27.

Calvert, J. D. (1988). Physical attractiveness: A review and reevaluation of its role in social skill research. *Behavioral Assessment, 10*, 29–42.

Campbell, A., Sapochnik, M., & Muncer, S. (1996). Sex differences in aggression: Does social representation mediate form of aggression? *British Journal of Social Psychology*.

Campbell, D. T., & Specht, J. C. (1985). Altruism: Biology, culture, and religion. *Journal of Social and Clinical Psychology, 3*, 33–42.

Campbell, J. D., Chew, B., & Scratchley, L. S. (1991). Cognitive and emotional reactions to daily events: The effects of self-esteem and self-complexity. *Journal of Personality, 59*, 473–505.

Cann, A., Calhoun, L. G., & Banks, J. S. (1995). On the role of humor appreciation in interpersonal attraction: It's no joking matter. *Humor: International Journal of Humor Research, 10*, 77–89.

Caprara, G. V. (1986). Indicators of aggression: The dissipation–rumination scale. *Personality and Individual Differences, 7*, 23–31.

Caprara, G. V. (1987). The disposition–situation debate and research on aggression. *European Journal of Personality, 1*, 1–16.

Caprara, G. V., Barbaranelli, C., Pastorelli, C., & Perugini, M. (1994). Individual differences in the study of human aggression. *Aggressive Behavior, 20*, 291–303.

Carey, M. P., Morrison-Beedy, D., & Johnson, B. T. (1997). The HIV-Knowledge Questionnaire: Development and evaluation of a reliable, valid, and practical self-administered questionnaire. *AIDS and Behavior, 1*, 61–74.

Carnevale, A. P., & Stone, S. C. (1995). *The American mosaic: An in-depth report on the future of diversity at work*. New York: McGraw-Hill.

Carroll, S. J., Perkowitz, W. T., Lurigio, A. J., & Waver, F. M. (1987). Sentencing goals, causal attributions, ideology, and personality. *Journal of Personality and Social Psychology, 36*, 107–118.

Carter, D. B., & McCloskey, L. A. (1984). Peers and the maintenance of sex-typed behavior: The development of children's conceptions of cross-gender behavior in their peers. *Social Cognition, 2*, 294–314.

Carver, C. S., Pozo, C., Harris, S. D., Noriega, V., Scheier, M. F., Robinson, D. S., Ketcham, A. S., Moffat, F. L., Jr., & Clark, K. C. (1993). How coping mediates the effect of optimism on distress: A study of women with early stage breast cancer. *Journal of Personality and Social Psychology, 65*, 375–390.

Cash, T. F. (1995). Developmental teasing about physical appearance: Retrospective descriptions and relationships with body image. *Social Behavior and Personality, 23*, 123–130.

Cash, T. F., & Duncan, N. C. (1984). Physical attractiveness stereotyping among black American college students. *Journal of Social Psychology, 122*, 71–77.

Cash, T. F., & Trimer, C. A. (1984). Sexism and beautyism in women's evaluation of peer performance. *Sex Roles, 10*, 87–98.

Caspi, A., & Herbener, E. S. (1990). Continuity and change: Assortative marriage and the consistency of personality in adulthood. *Journal of Personality and Social Psychology, 58*, 250–258.

Castellow, W. A., Wuensch, K. L., & Moore, C. H. (1990). Effects of physical attractiveness of the plaintiff and defendant in sexual harassment judgments. *Journal of Social Behavior and Personality, 5*, 547–562.

Cavoukian, A., & Doob, A. N. (1980). The effect of a judge's charge and subsequent recharge on judgments of guilt. *Basic and Applied Social Psychology, 1*, 103–114.

Chaiken, S., Giner-Sorolla, R., & Chen, S. (1996). Beyond accuracy: Defense and impression motives in heuristic and systematic information processing. In P. M. Gollwitzer & J. A. Bargh (Eds.), *The psychology of action: Linking motivation and cognition in behavior* (pp. 553–578). New York: Guilford.

Chaiken, S., Liberman, A., & Eagly, A. H. (1989). Heuristic and systematic processing within and beyond the persuasion context. In J. S. Uleman & J. A. Bargh (Eds.), *Unintended thought* (pp. 212–252). New York: Guilford.

Chaiken, S., & Maheswaran, D. (1994). Heuristic processing can bias systematic processing: Effects of source credibility, argument ambiguity, and task importance on attitude judgment. *Journal of Personality and Social Psychology, 66,* 460–473.

Chatterjee, J., & McCarrey, M. (1991). Sex-role attitudes, values, and instrumental-expressive traits of women trainees in traditional vs. non-traditional programmes. *Applied Psychology: An International Review, 40,* 282–297.

Chen, S., Shechter, D., & Chaiken, S. (1996). Getting at the truth or getting along: Accuracy-versus impression-motivated heuristic and systematic processing. *Journal of Personality and Social Psychology, 71,* 262–275.

Cheuk, W. H., & Rosen, S. (1992). Helper reactions: When help is rejected by friends or strangers. *Journal of Social Behavior and Personality, 7,* 445–458.

Christensen, L. (1988). Deception in psychological research: When is its use justified? *Personality and Social Psychology Bulletin, 14,* 664–675.

Christy, P. R., Gelfand, D. M., & Hartmann, D. P. (1971). Effects of competition-induced frustration on two classes of modeled behavior. *Developmental Psychology, 5,* 104–111.

Cialdini, R. B. (1994). Interpersonal influence. In S. Shavitt & T. C. Brock (Eds.), *Persuasion* (pp. 195–218). Boston: Allyn & Bacon.

Cialdini, R. B., Bauman, D. J., & Kenrick, D. T. (1981). Insights from sadness: A three-step model of the development of altruism as hedonism. *Developmental Review, 1,* 207–223.

Cialdini, R. B., Cacioppo, J. T., Bassett, R., & Miller, J. A. (1978). A low-ball procedure for producing compliance: Commitment then cost. *Journal of Personality and Social Psychology, 36,* 463–476.

Cialdini, R. B., Green, B. L., & Rusch, A. J. (1992). When tactical pronouncements of change become real change: The case of reciprocal persuasion. *Journal of Personality and Social Psychology, 63,* 30–40.

Cialdini, R. B., & Petty, R. (1979). Anticipatory opinion effects. In R. E. Petty, T. Ostrom, & T. Brock (Eds.), *Cognitive responses in persuasion.* Hillsdale, NJ: Erlbaum.

Cialdini, R. B., Schaller, M., Houlainhan, D., Arps, K., Fultz, J., & Beaman, A. L. (1987). Empathy-based helping: Is it selflessly or selfishly motivated? *Journal of Personality and Social Psychology, 52,* 749–758.

Cialdini, R. B., Vincent, J. E., Lewis, S. K., Catalan, J., Wheeler, D., & Darby, B. L. (1975). Reciprocal concessions procedure for inducing compliance: The door-in-the-face technique. *Journal of Personality and Social Psychology, 31,* 206–215.

Cioffi, D., & Holloway, J. (1993). Delayed costs of suppressed pain. *Journal of Personality and Social Psychology, 64,* 274–282.

Clark, L. F. (1993). Stress and the cognitive–conversational benefits of social interaction. *Journal of Social and Clinical Psychology, 12,* 25–55.

Clark, L. F., & Collins, J. E. II. (1993). Remembering old flames: How the past affects assessments of the present. *Personality and Social Psychology Bulletin, 19,* 399–408.

Clark, M. S. (1991). *Prosocial behavior.* Newbury Park, CA: Sage.

Clark, M. S., Ouellette, R., Powel, M. C., & Milberg, S. (1987). Recipient's mood, relationship type, and helping. *Journal of Personality and Social Psychology, 53,* 94–103.

Clore, G. L., Schwarz, N., & Conway, M. (1994). Affective causes and consequences of social information processing. In R. S. Wyer, Jr., & T. K. Srull (Eds.), *Handbook of social cognition* (2nd ed., pp. 323–417). Hillsdale, NJ: Erlbaum.

Coats, E. J., & Feldman, R. S. (1996). Gender differences in nonverbal correlates of social status. *Personality and Social Psychology Bulletin, 22,* 1014–1022.

Cohen, D. (1996). Law, social policy, and violence: The impact of regional cultures. *Journal of Personality and Social Psychology, 70,* 961–978.

Cohen, D., & Nisbett, R. E. (1994). Self-protection and the culture of honor: Explaining southern violence. *Personality and Social Psychology Bulletin, 20,* 551–567.

Cohen, D., Nisbett, R. E., Bowdle, B. F., & Schwarz, N. (1996). Insult, aggression, and the southern culture of honor: An "experimental ethnography." *Journal of Personality and Social Psychology, 70,* 945–960.

Cohen, S., Doyle, W. J., Skoner, D. P., Rabin, B. S., Gwaltney, J. M., Jr. (1997). Social ties and susceptibility to the common cold. *Journal of the American Medical Association, 277,* 1940–1944.

Cohen, S., Kaplan, J. R., Cunnick, J. E., Manuck, S. B., & Rabin, B. S. (1992). Chronic social stress, affiliation, and cellular immune response in non-human primates. *Psychological Science, 3,* 301–304.

Cohen, S., Tyrrell, D. A. J., & Smith, A. P. (1993). Negative life events, perceived stress, negative affect, and susceptibility to the common cold. *Journal of Personality and Social Psychology, 64,* 131–140.

Cole, S. W., Kemeny, M. E., & Taylor, S. E. (1997). Social identity and physical health: Accelerated HIV progression in rejection-sensitive gay men. *Journal of Personality and Social Psychology, 72,* 320–335.

Coleman, L. M., Jussim, L., & Abrams, J. (1987). Students' reactions to teachers' evaluations: The unique impact of negative feedback. *Journal of Applied Social Psychology, 17,* 1051–1070.

Collins, M. A., & Zebrowitz, L. A. (1995). The contributions of appearance to occupational outcomes in civilian and military settings. *Journal of Applied Social Psychology, 25,* 129–163.

Collins, N. L., Dunkel-Schetter, C., Lobel, M., & Scrimshaw, S. C. M. (1993). Social support in pregnancy: Psychosocial correlates of birth outcomes and postpartum depression. *Journal of Personality and Social Psychology, 65,* 1243–1258.

Colvin, C. R., Block, J., & Funder, D. C. (1995). Overly positive self-evaluations and personality: Negative implications for mental health. *Journal of Personality and Social Psychology, 68,* 1152–1162.

Comstock, G. A., & Paik, H. (1991). *Television and the American child.* San Diego: Academic Press.

Condon, J. W., & Crano, W. D. (1988). Inferred evaluation and the relation between attitude similarity and interpersonal attraction. *Journal of Personality and Social Psychology, 54,* 789–797.

Conger, J. A. (1991). Inspiring others: The language of leadership. *Academy of Management Executive, 5*(1), 31–45.

Conger, J. A., & Kanungo, R. N. (1994). Charismatic leadership in organizations: Perceived behavioral attributes and their measurement. *Journal of Organizational Behavior, 15,* 439–452.

Conway, M., Giannopoulos, C., Csank, P., & Mendelson, M. (1993). Dysphoria and specificity in self-focused attention. *Personality and Social Psychology Bulletin, 19,* 265–268.

Cook, S. W. (1985). Experimenting on social issues: The case of school desegregation. *American Psychologist, 40,* 452–460.

Cooper, J., Hall, J., & Huff, C. (1990). Situational stress as a consequence of sex-stereotyped software. *Personality and Social Psychology Bulletin, 16,* 419–429.

Cooper, J., & Scher, S. J. (1994). Actions and attitudes: The role of responsibility and aversive consequences in persuasion. In T. Brock & S. Shavitt (Eds.), *Persuasion* (pp. 95–111). San Francisco: Freeman.

Costanza, R. S., Derlega, V. J., & Winstead, B. A. (1988). Positive and negative forms of social support: Effects of conversation topics on coping with stress among same-sex friends. *Journal of Experimental Social Psychology, 24,* 182–193.

Cota, A. A., Evans, C. R., Dion, K. L., Kilik, L., & Longman, R. S. (1995). The structure of group cohesion. *Personality and Social Psychology Bulletin, 21,* 572–580.

Cowan, G., & Curtis, S. R. (1994). Predictors of rape occurrence and victim blame in the William Kennedy Smith case. *Journal of Applied Social Psychology, 24,* 12–20.

Cox, M., & Tanford, S. (1989). Effects of evidence and instructions in civil trials: An experimental investigation of rules of admissibility. *Social Behavior, 4,* 31–55.

Cramer, D. (1995). Life and job satisfaction: A two-wave panel study. *Journal of Psychology, 129,* 261–267.

Cramer, R. E., McMaster, M. R., Bartell, P. A., & Dragna, M. (1988). Subject competence and minimization of the bystander effect. *Journal of Applied Social Psychology, 18,* 1133–1148.

Crandall, C. S. (1988). Social contagion of binge eating. *Journal of Personality and Social Psychology, 55,* 588–598.

Crandall, C. S. (1995). Do parents discriminate against their heavyweight daughters? *Personality and Social Psychology Bulletin, 21,* 724–735.

Crandall, C. S., & Martinez, R. (1996). Culture, ideology, and antifat attitudes. *Personality and Social Psychology Bulletin, 22,* 1165–1176.

Crelia, R., & Tesser, A. (in press). Attitude heritability and attitude reinforcement: A replication. *Personality and Individual Differences.*

Crime rate down; murders by teens soar. (1995, May 22). *Albany Times Union,* A-2.

Crocker, J. (1993). Memory for information about others: Effects of self-esteem and performance feedback. *Journal of Research in Personality, 27,* 35–48.

Crocker, J., Cornwell, B., & Major, B. (1993). The stigma of overweight: Affective consequences of attributional ambiguity. *Journal of Personality and Social Psychology, 64,* 60–70.

Crocker, J., & Major, B. (1989). Social stigma and self-esteem: The self-protective properties of stigma. *Psychological Review, 96,* 608–630.

Crocker, J., & Major, B. (1993). *When bad things happen to bad people: The perceived justifiability of negative outcomes based on stigma.* Manuscript submitted for publication.

Crusco, A. H., & Wetzel, C. G. (1984). The Midas touch: The effects of interpersonal touch on restaurant tipping. *Personality and Social Psychology Bulletin, 10,* 512–517.

Cruse, D., & Leigh, B. C. (1987). "Adam's Rib" revisited: Legal and non-legal influences on the processing of trial testimony. *Social Behaviour, 2,* 221–230.

Crutchfield, R. A. (1955). Conformity and character. *American Psychologist, 10,* 191–198.

Csikszentmihalyi, M. (1993). Relax? Relax and do what? *The New York Times,* p. A25.

Cunningham, M. R. (1986). Measuring the physical in physical attractiveness: Quasi-experiments in the sociobiology of female facial beauty. *Journal of Personality and Social Psychology, 50,* 925–935.

Cunningham, M. R. (1989). Reactions to heterosexual opening gambits: Female selectivity and male responsiveness. *Personality and Social Psychology Bulletin, 15,* 27–41.

Cunningham, M. R., Roberts, A. R., Wu, C.-H., Barbee, A. P., & Druen, P. B. (1995). "Their ideas of beauty are, on the whole, the same as ours": Consistency and variability in the cross-cultural perception of female physical attractiveness. *Journal of Personality and Social Psychology, 68,* 261–279.

Curtis, R. C., & Miller, K. (1986). Believing another likes or dislikes you: Behavior making the beliefs come true. *Journal of Personality and Social Psychology, 51,* 284–290.

Cutler, B. L., Penrod, S. D., & Martens, T. K. (1987). Improving the reliability of eyewitness identification: Putting content into context. *Journal of Applied Psychology, 72,* 629–637.

Cutler, B. L., & Wolfe, R. N. (1989). Self-monitoring and the association between confidence and accuracy. *Journal of Research in Personality, 23,* 410–420.

da Gloria, J., Pahlavan, F., Duda, D., & Bonnet, P. (1994). Evidence for a motor mechanism of pain-induced aggression instigation in humans. *Aggressive Behavior, 20,* 1–7.

Dabbs, J. M., Jr. (1992). Testosterone measurements in social and clinical psychology. *Journal of Social and Clinical Psychology, 11,* 302–321.

Dabbs, J. M., Jr. (1993). Salivary testosterone measurements in behavioral studies. In D. Malamud & L. A. Tabak (Eds.), *Saliva as a diagnostic fluid* (pp. 177–183). New York: New York Academy of Sciences.

Dane, F. C. (1992). Applying social psychology in the courtroom: Understanding stereotypes in jury decision making. *Contemporary Social Psychology, 16,* 33–36.

Darley, J. M. (1995). Constructive and destructive obedience: A taxonomy of principal-agent relationships. *Journal of Social Issues, 51*(3), 125–154.

Darley, J. M., & Batson, C. D. (1973). From Jerusalem to Jericho: A study of situational dispositional variables in helping behavior. *Journal of Personality and Social Psychology, 27,* 100–108.

Darley, J. M., & Latané, B. (1968). Bystander intervention in emergencies: Diffusion of responsibility. *Journal of Personality and Social Psychology, 8,* 377–383.

Daubman, K. A. (1993). *The self-threat of receiving help: A comparison of the threat-to-self-esteem model and the theat-to-interpersonal-power model.* Unpublished manuscript, Gettysburg College, Gettysburg, PA.

Davis, C., Brewer, H., & Weinstein, M. (1993). A study of appearance anxiety in young men. *Social Behavior and Personality, 21,* 63–74.

Davis, J. H., Stasson, M. F., Parks, C. D., & Hulbert, L., Karneda, T., Zimmerman, S. K., & Ono, K. (1993). Quantitative decisions by groups and individuals: Voting procedures and monetary awards by mock civil juries. *Journal of Experimental Social Psychology, 29,* 326–346.

Day, D. V., & Bedian, A. G. (1991). Work climate and Type A status as predictors of job satisfaction: A test of the international perspective. *Journal of Vocational Behavior, 38,* 39–52.

Day J. D., Borkowski, J. G., Punzo, D., & Howsepian, B. (1994). Enhancing possible selves in Mexican American students. *Motivation and Emotion, 18,* 79–103.

DeBono, K. G., & Packer, M. (1991). The effects of advertising appeal on perceptions of product quality. *Personality and Social Psychology Bulletin, 17,* 194–200.

DeBono, K. G., & Snyder, M. (1995). Acting on one's attitudes: The role of a history of choosing situations. *Personality and Social Psychology Bulletin, 21*, 629–636.

DePaulo, B. M. (1992). Nonverbal behavior and self-presentation. *Psychological Bulletin, 111*, 230–243.

DeSteno, D. A., & Salovey, P. (1996). Jealousy and the characteristics of one's rival: A self-evaluation maintenance perspective. *Personality and Social Psychology Bulletin, 22*, 920–932.

de Weerth, C., & Kalma, A. P. (1993). Female aggression as a response to sexual jealousy: A sex role reversal? *Aggressive Behavior, 19*, 265–279.

Dean, K. E., & Malamuth, N. M. (1997). Characteristics of men who aggress sexually and of men who imagine aggressing: Risk and moderating variables. *Journal of Personality and Social Psychology, 72*, 449–455.

Dean-Church, L., & Gilroy, F. D. (1993). Relation of sex-role orientation to life satisfaction in a healthy elderly sample. *Journal of Social Behavior and Personality, 8*, 133–140.

Deaux, K., Reid, A., Mizrahi, K., & Ethier, K. A. (1995). Parameters of social identity. *Journal of Personality and Social Psychology, 68*, 280–291.

Denes-Raj, V., & Epstein, S. (1994). Conflict between intuitive and rational processing: When people behave against their better judgment. *Personality and Social Psychology Bulletin, 66*, 819–829.

Desmaris, S., & Curtis, J. (1997). Gender and perceived pay entitlement: Testing for effects of experience with income. *Journal of Personality and Social Psychology, 72*, 141–150.

Deutsch, F. M., & Lamberti, D. M. (1986). Does social approval increase helping? *Personality and Social Psychology Bulletin, 12*, 149–157.

Deutsch, F. M., Zalenski, C. M., & Clark, M. E. (1986). Is there a double standard of aging? *Journal of Applied Social Psychology, 16*, 771–785.

Deutsch, M., & Gerard, H. B. (1955). A study of normative and informational social influences upon individual judgment. *Journal of Abnormal and Social Psychology, 51*, 629–636.

Devine, P. G. (1989). Stereotypes and prejudice: Their automatic and controlled components. *Journal of Personality and Social Psychology, 56*, 5–18.

Devine, P. G., & Monteith, M. J. (1993). The role of discrepancy-associated affect in prejudice reduction. In D. M. Mackie & D. L. Hamilton (Eds.), *Affect, cognition and stereotyping: Interactive processes in group perception* (pp. 317–344). San Diego: Academic Press.

Devine, P. G., Monteith, M. J., Zuwerink, J. R., Elliot, A. J. (1991). Prejudice with and without compunction. *Journal of Personality and Social Psychology, 60*, 817–830.

Diener, E., & Diener, C. (1996). Most people are happy. *Psychological Science, 7*, 181–185.

Diener, E., Wolsic, B., & Fujita, F. (1995). Physical attractiveness and subjective well-being. *Journal of Personality and Social Psychology, 69*, 120–129.

Dion, K. K., Berscheid, E., & Hatfield (Walster), E. (1972). What is beautiful is good. *Journal of Personality and Social Psychology, 24*, 285–290.

Dion, K. K., & Dion, K. L. (1991). Psychological individualism and romantic love. *Journal of Social Behavior and Personality, 6*, 17–33.

Dion, K. K., & Dion, K. L. (1993). Individualistic and collectivistic perspectives on gender and the cultural context of love and intimacy. *Journal of Social Issues, 49*(3), 53–69.

Dipboye, R. L. (1992). *Selection interviews: Process perspectives.* Cincinnati: South-Western.

Ditto, P. H., & Griffin, J. (1993). The value of uniqueness: Self-evaluation and the perceived prevalence of valenced characteristics. *Journal of Social Behavior and Personality, 8*, 221–240.

Dixon, T. M., & Baumeister, R. F. (1991). Escaping the self: The moderating effect of self-complexity. *Personality and Social Psychology Bulletin, 17*, 363–368.

Doherty, K., Weigold, M. F., & Schlenker, B. R. (1990). Self-serving interpretations of motives. *Personality and Social Psychology Bulletin, 16*, 485–495.

Dollard, J., Doob, L., Miller, N., Mowerer, O. H., & Sears, R. R. (1939). *Frustration and aggression.* New Haven, CT: Yale University Press.

Donovan, S., & Epstein, S. (1997). The difficulty of the Linda conjunction problem can be attributed to its simultaneous concrete and unnatural representation, and not to conversational implicature. *Journal of Experimental Social Psychology, 33*, 1–20.

Dorian, B. J., Keystone, E., Garfinkel, P. E., & Brown, J. M. (1982). Aberrations in lymphocyte subpopulations and function during psychological stress. *Clinical and Experimental Immunology, 50*, 132–138.

Dovidio, J. F., Brigham, J., Johnson, B. T., & Gaertner, S. L. (1996). Stereotyping, prejudice, and discrimination: Another look. In C. N. Macrae , C. Stangor, & M. Hewstone (Eds.), *Stereotypes and stereotyping* (pp. 276–319). New York: Guilford.

Dovidio, J. F., & Gaertner, S. L. (1993). Stereotype and evaluative intergroup bias. In D. M. Mackie & D. L. Hamilton (Eds.), *Affect, cognition, and stereotyping: Interactive processes in group perception* (pp. 167–193). Orlando, FL: Academic Press.

Dovidio, J. F., Gaertner, S. L., Isen, A. M., & Lowrance, R. (1995). Group representations and intergroup bias: Positive affect, similarity, and group size. *Personality and Social Psychology Bulletin, 21,* 856–865.

Dovidio, J. F., Gaertner, S. L., Validzic, A. Matoka, K., Johnson, B., & Taylor, S. (in press-a). Extending the benefits of recategorization: Evaluations, self-disclosure, and helping. *Journal of Experimental Social Psychology.*

Dovidio, J. F., Kawakami, K., Johnson, C., Johnson, B., & Howard, A. (in press-b). On the nature of prejudice: Automatic and controlled processes. *Journal of Experimental Social Psychology.*

Downey, J. L., & Damhave, K. W. (1991). The effects of place, type of comment, and effort expended on the perception of flirtation. *Journal of Social Behavior and Personality, 6,* 35–43.

Downs, A. C., & Lyons, P. M. (1991). Natural observations of the links between attractiveness and initial legal judgments. *Personality and Social Psychology Bulletin, 17,* 541–547.

Drachman, D., DeCarufel, A., & Insko, C. A. (1978). The extra credit effect in interpersonal attraction. *Journal of Experimental Social Psychology, 14,* 458–465.

Drigotas, S. M., & Rusbult, C. E. (1992). Should I stay or should I go? A dependence model of breakups. *Journal of Personality and Social Psychology, 62,* 62–87.

Drigotas, S. M., Whitney, G. A., & Rusbult, C. E. (1995). On the peculiarities of loyalty: A diary study of responses to dissatisfaction in everyday life. *Personality and Social Psychology Bulletin, 21,* 596–609.

Driscoll, R., Davis, K. E., & Lipetz, M. E. (1972). Parental interference and romantic love: The Romeo and Juliet effect. *Journal of Personality and Social Psychology, 24,* 1–10.

Duggan, E. S., & Brennan, K. A. (1994). Social avoidance and its relation to Bartholomew's adult attachment typology. *Journal of Social and Personal Relationships, 11,* 147–153.

Dunham, R. B., Grube, J. A., & Castaneda, M. B. (1994). Organizational commitment: The utility of an integrative definition. *Journal of Applied Psychology, 79,* 370–380.

Dunning, D., & Stern, L. B. (1994). Distinguishing accurate from inaccurate eyewitness identification via inquiries about decision processes. *Journal of Personality and Social Psychology, 67,* 818–835.

Dutton, D. G., & Aron, A. P. (1974). Some evidence for heightened sexual attraction under conditions of high anxiety. *Journal of Personality and Social Psychology, 30,* 510–517.

Dutton, D. G., Saunders, K., Starzomski, A., & Bartholomew, K. (1994). Intimacy-anger and insecure attachment as precursors of abuse in intimate relationships. *Journal of Applied Social Psychology, 24,* 1367–1386.

Eagly, A. H. (1987). *Sex differences in social behavior: A social-role interpretation.* Hillsdale, NJ: Erlbaum.

Eagly, A. H. (1992). Uneven progress: Social psychology and the study of attitudes. *Journal of Personality and Social Psychology, 63,* 693–710.

Eagly, A. H. (1995). The science and politics of comparing women and men. *American Psychologist, 50,* 145–158.

Eagly, A. H., & Carli, L. (1981). Sex of researchers and sex-typed communications as determinants of sex differences in influence-ability: A meta-analysis of social influence studies. *Psychological Bulletin, 90,* 1–20.

Eagly, A. H., & Chaiken, S. (1993). *The psychology of attitudes.* New York: Harcourt, Brace.

Eagly, A. H., & Chaiken, S. (in press). Attitude structure and function. In G. Lindsey, S. T. Fiske, & D. T. Gilbert (Eds.), *Handbook of social psychology* (4th ed.). New York: Oxford University Press and McGraw-Hill.

Eagly, A. H., & Johnson, B. T. (1990). Gender and leadership style: A meta-analysis. *Psychological Bulletin, 108,* 233–256.

Eagly, A. H., Makhijani, M. G., & Klonsky, B. G. (1992). Gender and the evaluation of leaders: A meta-analysis. *Psychological Bulletin, 111,* 3–22.

Eagly, A. H., & Steffen, V. J. (1986). Gender and aggressive behavior: A meta-analytic review of the social psychological literature. *Psychological Bulletin, 100,* 309–330.

Eagly, A. H., & Wood, W. (1991). Explaining sex differences in social behavior: A meta-analytic perspective. *Personality and Social Psychology Bulletin, 17,* 306–315.

Eagly, A. H., Wood, W., & Chaiken, S. (1996). Principles of persuasion. In E. T. Higgins & A. W.

Kruglanski (Eds.), *Social psychology: Handbook of basic principles* (pp. 702–742). New York: Guilford.

Earley, P. C. (1993). East meets West meets Mideast: Further explorations of collectivistic and individualistic work groups. *Academy of Management Journal, 36,* 319–348.

Ebbeson, E. B., Kjos, G. L., & Konecni, V. J. (1976). Spatial ecology: Its effects on the choice of friends and enemies. *Journal of Experimental Social Psychology, 12,* 508–518.

Ehrhardt, A. A., Yingling, S., & Warne, P. A. (1991). Sexual behavior in the era of AIDS: What has changed in the United States? *Annual Review of Sex Research, 2,* 25–47.

Eisenman, R. (1985). Marijuana use and attraction: Support for Byrne's similarity-attraction concept. *Perceptual and Motor Skills, 61,* 582.

Eisenman, R. (1993). Belief that drug usage in the United States is increasing when it is really decreasing: An example of the availability heuristic. *Bulletin of the Psychonomic Society, 31,* 249–252.

Eisenstadt, D., & Leippe, M. R. (1994). The self-comparison process and self-discrepant feedback: Consequences of learning you are what you thought you were not. *Journal of Personality and Social Psychology, 67,* 611–626.

Ekman, P. (1985). *Telling lies.* New York: Norton.

Ekman, P. (1989). The argument and evidence about universals in facial expressions of emotion. In H. Wagner & A. Manstead (Eds.), *Handbook of psychophysiology: Emotion and social behavior* (pp. 143–164). New York: Wiley.

Ekman, P. (1992). Are there basic emotions? *Psychological Review, 99,* 550–553.

Ekman, P., Davidson, R. J., & Friesen, W. V. (1990). The Duchenne smile: Emotional expression and brain physiology II. *Journal of Personality and Psychology, 58,* 342–353.

Ekman, P., & Heider, K. (1988). The universality of a contempt expression: A replication. *Motivation and Emotion, 12,* 303–308.

Elkins, L. E., & Peterson, C. (1993). Gender differences in best friendships. *Sex Roles, 29,* 497–508.

Elliot, A. J., & Devine, P. G. (1994). On the motivational nature of cognitive dissonance: Dissonance as psychological discomfort. *Journal of Personality and Social Psychology, 67,* 382–394.

Ellsworth, P. C., & Carlsmith, J. M. (1973). Eye contact and gaze aversion in aggressive encounter. *Journal of Personality and Social Psychology, 33,* 117–122.

Elms, A. C. (1995). Obedience in retrospect. *Journal of Social Issues, 51* (3), 21–31.

Epstein, S. (1983). The unconscious, the preconscious, and the self-concept. In J. Suls & A. Greenwald (Eds.), *Psychological perspectives on the self* (Vol. 2, pp. 220–247). Hillsdale, NJ: Erlbaum.

Epstein, S., Pacini, R., Denes-Raj, V., & Heier, H. (1996). Individual differences in intuitive-experiential and analytical-rational thinking styles. *Journal of Personality and Social Psychology, 71,* 390–405.

Erber, R. (1991). Affective and semantic priming: Effects of mood on category accessibility and inference. *Journal of Experimental Social Psychology, 27,* 480–498.

Esses, V. M. (1989). Mood as a moderator of acceptance of interpersonal feedback. *Journal of Personality and Social Psychology, 57,* 769–781.

Esses, V. M., & Webster, C. D. (1988). Physical attractiveness, dangerousness, and the Canadian criminal code. *Journal of Applied Social Psychology, 18,* 1017–1031.

Estrada, C. A., Isen, A. M., & Young, M. J. (1995). Positive affect improves creative problem solving and influences reported source of practice satisfaction in physicians. *Motivation and Emotion, 18,* 285–300.

Ethier, K. A., & Deaux, K. (1994). Negotiating social identity when contexts change: Maintaining identification and responding to threat. *Journal of Personality and Social Psychology, 67,* 243–251.

Farnsworth, C. H. (1995, June 4). Canada puts different spin on sensational murder trial. *Albany Times Union,* pp. E-8.

Fazio, R. H. (1989). On the power and functionality of attitudes: The role of attitude accessibility. In A. R. Pratkanis, S. J. Breckler, & A. G. Greenwald (Eds.), *Attitude structure and function* (pp. 153–179). Hillsdale, NJ: Erlbaum.

Fazio, R. H., Jackson, J. R., Dunton, B. C., & Williams, C. J. (1995). Variability in automatic activation as an unobstrusive measure of racial attitudes: A bona fide pipeline? *Journal of Personality and Social Psychology, 69,* 1013–1027.

Fazio, R. H., & Roskos-Ewoldsen, D. R. (1994). Acting as we feel: When and how attitudes guide behavior. In S. Shavitt & T. C. Brock (Eds.), *Persuasion* (pp. 71–93). Boston: Allyn & Bacon.

Feingold, A. (1992). Good-looking people are not what we think. *Psychological Bulletin, 111,* 304–341.

Feingold, A. (1994). Gender differences in personality: A meta-analysis. *Psychological Bulletin, 116,* 412–456.

Feingold, A. J. (1995). *Gender stereotyping for sociability, dominance, character, and mental health: An examination using the bogus stranger paradigm.* Manuscript submitted for publication.

Felmlee, D. H. (1995). Fatal attractions: Affection and disaffection in intimate relationships. *Journal of Social and Personal Relationships, 12,* 295–311.

Fenigstein, A., & Abrams, D. (1993). Self-attention and the egocentric assumption of shared perspectives. *Journal of Experimental Social Psychology, 29,* 287–303.

Festinger, L. (1954). A theory of social comparison processes. *Human Relations, 7,* 117–140.

Festinger, L. (1957). *A theory of cognitive dissonance.* Evanston, IL: Row, Peterson.

Festinger, L., & Carlsmith, J. M. (1959). Cognitive consequences of forced compliance. *Journal of Abnormal and Social Psychology, 58,* 203–210.

Festinger, L., Schachtr, S., & Back, K. W. (1950). *Social pressures in informal groups.* New York: Harper.

Festinger, L., Schachter, S., & Back, K. W. (1950). *Social pressures in informal groups.* New York: Harper.

Fichten, C. S., & Amsel, R. (1986). Trait attributions about college students with a physical disability: Circumplex analyses and methodological issues. *Journal of Applied Social Psychology, 16,* 410–427.

Fiedler, F. E. (1994). *Leadership experience and leadership performance.* United States Army Research Institute for the Behavioral and Social Sciences.

Fiedler, K. (1996). Explaining and simulating judgment biases as an aggregation phenomenon in probabilistic, multiple-cue environments. *Psychological Review, 103,* 193–214.

Finn, J. (1986). The relationship between sex role attitudes and attitudes supporting marital violence. *Sex Roles, 14,* 235–244.

Fischer, G. J. (1986). College student attitudes toward forcible date rape: I. Cognitive predictors. *Archives of Sexual Behavior, 15,* 457–466.

Fischman, J. (1986, January). Women and divorce: Ten years after. *Psychology Today,* 15.

Fisher, A. B. (1992, September 21). When will women get to the top? *Fortune,* pp. 44–56.

Fisher, C. D. (1993). Boredom at work: A neglected concept. *Human Relations, 46,* 395–417.

Fiske, A. P. (1991). The cultural relativity of selfish individualism: Anthropological evidence that humans are inherently sociable. In M. S. Clark (Ed.), *Prosocial behavior* (pp. 176–214). Newbury Park, CA: Sage.

Fiske, S. T. (1993). Social cognition and social perception. In L. W. Porter & M. R. Rosenzweig (Eds.), *Annual Review of Psychology, 44,* 155–194.

Fiske, S. T., & Neuberg, S. L. (1990). A continuum model of impression formation, from category-based to individuating processes: Influence of information and motivation on attention and interpretation. In M. P. Zanna (Ed.), *Advances in experimental social psychology* (Vol. 23). New York: Academic Press.

Fiske, S. T., & Taylor, S. E. (1991). *Social cognition* (2nd ed.). New York: McGraw-Hill.

Forgas, J. P. (1993). On making sense of odd couples: Mood effects on the perception of mismatched relationships. *Personality and Social Psychology Bulletin, 19,* 59–70.

Forgas, J. P. (1994). Sad and guilty? Affective influences on attributions for simple and serious interpersonal conflict. *Journal of Personality and Social Psychology, 66,* 56–68.

Forgas, J. P. (1995). Mood and judgment: the Affect infusion model (AIM). *Psychological Bulletin, 117,* 39–66.

Forgas, J. P., & Fiedler, K. (1996). Us and them: Mood effects on intergroup discrimination. *Journal of Personality and Social Psychology, 70,* 28–40.

Forston, M. T., & Stanton, A. L. (1992). Self-discrepancy theory as a framework for understanding bulimic symptomatology and associated distress. *Journal of Social and Clinical Psychology, 11,* 103–118.

Forsythe, S., Drake, M. F., & Cox, C. E. (1985). Influence of applicant's dress on interviewer's selection decisions. *Journal of Applied Psychology, 70,* 374–378.

Frable, D. E. S. (1993). Dimensions of marginality: Distinctions among those who are different. *Personality and Social Psychology Bulletin, 19,* 370–380.

Frank, M. G., & Gilovich, T. (1989). Effect of memory perspective on retrospective causal attributions. *Journal of Personality and Social Psychology, 57,* 399–403.

Fredrickson, B. L. (1995). Socioemotional behavior at the end of college life. *Journal of Social and Personal Relationships, 12,* 261–276.

Freudenheim, M. (1992, October 14). Software helps patients make crucial choices. *New York Times,* p. D6.

Fricko, M. A. M., & Beehr, T. A. (1992). A longitudinal investigation of interest congruence and gender concentration as predictors of job satisfaction. *Personnel Psychology, 45,* 99–117.

Friedman, H. S., Hawley, P. H., & Tucker, J. S. (1994). Personality, health, and longevity. *Current Directions in Psychological Science, 3,* 37–41.

Friedman, H. S., & Miller-Herringer, T. (1991). Nonverbal display of emotion in public and private: Self-monitoring, personality, and expressive cues. *Journal of Personality and Social Psychology, 61,* 766–775.

Friedman, H. S., Prince L. M., Riggio, R. E., & DeMatteo, M. R. (1980). Understanding and assessing nonverbal expressiveness: The affective communication test. *Journal of Personality and Social Psychology, 39,* 333–351.

Friedman, H. S., Tucker, J. S., Schwartz, J. E., Martin, L. R., Tomlinson-Keasey, C., Wingard, D. L., & Criqui, M. H. (1995). Childhood conscientiousness and longevity: Health behaviors and cause of death. *Journal of Personality and Social Psychology, 68,* 696–703.

Friedman, H. S., Tucker, J. S., Tomlinson-Keasey, C., Schwartz, J. E., Wingard, D. L., & Criqui, M. H. (1993). Does childhood personality predict longevity? *Journal of Personality and Social Psychology, 65,* 176–185.

Fultz, J., Shaller, M., & Cialdini, R. B. (1988). Empathy, sadness, and distress: Three related but distant vicarious affective responses to another's suffering. *Personality and Social Psychology Bulletin, 14,* 312–325.

Funder, D. C., & Colvin, C. R. (1991). Explorations in behavioral consistency: Properties of persons, situations, and behavior. *Journal of Personality and Social Psychology, 59,* 149–158.

Funder, D. C., & Sneed, C. D. (1993). Behavioral manifestations of personality: An ecological approach to judgmental accuracy. *Journal of Personality and Social Psychology, 64,* 479–490.

Furnham, A. (1990). *The Protestant work ethic.* London: Routledge.

Furnham, A., Kirkcaldy, B. D., & Lynn, R. (1994). National attitudes to competitiveness, money, and work among young people: First, second, and third world differences. *Human Relations, 47,* 119–132.

Gaertner, S. L., Mann, J. A., Dovidio, J. F., Murrell, A. J., & Pomare, M. (1990). How does cooperation reduce intergroup bias? *Journal of Personality and Social Psychology, 59,* 692–704.

Gaertner, S. L., Mann, J. A., Murrell, A., & Dovidio, J. F. (1989). Reducing intergroup bias: The benefits of recategorization. *Journal of Personality and Social Psychology, 57,* 239–249.

Gaertner, S. L., Rust, M. C., Dovidio, J. F., Bachman, B. A., & Anastasio, P. A. (1993). The contact hypothesis: The role of a common ingroup identity on reducing intergroup bias. *Small Groups Research, 25*(2), 224–249.

Garcia, L. T. (1982). Sex role orientation and stereotypes about male-female sexuality. *Sex Roles, 8,* 863–876.

Garst, J., & Bodenhausen, G. V. (1996). "Family values" and political persuasion: Impact of kin-related rhetoric on reactions to political campaigns. *Journal of Applied Social Psychology, 26,* 1119–1137.

Geen, R. G. (1989). Alternative conceptions of social facilitation. In P. B. Paulus (Ed)., *Psychology of group influence* (2nd ed., pp. 15–51). New York: Academic Press.

Geen, R. G., & Gange, J. J. (1977). Drive theory of social facilitation: Twelve years of theory and research. *Psychological Bulletin, 84,* 1267–1288.

Geier, J. G. (1969). A trait approach to the study of leadership in small groups. *Journal of Communication, 17,* 316–323.

Geller, P. A., & Hobfoll, S. E. (1994). Gender differences in job stress, tedium and social support in the workplace. *Journal of Social and Personal Relationships, 11,* 555–572.

Gentile, D. A. (1993). Just what are sex and gender, anyway? A call for a new terminological standard. *Psychological Science, 4,* 120–122.

George, J. M. (1990). Personality, affect, and behavior in groups. *Journal of Applied Psychology, 75,* 107–116.

George, J. M. (1995). Leader positive mood and group performance: The case of customer service. *Journal of Applied Social Psychology, 25,* 778–794.

George, J. M., & Brief, A. P. (1992). Feeling good—doing good: A conceptual analysis of the mood at work–organizational spontaneity relationships. *Psychological Bulletin, 112,* 310–319.

Gibbons, F. X., Eggleston, T. J., & Benthin, A. C. (1997). Cognitive reactions to smoking relapse: The reciprocal relation between dissonance and self-esteem. *Journal of Personality and Social Psychology, 72,* 184–195.

Gigone, D., & Hastie, R. (1993). The common knowledge effect: Information sharing and group judgment. *Journal of Personality and Social Psychology, 65*, 959–974.

Gilbert, D. T., & Hixon, J. G. (1991). The trouble of thinking: Activation and application of stereotypic beliefs. *Journal of Personality and Social Psychology, 6*, 509–517.

Gilbert, D. T., & Malone, P. S. (1995). The correspondence bias. *Psychological Bulletin, 117*, 21–38.

Gilbert, D. T., McNulty, S. E., Giuliano, T. A., & Benson, J. E. (1992). Blurry words and fuzzy deeds: The attribution of obscure behavior. *Journal of Personality and Social Psychology, 62*, 18–25.

Gilbert, D. T., & Osborne, R. E. (1989). Thinking backward: Some curable and incurable consequences of cognitive busyness. *Journal of Personality and Social Psychology, 54*, 733–740.

Gilbert, D. T., Pelham, B. W., & Krull, D. S. (1988). On cognitive busyness: When person perceivers meet persons perceived. *Journal of Personality and Social Psychology, 54*, 733–740.

Gilbert, D. T., Tafarodi, R. W., & Malone, P. S. (1993). You can't not believe everything you read. *Journal of Personality and Social Psychology, 65*, 221–233.

Gillen, B. (1981). Physical attractiveness: A determinant of two types of goodness. *Personality and Social Psychology Bulletin, 7*, 277–281.

Gilovich, T., & Medvec, V. H. (1994). The temporal pattern to the experience of regret. *Journal of Personality and Social Psychology, 67*, 357–365.

Giner-Sorolla, R., & Chaiken, S. (1997). Selective use of heuristic and systematic processing under defense motivation. *Personality and Social Psychology Bulletin, 23*, 84–97.

Gladue, B. A. (1991). Aggressive behavioral characteristics, hormones, and sexual orientation in men and women. *Aggressive Behavior, 17*, 313–326.

Glass, D. C. (1977). *Behavior patterns, stress, and coronary disease.* Hillsdale, NJ: Erlbaum.

Glass, D. C. (1989). Psychology and health: Obstacles and opportunities. *Journal of Applied Social Psychology, 19*, 1145–1163.

Glenn, N. D., & Weaver, C. N. (1988). The changing relationship of marital status to reported happiness. *Journal of Marriage and the Family, 50*, 317–324.

Glick, P. C. (1983). Seventh-year itch. *Medical Aspects of Human Sexuality, 17*(5), 103.

Goethals, G. R., Cooper, J., & Naficy, A. (1979). Role of foreseen, foreseeable, and unforeseeable behavioral consequences in the arousal of cognitive dis-

sonance. *Journal of Personality and Social Psychology, 37*, 1179–1185.

Gold, J. A., Ryckman, R. M., & Mosley, N. R. (1984). Romantic mood induction and attraction to a dissimilar other: Is love blind? *Personality and Social Psychology Bulletin, 10*, 358–368.

Goldstein, A. G., Chance, J. E., & Schneller, G. R. (1989). Frequency of eyewitness identification in criminal cases: A survey of prosecutors. *Bulletin of the Psychonomic Society, 27*, 71–74.

Goldstein, M. D., & Strube, M. J. (1994). Independence revisited: The relation between positive and negative affect in a naturalistic setting. *Personality and Social Psychology Bulletin, 20*, 57–64.

Goleman, D. (1995, August 8). Brain may tag all perceptions with a value. *The New York Times*, pp. C1, C10.

Gorassini, D. R., & Olson, J. M. (1995). Does self-perception change explain the foot-in-the-door effect? *Journal of Personality and Social Psychology, 69*, 91–105.

Gordon, R. A. (1996). Impact of ingratiation on judgments and evaluations: A meta-analytic investigation. *Journal of Personality and Social Psychology, 71*, 54–70.

Gould, D., & Weiss, M. (1981). Effect of model similarity and model self-talk on self-efficacy in muscular endurance. *Journal of Sport Psychology, 3*, 17–29

Graham, S., & Folkes, V. (Eds.). (1990). *Attribution theory: Applications to achievement, mental health, and interpersonal conflict.* Hillsdale, NJ: Erlbaum.

Grant, P. R. (1993). Ethnocentrism in response to a threat to social identity. *Journal of Social Behavior and Personality, 8*, 143–154.

Graziano, W. G., Jensen-Campbell, L. A., & Hair, E. C. (1996). Perceiving interpersonal conflict and reacting to it: The case for agreeableness. *Journal of Personality and Social Psychology, 70*, 820–835.

Graziano, W. G., Jensen-Campbell, L. A., Shebilske, L. J., & Lundgren, S. R. (1993). Social influence, sex differences, and judgments of beauty: Putting the interpersonal back in interpersonal attraction. *Journal of Personality and Social Psychology, 65*, 522–531.

Greenberg, J. (1993a). Stealing in the name of justice: Informational and interpersonal moderators of theft reactions to underpayment inequity. *Organizational Behavior and Human Decision Processes, 54*, 81–103.

Greenberg, J. (1993b). The social side of fairness: Interpersonal and informational classes of organizational justice. In R. Cropanzano (Ed.), *Justice in the workplace* (pp. 79–103). Hillsdale, NJ: Erlbaum.

Greenberg, J., Pyszcynski, T., & Solomon, S. (1982). The self-serving attributional bias: Beyond self-presentation. *Journal of Experimental Social Psychology, 18,* 56–67.

Greenberg, J., & Scott, K. S. (1996). Why do workers bite the hands that feed them? Employee theft as a social exchange process. In B. M. Staw & L. L. Cummings (Eds.), *Research in organizational behavior* (Vol. 18, pp. 111–156). Greenwich, CT: JAI Press.

Greenberg, J., Solomon, S., & Pyszczynski, T. (in press). Terror management theory of self-esteem and cultural worldviews: Empirical assessments and conceptual refinements. *Advances in Experimental Social Psychology.*

Greenberg, J., Solomon, S., Pyszczynski, T., Rosenblatt, A., Burling, J., Lyon, D., Simon, L., & Pinel, E. (1992). Why do people need self-esteem? Converging evidence that self-esteem serves an anxiety-buffering function. *Journal of Personality and Social Psychology, 63,* 913–922.

Greenberg, J. A., & Baron, R. (1995). *Behavior in organizations: Understanding and managing the human side of work* (5th ed.). Boston: Allyn & Bacon.

Greenberg, M. A., & Stone, A. A. (1992). Emotional disclosure about traumas and its relation to health: Effects of previous disclosure and trauma severity. *Journal of Personality and Social Psychology, 63,* 75–84.

Greenwald, A. G., Klinger, M. R., & Schuh, E. S. (1995). Activation by marginally perceptible ("Subliminal") stimuli: Dissociation of unconscious from conscious cognition. *Journal of Experimental Psychology: General, 124,* 22–42.

Gregory, S. W., Jr., & Webster, S. (1996). A nonverbal signal in voices of interview partners effectively predicts communication accomodation and social status perceptions. *Journal of Personality and Social Psychology, 70,* 1231–1240.

Greer, A. E., & Buss, D. M. (1994). Tactics for promoting sexual encounters. *Journal of Sex Research, 31,* 185–201.

Griffin, D. W., & Bartholomew, K. (1994a). Models of the self and other: Fundamental dimensions underlying measures of adult attachment. *Journal of Personality and Social Psychology, 67,* 430–445.

Griffin, D. W., & Bartholomew, K. (1994b). The metaphysics of measurement: The case of adult attachment. In K. Bartholomew & D. Perlman (Eds.), *Advances in personal relationships: Vol. 5. Attachment processes in adulthood* (pp. 17–52). London: Jessica Kingsley.

Griffin, D. W., & Buehler, R. (1993). Role of construal process in conformity and dissent. *Journal of Personality and Social Psychology, 65,* 657–669.

Groff, D. B., Baron, R. S., & Moore, D. L. (1983). Distraction, attentional conflict, and drivelike behavior. *Journal of Experimental Social Psychology, 19,* 359–380.

Grossman, M., & Wood, W. (1993). Sex differences in intensity of emotional experience: A social role interpretation. *Journal of Personality and Social Psychology, 65,* 1010–1022.

Guimond, S., & Palmer, D. L. (1990). Type of academic training and causal attributions for social problems. *European Journal of Social Psychology, 20,* 61–75.

Gunter, B. G., & Gunter, N. C. (1991). Inequities in household labor: Sex role orientation and the need for cleanliness and responsibility as predictors. *Journal of Social Behavior and Personality, 6,* 559–572.

Gur, R. C., Mozley, L. H., Mozley, P. D., Resnick, S. M., Karp, J. S., Alavi, A., Arnold, S. E., & Gur, R. E. (1995). Sex differences in regional glucose metabolism during a resting state. *Science, 267,* 528–531.

Hackett, R. D., Bycio, P., & Hausdorf, P. A. (1994). Further assessments of Myer and Allen's (1991) three-component model of organizational commitment. *Journal of Applied Psychology, 79,* 15–23.

Hagborg, W. J. (1993). Gender differences on Harter's Self-Perception Profile for Adolescents. *Journal of Social Behavior and Personality, 8,* 141–148.

Halford, W. K., & Sanders, M. R. (1990). The relationship of cognition and behavior during marital interaction. *Journal of Social and Clinical Psychology, 9,* 489–510.

Hamberger, J., & Hewstone, M. (1997). Inter-ethnic contact as a predictor of blatant and subtle prejudice: Tests of a model in four West European nations. *British Journal of Social Psychology, 36.*

Hamilton, D. L., & Sherman, S. J. (1989). Illusory correlations: Implications for stereotype theory and research. In D. Bar-Tal, C. F. Graumann, A. W. Kruglanski, & W. Stroebe (Eds.), *Stereotyping and prejudice: Changing conceptions* (pp. 59–82). New York: Springer-Verlag.

Hamilton, G. V. (1978). Obedience and responsibility: A jury simulation. *Journal of Personality and Social Psychology, 36,* 126–146.

Hamilton, V. L., & Sanders, J. (1995). Crimes of obedience and conformity in the workplace: Surveys of Americans, Russians, and Japanese. *Journal of Social Issues, 51,* 67–88.

Hammock, D. S., & Richardson, D. B. A. (1992). Aggression as one response to conflict. *Journal of Applied Social Psychology, 22,* 298–311.

Hans, V., & Vidmar, N. (1982). Jury selection. In N. L. Kerr & R. M. Bray (Eds.), *The psychology of the courtroom* (pp. 39–82). New York: Academic Press.

Hansen, C. H., & Hansen, R. D. (1988). Finding the face in the crowd: An anger superiority effect. *Journal of Personality and Social Psychology, 54,* 917–924.

Harkins, S. (1987). Social loafing and social facilitation. *Journal of Experimental Social Psychology, 23,* 1–18.

Harkins, S., & Szymanski, K. (1989). Social loafing and group evaluation. *Journal of Personality and Social Psychology, 56,* 934–941.

Harmon-Jones, E., Simon, L., Greenberg, J., Pyszczynski, T., Solomon, S., & McGregor, H. (1997) Terror management theory and self-esteem: Evidence that increased self-esteem reduces mortality salience effects. *Journal of Personality and Social Psychology, 72,* 24–36.

Harrigan, J. A., Lucic, K. S., Kay, D., McLaney, A., & Rosenthal, R. (1991). Effect of expresser role and type of self-touching on observers' perceptions. *Journal of Applied Social Psychology, 21,* 585–609.

Harris, M. B., (1992). Sex, race, and experiences of aggression. *Aggressive Behavior, 18,* 201–217.

Harris, M. B. (1993). How provoking! What makes men and women angry? *Journal of Applied Social Psychology, 23,* 199–211.

Harris, M. B. (1994). Gender of subject and target as mediators of aggression. *Journal of Applied Social Psychology, 24,* 453–471.

Harris, M. B. (in press). Aggressive experiences and aggressiveness: Relationship to gender, ethnicity, and age. *Journal of Applied Social Psychology.*

Hart, A. J. (1995). Naturally occurring expectation effects. *Journal of Personality and Social Psychology, 68,* 109–115.

Hasart, J. K., & Hutchinson, K. L. (1993). The effects of eyeglasses on perceptions of interpersonal attraction. *Journal of Social Behavior and Personality, 8,* 521–528.

Hastie, R. (Ed.). (1993). *Inside the juror: The psychology of juror decision making.* Cambridge, England: Cambridge University Press.

Hatfield, E. (1988). Passionate and companionate love. In R. J. Sternberg & M. I. Barnes (Eds.), *The psychology of love* (pp. 191–217). New Haven, CT: Yale University Press.

Hatfield, E., & Rapson, R. L. (1992). Similarity and attraction in close relationships. *Communication Monographs, 59,* 209–212.

Hatfield, E., & Rapson, R. L. (1993). Historical and cross-cultural perspectives on passionate love and sexual desire. *Annual Review of Sex Research, 4,* 67–97.

Hatfield, E., & Sprecher, S. (1986). Measuring passionate love in intimate relations. *Journal of Adolescence, 9,* 383–410.

Hatfield, E., Sprecher, S., Pillemer, J. T., Greenberger, D., & Wexler, P. (1989). Gender differences in what is desired in the sexual relationship. *Journal of Psychology and Human Sexuality, 1,* 39–52.

Hatfield, E., & Walster, G. W. (1981). *A new look at love.* Reading, MA: Addison-Wesley.

Hecht, M. L., Marston, P. J., & Larkey, L. K. (1994). Love ways and relationship quality in heterosexual relationships. *Journal of Social and Personal Relationships, 11,* 25–43.

Heider, F. (1958). *The psychology of interpersonal relations.* New York: Wiley.

Heilman, M. E., Block, C. J., & Lucas, J. A. (1992). Presumed incompetent? Stigmatization and affirmative action efforts. *Journal of Applied Psychology, 77,* 536–544.

Heilman, M. E., Martell, R. F., & Simon, M. C. (1988). The vagaries of sex bias: Conditions regulating the undervaluation, equivalation, and overvaluation of female job applicants. *Organizational Behavior and Human Decision Processes, 41,* 98–110.

Heinberg, L. J., & Thompson, J. K. (1992). Social comparison: Gender, target importance ratings, and relation to body image disturbance. *Journal of Social Behavior and Personality, 7,* 335–344.

Helgeson, V. S. (1992). Moderators of the relation between perceived control and adjustment to chronic illness. *Journal of Personality and Social Psychology, 63,* 656–666.

Helson, R., & Roberts, B. (1992). The personality of young adult couples and wives' work patterns. *Journal of Personality, 60,* 575–597.

Henderson, J., & Taylor, J. (1985, November 17). Study finds bias in death sentence: Killers of whites risk execution. *Albany Times Union,* pp. A-19.

Henderson-King, D. H., & Veroff, J. (1994). Sexual satisfaction and marital well-being in the first years of marriage. *Journal of Social and Personal Relationships, 11,* 509–534.

Henderson-King, E. E., & Nisbett, R. E. (1996). Anti-Black prejudice as a function of exposure to the negative behavior of a single Black person. *Journal of Personality and Social Psychology, 71,* 654–664.

Hendrick, C., & Hendrick, S. S. (1986). A theory and method of love. *Journal of Personality and Social Psychology, 50,* 392–402.

Hendrix, W. H., Steel, R. P., & Schultz, S. A. (1987). Job stress and life stress: Their causes and consequences. *Journal of Social Behavior and Personality, 2,* 291–302.

Hepworth, J. T., & West, S. G. (1988). Lynchings and the economy: A time-series reanalysis of Hovland and Sears (1940). *Journal of Personality and Social Psychology, 55,* 239–247.

Hewstone, M., Bond, M. H., & Wan, K. C. (1983). Social factors and social attributions: The explanation of intergroup differences in Hong Kong. *Social Cognition, 2,* 142–157.

Higgins, E. T. (1996). The "self" digest: Self-knowledge serving self-regulatory functions. *Journal of Personality and Social Psychology, 71,* 1062–1083.

Hilton, J. L., Klein, J. G., & von Hippel, W. (1991). Attention allocation and impression formation. *Personality and Social Psychology Bulletin, 17,* 548–559.

Hinsz, V. B. (1995). Goal setting by groups performing an additive task: A comparison with individual goal setting. *Journal of Applied Social Psychology, 25,* 965–990.

Hixon, J. G., & Swan, W. B., Jr. (1993). When does introspection bear fruit? Self-reflection, self-insight, and interpersonal choices. *Journal of Personality and Social Psychology, 64,* 35–43.

Hochschild, A. (1989). *The second shift: Inside the two-job marriage.* New York: Viking.

Hogg, M. A., & Hains, S. C. (1996). Intergroup relations and group solidarity: Effects of group identification and social beliefs on depersonalized attraction. *Journal of Personality and Social Psychology, 70,* 295–309.

Hogg, M. A., Cooper-Shaw, L., & Holzworth, D. W. (1993). Group prototypicality and depersonalized attraction in small interactive groups. *Personality and Social Psychology Bulletin, 19,* 452–465.

Holtgraves, T., & Grayer, A. R. (1994). I am not a crook: Effects of denials on perceptions of a defendant's guilt, personality, and motives. *Journal of Applied Social Psychology, 24,* 2132–2150.

Holtzworth-Munroe, A., & Stuart, G. L. (1994). Typologies of male batterers: Three subtypes and the differences among them. *Psychological Bulletin, 116,* 476–497.

Hopkins, N., Reicher, S. & Levin, M. (in press). On the parallels between social cognition and the "new racism." *British Journal of Social Psychology.*

House R. J. (1977). A theory of charismatic leadership. In J. G. Hunt & L. L. Larson (Eds.), *Leadership: The cutting edge* (pp. 189–207). Carbondale, IL: Southern Illinois University Press.

House, R. J., & Podsakoff, P. M. (1994). Leadership effectiveness: Past perspectives and future directions for research. In J. Greenberg (Ed.), *Organizational behavior: The state of the science* (pp. 45–82). Hillsdale, NJ: Erlbaum.

House, R. J., Spangler, W. D., & Woycke, J. (1991). Personality and charisma in the U.S. presidency: A psychological theory of leader effectiveness. *Administrative Science Quarterly, 36,* 364–396.

Hovland, C. I., Janis, I. L., & Kelley, H. H. (1953). *Communication and persuasion: Psychological studies of opinion change.* New Haven, CT: Yale University Press.

Howell, J. M., & Avolio, B. J. (1992). The ethics of charismatic leadership: Submission or liberation? *Academy of Management Executive, 6,* 43–54.

Howell, J. M., & Frost, P. J. (1989). A laboratory study of charismatic leadership. *Organizational Behavior and Human Decision Processes, 43,* 243–269.

Hoyle, R. H., & Sowards, B. A. (1993). Self-monitoring and the regulation of social experience: A control-process model. *Journal of Social and Clinical Psychology, 12,* 280–306.

Huang, K., & Uba, L. (1992). Premarital sexual behavior among Chinese college students in the United States. *Archives of Sexual Behavior, 21,* 227–240.

Huesmann, L. R. (1988). An information processing model for the development of aggression. *Aggressive Behavior, 14,* 13–24.

Huesmann, L. R. (Ed.). (1994). *Aggressive behavior: Current perspectives.* New York: Plenum.

Huesmann, L. R., & Eron, L. D. (1986). *Television and the aggressive child: A cross-national comparison.* Hillsdale, NJ: Erlbaum.

Huesmann, L. R., & Guerra, N. G. (1997). Children's normative beliefs about aggression and aggressive behavior. *Journal of Personality and Social Psychology, 72,* 408-419.

Huesmann, L. R., & Miller, L. S. (1994). Long-term effects of repeated exposure to media violence in childhood. In L. R. Huesmann (Ed.), *Aggressive behavior* (pp. 153–186). New York: Plenum.

Hughes, C. F., Uhlmann, C., & Pennebaker, J. W. (1994). The body's response to processing emotional trauma: Linking verbal text with autonomic activity. *Journal of Personality, 62,* 565–585.

Hulin, C. L. (1991). Adaptation, persistence, and commitment in organizations. In M. D. Dunnette & I. M. Hough (Eds.), *Handbook of industrial and organizational psychology* (2nd ed. Vol. 2, pp. 445–506). Palo Alto, CA: Consulting Psychologists Press.

Hyde, J. S., & Plant, E. A. (1995). Magnitude of psychological gender differences: Another side to the story. *American Psychologist, 50,* 159–161.

Ickes, W., Reidhead, S., & Patterson, M. (1986). Machiavellianism and self-monitoring : As different as "me" and "you." *Social Cognition, 4,* 58–74.

Imrich, D. J., Mullin, C., & Linz, D. (1995). Measuring the extent of prejudicial pretrial publicity in major American newspapers: A content analysis. *Journal of Communication, 45,* 94–117.

Insko, C. A. (1984). Balance theory, the Jordan paradigm, and the Wiest tetrahedron. In L. Berkowitz (Ed.), *Advances in experimental social psychology* (Vol. 18, pp. d9–140). New York: Academic Press.

Isen, A. M., & Baron, R. A. (1991). Affect and organizational behavior. In B. M. Staw & L. L. Cummings (Eds.), *Research in organizational behavior* (Vol. 15, pp. 1–53). Greenwich, CT: JAI Press.

Istvan, J., Griffitt, W., & Weidner, G. (1983). Sexual arousal and the polarization of perceived sexual attractiveness. *Basic and Applied Social Psychology, 4,* 307–318.

Izard, C. E. (1991). *The psychology of emotions.* New York: Plenum.

Izard, C. E. (1993) Four systems for emotion activation: Cognitive and noncognitive processes. *Psychological Review, 100,* 68–90.

Jackson, L. A., & Grabski, S. V. (1988). Perceptions of fair play and the gender wage gap. *Journal of Applied Social Psychology, 18,* 606–625.

Jackson, L. A., Gardner, P., & Sullivan, L. (1992). Explaining gender differences in self-pay expectations: Social comparison standards and perceptions of fair pay. *Journal of Applied Psychology, 77,* 651–663.

James, W. J. (1890). *Principles of psychology.* New York: Holt.

Jamieson, D. W., & Zanna, M. P. (1989). Need for structure in attitude formation and expression. In A. R. Pratkanis, S. J. Breckler, & A. G. Greenwald (Eds.), *Attitude structure and function* (pp. 383–406). Hillsdale, NJ: Erlbaum.

Janis, I. L. (1982). *Victims of groupthink* (2nd ed.). Boston: Houghton Mifflin.

Jay, S. M., Ozolins, M., Elliott, C. H., & Caldwell, S. (1983). Assessment of children's distress during painful medical procedures. *Health Psychology, 2,* 133–147.

Jemmott, J. B. III, & Magloire, K. (1988). Academic stress, social support, and secretory immunoglobulin. *Journal of Personality and Social Psychology, 55,* 803–810.

Jensen-Campbell, L. A., Graziano, W. G., & West, S. G. (1995). Dominance, prosocial orientation, and female preferences: Do nice guys really finish last? *Journal of Personality and Social-Psychology, 68,* 427–440.

Jetten, J., Spears, R., & Manstead, A. S. R. (1996). Intergroup norms and intergroup discrimination: Distinctive self-categorization and social identity effects. *Journal of Personality and Social Psychology, 71,* 1222–1233.

Jex, S. M., Cvetanovski, J., & Allen, S. J. (1994). Self-esteem as a moderator of the impact of unemployment. *Journal of Social Behavior and Personality, 9,* 69–80.

Jockin, V., McGue, M., & Lykken, D. T. (1996). Personality and divorce: A genetic analysis. *Journal of Personality and Social Psychology, 71,* 288–299.

John, O. P., Cheek, J. M., & Klohnen, E. V. (1996). On the nature of self-monitoring: Construct explication with Q-sort ratings. *Journal of Personality and Social Psychology, 71,* 763–776.

Johnson, A. B., & Byrne, D. (1996, March). *Effects of proximity in familiarity and preferences for places of work.* Paper presented at the meeting of the Eastern Psychological Association, Philadelphia.

Johnson, B. T. (1994). Effects of outcome-relevant involvement and prior information on persuasion. *Journal of Experimental Social Psychology, 30,* 556–579.

Johnson, B. T., & Eagly, A. H. (1989). Effects of involvement on persuasion: A meta-analysis. *Psychological Bulletin, 106,* 290–314.

Johnson, B. T., & Eagly, A. H. (in press). Quantitative synthesis of social psychological research. In H. T.

Reis & C. M. Judd (Eds.), *Handbook of research methods in social psychology*. London: Cambridge University Press.

Johnson, B. T., Lin, H., Symons, C. S., Campbell, L. A., & Ekstein, G. (1995). Initial beliefs and attitudinal latitudes as factors in persuasion. *Personality and Social Psychology Bulletin, 21,* 502–511.

Johnson, J. C., Poteat, G. M., & Ironsmith, M. (1991). Structural vs. marginal effects: A note on the importance of structure in determining sociometric status. *Journal of Social Behavior and Personality, 6,* 489–508.

Johnson, R. A. (1993). *Negotiation basics: Concepts, skills, and exercises.* Thousand Oaks, CA: Sage.

Joiner, T. E., Jr. (1994). The interplay of similarity and self-verification in relationship formation. *Social Behavior and Personality, 22,* 195–200.

Joiner, T. E. Jr., & Schmidt, N. B. (1995). Dimensions of perfectionism, life stress, and depressed and anxious symptoms: Prospective support for diathesis–stress but not specific vulnerability among male undergraduates. *Journal of Social and Clinical Psychology, 14,* 165–183.

Jones, E. E. (1964). *Ingratiation: A social psychology analysis.* New York: Appleton-Century-Crofts.

Jones, E. E. (1979). The rocky road from acts to dispositions. *American Psychologist, 34,* 107–117.

Jones, E. E., & Davis, K. E. (1965). From acts to disposition: The attribution process in person perception. In L. Berkowitz (Ed.), *Advances in experimental social psychology* (Vol. 2, pp. 219–266). New York: Academic Press.

Jones, E. E., & McGillis, D. (1976). Corresponding inferences and attribution cube: A comparative reappraisal. In J. H. Har, W. J. Ickes, & R. F. Kidd (Eds.), *New directions in attribution research* (Vol. 1, pp. 389–420). Morristown, NJ: Erlbaum.

Jones, E. E., & Nisbett, R. E. (1971). The actor and the observer: Divergent perceptions of the causes of behavior. In E. E. Jones, D. Kanouse, H. H. Kelley, R. Nisbett, S. Valins, & D. Weiner (Eds.), *Attribution: Perceiving the causes of behavior* (pp. 79–94). Morristown, NJ: General Learning Press.

Jones, J. M. (1997). *Prejudice and racism.* New York: McGraw-Hill.

Jones, M. (1993). Influence of self-monitoring on dating motivations. *Journal of Research in Personality, 27,* 197–206.

Judd, C. M., Drake, R. A., Downing, J. W., & Krosnick, J. A. (1991). Some dynamic properties of attitude structures: Context-induced response facilitation and polarization. *Journal of Personality and Social Psychology, 60,* 193–202.

Judd, C. M., Ryan, C. S., & Parke, B. (1991). Accuracy in the judgment of in-group and out-group variability. *Journal of Personality and Social Psychology, 61,* 366–379.

Judge, T. A., & Watanabe, S. (1993). Another look at the job–life satisfaction relationships. *Journal of Applied Psychology, 78,* 939–948.

Jussim, L. (1991). Interpersonal expectations and social reality: A reflection–construction model and reinterpretation of evidence. *Psychological Review, 98,* 54–73.

Jussim, L. J., McCauley, C. R., & Lee, Y. (1995). Why study stereotype accuracy and inaccuracy? In Y. Lee, L. J. Jussim, and C. R. McCauley (Eds.), *Stereotype accuracy* (pp. 3–28). Washington, D.C.: American Psychological Association.

Jussim, L., Nelson, T. E., Manis, M., & Soffin, S. (1995). Prejudice, stereotypes, and labeling effects: Sources of bias in person perception. *Journal of Personality and Social Psychology, 68,* 228–246.

Kabanoff, B. (1991). Equity, equality, power, and conflict. *Academy of Management Review, 12,* 9–22.

Kahneman, D., & Miller, D. T. (1986). Norm theory: Comparing reality to its alternatives. *Psychological Review, 93,* 136–153.

Kameda, T., & Sugimori, S. (1993). Psychological entrapment in group decision making: An assigned decision rule and a groupthink phenomenon. *Journal of Personality and Social Psychology, 65,* 282–292.

Kamo, Y. (1993). Determinants of marital satisfaction: A comparison of the United States and Japan. *Journal of Social and Personal Relationships, 10,* 551–568.

Kandel, D. B. (1978). Similarity in real-life adolescent friendship pairs. *Journal of Personality and Social Psychology, 36,* 306–312,

Kanekar, S., Kolsawalla, M. B., & Nazareth, T. (1988). Occupational prestige as a function of occupant's gender. *Journal of Applied Social Psychology, 19,* 681–688.

Karau, S. J., & Williams, K. D. (1993). Social loafing: A meta-analytic review and theoretical integration. *Journal of Personality and Social Psychology, 65,* 681–706.

Karau, S. J., & Williams, K. D.(1995). Social loafing: Research findings, implications, and future directions. *Current Directions in Psychological Science, 4,* 134–140.

Karraker, K. H., & Stern, M. (1990). Infant physical attractiveness and facial expression: Effects on adult perceptions. *Basic and Applied Social Psychology,* 11, 371–385.

Kashy, D. A., & DePaulo, B. M. (1996). Who lies? *Journal of Personality and social Psychology, 70,* 1037–1051.

Katz, D., Johnson, B. T., & Nichols, D. R. (in press). Floyd Henry Allport: A founder of social psychology as a behavioral science. In G. Kimble & M. Wertheimer (Eds.) *Portraits of pioneers in psychology* (Vol. 3). Washington, DC: APA Books.

Katz, I. M., & Campbell, J. D. (1994). Ambivalence over emotional expression and well-being: Nomothetic and idiographic tests of the stress-buffering hypothesis. *Journal of Personality and Social Psychology, 67,* 513–523.

Keelan, J. P. R., Dion, K. L., & Dion, K. K. (1994). Attachment style and heterosexual relationships among young adults: A short-term panel study. *Journal of Social and Personal Relationships, 11,* 201–214.

Keller, L. M., Bouchard, T. J. Jr., Arvey, R. D., Segal, N. L., & Dawis, R. V. (1992). Work values: Genetic and environmental influences. *Journal of Applied Psychology, 77,* 79–88.

Kellerman, J., Lewis, J., & Laird, J. D. (1989). Looking and loving: The effects of mutual gaze on feelings of romantic love. *Journal of Research in Personality, 23,* 145–161.

Kelley, H. H. (1972). Attribution in social interaction. In E. E. Jones et al. (Eds.), *Attribution: Perceiving the causes of behavior* (pp. 1–26). Morristown, NJ: General Learning Press.

Kelley, H. H., & Michela, J. L. (1980). Attribution theory and research. *Annual Review of Psychology, 31,* 457–501.

Kelley, K., & Streeter, D. (1992). The role of gender in organizations. In K. Kelley (Ed.), *Issues, theory, and research in industrial/organizational psychology* (pp. 285–337). Amsterdam: North-Holland.

Kelman, H. C. (1967). Human use of human subjects: The problem of deception in social psychological experiments. *Psychological Bulletin, 67,* 1–11.

Kemeny, M. E., & Dean, L. (1995). Effects of AIDS-related bereavement on HIV progression among gay men in New York City. *AIDS Education and Prevention, 7,* 36–47.

Kenealy, P., Gleeson, K., Frude, N., & Shaw, W. (1991). The importance of the individual in the 'causal' relationship between attractiveness and self-esteem. *Journal of Community and Applied Social Psychology, 1,* 45–56.

Kenny, R. A., Schwartz-Kenney, B. M., & Blascovich, J. (1996). Implicit leadership theories: Defining leaders described as worthy of influence. *Personality and Social Psychology Bulletin, 22,* 1128–1140.

Kenrick, D. T., Groth, G. E., Trost, M. R., & Sadalla, E. K. (1993). Integrating evolutionary and social exchange perspectives on relationships: Effects of gender, self-appraisal, and involvement level on mate selection criteria. *Journal of Personality and Social Psychology, 64,* 951–969.

Kenrick, D. T., Montello, D. R., Gutierres, S. E., & Trost, M. R. (1992). Effects of physical attractiveness on affect and perceptual judgments: When social comparison overrides social reinforcement. *Personality and Social Psychology Bulletin, 19,* 195–199.

Kenrick, D. T., Neuberg, S. L., Zierk, K. L., & Krones, J. M. (1994). Evolution and social cognition: Contrast effects as a function of sex, dominance, and physical attractiveness. *Personality and Social Psychology Bulletin, 20,* 210–217.

Kent, R. L., & Moss, S. E. (1994). Effects of sex and gender role on leader emergence. *Academy of Management Journal, 37,* 1335–1346.

Kernis, M. H., & Waschull, S. B. (1995). The interactive roles of stability and level of self-esteem. *Advances in Experimental Social Psychology, 27,* 93–141.

Kessler, R. C., Kendler, K. S., Heath, A., Neale, M. C., & Eaves, L. J. (1992). Social support, depressed mood, and adjustment to stress: A genetic epidemiologic investigation. *Journal of Personality and Social Psychology, 62,* 257–272.

Kilbourne, J. (1994). Still killing us softly: Advertising and the obsession with thinness. In P. Fallon, M. A. Katzman, & S. C. Wooley (Eds.), *Feminist perspectives on eating disorders* (pp. 395–418). New York: Guilford Press.

Kilham, W., & Mann, L. (1974). Level of destructive obedience as a function of transmitter and executant roles in the Milgram obedience paradigm. *Journal of Personality and Social Psychology, 29,* 696–702.

Killeya, L. A., & Johnson, B. T. (in press). Experimental induction of biased systematic processing:

The directed thought technique. *Personality and Social Psychology Bulletin.*

Kilmann, R. H., & Thomas, R. W. (1977). Developing a forced-choice measure of conflict-handling behavior: The "MODE" instrument. *Educational and Psychological Measurement, 3,* 309–325.

King, L. A. (1993). Emotional expression, ambivalence over expression, and marital satisfaction. *Journal of Social and Personal Relationships, 10,* 601–607.

King, L. A., & Emmons, R. A. (1991). Psychological, physical, and interpersonal correlates of emotional expressiveness, conflict, and control. *European Journal of Social Personality, 5,* 131–150.

Kirchler, E., & Davis, J. H. (1986). The influence of member status differences and task type on group consensus and member position change. *Journal of Personality and Social Psychology, 51,* 83–91.

Kirkpatrick, L. A., & Epstein, S. (1992). Cognitive–experiential self theory and subjective probability: Further evidence for two conceptual systems. *Journal of Personality and Social Psychology, 63,* 534–544.

Kirkpatrick, S. A., & Locke, E. A. (1991). Leadership: Do traits matter? *Academy of Management Executive, 5*(2), 48–60.

Kirkpatrick, S. A., & Locke, E. A. (1996). Direct and indirect effects of three core charismatic leadership components on performance and attitudes. *Journal of Applied Psychology, 81,* 36–51.

Kite, M. E., & Johnson, B. T. (1988). Attitudes toward older and younger adults: A meta-analysis. *Psychology and Aging, 3,* 233–244.

Klein, S. B., Loftus, J., & Burton, H. A. (1989). Two self-reference effects: The importance of distinguishing between self-descriptiveness judgments and autobiographical retrieval in self-referent encoding. *Journal of Personality and Social Psychology, 56,* 853–865.

Klein, S. B., Loftus, J., & Plog, A. E. (1992). Trait judgments about the self: Evidence from the encoding specificity paradigm. *Personality and Social Psychology Bulletin, 18,* 730–735.

Kleinke, C. L. (1986). Gaze and eye contact: A research review. *Psychological Bulletin, 100,* 78–100.

Kleinke, C. L., Meeker, F. B., & Staneski, R. A. (1986). Preference for opening lines: Comparing ratings by men and women. *Sex Roles, 15,* 585–600.

Klesges, R., Klem, M., Hanson, C., Eck, L., Ernst, J., O'Laughlin, D., Garrot, A., & Rife, R. (1990). The effect of applicant's health status and qualifications on simulated hiring decisions. *International Journal of Obesity, 14,* 527–535.

Kolb, D. M., & Bartunek, J. M. (1992). *Hidden conflict in organizations.* Thousand Oaks, CA: Sage.

Kollock, P., Blumstein, P., & Schwartz, P. (1994). The judgment of equity in intimate relationships. *Social Psychology Quarterly, 57,* 340–351.

Kolodziej, M. E., & Johnson, B. T. (1996). Interpersonal contact and acceptance of persons psychiatric disorders: A research synthesis. *Journal of Consulting and Clinical Psychology, 64,* 1387–1396.

Konovsky, M. A, & Organ, D. W. (1996). Dispositional and contextual determinants of organizational citizenship behavior. *Journal of Organizational Behavior, 17,* 253–266.

Konovsky, M. A., & Pugh, S. D. (1994). Citizenship behavior and social exchange. *Academy of Management Journal, 37,* 656–669.

Kosmitzki, C. (1996). The reaffirmation of cultural identity in cross-cultural encounters. *Personality and Social Psychology Bulletin, 22,* 238–248.

Koss, M. P., Dinero, T. E., Seibel, C. A., & Cox, S. L. (1988). Stranger and acquaintance rape: Are there differences in the victim's experience? *Psychology of Women Quarterly, 12,* 1–24.

Koss, M. P., & Harvey, M. R. (1991). *The rape victim: Clinical and community interventions* (2nd ed.). Newbury Park, CA: Sage.

Kraus, S. J. (1995). Attitudes and the prediction of behavior: A meta-analysis of the empirical literature. *Personality and Social Psychology Bulletin, 21,* 58–75.

Kring, A. M., Smith, D. A., & Neale, J. M. (1994). Individual differences in dispositional expressiveness: Development and validation of the emotional expressivity scale. *Journal of Personality and Social Psychology, 66,* 934–949.

Krosnick, J. A. (1988). The role of attitude importance in social evaluation: A study of political preferences, presidential candidate evaluations, and voting behavior. *Journal of Personality and Social Psychology, 55,* 196–210.

Krosnick, J. A. (1989). Attitude importance and attitude accessibility. *Personality and Social Psychology Bulletin, 15,* 297–308.

Krosnick, J. A., Betz, A. L., Jussim, L. J., & Lynn, A. R. (1992). Subliminal conditioning of attitudes. *Personality and Social Psychology Bulletin, 18,* 152–162.

Krosnick, J. A., Boninger, D. S., Chuang, Y. C., Berent, M. K., & Carnot, C. G. (1993). Attitude strength: One construct or many related constructs? *Journal of Personality and Social Psychology, 65,* 1132–1151.

Krueger, J., & Clement, R. W. (1994). The truly false consensus effect: An ineradicable and egocentric bias in social perception. *Journal of Personality and Social Psychology, 67,* 596–610.

Kruglanski, A. W., & Webster, D. M. (1996). Motivated closing of the mind: "Seizing" and "freezing." *Psychological Review, 103,* 263–285.

Kubany, E. S., Bauer, G. B., Muraoka, M. Y., Richard, D. C., & Read, P. (1995). Impact of labeled anger and blame in intimate relationships. *Journal of Social and Clinical Psychology, 14,* 53–60.

Kulik, J. A., & Mahler, H. I. M. (1987). Effects of preoperative roommate assignment on preoperative anxiety and recovery from coronary-bypass surgery. *Health Psychology, 6,* 525–544.

Kunda, Z., Fong, G. T., Sanitioso, R., & Reber, E. (1993). Directional questions direct self-conception. *Journal of Experimental Social Psychology, 29,* 63–86.

Kunda, Z., & Oleson, K. C. (1995). Maintaining stereotypes in the face of disconfirmation: Constructing grounds for subtyping deviants. *Journal of Personality and Social Psychology, 68,* 565–579.

Kupersmidt, J. B., DeRosier, M. E., & Patterson, C. P. (1995). Similarity as the basis for children's friendships. *Journal of Social and Personal Relationships, 9,* 125–142.

Kurdek, L. A. (1993). The allocation of household labor in gay, lesbian, and heterosexual married couples. *Journal of Social Issues, 49(3),* 127–139.

Kutchinsky, B. (1991). Pornography and rape: Theory and practice? *International Journal of Law and Psychiatry, 14,* 47–64.

Kwon, Y.-H. (1994). Feeling toward one's clothing and self-perception of emotion, sociability, and work competency. *Journal of Social Behavior and Personality, 9,* 129–139.

LaPiere, R. T. (1934). Attitude and actions. *Social Forces, 13,* 230–237.

LaPrelle, J., Hoyle, R. H., Insko, C. A., & Bernthal, P. (1990). Interpersonal attraction and descriptions of the traits of others: Ideal similarity, self similarity, and liking. *Journal of Research in Personality, 24,* 216–240.

Lamm, H. & Myers, D. G. (1978). Group-induced polarization of attitudes and behavior. In L. Berkowitz (Ed.), *Advances in experimental social psychology* (Vol. 11, pp. 145–195). New York: Academic Press.

Lander, M. (1992, June 8). Corporate women. *Business Week, 74,* 76–78.

Langer, E., Blank, A., & Chanowitz, B. (1978). The mindlessness of ostensibly thoughtful actions: The role of "placebic" information in interpersonal interaction. *Journal of Personality and Social Psychology, 36,* 635–642.

Langis, J., Sabourin, S., Lussier, Y., & Mathieu, M. (1994). Masculinity, femininity, and marital satisfaction: An examination of theoretical models. *Journal of Personality, 62,* 393–414.

Langlois, J. H., Ritter, J. M., Roggman, L. A., & Vaughn, L. S. (1991). Facial diversity and infant preferences for attractive faces. *Developmental Psychology, 27,* 79–84.

Langlois, J. H., & Roggman, L. A. (1990). Attractive faces are only average. *Psychological Science, 1,* 115–121.

Langlois, J. H., Roggman, L. A., & Musselman, L. (1994). What is average and what is not average about attractive faces? *Psychological Science, 5,* 214–220.

Langston, C. A., & Cantor, N. (1989). Social anxiety and social constraint: When making friends is hard. *Journal of Personality and Social Psychology, 56,* 649–661.

Larson, D. G., & Chastain, R. L. (1990). Self-concealment: Conceptualization, measurement, and health implications. *Journal of Social and Clinical Psychology, 9,* 439–455.

Larson, R. W., Richards, M. H., & Perry-Jenkins, M. (1994). Divergent worlds: The daily emotional experience of mothers and fathers in the domestic and public spheres. *Journal of Personality and Social Psychology, 67,* 1034–1046.

Larwood, L. (1995). Attributional effects of equal employment opportunity: Theory development at the intersection of EEO policy and management practice. *Group and Organization Management, 20,* 391–408.

Lasswell, M. E., & Lobsenz, N. M. (1980). *Styles of loving.* New York: Ballantine.

Latané, B. (1981). The psychology of social impacts. *American Psychologist, 36,* 343–356.

Latané, B., & Darley, J. M. (1968). Group inhibition of bystander intervention in emergencies. *Journal of Personality and Social Psychology, 10,* 215–221.

Latané, B., & Darley, J. M. (1970). *The unresponsive by-stander: Why doesn't he help?* New York: Appleton-Century-Crofts.

Latané, B., & L'Herrou, T. (1996). Spatial clustering in the conformity game: Dynamic social impact in electronic groups. *Journal of Personality and Social Psychology, 70,* 1218–1230.

Latané, B., Williams, K., & Harkins, S. (1979). Many hands make light the work: The causes and consequences of social loafing. *Journal of Personality and Social Psychology, 37,* 822–832.

Lau, S. (1989). Sex role orientation and domains of self esteem. *Sex Roles, 21,* 415–422.

Lau, S., & Gruen, G. E. (1992). The social stigma of loneliness: Effect of target person's and perceiver's sex. *Personality and Social Psychology Bulletin, 18,* 182–189.

Laumann, E. O., Gagnon, J. H., Michael, R. T., & Michaels, S. (1994). *The social organization of sexuality: Sexual practices in the United States.* Chicago: University of Chicago Press.

Law, A., Logan, H., & Baron, R. S. (1994). Desire for control, felt control, and stress inoculation training during dental treatment. *Journal of Personality and Social Psychology, 67,* 926–936.

Lazarus, R. S. (1966). Psychological stress and the coping process. New York: McGraw-Hill.

Lazarus, R. S. (1993). From psychological stress to the emotions: A history of changing outlooks. *Annual Review of Psychology, 44,* 1–21.

LeDoux, J. E. (1995). Emotion: Clues from the brain. *Annual Review of Psychology, 46,* 209–235.

Leary, W. E. (1988, November 19). Novel methods unlock witnesses' memories. *The New York Times,* pp. C1, C15.

Lee, T. W., Ashford, S. J., Walsh, J. P., & Mowday, R. T. (1992). Commitment propensity, organizational commitment, and voluntary turnover: A longitudinal study of organizational entry processes. *Journal of Management, 18,* 15–32.

Lee, Y. T., & Ottati, V. (1993). Determinants of in-group and out-group perceptions of heterogeneity: An investigation of Sino-American differences. *Journal of Cross-Cultural Psychology, 25,* 146–158.

Lee, Y. T., & Ottati, V. (1995). Perceived in-group homogeneity as a function of group membership salience and stereotype threat. *Personality and Social Psychology Bulletin, 21,* 610–619.

Leippe, M. R., & Romanczyk, A. (1987). Children on the witness stand: A communication/persuasion analysis of jurors' reactions to child witnesses. In S. J. Ceci, M. P. Toglia, & D. F. Ross (Eds.), *Children's eyewitness memory* (pp. 155–177). New York: Springer-Verlag.

Leith, K. P., & Baumeister, R. F. (1996). Why do bad moods increase self-defeating behavior? Emotion, risk taking, and self-regulation. *Journal of Personality and Social Psychology, 71,* 1250–1267.

Lerner, Ma. J. (1980). *The belief in a just world: A fundamental delusion.* New York: Plenum Press.

Levenson, R. W. (1992). Autonomic nervous system differences among emotions. *Psychological Science, 3,* 23–27.

Levenson, R. W., Carstensen, L. L., & Gottman, J. M. (1994). The influence of age and gender on affect, physiology, and their interrelations: A study of long-term marriages. *Journal of Personality and Social Psychology, 67,* 56–68.

Levenson, R. W., Ekman, P., & Friesen, W. V. (1990). Voluntary facial action generates emotion-specific autonomic nervous system activity. *Psychophysiology, 27,* 363–384.

Levenson, R. W., Ekman, P., Heider, K., & Friesen, W. V. (1992). Emotion and autonomic nervous system activity in the Minangkabau of West Sumatra. *Journal of Personality and Social Psychology, 62,* 972–988.

Leventhal, G. S., & Anderson, D. (1970). Self-interest and the maintenance of equity. *Journal of Personality and Social Psychology, 15,* 57–62.

Levy, B., & Langer, E. (1994). Aging free from negative stereotypes: Successful memory in China and among the American deaf. *Journal of Personality and Social Psychology, 66,* 989–997.

Lewin, K., Lippitt, R., & White, R. K. (1939). Patterns of aggressive behavior in experimentally created "social climates." *Journal of Social Psychology, 10,* 271–299.

Liberman, A., & Chaiken, S. (1992). Defensive processing of personally relevant health messages. *Personality and Social Psychology Bulletin, 18,* 669–679.

Linville, P. W. (1987). Self-complexity as a cognitive buffer against stress-related illness and depression. *Journal of Personality and Social Psychology, 52,* 663–676.

Linville, P. W., & Fischer, G. W. (1993). Exemplar and abstraction models of perceived group variability and stereotypicality. *Social Cognition, 11,* 92–125.

Linville, P. W., Fischer, G. W., & Salovey, P. (1989). Perceived distributions of the characteristics of in-group and out-group members: Empirical evidence and a computer simulation. *Journal of Personality and Social Psychology, 57,* 165–188.

Linz, D., Donnerstein, E., & Penrod, S. (1988). Effects of long-term exposure to violent and sexually degrading depictions of women. *Journal of Personality and Social Psychology, 55,* 758–768.

Linz, D., & Penrod, S. (1992). Exploring the first and sixth amendments: Pretrial publicity and jury decision making. In D. K. Kagehiro & W. S. Laufer (Eds.), *Handbook of psychology and law* (pp. 3–20). New York: Springer-Verlag.

Locke, E. A. (1991). *The essence of leadership.* New York: Lexington Books.

Locke, M. (1995, May 25). Love better with age, study says. *Albany Times Union,* p. C-5.

Loftus, E. F. (1992). *Witness for the defense.* New York: St. Martin's Press.

Lorenz, K. (1966). *On aggression.* New York: Harcourt, Brace, & World.

Lox, C. L., & Rudolph, D. L. (1994). The Subjective Exercise Experiences Scale (SEES): Factorial validity and effects of acute exercise. *Journal of Social Behavior and Personality, 9,* 837–844.

Luks, A. (1988, October). Helper's high. *Psychology Today* pp. 39–40.

Lupfer, M. B., Clark, L. F., & Hutcherson, H. W. (1990). Impact of context on spontaneous trait and situational attributions. *Journal of Personality and Social Psychology, 58,* 239–249.

Lurie, A. (Ed.) (1993). *The Oxford book of modern fairy tales.* Oxford, England: Oxford University Press.

Luus, C. A. E., Wells, G. L., & Turtle, J. W. (1995). Child eyewitnesses: Seeing is believing. *Journal of Applied Psychology, 80,* 317–326.

Lyall, S. (1995, April 30). British watch trial of Simpson. *The New York Times,* p. 9.

Lynn, M., & Mynier, K. (1993). Effects of server posture on restaurant tipping. *Journal of Applied Social Psychology, 23,* 678–685.

Maas, A., & Clark, R. D. III (1984). Hidden impact of minorities: Fifteen years of minority influence research. *Psychological Bulletin, 95,* 233–243.

MacCoun, R. J., & Kerr, N. L. (1988). Asymmetric influence in mock jury deliberation: Jurors' bias for leniency. *Journal of Personality and Social Psychology, 54,* 21–33.

MacDonald, T. K., Zanna, M. P., & Fong, G. T. (1996). Why common sense goes out the window: Effects of alcohol on intentions to use condoms. *Personality and Social Psychology Bulletin, 22,* 763–775.

Mack, D., & Rainey, D. (1990). Female applicants' grooming and personnel selection. *Journal of Social Behavior and Personality, 5,* 399–407.

Macrae, C. N., Hewstone, M., & Griffiths, R. J. (1993). Processing load and memory for stereotype-based information. *European Journal of Social Psychology, 23,* 77–87.

Macrae, C. N., & Milne, A. B. (1992). A curry for your thoughts: Empathic effects on counterfactual thinking. *Personality and Social Psychology Bulletin, 18,* 625–630.

Macrae, C. N., Milne, A. B., & Bodenhausen, G. V. (1994). Stereotypes as energy-saving devices: A peek inside the cognitive toolbox. *Journal of Personality and Social Psychology, 66,* 37–47.

Maio, G. R., Esses, V. M., & Bell, D. W. (1994). The formation of attitudes toward new immigrant groups. *Journal of Applied Social Psychology, 24,* 1762–1776.

Major, B. (1989). Gender differences in comparisons and entitlement: Implications for comparable worth. *Journal of Social Issues, 45,* 99–115.

Major, B. (1993). Gender, entitlement, and the distribution of family labor. *Journal of Social Issues, 42(3),* 141–159.

Major, B., & Adams, J. B. (1983). Roles of gender, interpersonal orientation, and self-presentation in distributive justice behavior. *Journal of Personality and Social Psychology, 45,* 598–608.

Major, B., Carnevale, P. J. D., & Deaux, K. (1981). A different perspective on androgyny: Evaluations of masculine and feminine personality characteristics. *Journal of Personality and Social Psychology, 41,* 988–1001.

Major, B., & Deaux, K. (1982). Individual differences in justice behavior. In J. Greenberg & R. L. Cohen (Eds.), *Equity and justice in social behavior* (pp. 43–76). New York: Academic Press.

Major, B., Sciacchitano, A. M., & Crocker, J. (1993). In-group versus out-group comparisons and self-esteem. *Personality and Social Psychology Bulletin, 19,* 711–721.

Malamuth, N. M., & Brown, L. M. (1994). Sexually aggressive men's perceptions of women's communications: Testing three explanations. *Journal of Personality and Social Psychology, 67,* 699–712.

Malamuth, N. M., Linz, D., Heavey, C. L., Barnes, G., & Acker, M. (1995). Using the confluence model of sexual aggression to predict men's conflict with women: A 10-year follow-up study. *Journal of Personality and Social Psychology, 69,* 353–369.

Malle, B. F., & Horowitz, L. M. (1995). The puzzle of negative self-views: An exploration using the schema concept. *Journal of Personality and Social Psychology, 68,* 470–484.

Malle, B. F., & Knobe, J. (1997a). The folk concept of intentionality. *Journal of Experimental Social Psychology, 33,* 101–121.

Malle, B. F., & Knobe, J. (1997b). Which behaviors do people explain? A basic actor-observer asymmetry. *Journal of Personality and Social Psychology, 72,* 288–304.

Mansfield, E. D., & McAdams, D. P. (1996). Generativity and themes of agency and communion in adult autobiography. *Personality and Social Psychology Bulletin, 22,* 721–731.

Marazziti, D., Rotondo, A., Presta, S., Pancioloi-Guadagnucci, M. L., Palego, L., & Conti, L. (1993). Role of serotonin in human aggressive behavior. *Aggressive Behavior, 19,* 347–353.

Margolick, D. (1994, October 3). Remaking of the Simpson prosecutor. *The New York Times,* p. A10.

Margolin, G., John, R. S., & O'Brien, M. (1989). Sequential affective patterns as a function of marital conflict style. *Journal of Social and Clinical Psychology, 8,* 45–61.

Marks, N. L., & Miller, H. (1987). Ten years of research on the false-consensus effect: An empirical and theoretical review. *Psychological Bulletin, 8,* 728–735.

Markus, H., & Nurius, P. (1986). Possible selves. *American Psychologist, 41,* 954–969.

Maroney, D., & Golub, S. (1992). Nurses' attitudes toward obese persons and certain ethnic groups. *Perceptual and Motor Skills, 75,* 387–391.

Marsh, H. W. (1993). Relations between global and specific domains of self: The importance of individual importance, certainty, and ideal. *Journal of Personality and Social Psychology, 65,* 975–992.

Martin, C. L., & Parker, S. (1995). Folk theories about sex and race differences. *Personality and Social Psychology Bulletin, 21,* 45–57.

Maslach, C., Santee, R. T., & Wade, C. (1987). Individuation, gender role, and dissent: Personality mediators of situational forces. *Journal of Personality and Social Psychology, 53,* 1088–1094.

Masters, R. D., & Sullivan, D. G. (1989). Facial displays and political leadership in France. *Behavioural Processes, 19,* 1–30.

Mastekaasa, A. (1995). Age variation in the suicide rates and self-reported subjective well-being of married and never married persons. *Journal of Community and Applied Social Psychology, 5,* 21–39.

Matlin, M. W., & Zajonc, R. B. (1968). Social facilitation of word associations. *Journal of Personality and Social Psychology, 10,* 455–460.

Maupin, H. E., & Fisher, R. J. (1989). The effects of superior female performance and sex-role orientation on gender conformity. *Canadian Journal of Behavioral Science, 21,* 55–69.

Mayer, J. D., & Hanson, E. (1995). Mood-congruent judgment over time. *Personality and Social Psychology Bulletin, 21,* 237–244.

Mazzella, R., & Feingold, A. (1994). The effects of physical attractiveness, race, socioeconomic status, and gender of defendants and victims on judgments of mock jurors: A meta-analysis. *Journal of Applied Social Psychology, 24,* 1315–1344.

McArthur, L. Z., & Eisen, S. V. (1976). Achievements of male and female storybook characters as determinants of achievement behavior by boys and girls. *Journal of Personality and Social Psychology, 33,* 467–473.

McAdams, D., Hoffman, B., Mansfield, E., & Day, R. (in press). Themes of agency and communion in significant autobiographical scenes. *Journal of Personality.*

McCall, M. E., & Struthers, N. J. (1994). Sex, sex-role orientation and self-esteem as predictors of coping style. *Journal of Social Behavior and Personality, 9,* 801–810.

McClelland, D. C. (1986). Some reflections on the two psychologies of love. *Journal of Personality, 54,* 334–352.

McConnell, A. R., Sherman, S. J., & Hamilton, D. L. (1994). Illusory correlation in the perception of groups: An extension of the distinctiveness-based account. *Journal of Personality and Social Psychology, 67,* 414–429.

McCrae, R. R. (1996). Social consequences of experiential openness. *Psychological Bulletin, 120,* 323–337.

McCrae, R. R., & Costa, P. T., Jr. (1997). Personality trait structure as a human universal. *American Psychologist, 52,* 509–516.

McDaniel, M. A., Whetzel, D. L., Schmidt, F. L., & Maurer, S. D. (1994). The validity of employment interviews: A comprehensive review and meta-analysis. *Journal of Applied Psychology, 79,* 599–616.

McFarland, C., & Buehler, R. (1995). Collective self-esteem as a moderator of the frog-pond effect in reactions to performance feedback. *Journal of Personality and Social Psychology, 68,* 1055–1070.

McGonagle, K. A., Kessler, R. C., & Schilling, E. A. (1992). The frequency and determinants of marital disagreements in a community sample. *Journal of Social and Personal Relationships, 9,* 507–524.

McGuire, A. M. (1994). Helping behaviors in the natural environment: Dimensions and correlates of helping. *Personality and Social Psychology Bulletin, 20,* 45–56.

McGuire, W. J. (1990). Dynamic operations of thought systems. *American Psychologist, 45,* 504–512.

McKelvie, S. J. (1993). Perceived cuteness, activity level, and gender in schematic babyfaces. *Journal of Social Behavior and Personality, 8,* 297–310.

McKelvie, S. J., & Coley, J. (1993). Effects of crime seriousness and offender facial attractiveness on recommended treatment. *Social Behavior and Personality, 21,* 265–277.

McMullen, M. N. (1997). Affective contrast and assimilation in counterfactual thinking. *Journal of Experimental Social Psychology, 33,* 77–100.

Meeus, W. H. J., & Raaijmakers, Q. A. W. (1995). Obedience in modern society: The Utrecht Studies. *Journal of Social Issues, 51*(3), 155–175.

Mehrabian, A., & Piercy, M. (1993). Positive or negative connotations of unconventionally or conventionally spelled names. *Journal of Social Psychology, 133,* 445–451.

Meindl, J. R., & Lerner, M. J. (1984). Exacerbation of extreme responses to an outgroup. *Journal of Personality and Social Psychology, 47,* 71–84.

Melamed, S., Ben-Avi, I., Luz, J., & Green, M. S. (1995). Objective and subjective work monotony: Effects on job satisfaction, psychological distress, and absenteeism in blue-collar workers. *Journal of Applied Psychology, 80,* 29–42.

Mellers, B. A., Richards, V., & Birnbaum, M. H. (1992). Distributional theories of impression formation. *Organizational Behavior and Human Decision Processes, 51,* 313–343.

Mendolin, M., & Kleck, R. E. (1993). Effects of talking about a stressful event on arousal: Does what we talk about make a difference? *Journal of Personality and Social Psychology, 64,* 283–292.

Metz, M. E., Rosser, B. R. S., & Strapko, N. (1994). Differences in conflict-resolution styles among heterosexual, gay, and lesbian couples. *Journal of Sex Research, 31,* 293–308.

Meyer, J. P., & Allen, N. J. (1991). A three-component conceptualization of organization commitment. *Human Resource Management Review, 1,* 61–89.

Miceli, M. P., & Lane, M. C. (1991). Antecedents of pay satisfaction: A review and extension. In K. Rowland & O. R. Ferris (Eds.), *Research in personnel and human resources management* (Vol. 9, pp. 235–309). Greenwich, CT: JAI Press.

Michael, R. T., Gagnon, J. H., Laumann, E. O., & Kolata, G. (1994). *Sex in America: A definitive survey.* Boston: Little, Brown.

Mikolic, J. M., Parker, J. C., & Pruitt, D. G. (1997). Escalation in response to persistent annoyance: Groups versus individuals and gender effects. *Journal of Personality and Social Psychology, 72,* 151–163.

Mikulincer, M., & Florian, V. (1995). Appraisal of and coping with a real-life stressful situation: The contribution of attachment styles. *Personality and Social Psychology Bulletin, 21,* 406–414.

Mikulincer, M., Florian, V., & Weller, A. (1993). Attachment styles, coping strategies, and posttraumatic psychological distress: The impact of the Gulf War in Israel. *Journal of Personality and Social Psychology, 64,* 817–826.

Milgram, S. (1974). *Obedience to authority.* New York: Harper.

Miller, C. T., Rothblum, E. D., Barbour, L., Brand, P. A., & Felicio, D. (1990). Social interactions of obese and nonobese women. *Journal of Personality, 58,* 365–380.

Miller, C. T., Rothblum, E. D., Brand, P. A., & Felicio, D. M. (1995). Do obese women have poorer social relationships than nonobese women? Reports by self, friends, and coworkers. *Journal of Personality, 63,* 65–85.

Miller, D. T., & Ross, M. (1975). Self-serving biases in attribution of causality: Fact or fiction? *Psychological Bulletin, 82,* 313–325.

Miller, D. T., Turnbull, W., & McFarland, C. (1990). Counterfactual thinking and social perception: Thinking about what might have been. In M. P. Zanna (Ed.), *Advances in experimental social psychology* (Vol. 23, pp. 305–331). Orlando, FL: Academic Press.

Miller, M. L., & Thayer, J. F. (1989). On the existence of discrete classes in personality: Is self-monitoring the correct joint to carve? *Journal of Personality and Social Psychology, 57,* 143–155.

Miller, R. S. (1991). On decorum in close relationships: Why aren't we polite to those we love? *Contemporary Social Psychology, 15,* 63–65.

Miyake, K., & Zuckerman, M. (1993). Beyond personality impressions: Effects of physical and vocal attractiveness on false consensus, social comparison, affiliation, and assumed and perceived similarity. *Journal of Personality, 61,* 411–437.

Modigliani, A., & Rochat, F. (1995). The role of interaction sequences and the timing of resistance in shaping obedience and defiance to authority. *Journal of Social Issues, 51,* 107–123.

Monsour, M., Betty, S., & Kurzweil, N. (1993). Levels of perspectives and the perception of intimacy in cross-sex friendships: A balance theory explanation of shared perceptual reality. *Journal of Social and Personal Relationships, 10,* 529–550.

Monteith, M. J. (1993). Self-regulation of prejudiced responses: Implications for progress in prejudice-reduction efforts. *Journal of Personality and Social Psychology, 65,* 469–485.

Monteith, M. J. (1996a). Affective reactions to prejudice-related discrepant responses: The impact of standard salience. *Personality and Social Psychology Bulletin, 22,* 48–59.

Monteith, M. J. (1996b). Self-regulation of prejudiced responses: Implications for progress in prejudice-reduction efforts. *Journal of Personality and Social Psychology, 65,* 469–485.

Moore, C. H., Wuensch, K. L., Hedges, R. M., & Castellow, W. A. (1994). The effects of physical attractiveness and social desirability on judgments regarding a sexual harassment case. *Journal of Social Behavior and Personality, 9,* 715–730.

Moore, D. (1994). Entitlement as an epistemic problem: Do women think like men? *Journal of Social Behavior and Personality, 9,* 665–684.

Moore, J. S., Graziano, W. G., & Miller, M. G. (1987). Physical attractiveness, sex role orientation, and the evaluation of adults and children. *Personality and Social Psychology Bulletin, 13,* 95–102.

Moran, G., & Cutler, B. L. (1991). The prejudicial impact of pretrial publicity. *Journal of Applied Social Psychology, 21,* 345–367.

Moreland, R. L., & Beach, S. R. (1992). Exposure effects in the classroom: The development of affinity among students. *Journal of Experimental Social Psychology, 28,* 255–276.

Moreland, R. L., & Zajonc, R. B. (1982). Exposure effects in person perception: Familiarity, similarity, and attraction. *Journal of Experimental Social Psychology, 18,* 395–415.

Morgan, H. J., & Janoff-Bulman, R. (1994). Positive and negative self-complexity: Patterns of adjustment following traumatic versus non-traumatic life experiences. *Journal of Social and Clinical Psychology, 13,* 63–85.

Mori, D. L., & Morey, L. (1991). The vulnerable body image of females with feelings of depression. *Journal of Research in Personality, 25,* 343–354.

Morrison, E. W., & Bies, R. J. (1991). Impression management in the feedback-seeking process: A literature review and research agenda. *Academy of Management Review, 16,* 322–341.

Moscovici, S. (1985). Social influence and conformity. In G. Lindzey & E. Aronson (Eds.), *Handbook of social psychology* (3rd ed., Vol. 2, pp. 347–412). New York: Random House.

Moskowitz, D. S. (1993). Dominance and friendliness: On the interaction of gender and situation. *Journal of Personality, 61,* 387–409.

Muczyk, J. P., & Reimann, B. C. (1987). The case for directive leadership. *Academy of Management Review, 12,* 647–687.

Mugny, G. (1975). Negotiations, image of the other and the process of minority influence. *European Journal of Social Psychology, 5,* 209–229.

Mullen, B., Anthony, T., Salas, E., & Driskell, J. E. (1994). Group cohesiveness and quality of decision making: An integration of tests of the groupthink hypothesis. Special Issue: Social cognition in small groups. *Small Group Research, 25,* 189–204.

Mullen, B., Atkins, J. L., Champion, D. S., Edwards, C., Hardy, D., (1985). The false consensus effect: A meta-analysis of 115 hypothesis tests. *Journal of Experimental Social Psychology, 21,* 262–283.

Mullen, B., & Copper, C. (1994). The relation between group cohesiveness and performance: An integration. *Psychological Bulletin, 115,* 210–227.

Mullen, B., & Johnson, C. (1990). Distinctiveness-based illusory correlations and stereotyping: A meta-analytic integration. *British Journal of Social Psychology, 29,* 11–28.

Mullen, B., & Johnson, C. (1995). Cognitive representation in ethnophaulisms and illusory correlation in stereotyping. *Personality and Social Psychology Bulletin, 21,* 420–433.

Murnighan, K. (Ed.). (1993). *Handbook of social psychology in organizations.* Englewood Cliffs, N.J.

Murphy, P. L., & Miller, C. T. (1997). Postdecisional dissonance and the commodified self-concept: A cross-cultural examination. *Personality and Social Psychology Bulletin, 23,* 50–62.

Murphy, S. T., Monahan, J. L., & Zajonc, R. B. (1995). Additivity of nonconscious affect: Combined effects of priming and exposure. *Journal of Personality and Social-Psychology, 69,* 589–602.

Murray, S. L., & Holmes, J. G. (1994). Storytelling in close relationships: The construction of confidence. *Personality and Social Psychology Bulletin, 20,* 650–663.

Myers, D. G., & Diener, E. (1995). Who is happy? *Psychological Science, 6,* 10–19.

Nadkarni, D. V., Lundgren, D., & Burlew, A. K. (1991). Gender differences in self-depriving behavior as a reaction to extreme inequity. *Journal of Social Behavior and Personality, 6,* 105–117.

Neck, C. P., & Moorhead, G. (1995). Groupthink remodeled: The importance of leadership, time pressure, and methodical decision-making procedures. *Human Relations, 48,* 537–557.

Nemeth, C. J. (1995). Dissent as driving cognition, attitudes, and judgments. *Social Cognition, 13,* 273–291.

Neto, F. (1992). Loneliness among Portuguese adolescents. *Social Behavior and Personality, 20,* 15–22.

Newcomb, T. M. (1961). *The acquaintance process.* New York: Holt, Rinehart and Winston.

Newton, T. L., Kiecolt-Glaser, J. K., Glaser, R., & Malarkey, W. B. (1995). Conflict and withdrawal during marital interaction: The roles of hostility and defensiveness. *Personality and Social Psychology Bulletin, 21,* 512–524.

Niedenthal, P. M., & Bieke, D. R. (1997). Interrelated and isolated self-concepts. *Personality and Social Psychology Review, 1,* 106–128.

Niedenthal, P. M., Setterlund, M. B., & Wherry, M. B. (1992). Possible self-complexity and affective reactions to goal-relevant evaluation. *Journal of Personality and Social Psychology, 63,* 5–16.

Nilchaikovit, T., Hill, J. M., & Holland, J. C. (1993). The effects of culture on illness behavior and medical care: Asian and American differences. *General Hospital Psychiatry, 15,* 41–50.

Nisbett, R. E. (1990). Evolutionary psychology, biology, and cultural evolution. *Motivation and Emotion, 14,* 255–264.

Nisbett, R. E. (1993). Violence and U. S. regional culture. *American Psychologist, 48,* 441–449.

Nisbett, R. E., & Cohen, D. (1996). *Culture of honor: The psychology of violence in the South.* Boulder, CO: Westview Press.

Number of sexually active teens levels off, survey says. (1995, February 24). *Albany Times Union,* A-5.

Number of young U.S. killers triples over past decade. (1996, March 8). *Albany Times Union,* A-4.

O'Connor, J., Mumford, M. D., Clifton, T. C., & Gessner, T., et-al. (1995). Charismatic leaders and destructiveness: An historiometric study. *Leadership Quarterly, 6,* 529–555.

O'Grady, K. E. (1989). Physical attractiveness, need for approval, social self-esteem, and maladjustment. *Journal of Social and Clinical Psycholgy, 8,* 62–69.

O'Sullivan, L. F., & Allgeier, E. R. (1994). Disassembling a stereotype: Gender differences in the use of token resistance. *Journal of Applied Social Psychology, 24,* 1035–1055.

O'Sullivan, L. F., & Byers, E. S. (1992). College students' incorporation of initiator and restrictor roles in sexual dating interactions. *Journal of Sex Research, 29,* 435–446.

Oggins, J., Veroff, J., & Leber, D. (1993). Perceptions of marital interaction among black and white newlyweds. *Journal of Personality and Social Psychology, 65,* 494–511.

Ohbuchi, K., Chiba, S., & Fukushima, O. (1996). Mitigation of interpersonal conflicts: Politeness and time pressure. *Personality and Social Psychology Bulletin, 22,* 1035–1042.

Ohbuchi, K., Kameda, M., & Agarie, N. (1989). Apology as aggression control: Its role in mediating appraisal of and response to harm. *Journal of Personality and Social Psychology, 56,* 219–227.

Ohbuchi, K. I., & Takahashi, Y. (1994). Cultural styles of conflict management in Japanese and Americans: Passivity, covertness, and effectiveness of strategies. *Journal of Applied Social Psychology, 24,* 1345–1366.

Olczak, P. V., Kaplan, M. F., & Penrod, S. (1991). Attorneys' lay psychology and its effectiveness in selecting jurors: Three empirical studies. *Journal of Social Behavior and Personality, 6,* 431–452.

Oliner, S. P., & Oliner, P. M. (1988). *The altruistic personality: Rescuers of Jews in Nazi Europe.* New York: Free Press.

Olmstead, R. E., Guy, S. M., O'Malley, P. M., & Bentler, P. M. (1991). Longitudinal assessment of the relationship between self-esteem, fatalism, loneliness, and substance use. *Journal of Social Behavior and Personality, 6,* 749–770.

Olweus, D. (1986). Aggression and hormones: Behavioral relationship with testosterone and adrenaline. In D. Olweus, J. Block, & M. Radke-Yarrows (Eds.), *Development of antisocial and prosocial behavior* (pp. 51–72). New York: Academic Press.

Orive, R. (1988). Social projective and social comparison of opinions. *Journal of Personality and Social Psychology, 54,* 953–964.

Orpen, C. (1994). The effects of self-esteem and personal control on the relationship between job insecurity and psychological well-being. *Social Behavior and Personality, 22,* 53–56.

Osborne, J. W. (1995). Academics, self-esteem, and race: A look at the underlying assumptions of the disidentification hypothesis. *Personality and Social Psychology Bulletin, 21,* 449–455.

Osterman, K., Bjorkqvist, K., Lagerspetz, K. M. J., Kaukianainen, A., Huesmann, L. W., & Fraczek, A. (1994). Peer and self-estimated aggression and victimization in 8-year-old children from five ethnic groups. *Aggressive Behavior, 20,* 411–428.

Otto, A. L., Penrod, S. D., & Dexter, H. R. (1994). The biasing impact of pretrial publicity on juror judgments. *Law and Human Behavior, 18,* 453–469.

Page, N. R., & Wiseman, R. L. (1993). Supervisory behavior and worker satisfaction in the United States, Mexico, and Spain. *Journal of Business Communication, 30,* 161–180.

Pan, S. (1993). China: Acceptability and effect of three kinds of sexual publication. *Archives of Sexual Behavior, 22,* 59–71.

Paulhus, D. L., & Bruce, M. N. (1992). The effect of acquaintanceship on the validity of personality impressions: A longitudinal study. *Journal of Personality and Social Psychology, 63,* 816–824.

Paulhus, D. L., Bruce, M. N., & Trapnell, P. D. (1995). Effects of self-presentation strategies on personality profiles and their structure. *Personality and Social Psychology Bulletin, 21,* 100–108.

Paulus, P. B. (Ed.). (1989). *Psychology of group influence* (2nd ed.). Hillsdale, NJ: Erlbaum.

Pennebaker, J. W. (1988). Confession, inhibition, and disease. *Advances in Experimental Social Psychology, 22,* 211–242.

Pennebaker, J. W. (1993). Overcoming inhibition: Rethinking the roles of personality, cognition, and social behavior. In H. C. Traue & J. W. Pennebaker (Eds.), *Emotion, inhibition and disease* (pp. 100–115). Kirkland, WA: Hofgref & Huber.

Pennebaker, J. W., Hughes, C. F., & O'Heron, R. C. (1987). The psychophysiology of confession: Linking inhibitory and psychosomatic processes. *Journal of Personality and Social Psychology, 52,* 781–793.

Pennebaker, J. W., Rimé, B, & Blankenship, V. E. (1996). Stereotypes of emotional expressiveness of Northerners and Southerners: A cross-cultural test of Montesquieu's hypotheses. *Journal of Personality and Social Psychology, 70,* 372–380.

Peplau, L. A., Hill, C. T., & Rubin, Z. (1993). Sex role attitudes in dating and marriage: A 15-year follow-up of the Boston couples study. *Journal of Social Issues, 49*(3), 31–52.

Peplau, L. A., & Perlman, D. (1982). Perspective on loneliness. In L. A. Peplau & D. Perlman (Eds.), *Loneliness: A sourcebook of current theory, research, and therapy* (pp. 1–18). New York: Wiley.

Perron, J., & St.-Onge, L. (1991). Work values in relation to gender and forecasted career patterns for women. *International Journal for the Advancement of Counseling, 14,* 91–103.

Pessin, J. (1933). The comparative effects of social and mechanical stimulation on memorizing. *American Journal of Psychology, 45,* 263–270.

Petkova, K. G., Ajzen, I., & Driver, B. L. (1995). Salience of anti-abortion beliefs and commitment to an attitudinal position: On the strength, structure, and predictive validity of anti-abortion attitudes. *Journal of Applied Social Psychology, 25,* 463–483.

Pettigrew, T. F. (1969). Racially separate or together? *Journal of Social Issues, 24,* 43–69.

Pettigrew, T. F. (1997). Generalized intergroup contact effects on prejudice. *Personality and Social Psychology Bulletin, 23,* 173–185.

Pettigrew, T. F. (in press). The affective component of prejudice: Empirical support for the new view. In S. A. Tuch & J. K. Martin (Eds.), *Racial attitudes in the 1990s : Continuity and change.* Westport, CT: Praeger.

Petty, R. E., & Cacioppo, J. T. (1986). The elaboration likelihood model of persuasion. In L. Berkowitz (Ed.), *Advances in experimental social psychology,* (Vol. 19, pp. 123–205). New York: Academic Press.

Petty, R. E., Cacioppo, J. T., Strathman, A. J., & Priester, J. R. (1994). To think or not to think: Exploring two routes to persuasion. In S. Shavitt & T. C. Brock (Eds.), *Persuasion* (pp. 113–147). Boston: Allyn & Bacon.

Phelps, E. J. (1981). *The maid of the north.* New York: Holt, Rinehart, & Winston.

Phinney, J. S. (1996) When we talk about American ethnic groups, what do we mean? *American Psychologist, 51,* 918–927.

Pierce, C. A. (1992). *The effects of physical attractiveness and height on dating choice: A meta-analysis.*

Unpublished masters thesis, University at Albany, State University of New York, Albany, NY.

Pierce, C. A. (1996). Body height and romantic attraction: A meta-analytic test of the male-taller norm. *Social Behavior and Personality, 24,* 143–150.

Pierce, C. A. (1997). *Factors associated with participating in a romantic relationship in a work environment.* Manuscript submitted for publication.

Pierce, C. A., & Aguinis, H. (in press). Bridging the gap between romantic relationships and sexual harrassment in organizations. *Journal of Organizational Behavior.*

Pierce, C. A., Byrne, D., & Aguinis, H. (1996). Attraction in organizations: A model of workplace romance. *Journal of Organizational Behavior, 17,* 5–32.

Pilkington, N. W., & Lydon, J. E. (1997). The relative effect of attitude similarity and attitude dissimilarity on interpersonal attraction: Investigating the moderating roles of prejudice and group membership. *Personality and Social Psychology Bulletin, 23,* 107–122.

Pingitore, R., Dugooni, B. L., Tindale, R. S., & Spring, B. (1994). Bias against overweight job applicants in a simulated employment interview. *Journal of Applied Psychology, 79,* 909–917.

Pittman, T. S. (1993). Control motivation and attitude change. In G. Weary, F. Gleicher, & K. L. Marsh (Eds.), *Control motivation and social cognition* (pp. 157–175). New York: Springer-Verlag.

Planalp, S., & Benson, A. (1992). Friends' and acquaintances' conversations: I. Perceived differences. *Journal of Social and Personal Relationships, 9,* 483–506.

Platz, S. G., & Hosch, H. M. (1988). Cross-racial/ethnic eyewitness identification: A field study. *Journal of Applied Social Psychology, 18,* 972–984.

Pleck, J. H., Sonenstein, F. L., & Ku, L. C. (1993). Masculinity ideology: Its impact on adolescent males' heterosexual relationships. *Journal of Social Issues, 49*(3), 11–29.

Plesser-Storr, D. (1995). *Self-presentation by men to attractive and unattractive women: Tactics of ingratiation, blasting, and basking.* Unpublished doctoral dissertation, University at Albany, State University of New York, Albany.

Pliner, P., Chaiken, S., & Flett, G. L. (1990). Gender differences in concern with body weight and physical appearance over the life span. *Personality and Social Psychology Bulletin, 16,* 263–273.

Plous, S., & Williams, T. (1995). Racial stereotypes from the days of American slavery: A continuing legacy. *Journal of Applied Social Psychology, 25,* 795–817.

Powell, G. N. (1990). One more time: Do female and male managers differ? *Academy of Management Executive, 4*(3), 68–75.

Pratto, F. (1996). Sexual politics: The gender gap in the bedroom, the cupboard, and the cabinet. In D. M. Buss & N. Malamuth (Eds.), *Sex, power, and conflict: Evolutionary and feminist perspectives* (pp. 179–230). New York: Oxford University Press.

Pratto, F., & John, O. P. (1991). Automatic vigilance: The attention-grabbing power of negative social information. *Journal of Personality and Social Psychology, 61,* 380–391.

Pratto, F., Stallworth, L. M., Sidanius, J., & Siers, B. (1997). The gender gap in occupational role attainment: A social dominance approach. *Journal of Personality and Social Psychology, 72,* 37–53.

Prentice, D. A., & Miller, D. T. (1993). Pluralistic ignorance and alcohol use on campus: Some consequences of misperceiving the social norm. *Journal of Personality and Social Psychology Bulletin, 64,* 243–256.

Prentice, D. A., & Miller, D. T. (1996). Pluralistic ignorance and the perpetuation of social norms by unwitting actors. *Advances in Experimental Social Psychology, 28,* 161–209.

Priel, B., Gonik, N., & Rabinowitz, B. (1993). Appraisals of childbirth experience and newborn characteristics: The role of hardiness and affect. *Journal of Personality, 61,* 299–315.

Ptacek, J. T., & Dodge, K. L. (1995). Coping strategies and relationship satisfaction in couples. *Personality and Social Psychology Bulletin, 21,* 76–84.

Purdue, C., Dovidio, J. F., Gurtman, M., & Tyler, R. (1990). Us and them: Social categorization and the process of intergroup bias. *Journal of Personality and Social Psychology, 59,* 475–486.

Putnam, L. L. (1990). Reframing integrative and distributive bargaining: A process perspective. In B. H. Sheppard, M. H. Bazerman, & R. J. Lewicki (Eds.), *Research on negotiation in organizations* (Vol. 2, pp. 3–30). Greenwich, CT: JAI Press.

Pyzczynski, T., Wicklund, R. A., Floresku, S., Koch, H., Gauch, G., Solomon, S., & Greenberg, J. (1996). Whistling in the dark: Exaggerated consensus estimates in response to incidental reminders of mortality. *Psychological Science, 7,* 332–336.

Quadrel, M. J., & Lau, R. R. (1989). Health promotion, health locus of control, and health behavior:

Two field experiments. *Journal of Applied Social Psychology, 19,* 1497–1521.

Queen Victoria (1881, January). *Medical Aspects of Human Sexuality,* 86.

Quigley, B. M., Johnson, A. B., & Byrne, D. (1995, June). *Mock jury sentencing decisions: A meta-analysis of the attractiveness–leniency effect.* Paper presented at the meeting of the American Psychological Society, New York.

Quigley, B. M., & Tedeschi, J. T. (1996). Mediating effects of blame attributions on feelings of anger. *Personality and Social Psychology Bulletin, 22,* 1280–1288.

Radecki-Bush, C., Farrell, A. D., & Bush, J. P. (1993). Predicting jealous responses: The influence of adult attachment and depression on threat appraisal. *Journal of Social and Personal Relationships, 10,* 569–588.

Rahim, M. A. (1983). *Organizational conflict inventories.* Palo Alto, CA: Consulting Psychologists Press.

Rajecki, D. W., McTavish, D. G., Rasmussen, L., Schreuders, M., Byers, D. C., & Jessup, S. K. (1994). Violence, conflict, trickery, and other story themes in TV ads for food for children. *Journal of Applied Social Psychology, 24,* 1685–1700.

Raleigh, M. J., McGuire, M. T., Brammer, G. L., Pollack, D. B., & Yuwiler, A. (1991). Serotonergic mechanisms promote dominance acquisition in adult male vervet monkeys. *Brain Research, 559,* 181–190.

Reed, D., & Weinberg, M. S. (1984). Premarital coitus: Developing and establishing sexual scripts. *Social Psychology Quarterly, 47,* 129–138.

Reed, G. M., Kemeny, M. E., Taylor, S. E., & Visscher, B. R. (in press). Negative HIV-specific expectancies and AIDS-related bereavement as predictors of symptom onset in asymptomatic HIV-positive gay men. *Health Psychology.*

Regan, D. T., & Fazio, R. H. (1977). On the consistency between attitudes and behavior: Look to the method of attitude formation. *Journal of Experimental Social Psychology, 13,* 38–45.

Reis, H. T., Nezlek, J., & Wheeler, L. (1989). Physical attractiveness in social interaction. *Journal of Personality and Social Psychology, 38,* 604–617.

Reis, T. J., Gerrard, M., & Gibbons, F. X. (1993). Social comparison and the pill: Reactions to upward and downward comparsion of contraceptive behavior. *Personality and Social Psychology Bulletin, 19,* 13–20.

Reiss, A. J., & Roth, J. A. (Eds.). (1993). *Understanding and preventing violence.* Washington, DC: National Academy Press.

Rentsch, J. R., & Heffner, T. S. (1994). Assessing self-concept: Analysis of Gordon's coding scheme using "Who am I?" responses. *Journal of Social Behavior and Personality, 9,* 283–300.

Rhodes, G., & Tremewan, T. (1996) Averageness, exaggeration, and facial attractiveness. *Psychological Science, 7,* 105–110.

Rhodewalt, F., & Davison, J., Jr. (1983). Reactance and the coronary-prone behavior pattern: The role of self-attribution in response to reduced behavioral freedom. *Journal of Personality and Social Psychology, 44,* 220–228.

Ridley, M., & Dawkins, R. (1981). The natural selection of altruism. In J. P. Rushton & R. M. Sorrentino (Eds.), *Altruism and helping behavior* (pp. 19–39). Hillsdale, NJ: Erlbaum.

Riggio, R. E., & Throckmorton, B. (1988). The relative effect of verbal and nonverbal behavior, appearance, and social skills on valuations made in hiring interviews. *Journal of Applied Social Psychology, 18,* 331–348.

Riskind, J. H., & Maddux, J. E. (1993). Loomingness, helplessness, and fearfulness: An integration of harm-looming and self-efficacy models of fear. *Journal of Social and Clinical Psychology, 12,* 73–89.

Roberts, B. W., & Donahue, E. M. (1994). One personality, multiple selves: Integrating personality and social roles. *Journal of Personality, 62,* 199–218.

Robins, R. W., Spranca, M. D., & Mendelsohn, G. A. (1996). The actor-observer effect revisted : Effects of individual differences and repeated social interactions on actor and observer attribution. *Journal of Personality and Social Psychology, 71,* 375-389.

Rochat, F., & Modigliani, A. (1995). The ordinary quality of resistance: From Milgram 's laboratory to the village of Le Chambon. *Journal of Social Issues, 51*(3), 195–210.

Rodgers, J. L., Billy, J. O. B., & Udry, J. R. (1984). A model of friendship similarity in mildly deviant behaviors. *Journal of Applied Social Psychology, 14,* 413–425.

Rodin, M., & Price, J. (1995). Overcoming stigma: Credit for self-improvement or discredit for needing to improve? *Personality and Social Psychology Bulletin, 21,* 172–181.

Roese, N. J. (1997). Counterfactual thinking. *Psychological Bulletin, 121,* 133–148.

Roese, N. J., & Olson, J. M. (in press). Counterfactual thinking: The intersection of affect and function. *Advances in Experimental Social Psychology, 29.*

Rogers, R. W., & Ketcher, C. M. (1979). Effects of anonymity and arousal on aggression. *Journal of Psychology, 102,* 13–19.

Rosenbaum, M. E., & Levin, I. P. (1969). Impression formation as a function of source credibility and the polarity of information. *Journal of Personality and Social Psychology, 12,* 34–37.

Rosenberg, E. L., & Ekman, P. (1995). Conceptual and methodological issues in the judgment of facial expressions of emotion. *Motivation and Emotion, 19,* 111–138.

Rosenthal, A. M. (1964). *Thirty-eight witnesses.* New York: McGraw-Hill.

Rosenthal, D. A., & Shepherd, H. (1993). A six-month follow-up of adolescents' sexual risk-taking, HIV/AIDS knowledge, and attitudes to condoms. *Journal of Community and Applied Social Psychology, 3,* 53–65.

Rosenzweig, J. M., & Daley, D. M. (1989). Dyadic adjustment/sexual satisfaction in women and men as a function of psychological sex role self-perception. *Journal of Sex and Marital Therapy, 15,* 42–56.

Rosnow, R. L., Skleder, A. A., Jaeger, M. E., & Rind, B. (1994). Intelligence and the epistemics of interpersonal acumen: Testing some implications of Gardner's theory. *Intelligence, 19,* 93–116.

Ross, L. (1977). The intuitive psychologist and his shortcomings. In L. Berkowitz (Ed.), *Advances in experimental social psychology* (Vol. 10, pp. 173–220). New York: Academic.

Ross, L., & Nisbett, R. N. (1991). *The person and the situation: Perspectives of social psychology.* New York: McGraw-Hill.

Rotenberg, K. J., & Kmill, J. (1992). Perception of lonely and non-lonely persons as a function of individual differences in loneliness. *Journal of Social and Personal Relationships, 9,* 325–330.

Roth, D. L., Wiebe, D. J., Fillingim, R. B., & Shay, K. A. (1989). Life events, fitness, hardiness, and health: A simultaneous analysis of proposed stress-resistance effects. *Journal of Personality and Social Psychology, 57,* 136–142.

Rothman, A. J., & Hardin, C. D. (1997) Differential use of the availability heuristic in social judgment. *Personality and Social Psychology Bulletin, 23,* 123–138.

Rotton, J., & Kelley, I. W. (1985). Much ado about the full moon: A meta-analysis of lunar-lunacy research. *Psychological Bulletin, 97,* 286–306.

Rozin, P., Lowery, L., & Ebert, R. (1994). Varieties of disgust faces and the structure of disgust. *Journal of Personality and Social Psychology, 66,* 870–881.

Rozin, P., Millman, L., & Nemeroff, C. (1986). Operation of the laws of sympathetic magic in disgust and other domains. *Journal of Personality and Social Psychology, 50,* 703–712.

Rubin, J. Z. (1985). Deceiving ourselves about deception: Comment on Smith and Richardson's "Amelioration of deception and harm in psychological research." *Journal of Personality and Social Psychology, 48,* 252–253.

Rusbult, C. E. (1983). A longitudinal test of the investment model: The development (and deterioration) of satisfaction and commitment in heterosexual involvements. *Journal of Personality and Social Psychology, 45,* 101–117.

Rusbult, C. E., & Martz, J. M. (1995). Remaining in an abusive relationship: An investment model analysis of nonvoluntary dependence. *Personality and Social Psychology Bulletin, 21,* 558–571.

Rusbult, C. E., Morrow, G. D., & Johnson, D. J. (1990). Self-esteem and problem-solving behavior in close relationships. *British Journal of Social Psychology,*

Rusbult, C. E., Onizuka, R. K., & Lipkus, I. (1993). What do we really want?: Mental models of ideal romantic involvement explored through multidimensional scaling. *Journal of Experimental Social Psychology, 29,* 493–527.

Rusbult, C. E., & Zembrodt, I. M. (1983). Responses to dissatisfaction in romantic involvements: A multidimensional scaling analysis. *Journal of Experimental Social Psychology, 19,* 274–293.

Ruscher, J. B., & Hammer, E. D. (1994). Revising disrupted impressions through conversation. *Journal of Personality and Social Psychology, 66,* 530–541.

Rushton, J. P. (1989). Genetic similarity, human altruism, & group selection, *Behavioral and Brain Sciences, 12,* 503–559.

Rushton, J. P. (1990). Sir Francis Galton, epigenetic rules, genetic similarity theory, and human life-history analysis. *Journal of Personality, 58,* 117–140.

Rushton, J. P., & Nicholson, I. R. (1988). Genetic similarity theory, intelligence, and human mate choice. *Ethology and Sociobiology, 9,* 45–57.

Rushton, J. P., Russell, R. J. H., & Wells, P. A. (1984). Genetic similarity theory: Beyond kin selection. *Behavior Genetics, 14,* 179–193.

Russell, G. W. (1993). *The psychology of sport.* New York: Springer-Verlag.

Russell, J. A. (1994). Is there universal recognition of emotion from facial expressions? A review of cross-cultural studies. *Psychological Bulletin, 115,* 102–141.

Rutkowski, G. K., Gruder, C. L., & Romer, D. (1983). Group cohesiveness, social norms, and bystander intervention. *Journal of Personality and Social Psychology, 44,* 542–552.

Ryan, R. H., & Geiselman, R. E. (1991). Effects of biased information on the relationship between eyewitness confidence and accuracy. *Bulletin of the Psychonomic Society, 29,* 7–9.

Safir, M. P., Peres, Y., Lichtenstein, M., Hoch, Z., & Shepher, J. (1982). Psychological androgyny and sexual adequacy. *Journal of Sex and Marital Therapy, 8,* 228–240.

Salovey, P., Rothman, A. J., & Rodin, J. (in press). Social psychology and health behavior. In G. Lindsey, S. T. Fiske, & D. T. Gilbert (Eds.), *Handbook of social psychology.* New York: Oxford University Press and McGraw-Hill.

Sanders, G. S. (1983). An attentional process model of social facilitation. In A. Hare, H. Blumberg, V. Kent, & M. Davies (Eds.), *Small groups.* London: Wiley

Sanna, L. J., & Pusecker, P. A. (1994). Self-efficacy, valence of self-evaluation, and performance. *Personality and Social Psychology Bulletin, 20,* 82–92.

Santos, M. D., Leve, C., & Pratkanis, A. R. (1994). Hey buddy, can you spare seventeen cents? Mindful persuasion and pique technique. *Journal of Applied Social Psychology, 24,* 755–764.

Sarason, I. G., Sarason, B. R., & Pierce, G. R. (1994). Social support: Global and relationship-based levels of analysis. *Journal of Social and Personal Relationships, 11,* 295–312.

Sayers, S. L., Baucom, D. H., & Tierney, A. M. (1993). Sex roles, interpersonal control, and depression: Who can get their way? *Journal of Research in Personality, 27,* 377–395.

Schachter, S. (1964). The interaction of cognitive and physiological determinants of emotional state. In L. Berkowitz (Ed.), *Advances in experimental social psychology* (Vol. 1, pp. 48–81). New York: Academic Press.

Schaller, M., Crandall, C. S., Stangor, C., & Neuberg, S. L. (1995). "What kinds of social psychology experiments are of value to perform?" Comment on Wallach and Wallach (1994). *Journal of Personality and Social Psychology, 69,* 611–618.

Scheier, M. F., & Carver, C. S. (1987). Dispositional optimism and physical well-being: The influence of generalized outcome expectancies in health. *Journal of Personality, 55,* 169–210.

Scheier, M. F., & Carver, C. S. (1993). On the power of positive thinking: The benefits of being optimistic. *Current Directions in Psychological Science, 2,* 26–30.

Schleifer, S. J., Keller, S. E., Camerino, M., Thornton, J. C., & Stein, M. (1983). Suppression of lymphocyte function following bereavement. *Journal of the American Medical Association, 250,* 374–377.

Schmitt, B., Gilovich, T. K., Goore, N., & Joseph, L. (1986). Mere presence and social facilitation: One more time. *Journal of Experimental Social Psychology, 22,* 242–248.

Schmitt, D. P., & Buss, D. M. (1996). Strategic self-promotion and competitor derogation: Sex and context effects on the perceived effectiveness of mate attraction tactics. *Journal of Personality and Social Psychology, 70,* 1185–1204.

Schneider, B. H. (1991). A comparison of skill-building and desensitization strategies for intervention with aggressive children. *Aggressive Behavior, 17,* 301–311.

Schwartz, A. E. (1994, December 20). Americans on line seldom fond of disagreement. *Albany Times Union,* p. A-11.

Schwarzwald, J., Amir, Y., & Crain, R. L. (1992). Long-term effects of school desegregation experiences on interpersonal relations in the Israeli defense forces. *Personality and Social Psychology Bulletin, 18,* 357–368.

Scott, K. P., & Feldman-Summers, S. (1979). Children's reactions to textbook stories in which females are portrayed in traditionally male roles. *Journal of Educational Psychology, 71,* 396–402.

Sears, D. O. (1988). Symbolic racism. In P. A. Katz & D. A. Taylor (Eds.), *Eliminating racism: Profiles in controversy* (pp. 53–84). New York: Plenum.

Sedikides, C. (1992). Attentional effects on mood are moderated by chronic self-conception valence. *Personality and Social Psychology Bulletin, 18,* 580–584.

Sedikides, C. (1993). Assessment, enhancement, and verification determinants of the self-evaluation process. *Journal of Personality and Social Psychology, 65,* 317–338.

Sedikides, C., & Skowronski, J. J. (1991). The law of cognitive structure activation. *Psychological Inquiry, 2,* 169–184.

Sedikides, C., & Skowronski, J. J. (1997). The symbolic self in evolutionary context. *Personality and Social Psychology Review, 1,* 80–102.

Sedikides, C., & Strube, M. J. (in press). Self-evaluation: To thine own self be good, to thine own self be sure, to thine own self be true, and to thine own self be better. *Advances in Experimental Social Psychology.*

Segal, M. M. (1974). Alphabet and attraction: An unobtrusive measure of the effect of propinquity in a field setting. *Journal of Personality and Social Psychology, 30,* 654–657.

Segerstrom, S. C., Taylor, S. E., Kemeny, M. E., Reed, G. M., & Visscher , B. R. (1996). Causal attributions predict rate of immune decline in HIV-Seropositive gay men. *Health Psychology, 15,* 485–493.

Selye, H. (1956). *The stress of life.* New York: McGraw-Hill.

Seta, C. E., Hayes, N. S., & Seta, J. J. (1994). Mood, memory, and vigilance: The influence of distraction on recall and impression formation. *Personality and Social Psychology Bulletin, 20,* 170–177.

Seta, J. J., Seta, C. E., & Wang, M. A. (1991). Feelings of negativity and stress: An averaging–summation analysis of impressions of negative life experiences. *Personality and Social Psychology Bulletin, 17,* 376–384.

Shackelford, T. K., & Buss, D. M. (1996). Betrayal in mateships, friendships, and coalitions. *Personality and Social Psychology Bulletin, 22,* 1151–1164.

Shanab, M. E., & Yahya, K. A. (1977). A behavioral study of obedience in children. *Journal of Personality and Social Psychology, 35,* 530–536.

Sharp, M. J., & Getz, J. G. (1996). Substance use as impression management. *Personality and Social Psychology Bulletin, 22,* 60–67.

Sharpe, D., Adair, J. G., & Roese, N. J. (1992). Twenty years of deception research: A decline in subjects' trust? *Personality and Social Psychology Bulletin, 18,* 585–590.

Sharpsteen, D. J. (1995). The effects of relationship and self-esteem threats on the likelihood of romantic jealousy. *Journal of Social and Personal Relationships, 12,* 89–101.

Shaw, J. I., Borough, H. W., & Fink, M. I. (1994). Perceived sexual orientation and helping behavior by males and females: The wrong number technique. *Journal of Psychology and Human Sexuality, 6,* 73–81.

Shaw, L. L., Batson, C. D., & Todd, R. M. (1994). Empathy avoidance: Forestalling feeling for another in order to escape the motivational consequences. *Journal of Personality and Social Psychology, 67,* 879–887.

Sheeran, P., & Abraham, C. S. (1994). Unemployment and self-conception: A symbolic interactionist analysis. *Journal of Community and Applied Social Psychology, 4,* 115–129.

Sheppard, B. H., Bazerman, M. H., & Lewicki, R. J. (Eds.). (1990). *Research on negotiations in organizations.* Greenwich, CT: JAI Press.

Sherif, M. (1935). A study of some social factors in perception. *Archives of Psychology,* No. 187.

Sherif, M., Harvey, D. J., White, B. J., Hood, W. R., & Sherif, C. W. (1961). *Intergroup conflict and cooperation: The Robbers' Cave experiment.* Norman, OK: Institute of Group Relations.

Sherman, J. W., & Klein, S. B. (1994). Development and representation of personality impressions. *Journal of Personality and Social Psychology, 67,* 972–983.

Sherman, S. S. (1980). On the self-erasing nature of errors of prediction. *Journal of Personality and Social Psychology, 16,* 388–403.

Shiffrin, R. M. (1988). Attention. In R. C. Atkinson, R. J. Herrnstein, G. Lindzey, & R. D. Luce (Eds.), *Stevens' handbook of experimental psychology: Vol 2. Learning and cognition* (pp. 739–811). New York: Wiley.

Shinn, M., Morch, H., Robinson, P. E., & Neuner, R. A. (1993). Individual, group and agency strategies for coping with job stressors in residential child care programmes. *Journal of Community and Applied Social Psychology, 3,* 313–324.

Shotland, R. L., & Goodstein, L. (1983). Just because she doesn't want to doesn't mean its rape: An experimentally causal model of the perception of rape in a dating situation. *Social Psychology Quarterly, 46,* 220–232.

Showers, C. (1992). Compartmentalization of positive and negative self-knowledge: Keeping bad apples out of the bunch. *Journal of Personality and Social Psychology, 62,* 1036–1049.

Showers, C., & Ryff, C. D. (1993). *Self-differentiation and well-being in a life transition.* Manuscript submitted for publication.

Sidanius, J., Pratto, F., & Brief, D. (1995). Group dominance and the political psychology of gender: A cross-cultural comparison. *Political Psychology, 16,* 381-396.

Sigall, H., & Ostrove, N. (1975). Beautiful but dangerous: Effects of offender attractiveness and nature of the crime on juridic judgment. *Journal of Personality and Social Psychology, 31,* 410–414.

Sigelman, C. K., Thomas, D. B., Sigelman, L., & Robich, F. D. (1986). Gender, physical attractiveness, and electability: An experimental investigation of voter biases. *Journal of Applied Social Psychology, 16,* 229–248.

Sillars, A. L., Folwell, A. L., Hill, K. C., Maki, B. K., Hurst, A. P., & Casano, R. A. (1994). Marital communication and the persistance of misunderstanding. *Journal of Social and Personal Relationships, 11,* 611–617.

Silverstein, R. (1994). Chronic identity diffusion in traumatized combat veterans. *Social Behavior and Personality, 22,* 69–80.

Simon, L., Greenberg, J., & Brehm, J. (1995). Trivialization: The forgotten mode of dissonance reduction. *Journal of Personality and Social Psychology, 68,* 247–260.

Simon, L., Jones, E., Greenberg, J., Solomon, S., Pyszczynski, T., & Arndt, J. (in press). Cognitive-experimental system and mortality salience effects. *Journal of Personality and Social Psychology.*

Simpson, J. A. (1987). The dissolution of romantic relationships: Factors involved in relationship stability and emotional stress. *Journal of Personality and Social Psychology, 53,* 683–692.

Simpson, J. A., & Gangestad, S. W. (1992). Sociosexuality and romantic partner choice. *Journal of Personality, 60,* 31–51.

Singh, D. (1993). Adaptive significance of female physical attractiveness: Role of waist-to-hip ratio. *Journal of Personality and Social Psychology, 65,* 293–307.

Singh, D. (1995). Female judgment of male attractiveness and desirability for relationships: Role of waist-to-hip ratio and financial status. *Journal of Personality and Social-Psychology, 69,* 1089–1101.

Singh, R., & Tan, L. S. C. (1992). Attitudes and attraction: A test of the similarity–attraction and dissimilarity–repulsion hypotheses. *British Journal of Social Psychology, 31,* 227–238.

Skolnick, P., & Shaw, J. I. (1994). Is defendant status a liability or a shield? Crime severity and professional relatedness. *Journal of Applied Social Psychology, 24,* 1827–1836.

Skowronski, J. J., & Carlston, D. E. (1989). Negativity and extremity biases in impression formation: A review of explanations. *Psychological Bulletin, 105,* 131–142.

Smeaton, G., & Byrne, D. (1988). The Feelings Scale: Positive and negative affective responses. In C. M. Davis, W. L. Yarber, & S. L. Davis (Eds.), *Sexuality related measures: A compendium* (pp. 88–90). Lake Mills, IA: Graphic Publishing.

Smeaton, G., Byrne, D., & Murnen, S. K. (1989). The repulsion hypothesis revisited: Similarity irrelevance or dissimilarity bias? *Journal of Personality and Social Psychology, 56,* 54–59.

Smith, C. M., Tindale, R. S., & Dugoni, B. L. (1996). Minority and majority influence in freely interacting groups: Qualitative versus quantitative differences. *British Journal of Social Psychology, 35,* 137–149.

Smith, D. E., Gier, J. A., & Willis, F. N. (1982). Interpersonal touch and compliance with a marketing request. *Basic and Applied Social Psychology, 3,* 35–38.

Smith, E. R., Byrne, D., & Fielding, P. J. (1995). Interpersonal attraction as a function of extreme gender role adherence. *Personal Relationships, 2,* 161–172.

Smith, E. R., & Henry, S. (1996). An in-group becomes part of the self: Response time evidence. *Personality and Social Psychology Bulletin, 22,* 635–642.

Smith, E. R., & Zárate, M. A. (1992). Exemplar-based model of social judgment. *Psychological Review, 99,* 3–21.

Smith, G. E., Gerrard, M., & Gibbons, F. X. (1997). Self-esteem and the relation between risk behavior and perceptions of vulnerability to unplanned pregnancy in college women. *Health Psychology, 16,* 137–146.

Smith, K. D., Keating, J. P., & Stotland, E. (1989). Altruism reconsidered: The effect of denying feedback on a victim's status to empathetic witnesses. *Journal of Personality and Social Psychology, 57,* 641–650.

Smith, P. B., & Bond, M. H. (1993). *Social psychology across cultures.* Boston: Allyn & Bacon.

Smith, R. E., Smoll, F. L., & Ptacek, J. T. (1990). Conjunctive moderator variables in vulnerability and resiliency research: Life stress, social support and coping skills, and adolescent sport injuries. *Journal of Personality and Social Psychology, 58,* 360–370.

Smith, S. S., & Richardson, D. (1985). On deceiving ourselves about deception: Reply to Rubin. *Journal of Personality and Social Psychology, 48,* 254–255.

Sneddon, I., & Kremer, J. (1992). Sexual behavior and attitudes of university students in Northern Ireland. *Archives of Sexual Behavior, 21,* 295–312.

Snell, W. E. Jr., & Finney, P. D. (1993). Measuring relational aspects of the self: Relational–esteem, relational–depression, and relational–preoccupation. *Contemporary Social Psychology, 17,* 44–55.

Sniffen, M. J. (1991, September 30). Blacks make up 40% of death row. *Albany Times Union,* p. A-3.

Snyder, C. R., & Fromkin, H. L. (1980). *Uniqueness: The human pursuit of difference.* New York: Plenum.

Snyder, M. (1974). Self-monitoring of expressive behavior. *Journal of Personality and Social Psychology, 30,* 526–537.

Snyder, M., Gangestad, S., & Simpson, J. A. (1983). Choosing friends as activity partners: The role of self-monitoring. *Journal of Personality and Social Psychology, 45,* 1061–1072.

Snyder, M., & Ickes, W. (1985). Personality and social behavior. In G. Lindzey & E. Aronson (Eds.), *Handbook of social psychology* (3rd ed.) (Vol. 2, pp. 883–947). New York: Random House.

Snyder, M., & Simpson, J. A. (1984). Self-monitoring and dating relationships. *Journal of Personality and Social Psychology, 47,* 1281–l291.

Sommer, S. B., Bae, S. H., & Luthans, F. (1996) Organizational commitment across cultures: The impact of antecedents on Korean employees. *Human Relations, 49,* 977–993.

Sorenson, K. A., Russell, S. M., Harkness, D. J., & Harvey, J. H. (1993). Account-making, confiding, and coping with the ending of a close relationship. *Journal of Social Behavior and Personality, 8,* 73–86.

Spence, J. T. (1993). Gender-related traits and gender ideology: Evidence for a multifactorial theory. *Journal of Personality and Social Psychology, 64,* 624–635.

Sprecher, S., & Duck, S. (1994). Sweet talk: The importance of perceived communication for romantic and friendship attraction experienced during a get-acquainted date. *Personality and Social Psychology Bulletin, 20,* 391–400.

Sprecher, S., Sullivan, Q., & Hatfield, E. (1994). Mate selection preferences: Gender differences examined in a national sample. *Journal of Personality and Social Psychology, 66,* 1074–1080.

Srull, T. K., Lichtenstein, M., & Rothbart, M. (1985). Associative storage and retrieval processes in person memory. *Journal of Experimental Psychology: Learning, Memory, and Cognition, 11,* 316–345.

Stalling, R. B. (1992). Mood and pain: The influence of positive and negative affect on reported body aches. *Journal of Social Behavior and Personality, 7,* 323–334.

Stangor, C., & McMillan, D. (1992). Memory for expectancy-congruent and expectancy-incongruent information: A review of the social and social developmental literature. *Psychological Bulletin, 111,* 42–61.

Stangor, C., & Ruble, D. N. (1989). Strength of expectancies and memory for social information: What we remember depends on how much we know. *Journal of Experimental Social Psychology, 25,* 18–35.

Stasser, G., & Stewart, D. (1992). Discovery of hidden profiles by decision-making groups: Solving a problem versus making a judgment. *Journal of Personality and Social Psychology, 63,* 426–434.

Stasser, G., Taylor, L. A., & Hanna, C. (1989). Information sampling in structured and unstructured discussions of three- and six-person groups. *Journal of Personality and Social Psychology, 57,* 67–78.

Steele, C. M. (1997). A threat in the air: How stereotypes shape intellectual identity and performance. *American Psychologist, 52,* 613–629.

Steffen, V. J., & Eagly, A. H. (1985). Implicit theories about influence style: The effects of status and sex. *Personality and Social Psychology Bulletin, 11,* 191–205.

Stein, R. I., & Nemeroff, C. J. (1995). Moral overtones of food: Judgments of others based on what they eat. *Personality and Social Psychology Bulletin, 21,* 480–490.

Steiner, D. D., & Gilliland, S. W. (1996). Fairness reactions to personnel selection techniques in France and the United States. *Journal of Applied Psychology, 81,* 134–141.

Steinhauer, J. (1995, April 10). Big benefits in marriage, studies say. *The New York Times,* p. A10.

Stephan, C. W., & Stephan, W. G. (1986). Habla Ingles? The effects of language translation on simulated juror decisions. *Journal of Applied Social Psychology, 16,* 577–589.

Sternberg, R. J. (1988). *The triangle of love.* New York: Basic Books.

Stewart, J. E., II. (1980). Defendant's attractiveness as a factor in the outcome of criminal trials: An observational study. *Journal of Applied Social Psychology, 10,* 348–361.

Stice, E., & Shaw, H. E. (1994). Adverse effects of the media portrayed thin-ideal on women and linkages to bulimic symptomatology. *Journal of Social and Clinical Psychology, 13,* 288–308.

Stinson, L., & Ickes, W. (1992). Empathic accuracy in the interactions of male friends versus male strangers. *Journal of Personality and Social Psychology, 62,* 787–797.

Stone, A. A., Cox, D., Valdimarsdottir, H., Jandorf, L., & Neale, J. M. (1987). Evidence that secretory IgA antibody is associated with daily mood. *Journal of Personality and Social Psychology, 52,* 988–993.

Stone, A. A., Neale, J. M., Cox, D. S., Napoli, A., Valdimarsdottir, H., & Kennedy-Moore, E. (1994). Daily events are associated with a secretory immune response to an oral antigen in men. *Health Psychology, 13,* 440–446.

Stone, J., Wiegand, A. W., Cooper, J., & Aronson, E. (1997). When exemplification fails: Hypocrisy and the motive for self-integrity. *Journal of Personality and Social Psychology, 72,* 54–65.

Stoppard, J. M., & Gruchy, C. D. G. (1993). Gender, context, and expression of positive emotion. *Personality and Social Psychology Bulletin, 19,* 143–150.

Stradling, S. G., Crowe, G., & Tuohy, A. P. (1993). Changes in self-concept during occupational socialization of new recruits to the police. *Journal of Community and Applied Social Psychology, 3,* 131–147.

Strauman, T. J., Lemieux, A. M., & Coe, C. L. (1993). Self-discrepancy and natural killer cell activity: Immunological consequences of negative self-evaluation. *Journal of Personality and Social Psychology, 64,* 1042–1052.

Straus, M. A., & Gelles, R. J. (1988). Violence in American families: How much is there and why does it occur? In E. W. Nunnally, C. S. Coleman, & F. M. Cox (Eds.), *Families in trouble* (Series 3, pp. 141–162). Newbury Park, CA: Sage.

Strickland, B. R. (1992). Women and depression. *Current Directions in Psychological Sciences, 1,* 132–135.

Strube, M. J. (1989). Evidence for the Type in Type A behavior: A taxonometric analysis. *Journal of Personality and Social Psychology, 56,* 972–987.

Strube, M. J, Turner, C. W., Cerro, D., Stevens, J., & Hinchey, F. (1984). Interpersonal aggression and the Type A coronary-prone behavior pattern: A theoretical distinction and practical implications. *Journal of Personality and Social Psychology, 47,* 839–847.

Suls, J., & Fletcher, B. (1985). The relative efficacy of avoidant and nonavoidant coping strategies: A meta-analysis. *Health Psychology, 4,* 249–288.

Suls, J., & Rosnow, J. (1988). Concerns about artifacts in behavioral research. In M. Morawski (Ed.), *The rise of experimentation in American psychology* (pp. 163–187). New Haven, CT: Yale University Press.

Suls, J., & Wan, C. K. (1989). The effects of sensory and procedural information on coping with stressful medical procedures and pain: A meta-analysis. *Journal of Consulting and Clinical Psychology, 57,* 372–379.

Suls, J., Wan, C. K., & Sanders, G. S. (1988). False consensus and false uniqueness in estimating the prevalence of health-protective behaviors. *Journal of Applied Social Psychology, 18,* 66–79.

Swann, W. B., Jr., De La Ronde, C., & Hixon, J. G. (1994). Authenticity and positivity strivings in marriage and courtship. *Journal of Personality and Social Psychology, 66,* 857–869.

Swann, W. B., Jr., Griffin, J. J., Jr., Predmore, S. C., & Gaines, B. (1987). Cognitive–affective crossfire: When self-consistency meets self-enhancement. *Journal of Personality and Social Psychology, 52,* 881–889.

Swann, W. B., Jr., Stein-Serossi, A., & Giesler, R. B. (1992). Why people self-verify. *Journal of Personality and Social Psychology, 62,* 392–401.

Swim, J. K. (1994). Perceived versus meta-analytic effect sizes: An assessment of the accuracy of gender stereotypes. *Journal of Personality and Social Psychology, 66,* 21–36.

Swim, J. K., Aikin, K. J., Hall, W. S., & Hunter, B. A. (1995). Sexism and racism: Old-fashioned and modern prejudices. *Journal of Personality and Social Psychology, 68,* 199–214.

Symons, C. S., & Johnson, B. T. (1997). The self-reference effect in memory: A meta-analysis. *Psychological Bulletin, 121,* 371–394.

Tajfel, H. (1982). *Social identity and intergroup relations.* Cambridge, England: Cambridge University Press.

Tannen, D. (1994). *Talking from 9 to 5.* New York: William Morrow.

Taylor, S. E., & Brown, J. D. (1988). Illusion and well-being: A social psychological perspective on mental health. *Psychological Bulletin, 103,* 193–210.

Taylor, S. E., Buunk, B. P., & Aspinwall, L. G. (1990). Social comparison, stress, and coping. *Personality and Social Psychology Bulletin, 16,* 74–89.

Taylor, S. E., Helgeson, V. S., Reed, G. M., & Skokan, L. A. (1991). Self-generated feelings of control and adjustment to physical illness. *Journal of Social Issues, 47,* 91–109.

Teens top elderly as victims of crime. (1995, June 1). *Albany Times Union,* p. A-13.

Terry, D. J., & Hogg, M. A. (1996). Group norms and the attitude-behavior relationship: A role for group identification. *Personality and Social Psychology Bulletin, 22,* 776-793

Terry, R. L., & Krantz, J. H. (1993). Dimensions of trait attributions associated with eyeglasses, men's facial hair, and women's hair length. *Journal of Applied Social Psychology, 23,* 1757–1769.

Tesser, A. (1993). On the importance of heritability in psychological research: The case of attitudes. *Psychological Review, 100,* 129–142.

Tesser, A., & Martin, L. (1996). The psychology of evaluation. In E. T. Higgins & A. W. Kruglanski (Eds.), *Social psychology: Handbook of basic principles* (pp. 400-432). New York: Guilford.

Tetlock, P. E., Peterson, R. S., McGuire, C., Change, S., & Feld, P. (1992). Assessing political group dynamics: A test of the groupthink model. *Journal of Personality and Social Psychology, 63,* 403–425.

Thompson, D. (1992). The danger in doomsaying. *Time, 139*(10), 61.

Thompson, J. K., & Tantleff, S. (1992). Female and male ratings of upper torso: Actual, ideal, and stereotypical conceptions. *Journal of Social Behavior and Personality, 7,* 345–354.

Thompson, L. (1990). An examination of naive and experienced negotiators. *Journal of Personality and Social Psychology, 59,* 82–90.

Thompson, L. (1993). *Biases in negotiation: An examination of reception and transmission processes.* Unpublished manuscript, University of Washington, Seattle.

Thompson, S. C., Nanni, C., & Levine, A. (1994). Primary versus secondary and central versus consequence-related control in HIV-positive men. *Journal of Personality and Social Psychology, 67,* 540–547.

Thompson, S. C., Sobolew-Shubin, A., Galbraith, M. E., Schwankovsky, L., & Cruzen, D. (1993). Maintaining perceptions of control: Finding perceived control in low-control circumstances. *Journal of Personality and Social Psychology, 64,* 291–300.

Thornton, A., & Freedman, D. (1982) Changing attitudes toward married and single life. *Family Planning Perspectives, 14*(6), 297–303.

Tidwell, M. O., Reis, H. T., & Shaver, P. R. (1996). Attachment, attractiveness, and social interaction. *Journal of Personality and Social Psychology, 71,* 729–745.

Toch, H. (1985). *Violent men* (rev. ed.). Cambridge, MA: Schenkman.

Toi, M., & Batson, C. D. (1982). More evidence that empathy is a source of altruistic motivation. *Journal of Personality and Social Psychology, 43,* 281–292.

Tomaka, J., & Blascovich, J. (1994). Effects of justice beliefs on cognitive appraisal of and subjective, physiological, and behavioral responses to potential stress. *Journal of Personality and Social Psychology, 67,* 732–740.

Tooley, V., Brigham, J. C., Maass, A., & Bothwell, R. K. (1987). Facial recognition: Weapon effect and attentional focus. *Journal of Applied Social Psychology, 17,* 845–859.

Torestad, B. (1990). What is anger provoking: A psychophysical study of perceived causes of anger. *Aggressive Behavior, 16,* 9–26.

Traeen, B., Lewin, B., & Sundet, J. M. (1992). The real and the ideal: Gender differences in heterosexual behaviour among Norwegian adolescents. *Journal of Community & Applied Social Psychology, 2,* 227–237.

Trafimow, D., & Finlay, K. A. (1996). The importance of subjective norms for a minority of people: Between-subjects and within-subjects analyses. *Personality and Social Psychology Bulletin, 22,* 820–828

Triandis, H. C. (1995). *Individualism & collectivism.* Boulder, CO: Westview.

Triplett, N. (1898). The dynamogenic factors in pacemaking and competition. *American Journal of Psychology, 9,* 507–533.

Trivers, R. (1972). Parental investment and sexual selection. In B. Campbell (Ed.), *Sexual selection and the descent of man, 1871–1971* (pp. 136–179). Chicago: Aldine.

Tuckman, B. W., & Sexton, T. L. (1990). The relation between self-beliefs and self-regulated performance. *Journal of Social Behavior and Personality, 5,* 465–472.

Turner, M. E., Pratkanis, A. R., & Hardaway, T. J. (1991). Sex differences in reaction to preferential selection: Towards a model of preferential selection as help. *Journal of Social Behavior and Personality, 6,* 797–814.

Tversky, A., & Kahneman, D. (1973). Availability: A heuristic for judging frequency and probability. *Cognitive Psychology, 5,* 207–232.

Tversky, A., & Kahneman, D. (1982). Judgment under uncertainty: Heuristics and biases. In D. Kahneman, P. Slovic, & A. Tversky (Eds.), *Judgment under uncertainty* (pp. 3–20). New York: Cambridge University Press.

Tyler, T. R. (1994). Psychological models of the justice motive: Antecedents of distributive and procedural justice. *Journal of Personality and Social Psychology, 67,* 850–863.

U.S. Department of Justice. (1994). *Criminal victimization in the United States, 1992.* Washington, DC: Office of Justice Programs, Bureau of Justice Statistics.

U.S. Department of Labor. (1992). *Employment and earnings* (Vol. 39, No. 5: Table A-22). Washington, DC: U.S. Department of Labor.

Uchino, B. N., Kiecolt-Glaser, J. K., & Cacioppo, J. T. (1992). Age-related changes in cardiovascular response as a function of a chronic stressor and social support. *Journal of Personality and Social Psychology, 63,* 839–846.

Uchitelle, L. (1994, November 28). Women in their 50's follow many paths into workplace. *The New York Times,* A1, B8.

Udry, J. R. (1980). Changes in the frequency of marital intercourse from panel data. *Archives of Sexual Behavior, 9,* 319–325.

Ullman, C. (1987). From sincerity to authenticity: Adolescents' views of the "true self." *Journal of Personality, 55,* 583–595.

Unger, R. K. (1994). Alternative conceptions of sex (and sex differences). In M. Haug, R. Whalen, C. Aron, & K. L. Olsen (Eds.), *The development of sex differences and similarities in behavior.* Dordrecht, The Netherlands: Kluwer Academic.

Unger, R. K., & Crawford, M. (1993). Commentary: Sex and gender—The troubled relationship between terms and concepts. *Psychological Science, 4,* 122–124.

van de Vliert, E., Euwema, M. C., & Huismans, S. E. (1995). Managing conflict with a subordinate or a superior: Effectiveness of conglomerated behavior. *Journal of Applied Psychology, 80,* 271–281.

Van Dyne, L., Graham, J. W., & Dienesch, R. M. (1994). Organizational citizenship behavior: Construct redefinition, measurement, and validation. *Academy of Management Journal, 37,* 765–802.

Van Goozen, S., Frijda, N., & de Poll, N. V. (1994). Anger and aggression in women: Influence of sports choice and testosterone administration. *Aggressive Behavior, 20,* 213–222.

Van Lange, P. A. M., & Rusbult, C. E. (1995). My relationship is better than—and not as bad as—yours is: The perception of superiority in close relationships. *Personality and Social Psychology Bulletin, 21,* 32–44.

Vinokur, A. D., Price, R. H., & Caplan, R. D. (1996). Hard times and hurtful partners: How financial strain affects depression and relationship satisfaction of unemployed persons and their spouses. *Journal of Personality and Social Psychology, 71,* 166–179.

Vonk, R., & van Knippenberg, A. (1995). Processing attitude statements from in-group and out-group members: Effects of within-group and within-person inconsistencies on reading times. *Journal of Personality and Social Psychology, 68,* 215–227.

Waller, N. G., Kojetin, B. A., Bouchard, T. J. Jr., Lykken, D. T., & Tellegen, A. (1990). Genetic and environmental influences on religious interests, attitudes, and values: A study of twins reared apart and together. *Psychological Science, 1,* 138–142.

Walster, E., Walster, G. W., Piliavin, J., & Schmidt, L. (1973). "Playing hard-to-get": Understanding an elusive phenomenon. *Journal of Personality and Social Psychology, 26,* 113–121.

Wardle, J., Bindra, R., Fairclough, B., & Westcombe, A. (1993). Culture and body image: Body perception and weight concern in young Asian and Caucasian British women. *Journal of Community and Applied Social Psychology, 3,* 173–181.

Waters, H. F., Block, D., Friday, C., & Gordon, J. (1993, July 12). Networks under the gun. *Newsweek,* 64–66.

Watson, D. (1989). Strangers' ratings of the five robust personality factors: Evidence of a surprising convergence with self report. *Journal of Personality and Social Psychology, 57,* 120–128.

Watts, B. L. (1982). Individual differences in circadian activity rhythms and their effects on roommate relationships. *Journal of Personality, 50,* 374–384.

Wayne, S. J., & Ferris, G. R. (1990). Influence tactics, and exchange quality in supervisor–subordinate interactions: A laboratory experiment and field study. *Journal of Applied Psychology, 75,* 487–499.

Wayne, S. J., & Liden, R. C. (1995). Effects of impression management on performance ratings: A longitudinal study. *Academy of Management Journal, 38,* 232–260.

Wegner, D. M. (1992). The premature demise of the solo experiment. *Personality and Social Psychology Bulletin, 18,* 504–508.

Weigel, R. H., Kim, E. L., & Frost, J. L. (1995). Race relations on prime time television reconsidered: Patterns of continuity and change. *Journal of Applied Social Psychology, 25,* 223–236.

Weigel, R. H., Loomis, J. S., & Soja, M. J. (1980). Race relations on prime time television. *Journal of Personality and Social Psychology, 39,* 884–893.

Weinberg, M. S., Lottes, I. L., & Shaver, F. M. (1995). Swedish or American heterosexual college youth:

Who is more permissive? *Archives of Sexual Be-havior, 24*, 409–437.

Weinberger, M., Hiner, S. L., & Tierney, W. M. (1987). In support of hassles as a measure of stress in predicting health outcomes. *Journal of Behavioral Medicine, 10*, 19–32.

Weiner, B., Amirkhan, J., Folkes, V. S., & Verette, J. A. (1987). An attributional analysis of excuse giving: Studies of a naive theory of emotion. *Journal of Personality and Social Psychology, 52*, 316–324.

Weitzman, L., Eifler, D., Hokada, E., & Ross, C. (1972). Sex-role socialization in picture books for preschool children. *American Journal of Sociology, 77*, 1125–1150.

Weldon, E., & Mustari, L. (1988). Felt dispensability in groups of coactors: The effects of shared responsibility and explicit anonymity on cognitive effort. *Organizational Behavior and Human Decision Processes, 41*, 330–351.

Wells, G. L. (1984). The psychology of lineup identification. *Journal of Applied Social Psychology, 14*, 89–103.

Wells, G. L., & Luus, C. A. E. (1990). Police lineups as experiments: Social methodology as a framework for properly conducted lineups. *Personality and Social Psychology Bulletin, 16*, 106–117.

Wells, G. L., Luus, C. A. E., & Windschitl, P. D. (1994). Maximizing the utility of eyewitness identification evidence. *Current Directions in Psychological Science, 3*, 194–197.

West, S. G., Newsom, J. T., & Fenaughty, A. M. (1992). Publication in JPSP: Stability and change in topics, methods, and theories across two decades. *Personality and Social Psychology Bulletin, 18*, 473–484.

Whisman, M. A., & Kwon, P. (1993). Life stress and dysphoria: The role of self-esteem and hopelessness. *Journal of Personality and Social Psychology, 65*, 1054–1060.

Whitbeck, L. B., & Hoyt, D. R. (1994). Social prestige and assortive mating: A comparison of students from 1956 and 1988. *Journal of Social and Personal Relationships, 11*, 137–145.

Whitley, B. E., Jr. (1993). Reliability and aspects of the construct validity of Sternberg's triangular love scale. *Journal of Social and Personal Relationships, 10*, 475–480.

Whitley, B. E., Jr., & Greenberg, M. S. (1986). The role of eyewitness confidence in juror perceptions of credibility. *Journal of Applied Social Psychology, 16*, 387–409.

Wicker, A. W. (1969). Attitudes versus actions: The relationship of verbal and overt behavioral responses to attitude objects. *Journal of Social Issues, 25*, 41–78.

Wiebe, D. J., & McCallum, D. M. (1986). Health practices and hardiness as mediators in the stress– illness relationship. *Health Psychology, 5*, 425–438.

Williams, D. E., & D'Alessandro, J. D. (1994). A comparison of three measures of androgyny and their relationship to psychological adjustment. *Journal of Social Behavior and Personality, 9*, 469–480.

Williams, G. P., & Kleinke, C. L. (1993). Effects of mutual gaze and touch on attraction, mood, and cardiovascular reactivity. *Journal of Research in Personality, 27*, 170–183.

Williams, K. B., Radefeld, P. A., Binning, J. F., & Suadk, J. R. (1993). When job candidates are "hard-" versus "easy-to-get": Effects of candidate availability on employment decisions. *Journal of Applied Social Psychology, 23*, 169–198.

Williams, K. D., Harkins, S., & Latané, B. (1981). Identifiability as a deterrent to social loafing: Two cheering experiments. *Journal of Personality and Social Psychology, 40*, 303–311.

Williams, K. D., & Karau, S. J. (1991). Social loafing and social compensation: The effects of expectations of co-worker performance. *Journal of Personality and Social Psychology, 61*, 570–581.

Williams, K. J., Suls, J., Alliger, G. M., Learner, S. M., & Wan, C. K. (1991). Multiple role juggling and daily mood states in working mothers: An experience sampling study. *Journal of Applied Psychology, 76*, 633–638.

Williamson, G. M., & Clark, M. S. (1989). Providing help and desired relationship type as determinants of changes in moods and self-evaluations. *Journal of Personality and Social Psychology, 56*, 722–734.

Williamson, G. M., Clark, M. S., Pegalis, L. J., & Behan, A. (1996). Affective consequences of refusing to help in communal and exchange relationships. *Personality and Social Psychology Bulletin, 22*, 4–47.

Wilson, E. O. (1975). *Sociobiology.* Cambridge, MA: Harvard University Press.

Wilson, J. P., & Petruska, R. (1984). Motivation, model attributes, and prosocial behavior. *Journal of Personality and Social Psychology, 46*, 458–468.

Wilson, T. D., & Brekke, N. (1994). Mental contamination and mental correction: Unwanted influences on judgments and evaluations. *Psychological Bulletin, 116*, 117–142.

Wilson, T. D., & Klaaren, K. J. (1992). Effects of affective expectations on willingness to relive pleasant and unpleasant events. Unpublished data.

Wilson, T. D., & Kraft, D. (1993). Why do I love thee?: Effects of repeated introspections about a dating relationship on attitudes toward the relationship. *Personality and Social Psychology Bulletin, 19,* 409–418.

Wilson, T. D., & Schooler, J. (1991). Thinking too much: Introspection can reduce the quality of preferences and decisions. *Journal of Personality and Social Psychology, 60,* 181–192.

Winstead, B. A., Derlega, V. J., Montgomery, M. J., & Pilkington, C. (1995). The quality of friendships at work and job satisfaction. *Journal of Social and Personal Relationships, 12,* 199–215.

Wolf, N. (1992). Father figures. *New Republic, 207*(15), 22, 24–25.

Wolf, S., & Bugaj, A. M. (1990). The social impact of courtroom witnesses. *Social Behaviour, 5,* 1–13.

Wood, J. V., Giordano-Beech, M., Taylor, K. L., Michela, J. L., & Gaus, V. (1994). Strategies of social comparison among people with low self-esteem: Self-protection and self-enhancement. *Journal of Personality and Social Psychology, 67,* 713–731.

Wood, W. (1982). Retrieval of attitude-relevant information from memory: Effects on susceptibility to persuasion on intrinsic motivation. *Journal of Personality and Social Psychology, 42,* 798–810.

Wood, W., Christensen, P. N., Hebl, M. R., & Rothgerber, H. (in press). Sex-typed norms and the self: Why are men dominant and women communal? *Journal of Personality and Social Psychology.*

Wood, W., Pool, G. J., Leck, K., & Purvis, D. (1996). Self-definition, defensive processing, and influence: The normative impact of majority and minority groups. *Journal of Personality and Social Psychology, 71,* 1181–1193.

Wood, W., Wong, F. Y., & Cachere, J. G. (1991). Effects of media violence on viewers' aggression in unconstrained social interaction. *Psychological Bulletin, 109,* 371–383.

Wright, R. (1994, November 28). Feminists, meet Mr. Darwin. *The New Republic, 34,* 36–37, 40, 42, 44–46.

Wright, R. (1995, March 13). The biology of violence. *The New Yorker,* 68–77.

Wuensch, K. L., Castellow, W. A., & Moore, C. H. (1991). Effects of defendant attractiveness and type of crime on juridic judgment. *Journal of Social Behavior and Personality, 6,* 713–724.

Wyer, R. S., Jr., Budesheim, T. L., Lambert, A. J., & Swan, S. (1994). Person memory judgment: Pragmatic influence on impressions formed in a social context. *Journal of Personality and Social Psychology, 66,* 254–267.

Wyer, R. S., Jr., & Srull, T. K. (1994). *Handbook of social cognition* (2nd ed). Hillsdale, NJ: Erlbaum.

Yamagishi, M., & Yamagishi, T. (1989). *Trust, commitment, and the development of network structures.* Paper presented at the Workshop for the Beyond Bureaucracy Research Project, December 18–21, Hong Kong.

Yamagishi, T., & Yamigishi, M. (1994). Trust and commitment in the United States and Japan. *Motivation and Emotion, 18,* 129–166.

Yamaguchi, S., Okamoto, K. & Oka, T. (1985). Effects of coactor's presence: Social loafing and social facilitation. *Japanese Psychological Research, 27,* 215–222.

Yost, J. H., & Weary, G. (1996). Depression and the correspondent inference bias: Evidence for more effortful cognitive processing. *Personality and Social Psychology Bulletin, 22,* 192–200.

Youille, J. C., & Tollestrup, P. A. (1990). Some effects of alcohol on eyewitness memory. *Journal of Applied Psychology, 71,* 291–301.

Yovetich, N. A., & Rusbult, C. E. (1994). Accommodative behavior in close relationships: Exploring transformation of motivation. *Journal of Experimental Social Psychology, 30,* 138–164.

Yukl, G. (1981). *Leadership in organizations.* Englewood Cliffs, NJ: Prentice-Hall.

Yukl, G. (1994). *Leadership in organizations* (3rd ed.). Englewood Cliffs, NJ: Prentice-Hall.

Yukl, G., & Falbe, C. M. (1991). Importance of different power sources in downward and lateral relations. *Journal of Applied Psychology, 76,* 416–423.

Zaccaro, S. J., Foti, R. J., & Kenny, D. A. (1991). Self-monitoring and trait-based variance in leadership: An investigation of leader flexibility across multiple group situations. *Journal of Applied Psychology, 76,* 308–315.

Zaccaro, S. J., & McCoy, M. C. (1988). The effects of task and interpersonal cohesiveness on performance of a disjunctive group task. *Journal of Applied Social Psychology, 18,* 837–851.

Zajonc, R. B. (1965). Social facilitation. *Science, 149,* 269–274.

Zajonc, R. B. (1968). Attitudinal effects of mere exposure [monograph]. *Journal of Personality and Social Psychology, 9,* 1–27.

Zajonc, R. B., Adelmann, P. K., Murphy, S. T., & Niedenthal, P. M. (1987). Convergence in the physical appearance of spouses. *Motivation and Emotion, 11,* 335–346.

Zajonc, R. B., Heingartner, A., & Herman, E. M. (1969). Social enhancement and impairment of performance in the cockroach. *Journal of Personality and Social Psychology, 13,* 83–92.

Zajonc, R. B., Murphy, S. T., & Inglehart, M. (1989). Feeling and facial efference: Implications of the vascular theory of emotion. *Psychological Review, 96,* 396–416.

Zajonc, R. B., & Sales, S. M. (1966). Social facilitation of dominant and subordinate responses. *Journal of Experimental Social Psychology, 2,* 160–168.

Zammichieli, M. E., Gilroy, F. D., & Sherman, M. F. (1988). Relation between sex-role orientation and marital satisfaction. *Personality and Social Psychology Bulletin, 14,* 747–754.

Zárate, M. A., & Sandoval, P. (1995). The effects of contextual cues on making occupational and gender categorizations. *British Journal of Social Psychology, 34,* 353–362.

Zdaniuk, B., & Levine, J. M. (1996). Anticipated interaction and thought generation: The role of faction size. *British Journal of Social Psychology, 35,* 201–218.

Zebrowitz, L. A. (1996) Physical appearance as a basis of stereotyping. In M. Hewstone, N. Macrae, & C. Stangor (Eds.), *Foundations of stereotypes and stereotyping* (pp. 79–120). New York: Guilford.

Zebrowitz, L. A., Voinescu, L., & Collins, M. A. (1996). "Wide-eyed" and "Crooked-Faced": Determinants of perceived and real honesty across the life span. *Personality and Social Psychology Bulletin, 22,* 1258–1269.

Zeitz, G. (1990). Age and work satisfaction in a government agency: A situational perspective. *Human Relations, 43,* 419–438.

Zelli, A., Huesmann, L. R., & Cervone, D. (1995). Social inference and individual differences in aggression: Evidence for spontaneous judgments of hostility. *Aggressive Behavior, 21,* 405–417.

Ziller, R. C. (1990). *Photographing the self: Methods for observing personal orientations.* Newbury Park, CA: Sage.

Zillmann, D. (1979). *Hostility and aggression.* Hillsdale, NJ: Erlbaum.

Zillmann, D. (1988). Cognition-excitation interdependencies in aggressive behavior. *Aggressive Behavior, 14,* 51–64.

Zillmann, D. (1993). Mental control of angry aggression. In D. M. Wegner & J. W. Pennebaker (Eds.), *Handbook of mental control.* Englewood Cliffs, NJ: Prentice-Hall.

Zillmann, D. (1994). Cognition–excitation interdependencies in the escalation of anger and angry aggression. In M. Potegal & J. F. Knutson (Eds.), *The dynamics of aggression* (pp. 45–71). Hillsdale, NJ: Erlbaum.

Zillmann, D., & Bryant, J. (1984). Effects of massive exposure to pornography. In N. M. Malamuth and E. Donnerstein (Eds.), *Pornography and sexual aggression.* New York: Academic Press.

Zillmann, D., Rockwell, S., Schweitzer, K., & Sundar, S. S. (1993). Does humor facilitate coping with physical discomfort? *Motivation and Emotion, 17,* 1–21.

Zimbardo, P. G. (1977). *Shyness: What it is and what you can do about it.* Reading, MA: Addison-Wesley.

Zoglin, R. (1993). The shock of the blue. *Time, 142*(17), 71–72.

Zuber, J. A., Crott, H. W., & Werner, J. (1992). Choice shift and group polarization: An analysis of the status of arguments and social decision schemes. *Journal of Personality and Social Psychology, 62,* 50–61.

Zuckerman, M., DePaulo, B. M., & Rosenthal, R. (1981). Verbal and nonverbal communication of deception. In L. Berkowitz (Ed.), *Advances in experimental social psychology* (Vol. 14, pp. 1–59). New York: Academic Press.

Zuwerink, J. R., & Devine, P. G. (1996). Attitude importance and resistance to persuasion: It's not just the thought that counts. *Journal of Personality and Social Psychology, 70,* 931–944.

Zuwerink, J. R., Devine, P. G., & Monteith, M. J. (1996). Prejudice toward Blacks: With and without compunction? *Basic and Applied Social Psychology, 18,* 31–150.

Author Index

Abraham, C. S., 79
Abrams, D., 77
Abrams, J., 163
Abramson, J., 268
Acker, M., 228
Ackerman, P., 216
Adair, J. G., 20, 21
Adams, J. B., 93
Adams, N. E., 86
Adelmann, P. K., 162
Ader, R., 283
Affleck, G., 289
Agarie, N., 231
Agnew, C. R., 159
Aguinis, H., 155, 156
Aiello, J. R., 247
Aikin, K. J., 130, 131
Ajzen, I., 108, 110
Alavi, A., 94
Alicke, M. D., 268
Allen, N. J., 274
Allen, S. J., 83
Allgeier, E. R., 172
Alliger, G. M., 163, 239
Allport, F. H., 8, 101, 242
Allport, G. W., 8
Alvaro, E. M., 192
Amason, A. C., 278
Amir, Y., 140
Amirkhan, J. H., 231, 284
Amsel, R., 161
Anastasio, P. A., 141
Andersen, S. M., 158, 162
Anderson, C. A., 6, 26, 220, 221
Anderson, D., 93
Anderson, K. B., 26, 220, 221
Anderson, N. H., 40, 41
Anderson, P. B., 93
Anthony, T., 137, 250
Aplan, R. D., 174
Archer, J., 91, 93, 218, 228

Archibald, F. S., 165
Arms, R. L., 226
Arndt, J., 82
Arnold, S. E., 94
Aron, A. P., 167, 171, 173
Aron, E. N., 167
Aronoff, J., 29
Aronson, E., 121
Arps, K., 217
Arrow, H., 186
Arvey, R. D., 105
Asch, S. E., 185, 188
Asendorpf, J. B., 166
Ashford, S. J., 274
Aspinwall, L. G., 283
Atkins, J. L., 55
Aube, J., 87, 89, 144
Averill, J. R., 168
Avolio, B. J., 258
Aymami, R., 93

Bachman, B. A., 141
Bae, S. H., 274
Bailey, R. C., 170
Bandura, A., 85, 86, 220, 285
Banks, J. S., 163
Barbaranelli, C., 227
Barbee, A. P., 159
Barbour, L., 160
Bargh, J. A., 56, 111, 153
Barkow, J. H., 6
Barnes, G., 228
Baron, R., 253, 272
Baron, R. A., 6, 20, 26, 39, 44,
    64, 66, 215, 220, 221, 226, 229,
    231, 275, 276, 277, 278, 280,
    287
Baron, R. S., 187, 244, 282, 290
Barrick, M. R., 227
Bar-Tal, Y., 283
Bartell, P. A., 212

Bartholomew, K., 164, 165, 177
Bartunek, J. M., 280
Bass, B. M., 254
Bassett, R., 194
Batista, S. M., 174
Batson, C. D., 142, 143, 209,
    216–217
Baucom, D. H., 89
Bauer, G. B., 175
Baum, A., 6, 158
Bauman, D. J., 217
Baumeister, R. F., 39, 76, 77, 168,
    210–211
Baumrind, D., 20
Baxter, L. A., 174
Bazerman, M. H., 279
Beach, S. R., 154, 155
Beall, A. E., 169
Beaman, A. L., 194, 217
Beckwith, J. B., 87, 89
Bedian, A. G., 273
Bednar, L. L., 142, 143
Beehr, T. A., 273
Behan, A., 218
Belinsky, D., 284
Bell, B. E., 266
Bell, D. W., 103–104
Bell, P. A., 6
Bell, S. T., 40
Bem, S. L., 88, 89
Ben-Avi, I., 272
Benson, A., 164
Benson, P. L., 213
Benthin, A. C., 122
Bentler, P. M., 83
Berent, M. K., 108, 109
Berkowitz, L., 102, 220, 221,
    222
Berman, M., 93, 226, 229
Bernard, L. C., 284
Berndt, T. J., 164

Subject Index

Photo Credits